EDITION 11

A Systems Approach to Small Group Interaction

Stewart L. Tubbs

Darrell H. Cooper Professor of Leadership
and Former Dean of the College of Business
Eastern Michigan University

To my beloved Gail, Brian, Michelle, Connor, Kelly, John, Katherine, and James

The McGraw-Hill Companies

A SYSTEMS APPROACH TO SMALL GROUP INTERACTION, ELEVENTH EDITION

Published by McGraw-Hill, a business unit of The McGraw-Hill Companies, Inc., 1221 Avenue of the Americas, New York, NY 10020.

This book is printed on acid-free paper.

1 2 3 4 5 6 7 8 9 0 DOC/DOC 1 0 9 8 7 6 5 4 3 2 1

ISBN 978-0-07-353432-9
MHID 0-07-353432-3

Vice President & Editor-in-Chief: *Michael Ryan*
Vice President & Director of Specialized Publishing: *Janice M. Roerig-Blong*
Publisher: *David Patterson*
Senior Sponsoring Editor: *Debra B. Hash*
Marketing Coordinator: *Angela R. FitzPatrick*
Project Manager: *Erin Melloy*
Design Coordinator: *Margaite Reynods*
Cover Designer: *Studio Montage, St. Louis, Missouri*
Cover Image: *Ingram Publishing*
Buyer: *Susan K. Culbertson*
Media Project Manager: *Sridevi Palani*
Compositor: *MPS Limited, a Macmillan Company*
Typeface: *10/12 Garamond Light*
Printer: *R.R Donnelley*

Library of Congress Cataloging-in-Publication Data

Tubbs, Stewart L., 1943–
A systems approach to small group interaction / Stewart Tubbs. — 11th ed.
p. cm.
Summary: "The only book that integrates all important small group communication topics into a single comprehensive conceptual model, this text pioneered the systems approach for the group communication course. Each chapter begins with a brief preview, followed by a glossary of terms and a real life case study. The text material in each chapter is followed by several experiential exercises for skill development and two original readings"— Provided by publisher.
ISBN 978-0-07-353432-9 (pbk.)
1. Teams in the workplace. 2. Small groups. 3. Organizational behavior. I. Title.
HD66.T82 2011
658.4'036—dc23 2011037386

www.mhhe.com

About the Author

STEWART L. TUBBS is the Darrell H. Cooper Professor of Leadership and former dean of the College of Business at Eastern Michigan University, and was a visiting professor at Koc University in Istanbul, Turkey. He received his doctorate in communication and organizational behavior from the University of Kansas. His master's degree in communication and his bachelor's degree in science are from Bowling Green State University. He has completed postdoctoral work in management at Harvard Business School, Stanford Graduate School of Business, and the Center for Creative Leadership.

Dr. Tubbs has also taught at General Motors Institute and at Boise State University, where he was chair of the Management Department and later associate dean of the College of Business. Dr. Tubbs also served at the University of Kansas as assistant director of Community Leadership Development.

He has been named an Outstanding Teacher ten times and an Outstanding Scholar twice, has consulted extensively for Fortune 500 companies, and is past chair of the Organizational Communication division of the Academy of Management. He has also received the outstanding leadership award in London from the Academy of Business Administration and has been inducted into the Distinguished Alumni Hall of Fame by Lakewood High School in Lakewood, Ohio. Dr. Tubbs is the author of *Keys to Leadership: 101 Steps to Success* and coauthor, with Sylvia Moss, of *Interpersonal Communication*, as well as *Human Communication: Principles and Contexts, The Open Person* (with John Baird), and *Shared Experiences in Human Communication* (with Robert Carter). He is listed in *American Men and Women of Science, Contemporary Authors, Directory of American Scholars, International Who's Who in Education*, and *Outstanding Young Men of America*.

Dr. Tubbs would very much like to receive any feedback and suggestions that you have about the book. This is true for students and instructors alike. His e-mail address is Stu.Tubbs@emich.edu. If you prefer snail mail, send it to the Management Department, Eastern Michigan University, Ypsilanti, MI 48197. He may also be reached by phone at 734-487-5875.

Brief Contents

Contents

2 Communication Processes 42

7 Conflict Management 322

8 Consequences 356

Preface

"A Systems Approach to Small Group Interaction" has sold approximately a quarter of a million copies worldwide in its first ten editions. Thank you all for making this one of the most successful small groups books of all time! I believe that if you learn more about teams and small groups, you will enrich your life and improve your chances of success in your chosen career. Whether in families, public schools, hospitals, universities, businesses, or government, it seems that everybody is discovering the value of small group activities. An increasing number of teams are now operating online as virtual teams. The information contained in this book could be some of the most useful of any that you will encounter in your college career and for the rest of your life.

This book explores the myriad ways in which groups and teams can be used to help achieve successful results. Intended as a primary text for courses in group communication, this book is also used as a text in management, psychology, nursing, and education courses. This eleventh edition represents a substantial and dramatic revision.

Distinctions of *A Systems Approach to Small Group Interaction*, Eleventh Edition

This book's format—text, with student experiential exercises and selected readings—is unique among the small group texts available. Each chapter begins with a brief chapter preview, followed by a glossary of terms used in that chapter. Next is an opening case study designed to stimulate student class discussions. The case study is followed by the chapter text material. Following each chapter are several experiential exercises designed to offer opportunities to practice the small group interactions discussed in the chapter. Each chapter ends with two reading selections chosen for their direct relevance to the subjects discussed in that chapter. The readings offer further depth or illustrate applications of the chapter's concepts. Finally, each chapter now includes one or more sections labeled "Practical Tips," which are designed to help readers see the practical applications of the text material.

Plan of the Book, Including New Features

Based on extensive feedback from students and professors who have used the book, we have made approximately one hundred changes in the book since the tenth edition.

Chapter 1 addresses the basic question, What is small group interaction? It presents key definitions and offers a "systems approach" conceptual model that serves as the organizing framework for the remainder of the book. New in this edition are

- Case study exercise ranking the teams in the National Football League to compare individual decision-making to group decisions
- Material on the importance of groups to human beings
- Research from *The Wall Street Journal* showing the high level of dissatisfaction with groups and the dramatic increase of group and team courses in top university curricula
- Discussion of the need for more and better critical thinking skills among college graduates
- Practical Tips box showing virtual team tips
- Research on the amount of time college students spend socializing in small groups compared to how much time they spend studying
- Discussion of Gallup survey data from around the world showing the importance of socializing for well-being
- Material on the "See it, own it, solve it, do it" method of problem-solving
- Discussion of "emergent systems"

Chapter 2, "Communication Processes," deals with the unique aspects of communication in the small group setting. It covers language behavior, self-disclosure, and interaction roles. New in this edition are

- Research findings that communication mistakes cost an estimated $300 million a year in the United States alone
- Opening case exercise about computers revealing personal information about users
- Research from Princeton University on the effects of good looks on getting hired for a job
- Research on voters predicting election outcomes based on a few seconds of nonverbal exposure to the candidates
- Practical Tips box with tips for speaking up in meetings
- Practical Tips box on assertive and self-disclosure communication skills
- Research on confirming versus disconfirming communication styles
- Research on message redundancy and leadership effectiveness

- Practical Tips box on ways to communicate more effectively, from Dr. Frank Luntz
- Research findings about lying and nonverbal behaviors

Chapter 3, "Relevant Background Factors," discusses six characteristics of individual group members that will influence the group's functioning. They are personality, gender, age, health, attitudes, and values. New in this edition are

- The Netflix opening chapter case
- Information on the role of social groups in well-being
- Material on the three components of attitudes
- Discussion of attitudinal consistency
- Research on the breakdown of age on happiness
- Discussion of hedonic versus eudaimonic happiness
- Tips on diversity and group effectiveness
- Research on the influence of weight on earnings

Chapter 4, "Group Circumstances and Structure," discusses the group's physical environment, the group's size and structure, and different types of groups. New in this edition are

- New chapter opening case study about Hooters and hiring policy in relation to weight
- Discussion of new findings about group size and group effectiveness
- Research on social loafing
- Information on autonomous work teams
- Research on the influence of friendship groups on an individual's mood, smoking behavior, obesity, and so on

Chapter 5, "Leadership and Social Influence Processes," discusses status, power, leadership, group norms, and conformity pressures. New in this edition are

- A Practical Tips box on team leadership
- Research material on the importance of leadership skills to career success
- Research on flattery and its effect on an individual's power
- Research on "Multiplier" leaders versus "Diminisher" leaders
- Research on the importance of team skills to leadership worldwide
- New examples of groupthink
- Examples of President Obama's leadership style in meetings
- New Practical Tips box on dealing with peer-group conformity pressures
- Examples of groupthink applied to the wars in Iraq and Afghanistan

Chapter 6, "Decision-Making Processes," examines the various methods for organizing group problem solving. New in this edition are

- A new Practical Tips box on a hybrid model of brainstorming
- Research on applied innovation
- New material on fishbone diagrams
- Examples of "Gamestorming"
- Research findings from the *Journal of Applied Psychology* about errors in decision making
- A section on the use of checklists
- A section on a new form of decision making called "obliquity"
- Research findings on creativity from a worldwide study by IBM
- Material from Harvard University research on motivational communication
- The Kissinger model in White House decision making
- Material on the unintended consequences of decisions

Chapter 7, "Conflict Management," examines the sources, types, and desirability or undesirability of conflict. It also offers ideas on resolving conflict. New in this chapter are

- A Practical Tips box on managing conflict
- Research findings about Iconoclasts as nonconformists
- Conflict management tips

Chapter 8, "Consequences," is devoted to the outcomes of group activity. It covers solutions to problems, changes in interpersonal relations, improving information flow, increased risk taking, interpersonal growth, and organizational change. New in this edition are

- A Practical Tips box on how to get your ideas accepted
- Research on innovators and their willingness to pay a premium for electric vehicles
- Discussion of Toyota's use of continuous-improvement teams to become the world leader implementing organizational change
- Research findings about the impact of team-based learning on improved attitudes
- Research findings showing that students do improve their group interaction skills from taking small group courses
- Examples of Blockbuster and Borders failing to implement organizational change well
- Example of iPhones beating Nokia cell phones as a result of applied organizational change

- Significant changes in top business school curricula moving toward more interpersonal, group, and leadership communication courses as a result of advice from the companies who hire their graduates

Resources for Instructors and Students

A Systems Approach to Small Group Interaction is accompanied by an Online Learning Center (OLC), available at www.mhhe.com/tubbs11e. It contains the following tools to help students comprehend concepts and to assist instructors in managing the course

- Chapter Self-Quizzes allow students to assess their understanding of chapter concepts.
- Animations provide step-by-step explanations of communication models and exercises presented in the textbook.
- Videos dramatize key group communication concepts.
- PowerPoint Tutorial presents the basic steps to create and use PowerPoint effectively in a presentation.
- The instructor's side of the OLC contains the Instructor's Manual, the Test Bank, and PowerPoint slides.

Acknowledgments

I would like to thank the reviewers whose valuable suggestions helped guide each of the eleven editions. They are

Barbara Adler, Concordia College
Timothy Ashmore, Eastern New Mexico University
Barbara Blackstone, Slippery Rock University of Pennsylvania
Daniel Bloomingdale, Penn State University
Terry Chmielewski, University of Wisconsin–Eau Claire
Robert Cocetti, Kearney State College
Michael Cruz, University of Wisconsin–Madison
Dan Curtis, Central Missouri State University
Rolayne S. Destaphen, Sinclair College
Kathleen Edelmayer, St. Mary's College of Ave Maria University
Stephen Fadden, Santa Fe Community College
Richard Fiordo, University of North Dakota
Hank Flick, Mississippi State University
Gene Fowler, University of Colorado
Hal W. Fulmer, Georgia Southern University
Carla Gesell-Streeter, Cincinnati State Technical and Community College
Tim Harper, San Jose City College
William Harpine, University of Akron

James Hasenauer, California State University, Northridge
Dean Kroeker, Biola University
William Krug, Purdue University
Toni MacDonald, Oakland City University
Gail E. Mason, Eastern Illinois University
Julie Morgan, Eastern University
Lisa Newman, University of Cincinnati
Brad Overholser, Hope International University
David L. Palmer, University of Northern Colorado
Brian Polansky, University of Arkansas, Little Rock
Gale Richards, Arizona State University
Harry Russell, Mid-American Nazarene College
Tamela Sadler, Trevecca Nazarene University
Gary Selby, George Washington University
James M. Shull, Jr., Trevecca Nazarene University
Sandra Upton, Cornerstone University
David Walker, Middle Tennessee State University
Mary F. Webster, Benedictine University
Keith Williamson, Temple University
John W. Wilson, Jr., Corpus Christi State University
Julie R. Woodbury, St. Cloud State University
Alan E. Yabui, Bellevue Community College
Raymond Zeuschner, California Polytechnic State University

Finally, I would especially like to thank senior sponsoring editor Deb Hash, project manager Erin Melloy, and design coordinator Margarite Reynolds of McGraw-Hill for their wonderful professional advice and Vivek Khandelwal and Sridevi Palani for their work on the production of the book and website.

Stewart L. Tubbs
Ann Arbor, Michigan

EDITION 11

A Systems Approach to Small Group Interaction

CHAPTER 1

What Is Small Group Interaction?

Preview

Chapter 1 lays the groundwork for the rest of the book. It begins with a definition of *small group interaction*. It includes a section that explains why studying small groups is useful and a section on empowerment. Chapter 1 also introduces systems theory along with a general systems model. The Systems Model of Small Group Interaction identifies three categories of variables: relevant background factors, internal influences, and consequences. Ten general systems concepts that apply to the model are explained briefly.

Glossary

Cycles A cycle is characterized by the results of group interaction being fed back to the group and becoming input for future interactions. For example, a team's success adds strength to the group's cohesion in future activities.

Differentiation Differentiation is the specialization that occurs among people in small group communication.

Dynamic Equilibrium Dynamic equilibrium is reached at the point at which the forces to change and the forces to resist change are equal.

Empowerment Empowerment is a leadership style that enables group members to utilize their talents, abilities, and knowledge more effectively.

Equifinality Equifinality is the potential for adaptation that groups possess. This allows for various possible approaches to achieve a goal.

Feedback Feedback is information groups receive and use to modify themselves.

Input Input is the raw material of small group interaction. It includes six relevant background factors: personality, gender, age, health, attitudes, and values. It also includes information the group receives from outside the group.

Integration Integration in small group communication is synonymous with organization. It is the coordination of the various parts of the group.

Negative Entropy Entropy is characterized by all systems moving toward disorganization or death. Negative entropies are the forces that maintain the organization of a system.

Output Output includes solutions, interpersonal relations, improved information flow, risk taking, interpersonal growth, and organizational change. It is sometimes called the end result of group interaction.

Throughput Throughput refers to all the actual verbal and nonverbal behaviors that occur in the course of a group discussion.

Virtual Teams A virtual team is one in which members communicate with each other through computers and may or may not be located near one another.

CASE STUDY

NFL RANKING EXERCISE

Step 1 Individual Task

Rank order the following National Football League teams according to your perception of their popularity. Later, you will learn how accurate your ranking is based on actual rankings from 2009.

continued

This ranks NFL teams in order of popularity, factoring in local and national television ratings, the amount of traffic the teams' official websites draw and how many times the teams are mentioned on the Internet.

_______________ Chicago Bears
_______________ Dallas Cowboys
_______________ Green Bay Packers
_______________ Indianapolis Colts
_______________ Minnesota Vikings
_______________ New England Patriots
_______________ New Orleans Saints
_______________ New York Giants
_______________ Philadelphia Eagles
_______________ Pittsburgh Steelers

Step 2

On a scale from 1 (not at all confident) to 5 (very confident), rate how confident you are in your individual rankings.

_______ 1 _______ 2 _______ 3 _______ 4 _______ 5

Step 3 Group Task

Now rank order the National Football League teams as a group of five people.

_______________ Chicago Bears
_______________ Dallas Cowboys
_______________ Green Bay Packers
_______________ Indianapolis Colts
_______________ Minnesota Vikings
_______________ New England Patriots
_______________ New Orleans Saints
_______________ New York Giants
_______________ Philadelphia Eagles
_______________ Pittsburgh Steelers

Step 4

Your instructor has the actual rankings. Compare your individual rank score to the actual rank for each team and subtract your rank from the actual rank, ignoring whether it is a plus or minus number. Then total the difference scores. For example: 2 − 1 = 1

10 − 3 = 7

1 + 7 = 8

Step 5

Repeat step 4 using the group rankings.

Step 6

Add the individual scores and divide by the number of people in the group to find the average difference score for individuals.

Step 7

Compare the average individual score to the group score. The smaller score is better.

Which was better, the average individual score or the group score?

Discuss why you think this happened. Do you think these results are typical of the difference between average individual scores and group scores? Why or why not?

Step 8

Compare your individual ranking difference scores to your individual level of confidence, keeping in mind that the lower the ranking difference scores (when compared to the actual scores), the better your answers.

How do the individual confidence scores compare to the accuracy of the individual scores?

Discuss the differences between individual and group problem solving.

How to Use Case Studies

The case study method originated many years ago at Harvard Medical School. At the end of each week, physicians shared their most interesting and challenging cases that week to help teach each other from their first-hand experiences. The case studies in this book are designed to stimulate student discussion and to illustrate the very rich nature of the principles of small group interaction in the real world. We encourage you to read each case and to use it to help you bridge the gap between the theoretical concepts in each chapter and their very practical applications. You will soon learn that there is almost no limit to the variety and complexity of the challenges of small group interaction. As you have seen from just the first case, it is truly a fascinating subject.

Source: David Biderman, "The Popularity Index," *The Wall Street Journal*, Thursday, September 9, 2010, p. D10.

The opening case study powerfully illustrates just one powerful example of the influence that groups can have on our behavior and on our lives. In fact, a major comprehensive national study of college and university experiences concluded that, "Undergraduate education is fundamentally a social experience" (Arum & Roksa, 2011, p. 59) and that 51 percent of college students' time is spent socializing, compared to only 9 percent attending classes (p. 97). So, small groups play an incredibly important part in shaping college students' lives. Furthermore, the Gallup Organization has collected data on millions of adults in 132 countries and has found that "each hour of social time quickly decreases the odds of having a bad day" (Rath & Harter, 2010, p. 39). It has been astonishing to see the growth of interest in small groups and teams since the last edition of this book. In fact, the editor of one professional journal reports that she had more research articles submitted on the subject of groups or teams (24 percent) between 2007–2009 than any other research topic! Leadership was secondmost (17 percent), and both of these topics are covered in this book (Morrison, 2010, p. 934). More and more people and organizations are coming to the realization that teams are the way of the future.

You may be interested to know that this book is the product of a virtual team. It began with the author, who is located in Ann Arbor, Michigan, providing a proposal to the editors located in New York City. They contacted reviewers, who are very knowledgeable about the subject and who teach in universities all over the world. The reviewers had several telephone conferences discussing things that students liked and disliked about the previous edition of this book. These telephone conferences were recorded and provided to the author. Once the manuscript was completed, utilizing the inputs from the reviewers, students, and editors, and up-to-date information from sources worldwide, it was sent to production facilities in Burr Ridge, Illinois. Ultimately, the books were manufactured and warehoused in Blacklick, Ohio. Meanwhile marketing materials were sent to sales representatives all over the world. In fact, the author once presented a paper at a conference in Taiwan and met the local McGraw-Hill representative there. If you look at the title page, you will see the major cities that have regional offices all over the world. The author is greatly indebted to all the members of this virtual team, yet he has never met face to face with any one of them! All our communication has been via email, telephone, or in a very few cases regular (snail) mail.

In this book, we will be looking at many group situations. Beginning with our family group and continuing throughout our lives, groups have a very significant impact on all of us. As you read this book, you should gain a great deal of information that will help you function more effectively in your groups and on your teams.

A Definition

If you were going to define the term *small group interaction,* how would you do it? First, you would probably want to consider size. Would two people constitute a group? How about 50 people? Most (although not all) experts agree that a group consists of at least three people. Because this book is about small groups, we can arbitrarily consider *small* to range from 3 to about 15 people. Lencioni (2007) suggests a range of 3 to 12.

Although companies and groups are different entities, they are correlated in some ways. Both contain members working together to accomplish goals. Now the important question is, does size matter? According to a recent poll of 2,000 top executives and managers, 54 percent of people in small companies (fewer than 50 employees) like their jobs a lot, versus 44 percent of people in big companies (1,000+ employees). This is analogous to group size. It seems to imply that members of smaller groups, like members of smaller companies, are more content (Coy, 2007b).

But size is only one consideration. Forsyth (2009) has proposed five different considerations in identifying a group. They are (1) interaction (Do group members communicate with each other?), (2) structure (How are the members organized into certain roles, such as moderator and note taker?), (3) Group cohesion (How strongly do the members feel a sense of unity?), (4) social identity (Do the group members share a perception of being members of the group? Is this membership important to their self-identity?), and (5) goals (What is it that the group is working to accomplish?). A group may be defined in any of the above ways.

What do we mean by *interaction?* Interaction simply means communication. This includes talking and listening, head nods, gestures, glances, pats on the back, smiles, frowns, and any other behavior to which people assign meaning. Because communication occurs in an ever-changing context, we use the term *process* of communication. The process of communication is often compared to a movie or a video as opposed to a snapshot of group behavior. In fact, these days most people agree that the speed of the video seems to be increasing.

To summarize, *small group interaction* is the process by which three or more members of a group exchange verbal and nonverbal messages in an attempt to influence one another.

What is the difference between a group and a team? The term *group* is more general. A team is a type of group. Francis and Young (1992) define a *team* as "a high-performing task group whose members are actively interdependent and share common performance objectives" (p. 9). The word *team* also has come to connote closer cooperation and cohesiveness than the term *group.* So when we use the word *team,* it implies closeness as well as cooperation.

It is important to study teams. However, this is not what usually happens. Managers spend 50 percent or more of their time in meetings, but Bain & Company research shows that two-thirds of meetings end before participants can make important decisions. Not surprisingly, 85 percent of survey respondents are dissatisfied with the efficiency and effectiveness of their companies' meetings, according to Blenko, Mankins, and Rogers (2010).

This finding is but one reason that Harvard Business School is changing their MBA curriculum to offer more courses teaching teamwork. Companies hiring their graduates say that team skills, even from Harvard graduates, are not as good as they need to be in the workplace (Middleton & Light, 2011, p. B8).

A handbook of career tips contains the following observation: "As we move into the next millennium, individual effort is still critical, but the nature of work has changed. The one-person show has given way to casts of tens, hundreds, even thousands of brain-powered workers required for massive, technically complex projects. We are in the 'we millennium.'"

VIRTUAL TEAMS

A *virtual team* is one that does not meet face-to-face but works through electronic means. Because virtual teams are becoming so popular, multinational companies are now hiring sociologists to unlock the secrets of teamwork among colleagues who have never met. This will become an important field of study as teams continue to meet as one virtual team regardless of location. Soon we may all have team members and even managers and subordinates in other countries! We'll need to learn and understand how to adapt to these changes (Engardio, 2007).

Virtual teams are forming everywhere in response to the increasingly popular question, "How quickly are you able to do it for me?" Cisco is following the trend. According to Cisco CEO John Chambers, "Those companies that capitalize on virtualized resources, such as access to information, access to other potential virtual team members, and swift problem solving to achieve an immediate goal, will become part of virtual teams that lead Cisco and other companies in the future." This means that tasks that used to take Cisco 45 days of intense information gathering and meetings now take only 8 days thanks to electronic interactions, social networking resources, and virtual teams (Babcock, 2007).

Another sign that virtual teams are increasing in number can be found in a *BusinessWeek* poll. According to a poll of 2,000 executives and managers, 9 percent of Americans are currently on a first-name basis with someone who works in India. This may not seem like a lot now, but the prediction is that in 10 years 30 percent of us will be on a first-name basis with someone in India. This implies that we are going to be doing a lot of teaming with India (and many other countries). This means that virtual teams will become the norm rather than the exception (Coy, 2007a).

Communication is an important aspect to every group and every business. Companies are always thinking of new ways to improve communication. One recent term is collaboratory. A collaboratory, as defined by William Wulf (1989), is a "center without walls, in which team members can collaborate without regard to physical location, interacting with colleagues, accessing instrumentation, sharing data and computational resources, accessing information in digital libraries" (Armano, 2010). Would you believe that video games could be the next communication gap filler? According to *BusinessWeek,* companies like Johnson and Johnson are using online games to improve internal communications. They're hoping that the games will strengthen the team environment and promote increased communication.

In spite of all the progress, that some team projects will fail is inevitable. However, forward-thinking teams have devised a way to help improve a project's chances of success! According to an article in the *Harvard Business Review,* teams are now performing what they call a *premortem,* which helps teams identify risks at the outset. A premortem is the hypothetical opposite of a postmortem.

Whereas a postmortem is a medical exam that takes place after a patient's death, so that professionals and family members can learn what caused the death, a premortem enables team members to assess the situation before the actual death (or failure) has occurred. For example, in a business-setting premortem, a team can assume that the project they are planning has already failed and then generate as many reasons for the failure as possible. They then use the hypothetical reasons to help the team avoid those pitfalls in the actual project! The premortem exercise can actually help silent members of a team speak up before problems happen, which in turn will help strengthen the team itself (Klein, 2007).

Suffice it to say that virtual teams are going to be an increasingly important part of our lives from now on.

WHY STUDY SMALL GROUPS?

One recent book lists the problems that many people have with meetings:

1. They're usually about abstract concepts, not real things.
2. They usually convey an abysmally small amount of information per minute.
3. They drift off-subject easier than a Chicago cab in a snowstorm.
4. They require preparation that takes time that people don't have.
5. Their agendas are too vague.
6. They usually include one person who wastes everybody else's time.
7. They procreate. One meeting leads to another, etc. (Fried & Hansson, 2010, p. 108)

Modern organizations are undergoing a radical transformation designed to better utilize human potential, primarily through the increased use of small groups. Just in the past few years, the U.S. Department of Labor has identified teamwork as one of five workplace skills that should be taught more aggressively in schools (LaFasto & Larson, 2001, p. xvii). In another article, Taylor (2010) reports on a survey of nearly 500 employers who report that the top job skills found to be lacking are (1) communication, (2) critical thinking, specifically critical thinking, problem-solving skills, and the ability to think independently, and (3) valuing a strong work ethic. As a result, several universities are changing their curriculum to strengthen emphasis on these skills. Some of the universities include Harvard, MIT, George Washington University, Villanova, and the University of California, San Francisco. Pfeffer and Fong (2002) argue that most universities, especially business schools, "have an overemphasis on analysis at the expense of both integration and developing wisdom as well as leadership and interpersonal skills" (p. 80). According to a poll by *BusinessWeek,* 9 out of the top 25 best companies for entry-level employment listed communication/leadership skills as the desirable trait for new hires (Gerdes, 2007). A further article, by Fernandez-Araoz (1999), offers some of the questions that must be asked when hiring new employees for any kind of organization: "Describe a time you led a team to be more effective. What did you do? How did the team and the organization benefit from your actions? Describe a time you were asked to lead a particularly challenging team project. How did you overcome the obstacles you faced?" (p. 119). These questions indicate the importance of knowing how to work successfully in small groups or teams.

According to a *Wall Street Journal* survey of employers, the following were the most highly valued attributes that recruiters were seeking in people that they wanted to hire (Safon, 2007):

Communication and interpersonal skills	89%
Ability to work well in teams	87%
Analytical and problem-solving skills	84%
Leadership potential	73%

All of these attributes will be discussed in this book.

The Gallup Organization surveyed the attitudes of over 1 million workers and 80,000 managers and reported in Buckingham and Coffman (1999) that employees of all types of organizations, both for-profit and not-for-profit, are looking for work in which they can play a meaningful role through decentralized decision making involving teams. We all want our opinions to count.

According to the book *Mobs, Messiahs, and Markets,* "Scientific studies show that our brains are hardwired to work best in small groups. Smaller groups foster greater cooperation and mutual trust, according to simple rules of conduct and easily understood hierarchies. In larger groups, however, everything changes: The crowd mentality takes over" (Rajiva & Bonner, 2007, p. 7).

In your lifetime, and in your career, you will undoubtedly be very much affected by these organizational changes. The exciting thing about all this is that the world of work will be more enriching and interesting than it was for your parents' generation. However, the challenge is for you to improve your proficiency in small group situations. This book is dedicated to that end.

In over 30 years of college teaching, the one question that I have heard most from students is, "How can I become a success?" Students are often surprised by the answers. The effective use of small groups has been found to be essential to career success. After an extensive examination of successful people, Whetton and Cameron (2010) identified what they consider the nine most important skills required for career success:

1. Developing self-awareness
2. Managing personal stress
3. Solving problems analytically and creatively
4. Coaching, counseling, and establishing supportive communication
5. Gaining power and influence
6. Motivating others

PRACTICAL TIPS

Ron Ashkenas, writing in the *Harvard Business Review Daily Alert* (2010), argues that group meetings meet three basic human needs. He writes,

> ***They encourage social interaction.*** *Most people don't enjoy working alone; they want contact and relationships with other people. Meetings make them feel part of a community, and give them an outlet for sharing their personal feelings and opinions, not only on work issues but also on personal or political topics.*
>
> ***They keep everyone in the loop.*** *As firms have become more matrixed and interdependent, meetings serve as the informal loom that weaves together the organizational threads. People need to know what's going on in other parts of the organization.*
>
> ***They often represent status.*** *Membership on multiple committees means that you are important, your opinion is valued, and you have a seat at a decision-making table. Attendance means that you are part of the leadership team.*
>
> *These psychological drivers of meetings are very powerful—and usually trump all of the logical and rational "meeting management" advice that is doled out in courses and articles. In other words, what seems like wasted or unproductive time for many managers is actually fulfilling important personal and organizational needs.*

7. Empowering and delegating
8. Managing conflict
9. Building effective teams and teamwork

All nine of these topics are covered in this book. In other words, this book is devoted to improving your understanding of the major action skills required for career success. However, the important thing to remember is that we are talking about utilizing these as behavioral skills, not just knowing about them. Like all skills, development begins with new information and proceeds with practice, and more practice, with continual modification and improvement based on feedback from previous performance.

Small groups can help you in college as well as in your career. For example, Fiske (1990) reported a Harvard University study conducted at 21 universities that showed that students who study in small groups learn more effectively than those who don't. Also, small group study experiences correlate with overall satisfaction in college (p. A1). In another set of studies, Cooper (1998) states the following: "The meta-analysis shows that small-group learning promotes greater student involvement, increased student achievement, increased persistence through courses and programs, and more favorable learning-related attitudes" (p. 3). For years the Harvard Business School has required that its students form study groups and remain in those groups throughout the course. This makes sense, as the Connecticut General Life Insurance Company found that the average employee spends over 700 hours a year in meetings—that is, almost two out of every five working days are spent in small group meetings.

TABLE 1.1 The Value of People's Time

Yearly Salary	Weekly Salary	Weekly Benefits (40% of Total Salary)	Weekly Total	Value per Hour	Value per Minute
$ 10,000	$ 192.31	$ 76.92	$ 269.23	$ 6.73	$0.11
20,000	384.62	153.85	538.47	13.46	0.22
30,000	576.92	230.77	807.69	20.19	0.34
40,000	769.23	307.69	1,076.92	26.92	0.45
50,000	961.54	348.62	1,346.16	33.65	0.56
60,000	1,153.85	461.54	1,615.39	40.38	0.67
70,000	1,346.15	538.46	1,884.61	47.12	0.79
80,000	1,538.46	615.38	2,153.84	53.85	0.90
90,000	1,730.77	692.31	2,423.08	60.58	1.01
100,000	1,923.08	769.23	2,692.31	67.31	1.12

Learning to work effectively in small groups can save you time and money. Table 1.1 shows the value of people's time as their salaries increase. If we can learn to improve our meeting effectiveness and thus cut the number and length of meetings, it can yield measurable savings. Westinghouse reportedly installed electronic numerical keypads in meeting rooms and had each group member enter his or her salary into the computer as he or she came into the room. The computer then gave a continuous readout of the cost of the meeting as time went on. Over a few months' time, corporatewide, Westinghouse cut its meeting times in half simply by making participants aware of the cost of each meeting and the cost of each person's comments. Evidently, this feedback made people weigh the real value of their comments and encouraged them to waste less time.

Leaders are increasingly learning to improve their use of small groups to achieve organizational goals. Few leaders in today's complex society can succeed on their own, without the help of competent and committed team members.

Daniel Pink writes in his best-selling book *Drive* (2009) that hiring decisions are often made by leaders in cooperation with employee teams (he calls them "grouplets"). Other organizations like Whole Foods; W. L. Gore & Associates, the makers of GORE-TEX fabric; and Google are actively involving teams of future colleagues in the hiring decisions. Universities have been doing this for decades. Research has shown that teams that organize themselves achieve superior results compared to "inherited" teams. One significant advantage of using teams is not only the improved quality of the decisions, but also the increased motivation of group members to do their best on the job (Pink, 2009, pp. 104–106).

In another study, employees who were seen acting like "the Lone Ranger" on the job often failed, while those who excelled at building teams early in their time on the job succeeded (Louis, 1990). Clearly, more and more organizations are moving toward a stronger emphasis on teamwork. In fact, many believe that to get a job within the next few years you will need to have some team-based experience on your résumé.

TABLE 1.2 Individualism versus Collectivism in Selected Countries

Individualism Score*	Country	Individualism Score*	Country
91	United States	53	Spain
90	Australia	48	India
89	Great Britain	46	Japan
77	Canada	46	Argentina
75	Denmark	38	Brazil
74	Italy	32	Mexico
74	Belgium	25	Hong Kong
71	Sweden	20	Singapore
70	Switzerland	17	Taiwan
70	France	16	Venezuela
55	Israel		

*Highest individualism score = 100.
Source: Frank L. Acuff, *How to Negotiate Anything with Anyone Anywhere Around the World* (New York: American Management Association, 1997), p. 70. Reprinted by permission of the American Management Association.

As you read further in this book, you will find that a strong understanding of group dynamics and the skills to use that understanding will be among the most important factors in your success as a leader and as a person. Although this book is primarily about problem-solving groups, its focus is broader than that. The lessons presented here also apply to your friendship groups, your family, and your classroom groups.

Just in case you think that these skills are easy to acquire, Acuff (1997) found in his research that Americans are the most individualistic and least team-oriented culture in the world. Therefore, it is harder for Americans to work together in teams than it is for any of the other nationalities he studied. His findings are presented in Table 1.2.

Empowerment

Modern organizations are basing multibillion-dollar decisions, in part, on the use of teams. Among the many companies using teams are Google, Apple, IDEO, Westinghouse, Toyota, Ford, General Electric, General Mills, and AT&T. More and more organizations are moving toward greater teamwork and empowerment in an all-out attempt to remain competitive in today's global economy. Your own future jobs and career no doubt will be dramatically affected by this national trend.

Empowerment is a leadership style that enables the leader more effectively to utilize the talents, abilities, and knowledge of others and, at the same time, to increase his or her available time to work on more strategic activities, rather than on "putting out fires." Stephen Covey (1991) writes:

> Empowerment basically means, "Give a man a fish and you feed him for a day. Teach him how to fish and you feed him for a lifetime." When you fully empower people, your paradigm of yourself changes. You become a servant. You no longer control others; they control themselves. You become a source of help to them (p. 256).

Team empowerment mediates the relationships of team context and team atmosphere with job satisfaction and organizational commitment. Better outcomes will be achieved when team members perceive a supportive team atmosphere and an empowering team context with clear and jointly developed goals, an appropriate mix of skills and expertise, and rewards linked to team performance (Proenca, 2007).

At Tropicana Products, Inc., in Bradenton, Florida, sales employees have been empowered to conduct promotions analyses that had previously been conducted at much higher levels in the company. Using online information, employees can analyze external data gathered from checkout scanners at retail grocery stores. This is an attempt to move decision making downward in the organization and to better utilize employees (Portnoy, 1992).

Empowerment has certain inherent advantages. For example, it leads to greater productivity, quicker responses to problems, improved quality of communication

PRACTICAL TIPS

Being in a small group isn't as easy as it sounds. Sometimes working in a group is harder than working toward the goal. Although many teams succeed, many others fail. According to research done by Don Carew and Eunice Parisi-Carew over the past 10 years, these are the top 10 reasons most teams fail:

1. Lack of a sufficient charter that defines the team's purpose and how it will work together to achieve that purpose
2. Inability to decide what constitutes the work for which team members are interdependent and mutually accountable
3. Lack of mutual accountability
4. Lack of resources to do the job, including time
5. Lack of effective leadership and lack of shared leadership
6. Lack of norms that foster creativity and excellence
7. Lack of planning
8. Lack of management support
9. Inability to deal with conflict
10. Lack of training on all levels on group skills

Keep in mind that these reasons aren't included here to discourage teams from forming; they're simply here to remind team members of what to avoid so they don't make the same common mistakes as many other teams (Blanchard, 2007, pp. 169–70).

between groups, increased individual motivation, and improved overall organizational effectiveness.

Empowering employees also works best if they are held accountable for their decisions. Connors and Smith (2011) suggests four practical ways to encourage accountability through empowerment.

1. *See it.* Look for ways to improve the way work processes can be improved.
2. *Own it.* Take the initiative and the responsibility for fixing the poor practice.
3. *Solve it.* Find a solution, then ask your boss, "What else can I do?"
4. *Do it.* Practice the new process until it becomes "the new normal." (pp. 22–23)

On the other hand, there are some potential challenges and disadvantages as well. Empowerment can cause frustration, since traditional sources of authority have been changed. Ambiguity as to who is responsible for what can also occur. New behaviors must be learned, new relations between groups must be established, and new levels of trust must be developed. Covey (1991) writes, "Technique is relatively unimportant compared to trust, which is the result of our [behaviors] over time. When trust is high, we communicate easily, effortlessly, instantaneously. We can make mistakes and others will still capture our meaning. But when trust is low, communication is exhausting, time-consuming, ineffective, and inordinately difficult" (p. 18). (See also Kouzes & Posner, 2010.)

Kirkman and Rosen (1999) studied 112 teams in four organizations. They wanted to see if empowerment was an important factor in the teams' success. They found strong support for the notion that empowerment does in fact lead to better team outcomes. They also found evidence that empowerment has four very closely related dimensions:

1. *Potency.* This means that teams feel that they have some degree of power to accomplish a goal.
2. *Meaningfulness.* This refers to a team's experiencing its tasks as important, valuable, and worthwhile.
3. *Autonomy.* This is the degree to which team members experience freedom, independence, and discretion in conducting their business.
4. *Impact.* This is when a team produces work that they feel is significant.

A Conceptual Orientation for Small Groups

Small group interaction is very complicated and involves a large number of factors that act and interact simultaneously. In addition, these factors are in a continual state of flux. Think of the difficulty of trying to describe and analyze all the behaviors that occur at just one party! We have all been to parties that generated far more reactions than we would have imagined. Any attempt to provide a conceptual orientation for small group interaction or any social process must be highly simplified.

GENERAL SYSTEMS APPROACH

Scholars in many disciplines are becoming increasingly aware that situations in the world, and even in small groups, are influenced within complex systems of forces. For example, since ethanol has been used as a supplement to gasoline (to reduce dependence on foreign oil), the price of the corn used to make ethanol has skyrocketed, sending a ripple effect through the economy and increasing the cost of everything from beef cattle (which eat corn) to all other corn-based products. These effects were mostly unanticipated by those trying to improve fuel economy.

In another example, Tom Brokaw, the famous NBC news anchor, writes in his 2007 best-selling book *Boom!* that many of the social and political trends in the current decade grew out of the 1960s and the values shaped during the Vietnam War era. Even the important topic of ethics is now being viewed as occurring in a system of social forces (see, for example, Stanwick & Stanwick, 2009).

The remainder of this book is organized around the idea that small group interaction can most adequately be thought of as occurring in a system of interdependent forces, each of which can be analyzed and set in relation to other forces. This idea represents a so-called general systems theory of thinking about small groups.

The general systems theory originated with Ludwig von Bertalanffy, a theoretical biologist, as a way to think about and study the constant, dynamic adjustments of living phenomena. An *open system* such as a group is defined as an organized set of interrelated and interacting parts that attempts to maintain its own balance amid the influences of its surrounding environment.

Another example of the systems approach is the rise in the use of rapid-delivery systems such as UPS and Fedex Office on account of the rapid increase of e-commerce. As more and more people order goods over the Internet, these rapid-delivery firms have experienced an explosive growth in their businesses. In fact, some investment experts believe that investing in these companies is the surest way to make money from the Internet (Bott, 1999).

Finally, as suggested by the open systems model, the consequences, or outputs, of the group are fed back into the system through the feedback loop. The example of United Airlines Flight 93 on September 11, 2001, demonstrates the power of feedback. If the passengers had not learned of the earlier suicide crashes into the World Trade Center buildings and the Pentagon, a group of them might not have taken any action to overcome the hijackers (Beamer, 2002). To read more details about this story and the members of the group, log onto http://www.cnn.com/2001/US/09/12/plane.phone.call/.

Katz and Kahn (1978) describe an open system this way: "Activities can be examined in relation to the *input* into the system, the *transformation of energies within the system,* and the *resulting product* or *output*" (italics added; p. 17). They also say that "our theoretical model for the understanding of [social] organizations is that of an input–output system in which the return from the output reactivates the system" (p. 16). Adams and colleagues (1999) put it this way: "Our challenge became to blend the best ideas, concepts, and practices, regardless of their origin, into an overall approach that actually produced the enduring changes and outcomes that both theorists and practitioners envisioned . . . the Whole Systems Approach" (pp. 54–55). (This entire process of multiple causation is indicated by the two-headed arrows in the Tubbs Model of Small Group Interaction—see

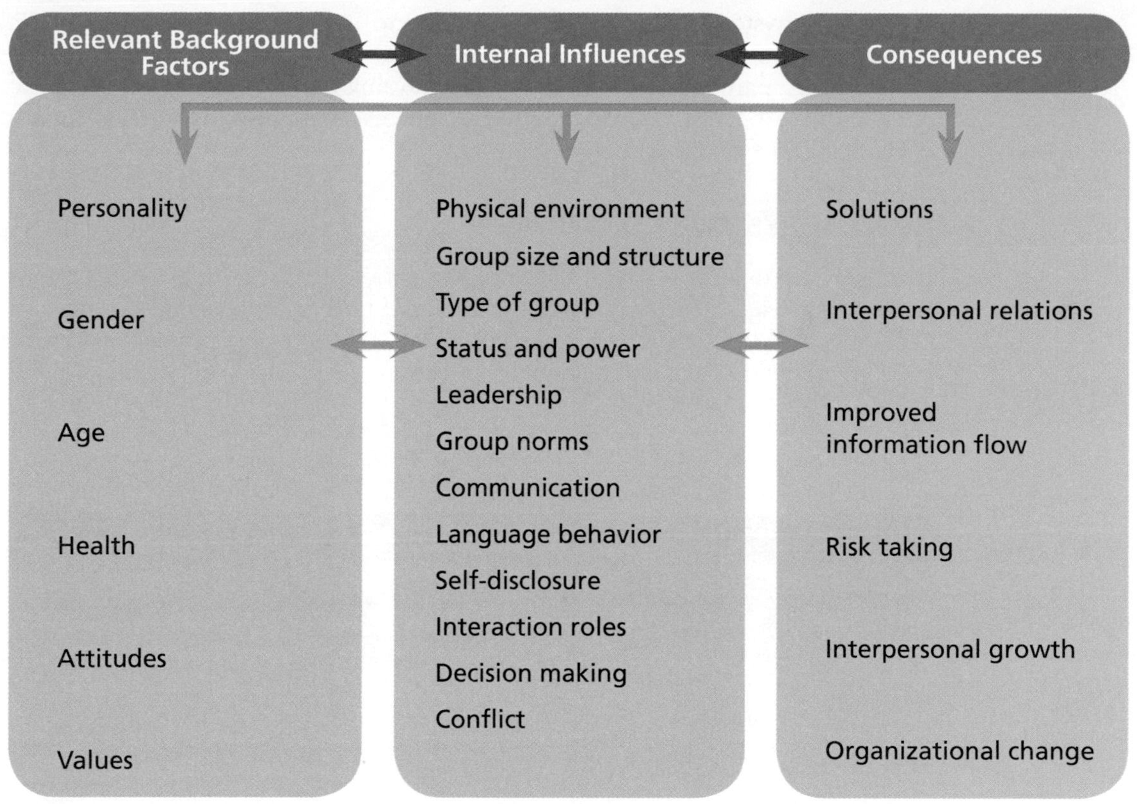

FIGURE 1.1 The Tubbs Model of Small Group Interaction

Figure 1.1.) Keep in mind that the model appears to be static, like a photograph. But in reality, small group behaviors are like a movie, with each of the parts *moving* in relation to the others.

Brooks (2011) puts it well when he describes systems as follows:

> Emergent systems exist when different elements . . . produce something that is greater than the sum of the parts. . . . out of their interaction something entirely new emerges. For example, air and water come together, and sometimes a hurricane emerges. Sounds and syllables come together and produce a story that has an emotional power that is irreducible to its parts (p. 109).

Different levels of systems analysis and the type of system studied include:

- Astronomy—universal systems
- Ecology—planetary systems
- Political science—political systems
- Sociology—social systems
- Psychology—human systems
- Physiology—organ systems
- Molecular biology—microscopic systems

General systems theory has been applied to many different fields of study, including biology, engineering, mathematics, and psychiatry. Systems analysis has become a particularly popular way of analyzing human behavior in organizations and has been described in several sources (Katz & Kahn, 1978; Hughes et al., 2006; Kusy & Holloway, 2009).

GENERAL SYSTEMS CONCEPTS

With some of this background in mind, let us look briefly at 10 general systems concepts that apply to small group communication and are suggested by our general systems model (Katz & Kahn, 1978, pp. 23–30). All processes consist of a cycle of inputs that lead to outputs, or outcomes.

CASE STUDY

THE SYSTEMS APPROACH IN AN AIRLINE COMPANY

Researchers at the Gallup Organization have found that organizations are a complex set of systems. The way employees are treated by their leaders is reflected in the ways that they treat customers. Customers who are treated well tend to come back. When customers are loyal and make repeated purchases, the company's financial health increases. In other words, leadership behaviors are leading indicators of success, and financial results are lagging indicators.

For example, one U.S. airline was aggressively trying to increase revenues and passenger market share while also managing costs and achieving operational goals such as percentage of on-time arrivals. The advertising department was working on increasing passenger volume. They launched an ambitious advertising campaign designed to fill more airplane seats, which turned out to be extremely successful. They claimed to be "New and Improved," with better service, friendlier flight attendants, better foods, and faster lines at the airport.

However, this ad campaign was a complete surprise to the airline's in-flight and operations employees. They received no advance notice, training, funding, or resources to achieve the advertised results. Since they had had staff cuts, they were already stretched too thin. The result was an even bigger gap between customer expectations and the actual services performed. This sudden increase in customer volume, combined with reduced flight and ground crews and inadequate catering, created a terrible experience for passengers. The result was even greater customer dissatisfaction and eventual bankruptcy for the airline (Fleming & Asplund, 2007).

The authors conclude that "customers do not experience your company through a series of corporate functions; instead, they experience it through a series of processes. A *process* is defined as 'a series of steps or activities that take inputs, add value, and produce an output'" (Fleming & Asplund, 2007, p. 230; see also de Janasz, Dowd, & Schneider, 2009).

Input. *Input* refers to the raw material of small group interaction. It includes all six of the relevant background factors depicted in the model (see Figure 1.1). It also includes information the group receives from outside the group. For example, problem-solving group members in the midst of a discussion may notice that they are running short on time. This new information will probably influence the group to change procedures (for example, to stop talking about side issues) and focus more directly or efficiently on solving the problem at hand. Chapter 3 discusses relevant background factors in greater depth.

A system that has inputs from outside is called an *open system*. An open system is said to interact with its environment, as opposed to remaining isolated. Gross (1995, p. 113) identifies four phenomena characteristic of open systems:

1. Entries and exits, which transform outsiders into members and members into outsiders.
2. Multiple membership, which results in members' loyalties to outside groups.
3. Resource exchange, which involves the absorption of inputs in the production process and in the delivery of output produced.
4. Mutual or reciprocal influence on the part of both members and outsiders.

Anyone who has ever felt torn between two different groups will be able to understand the relevance of Gross's four points.

Throughput. *Throughput* refers to the internal influences depicted in our model. It means all of the actual verbal and nonverbal behaviors that occur during a group discussion. It includes the process of creating and modifying ideas in the course of a discussion. Throughput is the heart, and in some cases the entirety, of what most small group communication books discuss. Chapters 2 and 4–7 discuss these variables in detail.

Output. *Output* refers to the consequences section of our model. Outputs are sometimes called the end results of group interaction. However, as we shall soon see, end results imply a beginning and an end, which is somewhat misleading, because groups often have an ongoing life history, during which these outputs, or consequences, are continually being modified on the basis of continuing interaction. Chapter 8 is devoted to discussing the consequences, or outputs, of small group interaction.

Cycles. Often the outputs of group interaction are fed back to the group and become inputs for future interactions. For example, a severe personality conflict in one meeting of a group may reduce the level of cohesiveness or interpersonal closeness of group members. As a result, some members may refuse to attend future meetings, some may attend but will not participate as openly, and some may try harder the next time to be more diplomatic in their remarks in order to avoid a recurrence of the conflict. The arrows at the top of our model (see again Figure 1.1) indicate what is commonly called a *feedback loop*. This loop represents the cyclical and ongoing nature of group processes and also implies that the process does not begin and end anew with each group meeting, but rather builds on all the past experiences of each group member.

Negative Entropy. The entropic process is a universal law of nature in which all systems eventually move toward disorganization or death. Recently, we have seen the entropic process overtake hundreds of dot-com companies, several airlines, several hundred banks, Bear Stearns, Hudson's Department Stores, and many other organizations. To combat the process of disorganization and/or death, a system must employ negative entropy. If you have ever been in a meeting that seemed to be completely out of control and was a total waste of time, you know how easily entropy can overtake a group.

Max DePree (1989), former chairman of the board of Herman Miller Furniture Company, writes:

> Some months ago, I was on what is known in the financial industry as a "dog and pony show." Our team was in Boston making a presentation to some sophisticated financial analysts. After the presentation and during the question-and-answer period, one of the analysts said to me, "What is one of the most difficult things that you personally need to work on?" He seemed very surprised when I said, "The interception of entropy."
>
> I am using the word "entropy" in a loose way, because technically it has to do with the second law of thermodynamics. From a corporate management point of view, I choose to define it as meaning that everything has a tendency to deteriorate. One of the important things leaders need to learn is to recognize the signals of impending deterioration (p. 98).

Feedback. All systems must receive feedback to modify themselves. Think of a bowling game in which you saw the ball go down the lane and through a black cover, and you never saw which pins you hit and never heard the sound of the ball striking the pins. You would never play a second game. Or imagine going to school year after year and never getting an assignment or any grades or comments from an instructor. We all want feedback on our performance. In a rather amusing example of how feedback can modify a group's behavior, the City Council of Boise, Idaho, decided to change its meetings from Monday nights to Tuesday nights because of *Monday Night Football*. The council had been meeting on Monday nights since 1929. However, because the public turnout was so poor, the council decided to modify its meeting time in response to the feedback that the televised football games were just too much competition. (As of 2011, NFL football games were the highest rated television shows on record.)

Dynamic Equilibrium. Management and labor have reached an unspoken agreement in virtually every organization on what constitutes "a fair day's work for a fair day's pay." This is an example of an equilibrium. Similarly, students and teachers often negotiate throughout the course of a term. However, should students fail to read their assignments, teachers will often react by throwing "pop" quizzes, thus upsetting the equilibrium. Once the students change their performance, equilibrium returns. Similarly, when an organization finds itself losing market share or profit margins, it often has to upset the fair-day's-work-for-a-fair-day's-pay equilibrium. One year General Motors decided to eliminate the cost of living allowance (COLA) for its salaried workers. This seemed to change the "fair day's pay" side of the equation. Salaried employees decided not to work so hard, thus restoring their feeling of equilibrium. In groups, we each decide whether membership is worth what we are putting into it. If not, we slack off and may even eventually quit the group to find one that more nearly meets our sense of equilibrium. In another example of the dynamic nature of business, according to a survey conducted by Penton Publishers, each day in the United States, 2,621 corporations go out of business or are acquired, 3,196 are formed, 1,984 change addresses, 704 change phone numbers, and 8 change names. If you would like to learn more about this, see www.penton.com.

Differentiation. Ever since the Industrial Revolution began, organizations have become increasingly more specialized. It is no longer adequate to have generalists; organizations must now have specialists in production, inspection, materials handling, transportation, legal affairs, accounting, payroll, sales, engineering, plant layout, maintenance, management information systems, distribution, service, real estate, finance, public relations, and labor relations, for example. In groups, we also see different people gravitating toward certain roles. In addition, it is a rare group in which all members' attitudes are the same toward any topic.

Denison, Hart, and Kahn (1996) found that as organizations get larger, they become more and more decentralized and, ironically, participation in decision making increases because of the increased need for individual departments to work independently of one another.

Integration. As groups and organizations become more complex and differentiated, the need for integration and coordination of the various parts increases. Without integration, the group or organization becomes chaotic. Imagine being in a hospital in which the lab results or X rays couldn't be communicated to the physician for interpretation or the pharmacy couldn't get your prescription in order to obtain your medication. Or worse yet, imagine a scenario in which the emergency room wasn't accessible because the driveways were blocked for repair. In groups, if too many subgroups talk at once, coordination soon breaks down, as it does if each person is trying to follow a different agenda (or no agenda). Integration, then, is synonymous with organizing.

Equifinality. You have undoubtedly heard the expression "There is more than one way to skin a cat." This expression captures part of the meaning of the concept of *equifinality:* Although two groups may have different members, leadership styles, decision-making methods, and so on, they may still arrive at the same solution to a given problem. There is an incredibly large number of combinations of all the variables in our small group model. These combinations may in some cases interact in such a way as to produce the same group consequences, but from dramatically different processes. Conversely, two groups may use the same

Homans (1950)	External system		Internal system	
Stogdill (1959)	Member inputs	Mediating variables	Resultant variables	
Thibaut and Kelley (1959)	Exogenous variables	Endogenous variables	Resultant variables	
McGrath and Altman (1966)	Properties of group members	Conditions imposed on group	Interaction process	Performance
Kibler and Barker (1969)	Antecedents	Messages	Consequences	
Fisher (1971)	Inputs	Mediating variables	Outputs	
Gouran (1973)	Context of communication	Communication behaviors	Group outcomes	
Tubbs (1978, 2012)	Relevant background factors ↔	Internal influences ↔	Consequences	
Brilhart and Galanes (1992)	Input	Throughput	Output	
Hughes et al. (1993)	Input	Process	Output	
Wilson and Hanna (1993)	Inputs	Processes	Outputs	
Ellis and Fisher (1994)	Entry elements	Process elements	Outcomes	
Denison, Hart, and Kahn (1996)	Context	Process	Outcomes	

FIGURE 1.2 Synthesis of Group Models

procedures but end up with different outcomes. Thus, equifinality refers to both the unpredictability and potential for adaptation of groups.

The systems approach is used in all types of professional fields, including biology. However, for many people, the systems approach is challenging. Take, for example, Dr. Roger M. Perlmutter, the mastermind behind R&D at Amgen, the world's number-one biotech company. When asked about the challenges of the systems approach in a *BusinessWeek* interview, Perlmutter said that the hardest part was working in teams: "That's not easy for most scientists. Individual scientists view themselves as artists. The idea of working with other people is very unsatisfying." However, it is through teams that Amgen is working to develop drugs to treat anemia, rheumatoid arthritis, and infections (Weintraub, 2003).

For readers who are familiar with small group literature, a synthesis of different small group models is presented in Figure 1.2. You will note the considerable similarity of conceptual approaches that span more than 60 years of writing. Note, however, that the Tubbs Model was the first to explicitly emphasize the dynamic and simultaneous interaction of all the component parts.

REVIEW OF THE SYSTEMS APPROACH

As an undergraduate, and then as a graduate student, I took a total of nine courses in group dynamics. In each course, I always felt a certain sense of discomfort with my inability to get an overall "feel" for the big picture of small group interaction. Each textbook took a different approach, and some approaches contradicted others. Few, if any, of the books had a conceptual model that explained the relationships of all the important variables related to small groups.

As a result, when I began to teach my first small groups course, I had difficulty picking out a textbook. As I studied various group communication texts, I found that all of them covered many of the same topics, such as leadership, communication, and problem solving. I found, however, that the topics were like so many playing cards that could be shuffled and reshuffled to form a book's table of contents. There was no conceptual model that integrated the topics in a meaningful way. It was only when I studied advanced theoretical books on groups that I found conceptual theories and models that did a better job of tying all the important topics together. These books, however, were not intended for beginning undergraduate students. When I tried using them as texts, students were very unhappy with the choices.

At about the same time, I began to study more and more of the literature on organizational behavior. I read the late Rensis Likert's (1967) now-classic text, which organized the variables in that discipline into three categories: (1) causal variables, (2) intervening variables, and (3) end-result variables. This was the closest I had come to finding the conceptualization that made sense. But Likert's model seemed to be lacking, too, as it implied a beginning and an end (for example, causal, intervening, and end-result variables).

Finally, I found in the general systems literature the missing link, which at that time had never been applied in a small group text. The systems approach advanced the idea that all the various component parts of the model are interrelated and that a change in one often creates changes in other parts of the system. In addition, in an open system, so-called end results are fed back into the beginning of the group and become causal variables for future behaviors. Berryman (1995) defined the fundamentals of systems thinking as a change to a relationship-and-process viewpoint. People in groups and groups in organizations both function within the context that surrounds them. They interrelate within themselves and outside of themselves.

Over time, I began to develop my own materials (as many professors do), and I eventually developed an open systems model of small group interaction (Figure 1.1). This model conceptualized the small group field and could be adapted for a text written for the introductory student. This systems model grew out of the conceptual groundwork that had been laid by several other authors. Figure 1.2 summarizes those authors' models.

The Tubbs Model of Small Group Interaction organizes the important small group variables into three major categories: (1) relevant background factors, (2) internal influences, and (3) consequences. This model offers several advantages over previous introductory books on small group interaction. First, it helps students grasp the conceptual overview that I had not found in books when I was a student. Second, this model shows the dynamic interactive nature of all the variables in the model and avoids the cause-and-effect thinking of earlier models. Third, it explicitly shows how consequences, or outputs, of one small group experience can become background factors or inputs for the next group experience.

This model is reinforced throughout the text with real-life case studies, student exercises, and carefully selected readings. I hope that this combination of theory and application will be useful to you.

The movie *Blackhawk Down* provides an excellent example of the systems model of group behavior. In the movie, a group of American soldiers from various backgrounds work on the task of helping to liberate Somalia from warlords. It illustrates the various *relevant background factors* of the group members, as well as the external forces impacting the group, the dynamic interplay of the many *internal influences* of the group's workings (for example, their frequent conflicts), and the ultimate *consequences* of the group's activities. If you get a chance, rent this film and see how well it illustrates the model on which this book is based.

Chapter 2 discusses (1) communication, (2) language behavior, (3) self-disclosure, and (4) interaction roles. Communication is the most important topic in this book. Thus, we have dedicated a significant amount of coverage to it. Virtually every human behavior has the potential to communicate, and so communication permeates all aspects of group behavior.

Language behavior focuses on the verbal part of communication and the intimate relationship between words and thoughts. This body of knowledge is often referred to as *semantics*. Chapter 2 includes a discussion of several language-related communication difficulties and practical methods for improvement.

PRACTICAL TIPS

Peter Senge at the Massachusetts Institute of Technology offers the following applications of the systems approach:

1. ***Think in systems.*** Successful leaders are often "systems thinkers." They focus less on day-to-day events and more on underlying trends and forces of change. This needs to be taught to others as a way of thinking about problems.
2. ***See interrelationships, not things, and processes, not snapshots.*** Focus not on static things and on isolated events, but on these events as part of an ongoing process. We need to see the interrelationships of these events.
3. ***Move beyond blame.*** It is often poorly designed systems that cause failure, not poorly motivated individuals. Systems thinking shows us that the outside forces and the individuals are part of the same system.
4. ***Focus on areas of high leverage.*** Small, well-focused actions can produce enduring changes if they are well leveraged. Announcing something in a group meeting is a more highly leveraged activity than telling each person individually.
5. ***Avoid symptomatic solutions.*** Look for underlying causes and address those rather than the symptoms. (Senge, in Costin, 1996, pp. 45–46)

Self-disclosure refers to the amount of information we reveal about ourselves to others. Too little self-disclosure results in isolation from others. However, too much self-disclosure with virtual strangers is inappropriate. The contexts of appropriate self-disclosure as a method for personal growth and development are discussed in Chapter 2. Several categories of interaction roles are also examined in Chapter 2.

RELEVANT BACKGROUND FACTORS

Relevant background factors are attributes of the individual participants that existed prior to the group's formation and that will endure in some modified form after the group no longer exists. These background factors influence the group's functioning; in turn, the group process affects the group's outcomes or results.

Let us look at a few of these background factors. Each of us has a distinct personality. The mix of personalities will undoubtedly have some influence on the "chemistry" or working relationships within the group. Team Technology calls this mix *team dynamics,* which is defined as the "often-unseen 'natural forces' that strongly influence how a team reacts, behaves, or performs" (2004). For example, when filming *The Godfather III,* Al Pacino and Diane Keaton broke off their long-running relationship, which caused severe setbacks in shooting the movie. This illustrates both personality conflict and the influence of sex or gender on the group's functioning. Obviously, any group that includes both sexes involves a very volatile element. In fact, many companies have policies that do not allow husbands and wives to work in the same department. Any time the two sexes interact, there is the potential for romantic relationships to influence the group's functioning.

Age is certainly a factor important to group activities. Age itself is probably not as important as the different attitudes that tend to be associated with different age groups. Therefore, groups containing members of a similar age group tend also to be somewhat more similar or homogamous in attitudes. For example, how different would a group discussion of Kanye West or The Black Eyed Peas be if your parents were in the group?

Health also plays a role in influencing groups. If individuals are suffering from health problems, their energy level and the stamina with which they address problems often are reduced. In one work group, a member who had chronic pneumonia was consistently the most outstanding contributor at each meeting of the group that she was able to attend. However, her frequent health-related absences handicapped the group.

Values also exert a powerful influence in groups. Think about a discussion on the subject of abortion, religion, gun control, or racism. How quickly do the values of the group members come into play and how will they most likely affect both the group's processes and its outcomes? Keep in mind that all six of these relevant background factors are constantly interacting with one another. For example, values and attitudes are closely related, as are age and health, and gender and personality. And all of these factors (except gender) are constantly changing over the course of our human experiences. The relevant background factors are the subject of Chapter 3.

INTERNAL INFLUENCES

The second set of variables in the model are *internal influences*. These factors influence the actual functioning of the group. Imagine how physical environment plays a role when the group meets in a quiet conference room with comfortable furniture compared with meeting in a noisy corner of a room with poor ventilation, poor lighting, and a high temperature. Similarly, imagine the way a group interacts when there are only 4 or 5 members as compared with 15 or 20. Typically, the smaller the group, the higher the individual satisfaction of group members with the discussion.

The *type of group* refers to a group's general nature. A group may be, for example, an educational group, a social group, or a work group. Obviously, each of these would perform differently. Chapter 4 discusses in greater depth the factors of physical environment, group size and structure, and group type. Group dynamics, which include a variety of critical elements that affect group process, are explored. These include individual personalities, group process, environmental layout, and technologies utilized in the group setting (Team Technology, 2004).

Take the example of *virtual groups*. Virtual groups and teams are generally small entities that come together to accomplish certain goals. They behave in many ways like face-to-face small groups but have some differences. Virtual groups are increasing in use and number and are taking the place of face-to-face groups within many contexts. A *Workforce Magazine* survey of Fortune 500 companies studied the effectiveness of small virtual groups and teams and found that they result in a 75 percent improvement in productivity and efficiency, a 63 percent increase in customer satisfaction, and a 38 percent improvement in group member work–life balance (VirtualConnection.biz, 2003). We will explore virtual groups and how their members interact within the context of each aspect of the Tubbs Model of Small Group Interaction.

One recent study of virtual teams resulted in the following observation: "Our findings reveal that trust is culture bound and therefore calls for cultural awareness and special precautions. The advantages gained in outsourcing relationships that could demonstrate trust between partners are improved communication, enhanced capabilities of problem solving and decision making, improved efficiency and quality outcomes, as well as the mitigation of opportunistic behavior" (Siakas & Siakas, 2008, p. 59).

Chapter 5 is devoted to three very important topics: (1) status and power, (2) leadership, and (3) group norms. Status and power strongly influence group outcomes. If a group such as the president's cabinet is meeting to discuss a problem, obviously, the president has the highest status and resulting power. Similarly, if the Pittsburgh Steelers or the Green Bay Packers are having a team meeting, Ben Roethlisberger or Aaron Rodgers will have an especially high level of status within the group, and their opinions will most likely be more powerful than those of other members of the group.

Leadership is probably one of the two most important internal influences, and this book devotes considerable attention to it. As mentioned earlier in this chapter, many people learn how to improve their own leadership skills by studying small group interaction. The trend of the present, and most definitely of the future, is for greater participative leadership that heavily utilizes group interaction. For example, Dumaine (1993) writes, "Managers who master skills such as team building ... will likely be in the best position to get tomorrow's top corporate jobs. That's because the role of the top executive is becoming more like that of a team player and broker of others' efforts, not that of an autocrat" (p. 81).

The third topic in Chapter 5 is group norms. These are unwritten rules that strongly influence our behaviors. Usually, norms are so much a part of our thinking that we become aware of them only when someone violates them. For example, if someone dresses (or undresses) in a fashion that is completely inappropriate, this violates our sense of what is comfortable (or *normal*). The pressure to conform to group norms is a powerful influence on every small group.

Chapter 6 covers the important topic of decision making. Many traditional small group books have been exclusively devoted to the topic of decision making. The skills covered in Chapter 6 will serve you throughout your entire lifetime as you solve literally thousands of problems.

Conflict is something all of us experience. Chapter 7 discusses the dynamics of conflict and attempts to better equip you for managing conflicts in your life, especially in small group situations.

CONSEQUENCES

Chapter 8 looks at the reasons we engage in small group activities in the first place—that is, the benefits we get from groups. These benefits are the raison d'être of a group, the reason the group was formed. These are (1) solutions to problems, (2) improvements in interpersonal relations, (3) improvements in the flow of information between and among people, and (4) organizational change. Each of these end results, or consequences, of group interaction is a worthwhile goal.

Appendix A offers guidelines for preparing an oral presentation. It also discusses three group formats: (1) the panel discussion, (2) the symposium, and (3) the forum discussion.

Finally, Appendix B offers several forms for observing and analyzing small group interaction. This material has been added in response to requests from readers like you.

As you read this book, keep in mind the consequences that are possible. As you focus on what is often referred to as "the bottom line," you will better understand how the systems approach ties all these variables together.

EXERCISES

1. Interpersonal Perceptions

Separate into groups of five, and fill out the Preliminary Scale of Interpersonal Perceptions on each of the other four group members. Pass the completed scales to each person in the group. Examine the feedback you get, and discuss it with the others in the group. You may want to share with one another the behaviors that led to these perceptions.

PRELIMINARY SCALE OF INTERPERSONAL PERCEPTIONS

Group Member's Name ______________________________

On the scale below each question, circle the number that best describes the way you see this person's participation in group discussion. Try to distinguish between those areas where the person rates high and those where he/she rates less well.

1. How well does this person understand himself/herself in relation to this group? (Circle one numeral)

5	4	3	2	1
He/she has a very good understanding				He/she has very little understanding

2. How effective do you think this person is in contributing ideas, insights, and suggestions that help the group solve problems and achieve its goals? (Circle one numeral)

5	4	3	2	1
He/she is exceptionally effective				He/she is very ineffective

3. How effective do you think this person is in performing functions that build the group and keep it working well? (Circle one numeral)

5	4	3	2	1
He/she is exceptionally effective				He/she is very ineffective

4. In your opinion, how able is this person to express himself/herself freely and comfortably in the group? (Circle one numeral)

5	4	3	2	1
He/she is exceptionally free and comfortable				He/she is very restricted and tense

5. To what extent do you feel that this person really understands your ideas and feelings? (Circle one numeral)

5	4	3	2	1
He/she has a very good understanding				He/she has very little understanding

2. Group Consensus Activity

Form into groups of five, and read and discuss the following article on cloning. Then answer the questions that follow the article.

CLONING CLAMOR

Connie Cass, The Associated Press

WASHINGTON—Suddenly, it seemed possible to ponder the imponderable: Could humans be copied and mass-produced? Could parents one day choose designer embryos?

Fertility researcher Jerry Hall says his research—cloning human embryos—is all part of helping couples who can't have babies. But to some, it eerily echoes science fiction and crosses an ethical boundary. The Vatican branded his experiment "perverse."

Hall says such far-fetched ideas as mass-producing humans may never be possible and certainly can't be done now.

At a news conference Monday, the George Washington University researcher seemed puzzled that his experiments on short-lived embryos in a petri dish raised such specters.

"We did not implant these into any women; we did not intend to implant them," Hall said. "No child has been born from this procedure."

Nevertheless, some ethicists say Hall crossed a line when he conducted the first known cloning of human life. They fear that other scientists will now charge across that same divide.

"Once you start tampering with the reproductive process, it's hard to decide about where to stop," said Ray Moseley, director of the Medical Humanities Program at the University of Florida College of Medicine.

Cynthia Cohen, head of the National Advisory Board on Ethics and Reproduction, said the research raises "chilling" possibilities for the future. She and others called for a moratorium on further human embryo research until clear limits can be set.

"The fact that there is a total moral vacuum in this whole area is now finally being realized," Cohen said. (*Ann Arbor News,* October 26, 1993, p. A4. Reprinted by permission of the Associated Press.)

What are the implications of this case for the cloning of humans? Would clones be human? Would they have souls? What rights should they have? Is it desirable to clone humans? What should be U.S. policy toward the cloning of humans?

3. Group Decision Making

Separate into groups of five or so. Read the case described below, and decide as a group what you would do in the situation. Then discuss your group processes.

The "Baby Jessica" Story: "Baby Jessica" was adopted shortly after her birth in 1990 by Jan and Roberta DeBoer of Ann Arbor, Michigan. Her birth mother, Cara Schmidt, of Blairstown, Iowa, signed the paperwork giving Jessica up for adoption. She was not married at the time. Later, Dan Schmidt found out that he was the father and filed suit for custody of Jessica. Subsequently the Schmidts got married. A legal battle that lasted two-and-a-half years followed. In late 1993 the Schmidts were awarded custody of Jessica. She was shown on national television crying and screaming while being taken from the DeBoers' home. Public opinion polls showed that respondents were strongly in favor of the DeBoers' keeping Jessica.

READINGS: Overview

The Tubbs Model presented in Figure 1.1 shows the interrelated nature of 24 variables relevant to the study of small group interaction. The reading below, by Wilson, offers excellent insights into some of the main reasons why people join groups. It is also interesting to note that these reasons fit quite comfortably within the systems approach to studying small group interaction, which is the conceptual model around which this book is structured.

The second reading, by Lipnack and Stamps, shows the complexity of systems theory and its relationship to small groups.

Reading 1.1 Motivations for Member Participation in Groups

Gerald L. Wilson

Examine your motives for being a member of a particular group. Do you have a group in mind? If not, stop for a moment and pick one. Now think both of yourself and the other members. A good question to ask yourself is, "What things do members of the group receive that keep them in the group?" See how many different motivations you can list.

Now check your list against the following items. Although the wording may be a little more "academic sounding" than yours, see if your ideas match these. People are motivated to belong to groups because of (1) attraction to others in the group, (2) attraction to the group's activities, (3) attraction to the group's goals, (4) attraction to being affiliated with the group, and (5) attraction to needs outside the group. We will take up each of these ideas, with illustrations of each and suggestions for group development. The motives for belonging that a person brings to a group affect the development potential and direction of the group. These motives can be used to develop other members' motivation to participate. And, in doing so, the development of the group is affected. The subsequent sections examine these motives.

ATTRACTION TO OTHERS IN THE GROUP

Ask any group of people to describe why they are attracted to one another, and you are likely to get a variety of answers. You can gain an appreciation of the complexity of this issue by considering someone you know in a group, to whom you are attracted. Now take a moment to think of several of the reasons you like to be with that person.

From Gerald L. Wilson, *Groups in Context,* 7th ed. (New York: McGraw-Hill, 2005). Reproduced with permission of The McGraw-Hill Companies.

Do you find the person physically attractive?

Do you have similar interests?

Do you have attitudes and values that seem to match reasonably closely?

Do your important values match closely?

Do you see yourselves as having similar personality characteristics?

Are you of similar economic status, race, and so forth?

Do you see the person as having abilities similar to yours?

Count the number of times you said yes to one of these questions. You are likely to have done so several times, because attraction is a complex issue. People are attracted to groups for a variety of reasons. Pete Wells belongs to the Rotary because the members he knows represent an image he admires. Yuka Ando belongs to a study group at her church because several of its members are interested in tennis. Sally Williams belongs to a group investigating computer needs in her department because she enjoys the people who volunteered. Motivations for being part of a group are varied, and they are not always related to the task of the group.

Attraction is related to pleasing physical characteristics, similarities in attitude, belief, personality, race, economic status, and perceived ability of the other person. Perhaps the strongest of these—and the most often studied—is perceived similarity of attitude. Theodore Newcomb conducted the classic study that demonstrated the strength of similarity. He invited seventeen male students to live in the same house rent-free for two years. After they occupied the house, he gave them a series of tests to measure attitudes and values. He also checked the room assignments and likings of group members. He discovered that liking was based on proximity—how physically close to one another they were situated in the house. Later, when he retested the interpersonal attractions, he found a shift. Those who perceived themselves to be similar in attitudes had developed attractions. Newcomb concluded that people initially got to know those closest to them. When they were able to know others, they were attracted to those who were similar. Similarity is a good starting place when you look at why members are attracted to groups.

Attraction is also related to personality similarity. Byrne, Griffitt, and Stefaniak, for example, had 151 subjects respond to items on a scale that measures personality characteristics. Then they examined a stranger's responses that agreed with their choices—25 percent, 50 percent, or 80 percent of the time. Next the subjects rated the stranger's attractiveness. The more the stranger agreed, the more the person was liked.

The details of these two studies are presented for two reasons. First, it is useful for you to have an appreciation of how researchers approach and examine these issues. Second, the kind of evidence that supports these generalizations is important. There is also support to show that attraction is related to economic similarity, race, and similarity of ability. The findings related to similarity of ability are interesting. Initially people were attracted to those who had previously been successful at a given task. However, when they had the opportunity to shift from their initial choices, in time unsuccessful people chose unsuccessful partners.

ATTRACTION TO GROUP ACTIVITIES

Sometimes people belong to a group because they enjoy some aspect of the task. This is not always the same thing as valuing the goal of the group. For example, imagine an athletic woman joining the sorority softball team to participate in its athletic program but not really embracing its primary goal of socializing. Some people belong to a civic group to socialize with its members rather than to work toward its goals. You can imagine how important it could be to realize that particular members are not especially interested in the group's goal. If you try to motivate such people by emphasizing goal commitment, your success is likely to be minimal. On the other hand, you may be able to link achievement of their needs to the group goal and be successful. For example, a sorority might show how other athletes are attracted to groups with strong social programs. This may give the woman who joined to participate in athletics a reason to support the social program, too.

ATTRACTION TO GROUP GOAL

Perhaps the most important reason for a member to belong to a group from the standpoint of group development is attraction to the goal. Goal attraction contributes more to a group than mere achievement of particular ends. Members who are committed to the goal may also work hard on being able to get along. They may even be able to put aside differences and hostilities because they value the goal. Sherif and Sherif vividly demonstrated this aspect of goal achievement in their famous boys' camp experiment. They created hostility between two groups of boys through various manipulations. For example, they invited both groups to a party at which half of the refreshments were badly damaged. They invited one group earlier than the other so that they had an opportunity to serve themselves the undamaged portion of the food. This they did; the other group became predictably angry. Next they tried to manage the conflict by creating a goal to which they thought both groups would be attracted. They arranged a baseball game in which their camp would play a neighboring camp. The embracing of this attractive goal served to ease much of the hostility and created a new group loyalty.

ATTRACTION TO BEING AFFILIATED WITH THE GROUP

Groups allow people to interact and thereby fulfill a need to affiliate with others. You undoubtedly know of people who do not really care about the task of the group, are not really interested in the group's goals, and may even not wish to get involved with the members on a personal level, but who attend some of the group meetings. You might suspect that affiliation with the group per se is rewarding—and it is. These people like to be able to say that they are members. Perhaps they believe that belonging to these groups gives them prestige. The aim of their attendance at a few meetings is to keep themselves in good standing so they can say they belong.

Need for affiliation when it is a member's sole attraction to the group may present a difficult problem for the leader. How do you interest the person in the group's goals? If you cannot do this, then the member's presence may be disruptive. Your group can suffer significantly if you have several of these members. Imagine a PTA member who attends an occasional meeting. This person is uninformed. He or she may want to discuss an ongoing issue, but the effort is more disrupting than helpful. The next section . . . presents some specific suggestions for making productive members out of people who have this type of need.

ATTRACTION TO NEEDS OUTSIDE THE GROUP

Finally, it is clear that people belong to groups for reasons that may have nothing to do with the group's task, goals, or members. Perhaps you know of a fellow student who has joined groups to bolster her or his employment résumé. Some people belong to religious groups merely because it is the socially acceptable thing to do. Sometimes businesspeople belong to civic organizations because they think it will be good for business.

You can imagine the problems it might create for your group if you have members who are pursuing goals primarily outside the group. They may be totally unreliable, may attend only rarely, and can even be disruptive when they do attend.

ENCOURAGING GROUP DEVELOPMENT: APPLYING MEMBERS' MOTIVATIONS TO ENCOURAGE PARTICIPATION

People perceive their membership as satisfying some need, and this can serve as an important source of motivation for those providing leadership.

The problem for members and leaders who wish to develop their group is finding out what motivates various members. If you find that you have a number of people who are motivated by a particular need (say affiliation), you might try to get them to value the group members more. Perhaps you could invite them to a group social function. This may promote cohesiveness and may also develop their commitment to members and the group, thereby enhancing productivity.

Sometimes it is the activities of the group that interest the member, with goal achievement being of little concern. Of course, if the group's activities are only task related, this is not a problem. One method of using this attraction to motivate is to link the activities to goal attainment. For example, if the person's primary motivation is to participate in your group's philanthropic effort, you might be sure that you devote some time in each of your meetings to this issue. You might emphasize how important you think this activity is and tell the person how much you appreciate his or her contributions in this area. You would also want to show how accomplishment of this philanthropic activity is related to the overall task.

Still others may belong to your group to try to fulfill their need for affiliation with others. These people may not care much about the group's goals or task or even the particular attributes of its members. If this is a chronic problem that is in fact disrupting the group, you may need to make the problem an agenda item. The group's members need to affirm their commitment to the tasks and goal. The group might decide, for instance, that regular attendance and work on the task are necessary for continued membership in the group. If these people enjoy the affiliation with the group enough, they may be motivated to embrace and work on the task in order to meet that need.

A Question of Ethics and Responsibility

Motivations for Joining a Group You find yourself elected to lead your neighborhood association. You called the group together for its first formal meeting. You met in the clubhouse. The room was arranged in such a way that people could decide to sit in a close circle or spread out. Members chose to spread out. You found it difficult to talk in this arrangement, so you suggested that they move into a closer circle of chairs. Members introduced themselves and told what they did to ocuppy their time. It turns out that three members are close neighbors and socialize with each other frequently. Yuka, a 24-year-old, works as a speech pathologist at a local hospital. Carol, aged 60, works in her home, while Isabel, a 29-year-old, works at a local bank as a marketing manager. Juan, 40 years old, is from a nearby state and owns a franchise for a fast-food restaurant. Doug, 50 years old, is coordinator of recreation for the Parks Department.

It appears that you have a diverse group. Some members know each other, while others do not. Age and place in life vary significantly. Some members have grown children, while others have youngsters. What problems do you anticipate in your attempt to develop this group? What strategies will you use to accomplish your objectives of completing some worthwhile tasks for the neighborhood and getting this group to pull together?

Finally, some members may belong to a group for a goal that is outside the group's purpose. They may wish to receive the benefits that outsiders might attribute to them because of their membership in the group. If the members are not genuinely interested in the task and in this case may not even particularly value the members, then your group may have to make membership contingent upon maintaining involvement. This is hard to do, but it is one of the more practical solutions to this kind of problem.

Reading 1.2 Holism for the Left Brain

Jessica Lipnack and Jeffrey Stamps

"Network" is a general concept like "system." Networks of molecules, neurons, waterways, transportation, television stations, and computers share common features, such as nodes (members) and links.

Consider the next few pages an extremely short course in systems thinking. Use it to help you simplify complexity. Each of the network concepts has an analog in general systems theory. By associating these concepts with one another, we leverage the phenomenal power of such complexity-busting tools as the systems principle of hierarchy:

Network Principle	Systems Principle
Network	System

From Jessica Lipnack and Jeffrey Stamps, *The Teamnet Factor,* © 1993. Reprinted by permission of John Wiley & Sons, Inc.

Purpose	Synergy
Members	Holons
Links	Relationships
Leaders	Representation
Levels	Hierarchy
Co-opetition	Complementarity
Phases	Logistic growth curve

NETWORKS ARE SYSTEMS

Systems theory the world around permeates advanced management techniques, such as the quality movement and sociotech approaches. When W. Edwards Deming, the father of the quality movement, turned to science, he did not borrow from the traditional reductionism of Frederick Winslow Taylor. Rather, he viewed science holistically, as do other great systems scientists, such as Herbert Simon and Kenneth Boulding. Deming's business systems model is very straightforward:

> Every value-producing organization receives inputs from suppliers and provides outputs to customers.

Networks are systems, pure and simple. Anywhere a systems concept will work, so will a network concept. Indeed, for many systems, particularly social systems, networks are an easier sell.

In the social world, people do not much love the word "system." It's easy—and often justified—to hate "the system." Some people hate it so much that they are blind to their aversion.

Little wonder. Most traditional systems are "black boxes." Think of the tax system or the international monetary system or even the municipal garbage system. Most systems portray themselves as beyond the comprehension and control of ordinary mortals. Traditional systems science is much the same. It also offers an obfuscating self-portrait of systems as black boxes, unfortunately too complicated for just anyone to understand.

With networks, you can take the wraps off systems. Instead of "black box" systems, create "glass box" networks. Make the outer boundary of the whole transparent. See inside to the parts—the members—and to the relationships—the links—between the parts. The more clearly you lay out the network-system elements, the easier it is to understand. (See Figure A.)

It is difficult to "see" a physically distributed organization. Turn this liability to advantage by promoting "whole systems awareness." Emphasize how all the parts interrelate. A systems view enables you to grasp a network as naturally as the hand of a friend.

Principle 1: Synergy Becomes You

"The whole is more than the sum of the parts." This systems principle is so popular that it's almost a cliché. In networks, purpose is the "more than" that defines

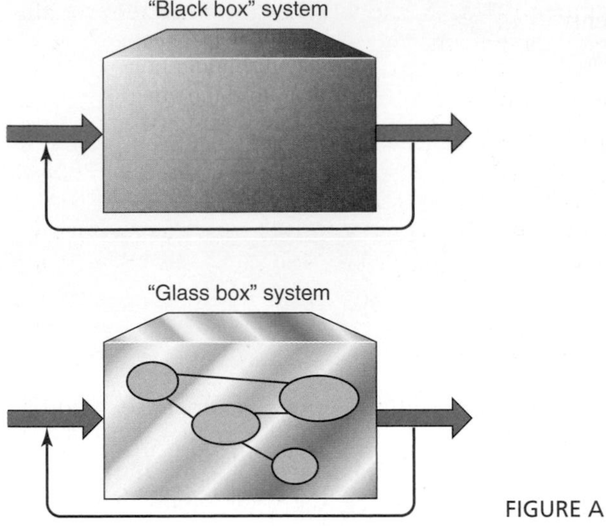

FIGURE A

the whole, what Buckminster Fuller called "synergy." Purpose is what enables a group of independent people to do something together that they cannot do alone. Together, synergy is possible; in isolation, it is not.

> To function, your system—no matter how minimal—has to have some synergy or purpose.

Purpose relates very practically to how people become legitimized in networks. In a simple hierarchy, you gain legitimacy from the authority structure, with its system of rewards and punishments. In bureaucracies, control comes from charters and all manner of legalities and policies. In networks, legitimacy is an altogether different animal. You gain real legitimacy through contribution to the shared purpose.

Develop purpose as a resource for your team, just as people develop procedures and policies using law as a resource. Encourage your members to participate in planning and decision making to internalize the purpose for themselves. Externalize the purpose through explicit plans, information access, and the creation of symbols—logos, nicknames, acronyms. Instead of controlling one another through one-way orders or endlessly detailed policies, boundary crossing teamnet members exercise control through their shared process.

Principle 2: The Best Member Is a Holon

Each of us is a whole person who plays a part in businesses, families, and communities.

What sorts of things are simultaneously wholes and parts? Everything. Arthur Koestler, the author and systems thinker, coined the word "holon" to stand for this whole/part characteristic of everything. This "systems within systems" feature of nature is fundamental to understanding complexity.

View teamnet members as holons. The autonomy of teamnet members means that they are independent parts; they have their own integrity and own life processes of survival and growth. This is true whether the members are alliances of firms or individual peers on a team.

Parts and wholes have names. Companies, departments, divisions, functions, projects, programs, and teams all have names. From a systems perspective, these names label categories. They differentiate the parts of complex systems. Bureaucratic boxes and network nodes both function as categories; they both collect people, things, and activities into coherent clusters. In real life, we are all parts of many categories, many social clusters, many boxes. Sometimes, the same name represents both a bureaucratic box and a network node: an engineering group is both a node in the product development boundary crossing teamnet, and a bureaucratic departmental box at the same time.

There are important differences here. While you play multiple roles in multiple networks, in hierarchies you appear in one and only one box. As a network member, you are relatively independent and demonstrate strong tendencies to autonomy. In a bureaucracy, you are relatively dependent and look for precision fit. When it comes to the independence–dependence continuum, network nodes and bureaucratic boxes lean to opposite poles.

Principle 3: The Interconnected Web of Relationships

Relationships are elusive things. For some people, they are real; for others, they are not. Some people literally cannot see relationships, even indirectly. These people do well in organizations with a rule to govern every aspect of behavior. They don't fare well in teamnets. Relationships are at a network's core.

There are so many relationships involved in life, and so many different kinds of them everywhere you look. To simplify this vast interconnected scheme, traditional organizations have many one-way signs. Hierarchies and bureaucracies take an extremely limited approach to how parts interconnect. Generally speaking, orders and information flow in a minimal number of formal channels. Information flows up and commands flow down. This traffic pattern gives rise to the walls, stovepipes, silos, and other hard-to-penetrate boundaries in organizations.

By contrast, in networks, connections are many rather than few. Information and influence flow both up and down the levels through links, as well as horizontally within levels. What is the situation with your boundary crossing teamnet? Do information and influence flow along a two-way highway, or are people stopped for going against the traffic?

Systems thinking has historically emphasized relationships. Peter Senge's book *The Fifth Discipline* is an excellent example of a systems approach to complexity for business based on understanding processes and relationships. Gregg Lichtenstein, one of the leading facilitators of flexible business networks, wrote about "the significance of relationships in entrepreneurship" for his doctoral dissertation in social systems science. June Holley and Roger Wilkens have developed a systems dynamics model of flexible networks to guide the development of networks of small manufacturers in southern Ohio.

Principle 4: Representative Leadership

Nothing in groups is as complicated as leadership. One way to simplify complex wholes is to grasp a part that represents the rest. For example, Wall Street is shorthand for America's financial system; the White House stands for the executive branch of government; the Oval Office represents the White House. In the search for simple ways to "grasp a group," leaders come in handy. Leaders are people who stand for a group.

All organizations have leaders, even self-directed groups, where leadership comes from within rather than from without. Networks are rife with leaders. By definition, leaders are partial representatives whose views others need to supplement.

To Americans, hierarchies in the social sense are single-pointed pyramids. As unfortunate as the burden is impractical, in a hierarchy everything supposedly comes together at the top in one perfect person. In a hierarchy, the rule is the fewer the leaders the better—with as little change as possible for as long as possible.

The same is not true in networks. As we stress repeatedly, the more leaders, the better. In the best of networks, everyone is a leader. Everyone provides guidance in specific realms of expertise, their talents and knowledge all contributing to the success of the group. People alternate between leadership and followership roles in fast-moving networks with many parallel interconnected activities.

Principle 5: Hierarchical Levels

While in some ways boundary crossing teamnets are very different from hierarchies, in others they are the same. Do not despair. This is not some sort of depressing truth that makes us want to say, "See? I knew there was nothing different here, after all." Consider it instead a great source of comfort. Since you already know a great deal about hierarchies, draw on your experience as a source of strength.

Were you schooled in the analytic, "break-it-down," mechanistic, one-size-fits-all strategy approach to anything complicated? We were, and so was nearly everyone else in the West. This half-brained approach to thinking has its strengths but also its limitations in solving life's problems. From a systems perspective, it ignores the parallel value of synthesis, the "build-it-up" holistic strategy, critical for all living systems, including human ones.

> What systems am I part of? What environments is the team part of? What contexts is the company part of? What systems . . .

One of the great ironies of systems science lies in the term *hierarchy*. Hierarchy is the most common principle threading through the multitude of systems theories. Every comprehensive systems theory uses it, regardless of its native discipline. According to Herbert Simon, the father of information science, hierarchy is nature's "architecture of complexity." Confusion over the word, which literally means *priestly rulership,* has kept this idea from being widely understood where it is needed most, in human affairs.

Hierarchy is what we mean by levels.

The social use of the term *hierarchy* includes the scientific one, levels of organization. Unfortunately, when people apply the word to organizations, they also add another characteristic: vertical control. In social hierarchies, the higher you are, the better off you are and the more power you have; the lower you are, the worse off you are and the less power you have.

As true as this may be in your local hierarchy, let us say most emphatically that top-down is only one of many possible relationships between levels. Exclusive one-way control is not natural in nature's hierarchies. Rather than dominating one another, levels are interdependent. More inclusive levels have critical dependencies on lower levels. Molecules would have a tough time without atoms. Organisms wouldn't be much without cells, which rely on molecules. The life of cells follows its own rules quite apart from an organism's life, which has its own special rules. These are all examples of hierarchy in the natural scientific sense.

Complex boundary crossing teamnets are "systems of systems within systems." Every teamnet is a hierarchy of wholes and parts. Teamnet members are systems of systems. The systems principles of segmentation and inclusion apply every time a group splits up into task teams or an alliance jells.

Love and Marriage, Horse and Carriage: The Complementarity of Co-opetition

Co-opetition brings the complements of cooperation and competition into one word. This dynamic between the self and others is one of many ways complementarity, the second fundamental principle of systems (after hierarchy), shows up in networks. When you see your teamnet as both structure and process, you see complementary views of the same thing.

Both hierarchy and complementarity appear everywhere in nature and society. They are grand boundary crossing concepts that cross many terrains of knowledge. Physicists use complements like positive and negative charges, matter and antimatter, and right and left spins. They see fundamental reality as both particles and waves at the same time. In biology, we see life and nonlife, birth and death, male and female, as basic complements. In society, people struggle between self and group, a natural dynamic that is central to families, communities, and nations alike.

Tension erupts when complements begin to grate against one another. In reality, the tension of duality is always there. When the system begins to shake, stress becomes noticeable as relationships form, break, and re-form. You can use the principle of complements as a simple tool in many teamnet situations. For example, you can take a complementary approach to conflict, using such simple homilies as "There are two sides to every story."

Phases of Growth

The teamnet concept of process derives from a key pattern recognized by general systems theory. *General systems*—initiated half a century ago by the biologist Ludwig von Bertalanffy and the economist Kenneth Boulding among others—is a scientific discipline that focuses on common patterns, mathematical and otherwise, found in physical, biological, and social systems.

The *S curve,* also known as the *logistic growth curve,* which we use to represent the change process, appears in the original paper von Bertalanffy wrote establishing the field of general systems. It was his first example of an *isomorphy,*

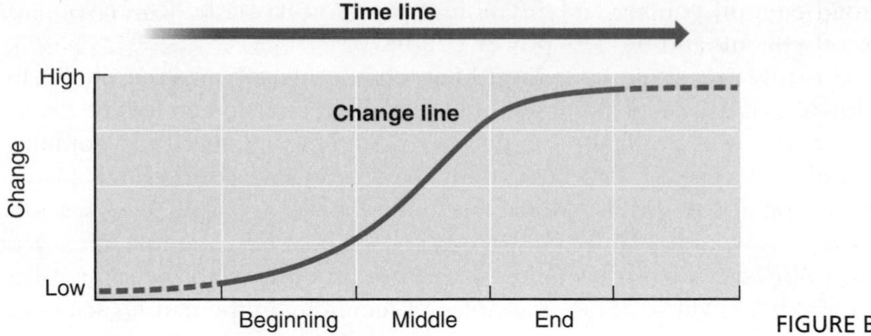

FIGURE B

a general principle that holds across scientific disciplines. An isomorphy is a boundary crossing principle.

To track the cumulative progress of some change over time, add a second dimension to the simple time line. Now, the straight-arrow process path looks like an S curve. It generates a plane of change, a very typical result when you plot change data against time.

The S curve does equally well at charting the growth of bacteria in a petri dish and the rate at which new technology spreads, for example, the penetration of a cable television franchise into a new area. *Limits to growth* is the common factor in these processes, a major law of all life on this planet.

> The S curve charts the common dynamic when change starts small, develops slowly, then "suddenly" takes off, rapidly filling out the available opportunity, slowing as it reaches limits, and stabilizing into a new slow- to no-growth pattern.

Well understood in a wide variety of disciplines, the S curve represents great acquired knowledge, available to those who want to deepen their understanding of process. (See Figure B.)

The S curve becomes the *stress curve* when you pay attention to the turbulence associated with the two bends in the curve.... The stress curve is a very handy pocket tool for anyone involved with teamnets. Use it as an extremely valuable process aid to plan meetings and conferences of all sizes. Look to the points of turbulence in the process. Use them as alpine skiers do the bumps on the downhill trial: racers anticipate and prejump the bump, leveraging momentum from the bump's back side rather than being thrown for a loop by flying off the front.

SMARTER GROUPS

Human evolution has progressed by substituting brain for brawn.

We see the possibility of much smarter groups as new forms of teamnets integrate with the electronic world of technology networks. Remember:

> Only a few generations of humans have had instantaneous electronic communications, and only now are we launching groups linked with the historically unique cognitive (digital) technology of computers.

In the broad cultural context, electronic and digital technology stimulates and shapes the sociological response of global networks. Networks are the unique response to the driving forces of information, just as hierarchy developed in the agricultural era and bureaucracy matured in the industrial era.

But we don't have to wait for tomorrow for smarter groups. Most people have at some time or another been a member of a group that really "clicks"—a family, work, political, religious, or volunteer effort. Most people intuitively know the tremendous personal satisfaction that is possible with high group performance. Only a small but critical general improvement in people's ability to think and act collectively may have a great impact on solving all the world's problems.

CHAPTER 2

Communication Processes

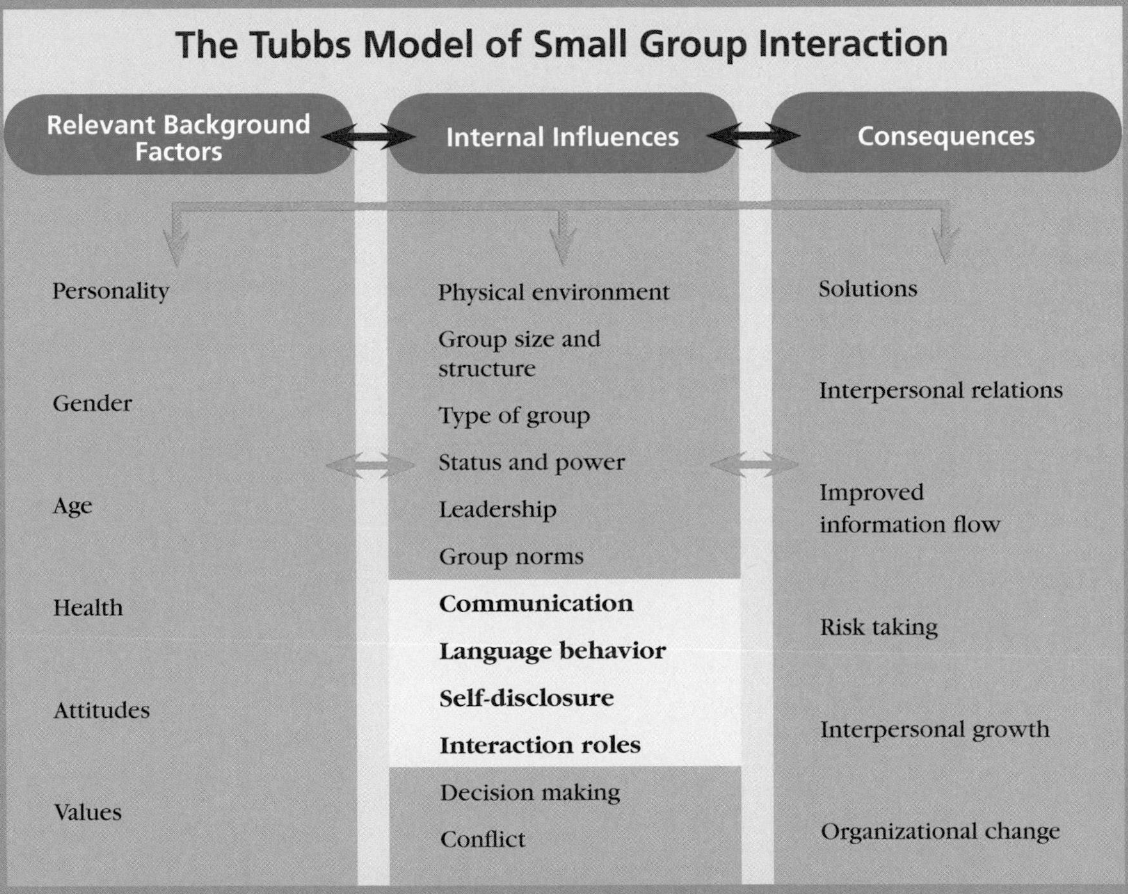

Concepts in **boldface** in gray panels are the emphases of this chapter.

Preview

Chapter 2 focuses on four of the internal influences of the system's Model of Small Group Interaction: communication, language behavior, self-disclosure, and interaction roles. This chapter concentrates on the important topic of communication. Because communication is one of the most important aspects of group interaction, a thorough discussion of it is necessary. This chapter defines communication and discusses several different types. The topic of language behavior is presented, along with four specific problems that groups often confront: bypassing, inference making, polarizing, and signal reactions. In a group, members must decide how much to share or contribute; therefore, this chapter examines self-disclosure. Interaction roles is the last of the internal influences discussed in Chapter 2. One often establishes several roles in day-to-day living. Three types of these are group task roles, group maintenance roles, and individual roles. Research at UCLA by Foreman (1999) shows that even graduate students at some of the top universities in America demonstrate a lack of skill in small group communication. She writes, "They may study the intricacies of team building, but they rarely learn how to coordinate the efforts of several people in the composition of a report or presentation" (p. 11). This chapter addresses some of those communication skills. If you are into Web surfing as one form of your communication, be careful. There is new software organizations can use to monitor your activity to see if it complies with their desires. To check it out, go to www.littlebrother.com.

Glossary

Appropriateness Appropriateness includes several factors that help determine the timing and extent of self-disclosure.

Bypassing Bypassing is a misunderstanding that occurs when the sender and the receiver miss each other with their meaning.

Content and Process Content of a group discussion includes comments about the *topic* of the discussion. Process is the *manner* in which the discussion is conducted.

Defensive–Supportive Communication Defensive communication occurs when a psychological barrier is created, known as a *defense mechanism*. This barrier acts to reduce effective communication. Supportive communication minimizes these types of problems.

Emotional Intelligence Personal and interpersonal skills that enable one to induce desired responses in others.

Group-Building and Maintenance Roles Group-building and maintenance roles help the interpersonal functioning of the group and alter the way of working by strengthening, regulating, and perpetuating the group.

Group Task Roles Group task roles are identifiable behaviors that are directed toward accomplishing the group's objective.

Individual Roles Individual roles are roles that are designed to satisfy an *individual's* needs rather than to contribute to satisfying the needs of the group.

Inference Making Inference making refers to going beyond observations and what we know. Inferences have only a low probability of coming true.

Intentional–Unintentional Communication Intentional communication occurs when we communicate what we mean to. Unintentional communication occurs when we communicate something different from what we intend, as when we accidentally offend someone.

Polarizing Polarizing is the exaggeration that occurs when people attempt to make a point.

Signal Reactions Signal reactions are learned responses to certain stimuli, such as emotional reactions to offensive swear words or racial slurs.

Verbal–Nonverbal Communication Verbal communication is the use of words to get across a message. Nonverbal communication is the use of physical actions, such as facial expression or tone of voice, to get across a message.

CASE STUDY

COMPUTERS GIVING AWAY YOUR LOCATION

How do you feel about Google Inc. and Apple Inc. collecting and storing information about your user location? iPad and iPhone users can have their locations traced from their usage.* This raises questions about how long the data are stored, who has access to the information, and how is it being used. These companies say that the data are used to improve service to customers. The information can also be used to locate a missing person, and it can be used to reconstruct a crime after-the-fact. Representative Joe Barton of Texas said that Apple apparently lied to him and another lawmaker last year when it said that its phones do not collect and transmit location-based data even when location services such as mapping are turned off.** Also, what if hackers got hold of the information? How might it be used in cases where there is a breach of security?

In addition, how would you like to have a tracking device in your jeans or even in your underwear? Wal-Mart has now rolled out sophisticated electronic ID tags in their 3,750 U.S. stores to track individual pairs of jeans and underwear.*** Supporters say that this will provide much better inventory control, but others question privacy concerns. The removable electronic "smart tags" that are routinely hand-scanned and then cut off clothing when sold have been replaced by radio-frequency ID (RFID) tags. Wal-Mart spokespeople say that this will transform their business and result in further cost savings to customers. Previously, these RFID tags were used to track pallets of merchandise traveling through their supply chain (exactly as FedEx or UPS tracks packages). Advocates predict that this practice will become standard across the retail industry. However, Katherine Albrecht, author of the book *Spychips*, argues that unscrupulous marketers or even criminals potentially could use this information to hurt customers, again through breaches in security or by stealing items of clothing. Although the tags may be removed (if one can find them), they cannot be turned off. Others argue that the new electronic personal ID

**Source:* Amir Efrati and Jennifer Valentino-DeVries, "Computers, too, can give away location," *The Wall Street Journal*, April 27, 2011, p. B1.

***Source:* YukariI watani Kane and Jennifer Valentino-DeVries, "Jobs tries to calm iPhone imbroglio," *The Wall Street Journal*, April 28, 2011, pp. A1, A2.

****Source:* Miguel Bustillo, "Wal-Mart radio tags to track clothing," *The Wall Street Journal*, July 23, 2010, pp. A1, A14.

cards (now used in Washington and New York for ease in border crossing) could also be secretly scanned to obtain private information, or credit card information, and lead to identity theft. But Sanjay Sarma, a professor at Massachusetts Institute of Technology, argues that these privacy concerns are far outweighed by the benefits. A pilot study at American Apparel, Inc. found that stores equipped with this new technology saw sales increase by 14.3 percent, according to Avery Dennison Corp., a maker of these RFID chips. Wal-Mart also expects that these tags will cut down on employee theft. Numerous European retailers have already implemented this technology. On the other hand, using more advanced technology in kiosks and smart phones, people even will be able to know what you are trying on in the dressing rooms.

What do you think about these issues?

Communication

EMOTIONAL INTELLIGENCE

Everyone knows the importance of intelligence. Surprisingly, however, recent research shows that IQ scores account for only about 4 percent of variance in job performance, and that IQ contributes only about 20 percent to life success (Tierney, 2007). One of the most exciting areas of recent research in the behavioral sciences is labeled "emotional intelligence." Harvard researcher Daniel Goleman has written several best-selling books on this subject (Goleman, 1997, 1998a; Cherniss & Goleman, 2001; Goleman, Boyatzis, & McKee, 2002). In Goleman's book *Emotional Intelligence,* he states that leaders must have strengths in "building consensus, being able to see things from the perspectives of others . . . and promoting cooperation, while avoiding conflicts" (Odell, 2003). Ironically, what they are calling emotional intelligence is a combination of intrapersonal communication (personal competence) and interpersonal communication (social competence). Whereas the ability to gather, interpret, analyze, and respond to data may be a function of technical competency, the ability to receive, interpret, analyze, and respond to messages, both external and internal, is regulated by one's emotional intelligence (EI) (Myers & Tucker, 2005).

Goleman and his colleagues (Cherniss & Goleman, 2001, p. 28) break down these competencies as follows:

Self	*Other*
(Personal competence)	(Social competence)
Self-awareness	Social awareness
Emotional self-awareness	Empathy
Accurate self-assessment	Service orientation
Self-confidence	Organizational awareness
Self-management	Relationship management
Emotional self-control	Developing others

(*Continued*)

Trustworthiness	Influence
Conscientiousness	Communication
Adaptability	Conflict management
Achievement drive	Visionary leadership
Initiative	Catalyzing change
	Building bonds
	Teamwork and collaboration

In their best-selling book, *Influencer,* Kerry Patterson and colleagues (Patterson et al., 2008) refer to two parts of our brains as the "know" and the "go" systems. They offer the following eloquent insights about emotional intelligence:

> As our "go" system kicks in and blood flows out of the brain and toward our arms and legs, we start relying on a much smaller part of our brain (the amygdala) to take over the job of "thinking." When the amygdala takes control, we no longer process information in a cool, calm, and collected way. Rather than cogitating, ruminating, and completing other high-level cognitive tasks, the amygdala or "reptilian brain" is made for speed. It's wired for quick, emotional processing that, when activated, triggers reflexive responses including fight and flight. The amygdala instinctively moves us to action. We see a tiger and bang, we're off and running. This hot/go system develops very early . . .
>
> The second system, known as the "cool" or "know" system, serves us well during more stable times. It's emotionally neutral, runs off the frontal lobe [of the cerebral cortex], and is designed for higher-level cognitive processing. Consequently, it helps us thrive, rather than survive. It's the part of our brain that we're using . . . while chatting with a friend.
>
> . . . the "go" system often turns on at the mere hint that you're about to fall under attack. Heaven forbid you think complexly and clearly in such a case. (pp. 130–31)

The remainder of this chapter will focus on some of the specifics of communication, especially in the group setting.

COMMUNICATION DEFINED

Communication as a topic has piqued the interest of millions. Kevin Basik, captain and instructor at the Air Force Academy and Foundational Leadership Program chief, believes that leadership communication may be an innate ability that individuals have but that it does not develop if it is not fostered. He feels that "effective communication" and understanding one's own shortcomings (business intelligence and emotional intelligence) make an effective leader and group member. On many occasions, individuals in positions of influence are incredibly intelligent and talented but do not have the communication skills necessary to motivate a team (Doerhman, 2004, p. 1).

Communication within the small group or team is both similar to and different from communication in other settings. *Group communication* is defined as the process of creating meanings in the minds of others. These meanings may or may not correspond to the meanings we intend to create. Group communication involves the sending and receiving of messages between and among the participants. Group communication includes both verbal and nonverbal message stimuli. In all these ways, group communication is similar to communication that occurs in other contexts, such as interpersonal communication (informal communication between two or more people), public communication (formal communication between a speaker and an audience), organizational communication (communication in an organizational setting), or mass communication (in which a source attempts to communicate with large numbers of people, usually through some electronic or written medium). This chapter will focus on communication principles as they relate to the small group context.

O'Hair, Friedrich, and Shaver (2010) identify six key components of effective communication skills:

1. Creative insight is the ability to ask the right questions.
2. Sensitivity means [a person] practices the golden rule.
3. Vision means being able to create the future.
4. Versatility is the capacity for anticipating change.
5. Focus is required to implement change.
6. Patience allows . . . people to live in the long term. (pp. 4–5)

As you practice communicating in groups, it would be wise to keep these six important components in mind.

Communication among group members also may depend on the nature of the group. Some groups are highly structured. In such groups, there is a leader and there are followers. In an unstructured group, the lines between leadership and followership are not so well defined. These various group environments have very different kinds of communication. One study (Courtwright, Fairhurst, & Rogers, 1989) compared the communication between work groups in structured, "authority-based" plants and less structured, "self-managing" plants.

Authority-based groups are highly structured. They are group environments that we think of as being *traditional.* In an authority-based group, orders come from the top, and no one in the *lower ranks* questions the leader. Authority-based groups are mechanical systems. In a mechanical system, the communication moves in one direction, from leader to subordinate, and tends to be one-sided. In other words, "no questions asked."

Courtwright and colleagues (1989) confirmed such types of communication in their study. Words such as *initiate, define, structure, dominate,* and *inform,* used by management, were indicative of the authority-based, top-down direction of communication. This study also discovered that competitive and argumentative communication was common in such systems. Its findings reflect "a greater overall level of disagreement, conflict, and managerial attempts to dominate" (p. 797) in a mechanistic system.

Self-managing groups are organic systems. They are less structured, less traditional task groups. Communication in self-managing groups is more discussion-oriented, with more "question-and-answer interactions" occurring between group leaders and subordinates. According to Tubbs (1994b), "Self-managed teams represent the farthest level of advancement in the employee involvement continuum" (p. 3).

In organic systems, communication flows through a group like blood through the circulatory system of a living thing. This circulatory process is vital to the life of the group. This vitality is dependent on effective communication between group members and the leadership, whether a system is authority-based or self-managing.

Additionally, Dr. Kerry Bunker, Sharon Ting, and Kathy Kram, authors of the book *The Young and the Clueless,* write about young businesspeople who are incredibly intelligent but need the skills necessary to effectively motivate teams because of a general lack of interpersonal business experience. More organizations are now putting new management training programs in place to prepare new leaders for their roles. Examples include LexisNexis and USAA. These programs include communication, coaching, and "conflict resolution" segments (Doerhman, 2003, p. 1). In another example, to develop the necessary skills early, organizations such as the University of Colorado at Colorado Springs have developed programs for college students and minority-group members to work with high school students on leadership skills including communication in general, interpersonal communication, and conflict resolution through effective communication (Doerhman, 2003, p. 1).

In the next section we will examine a few important types of communication that you should be aware of—namely, intentional and unintentional communication, verbal and nonverbal communication, and defensive and supportive communication.

INTENTIONAL–UNINTENTIONAL COMMUNICATION

Most of the time, we communicate for a purpose. It may be to get our point across, to persuade another, to prompt action, or simply to have fun. These types of messages are known as *intentional;* that is, we intend to communicate in order to achieve our purpose. However, we also may transmit messages that are *unintentional.* The slip of the tongue, or Freudian slip, is one well-known example of unintentional communication. Extensive new research has shown that unintentional communication errors (also called "toxic behaviors") cost American organizations an estimated $300 million a year in employee lost productivity, due to stress, and voluntary employee turnover (Kusy & Holloway, 2009; Pearson & Porath, 2009).

In her best-selling book *Slander* (2002), Ann Coulter quotes the famous anthropologist Margaret Mead, who described the tribesmen of New Guinea in the following way: "The natives are superficially agreeable, but they go in for cannibalism, headhunting, infanticide, incest, avoidance and joking relationships, and biting lice in half with their teeth" (p. 1). By analogy, Coulter compares this to the unintentional ways that members of the television and newspaper media distort the news according to their own (liberal) bias. She cites the following statistics: "In the 1992 presidential election, a mere 43 percent of Americans voted for Bill Clinton. That same year, 89 percent of Washington bureau chiefs reported voting for Clinton. Only 7 percent voted for George Bush. . . . A higher percentage of the Washington press corps voted for Clinton in 1992 than did 'Registered

Democrats'" (p. 56). On the other side of the coin, authors and former Democratic Party strategists James Carville and Paul Begala (2002) write an equally compelling argument to support their view that there is a conservative bias in well-known radio shows such as those hosted by Rush Limbaugh, Sean Hannity, Pat Buchanan, and others.

All of us can sympathize with a situation in which someone says something quite different from what he or she had intended to say. According to Freud, our id, or pleasure center, leads us to reveal what we really feel, whereas our ego—the rational, data-processing part of our personality—tends to limit or censor what we utter. When the id forces win out over the rational ego forces, the Freudian slip results. Freud (Ruch, 1972) stated that such unintentional verbal messages more than likely result when we are "distracted, confused, embarrassed, or simply not psychically engaged [or] when the thought is insufficiently worked out or the problem particularly complicated" (p. 102).

In a humorous example, in 2004 actress Heather Locklear was interviewed on the TV show *Live with Regis and Kelly* and accidentally used her ex-husband's name in place of her husband's name. Further reports state that she had been complaining about her husband earlier in the interview. Her slip was then interpreted as Locklear's expression of unhappiness with her current spouse. This adds meaning to her slip (*Los Angeles Times,* 2004)!

Unintentional messages may be transmitted by action as well as by words. People who cross their arms in front of themselves while rearing back in their chairs may be unknowingly communicating disapproval of events occurring in a group discussion. Frequently, group members direct their remarks (through eye contact) to those members whom they prefer or that they feel have influence in the group. This is often done unconsciously and unintentionally.

The use of time is something that can cause unintended communication reactions. Sometimes group members differ in their views of time, that is, what constitutes slow or rapid progress. A group's interaction pattern clearly affects the group's success (Bluedorn & Standifer, 2006). Groups that are open to new ideas, have a history of collaboration, and focus on the group's success, rather than on individual performance goals, are likely to develop better results. On the other hand, groups that are characterized by close-minded insularity, little collaboration, and a strong concern with achieving individual performance goals at the expense of group goals are likely to develop dysfunctional interaction patterns (pp. 363–64). These are all examples of unintentional communication.

Communication is not a one-way process, especially in groups. Members react to messages. They respond to one another. This response is called *feedback.* Stech and Ratliffe (1985, p. 22) say that providing feedback is just as complicated as sending the message. Like the intended message, feedback also has content and relationship levels. When person 2 gives feedback to person 1, that feedback is actually person 2's intended message. In an ongoing interaction, the two people continue to shift roles as sender and receiver, alternately providing each other with messages and feedback. O'Hair, Friedrich, and Shaver (2005) remind us that "the focus of feedback is not to pass judgment, but to report specific events or behavior, their effects, and what to do about them. Subjective interpretations . . . should be minimized" (p. 265).

Groups are one context in which we get feedback on behaviors that helps us eliminate unintentional cues. The gap between what we intend to communicate and what is actually received is called the *arc of distortion*. The larger the gap, the less effective we are in our relations with others. We can reduce the gap if we are receptive to feedback from others and if others are willing to share their impressions with us. In order for the arc to be reduced, the feedback must be of high quality. Most experts would agree that effective feedback should (1) be clear and understandable, (2) come from a trusted person, and (3) be as immediate as possible.

Feedback is usually best when it is immediate. For example, Williams (1996) advises that if we see a problematic behavior in the group, the best time to address it is right away. Often if the problem is not addressed, we tend more and more to avoid dealing with it as the problem grows (p. 208). For example, in one group, whenever one member (Bob) was bored or upset with the group's progress, he would indicate his feelings by his facial expressions. It was noticed by everyone in the group. Finally, the leader asked Bob a question that he knew pertained to something that Bob liked to talk about. Bob perked up immediately. So feedback can be subtle as well as direct. However, if nobody provides a problem member like Bob with any feedback, his behavior can become more and more disruptive to the rest of the group. After a while, if someone does address the problem, the feedback tends to be somewhat angry and less likely to help matters improve. Instead, it is likely to make Bob defensive and the problem then can become worse.

VERBAL–NONVERBAL COMMUNICATION

Research at Columbia University has shown that people who are lying tend to shrug their shoulders nearly four times as often as people telling the truth. In addition, liars talk faster and with a higher pitch compared to those telling the truth. Liars press their lips together and involuntarily smirk when they think they have gotten away with a lie. Finally, liars tend to show cognitive impairment with great nonfluencies in speech (Carney, 2010, pp. 32–33). So, watch for these communication behaviors if you suspect a person of not telling the truth.

As discussed above, we communicate not only with words (verbal messages) but by nonverbal means as well. Later in this chapter, we will discuss verbal cues, in the section on language behavior. Visual and vocal nonverbal cues will vary as a part of the process of discussion and will influence the eventual results of the discussion. There are many types of nonverbal cues, falling under the subheadings of visual and vocal cues. Researchers at the University of California at Santa Cruz (2004) define nonverbal communication as "facial expressions, tones of voice, gestures, eye contact, spatial arrangements, patterns of touch, expressive movement, cultural differences, and other 'nonverbal' acts." The primary aspects of nonverbal communication will be discussed in the next section.

Visual Cues

Visual cues are highly influential in interpersonal communication. *Facial expression* and *eye contact* are probably the two most important types of visual cues. Those who avoid looking at us communicate disapproval or disinterest. Those who look at us may still indicate a negative reaction on the basis of their facial expression. In Clearwater, Florida, police are running community programs regarding security issues. Bill Hardin, a Clearwater police officer, originally worked in the Navy in weapons analysis and intelligence and is now running the city's security program. Hardin is working to make residents aware of terrorism threats and teaches them to watch for suspicious body language (Cosdon, 2004). Since 9/11, officials and airport security workers have been taught how to identify suspicious airline passengers based on observation of visual cues such as facial espression and eye contact. The Federal Bureau of Investigation has taken a lead in training federal employees on the use of what they call "behavior profiling" (Davis et al., 2002). Joe Navarro, FBI counterterrorism agent, teaches courses in nonverbal communication for the FBI Academy in Quantico, Virginia. These programs are now open to community groups such as those led by Bill Hardin (Cosdon, 2004). Many experts in the field feel that watching visual cues is "more accurate than lie-detector tests," while others feel that this type of analysis is equivalent to phrenology and not a reliable method for detecting suspicous individuals (Davis et al., 2002). Either way, it is an evolving and compelling new science.

Researchers at Princeton University found that people make very quick judgments about a person's trustworthiness, competence, aggressiveness, and even likability within a fraction of a second. And people don't usually change their initial perceptions. In one study, subjects were shown pictures of pairs of political opponents. They were able to predict with 70 percent accuracy who would win the election (Bellew & Ridley, 2007).

We are extremely suspicious of people who won't look us in the eye. Speakers rated as "sincere" make eye contact three times more often than "insincere" speakers. So how do you make sincere eye contact? For 90 percent of Americans, sincere personal eye contact means using your right eye to look into the other person's right eye; the left eye is used only for depth perception.

To test this theory, use your left eye to look at someone else's left eye. Feels awkward, doesn't it? In most situations, sincere, respectful eye contact involves using your right eye to look into your counterpart's right eye.

Maintaining honest eye contact doesn't mean you should stare like an unblinking lizard, however. Sincere speakers blink 10–20 times a minute. In contrast, when Richard Nixon attended his first Watergate press conference, he blinked up to 40 times a minute. It is especially important to avoid excessive blinking when facing a news camera, where bright lights may naturally trigger a lot of blinking (Stein, 2007).

Probably the most rewarding cue is a smiling face and a head nod in combination with direct eye contact. From these and other cues, we infer support, confirmation, and agreement. Dr. Paul Ekman, a psychologist from the University of California at San Francisco, created the Facial Action Coding System (FACS) in 1978. Ekman studied "microexpressions," which are tiny movements of the face that add up to what we normally describe as composite facial expressions (Davis et al., 2002). Richmond and McCrosky (2000) emphasize the importance of the face: "The face is rich in communicative potential. It is the primary site for communication of emotional states; it reflects interpersonal attitudes; it provides nonverbal feedback on the comments of others; and some say it is the primary source of information next to human speech" (p. 52).

Although facial expression is usually a critical factor in nonverbal communication, there are some rare occasions in which other factors may take precedence. Mary Kay Ash, founder and chief executive officer of Mary Kay Cosmetics, cites the following example:

> I remember how offended I was when I was having lunch with my sales manager, and every time a pretty waitress walked by, his eyes would follow her across the room. I felt insulted and kept thinking to myself, "The waitress's legs are more important to him than what I have to say. He's not listening to me. He doesn't care about me." (quoted in Boone & Kurtz, 1994, p. 509)

One study confirmed the finding that the general tendency to look into a person's eyes can be preempted by other factors. Wahlers and Barker (1973) conducted an interview study and found that braless women got significantly less eye contact from males than their bra-wearing counterparts.

Eye contact, however, is a powerful type of nonverbal cue. Argyle (1967) estimates that in group communication we spend 30–60 percent of the time exchanging mutual glances with others. Many of these glances may last less than a second. He summarizes several unstated rules about visual interaction:

> a. A looker may invite interaction by staring at another person who is on the other side of a room. The target's studied return of the gaze is generally interpreted as acceptance of the invitation, while averting the eyes is a rejection of the looker's request.
>
> b. There is more mutual eye contact between friends than others, and a looker's frank gaze is widely interpreted as positive regard.
>
> c. Persons who seek eye contact while speaking are regarded not only as exceptionally well-disposed by their target, but also as more believable and earnest.
>
> d. If the usual short, intermittent gazes during conversation are replaced by gazes of longer duration, the target interprets this as meaning that the task is less important than the personal relation between the two persons. (pp. 115–16)

Several other principles have been borne out by experimental studies, as well as by systematic observation of ongoing behaviors. For example, females consistently make more eye contact than do males (Mehrabian, 1971). Also, we are able to assert dominance over others almost exclusively with eye contact in a matter of seconds when we first encounter one another (Strongman & Champness, 1968). We tend to direct our comments toward those from whom we expect or would like feedback. Conversely, avoiding eye contact is a way of protecting ourselves from the contact of others.

Facial expression, eye contact, and body positioning all reveal clear information about our present attitudes and feelings. We give approval and show disdain, all without saying a word. Sometimes our nonverbal responses to people lead others to make decisions about those people. This is reflected in the body of research investigating group members' nonverbal responses to leaders. The data demonstrate the existence of a social mechanism leading to the devaluation of leadership. Butler and Geis (1990) report that when some group members displayed unfavorable nonverbal responses to a leader, the remaining group members tended to rate that leader's contributions as less valuable. When favorable nonverbal cues were given, the leader's contributions were rated higher. Their study hypothesized and found that competent, assertive women in leadership roles elicit significantly more negative responses than do men in the same positions. This is thought to be a result of female leaders' breaking with the stereotypic submissive, "feminine" behaviors. When women served in stereotypic masculine roles (leadership), they received nonverbal disapproval from their peers. This disapproval was passed on to other group members, who assessed the female leaders as making less valuable contributions. This behavior has much to do with the elements of social influence and conformity discussed in Chapter 5.

Hand gestures are another type of visual cue. Barnlund (1968) states, "Next to the face, the hands are probably the most expressive part of the human body." Hand gestures are an effective way to bridge communication gaps in many situations. Let's look at the handshake as an example. A high school student at the Hillary Mullet Patrick Henry High School of Roanoke, Virginia, took a trip in February 2004 to Burkina Faso. The locals shook his hand, a gesture unfamiliar to them. The locals did know that this would be known as an accepted gesture by the student and would promote goodwill. The high school student noted that communicating with the natives of Burkina Faso was very difficult. He said that he utilized gesturing and facial expressions frequently to communicate (p. 6). On the flip side, in the employment setting, handshakes can speak volumes. The "limp fish" handshake can be very negative and project a poor first impression (Seebach, 2004).

Entire books have been devoted to the study of the use of hands in communication. It was once thought that hand gestures could be taught as a means of developing greater expressiveness. For example, the outstretched hands with the palms up would indicate a request for help, whereas the clenched fist would indicate a threat. For instance, Jon Stewart of Comedy Central's *Daily Show* made a comment regarding a hand gesture used by Democratic candidates for the last several decades. The gesture consists of a fist with the "thumb resting on top of the index finger." The director of the Center for Nonverbal Studies in Spokane, Washington, calls this the "rolling fist thumb show." The gesture dated all the way back to John F. Kennedy and was used both by President Bill Clinton and Senator John Kerry. David B. Givens, who wrote *Dictionary of Gestures, Signs, and Body Language Cues,* believes that the fist is a display of authority and the thumb is placed in a way that is read as compassion combined with authority. President George W. Bush used different gesturing according to Givens. Givens says that Bush used two primary hand gestures—palms up or palms down. The palms-down gesture meant, "I am adamant about this and I am certain," while the palms-up gesture meant that Bush was "softer on something" (Collington, 2004). The study of gestures today is more descriptive and leans less in the direction of trying to prescribe which gestures should be used in certain situations.

In one company, for example, a union grievance was filed on the basis of a gesture of an employee's boss. The grievance charged: "Animus toward the grievant can be demonstrated by the Department Head's handling of the application. . . . The application was tossed across the desk by the Department Head in the direction of the grievant. The Department Head's manner was offensive, embarrassing and unprofessional to both the grievant and the [union president]" (grievance dated 2011). This grievance went through several steps of the grievance procedure and tied up dozens of hours of managerial time for the better part of a year. There were also threats of legal action.

Correct use of gestures is especially critical within multicultural contexts. Axtell (1991) notes that military forces sent to Saudi Arabia during Operation Desert Storm were issued a 40-page booklet on gestures and body language among the Arabs. It offered such advice as the following: Avoid crossing the legs so that the sole of the shoe is pointed at someone, "don't be upset if Arabs stand very close, even touch you, when conversing, . . . [and be aware that] the 'O.K.' gesture (thumb and forefinger forming a circle) may be interpreted there as giving a curse" (pp. 12–13). In addition, in the Iraq war, American troops saw children appearing to be friendly, waving to them and giving them the "thumbs up" gesture. However, they didn't know that "in Iraq, the 'thumbs up' sign traditionally was the equivalent of the American middle-finger salute" (Woodward, 2006, p. 290). In Japan, putting your pointer fingers up by your ears means that you are "angry," and in France, pulling at the skin under your eye with your pointer fingers means that you "don't believe" what the recipient of the gesture is saying to you (University of California at Santa Cruz, 2004). In general, gestures are used more by Italians and Japanese, while in the United States, males use larger gestures than females (Seebach, 2004).

Physical appearance includes facial attractiveness as well as body shape and size and style of dress. In one study of physically attractive versus unattractive people, Widgery (1974) found that on the basis of faces alone, more-attractive people are consistently assumed to have higher credibility than their homelier counterparts. Recent research has confirmed these earlier findings. A 2010 *Newsweek* poll found that 64 percent of those polled felt that good-looking people had an advantage in virtually all aspects of social interaction. The survey was conducted by Princeton Research Associates. Walster and colleagues (1966) found that among 752 college students at a first-year dance, physical attractiveness was by far the most important factor in determining the extent to which a date would be liked by his or her partner. B. F. Skinner argued that beauty is a form of reinforcer, because it encourages us to look once again. Certainly, most fashion models of both sexes are reinforcing to look at!

A recent naturalistic study of schoolchildren's conversations recorded 590 comments regarding people's appearance in 22 hours of observation (Newman, Gabriel, & Jones, 2001); the ova and sperm of professional models are now available for purchase on the Internet; and in a recent survey of 107 plastic surgeons, respondents reported performing an average of 672 cosmetic and reconstructive surgeries in 2004 (American Academy of Facial Plastic and Reconstructive Surgery [AAFPRS], 2005). Physical appearance and beauty are unmistakably pervasive and powerful agents in the social world, and they influence our conversation, reproductive decisions, and perceptions of ourselves and others.

Body shape has been described in three basic categories by Sheldon (1954). The mesomorph is muscular and athletic looking and would be considered the most attractive. The ectomorph is tall, thin, and fragile looking. The endomorph is soft, round, and fat. Three representative examples of the respective body types would be Arnold Schwarzenegger, Pee Wee Herman, and the late John Candy. Our body shapes are usually some mixture of these three types. Jack LaLanne, the physical fitness personality, once said on a television show that if you raid the refrigerator every night, even if you are alone, your body itself communicates to everybody every day that you eat too much. So you're not fooling anybody.

Style of dress also communicates much about us. We are often judged as, for instance, "conservative" or "weird" on the basis of our clothing choices. Lefkowitz, Blake, and Mouton (1955) conducted an interesting study of the influence of a person's dress on jaywalking behavior. They collected data on jaywalking on three different days for three different one-hour periods. They wanted to determine whether pedestrians (these happened to be in Austin, Texas) would violate the "wait" signal more if they saw someone else violate it than if there were no violator. They were also interested in any differential effects that would result from differences in the violator's dress. The experimenters made use of a confederate who jaywalked while dressed in one of two ways. First, he dressed in a high-status manner, with a freshly pressed suit, shined shoes, white shirt, tie, and straw hat ("Mr. Clean"). The low-status dress consisted of an unpressed blue denim shirt, soiled and patched pants, well-worn shoes, and no hat ("Mr. Dirty"). Observations were made on 2,103 pedestrians who crossed the intersection during the hours of the experiment.

The study yielded several interesting results. Ninety-nine percent of the pedestrians obeyed the "wait" signal when no confederate was present or when the confederate also obeyed. When Mr. Dirty jaywalked, 4 percent of the other pedestrians also violated the signal. When Mr. Clean jaywalked, 14 percent of the other pedestrians also disobeyed.

The move toward more casual dress in the workplace has also created some interesting nonverbal issues. Bounds, Quick, and Nelson (1999) cite the following example: "In her black business suit, Heather Vandenberghe was the picture of professionalism this summer when she made a presentation to her board. Except for one thing: She also happened to be wearing a hot-pink tube top and black, high-heeled sandals" (p. B1). Bounds et al. went on to say that today people take more risks and are more "fashion-forward." This fashion trend was amplified by TV lawyer Ally McBeal, played by Calista Flockhart, who was often shown in the courtroom wearing micro-miniskirts and very high heels. Also, World Cup soccer player Brandi Chastain was seen all over the world when she celebrated by taking off her jersey and kneeled in shorts and sports bra. This laid-back look has swept all over America. At an Atlanta public-relations firm GCI Group, "some employees have such a relaxed sense of dress that Vice President Bill Crane says he knows who has belly-button rings" (p. B4).

In addition to clothing, aspects of physical appearance, such as hairstyles and jewelry, send visual cues. For instance, a person with multicolored or spiked hair and a punk rock appearance would not get very far in a job interview in most companies. In Santa Cruz, California, one food worker at the boardwalk amusement park was not allowed to wear a nose ring at work because doing so was against the law. Originally, the law also prohibited workers with pierced body parts and colorful hairdos. One woman reportedly changed her hair from fire-engine red back to brown. As it is, applicants for jobs have to "tuck their long hair under hats; no dangling earrings are allowed; and tattoos can't show because of possible gang connections" (Associated Press, 1992). In another example, at Oberson Middle School in Concord, New Hampshire, two eighth-grade female students were sent home from school because they both had nose piercings. The school passed the judgment that the nose piercings interfered with the learning process and sent the wrong message to other students. Piercings were also considered to violate the school dress code (Reed, 2004). What do you think about the school's dress code? What influence do you think factors such as these have on group dynamics?

To summarize, our physical appearance, including facial attractiveness, body shape, and choice of clothing, will determine to some extent our influence on others.

Body movements are another influential type of nonverbal cue. Each of us can probably remember having someone say, "You seem kind of down today," as a reaction to our slumped shoulders and slightly bowed head. Probably one of Peter Falk's most memorable roles was his slouchy interpretation of the TV detective Columbo. Although there were a wealth of other cues (gestures, raincoat, cigar), his body movements stood out very vividly, as did John Wayne's swagger and Paris Hilton's sassy walk.

Body orientation is an important factor in small group interaction. During the 2004 presidential debates, the candidates' wives expressed a nonverbal message of unity and camaraderie. They were both dressed the same (white suits), eliminating attire as a variable. Laura Bush gave Teresa Heinz Kerry a hug, and they moved into a conjoined hug (Stanley, 2004). This sent a very positive message to the very intimate debate audience. Richmond and McCroskey (2000) define body orientation as "the degree to which a communicator's shoulders and legs are turned in the direction of, rather than away from, the addressee" (p. 83). Mehrabian (1971) found that a seated communicator who leaned forward was perceived as having a more positive attitude than one who leaned backward and away from the person judging. Higher-status persons tend to be more relaxed in staff meetings than lower-status individuals, who sit straighter in their chairs. Body position may also add to our perception of a person as uptight. Schutz (1971) described this in the context of an encounter group:

> If a person is holding himself tight, I would either move on to someone else and count on the group interaction to loosen him up so that he can work better later, or perhaps choose to try to help him break through that defense. . . . A first step is to ask the person to relax by unlocking his arms and legs if he has them crossed, perhaps to stand up and shake himself loose, jiggle and breathe very deeply for several minutes. (p. 212)

Inclusiveness is another important aspect of body orientation. In a small group discussion, subgroups frequently form that are usually annoying to at least some in the group. Subgroups may be the result of one person's directing comments to only one or two others. *Directing comments* refers to body orientation

CASE STUDY

INSTANT MESSAGING IN PERSON

A software trainer named Stefani Pine created an idea called the "Zipit." This term refers to a small group of single individuals who gather regularly at the bar. No verbal communication is allowed except to order food or drinks from the bar. Participants must communicate with each other in writing or by using visual cues or gestures. Pine refers to the type of communications fostered by Zipit gatherings as "instant messaging in person" (Finney, 2004).

1. What challenges would the Zipit gathering offer in meeting new people?
2. What benefits would it offer?
3. What types of visual cues would be utilized?
4. Do you think that you would be comfortable participating in a Zipit gathering?

and the direction of eye contact. Those who feel excluded from the discussion will sooner or later begin to withdraw their participation from the group, and the benefit of their contributions will be lost. Thus, body orientation can be a potent factor in determining the discussion's outcome.

Visual symbolism can also speak volumes without saying a word. For example, in the courtroom, signaling, symbolic references, or any form of nonverbal communication is strictly prohibited. In Redwood City, California, convicted murderer Scott Peterson's attorney had a complaint filed against him by the prosecutor for nonverbally communicating with the jury. Peterson's attorney had created a replica of Peterson's boat and placed it outside the court. The prosecutor claimed that Peterson's attorney was trying to "engage in nonverbal communication" with the jury through this action in an attempt to influence them (Associated Press, 2004).

We all express ourselves nonverbally. A columnist for the *Roanoke Times and Work News* recommends videotaping oneself to understand how our verbal expressions look to others. Often we do not realize how much our expressions say about us, and in many cases they may be inaccurate (Miller, 2004).

Vocal Cues

In addition to verbal messages and visual cues, vocal cues affect small group interaction. There is usually some confusion between the terms *vocal cues* and *verbal cues*. Perhaps it would be helpful to remember that vocal cues are lost when a verbal (word) message is written down. Vocal cues include regional dialects, methods of pronunciation, and the five major factors of (1) volume, (2) rate and fluency, (3) pitch, (4) quality, and (5) inflection.

Try to imagine the sound of your voice saying, "Now that we are all here, we can get the meeting started." Now think of how it would sound as stated by David

Letterman, Chris Rock, Jay Leno, Dr. Phil, Jennifer Lopez, Tom Cruise, Penelope Cruz, Simon Cowell, Oprah Winfrey, Bart Simpson, or some of your own friends. Imagine something said in a sarcastic versus a serious tone. In 2004, Kurt Koller created the website "Sarcasm.com"; he defines sarcasm as "the ability to quickly come up with comments that hit close to home but that have a humorous edge to them" (Johnson, 2003). There are also differences in vocal cues across genders. Susan Golant, author of *You Don't Say: Navigating Nonverbal Communication Between the Sexes,* analyzed communication differences in the workplace. She goes a step further to discuss "vocal cues—pitch, tone, inflection, rate of speech, pausing, etc." (Seebach, 2004). Each person's voice is unique; sometimes voiceprints are used like fingerprints for identification. This individuality results from the complex combination of vocal cues mentioned above. Speaking with adequate *volume,* or loudness, is the first responsibility of any communicator. Conversely, the first responsibility of listeners is to let speakers know they can't be heard. Speakers should be asked to speak more loudly and to repeat the part that was missed. This requires some tact, however. The intent should be to communicate, "I want to know what you're saying," rather than, "Listen, dummy, I'm important and you're not taking my listening convenience into sufficient account."

Groups tend to have more problems with adequate volume than, say, individuals involved in personal conversations. As the size of the group increases, the hearing difficulties may also increase, because there are more potential sources of interfering noise, and the distance from the speaker to any given member in the group tends to be greater.

A second critical vocal cue is *rate and fluency.* Rate refers to words uttered per minute (WPM), and fluency refers to the lack of interruptions (which may influence the rate). We have all suffered the unpleasantness of listening to a person who injects long pauses in the middle of sentences or who frequently throws in distracting verbal fillers such as "ah," "um," "er," "why I," "and-uh," "You know what I'm saying," and "like," among others. An average speaking rate is between 125 and 175 WPM. If the person is able to articulate well—that is, to speak distinctly—a faster rate seems to be more interesting to listen to. Studies in listener comprehension indicate that we can understand rates two to three times the normal speed with little difficulty. In group discussion, the fluent speaker is usually more pleasant to listen to.

Vocal pitch refers to the frequency in cycles per second (CPS) of the vocal tones. Melanie Griffith and Chris Rock have high-pitched (or high-frequency) voices; James Earl Jones has a lower-pitched voice. There is probably no such thing as the perfectly pitched voice; however, most successful professional announcers seem to have lower-pitched voices (such as Joe Buck and Al Michaels).

Vocal quality refers to the resonance of the voice. Different examples would include crispness (Britney Spears), hoarseness (Vin Diesel), harshness (Fran Drescher), nasality (Sylvester Stallone), and huskiness (Debra Winger). Vocal quality may determine the extent to which people want to listen to us for any length of time. The late Johnny Carson's laugh was once described as being "like the sound of cracking plastic." The voice of comedian Jerry Lewis was once compared to "the sound of scratching your fingernail across a blackboard." On the other hand, some people who try to make their voices sound deeper and more resonant come across as phony and artificial.

It is now possible to medically change the way that your voice sounds. In June 2004, *USA Today* published an article addressing the seemingly new practice of "voice lifts." Surgery has been available to correct *voice-quality* medical concerns, but it is now available cosmetically to help people actually sound younger. Robert Thayer Sataloff founded "voice medicine" technology. He is chair of otolaryngology at the Graduate Hospital in Philadelphia. He says that "some people who pay $15,000 for a face lift might not get the full benefit if they open their mouth and sound like they're 75"—they need a "voice lift" (Puente, 2004). The surgery actually squeezes the vocal cords close together to restore their youthful condition since they get more relaxed with age.

A 2004 *Wall Street Journal* article addressed examples of vocal style and job growth. In one example, an employee was promoted but sounded so young that she had a hard time gaining the respect of her colleagues. There is now an actual business in coaching "speech flaws" including all aspects of vocal quality (Lublin, 2004).

Inflection refers to the relative emphasis, pitch changes, and duration in uttering different word parts in a sentence. The southern American's accent is characterized by a drawn-out vowel sound—for example, "Atlanta" (northern pronunciation) versus "Atlaaanta" (southern pronunciation). Inflections also include the rise in vocal pitch at the end of an interrogative sentence:

Are you coming?

Duration in uttering different word parts in a sentence is a very revealing vocal cue. Frieda Goldman-Eisler, a 1950s London psychologist, found through her dedicated research that 50 percent of our speaking time is filled with silence. The silence is filled with vocal cues called *disfluencies*, which are "filler words" such as "um" or "uh." The number of disfluencies used by a speaker can be assessed to measure the discomfort level of the speaker. The more uncomfortable a speaker is, the more disfluencies she or he uses when talking. Conversely, the more relaxed a speaker is, the less disfluencies she or he uses. Studies revealed that alcohol consumption increases relaxation and therefore decreases use of disfluencies. This does not suggest that a martini before a speech is a good idea, but it is interesting research! It is also important to note that every culture has its own filler words. For instance, the French say "euh," Americans say "um" or "uh," the Turkish say "mmm," and the Japanese say "eh-to." These disfluencies are also creating new challenges for voice technology systems that must recognize cross-cultural disfluencies that occur with the natural speech process (Erard, 2004).

Probably the most critical thing to remember about vocal inflections is that they may indicate a lot of the emotional tone of a statement. The statement "Oh, great!" can be said with true enthusiasm or great disgust. We can use our voices to indicate sarcasm, ridicule, and superiority, and what we convey may be counterproductive to the group's progress.

Leathers (2002) reports that several emotions can be reliably detected in most speakers. He had groups of students rate 10 different vocal messages according to the emotions they conveyed (for example, disgust, happiness, sadness, bewilderment, surprise, or anger). Although Leathers used this technique for the purpose of research, the practical aspect is that vocal cues do accurately convey emotions. As we become more aware and in control of our nonverbal cues, we may improve our effectiveness in groups. For example, several students complained about a professor whose tone of voice was quite abusive to them. They were considering quitting his class because of this. When he was told, he was shocked. He had been unaware of the negative effect his vocal tone had on his teaching effectiveness.

Clearly, not all the cues are exhibited in the small group setting. However, as we become more aware of our nonverbal behavior overall, we can begin to change some of the cues that appear to need improvement. We can also begin to develop our sensitivities to the nonverbal behaviors of others. For example, if a meeting has been going on for a long time, you may detect fatigue and low levels of energy through bored facial expressions, yawns, or unenthusiastic vocal tones. These cues may indicate that the group needs to take a break in order to continue at peak efficiency. A person not sensitive to these cues may try to keep pushing a tired group, only to accomplish less and less.

In summarizing this section on verbal and nonverbal cues, we need to point out that all these cues are perceived as a whole. In reality, we do not dissect them as we have done in this analysis. For example, it has been found that when we say one thing but nonverbally indicate something else (as with "I really appreciate that" spoken sarcastically), the *nonverbal* message is more likely to be believed. In this same context, subjects in one study who were told to lie showed several nonverbal changes. There were more errors in their speech, they had less direct eye contact, and they talked less than they had when they were telling the truth (Mehrabian, 1971). Obviously, nonverbal communication plays a significant role in small groups. Communication experts agree that whether you say anything or not, "you can't not communicate." Thus, we need to keep in mind the importance of both verbal and nonverbal messages.

Nonverbal communication takes a different form at the organizational level. Ornstein (1989) asserted that people are often unaware of the nonverbal communication that results from the layout and decor of an office. Definite relationships have been established between office design and various organizational behaviors, attitudes, and impressions. An open-office layout, as opposed to the conventional, individual-office design, is often conducive to communication in the workplace and can lead to greater employee satisfaction. If employees are comfortable in their offices, they feel that their managers are concerned about their well-being, and they will be more satisfied in their jobs. Other elements of the workplace that affect employee behaviors and attitudes include seating arrangement, lighting, temperature, noise, and the presence of artwork. The decor and layout of corporate offices lead to the impressions that people have about that corporation: "Not only is office configuration important in conveying information about the organization's values, but the physical layout of the offices themselves . . . also serves to reinforce the company's values" (Ornstein, 1989, p. 144).

Ornstein made suggestions to managers about what they should consider when implementing changes in office layout: (1) Managers should seek input from employees who will be affected by the change; (2) they should thoroughly analyze the work to be performed in the space under consideration; (3) they should consider the values, goals, and behaviors they want to reinforce by their selection of office design; and (4) they should consider the influence office design has on outsiders who have cause to visit the facility.

More recently, newspaper columnist Joyce Gannon (2003) addressed the effects of space on perception of the organizational environment. The original facility purchased for the H.J. Heinz Corporation's North American headquarters was dark and drab. Since then, the facility has undergone a substantial transformation. Gannon comments that it is very open and bright, with open-cube spaces, glass walls and doors, café areas, and skylights. Heinz embraced the concept of openness with the goal of opening lines of communication and increasing productivity. Heinz also felt that the special design broke down hierarchical boundaries. According to David Ross of the Design Alliance, Heinz once said that this openness "enhances morale and helps better communicate to people what's going on with the business" (Gannon, 2003). Business places and environments of today have become open spaces to promote cross-functional work styles and to inspire creativity.

Recent research has put the new workspace and organizational design to the test. A study by BOSTI Associates of Buffalo, New York, found that the following items were highest on employee environmental wish lists: "distraction-free work" and "interactions with co-workers" (Downey, 2004, p. 40). A facility design and planning company called Flad and Associates in Madison, Wisconsin, put these elements into play when constucting its own facility. It studied "interaction generators" to discover what sparked positive worker interactions and communications in the workplace. Flad then created "interactive spaces" to facilitate communication. These spaces can be found outside the elevator, near the bathroom, in any corner, and near the kitchen area. The Flad sales force works closely together in an open atmosphere that promotes teamwork and higher productivity (Downey, 2004). In another example, Sun Microsystems has created shared workspaces and associate-driven hours to promote flexibility and work–life balance (Hudson, 2004).

The U.S. government has also joined the circles of contemporary research on the subject. In 2003, the American Institute of Architects and the National Institute of Health and General Services Administration (GSA) Public Buildings Service division took the current research a step further by studying workers' physical reactions to different office spatial environments. In this study, federal employees wore heart monitors for a full day to test stress in different types of environments. Another study by the University of Wisconsin at Madison's neuroscience department and the GSA monitored participant reactions to images of different types of buildings. This new line of study is the first in a century and a half to look closely at environments and individual health in the workplace (Smith, 2003).

DEFENSIVE–SUPPORTIVE COMMUNICATION

For several years, it has been an established fact that when someone threatens us psychologically, we react by throwing up a barrier against that threat.. That barrier is referred to as a *defense mechanism.* Once that defensive barrier has been erected, effective communication is reduced. Thus, it is valuable to learn how we can avoid arousing others' protective psychological shields. In a classic article, Gibb (1961) described six differences between what he called defensive and supportive communication climates. More recently, Whetton and Cameron (2005) have refined Gibb's concepts as we see below.

Supportive Climates	*Defensive Climates*
Description	Evaluation
Problem orientation	Control
Spontaneity	Strategy
Empathy	Neutrality
Equality	Superiority
Provisionalism	Certainty

Sharon Ellison (2004), speaker and communication expert, and founder of PNDC (Powerful Non-Defensive Communication) Enzine, has expanded research in defensive and supportive communication climates. (You can read more about PNDC Enzine and Sharon Ellison at www.pndc.com.) Ellison has spent her life studying communication methodology with the purpose of eliminating power boundaries and general defensiveness in communication settings. Her goal is to help people solve conflict more productively through nondefensive communication. Ellison, author of *Taking the War out of Our Words,* feels strongly that we have "transferred military logic into our everyday conversational practices." According to her theory, defensive communication choices parallel the choices that people have in war. The three choices that people have in war, and in defensive communication climates, says Ellison, are "surrender, withdrawal, and attack." If *surrendering,* a communicator can either surrender through "betrayal," by taking responsibility for something he or she is not responsible for, or through "sabotage," by faking responsibility and then responding in a passive-aggressive fashion. When *withdrawing,* a communicator will either "escape" (avoid the situation) or "entrap," which forces the enemy to do something wrong through actual entrapment. If *attacking,* the communicator can either "justify" (rationalize) or "blame" (attack and judge) the enemy (Ford, 2004). Ellison focuses on taking the "war" out of the communication climate.

In a laboratory simulation involving 50 zero-history undergraduates, researchers found that group members' average scores on extraversion, agreeableness, and openness personality factors all correlated positively with the rate at which they generated supportive communication. Further, the rate of supportive communication correlated positively with the percentage of members who reported that the consensus decision rule had been applied. In addition, the percentage reporting consensus correlated positively with average ratings of satisfaction, self-representation, other representation, and fairness (Sager & Gastil, 2006).

Description Versus Evaluation

When we feel we are being evaluated, especially when someone is criticizing us, we are likely to rise to our own defense. However, when we feel that a person is objectively describing us without adding an evaluation, we are not as likely to become defensive. Perhaps you have experienced the following situation: You ask a fellow group member for information—"Bill, have you got the research data we need for the class presentation?"—and you get an answer something like "I didn't know I was supposed to get that information." The original question is intended to solicit information, but the answer is an attempt to defend against a perceived criticism. Tone of voice can add an element of criticism or evaluation even when we are not intending it.

Problem Orientation Versus Control

When someone tries to control or coerce us, we become more uncomfortable than when a person seeks to solve a problem without forcing us to go along with the solution. O'Toole (1999) argues that there must be at least 35 theories as to why people resist being told what to do. It does seem to be a basic human characteristic to dislike others trying to control us. Think of how you would react to the following two approaches: (1) "Doris, what is your advice on how to attack this problem?" and (2) "Doris, I think this would be a good project for you to tackle. Why don't you work on it and report back to the group at our next meeting?" The first approach is more of a problem orientation; the second is more controlling.

Spontaneity Versus Strategy

A person who has a preset plan usually turns us off, as opposed to one who reacts spontaneously to situations. Strategy often implies a gimmick or even some deception. I once went to a three-hour deans' council meeting to decide on budget allocations for the upcoming academic year. Each dean presented his or her case for why he or she needed more money. However, at the end of the meeting, the provost handed out his decision regarding the budgets for the upcoming year. All the deans felt betrayed since the decision had already been made, and the provost had let us waste three hours. We would have accepted it much more if he had simply given us his decision at the beginning of the meeting. Pseudo-participative decision making is even worse than autocratic decision making.

Empathy Versus Neutrality

When a person is neutral toward us, as opposed to empathic or sympathetic, this usually makes us more defensive. We all want to feel that someone cares about how we feel. Ford Motor Company once had a terrible explosion at its Dearborn facility in which several workers were killed and several others were badly burned. William Clay Ford, Jr., chair of the board, personally went to the site of the explosion, against the advice of his public relations staff. He stayed with the families in the hospital, and he went to the homes of those workers who had been killed. When he spoke to the press, he said that this was the worst day of his life and that Ford was a family and these were like members of his family who had been injured. His genuine feelings of warmth and support for these families were an outstanding example of leadership and empathy.

Equality Versus Superiority

When a person acts in a superior manner instead of treating us as equals, we say that person is on an ego trip. Such superior behavior is deflating to our

PRACTICAL TIPS

Communication expert Jodi Glickman offers the following practical advice on how to speak up in meetings:

Often people don't speak up because they're afraid of being seen as wrong, uninformed, or [having a] dumb idea. A great way to sidestep this inherent fear is to depersonalize your idea, putting a question to the group. When you think you might have a good idea but aren't too confident about it, go ahead with a comment such as:

Have we thought about . . . getting Steve involved in the PR campaign directly?

Did anyone mention . . . the Brealy report? I seem to recall it covered some of the same topics Andrew has raised here.

Another option we may want to consider . . . is pushing back the deadline until October.

Is it worth going back to . . . last week's minutes from the meeting to review the things we agreed on?

This way, you're contributing to the conversation and adding value to the group—but not taking over the conversation. By using a more informal question, you'll be able to make your idea heard, without overstating your position. (Glickman, 2010)

self-esteem and arouses our defenses. Nobody likes someone who acts like they are better than we are. When Al Dunlap was CEO of Sunbeam, he often acted in an arrogant manner (Dunlap, 1996). He seemed to take pride and pleasure in putting people out of their jobs. When he was fired, most people felt that it couldn't have happened to a more deserving person.

Provisionalism Versus Certainty

Finally, when someone acts as a "know-it-all," this attitude of certainty or dogmatism is less pleasant than that of a person who has an open mind and acts with a degree of provisionalism. I once knew an economist who would make predictions about what the economy was going to do in the next year. He was so cocky and sure of himself that he would argue with others who questioned his predictions. It turned others off so much that when his predictions turned out to be wrong, others would tape the newspaper clippings to his office door just to make him look bad. It is so much more appealing when someone says, "In my view the future will be such and so. But certainly nobody can predict the future with any certainty. What do you think?"

Gibb found that groups with defensive climates got more bogged down in worthless, ego-protecting discussion and accomplished less than did those with more supportive climates. This viewpoint is confirmed and explained even more strongly by Goleman, Boyatzis, and McKee (2002).

Sometimes it may become necessary to criticize a group member. This is difficult and embarrassing for everyone involved. In fact, Weisinger (1989) described criticism within a group as "one of the most difficult criticism encounters" (p. 245). When one member of the group is criticized, the other members of the group are less likely to contribute, for fear of being put down. Weisinger (pp. 246–48) offered three strategies for criticizing group work or group members while still maintaining a supportive environment for the group:

1. Direct critical comments to the work, and not to the person who performed it.
2. Turn individual criticism into a group criticism by making the statement general.
3. Present the criticism in a way that forces the group members to come up with answers to the problem.

The first strategy depersonalizes the criticism by addressing it to the task rather than the person. It's the difference between saying "This could use some more work" and "You did this wrong. You must redo it." The latter is more likely to bring about feelings of resentment and defensiveness than the former. The second strategy aims the criticism at the whole group, as a general request for change. Rather than saying, "You are not spending enough time on the project," say, "We could all stand to commit ourselves more to the project." Although there is a chance that the person for whom the comment was intended will miss it altogether, such a strategy maintains the supportive nature of the group and will help to encourage the other members of the group. The purpose of the third strategy is to involve the group members in the solution process. Instead of laying harsh criticism on the members of the group ("Your sales records are rotten! The company is ready to fold"), invite them to come up with a solution to the problem ("Sales are down throughout the company. Does anyone have any ideas on how to remedy the situation?").

A specific line of research on supportive versus defensive communication has investigated confirming versus disconfirming aspects of communication. Dance and Larson (1976) defined these concepts in the following way: "Confirmation, as used in an interpersonal sense, refers to any behavior that causes another person to value himself more. Its opposite, disconfirmation, refers to any behavior that causes another person to value himself less" (p. 77).

The confirmation–disconfirmation literature has expanded within recent years. Although the basic thrust of the theory remains the same—that is, that communication with others is potentially confirming or disconfirming—the role of such behavior in communication has been continually refined.

LaFasto and Larson (2001) divide communication patterns into four types:

1. Explicit rejection (disconfirming)
2. Implicit rejection (disconfirming)
3. Explicit acceptance (confirming)
4. Implicit acceptance (confirming)

Explicit rejection involves either a negative evaluation or an overt dismissal of the person or his or her message. For example:

A: I can't understand how they can just sit on their duffs and not do anything about it. Time is running out.

B: Yeah, well, I don't see you doing anything about it.

Implicit rejection involves four more subtle types of disconfirmation:

1. Interruptions—when a speaker cuts you off in midsentence
2. Imperviousness—when a speaker ignores what you say as if you had never said it
3. Irrelevant response—when the speaker starts off on a totally unrelated topic in response to your initial comment
4. Tangential response—when a person gives some acknowledgment of your initial comment but immediately launches off on a new irrelevant topic

Explicit acceptance involves a positive evaluation of either the person or his or her communication extent. For example:

A: So I just told him straight out that HE WASN'T GOING TO PULL THAT KIND OF STUFF WITH ME.

B: That took guts.

Implicit acceptance involves either a direct acknowledgment of a person's remark, an attempt to clarify the remark by asking for more information, or an expression of positive feeling. For example:

A: What I meant to say was that I've known him for a long time, and I've never seen him do anything like that.

B: Oh, well, now I understand.

The importance of confirmation–disconfirmation literature lies in its specific identification of communication patterns that seem to help or hinder communication effectiveness in most situations. Cissna (1976), who summarized studies in widely differing situations, found that the only factor that appeared in all these studies was the confirmation–disconfirmation factor. Thus, this factor may be one of the most pervasive dimensions in human communication.

Stephen Covey (1990), in his best-selling book *The Seven Habits of Highly Effective People,* lists as one of the habits: "Seek first to understand, then to be understood." This is excellent advice and is totally consistent with the notion of confirming types of communication. In his follow-up best-seller, *Principle-Centered Leadership,* Covey (1991) states:

> Technique is relatively unimportant compared to trust, which is the result of our trustworthiness over time. When trust is high, we communicate easily, effortlessly, instantaneously. We can make mistakes and others will still capture our meaning. But when trust is low, communication is exhausting, time-consuming, ineffective, and inordinately difficult. (p. 18)

New research by Seligman (2011) supports and confirms these four communication behaviors, but calls them, respectively:

1. Active and destructive
2. Passive and destructive
3. Active and constructive
4. Passive and constructive (pp. 48–49)

CONTENT AND PROCESS OF COMMUNICATION

One rather difficult distinction to make about group discussion is the difference between the content of the discussion and the process. Suppose a small group of students is discussing the topic "How can political corruption in the United States be reduced?" in front of the class. When the discussion is over, the professor asks the others in the class to comment on the discussion. Comments on the *content* of the discussion might include the following:

- "I think political corruption will always be with us."
- "I think politics are no more dirty now than in the past."
- "The political system has shown its strength by catching its own offenders."

These comments are typical of an untrained observer. They all deal with the topic of the discussion, and the observer frequently gets into the heat of the topic.

Comments about the *process* of the same discussion are quite different, as illustrated by the following:

- "Joe dominated the group while the others couldn't get a word in edgewise."
- "Most of your comments were based on opinions. Few actual facts were brought out."
- "I think you got bogged down in defining the problem and never really got to any conclusion as to how to solve the problem."

These comments deal with the process or manner in which the discussion was conducted. This type of observation usually requires more insight into group interaction. It allows both participants and observers to learn from one discussion some principles of group interaction that can be generalized to other discussions. Thus, it is important to be able to distinguish the discussion content from the discussion process.

Two students were asked to describe the group processes in their small group's discussion of the ethics of cloning humans (Exercise 2 in Chapter 1). Notice the differences in their descriptions:

STUDENT 1

I feel a certain resentment toward the idea of *producing* life, which I consider cloning to be. I especially feel a resentment toward producing beings to act as slaves or to be

PRACTICAL TIPS

Dr. Karl Albrecht (2004) developed a "Power Thinking Course" and has several tips for better listening in his "thinking" list:

1. Pay attention to differences in thinking styles; remember that each person has his or her own unique way of constructing reality.
2. Listen for the subtext: facts, feelings, values, and opinions.
3. Suspend judgment when hearing something new.
4. Explain things in the other person's thinking pattern, not always your own.
5. Remember that "truth" is relative to the individual brain-mind system in which it arises, and to the language system used to construct it.
6. To change the way you're feeling, change what you're doing.

used by us in any way. My group discussed the idea of controlling the traits of cloned human beings for specialized purposes. I do not feel that God appreciates his children tampering with the miracle of life.

STUDENT 2

The group started with the usual "I guess we're supposed to's" and, after only a minimal amount of paper shuffling, got down to the subject at hand.

Of the five-person group, only four participated. It was interesting to note who assumed the leadership role, for how long, for what reasons, how effectively, and so on. I feel that the member who occupied this role initially usually does not do so in other groups—that members who seemed to know something about this subject successfully opened the discussion and maintained it by asking others questions. What I looked for but did *not* see was direct eye contact, an authoritative tone of voice (I didn't say authoritarian), and backbone enough to justify occupying the leader's role. I think she was assuming this behavior to get a good grade.

Notice how student 1 discusses only the *topic* of the discussion content. Student 2, however, really discusses the group's *process,* or behavior, and therefore does a much better job of fulfilling the assignment.

Finally, in a comprehensive study, Insko and colleagues (1993) found that communication within groups led to significantly greater cooperation and less competition than was the case when individuals worked independently and did not communicate with one another.

Listening

In the ancient Greek play *Antigone,* Sophocles (495–406 B.C.) tells the story of Creon, the king of Thebes, who refuses to listen to the requests of his subjects when they ask him to grant mercy to his niece, Antigone. This stubbornness, born out of fear, eventually proves to be the cause of Creon's self-destruction. Ineffective listening has been a problem for centuries. The problem of poor listening is so chronic that one author (Isaacs, 1999) has said that "people don't listen, they reload" (p. 18).

How many times have you been annoyed by someone in a meeting who makes a point that someone else just stated a few minutes before, but the second

PRACTICAL TIPS

The following are 10 rules for communicating effectively, adapted from Frank Luntz (2007):

1. Use small words (simplicity).
2. Use short sentences (brevity).
3. Remember that credibility is key.
4. Use repetition—consistency matters.
5. Offer something fresh and new (novelty).
6. Use alliteration—sounds matter.
7. Speak aspirationally: Appeal to people's best motives.
8. Visualize: Use the word "imagine."
9. Ask questions.
10. Provide context and explain the relevance of your information.

speaker doesn't realize it because she or he wasn't listening? Meetings can sometimes be boring (chair of the bored), unproductive, and lengthy. As a result, people's attention may fade. When that happens, the group's productivity is reduced. Research on managerial communication has found that employees most value supervisors who (1) are goal-oriented, (2) use a team approach, and (3) are supportive. This type of supervisor backs the employee rather than looks for the employee's mistakes. Employees also value supervisors who listen to the employee's side of an issue before making up their own mind on the issue. A substantial body of research has found that when we can make the other person feel really understood, we are often seen as effective communicators. One additional finding is that repeating your comments (or message redundancy) helps get your message across. Nely and Leonardi (2011) studied 13 managers in six companies for over 250 hours and found that planned redundancy (repetition) of comments was significantly more effective than for those who did not use redundancy. They found that "the managers who were deliberately redundant moved their teams forward faster and more smoothly" (p. 38). You may have noticed this in your meetings, when you have a momentary distraction and miss an important comment. If the person repeats the comment, it is helpful.

What if you are part of a sales team? One of the most important aspects of successful selling is first to find out what the customer's needs are before trying to determine what product or service will best fit his or her needs. Similarly, most experts who have studied negotiation teams agree that when you are talking, you are giving away information; when you are listening, you are gaining information. Which do you suppose is better in a negotiation? I have noticed in several collective bargaining committee negotiations that those who listen carefully tend to be more successful in seeing ways to find common ground in resolving the conflict.

In problem-solving teams, what do you suppose is one of the most important communication skills for synthesizing various member contributions? You guessed it: listening. Note the excitement of Bill Gates, CEO of Microsoft, as he talks about being part of a really effective team early in his career. "We didn't obey a 24-hour clock. We'd come in and [work] for a couple of days straight, . . . when it was time to eat, we'd get in our cars and kind of race over to the restaurant and sit and talk about what we were doing. Sometimes I'd get so excited about things, I'd forget to eat" (Lipman-Blumen & Leavitt, 1999, p. 8).

Whether you are interested in improving your communication skills as a manager, as a member of a sales team or a negotiation team, or as a team problem solver, listening is one common denominator for success. Remember the old adage, "None of us is as smart as all of us" (Blanchard, 1999). For more on the subject of listening, see Tubbs and Moss (2008) and Chapter 5, and log onto http://www.listen.org/quotations/quotes_caring.html.

Language Behavior

Words are the only things that last forever. —Winston Churchill

A few years ago, the comedian Michael Richards, best known as Kramer on the sitcom *Seinfeld,* had a meltdown at the Laugh Factory in Los Angeles. In response to an African American audience member's heckling, Richards started using the "n" word repeatedly and made many other racial comments. Months earlier, Mel Gibson had a similar race-related incident: When he was pulled over by the police in Los Angeles, he began yelling anti-Semitic comments (Hamilton, 2006). In both instances, these outbursts may have permanently tainted society's perception of these celebrities.

The study of the interaction between verbal symbols and the thought patterns associated with them is referred to as *general semantics.* The Institute of General Semantics (IGS), a not-for-profit member-based organization, describes general semantics as "the study of how we perceive, construct, and *communicate* our life experiences." IGS strives to "seek more effective inter-personal, intra-personal, and inter-cultural relationships by focusing on the impact of language and symbols on individuals and societies' behavior" (2004). General semantics is also the application of the way people process information in a particular system. General semantics sees the world as a system of many dimensions that connect the human race with its environment. Events can be peeled apart at multiple levels by a process called *abstracting,* which looks at the multiple causes behind events. People use general semantics to understand how people adapt to their environments and to understand the causes behind events (Kenyon, 2004).

For an additional viewpoint, Stockdale (2004) defines general semantics as "an inter-disciplinary discipline that makes it easier for you to live with yourself, you to live with others, and others to live with you. . . . In general semantics, we deal with matters that affect how you prepare for the inevitable accidents waiting to happen in your life and then how you respond when they do happen." General semantics pulls together the external world, the internal world, the nonverbal world, and the verbal world. The nonverbal world consists of information collected by the senses, while the verbal world consists of words, symbols, values, and assumptions or anything that can be described through language. The sphere of communication includes the external and internal worlds that can be described through language and the world that is "not words" (Stockdale, 2004).

If you think that something is "mere semantics," think again. When AT&T and Cingular Wireless merged in 2005, AT&T and its owners, ABC, spent over $4 million to increase brand awareness of Cingular. This has made it the most popular among the younger generation by using voting for *American Idol* as one of its tools (Hood, 2006).

If you have ever become bogged down in a group discussion because of a difficulty in defining terms or language problems, as in the case study at the beginning of this chapter, you will immediately see the relevance of this topic to the study of small group interaction. In fact, some discussions may even focus on the problem of choosing the appropriate verbal symbol to represent a concept. By 2008, the ever-growing popularity of text messaging had led to the formation of a new "language" for the individuals who use cell phones far more than traditional land lines. Those who mainly fit into this group are teenagers and young adults across the globe. They have created an abbreviated version of their existing languages to type faster. Below are some examples of English-language text-messaging shorthand (http://www.netlingo.com):

CUL8R—see you later

BRB—be right back

2BZ4UQT—too busy for you cutie

@TEOTD—at the end of the day

LOL—laughing out loud

P911—parent alert

TNX—thanks

New products frequently have several proposed names that may be market-tested for consumer response. In her excellent book *Team Talk,* Anne Donnellon (1996) contends that the verbal interaction in teams is their defining characteristic. An excerpt of her work is included at the end of this chapter. Each of us will undoubtedly be involved with language problems of one sort or another in group discussions. Our discussion will focus on four specific language problems that frequently plague groups: (1) bypassing, (2) inference making, (3) polarizing, and (4) signal reactions.

BYPASSING

> If your language is confused, your intellect, if not your whole character, will almost certainly correspond. —Sir Arthur Quiller-Couch

A French organization called *Communiqué* (2003) focuses on the importance of effective communication skills. It states that "good communication can be a matter of life or death." Consider the following real events. In January 1990, an Avianca Airlines passenger plane crashed on Long Island, New York, killing 73 people. A subsequent investigation attributed the crash to a miscommunication between the pilots and the air traffic controllers. One report indicated that "Avianca pilots were not trained to use the term 'fuel emergency.' … Controllers testified that the plane received no priority to land that night because the term 'fuel emergency' was not used" (Associated Press, 1990a). In another historical example, in the 1970s, two jets collided while one was landing and one was taking off because both made assumptions based on the communication instructions from air traffic control. In this accident, 576 people were killed. Imagine the potential consequences of incorrect information given to 911 operators or misunderstood instructions given to ambulance drivers (Communiqué, 2004).

These cases illustrate situations in which a misunderstanding occurred because of a language problem. This sort of misunderstanding is referred to as *bypassing*. It is defined as "the miscommunication pattern which occurs when the *sender* (speaker, writer, and so on) and the *receiver* (listener, reader, and so forth) *miss each other with their meaning*" (Haney, 1992). To illustrate this concept, Monster.com has a section called "Work Abroad" that discusses cultural differences encountered by traveling business officials (www.workabroad.monster.com). One excerpt focuses on mistakes in translation or in language use, which is a basic type of bypassing. In one example, the writer tells the story of a meeting in France with his distributor and a potential customer who spoke only French. The distributor was bilingual and was able to act as translator; however, he was not a very good translator. The meeting dragged on for 20 minutes before they realized that they were talking about completely different things (Falkoff, 2004). In another example, the writer was teaching English in Japan. One of his students, only four years old, tried to communicate with him in his newly learned English but was having difficulty. The teacher, in efforts to console the boy, told him "it's OK, it's OK, it's just fine" in Japanese. The student then proceeded to urinate just standing there! The writer's efforts to console the child had resulted in him telling the boy that it was "OK" to do so (Falkoff, 2004)!

Naoki Kameda, professor at Commerce Doshisha University in Japan, wrote an article called "Miscommunication in Japanese-U.S. Trade Relationship." He describes examples of common miscommunications, or "bypasses." For example, when a Japanese businessperson says that a deal is "very difficult," it means that it will be impossible to reach a compromise and negotiations are off. The American understanding of this phrase is that there is still room for discussion. Also, when using the phrase "I suspect," meaning "I think," the Japanese interpret it to mean "I am suspicious." There is a significant difference in the understanding of time as well. "Soon" may have ambiguous meanings. The writer said that he thought that "soon" meant a day or two, but Japanese business counterparts thought that it meant two to three hours instead of a day or two!

One very critical communication context is between investors and their financial advisor or broker. As it turns out, a lot of bypassing occurs in these small group meetings (usually involving a couple and their advisor). Instead of using plain English, financial experts tend to speak in financial language or "Finglish." A survey of 800 investors conducted by the financial firm Investco, Ltd., found that investors hate the technical financial jargon that advisors use. In fact, the Securities and Exchange Commission has now published their *Plain English Handbook* to help improve these communication problems. The book explains that using such terms as (1) equities, (2) fixed income investments, (3) dollar cost averaging, and (4) asset allocation, among many others, causes many investor couples to come out of meetings with their heads spinning with confusion. Recently, Brett Arends, a personal financial columnist for the *Wall Street Journal*, has suggested that advisors should communicate more clearly using common English terms to educate, rather than to impress their clients. He suggests using the terms (1) stocks, rather than equities; (2) bonds, rather than fixed income investments; (3) automatic monthly investments, rather than dollar cost averaging; and (4) diversifying investments, rather than asset allocation (Arends, 2011, p. R1).

In group discussions, the entire focus of the discussion may be diverted by a difference in interpretation of a given word. Note the incredible problems that arose in one group as seen by one participant:

> At the start of our meeting I introduced a definition of communication (communication is an expression of ideas). Although the basics were appreciated, Ed and Al requested a revision, as the statement was too simple. They decided to drop the words "an expression of ideas." I didn't believe this was a very good revision and said so. A slight altercation developed lasting about five minutes. It was resolved that other ideas would be considered.
>
> After sufficient waiting (about 30 seconds), I realized no great ideas were forthcoming, so I subtly suggested that my idea be reconsidered. This time Pete and John were on my side. Still, my full idea could not survive Al and Ed, so it was given new form. . . . In the process of getting a communication definition, they had to satisfy me that their changes were justified, while I was attempting to show my original as the best. "Well, you haven't done any better," was surprisingly effective. While I had been using sword points, the best they could muster was a safety pin.
>
> After the mutilation of my last idea, I decided I would not volunteer any more material and thus "watch them squirm."

It seems hard to believe that such intense reactions could result from a difference of opinion over the definition of the term *communication*. However, this reaction is more typical than atypical.

The diagram in Figure 2.1 helps us understand the relation between an object (or referent) and a symbol used to represent that object. As Figure 2.2 shows, the symbol may vary, but the object remains the same. The object has a word to represent it, but that word and the object do not necessarily have an inherent relationship. It is a little like selecting a name for a newborn baby. At first, the choice seems arbitrary, but after a few years, it seems impossible to think of that person having a different name. The relationship is indirect between symbol and referent; it exists only in the mind. Because each of us has a different brain and nervous system, the relationship between any given referent and any given word will vary to some extent from person to person.

PRACTICAL TIPS

Here are a few suggestions on how to avoid bypassing:

1. Be person-minded, not word-minded.
2. Question and paraphrase.
3. Be receptive to feedback.
4. Be sensitive to contexts.

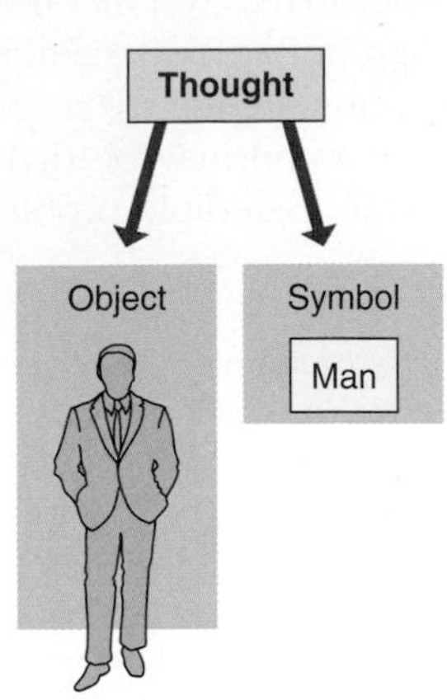

FIGURE 2.1 The Relationship between an Object and the Symbol for the Object

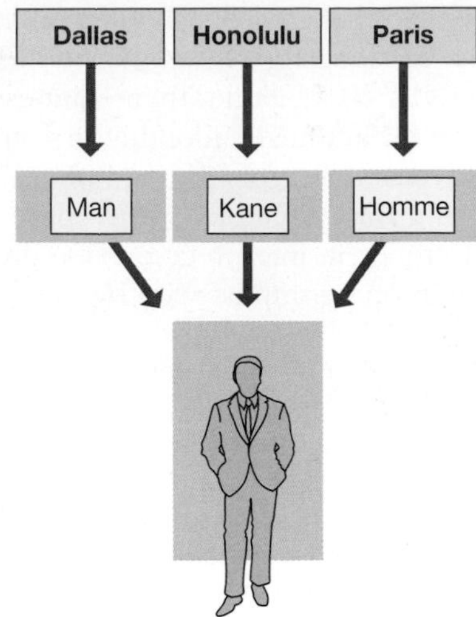

FIGURE 2.2 The Same Object May Be Represented by More Than One Symbol

Part of the bypassing problem is that we frequently assume that words "contain" meaning. A different view is that words are symbols arbitrarily designated to represent concepts or referents. Over time, we begin to associate the word with its referent so strongly that they become inseparable. It is easy enough to say that the word is not the thing and that we should be able to separate the symbol from the referent, but it is difficult in practice not to respond emotionally when another person refers to us as a *fascist pig, a n_ _ _ _r, a stupid hillbilly,* or *a honky*. In fact, Ted Danson and Whoopi Goldberg created quite a controversy when they used racial slurs in a comedy skit (Danson also appeared in blackface). Even in comedy, there are limits to what can be said and done.

Two problems related to bypassing occur when (1) we use the same word to mean different things (dress "casually") or (2) different words are used to express essentially the same idea. For example, we may argue that company employees are not performing properly because of a "communication problem" as opposed to a "lack of motivation." It may be that we are really talking about related problems (that is, employees would be better motivated to perform [motivation problem] if they could suggest some new job procedures to their supervisors [communication problem]), but the issue may be clouded by arguments over the labels used to describe the situation.

Haney (1992) suggests two outcomes that can result from bypassing. On the one hand, we may have apparent agreement when, in fact, we are calling different things by the same name (dressing casually). On the other hand, we may have actual agreement but apparent disagreement, as in the employee problem described above. Given these possible outcomes, Haney suggests some guidelines that we reproduce (slightly modified) in the Practical Tips box to remedy the potential difficulties.

McCormack (1984), in his best-selling book *What They Don't Teach You at Harvard Business School,* confirms Haney's advice when he writes, "Insight demands opening up your senses, talking less and listening more. I believe you can learn almost everything you need to know—and more than other people would like you to know—simply by watching and listening, keeping your eyes peeled, your ears open. And your mouth closed. . . . Watch your listen/talk ratio" (pp. 8–9). These points also corroborate the ancient rhetorician who observed, "We have two ears and only one tongue, so that we might listen more than we speak."

In a nutshell, these guidelines focus on the ideas that not all of us use words precisely the same way and that all words have the potential for multiple usage and interpretation. When you suspect that there may be a difference in word usage, ask questions, and be willing to try to restate or paraphrase the person's message. Remember to use different words in your restatement to see if the basic intent is understood. Also, be receptive to feedback. If we are too impervious or insensitive to allow for the possibility that we may not have stated something perfectly clearly, then we are unlikely to get much feedback to that effect. However, if we are willing to admit to fallibility, we invite feedback and can benefit from that information. Finally, we can often guess the intended meaning of a given statement on the basis of its use in a given context. For example, one supervisor frequently bade good-bye to his employees with the common phrase "Well, take it easy now." It was quite obvious from the context that he meant this only as a casual expression. He did *not* intend employees to work less hard. By employing the four Practical Tips shown in the box, we can reduce the frequency of bypassing.

CASE STUDY

LANGUAGE AND CROSS-CULTURAL POLITICS

In 2003, North Korea issued a statement prior to the 2003 nuclear weapons talks that was translated incorrectly in English to mean that they had already begun nuclear weapons production with the "reprocessing of spent nuclear rods." In the original North Korean statement, however, it was clearly stated that production and reprocessing had *not* begun. This misunderstanding in translation created a very large problem and weakened political ties between the United States and North Korea (Cho & Struck, 2003, p. A2).

1. What do you think could have been done to prevent the linguistic difficulties presented by the case?
2. What do you think the United States could have done to ease the tension created by the situation?
3. What examples can you think of that illustrate bypassing in a small-scale group context?

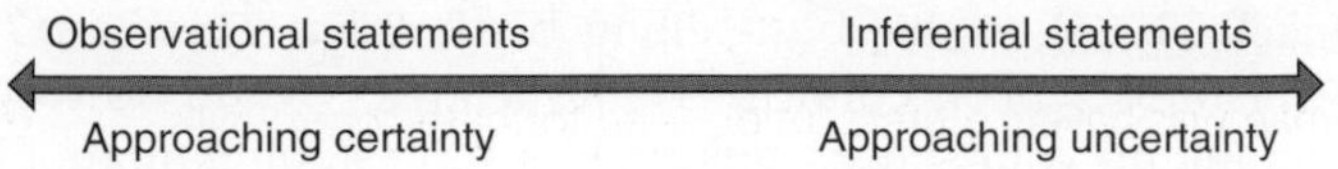

FIGURE 2.3 Inferences versus Observations

INFERENCE MAKING

TheScienceDesk.com (2004) describes *inference* as logical "explanation of an observation." Direct observation is the "noticing of phenomena, events, or processes without any intervening factors between the observer and what is being observed." Indirect observation includes an intervening factor. We make observations by using our senses. Inferences are used to surmise and suggest causes that relate to the observations themselves, and they generally include more investigation to prove or disprove the assumptions (Glencoe.com, 2004). In understanding evolution, for example, inferences are made based on scientific findings such as fossil records. Direct observation cannot be used in this case (*Daily Herald,* 2004).

Sir Francis Bacon championed inductive reasoning, based on Aristotle's system of using the senses to observe similarities and differences between things. Bacon's most important and original contribution to the theory of induction, however, was his argument that it must entail not only detailed observations of nature, including similarities and differences, but also (going beyond Aristotle) the discovery of causal relationships by experiment. This was the method for discovering the essential nature of things and thus made generalization possible without complete enumeration (Locke, 2007).

Each of us makes numerous inferences every day. For example, we infer (1) that the sun will rise tomorrow, (2) that a chair won't collapse when we sit down, (3) that the sun is shining on the other side of town, because it is shining at our location, (4) that a car coming at us from a side street will stop at the stop sign and not run into the side of our car, and (5) that a person who consistently fails to show up for a group discussion is not committed to our group task. In each of these five cases, there is some probability that our inference will be borne out by the actual events. However, these five examples illustrate quite a range from most probable (number 1) to least probable (number 5).

Statements of inference go beyond what we know through observations. They represent only some degree of probability of coming true. This idea is illustrated in the diagram in Figure 2.3.

One of the major problems in groups is being able to recognize our own inference making. You can test your own ability on the following sample story. True (T) means that the inference drawn is definitely true on the basis of the information in the story. False (F) means that the inference is definitely wrong on the basis of the information in the story. A question mark (?) means that you cannot be certain of the inference on the basis of the story.

SAMPLE STORY

A customer handed the pharmacist a prescription for birth control pills. "Please fill this quickly. I have someone waiting in the car."

The pharmacist hurried to fill the order.

STATEMENTS ABOUT THE STORY

1. A woman was having a prescription filled for birth control pills. T F ?
2. She did not want to become pregnant. T F ?
3. She was in a hurry to have the order filled. T F ?
4. The pharmacist did his best to speed up the order. T F ?

If you answered T to any of the statements, you probably assumed or inferred that the customer and the pharmacist were female and male, respectively. Yet there is no statement in the story to support that assumption. Actually, a man is ordering birth control pills for his wife. The pharmacist, a female, cannot do "his" best to fill the order.

Another way of describing inference making is to say that it involves certain assumptions or conclusion drawing (sometimes jumping to the wrong conclusion). This becomes a problem in groups when we react to each other on the assumption that a person is behaving a certain way for the reason that seems obvious or apparent. However, the person may be acting that way for reasons other than the obvious. For example, one person may attack another by saying, "I'm sick and tired of your holding us back in our work." On the surface, this appears to be a comment intended to help the group get more accomplished. Beneath the surface, however, it may be part of an effort to undermine the other person's status in the group and may be a part of the struggle between the two for leadership in the group. These levels can be diagrammed as shown in Figures 2.4 and 2.5. Although it is helpful to recognize that all behaviors are motivated and that they may be motivated by multiple causes, it is also dangerous to attempt to infer too much. Even if we make such an inference, we must recognize the possibility of error.

On the other hand, it is often difficult to analyze the group process without making some inferences. For example, one encounter group was having its last meeting, and the discussion somehow got around to the subject of death. After a somewhat extended discussion on this subject, the group leader intervened by saying, "I wonder if this discussion of death is motivated by the reluctance we are all feeling tonight about saying good-bye for the last time." Although this comment was initially rejected by the group, it turned out that a lot of people were

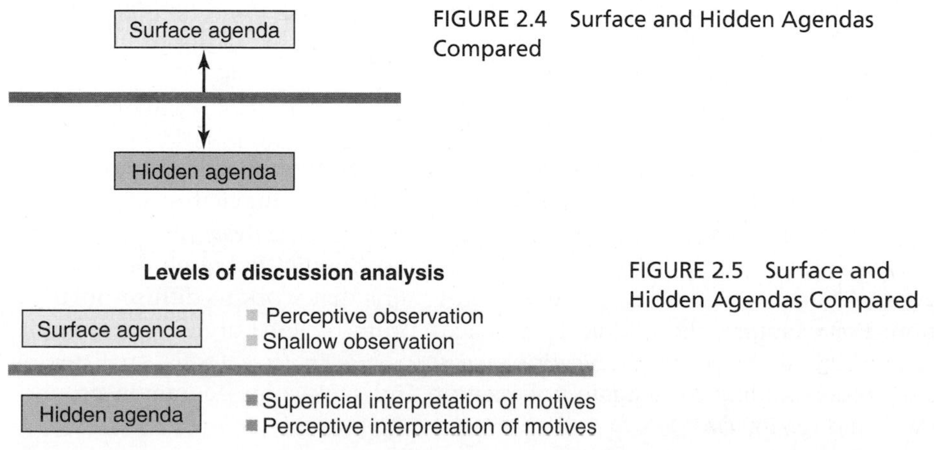

FIGURE 2.4 Surface and Hidden Agendas Compared

FIGURE 2.5 Surface and Hidden Agendas Compared

PRACTICAL TIPS

Communication expert Dr. Frank Luntz (2011) offers these practical tips for successfully communicating in a team.

1. Don't mistake volume for enthusiasm. Shouting is one of the worst mistakes communicators make in demonstrating passion.
2. Absolutes are deal breakers. Avoid words like always, everyone, all the time or never, because they sound too over-generalized.
3. Use clarity. Avoid using technical jargon to impress others. This can confuse rather than clarify.
4. Maintain eye contact. People who look above you or around you appear to be deceptive.
5. Avoid texting, phoning, or e-mailing, etc. during meetings. It is rude and gives the impression that you are not engaged in the discussion. (Luntz, 2011, pp. 26, 48)

reluctant to end the friendships that had grown out of this group, and the topic of the discussion shifted to directly expressing and resolving those feelings.

Some inference making may be useful to the group, whereas at other times it may be harmful. A person who tries to read too much into behaviors may become a "psychopest." For example, a person crossing her or his arms across the chest may do this for no other reason than increased comfort. An overinterpretation might be that the person is becoming defensive and is trying to put up a barrier between the self and others. In attempting to analyze behaviors, it is wise to recognize that analyses often involve inferences that go beyond what we have observed and involve some probability for error.

POLARIZING

Perhaps one of the most common problems in groups is polarization. The University of Colorado Conflict Research Consortium (2004) defines *polarization* as "the process that causes people who had been staying neutral to take sides in a conflict." It is difficult to express differences in viewpoint without tending to overstate or exaggerate to make our point. When this happens, it encourages the others to exaggerate a bit more in the opposite direction to make their point. Before long, the sides are so far apart that constructive discussion of the issues is often discontinued. Because of this exaggeration, polarization is often seen as a major phase of "conflict escalation." With the exaggeration comes stereotyping. Next comes "segregation," which ends inevitably in "destruction." If conflict escalation can be halted at the polarization phase, the final phases can be avoided (Univeristy of Colorado Conflict Research Consortium, 2004). There are additional societies and groups that work to diffuse polarization. For example, the Middle East Peace Forum of Pittsburgh, Pennsylvania, is working to help communication across groups with a focus on listening and understanding to mitigate polarization and seek some "common ground" (Wahrhaftig, 2004).

There are steps that you can take to prevent or dissolve polarization. Consider the following example:

KYLE: I can't see why a woman should get a job just to avoid the boredom of housework when a man who needs to support his family goes without a job.

SUE: Just because your masculinity is threatened is no reason to keep women out of work!

KYLE: My masculinity? You women's libbers are always hung up on trying to be the dominant sex!

SUE: You men are all alike. You can't stand being bettered by anyone, especially a woman. You want us to tell you how brilliant you are because you know what day of the week it is.

This exchange actually occurred in a student discussion. The topic was "How can greater job equality be achieved in this country?" The discussion had been progressing well until this polarization occurred.

Polarization has three distinct characteristics. First, the statements get more intense emotionally. Second, they go from being specific to being more general ("You men are all alike!"). Third, they tend to move away from the topic at hand (job equality) to other issues ("You can't stand being bettered by anyone").

A simple technique usually nips polarization in the bud. It is described by Rogers and Roethlisberger (1952) in the following way:

> The next time you get into an argument with . . . a small group of friends, just stop the discussion for a moment and, for an experiment, institute this rule. "Each person can speak up for himself only *after* he has repeated the ideas and feelings of the speaker accurately and to that speaker's satisfaction." You see what this would mean. It would simply mean that before presenting your own point of view, it would be necessary for you to achieve the other speaker's frame of reference—to understand his thoughts and feelings so well that you could summarize them for him. Sounds simple doesn't it? But if you try it, you will discover that it is one of the most difficult things you have ever tried to do. (p. 48)

After you have tried this restating exercise, notice the effects. First, the tendency for statements to gain emotional intensity is significantly reduced. The calmness is quite dramatic when compared with the interchange between Kyle and Sue above. Second, the discussion tends to stay with manageable specifics rather than move to gross generalities that are quite frequently based on stereotypes (men are not all alike any more than women are all alike). Third, the discussion is more likely to remain focused on the group's discussion topic than to go off on a tangent that may be much less relevant to the group's task. This simple technique actually can be quite potent in reducing the problem of polarization.

SIGNAL REACTIONS

Consider the following situation:

> In 1999, Crayola changed the name of one of its colors from "Indian Red" to "chestnut." They said it was "to avoid misunderstandings over the color's origin."

> The color had originally been named after a reddish brown pigment commonly found near India. However, native Americans thought it described the skin color of American Indians. This was only the third time in the company's 96-year history that a color has been changed. Company officials sifted through over 250,000 suggested names in selecting the new label. (Associated Press, 1998)

Signal reactions are learned responses to certain stimuli. Perhaps the best-known example of a signal reaction is the salivation of Pavlov's dogs. Ivan Pavlov was a Nobel Prize–winning Russian physiologist. He accidentally stumbled onto a very important concept of learning known as *classical conditioning*. He noticed that the carefully calibrated measurements of his test animals' salivation started to break down because the experienced dogs began to salivate in anticipation of the food when he opened the door to the room before he fed them. His coming through the door was the *conditioned stimulus*—the signal that triggered the salivation response. Eventually, he brought the salivation response under stimulus control by associating a bell with food so that the dogs learned to salivate at the sound of the bell even when the food was *not* present.

Philosopher Alfred Korzybski said that "general semantics is not any philosophy, or psychology, or logic, in the ordinary sense. It is a new extensional discipline which explains and trains us how to use our nervous systems most efficiently" (Kenyon, 2004). Korzybski believed that the signal response was an animal-like response. He wrote (1948):

> In Pavlov's experiments a dog is shown food and a bell rung simultaneously. At the sight of food, saliva and gastric juice flow. Associations soon *relate* the ringing of a bell and the food, and, later, simply the ringing of the bell will produce the flow. In another animal some other signal, a whistle, for instance, would produce similar effects. In different people, through experience, associations, relations, meanings, and s.r. [stimulus response] patterns are built around some symbol. Obviously in grown-up humans the identification of the symbol with the thing must be pathological. (p. 249)

Actually, Korzybski was a little extreme in saying that we are pathological to allow such strong connections between signal and response. One study showed that the repetitive sound of a gong produced marked emotional responses in former sailors (as measured by their perspiration levels) but very little emotional reaction among former soldiers. Edwards and Acker (1962) write, "This signal was used as a call to battle stations aboard U.S. Navy ships during the war, and it continued to elicit a strong autonomic response from the Navy veterans, even though more than fifteen years had elapsed since this stimulus had signaled danger." Although this study did not involve reactions to verbal symbols, it does demonstrate the natural, not pathological, tendency toward strong signal reactions.

A study that directly tested emotional reactions to verbal symbols also proved that strong physiological reactions to symbols are typical rather than pathological. College students were exposed to various words on a screen, and their perspiration was measured as an index of their reactions. There were no significant differences between reactions to positive words, such as *beauty, love,* and *kiss,* and negative words, such as *cancer, hate,* and *death*. However, some words did cause significant responses. These were referred to as *personal* words and included the

PRACTICAL TIPS

Idea-Killer Phrases

- "That's ridiculous."
- "We tried that before."
- "That will never work."
- "That's crazy."
- "It's too radical a change."
- "We're too small for it."
- "It's not practical."
- "Let's get back to reality."
- "You can't teach an old dog new tricks."
- "We'll be the laughingstock."
- "You're absolutely wrong."
- "You don't know what you're talking about."
- "It's impossible."
- "There's no way it can be done."

Igniter Phrases

- "I agree."
- "That's good!"
- "I made a mistake. I'm sorry."
- "That's a great idea."
- "I'm glad you brought that up."
- "You're on the right track."
- "I know it will work."
- "We're going to try something different today."
- "I never thought of that."
- "We can do a lot with that idea."
- "Real good, anyone else?"
- "I like that!"
- "That would be worth a try."
- "Why don't we assume it would work and go from there."

person's first and last names, father's and mother's first names, major in school, year in school, and school name. Subjects were significantly aroused by these personal words (Crane, Diecker, & Brown, 1970).

Certainly, nobody would argue that these college students were pathological or that they "confused" their own names with themselves as physical beings. Yet these studies collectively indicate that all of us learn to react to certain verbal and nonverbal stimuli in some strong and predictable ways. When the response becomes habitual, it is like a reflex action. At this point, the so-called signal reaction, or automatic response, may create problems.

An example of a signal reaction occurred in Sacramento, California. Holes in the pavement used to access utilities are commonly referred to as *manholes.* However, because the Sacramento city council has a majority of women, the term *manholes* was thought to be sexist. A major contest was held to come up with a gender-neutral term. Some examples included "sewer viewer," "peopleholes," and "peepholes." The council finally decided on the term *maintenance hole.* This appears to be a signal reaction to the term *manhole* (Associated Press, 1990c).

In group discussions, certain phrases may produce signal reactions that are counterproductive. Such phrases have been referred to as *idea killers* (Tubbs & Moss, 2008) or communication stoppers. On the other hand, *igniter* phrases seem to promote group productivity.

Other specific terms that are likely to produce signal reactions to one degree or another are such insults as *weirdo, fag, honky, racist,* and *male chauvinist pig,* and many swear words. Swear words have different levels of offensiveness that vary from culture to culture. Profane words have been classified as (1) religious, (2) excretory, and (3) sexual (Bostrom & Rossiter, 1969). In our culture, the sexual words are usually the most offensive; in Italy, where the Roman Catholic Church is very strong, religious words are considered much more offensive; and in Germany, excretory swear words are considered to be the worst. The 2 Live Crew album "As Nasty As They Wanna Be" was declared obscene by a federal court judge in Florida in part because of the use of swear words. This is a vivid example of the emotional impact created by language. One writer expressed her reaction by stating, "But incitement to rape, even if it rhymes and has a rap beat, cannot be defended, whatever its rhythms. . . . Exhortations to sexual violence do not have to be tolerated" (Beck, 1990, p. 7A).

Several studies indicate that those who swear may reduce their credibility in the eyes of others (Bauduin, 1971). Clearly, swear words and insulting terms may produce signal reactions and should be avoided. It also seems advisable to avoid communication stoppers and idea killers whenever possible.

Self-Disclosure

Perhaps one of the greatest dilemmas facing a group member is the choice between openly expressing his or her thoughts and feelings and concealing or distorting inner feelings, thoughts, and perceptions. In a discussion on racial equality, we may not openly reveal our true feelings for fear of sounding like racists or bigots. Nobody wants to be labeled a racist if it can be avoided! On the other hand, if every person in the group conceals his or her thoughts, there will be little said and, therefore, little accomplished. The question is not *whether* to reveal or conceal, but *how much* to reveal or conceal. *Self-disclosure* has been defined by Tubbs and Baird (1980) as "a process, whereby an individual voluntarily shares information in a personal way, about his or her 'self' that cannot be discovered through other sources" (p. 15; see also De Janasz, Dowd, & Schneider, 2009).

You may wonder why a person should bother to let him- or herself be known to others. Experts who studied mentally disturbed individuals concluded that a great deal of human energy is consumed in attempts to keep themselves from being known by others. That energy could be used for other purposes, but neurotic individuals are so "wrapped up in themselves" that they are seldom able to devote sufficient energy to other problems (such as a group problem-solving discussion). All of us are periodically faced with such situations. When we get bad news from home or from a friend, it is much harder to concentrate on such mundane problems as how to budget our study time for tomorrow's exam. However, the mentally unhealthy person is habitually in this state of mind.

Part of returning to mental health involves sharing oneself with others. Jourard (1964) states:

> Self-disclosure, or should I say "real" self-disclosure, is both a symptom of personality health . . . and at the same time a means of ultimately achieving healthy, personality. . . . I have known people who would rather die than become known. . . . When I say that self-disclosure is a symptom of personality health, what I mean really is that a person who displays many of the other characteristics that betoken healthy personality . . . *will also display the ability to make himself fully known to at least one other significant human being*. (p. 24)

Countless students in group discussions feel that they don't know what to contribute. They often feel that they have no good or new ideas to add to what has already been said. Yet as we will see in the last section of this chapter, numerous roles may be adopted by group members, several of which involve some degree of self-disclosure. For example, if an idea is initiated by another, you may make a substantial contribution by offering your *reaction* to the idea (opinion giving)—by encouraging or showing agreement or disagreement. Counterproductive role behaviors may also involve self-disclosure (for example, aggressing, reporting a personal achievement, confessing a personal ideology that is irrelevant to the discussion topic, or seeking sympathy from the group).

Self-disclosure is not always desirable. An optimum amount of self-disclosure seems a desirable goal to achieve. Some of us are too closed (concealers); others of us "wear our hearts on our sleeves" (revealers). Culbert (1968) describes the problem of overdisclosing rather vividly:

> The revealer is likely to react by immediately disclosing any self-information to which he has access. The revealer, too, is attempting to master the problem, but for him mastery seems to be attained by explicitly acknowledging and labeling all the relevant elements comprising the situation. While a concealer runs the risk of having insufficient external feedback, a revealer runs the risk of overlabeling the limited number of objective elements present or of labeling them so early that their usefulness in the relationship is nullified. (p. 19)

Encounter groups usually proceed under the assumption that people have learned to be too closed too often. Thus, participants are encouraged to share their feelings and perceptions as openly and honestly as they can. Much of the self-disclosure involves giving feedback to others concerning the ways in which they "come across." This feedback is often useful in reducing the size of the arc of distortion discussed earlier in this chapter.

PRACTICAL TIPS

Self-Disclosure and Assertive Communication

Psychologist Martin Seligman (2011) has devoted his entire forty-year career to studying what makes people feel psychologically well.* One important set of wellness skills is how to deal with situations in which you feel the need to stand up for yourself. Possible reactions can range on a continuum from one extreme of being nonassertive and saying or doing nothing in an uncomfortable situation, to the opposite extreme of being aggressive and telling the other person off. Neither extreme is as good as a middle ground approach such as learning how to address the situation in an assertive manner. Below are five assertive communication skills:

1. Identify and work to understand the situation.
2. Describe the situation objectively and accurately (without exaggeration or sarcasm).
3. Express your concerns.
4. Ask the other person for his or her perspective and work toward an acceptable change.
5. List the benefits that will follow when the change is implemented.

Source: Martin Seligman. *Flourish*. New York: Free Press, 2011, p. 174.
*If you would like to learn more about how to increase your wellness, go online to www.authentichappiness.org.

THE JOHARI WINDOW

Perhaps the most useful model for illustrating self-disclosure in groups is the Johari window (named for its originators, Joe Luft and Harry Ingham) (Luft, 1984). See Figure 2.6 for a diagram of this model.

The Johari window classifies an individual's relating to others according to four quadrants (or windowpanes). The size of each quadrant represents the person's level of self-awareness. Quadrant 1, the *open quadrant,* represents our willingness to share with others our views on such things as current national or world events, current movies, sports, and what is generally referred to as *cocktail party conversation.*

Quadrant 2 is referred to as the *blind quadrant* or the "bad-breath" area. This area represents the things others may know about us that we do unintentionally and unknowingly. We may continually dominate meetings or bore people with long-winded accounts of how good our high school was. Conversely, we may annoy people by our silence, because they may feel that they have opened themselves up to the group while we have "played our cards pretty close to the chest" by revealing little. Group members seem to resent both those who talk too much and those who talk too little.

Quadrant 3 is the *hidden area* that is most likely to be changed (reduced) by self-disclosure. It represents the feelings about ourselves that we know but are unwilling to reveal to others. It may represent our greatest fears, some

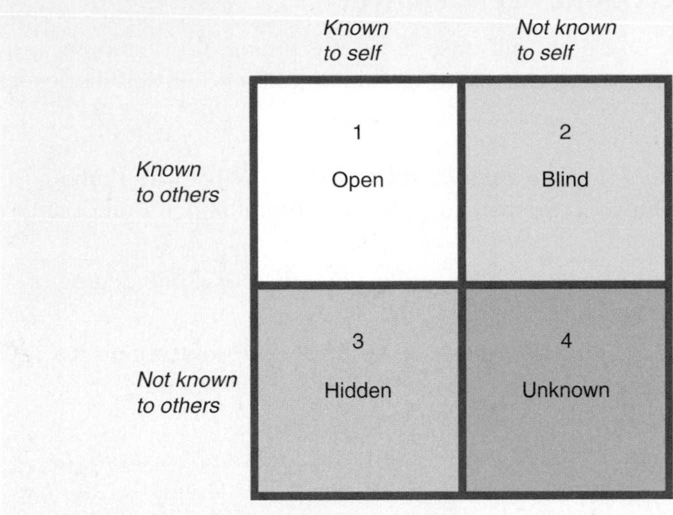

FIGURE 2.6 The Johari Window

From *Group Processes: An Introduction to Group Dynamics,* by Joseph Luft, Mayfield Publishing Company. Copyright © 1963, 1970 by Joseph Luft. Reproduced with permission of The McGraw-Hill Companies.

past experiences we would like to forget, or our secret sexual fantasies, among other things.

Quadrant 4 is called the *area of the unknown.* It represents all the areas of potential growth or self-actualization. This includes almost anything outside our experience, such as the sport we've never played, the places we have never seen, the hobby we haven't taken the time to try, the organization we have never joined, and the style of behaving we have never been willing to risk.

Luft advocates changing the shape of the window so that quadrant 1 enlarges while all the others become smaller. I once participated in an encounter group in which we tried to grow interpersonally along the lines suggested by this model. One participant introduced herself as "Mickey" and told us what city she was from and so on. She was dressed in slacks and a sweater. Only after 15 weeks did we find out that she was a nun. She had been trying to develop herself as a person without having the rest of us react to her role rather than to her. Thus, her unknown quadrant was diminished by her efforts to try new, less inhibited behaviors. She also reduced her blind quadrant by asking for interpersonal feedback. We might have been more inhibited in our feedback had we known that she was a nun. She also destroyed the stereotypes most of us had about nuns.

Open communication for many years has been regarded as the ultimate strategy for improving employee morale and productivity. In an open-communication setting, superiors and subordinates talk with one another freely and openly about company goals, work stressors, and other job-related issues. However, Eisenberg and Witten (1987), among others, disagree that open communication is the ultimate strategy. They argue that there are situations when managers and employees have successfully chosen to be more or less open. These decisions stem in part from concern for serving personal goals, as well as those of the company.

WHEN IS SELF-DISCLOSURE APPROPRIATE?

Within this framework questions still arise as to the timing and extent of self-disclosure. Luft (1969) proposes the following guidelines for when self-disclosure is appropriate:

1. *When it is a function of the ongoing relationship.* What one shares with another belongs in the particular relationship; it is not a random or isolated act.
2. *When it occurs reciprocally.* This implies that there is some degree of interdependence and mutuality involved.
3. *When it is timed to fit what is happening.* The self-disclosure grows out of the experience that is going on between or among the persons involved. The timing and sequence are important.
4. *When it concerns what is going on within and between persons in the present.* Some account is taken of the behavior and feelings of the participants individually and of the persons collectively. There is a recognition of the relationship as an emergent phenomenon in addition to the individual selves.
5. *When it moves by relatively small increments.* What is revealed does not drastically change or restructure the relationship. The implication is that a relationship is built gradually except in rare and special cases.
6. *When it is confirmable by the other person.* Some system is worked out between the persons to validate reception of that which has been disclosed.
7. *When account is taken of the effect disclosure has on the other person(s).* The disclosure has not only been received, but there is evidence of its effect on the receiver.
8. *When it creates a reasonable risk.* If the feeling or behavior were really unknown to the other, it may have been withheld for a reason bearing on differences that have yet to be faced by the participants.
9. *When it is speeded up in a crisis.* A serious conflict jeopardizing the structure of the relationship may require that more quadrant 3 material be quickly revealed to heal the breach or help in the reshaping of the relationship.
10. *When the context is mutually shared.* The assumptions underlying the social context suggest that there is enough in common to sustain the disclosure. (pp. 132–33)

Probably the most difficult problem for participants in any type of professional development program to resolve when they go "back home" is knowing how to apply what they have learned without overdoing it. One encounter graduate asked, "How do I use this openness with my boss when he hasn't read the book?" The concern was warranted. It may be quite difficult to put any new behaviors into practice when the others "back home" haven't changed and are still as closed and perhaps as devious as ever.

The most logical advice would be to try to use what you can, when you can. Not all of our learnings will be usable all the time. But certainly some new behaviors (such as increased openness and sensitivity) will be appropriate some, if not most, of the time. Experiences in groups frequently teach us lessons we can't possibly unlearn. Once we have experienced a greater level of personal intimacy with others, day-to-day superficiality may compare rather badly. Schutz (1971) puts it this way:

> Relating to people more honestly is certainly possible. Find someone you have withheld something from and tell it to him. See what happens. Next time you feel like touching someone, do it. Next time you are hurt or frightened, express it. When you catch yourself trying to protect an image, stop, and see if you can be real instead. If you're embarrassed to pay someone a compliment, do it anyway. If you want to know how people respond to you, ask them. (p. 284)

Another way to put it is that the competent communicator has a higher level of rhetorical sensitivity. That is, he or she learns when and with whom to disclose and when and with whom to refrain from disclosure. Total disclosure at all times with all people is obviously not desirable.

Interaction Roles

Each of us is required to enact multiple roles in our everyday living. Usually, we are able to function effectively in these different roles, which require or expect certain behaviors. We are, at different times, student or teacher, son or daughter, friend, counselor, leader or follower, spouse, parent, manager or employee. It is important to realize that roles are simply sets of identifiable behaviors. When we say that a person is assuming a role, this does not imply that he or she is faking it or acting in a way that is not within that person's true character. In fact, some studies indicate that the more interpersonally sensitive person is one who is able to develop a considerable degree of role flexibility. It is desirable to learn to widen our repertoire of roles and to discover those roles we most enjoy.

A student relatively new to the small group field indicated an awareness of a few interaction roles:

> This group discussion was a real experience for me. I have never been mixed in with a complete group of strangers and have things work out so smoothly. In most groups you get a few quiet shy ones, who don't say anything, and opposed to them, there's usually one big mouth, normally found in a group, who says everything and has all of the ideas without giving anyone else a chance to give their opinion. It was good to work in a group that was well balanced and one in which everyone participated.

As we mentioned in the discussion of leadership, different functions can be performed by any group member. This is another way of saying that individuals assume different roles in helping the group move toward its goal. In Chapter 4 we will discuss task roles and socioemotional functions or roles. Benne and Sheats (1948) proposed a classification of roles into three broad categories: (1) task roles, (2) group-building and maintenance roles, and (3) individual roles (see also Tubbs and Moss, 2008). Although other sets of categories have been developed for research purposes, this time-tested approach is still one of the most useful for learning to identify roles and to develop role flexibility.

GROUP TASK ROLES

Group task roles are directed toward accomplishing the group's objective through the facilitation of problem solving. They include the following roles:

- *Initiating–contributing.* Proposing new ideas or a changed way of regarding the group goal. This may include a new goal or a new definition of the problem. It may involve suggesting a solution or some way of handling a difficulty the group has encountered. It may also include a new procedure for the group to organize its efforts better.
- *Information seeking.* Asking for clarification and for authoritative information and facts relevant to the problem under discussion.
- *Opinion seeking.* Seeking information related not so much to factual data as to the values underlying the suggestions being considered.
- *Information giving.* Offering facts or generalizations based on experience or authoritative sources.
- *Opinion giving.* Stating beliefs or opinions relevant to a suggestion made. The emphasis is on the proposal of what ought to become the group's values rather than on factors or information.
- *Elaborating.* Expanding on suggestions with examples or restatements, offering a rationale for previously made suggestions, and trying to determine the results if a suggestion were to be adopted by the group.
- *Coordinating.* Indicating the relationships among various ideas and suggestions, attempting to combine ideas and suggestions, or trying to coordinate the activities of group members.
- *Orienting.* Indicating the position of the group by summarizing progress made and deviations from agreed-upon directions or goals or by raising questions about the direction the group is taking.
- *Evaluating.* Comparing the group's accomplishments with some criterion or standard of group functioning. This may include questioning the practicality, logic, or procedure of a suggestion.
- *Energizing.* Stimulating the group to action or decision, and attempting to increase the level or quality of activity.
- *Assisting on procedure.* Helping or facilitating group movement by doing things for the group—for example, performing routine tasks, such as distributing materials, rearranging the seating, or running a tape recorder.
- *Recording.* Writing down suggestions, recording group decisions, or recording the outcomes of the discussion. This provides tangible results of the group's effort.

GROUP-BUILDING AND MAINTENANCE ROLES

The roles in this category help the interpersonal functioning of the group. They alter the way of working by strengthening, regulating, and perpetuating the group. This is analogous to preventive maintenance done to keep a mechanical device, such as a car, in good working order. Group-building and maintenance roles include the following:

- *Encouraging.* Praising, showing interest in, agreeing with, and accepting the contributions of others; showing warmth toward other group members; listening attentively and seriously to the ideas of others; showing tolerance for ideas different from one's own; and/or conveying the feeling that one feels the contributions of others are important.
- *Harmonizing.* Mediating the differences among the other members, attempting to reconcile disagreements, and/or relieving tension in moments of conflict through the use of humor.
- *Compromising.* Within a conflict situation, yielding status, admitting a mistake, disciplining oneself for the sake of group harmony, or coming halfway toward another position.
- *Gatekeeping and expediting.* Attempting to keep communication channels open by encouraging the participation of some or by curbing the participation of others.
- *Setting standards or ideals.* Expressing standards for the group and/or evaluating the quality of group processes (as opposed to evaluating the content of discussion).
- *Observing.* Keeping a record of various aspects of group process and feeding this information, along with interpretations, into the group's evaluation of its procedures. This contribution is best received when the person has been requested by the group to perform this function. The observer should avoid expressing judgments of approval or disapproval in reporting observations.
- *Following.* Going along with the group, passively accepting the ideas of others, and/or serving as an audience in group discussion.

INDIVIDUAL ROLES

Individual roles are designed more to satisfy an individual's needs than to contribute to the needs of the group. These are sometimes referred to as *self-centered roles.* They include the following:

- *Aggressing.* Deflating the status of others, disapproving of the ideas or values of others, attacking the group or the problem it is attempting to solve, joking maliciously, resenting the contributions of others, and/or trying to take credit for others' contributions.
- *Blocking.* Resisting, disagreeing, and opposing beyond reason, and/or bringing up dead issues after they have been rejected or bypassed by the group.

- *Recognition seeking.* Calling attention to oneself through boasting, reporting on personal achievements, acting in inappropriate ways, and/or fighting to keep from being placed in an inferior position.
- *Self-confessing.* Using the group as an opportunity to express personal, non-group-related feelings, insights, and ideologies.
- *Acting the playboy.* Showing a lack of involvement in the group's task and/or displaying nonchalance, cynicism, horseplay, and other kinds of goofing off.
- *Dominating.* Trying to assert authority or superiority by manipulating others in the group. This may take the form of flattering, asserting a superior status or right to attention, giving directions authoritatively, and/or interrupting others.
- *Help seeking.* Attempting to get sympathy from other group members through expressions of insecurity, personal inadequacy, or self-criticism beyond reason.
- *Special-interest pleading.* Speaking on behalf of some group, such as "the oppressed," "labor," or "business," usually cloaking one's own prejudices or biases in the stereotype that best fits one's momentary need.

It is generally desirable to learn to perform the task roles and the group-building and maintenance roles and to avoid the individual roles. However, even the first and second sets of roles may be misused and abused. For example, there is a fine line between initiating and dominating, between encouraging and flattering, and between opinion giving and recognition seeking. The way in which a role is enacted can make a crucial difference in whether the behavior is viewed as constructive or self-serving. Consider the following example. In a *New York Times* article called "Fear in the Workplace: The Bullying Boss" (Carey, 2004), the workplace bully phenomenon was analyzed through the study of group dynamics. The bullying boss is generally one who communicates all criticisms and irritations aggressively and outwardly. The Workplace Bullying and Trauma Institute of Bellingham, Washington, typifies the workplace bully: (1) the "snake," who speaks badly of you behind your back; (2) the "screamer", who publicly expresses disapproval; (3) the "nitpicker," who uses "insinuation and insult"; and (4) the "gatekeeper," who controls employee access to success and resources (Carey, 2004). Many people bully to hold down a subordinate whom they perceive as a threat, or they might bully to inflict blame. Some bully simply to show their power over subordinates. So what do group members do? Dr. Hornstein of Columbia University suggests looking for bully boss behavior patterns to conquer them. He recommends that one "stick with the substance, not the process" of how the message is delivered. Although research shows that bullied employees are still effective and productive in most cases, no one wants to be the recipient of this type of behavior (Carey, 2004).

In another example, one student attempted to be a gatekeeper by asking silent group members if they had any ideas they would like to contribute. After his attempts were rebuffed, he wrote the following analysis of his behavior:

> On one occasion, I tried to involve another group member in the discussion against his will. The conflict was resolved in a later discussion, but my bad feelings during the intervening period made me realize that this was an area for attention. . . .

> This "expansiveness" and disregard for another person's feelings is an amazing trait to find in myself, because it is something I dislike in other people. It has caused me to resolve that (1) I will not be "overbearing" with quiet people, (2) I will listen more, (3) I will attempt to be more aware of the feelings of others.

Even behaviors motivated by the best intentions may go astray in their attempt at producing a desired contribution to the group effort.

Virtual Small Group Communication

We are surrounded by networks of communication media. We can communicate in person, with words, on the phone, through the Internet, through text messages, pictures, and music. New technologies have emerged that facilitate small group communication across the globe. These include online meetings, user groups, videoconferencing, teleconferencing, webinars, or combinations of these. The use of virtual meeting technologies has exploded in recent years. The concept of the virtual meeting is becoming commonplace in today's global workplace. It has many benefits and some challenges that must be overcome to successfully integrate the technology.

With the explosion of virtual meeting environments comes a new type of communication and etiquette. Some of the challenges of this new type of communication are mentioned here. First, in many cases, virtual meeting environments do not allow users to really see expressions on the faces of their peers or group members, allowing body language to remain nearly invisible. Some videoconferencing technologies help overcome this obstacle, but resolution difficulties may prevent a clear view of facial expression. Second, although vocal tone is now available through Web-conferencing and telephone-conferencing components, it may be distorted based on the integrity of the technology. Last, use of online tools gives some individuals a sense of courage to write things that they would not say, leading to rifts and explanation of perceived *written* tone (*Post-Tribune* wire report, 2004).

To clarify any misunderstandings that may result from the use of online communication media, Springfield, Illinois, *State Journal Register* news service writers suggest methods for creating "warmth" in online meetings. They recommend following up any type of technology-driven meeting with faxes to the participants and creating simple, to-the-point professional emails. For conference calls, they recommend treating the calls just as face-to-face group meetings are treated. Participants should be on time and should give their undivided attention (Copley News Service, 2004).

Currently, there are numerous software packages available to communicate within small groups virtually, or online, from Microsoft *Live Meeting* and Global Crossing. In August 2004, the two giants formed an alliance creating multinational virtual meeting communication tools. The latter has been in business for 25 years in a variety of media. Both offer Web-conferencing, allowing an audio and visual component to bring distant group members closer together to meet goals. The customer-focused goal of the alliance is to increase productivity across continents, states, or any other distant location, with an emphasis on effective group work and teamwork. Business travel, which is very expensive and limited in many companies because of the 2008 economic downturn, is now not a necessity in many cases thanks to the products offered by organizations such as Microsoft and Global Crossing (PR Newswire, 2004).

Communication technologies are allowing groups to meet where it was never before possible. With just a few reminders and thoughtful group participation, virtual meetings, whether only online, or with video- or teleconference capabilities, can create success from around the globe. We will be exploring virtual groups further in the following chapters.

Ethical Considerations

In the movie *Class Action,* starring Gene Hackman and Mary Elizabeth Mastrantonio, a burn victim sues an auto manufacturer for a defective fuel tank that exploded during a rear-end collision. During the course of the trial, it is revealed that the manufacturer was aware of the defect but calculated the costs of conducting a recall versus the estimated costs of claims from accident victims and their families. Since the claims were projected to cost less, they opted not to fix the defect. This movie is based on a true story, which seems to be a clear case of poor business ethics. Most cases may not be as clear. Although you and I may not ever get involved in a major case such as this, we are faced with ethical choices every day. Should we plagiarize off the Internet? Should we cheat on an exam? and so on.

The tension between ethics and self-interests has been central to philosophy since the time of Socrates in the Western world, and Confucius in the East. Plato, a student of Socrates, once wrote, "Good people do not need laws to tell them to act justly, while bad people will find a way around the laws."

One definition of *ethics* is "the study of the general nature of morals and of the specific moral choices made by a person" (Tubbs & Moss, 2008). Business schools have taught ethics for years, but especially so in recent years due to some of the scandals involving such corporations as Enron, WorldCom, and Tyco. There are four classic ethical schools of thought that are often taught in communication and business courses. However, people do not always agree as to which one applies the best in any given case (Donaldson & Werhane, 2008).

ARISTOTLE: THE RULE OF THE GOLDEN MEAN

Aristotle was a Greek philosopher who wrote in the fourth century B.C. His philosophy encouraged moderation in all things. For example, eating too much or too little is not as good as eating a healthy average (or mean) amount. He argued that the same is true of courage: It is better to have an average amount than to be either lacking in self-confidence or arrogant. In China, Confucius came up with a very similar philosophy about the same time as Aristotle. Chinese children are taught that a high tree can break more easily but that a small tree will not get enough sunlight to grow. Humans who have too strong of a desire will often be disappointed in chasing unrealistic dreams. If people have a more reasonable amount of desire, they are more likely to be satisfied with their life (Ying Wang, 2008). How do you think this philosophy might be applied to the auto manufacturer case described above? How do you think it applies to participating in small groups?

KANT: THE CATEGORICAL IMPERATIVE

The 18th-century German philosopher Immanuel Kant argued that there is one ethical principle, namely, the respect for and dignity of each human being. He said that we should all obey universal laws, which he called "a command or obligation to act [an imperative] that is absolute [categorical] with no exceptions or conditions." The Ten Commandments are good examples. "Thou shalt not kill," period! No exceptions. This principle seems much easier to apply to the case above. However, are there ever any exceptions to the rules? What about killing in self-defense? Have you ever discussed this question with friends?

BENTHAM AND MILL: UTILITARIANISM

The 18th-century English philosophers Jeremy Bentham and John Stuart Mill believed that morals are based on outcomes, not intent. In business this is referred to as the *bottom line*. For example, it doesn't matter what a firm intends to do; what matters is what actually results. They argued that "actions are right in proportion to the extent to which they promote happiness." To be moral is to see the greatest happiness for the most people. So, utilitarians believe that there are no absolute rules about right or wrong; rather, what's important is what gets the job done. How do you think this philosophy might apply to the auto manufacturer case?

RAWLS: JUSTICE AND THE VEIL OF IGNORANCE

John Rawls, a contemporary philosophy professor at Harvard, believes that things should be shared equally by all members of a society. This means that those who have more should protect the less fortunate by "accidents of birth." An example of this is the recent donations from U.S. citizens, who have given financial support to the victims of the 2004 tsunami in Indonesia, Thailand, and India. Do you think that this philosophy implies that auto manufacturers with deep pockets should be sued for gigantic amounts to spread the wealth? Or is increasing shareholder value good for all?

Issues like these were the subject of the first-ever "Ethos Week," held at Eastern Michigan University's College of Business in 2007. *Ethos* is the ancient Greek word for "ethics." The headline speaker was Randy Cohen, "The Ethicist" from *The New York Times* and author of *The Good, The Bad and the Difference* (Cohen, 2000). Cohen asked two questions: (1) What is the right thing to do, and (2) How do we get people to do right? He believes that the first question is easy. The difficulty is with the second question. He disagrees with Plato that people are either good or bad, asserting that most people can be either good or bad but are strongly influenced by differing circumstances. So, we need to build ethical communities that have ethical norms to encourage good deeds. Writer Upton Sinclair once said, "It is difficult to get a man to understand something when his salary depends upon his not understanding it." In other words, an organization's culture and reward systems will strongly shape people's behaviors.

All those who attended Ethos Week signed a banner and were asked to stand and recite the Ethos Mission Statement while holding their Ethics Honor Society pins. Participants were then asked to put the pins on, automatically inducting them into the society. These were all steps intended to help build an ethical community in the College of Business. Dr. David Mielke, dean of the EMU College of Business, said, "Like other schools, we seek to achieve academic excellence, but we are equally committed to fostering an environment where students can learn to be ethical leaders in their future careers. Ethos Week is a fundamental component of our program, raising student awareness of ethical considerations in a variety of business and personal contexts."

Does your school have any programs dedicated to fostering ethical behavior?

REVIEW OF THE SYSTEMS APPROACH

As discussed in Chapter 1, systems theory defines the world as a series of interrelationships between elements. Systems theorist Yaneer Bar-Yam (2004) defines the human race as an "organism" that should be adaptable and responsive to all changes in the environment. He believes that there are connections across the world between the human race and the economy, transportation, and communication technologies. These elements respond to leadership and politics, socialization, organizations or corporations, and environmental issues (Bar-Yam, 2004). Just as the human race as a whole can adapt in ways that are much more complex than the individual, small groups can create solutions and processes that are much more complex than the work of only one group member. In a group, an aggregate result is achieved. Groups can respond better to challenges than can the individual group member (Odell, 2004). Within small groups, several elements are at work making the group a microcosmic system in and of itself. Methods and interpretations of communication elements within a small group are critical elements in small group functioning.

In this chapter, we examined some issues close to the hearts of many modern communication scholars. The chapter began with an analysis of four critical communication issues. We looked at the differences between intentional–unintentional, verbal–nonverbal, and defensive–supportive communication, and between the content and process of communication. Although these concepts apply to all communication contexts, our examples and specific applications focused on the small group context. These issues have considerable overlap with topics discussed in other chapters in this book. For example, how does one express leadership behavior, or establish a group norm, or manifest one's personality, or express one's values? All of these become manifest through behaviors that communicate to others in the group.

The systems perspective fits very well with the emphasis in communication theory on the transactional model of communication. Many authors stress that the participants in any communication event are highly dependent on one another: They are simultaneously influencing one another and are both senders and receivers at all times. Some experts go so far as to state that "the process of your creating a message may affect you *more* than it does the person receiving it" (p. 402). The transactional point of view can be summarized by stating that a person's communication can be defined only *in relation to* some other or others.

In this chapter, we discussed both verbal and nonverbal communication. The systems nature of nonverbal communication is wonderfully illustrated in an article about fights breaking out over space in aerobics classes (Wood, 1993). The primary conflict developed when one person in the exercise group encroached on the exercise space of another. One factor in the mix was the territoriality of an individual. Some people are much more territorial than others. A second factor was gender. Men are generally more aggressive than women. A third factor was the person's level of skill and the resulting body shape. As one person stated, "If you don't know the routine by heart or if your body fat is higher than 2 percent, it's best not to go [in the front row]" (p. D2). This situation is a perfect example of the systems nature of small group interaction. The type of group and the personalities, genders, body shapes, and ability levels all interacted to produce the outcome (poor interpersonal relations). "Verbal and nonverbal communication should be treated as a total and inseparable unit." We might add that each of the communication types discussed in this chapter is, similarly, related to all the others.

In the second section of this chapter, we examined four problems related to language behavior: bypassing, inference making, polarizing, and signal reactions. Each of these problems is related to both the background factors of the individuals and the eventual consequences of group discussion. We saw that background factors were related to signal reactions in a study showing that former sailors experienced a physiological reaction to an alarm bell they had not heard for 15 years. We also saw that similar reactions can be elicited by such verbal stimuli as our own names or our parents' names. The influence of language on group productivity was illustrated with a discussion of idea killers, such as "It's impossible," "That's crazy," or "That will never work." The net effect of this type of statement is a decrease in potential group productivity in terms of both idea generation and interpersonal relations, as we saw in the case study at the beginning of this chapter.

The third section of this chapter dealt with self-disclosure, answering the question "How much should I reveal and how much should I conceal in a group?" The Johari window was offered as a useful model for understanding one's relationship to others. The chapter included guidelines for appropriate self-disclosure. Obviously, appropriate self-disclosure will vary considerably from group to group. High self-disclosure is probably appropriate in an encounter group with a highly supportive atmosphere and a norm of openness and trust. However, social groups, educational groups, work groups, and especially problem-solving groups are hardly the place for a high degree of very personal self-disclosure. Personality also interacts with self-disclosure. If we open up to those who are highly Machiavellian, they will turn around and use our revelations to benefit themselves and possibly to harm us. Appropriate self-disclosure, then, is very much contingent on a number of relevant variables. For this reason, Tubbs and Baird (1980) have developed a contingency model of self-disclosure that suggests how much to disclose and under what circumstances. For example, self-disclosure should follow the natural evolution of a relationship. As we get to know each other more, deeper levels of sharing information are appropriate. Too much self-disclosure too soon will be perceived as inappropriate.

The final section discussed roles members adopt in groups. Group task and group maintenance roles were described as roles that contribute to the group's needs. Individual, or self-centered, roles were identified as communication behaviors that are typically *not* useful to the group. Roles undoubtedly interact with a person's personality traits. For example, a person who is dominant and achievement-oriented will probably adopt group task roles quite comfortably. Affiliators will naturally gravitate toward group maintenance roles. Finally, hostile or acquiescent personality types will be tempted to adopt the self-centered roles of aggressing and blocking or help seeking and special-interest pleading, respectively. One of the reasons for studying different types of roles is to increase our ability to adopt different roles in accordance with the demands of the situation.

The readings for this chapter deal with improving management communication skills and with defensive communication.

EXERCISES

1. Case Study Discussion

The following excerpt discusses a 1994 article by George F. Will on the National Endowment for the Arts (NEA).

> TAXPAYER SUPPORT FOR THE ARTS
> The NEA was created in 1965. By 1993 it was spending $175 million a year of taxpayers' money. The NEA has funded, for example,
>
> - "Dinner Party," a table with 39 place settings of vaginas on dinner plates.
> - the artist who inserted a speculum into a vagina and invited members of the audience to come on stage to view her cervix with a flashlight.
> - a Chicago film project that was publicized with a poster announcing "Sister Serpents F_______ a Fetus."
> - three Wyoming women for a display of 70 cows painted . . . with feminist thoughts.
>
> New York City spends $87.3 million a year to support 431 arts groups. Mr. Will concludes that "subsidized arts are pork for the articulate, for people nimble and noisy in presenting their employment or entertainment as an entitlement." (*Newsweek,* January 10, 1994, pp. 64–65)

In groups of five, discuss the pros and cons of taxpayer subsidies for the National Endowment for the Arts. See if you can reach a consensus on this issue.

2. Self-Disclosure Exercise

Pair off with someone you feel close to. Talk about the topics listed below. *Feel free to stop if you feel things are getting too close for comfort. Take turns discussing each topic before moving on to the next.

a. Your hobbies and interests
b. Your attitude toward your body—likes and dislikes
c. Your family's financial status
d. Attitudes toward your parents and others in your family
e. Attitudes toward religion
f. Your love life, past and present
g. Personal problems that really concern you
h. Your reaction to your partner on the basis of this exercise

*The topics are similar to those developed by Sidney Jourard (1964) and published in *Self-Disclosure: An Experimental Analysis of the Transparent Self* (New York: Wiley, 1971), pp. 177–78.

3. Member Roles Exercise

Have a group discussion using the fishbowl format (a group of observers surrounding a group of discussants). Try to identify the roles each member plays by placing a check mark in the appropriate box in the chart shown in Figure 2.7.

Roles	Members							
	A	B	C	D	E	F	G	H
Group Task Roles:								
1. Initiator-contributor								
2. Information seeker								
3. Information giver								
4. Coordinator								
5. Orientor								
6. Evaluator								
7. Energizer								
8. Opinion giver								
Group-Building Roles:								
9. Encourager								
10. Harmonizer								
11. Compromiser								
12. Gatekeeper and exploiter								
13. Standard setter								
14. Follower								
Self-Centered Roles:								
15. Aggressor								
16. Blocker								
17. Recognition seeker								
18. Playboy (playgirl)								
19. Dominator								
20. Help seeker								

FIGURE 2.7 Member Roles Exercise Chart

These observations should be fed back to the group members and discussed in a supportive way. For a variation, some group members can be briefed in advance to act out certain roles to test the observers' abilities to recognize the behavior.

READINGS: Overview

Much has been written about the importance of language behavior in and outside small groups. In the first reading, Arizona Senator John McCain describes the powerful role that communication plays in one's very survival. In the second reading, Anne Donnellon demonstrates the successes that resulted from using certain communication behaviors. Both readings further illustrate concepts discussed in this chapter.

Reading 2.1 Communication

John McCain

Nothing crushes your spirit more effectively than solitary confinement. Having no one else to rely on, to share confidences with, to seek counsel from, you begin to doubt your judgment and courage. The loneliness robs you of everything—everything but time. When you are in solitary confinement you have nothing to think about other than time and just making it through another day. So needless to say, keeping track of the date is not difficult for a man held at length in solitary confinement.

In the five and a half years I was a prisoner of war in Vietnam, Christmas was always the most difficult time of year for me. I distinctly remember Christmas Eve 1969. I had been a POW for more than two years already, most of which was spent alone in my cell. Like many other cells in the Hanoi Hilton, mine was a small, empty room, roughly seven feet by ten feet with a concrete slab on the floor, which served as my bed. The walls were eighteen inches thick and the windows of each cell were boarded up so that the POWs could not communicate with each other. I remember there being a single, naked lightbulb dangling on a cord in the center of the ceiling and a small loudspeaker in the corner on which the Vietnamese would play various propaganda pieces.

It was about eight o'clock on Christmas Eve 1969. I was in pretty bad shape, having received some severe beatings from the North Vietnamese. On top of that, I had still not recovered from the injuries I received when I was shot down two years earlier. I was cold. I was injured. And as I lay there in my cell listening to Hanoi Hanna report on "latest heroic victory over the American imperialists," I had some real serious doubts of my chances for survival.

Then the prison guards began to play a series of Christmas songs over the camp's public address system, the last of which was Dinah Shore singing "I'll Be Home for Christmas." As I lay there listening to that particular song, my spirits dropped to the lowest possible point. I was not sure if I would survive another night, let alone ever return home for another Christmas with my family.

It was then that I heard the tapping on my wall.

Despite the strict rules against it, the POWs communicated to each other by tapping on the walls of our cells. The secretive tap code was a simple system. We divided the alphabet into five columns of five letters each. The letter K was dropped. A, F, L, Q, and V were the key letters. Simply tap once for the five letters in the A column, twice for F, three times for L, and so on. After indicating the column, pause for beat, then tap one to five times to indicate the right letter. For example, the letter C is sent as: tap . . . tap tap tap.

We became so proficient at the tap code that in time the whole prison system became a complex information network. With each new addition to our population, word quickly passed from cell to cell about every POW's circumstances and information from home. The tap code was my sanity's saving grace. That daily personal contact through the drumming on my wall made my isolation more bearable. It affirmed my humanity and kept me alive.

The cell on one side of me was empty but in the other adjacent room was a guy named Ernie Brace. Ernie was a decorated former marine who had flown more than one hundred combat missions in the Korean War. He had volunteered as a civilian pilot to fly missions to secretly supply CIA-supported military units in the Laotian jungle. During one such operation in 1965, he was captured and handed over to the North Vietnamese. He was brutally tortured and kept in solitary confinement for three years at a remote outpost near Dien Bien Phu before he was even brought to the Hanoi Hilton in 1968.

As soon as I heard the tapping that Christmas Eve, I knew it was Ernie. I got up and pressed my ear against the cold stone wall of my cell. At first it was difficult to make out the faint tapping of my neighbor. But it soon became very clear.

"We'll all be home for Christmas," Ernie tapped. "God Bless America."

With that I began to cry.

When you are imprisoned, the enemy can take almost everything from you but they cannot take your spirit. Those unspoken words coming from Ernie—who, due to his work with the CIA, had the least chance of getting out of the camp alive—were a poignant affirmation that as Americans, we possessed a divine spark that our enemies could not extinguish—hope.

"We'll all be home for Christmas. God Bless America."

That simple message, in my darkest hour, strengthened my will to live. Ernie helped me realize that we would get home when we got home. Until then, we had to manage our hardships as best we could. Without his strength, I doubt I would have survived solitary confinement with my mind and self-respect intact.

It was long ago and far away. But around the holidays, when I hear "I'll Be Home for Christmas," I am always reminded of that time, that place, and the words of my friend Ernie Brace. He kept me going and lifted my spirit when they were in their greatest need of lifting. When I hear that song I think of Ernie. I think about my friends that never made it home for another Christmas. And I think of what a blessing it is to be an American.

Reading 2.2 Team Talk

Anne E. Donnellon

Typically, it is the primary medium through which information is exchanged, decisions are made, and plans are formulated. Beyond these obvious functions, team talk plays other powerful, though subtle, roles. The way a team talks reveals where the team is coming from and where it is headed. More important, talk is a tool for changing a team's destination, and it can even alter a team's point of origin. The purpose of this article is to explain how to analyze team dynamics through talk.

TEAM DYNAMICS

What are the important dynamics in teams, and how does talk affect these? A common assumption is that a team's character or its typical dynamics are formulated by accumulating the individual traits and values of each team member (see Figure A). But it is far more complicated than that. Teams are work groups characterized by the interdependence (and, in the case of cross-functional teams, the diversity) of their members. These two features create several important dynamics in teams:

1. *Identity crises.* Team members typically come into teams identifying more strongly with their functional group, yet the team's shared goals impose a new common identity on them, which may conflict with their functional identity.
2. *A requirement to manage interdependence.* By virtue of their team membership, individuals who are trained and socialized to think and act independently must learn how to act when they are interdependent.
3. *A requirement to manage power differences.* To manage differences and interdependence without threatening a precarious team identity, teams need to manage the power differences among team members.
4. *A potential for social closeness.* Given the shared identity and diversity of team members, how close are team members socially?
5. *The inevitability of conflict.* Differences of perspective, opinion, and interests within a team inevitably create conflict; whether it is constructive or destructive, conflict is critical to team effectiveness.
6. *A requirement for negotiation.* To resolve the crises and conflicts created by diversity and interdependence, teams need to negotiate.

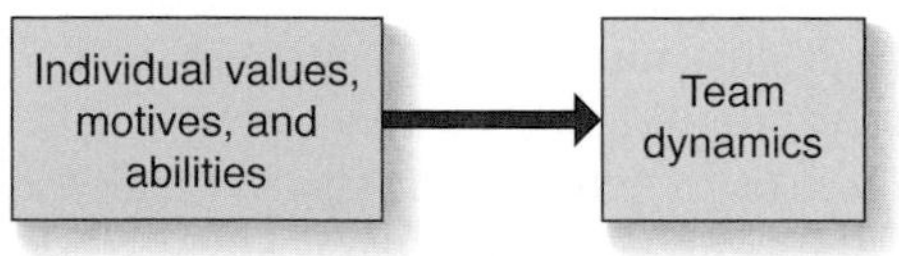

FIGURE A A Commonly Assumed Relationship Between Individuals and Teams

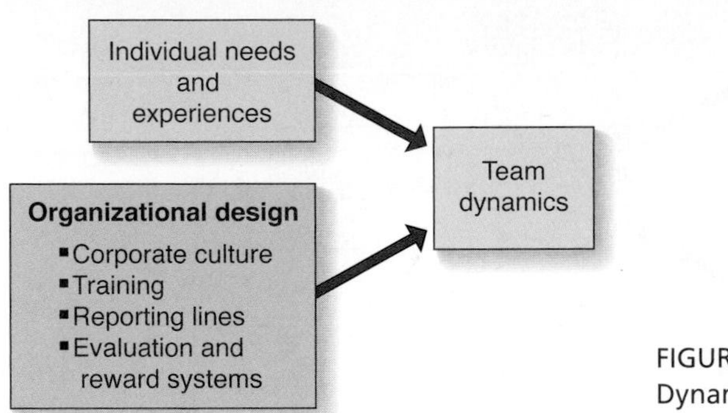

FIGURE B Factors Shaping Team Dynamics

Obviously, some of these dynamics start as struggles within individuals, such as the problem of where you identify or how to cope with being dependent on someone who is different from you. Others—like conflict and negotiation—clearly occur among team members. Virtually all these internal dynamics of teams are amplified, if not created, by organizational factors (see Figure B for a depiction of these relationships). For example, organizations with strong functional subcultures amplify the identity crises that team members experience when they join cross-functional teams. Organizations with evaluation and reward systems that focus on individual performance increase the likelihood of conflict in teams, and the probability that team members will use differences in power to influence one another in directions that make their own individual performance look better.

Yet teams typically do not examine their dynamics or diagnose and treat their causes. Instead team members tend to blame one another for the problems the team experiences: "He's incompetent," "She's always got a different opinion from the rest of us," "He talks a good game but doesn't follow through," "She doesn't speak up in meetings but always manages to impose her views." Such judgments of individual blame are based on the observed behavior of team members, a significant proportion of which is talk. This is ironic because closer attention to the language that teams use as they do their work would enable team members to recognize the many factors, other than individual motives and abilities, that shape the behavior.

Listening to teams as they work, you can hear them struggling with conflicting identities and using the differences of power among them to resolve disputes. You can hear and assess the dynamics of the team by listening to the language the team uses. These dynamics occur in the talk of teams. Talk thus reveals the team dynamics as well as the pressures of the organization on the team and its members. But team talk does more than just reveal team dynamics; it creates them. The language that team members use as they work together has consequences. If certain team members consistently remind others of their power differential, those differences create differences in the contributions of team members, as the less powerful defer to the more powerful. When team members negotiate with one another as if the situation would create winners and losers, other members adopt similar language. Language thus creates thoughts, feelings, and behavior in team members, which affect the way the team uses

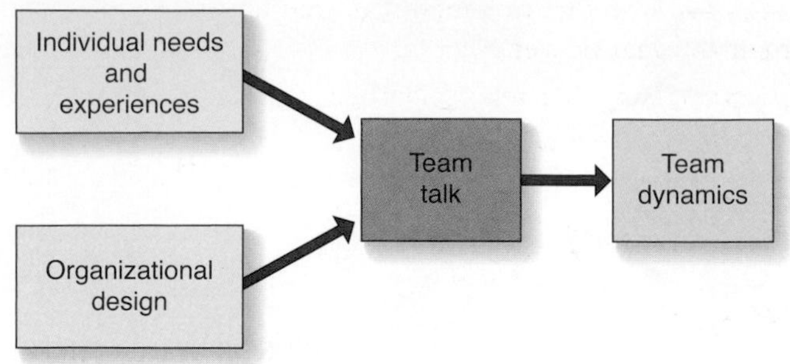

FIGURE C The Role of Team Talk in Team Dynamics

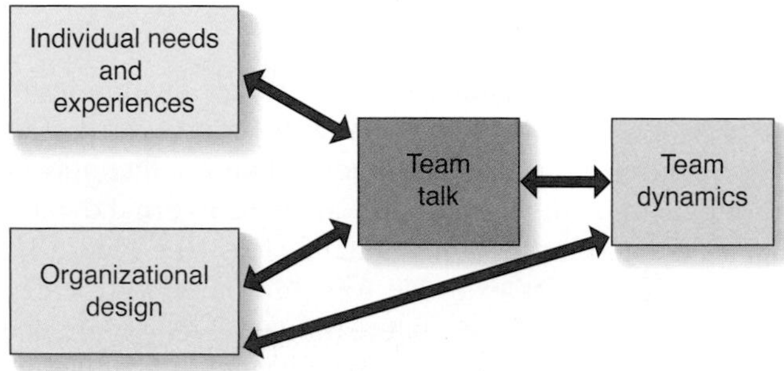

FIGURE D The Cyclical Relationship of Organizations, Teams, and Language

power, manages conflict, and negotiates. The way this occurs is explained more fully later in the chapter. Figure C depicts the distinctive role of team talk in shaping team dynamics.

Team talk, because it is so influential in shaping team dynamics, also influences the organization. As teams deliver their joint products or outcomes, organizations are influenced by them. For example, one organization overcame stagnant growth through the introduction of teams; it also gradually changed many of its structures and systems in response to team initiatives to ensure that its teams would flourish. In another organization in this study, poor team dynamics not only contributed significant loss of return on investments, they also ended up costing the organization its survival as an independent division. Team dynamics thus shape the organization. Figure D depicts the full set of relationships among organizations, individuals, teams, and language.

KEY DIMENSIONS OF TEAM TALK

Let's look specifically now at how important team dynamics are revealed and shaped by language. The distinctive dynamics of teams discussed on the previous page identify six key categories or dimensions of team talk:

1. *Identification* (with what group team members identify).
2. *Interdependence* (whether team members feel independent from or interdependent with one another).

3. *Power differentiation* (how much team members use the differences in their organizational power).
4. *Social distance* (whether team members feel close to or distant from one another socially).
5. *Conflict management tactics* (whether members use the tactics of force or collaboration to manage their conflicts).
6. *Negotiation process* (whether the team uses a win–lose or win–win process).

The types of words, sentences, and patterns of speech that a team uses repetitively create a sense of how team members think and feel about each other and about their task. Listeners form these impressions often without thinking about what they are hearing or even about what it means. To be more systematic about diagnosing a team's problems, imagine that each of these dimensions is a continuum and that you can analyze a team's talk and place it at some point along each continuum. To do this, you need to know which language or linguistic forms produce the meanings of different points along each continuum. Table A presents the linguistic forms that research has found to produce specific social meanings. These linguistic forms help us form crude assessments about whether a team is at one end of the continuum, the other, or somewhere between, as Figure E indicates. At one end of the dimension is the kind of talk you would expect to hear in a real team, and at the other is the kind of language you would expect from people who were a team in name only.

Doing this kind of interpretive work sounds more complicated than it is. In fact, we make such interpretations of people's talk continually and unconsciously every day. The approach taken here is simply a more mindful and systematic

TABLE A Dimensions, Forms, and Examples of Team Talk

Dimensions and Forms	Examples
I. Identification	
A. Inclusive pronouns refer to functional groups	"we" "our" "us"
Reference to functional groups	marketing, engineering
B. Inclusive pronouns referring to team	"we" "our" "us"
II. Interdependence	
A. Explicit reference to independence	"We can design this product without your input."
Assertions of individual intent	"I'm going to tell the customer to expect it Tuesday."
Failure to respond to questions	
B. Acknowledgment of mutual interests	"If we can pull this off, our careers will be made."
Expressions of own needs	"I need to know your opinion before I go on."
Soliciting of others' views and needs	"How do you feel about my idea?"
Proposals of joint action	"Let's review our progress to date."
Explicit reference to interdependence	"We need to decide whether this meets our goals."

TABLE A Dimensions, Forms, and Examples of Team Talk—Continued

Dimensions and Forms	Examples
III. Power Differentiation	
A. Certainty	"I believe we are doing this the wrong way."
Challenges	"Why do you think that?"
Challenges to competence	"Do you have an agenda for this meeting?"
Corrections	"That's not right."
Directness	"I want you to have these data tomorrow."
Interruptions	
Leading questions	"Did you tell us you would have that report today?"
Orders	"Tell me what happens at that meeting."
Repetition of questions	
Topic change	"Moving right along. What about X?"
Verbal aggression	"If you can't do this, we'll have to find someone else."
Excessive or asymmetrical politeness	"Would you be so kind as to . . . ?"
B. Apologies	"Sorry. My other meeting ran over time."
Disassociations of self from request	"The team will need you to take this to management."
Disclaimers	"I'm no engineer, but . . . "
Indirect questions	"Is there a way this could be done quickly?"
Hedges	"I'm thinking out loud here, but . . . "
Politeness	"John, could you please tell us more about that?"
Stating one's debt to other	"I am indebted to you for your participation."
IV. Social Distance	
A. Accounts using formal language	"Our perspectives are convergent."
Formal forms of address	"Mrs. Smith . . . "
Excessive politeness	"Would you be so kind as to . . . ?"
Impersonal requests or assertions	"Is it possible for you to review this quickly?"
Literal response to question about relationship	Q: "What does your other commitment do to our 4:30 meetings?" A: "Shortens them."
B. Casual style, using of slang	"What's up?"
Use of nicknames	
Slurring of pronunciation or ellipsis	"Whatta ya gonna do?" "Dunno."
Claiming commonalities in group membership	"We're all part of the team."
Claiming common views	"I see what you mean."
Displaying knowledge and concern for others' wants	"You're asking whether you need to file that form."
Empathy	"I understand your dilemma."
Expressions of liking or admiration	"I knew you could do it."
Expressions of reciprocity or cooperation	"I'll owe you."
Familiar address	"Pal."
Similar language	

TABLE A Dimensions, Forms, and Examples of Team Talk—Continued	
Dimensions and Forms	**Examples**
V. Conflict Management Tactics	
A. Directives	"Do it in the format she needs."
Threats	"We'll have to take this up with your boss."
Acquiescence	"Okay."
Use of power differences	
Voting	"How many think we should pursue this?"
B. Expression of interest, problem, need	"To get you timely feedback, I need the specs soon."
Questions seeking others' needs	"What do you need to know from us to do it?"
Synthesis of interests	"If you drop that requirement, I can meet your others."
Nonthreatening tone to debates	"We could look at these data another way."
Restatement of dissenting views	"You are saying you're not persuaded we need this."
Analysis of implications or consequences	"If we go that route, what are associated costs?"
VI. Negotiation Process	
A. Expressions of positions	"We have always said we need A before B."
Lexicon of debt, concession	"We'll be selling everyone out."
Use of power differences to win	
B. Reframing or reinterpreting in light of others' ideas	"So, as long as I cover the costs, I can speed up the . . . "
Exploration of implications	"How would it affect you if I . . . ?"
What-if questions	"What if we justified the additional costs?"
Using objective criteria for resolution	"What data would we all need to persuade us?"

focus on the kind of language that makes a difference in team work. Each of the key dimensions of team talk is explained in greater detail below.

Identification

Organizational groupings provide people with a common identity. From this common identity, group members develop shared values and similar patterns of behavior. The challenge for work teams, especially of professional-level employees, is the management of multiple identities. Professionals tend to identify strongly with their disciplines (and functional department), which often have different values and ways of acting and talking, and interpret the cross-functional task in very different, sometimes mutually contradictory, ways. On the other hand, the team task creates a new grouping and imposes a new shared identity for team members.

In their interaction, we would expect that members of real teams would display at least as much identification with the team and other team members as with their functional departments. Repeated references to functional groups and identifications with the functional department, especially in the absence of team identification, would usually indicate that this is a nominal team. The primary linguistic forms of identification are the inclusive plural pronouns "we" and "you"

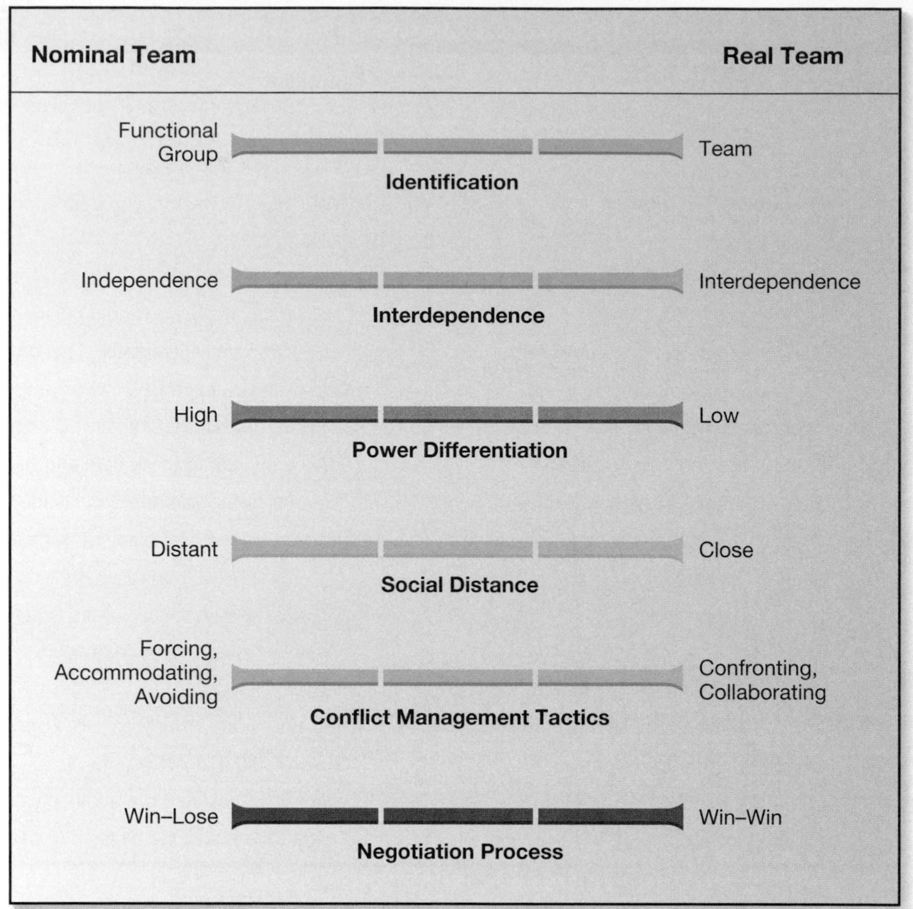

FIGURE E Key Dimensions of Team Interaction

and the exclusive "they." Obviously, analysis of the linguistic context of these forms is required to determine whether such pronouns refer to the team or the functional group.

Interdependence

Interdependence is a central defining characteristic of work teams because team members, by virtue of their shared responsibility, are dependent upon one another. However, this interdependence is not always perceived by all of the members of the team. In fact, the primary distinction between a real team and a nominal team is the common perception of interdependence among members of a real team. When team members feel themselves to be interdependent in the process of achieving the task and goals, they not only reflect this in their talk but they also use it. The linguistic signs of interdependence remind other team members of their mutual dependencies and solicit appropriate contributions to the necessary integration. Forms that mark such interdependence include acknowledgment of mutual interests and expressions of one's own needs, proposals for joint action, and solicitation of others' views, needs, and preferences.

At the opposite end of this continuum, the interaction of nominal teams is notable for both the absence of such interdependence talk as well as the presence of linguistic signs of perceived independence from other team members. Forms that express independence include assertions of individual intent and challenges to the other, and failures to respond to the questions of others.

Distinctions along this dimension are subtle, however, and depend upon the rest of the conversation for interpretation. For example, "expressions of own needs" could indicate independence, even selfishness or defiance of the team, in a statement like "I need that information tomorrow regardless of the team's schedule." To reflect perceptions of interdependence, the expression of one's own needs must occur in the context of expressed mutual interest or interdependency. Similarly, an "assertion of individual intent" could reflect a perception of interdependence if the statement is made after a joint team decision, as a summation of one's own role in the plan developed together.

Power Differentiation

Research on groups has repeatedly found that the display of power differences within groups produces numerous negative effects, from the suppression of opinions to conformity of behavior. Given that groups solve problems better and make decisions more effectively than individuals because multiple perspectives and sources of knowledge and skill are brought to bear on the problem, the persistent use of power differences in teams is likely to affect teams' performance negatively.

Theoretically, the task interdependence that characterizes teams should motivate team members to contribute whatever they can to the team's efforts, regardless of their relative power. Of course, the power distribution within the larger organization is likely to be reflected in the interaction of all teams to some extent, as members employ conversational tactics to preserve their status and to influence others. However, real teams are likely to deemphasize these differences—either deliberately, to avoid suppressing valuable contributions, or unconsciously, because organizational identities are less important than the team identity. Members of nominal teams are likely to use forms that reflect perceived differences of power because they are more oriented to the organization than to the team, more accustomed to using the power differences, and less concerned with threats to the team and its goals. The linguistic forms that show perceptions of power differences (between speaker and listener) are numerous, since this subject has been extensively researched.

The forms of talk that emphasize differences of power between speaker and listener include dominating the floor, interruption, questioning, demands and directives, topic changes, and challenges. These forms are easy to recognize and, when they are repeatedly used by the same people, are typically interpreted as displays and use of power. When team members with greater organizational power refrain from using such forms of talk, they are minimizing the differences of power among members of the team. The linguistic forms that actively minimize the power differences between speaker and listeners include apologies, disclaimers, hedges, indirect questions and requests, and politeness.

Social Distance

Since power differentiation in team interaction suppresses contributions or reduces commitment to team goals, there must be another process by which team members can influence one another. Social exchange theory suggests that linguistic displays of social closeness may fulfill this function. By signaling closeness or inclusion, speakers invite reciprocal feelings and the accommodation that such relationships require.

In one model of social influence, researchers demonstrated how linguistic forms of social closeness produce social calibration and compliance by minimizing attention to disparities in the social exchange. The model implies, for example, that addressing a team member by her nickname signals a closeness that, if warranted and desirable, can distract her from calculating whether the request for support is reasonable and can instead motivate similar feelings of closeness and obligation. In team work, this effect would serve multiple purposes: (1) reducing the attention given to calculating, monitoring, and altering social debts, (2) increasing the attention that could be focused on task accomplishment, and (3) reinforcing team identity.

In the conversation of a real team, where there is a shared identity, a common perception of interdependence, and a commitment to the task, we would expect to observe linguistic forms of social closeness. These include an informal style of speech, claims of common group membership, claims of common views, displays of knowledge of or concern for others' wants, expressions of liking or admiration, nicknames, presumptive requests or statements, similar word use, empathy, and humor.

We might see nominal teams expressing social closeness, for reasons other than a shared identity and the need to influence one another without use of power differentiation. For example, the team members might know and like one another. However, it is more likely that such groups would not display social closeness because even if some team members are close, the presence of less familiar people establishes a level of social interaction at a more socially neutral level. Social distance could be shown by the absence of closeness forms or by specific linguistic forms such as formal language, disagreement, disconfirmation, failure to acknowledge or respond to others' comments, and literal response to questions about relationship.

Conflict Management Tactics

To say that team work inherently involves diversity and interdependence is to acknowledge that conflict is both inevitable and desirable. It also means that conflict management will be a common and critical task for teams and that the amount of conflict does not distinguish real teams from nominal teams. The absence of conflict in a group may be more problematic than its presence. Therefore, it is the tactics for managing the conflict that distinguish a real team from a nominal one.

Researchers have identified five different types of tactics used to manage conflict that vary in terms of their assertiveness and cooperativeness, including avoidance, accommodation, forcing, compromise, and collaboration. Avoidance of conflict in teams is a common but disastrous approach to managing differences: it does not exploit the differences that teams are designed to take into account. Accommodating is the willingness to meet the needs of the other, even at the expense of your own. If team members make concessions that ignore or minimize their own perspective or expertise, chances are that the team's outcomes will be less than optimal. Similarly, if team members try to manage conflicts by forcing their opinions, this behavior will have the same negative effect. Compromise is seen by many managers as the optimal approach to managing conflicts because it seems fair to give up something to get something. Compromise also takes less time than collaboration, which attempts to meet all parties' concerns and needs as fully as possible. In the context of team work, in which differences need to be integrated into a whole that is greater than the sum of its parts, compromise is not desirable because one or more perspectives may not be fully considered. Only the tactics of collaboration can provide the basis for integration, by surfacing differences and discovering overlapping interests.

The linguistic forms that constitute tactics of forcing, avoiding, and accommodating are similar to those that differentiate power. Forcing also includes commands, directives, and threats. The linguistic signs of accommodation and avoidance are typically the absence of self-assertive behavior in the context of forcing behavior. Compromise can be seen in the delaying or redirecting of conflictual decisions, and in voting. Repeated use of such forms identifies a team as nominal rather than real. Teams that are focused on integrating their differences (that is, real teams) use confrontation and collaboration tactics of soliciting all members' views and preferences, redefining the problem to take those views into account. Consensus and dissent are explicitly sought. On real teams, we would not expect to find conflicts delegated to the hierarchy for resolution.

Negotiation Process

When teams focus on resolving their conflicts to achieve mutual agreements, they are negotiating. Negotiation theorists have identified two distinct processes for resolving differences among negotiators: win–lose and win–win. The former focuses on the competitive aspect of the negotiation, treating it as a distribution of wins and losses among the negotiating parties. The latter seeks to "integrate the parties and hence yield high joint benefit." These two types of process are the endpoints on a continuum of team negotiation.

Some organizational team work amounts to win–lose negotiation, typically as a result of competitive pressures outside the team, such as resource scarcity or rigid functional accountability. Linguistically, a win–lose orientation is manifest through explicit expressions of positions rather than interests, use of power differences to win, and words that refer to dividing things, or to debt, concession, winning, and losing. A win–win negotiation process, especially in the early stages, may include assertions of individual interests that are difficult to distinguish from assertions of positions. However, a win–win orientation ultimately is shown through talk such as the elaboration of the others' ideas, exploration of the implications of the others' ideas, and reevaluation or refraining of one's own interests in light of the others'.

CHAPTER 3

Relevant Background Factors

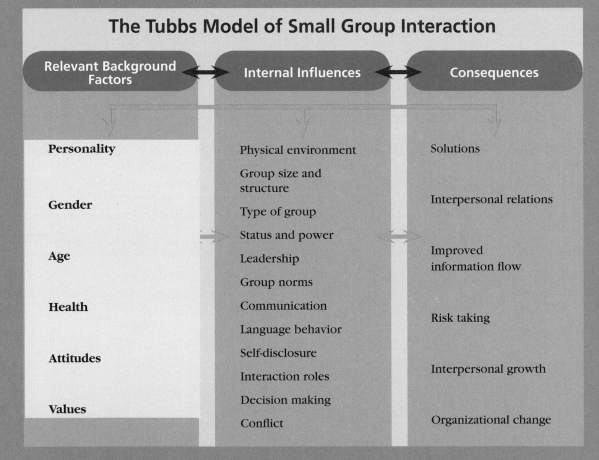

The Tubbs Model of Small Group Interaction		
Relevant Background Factors ↔	**Internal Influences** ↔	**Consequences**
Personality	Physical environment	Solutions
Gender	Group size and structure	Interpersonal relations
Age	Type of group	Improved information flow
Health	Status and power	Risk taking
Attitudes	Leadership	Interpersonal growth
Values	Group norms	Organizational change
	Communication	
	Language behavior	
	Self-disclosure	
	Interaction roles	
	Decision making	
	Conflict	

Concepts in **boldface** in gray panels are the emphases of this chapter.

Preview

Chapter 3 details the six relevant background factors that are part of the Tubbs Model of Small Group Interaction. These factors—personality, gender, age, health, attitudes, and values—relate directly to why we do what we do when placed in small group situations. The chapter also discusses Maslow's hierarchy of needs. These needs tend to explain further the six relevant background factors. By the way, universities are now looking at some of these factors to determine college admissions. If you would like to look into this, see www.AdmissionsEssays.com.

Glossary

Affection Affection refers to the friendship and closeness between people.

Attitudes An attitude is a mental state that exerts influence over an individual's behaviors. Attitudes have three components: (1) a cognitive component, which refers to a concept, (2) an affective component, which is emotion, and (3) a behavioral component, which is the readiness to act.

Consistency Theories Consistency theories all are based on the assumption that human beings have a strong psychological need for consistency. This is often referred to as a need to maintain cognitive balance.

Control Control is our need to influence, lead, and develop power over others or to be influenced, be led, or have others exert power over us.

Inclusion Inclusion is our need for belonging, feeling a part of, and being together with others.

Values Values are fewer in number than attitudes and serve as important predictors of behavior. They appear to be more stable and long-lasting than attitudes.

CASE STUDY

NETFLIX

Entrepreneur Reed Hastings got the idea for a Web-based movie rental business called "Netflix" in 1997 after he was charged a huge late fee for renting *Apollo 13* from his local video store. He thought, "There has to be a better way." Later, he drove to his local gym where customers are charged with a flat fee, rather than a fee based on the time spent in the gym. And so he created his own business using the gym's business model—that is, renting unlimited movies on a flat-fee monthly basis, with no penalties for keeping movies beyond a certain time. At that time, renting movies by mail instead of at the video store "struck most people as somewhat ludicrous" (Cook & Taylor, 2006, p. 1).

But having a great idea is not enough. Hastings then gathered a group of friends, along with his wife, lawyer, and others, to thoroughly discuss his idea and to develop a full-fledged business plan that he could take to a bank or other funding source to launch the company. One by one, they went through the list of possible customer objections, systematically coming up with answers to each. They had to design a mailer package that was small, lightweight, and convenient. They mapped the processing logistics of each package. They

continued

started by acquiring intimate knowledge of the U.S. Postal Service operations. Next, they customized their software and operational technologies to automate their picking, packing, and shipping processes and then linked those to their website. They also concocted the idea of offering 10 free movie rentals with the purchase of any new DVD player sold by the big-three manufacturers—Panasonic, Sony, and Toshiba. Combined, the big three had an 85 percent market share. Once new DVD player owners used the 10 free rentals, they were "hooked" (Cook & Taylor, 2006).

Once Hastings went to the funding sources, they in turn convened their loan committee to make sure that their decision to fund this new business was a sound one. The rest is history. In fact, Netflix is so successful that competitors like Blockbuster have added the same flat-fee, no-penalty type of service to their business model to supplement their local rental stores (Shell & Moussa, 2007). By 2006, Netflix was worth twice as much as Blockbuster, with over 4 million customers and a market value of over $1.5 billion (Cook & Taylor, 2006; see www.marketingprofs.com/6/cooktaylor1.asp?sp=1).

Notice that a key part of Hastings's business launch included gathering a group of interested and knowledgeable friends to think through the original idea. And the lending institution did the same thing to thoroughly explore their decision to loan him the money to start the business.

Our daily life involves dozens of groups including our family, friends, classes, teams, fraternity or sorority groups, church groups, and many others. Groups are a fundamental element of our society. In this book, we will explore many ways in which you can learn to become more productive and effective in the groups to which you belong.

1. What does this case study tell you about the potential influence that groups can have on individual behavior?
2. Identify and discuss as many examples as you can that you have observed of group influence on college students' behaviors.
3. From your own experience, how do you think that groups can be used to have positive influences on college students? What about people in other age groups?
4. What would you most like to learn from this course?
5. What expectations or concerns do you have?
6. Now that Netflix has moved to streaming online video, what do you think will be the next innovation that Reed Hastings should pursue to keep Netflix ahead of the competition?

This case clearly illustrates just one important example of the role groups play in life. Hastings had an idea, but needed to clarify and flesh-out his idea by using multiple groups to help him bring that idea to reality. As it turns out, Netflix has been an astonishing success with over 25 million subscribers by 2012.

In this chapter we will examine six relevant background factors: personality, gender, age, health, attitudes, and values. One of the basic premises of systems theory is that all these factors are interrelated, so that a change in one part of the system creates changes in other parts of the system.

Diversity: Groups in Context

Perhaps you wondered why Reed Hastings and his colleagues acted they way they did, or more generally, why anybody behaves the way they do. This question has intrigued people for centuries.

Most experts agree that our behavior is a result of a combination of *nature* and *nurture*. Associate Professor in Human Development Dario Maestripieri conducted a study, published in 2003, which revealed that baby rhesus macaques who are raised by a surrogate mother actually display behaviors that are more similar to those of the biological mother. This example indicates that *nature,* or genetics, is a critical factor in behavior. Maestripieri believes that many social and personality aspects of individuals are genetically determined and can actually produce a predisposition toward certain types of behavior that will reveal itself depending on environmental factors (Harms, 2003).

In recent and controversial studies, DNA testing has been utilized in attempts to pinpoint predispositions toward "antisocial behaviors" in individuals. The concept of DNA testing relies heavily on the belief that nature, or genetics, plays the key role in shaping behavior (Williams, 2003). Gene Robinson, neuroscience program director at the University of Illinois, wrote an article for *The New York Times* in 2004 called "The Behavior of Genes." Robinson states that certain elements of personality and behavioral tendencies may be inherited and can be identified through DNA. There is ample concern that such DNA testing violates human rights and would be unethical if used for instrumental purposes such as granting insurance, medicine, and employment (Robinson, 2004).

Many others believe in a more well-rounded view of the shaping of human behavior. Dr. Michel Rutter of the Institute of Psychiatry in London, for example, feels strongly that development plays a strong role in the emergence of genetic factors and should not be ignored. People with a genetic predisposition for antisocial behavior may never exhibit this behavior, depending on the contexts in which they develop (Williams, 2003).

It is important to remember that all behavior occurs in some context. The UCLA Center for Society and Genetics describes human nature as "the collection of psychological mechanisms typically shared by members of the human species that give rise to human behavior" and that "humans respond different ways to different conditions," or contexts (2005). Bennis and Thomas (2002) examine this phenomenon in their book *Geeks and Geezers.* They interviewed highly successful people under age 35 and over age 70 to learn more about how their experiences influenced the way they think. They found that context was one of the most important predictors of their viewpoint.

Michel Rutter asserts that human nature can be nurtured differently across different cultures, resulting in a difference in displayed behaviors (Williams, 2003). Understanding cultural differences in behavior is critical for our study as the United States continues to become more and more diverse. In order to celebrate this growing diversity and promote understanding of behaviors across cultures, children must be encouraged to accept and foster diversity at an early age. For instance, Crooked Creek Elementary School in Indianapolis focuses on diversity to teach children to understand individual differences very early in life (Banes, 2005). Respect for different types of diversity is critical in today's multinational environment. Take religious diversity, for example. Respect for religious diversity in the current climate is critical for peace and acceptance of those who have different beliefs, in the United States and abroad. Furthermore, our world has become increasingly interdependent. Ohmae (1999) writes in his book *The Borderless World,* "This forced isolation [of the United States has been] even harder to enforce with the emergence of the Triad (the United States, Europe, and Japan), a long-standing tri-lateral economic alliance that recently has been joined by such aggressive economies as Taiwan, China, Singapore, and Ireland" (p. xvi).

Rosen and colleagues (2000) remind us that if the world were a village of 100 people, there would be 56 Asians, 21 Europeans, 9 Africans, 8 South Americans, and 6 North Americans. There would be 30 Christians, 18 Muslims, 13 Hindus, 6 Buddhists, 5 animists, and 21 without any religion (p. 175). In the 1990s, the number of minorities in the United States doubled, with Hispanic Americans, Asian Americans, and African Americans making up 30 percent of the population. And these groups are expected to become the majority by the year 2050 (Holmes, 2003a). According to the data released in 2004 from the 2000 census, the largest minority group in the United States is Hispanic (Holmes, 2004b), with Asians being the fastest-growing minority population. The largest Asian populations are in California, New York, New Jersey, and Hawaii, with rapidly growing populations in Florida, Georgia, and Virginia. Additionally, Multicultural Marketing Resources Inc. conducted a study in 2004 which revealed that Asian Americans have the highest household incomes in the United States, make more purchases, and own more businesses than any other ethnic group (Holmes, 2004a). Recent research on group diversity has shown that homogenous teams tend to be more comfortable with each other, but diverse teams tend to solve problems more effectively. "Generally speaking, people would prefer to spend time with others who agree with them rather than disagree with them," says Katherine Phillips, professor at Northwestern University. But this unbridled affirmation does not always produce the best results. "When you think about diversity, people tend to view conversations as a potential source of conflict that can breed negative emotions, and it is these emotions that can blind people to diversity's upsides: new ideas can emerge, individuals can learn from one another, and they may discover the solution to a problem in the process" (Phillips et al., 2009).

The focus in recent years has been on developing global leadership competencies—that is, interpersonal and intellectual skills that work in any culture and in our culture with many diverse others. One team of researchers (McCall & Hollenbeck, 2002) studied hundreds of successful and unsuccessful leaders who worked in other countries. Their conclusion was this:

> The essence of development is that diversity and adversity beat out repetition every time. The more dramatic the change in skills demanded, the more severe the personnel problems, the greater the bottom-line pressure, and the more sinuous and unexpected the turns in the road, then the greater the opportunities for learning. . . . [Diversity and exposure] to other people are the best teachers. (p. 109)

So what else are businesses doing to respond to the multicultural climate in the United States, to appeal to the diverse market, and to leverage diversity in their organizations? Organizations are focusing on increasing multilingual employees in the workplace, attracting and recruiting diverse populations, and retaining diverse individuals within the workplace. Diversity initiatives are now linked to the bottom line of companies. As Linda Rush, Raytheon's director of global diversity, said, "When you have a team where everyone looks alike and thinks alike, they come up with the same solution. Diverse teams make better decisions, and solve problems faster and better" (Holmes, 2004b).

Companies are attempting to hire individuals who speak multiple languages to communicate with the diverse population in the United States and abroad. With the increase in Hispanics in the United States, many businesses have hired individuals who speak both Spanish and English. Some have also introduced "English as a Second Language" (ESL) training within their companies. Online courses are now available and offered by businesses for a more economical method of this type of language training (Holmes, 2004c).

As a secondary benefit, this practice opens companies up to hiring a more diverse workforce by creating a comfortable environment for individuals with language barriers. Recruiting a diverse workforce is a necessity today. Tamara Holmes wrote, "Today, firms are focusing on providing management with specific skills that are designed to attract and retain a diverse workforce." Companies are utilizing minority-specific job fairs and encouraging employee referrals from members of minority groups to reach out to other diverse employees (Holmes, 2004c).

Most people assume that multicultural conflicts arise because of different styles of communication. However, according to research, communication difference is only one of the four categories that can create barriers to a team's success. The four categories that suppress group cohesiveness are (1) direct versus indirect communication, (2) trouble with accents and fluency, (3) differing attitudes toward hierarchy and authority, and (4) conflicting norms for decision making (Brett, Behfar, & Kern, 2006).

In addition to diversity based on ethnic and cultural differences, there are key dimensions and needs that differentiate individuals. Based on decades of research on a sample of 46,000 people from more than 40 countries, Hampden-Turner and Trompenaars (2000) identified six dimensions that distinguish people. They are as follows:

1. Universalism (rules, laws, and generalizations)	Particularism (exceptions, special circumstances, unique relations)
2. Individualism (personal freedom, human rights, competitiveness)	Communitarianism (social responsibility, relations, cooperation)

continued

3. Specificity (atomistic, reductive, analytic, objective)	Diffusion (holistic, elaborative, synthetic, relational)
4. Achieved status (what you've done; your track record)	Ascribed status (who you are; your potential and connections)
5. Inner direction (conscience and convictions are located inside)	Outer direction (examples and influences are located outside)
6. Sequential time (time is a race along a set course)	Synchronous time (time is a dance of fine coordinations) (p. 11)

As you can imagine, when working with others who vary all along all six of these dimensions, it makes effective communication quite a challenge. On the other hand, working and socializing with people from different ethnic and cultural backgrounds can be one of life's richest rewards.

CASE STUDY

THE NATIONAL OCEANOGRAPHIC AND ATMOSPHERIC ADMINISTRATION ON DIVERSITY

The National Oceanographic and Atmospheric Administration (NOAA) takes diversity very seriously. It has a robust diversity strategy, which converges across aspects of inclusion, supportiveness, openness, and challenging and innovative work. These elements are critical to the NOAA at the personal, interpersonal/group, and organizational level. The NOAA works to respect all individuals, ensure equal opportunity, reduce climate barriers, and integrate diversity into the workplace. Each employee is accountable for respecting peers, promoting a culture of involvement, and welcoming fresh ideas (National Oceanographic and Atmospheric Administration, 2007).

The NOAA views diversity through a lens of dimensions. These dimensional categories are personality, internal dimensions, external dimensions, and organizational dimensions (National Oceanographic and Atmospheric Administration, 2007). The lens of diversity that is presented places individuals at the center, as they are held responsible for actively contributing to the NOAA strategy of diversity. You can read more at the NOAA website on diversity, http://www.nws.noaa.gov/eeo/index.php.

- *Personality*
- *Internal dimensions*
  Age
  Gender

Sexual orientation
Physical ability
Ethnicity
Race

- *External dimensions*
  Geographic location
  Income
  Personal habits
  Recreational habits
  Religion
  Educational background
  Work experience
  Appearance
  Parental status
  Marital status
- *Organizational dimensions*
  Work content/field
  Division/department/unit/group
  Seniority
  Work location
  Union affiliation
  Management status

Source: National Oceanographic and Atmospheric Administration, 2007; http://www.nws.noaa.gov/eeo/index.php.

Behaving in specific ways is usually seen as an attempt by the individual to meet certain needs. For example, have you ever been in a group situation and wondered why you were there? Suppose you look out a classroom window and see a beautiful sky; it is a great day for being outside. You begin to experience competing needs—the need to go outside and have fun and the need to accomplish whatever the group's purpose is (such as studying for an upcoming exam). Whichever need is more intense will most probably determine the behavior you pursue.

Probably one of the best-known models for explaining people's needs is Abraham Maslow's (1970) hierarchy of needs (see Figure 3.1).

Physiological needs must be met in order to survive. Some groups were formed in the days of the cave dwellers to fight off saber-toothed tigers, as well as unfriendly cave people, and to help gather food.

Security needs often motivate the formation of groups by individuals who lack sufficient power on their own. This is demonstrated by the union movement, which resulted from the fact that there were far more workers than jobs.

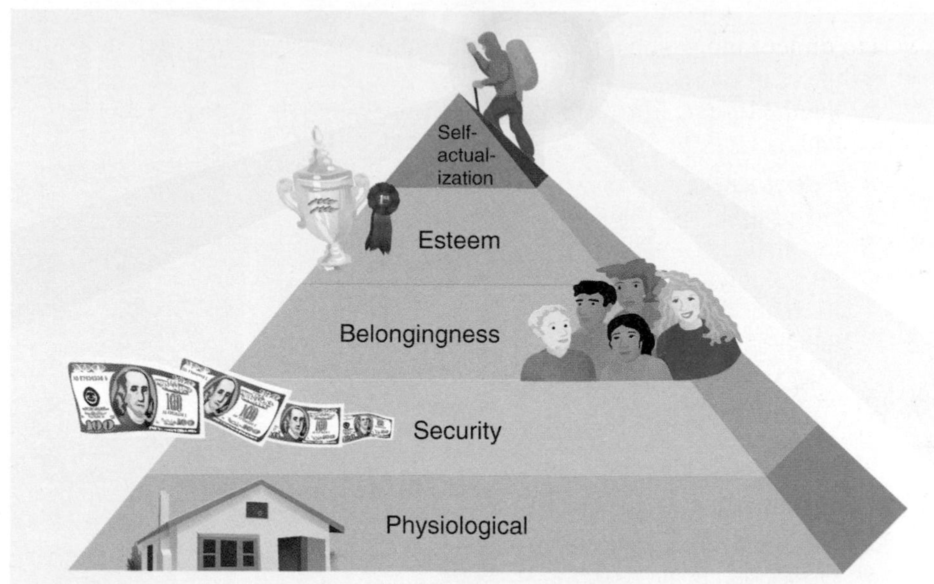

FIGURE 3.1 Maslow's Need Hierarchy

With 10 people waiting to fill each job, workers were somewhat hesitant to make demands of bosses. Unions helped workers gain power and, eventually, job security.

Belongingness needs are easy for most people to identify with. Think about what you felt like during your first week at college. One student member of a first-year discussion group wrote about this belongingness need not being fulfilled:

> During our discussion, I felt like I wasn't even supposed to be in my group. The others seemed like they were all very familiar with each other and discussed almost entirely among themselves. They took over the discussion basically by looking only at each other and asking a lot of questions of each other (and cracking a lot of really funny jokes). I tried to contribute but felt ignored. It was very uncomfortable and I became quiet after a few more attempts to contribute. I'm glad I didn't receive a grade on that discussion because I was annoyed at how little I participated.

Social needs in organizations can be satisfied by positive teamwork and membership in an established organizational culture. Eventually, the feelings of aloneness begin to subside as people develop their own circles of friends (social groups).

Esteem needs may also be met by groups. Often people are attracted to certain fraternities or sororities because of the prestige of membership, which adds to their feeling of self-esteem. All people need to feel that they are important, and being a part of a group or organization is one very good way to accomplish that goal. Esteem needs can also be satisfied through recognition, rewards, and status. Dave Russell (2004) of Envision Software expanded on satisfying esteem needs in his article "Break the Golden Rule Rewarding Top Performers." Russell reminds us that people are motivated by different types of reward and recognition. You can consider cash, training opportunities, or additional time away from work. The key is to understand which type of reward is most meaningful for each individual within the organization.

Self-actualization needs are the highest-level needs Maslow identified. A person may be attracted to a group because of the need for self-development. Encounter groups are one particular type of group devoted to the growth and development of members. Educational groups or work groups also may help individuals achieve a higher level of human potential.

Maslow argued that the needs lowest on the hierarchy must be satisfied before the higher-level needs are activated. For example, we worry less about self-actualization in a job when we are unemployed and the bills haven't been paid. However, further research has found that several needs may be experienced and met at once, or in different orders. Maslow's theory helps us to understand what types of behaviors motivate individuals. In some cases, an individual may naturally have stronger esteem needs while someone else may have strong self-actualization needs. Satisfying these individual needs can motivate behavior (Envision Software, 2004).

To fully understand Maslow's needs hierarchy within a work group, you can rework his diagram to show the following (Todd, 2005):

- *Self-actualization:* I am contributing to the group and growing as a result.
- *Esteem:* I am valued, recognized, and rewarded in a way that is meaningful to me.
- *Belongingness:* I am a member of the group and the organization.
- *Security:* I am safe at work and safe in my work group.
- *Physiological:* I am secure in my job and comfortable with the environment.

Probably one of the reasons Maslow's theory has been so popular is that it seems intuitively valid. It is important to have an understanding of what motivates people (including ourselves). When we are in a group and one person talks a lot, it may be that he or she is trying to meet a belongingness need. If people brag, they are probably trying to satisfy an esteem need. If they consistently offer creative ideas that seem quite unusual, they may be trying to meet a self-actualization need. Recent research by the Gallup Organization across 132 countries shows that all people seem to have five areas of well-being: (1) career, (2) social, (3) financial, (4) physical and health, and (5) community (Rath & Harter, 2010, pp. 153–56). These seem to correspond somewhat to Maslow's intuitive model.

Personality

FIRO-B

Because each of us is a member of numerous groups throughout our lives, have you ever wondered what motivates us to join groups in the first place? Although there are many personality theories, one seems particularly relevant to small group behavior. Schutz (1958, 1967, 1971) hypothesized that most people share three needs that groups help fulfill: needs for inclusion, control, and affection. Schutz's theory is called the *FIRO-B theory*. FIRO-B stands for Fundamental Interpersonal Relations Orientation—Behavior. It means that individuals relate or orient themselves to others in ways that can be identified, measured, and predicted. Many assessment organizations have provided FIRO-B assessment services to their clients as a premium product. In 2004, one assessment company, CPP, Inc., started offering a FIRO-B analysis profile to go with its current assessment package to help its clients (mostly managers, consultants, and trainers) understand work group interactions in the organizational environment (Wire Feed, 2004). CCP defines FIRO-B to be "the 15-minute tool for improving organizational relationships and individual effectiveness" (FIRO-B, 2004). This tool helps individuals understand their own needs and motivations and those of others in their group's organizations. If you are trying to lead a work group, it is very useful to be able to understand what motivates you and your group's members.

Schutz's work began at the Naval Research Laboratory in Washington, DC. The FIRO-B test has been used to select submarine crews and astronaut teams, whose members need personality styles that will help them work more efficiently together under high-stress conditions. The major premise of Schutz's theory is that people need people and that we join groups to help fill this need. Each person, from childhood on, develops a fundamental interpersonal relations orientation with differing levels of needed inclusion, control, and affection.

All of us have felt the need for inclusion. If you have ever been in a physical education class in which teams were chosen, you know this feeling. Do you remember waiting to be chosen and fearing not being chosen? Some people have also experienced the need for control. If you are trying to lead a group and several conversations are going on simultaneously, the need arises to control the discussion. Finally, if a group pays a lot of attention to certain members, this can make us feel the need to have some attention and affection directed our way, too. These are important needs in all people, but obviously they vary in intensity from person to person.

INCLUSION

Inclusive groups are more productive, have more group unity, promote better customer satisfaction, accomplish more goals, transfer knowledge more effectively, and possess more group confidence (Ferdman, 2003). *Inclusion* refers to our need for belonging—for feeling a part of and being together with others. Bernardo Ferdman of Alliant International University defines *inclusiveness* as "feeling accepted, recognized, and respected as a person." Ferdman spent time asking groups of people from five countries what *inclusion* feels like. Most of the people who responded to Ferdman described their experience of *exclusion* instead (Ferdman, 2003)! Have you ever been in a group in which you felt ignored? Perhaps you have felt this way in this very class, especially on the first or second day. This is because you were not being responded to as much as your need for inclusion required. Other people may not necessarily disagree with what you are saying; they just may not be responding. Such behavior violates our need to be included in the group. On a more basic level, it also makes us doubt our self-worth. If this exclusion happens over and over, most of us will begin to doubt our intrinsic worth as people.

On the job, if people go to lunch and don't invite us, our need for inclusion may not be met. On the other hand, if we prefer to do things on our own and people are constantly around us, this violates our *low* need for inclusion. Most of us want to be included in some groups and prefer to avoid others. If we are ignored by the attractive groups and sought after by the unattractive groups, this also violates our need for inclusion. O'Toole (1999) writes, "Inclusion. In a word, that's the secret to enlisting followers. Leaders create followers by including them in the process." He goes on to say, "Exclusion is thus the ultimate expression of disrespect for an individual in an organizational context" (pp. 145–46).

The late, great entertainer Sammy Davis, Jr., experienced exclusion when he first went into his group in the U.S. Army in 1942. Here is his gripping description of the incident:

> It was impossible to believe they were talking about me.
>
> "Yeah, but I still ain't sleepin' next to no nigger." . . . The corporal beckoned from the doorway. "Okay, c'mon in," he snapped, "on the double." We picked up our gear and followed him through the door. I felt like a disease he was bringing in. . . . I looked around the barracks. The bed nearest was empty. All the cots were about two feet apart from each other except ours, which were separated from the rest by about six feet—like we were on an island. . . . A sergeant came in and from the center of the barracks announced, "I'm Sergeant Williams. I'm in charge of this company. . . . There is only one way we do things here and that's the Army way! There will be exactly three feet of space, to the inch, between every bed in this barracks. You have sixty seconds to replace the beds as you found them. *Move!*" (Davis & Boyar, 1989, pp. 6–7)

It has been projected that 85 percent of people entering the workforce in the year 2050 will be females and people of color. If this 85 percent feels excluded, organizations will not succeed. Billy Dexter, president of the Hudson Highland Group, says that there are three primary reasons why inclusion in organizations is critical. The first is so that organizations can reflect or mirror the demographics of the United States, the population that they serve or sell to. The second is so that organizations may effectively market and increase their appeal to diverse populations. The final reason is to attract and retain key talent. In order to create this inclusive workplace culture, the initiative must be driven from the top of the organization down through the ranks. Upper management must support diversity and inclusive programs if they are to succeed across the organization (Holmes, 2003a).

According to a *New York Times* survey conducted by the Beta Research Corporation in 2003, companies that are able to "brand" themselves as inclusive and diverse actually have a competitive edge in the market. This survey assessed opinions across 500 hiring managers and 350 minority job seekers from three

Community Connect websites. The findings of this survey include the following results from both hiring managers and minority job seekers (Holmes, 2003a):

Hiring Managers

- In 92 percent of the organizations with diversity and inclusion programs surveyed, upper management fostered diversity as a company goal.
- Sixty-five percent of hiring managers feel that their programs are successful and have made a difference in the organization.
- Seventy percent of the hiring managers at these organizations feel that the inclusion efforts actually increase the performance of the business, and therefore affect the bottom line.

Minority Job Seekers

- Ninety-one percent of minority job seekers feel that organizations with diversity and inclusion programs are better places to work.
- Ninety-seven percent of minority job seekers prefer diverse workplaces and feel that these environments will offer better opportunities for advancement.
- Sixty-five percent of minority job seekers feel that an organization that has a solid branding or reputation for inclusion will attract more qualified minority and nonminority candidates.

With advances in technology, the *digital divide* may raise additional exclusion issues. The digital divide is the exclusion of certain groups of people from technology, either through lack of education, access limitations, disability, or any of the elements of diversity that we have discussed. Kees Brants and Valerie Frissen wrote an article for the European Media and Technology in Everyday Life Network in 2003, titled "Inclusion and Exclusion in the Information Society." This article addresses the Internet and exclusiveness on the basis of race, gender, socioeconomic class, and age. There is a sense that older populations have had less access to computer or technology training and are therefore excluded from the Internet network. There is also the belief that certain ethnic groups, women, and some lower economic classes do not have appropriate Internet access or representation in virtual space. Alternatively, others feel that the Internet has the power to increase sharing across diverse groups and create inclusiveness by bringing together people and opinions in an idea-sharing environment where this was once not possible. Some studies suggest that the potentially excluded groups are not gaining more access to the Internet and that the digital divide is widening (Brants & Frissen, 2003).

The inclusion issue raises its head over and over throughout our lives. Each time we take a new job, join a new work group, or meet a new group socially, we feel excluded. Problems occur when we are not sensitive to someone who is new in the group. That person is experiencing the feeling, but we may not be tuned into his or her needs. Often, when a person arrives late for a meeting, the others do not make any attempt to orient that person or to bring him or her up to date. All of us have a need for inclusion that must be met before we are able to function fully in a group. Keep in mind that this need recurs, much as our need to eat.

CONTROL

Control refers to our need to influence, lead, and develop power over others or to be influenced, led, or have others exert power over us. If you have ever been in a group with no appointed leader, you know how uncomfortable it is to break the ice and get the discussion started. Those who attempt to get the group organized are trying to exert control over the others. At first, this may be welcomed, but often people begin to resent the control takers and will eventually ask them to stop being so pushy, with such comments as "Who made you boss?" The issue of who is in control remains throughout the life of any group. Especially as membership changes, the pecking order is reshuffled and has to be reestablished. Here is an account of a class exercise in which resentment of a control taker is very obvious.

> The group consisted of seven people. The purpose of the class exercise was to form a manufacturing company and produce products. One individual chose himself as General Manager and also appointed an Assistant General Manager. The remaining members formed the assembly line workers. . . . The General Manager was a very forceful, energetic individual. He chose his own Assistant and appointed himself almost before we had formed the group. He is a very impatient individual. His entire manner left everyone in doubt as to the final outcome of the exercise. . . . The practice run was a complete disaster. We didn't know what the product was, let alone how to build it. Step-by-step instructions were available for everyone to read, but we weren't given time to read them. The General Manager didn't pay attention to his duties. He was more interested in production line speed than he was in purchasing materials or financial matters. He couldn't get quality products because of the haphazard organization of the work force. We had to start over again and again. The third time through, we got fairly decent quality. By that time it was too late. Dissension in the ranks of the group was rampant. . . . We were not motivated to do a good job, the only challenge was to beat the opposition (i.e., management).

Control, power, and leadership are closely related subjects. Why do you suppose so much has been written about them? Who is in control seems to be one of life's basic issues. The *Working Manager* defines control as "one symptom or use of power" (TheWorkingManager.com, 2005). Power is what makes you listen to one person and not another, making power very closely related to leadership. Power can be derived from 11 primary sources, according to the *Working Manager*. Some of the most critical sources are "role" or position, "network" within the organization, dedication, expertise, customer base, leadership, creativity, and politics (West, 2005).

Some studies have shown that whenever two people meet for the first time, a dominant–submissive relationship is established within the first 60 seconds. The perception of who is dominant between two people has been found to correlate over 90 percent with carefully constructed personality tests measuring the same phenomenon. Some books on power and control go to extreme lengths to help people gain control over others. For instance, Korda (1975) suggests that in order to gain and hold control over others, you should position your desk with your back to a window so that the other person has to look into the sunlight, thus putting him or her at a disadvantage.

The control issue is relevant to every organization on a daily basis, from the formal organization and the so-called span of control to who talks the most in meetings. Supervisors typically talk more than subordinates. They also usually control the topic of conversation. Control is often demonstrated in rather subtle ways, too. I once saw a professor throw a report on a secretary's desk. He said, "Sandy, I need to have this typed for the 3 o'clock class today." You could tell by her expression that she did not like the way he talked to her. Later that day, he came to pick up the finished report. She said, "Gee, Dave, I'm really sorry. I just didn't have time to get it done. Dr. Jenkins [the department head] had me on another project all day." She was giving Dave a lesson in organizational control. Any experienced supervisor knows how much control his or her subordinates have if they choose to use it.

Management control within organizations and groups has changed with the times. The use of information technology within organizations has changed the control relationship between managers and their subordinates dramatically. The use of information technology has empowered employees with access to information resources that they never had before. In organizations, control and power are generally interchangeable and defined as the amount of control one person has over a particular process or resource. Workers have begun to possess institutional knowledge that gives them leverage and empowerment when working with management.

The control–empowerment matrix shows the balance of employee empowerment and management control in organizations with different levels of information technology utilization (Reilley, 2004). An adaptation of this matrix is illustrated below:

Control–Empowerment Matrix	**Management Control**	
Employee Empowerment	**High**	**Low**
Low	*Panopticon*	*Taylorism*
High	*High-level bureaucracy*	*Networked organization*

According to this diagram, when management control is high and employee empowerment is low (*panopticon*), technology is generally used for surveillance and shadowing activities, such as quality assurance, or call monitoring in inside sales, telemarketing, or customer service roles. When there is low management control and low worker empowerment (*Taylorism*), the environment is generally automated or static, as in a production environment. When management control is high and worker empowerment is high (*high-level bureaucracy*), technology is generally used most effectively in a structured environment where employees and management both hold high levels of responsibility. Alternatively, when management control is low and employee empowerment is high (*networked organization*), complex information technology processes with subject matter experts and institutional knowledge evolve. This type of organization uses work groups or teams to run the technology, much like Web pages and interactive Internet media. This structure is flexible and can adapt (Reilley, 2004). Technology has changed the face of management control and employee empowerment and will continue to do so as technology evolves and the technological organization becomes forefront.

AFFECTION

Affection refers to the friendship and closeness among people. Often our best friends are co-workers. Why is it that when we have time off from the job, we organize bowling leagues, golf outings, and softball leagues with co-workers? Some of these activities, such as the company picnic or Christmas party, may be more or less required. But for the most part, we socialize off the job as well as on because we want to; picture the many winning-team locker-room scenes with the champagne pouring over people's heads and players hugging each other as extreme examples of this affection.

Schutz (1967) compares inclusion, control, and affection in the following way: "A difference in inclusion behavior, control behavior, and affection behavior is illustrated by the different feelings a man has in being turned down by a fraternity, failed in a course by a professor, and rejected by his girl. . . . Inclusion is concerned with the problem of in or out, control is concerned with top or bottom, and affection with close or far." In each of these areas, we have both the need to receive these behaviors from others and the need to express such needs toward others. Wanted inclusion might be hoping to be asked to go to lunch or for coffee or to have a beer with the group; expressed inclusion might be inviting someone else to go. A compatible need level exists when a person's wanted and expressed needs are at about the same level of intensity. Compatibility among individuals seems to occur when their needs are similar on the inclusion and affection dimensions and complementary or different on the control dimension. A group may suffer from too many power struggles if members are all high in need to control. Compatibility on these three dimensions tends to reduce conflict and increase group cohesiveness and satisfaction.

A carefully controlled laboratory study substantiated Schutz's predictions. Research in carefully constructed groups that were neutral, compatible, or incompatible on the basis of FIRO-B scores shows the following results. When the groups were allowed to work on a problem-solving task, the compatible groups completed their tasks significantly more quickly than did the neutral groups, which were significantly more efficient than the incompatible groups.

FIRO-B also has been found to be useful in organizational development. Varney and Hunady (1978) conducted a study in a 50-year-old heavy-metal production plant with 900 employees and 95 managers. They used the FIRO-B test as a tool to give feedback to the work groups regarding their own individual needs and to give them insight into each other. The plant manager originally described the organization's needs in the following summary:

> There is a considerable amount of disagreement and disharmony among members of the management staff, resulting in a failure on the part of individuals as well as the team as a whole to accomplish set tasks. The performance indicators for the plant are in almost all cases below the normal, and we ranked among a total of six plants in our division as the lowest performer. The basic problem seems to be that people cannot work together when it comes to sorting out problems, and they spend a lot of time blaming each other for the failures that occur. (p. 445)

As a result of the study, the researchers reported numerous changes in the behavior of the employees involved in the study. They concluded, "FIRO-B is a powerful stimulus to change. In the research reported here, we have demonstrated the value of the use of a 'high energizer' such as the FIRO-B in team-building interventions" (p. 445).

Sulloway (1996) argues in his controversial book *Born to Rebel* that birth order is an important influence on personality. He summarizes his study of 6,000 famous people as follows:

1. *Openness to experience*. Firstborns are more conforming and traditional, and more closely identified with parents.
2. *Conscientiousness*. Firstborns are more responsible, achievement oriented, and organized.
3. *Agreeableness*. Laterborns are more easygoing, cooperative, and popular.
4. *Neuroticism*. Firstborns are more jealous, anxious, and fearful.
5. *Extraversion*. Firstborns are more extraverted, assertive, and likely to exhibit leadership. (p. 73)

Although there are many exceptions to these conclusions, you can easily see how different personalities in a group may have a hard time agreeing.

MYERS-BRIGGS TYPE INDICATOR (MBTI)

One of the most popular methods of measuring personality, the MBTI, is based on the work of the psychologist Carl Jung and has been developed and expanded by Isabel Briggs Myers (1993) and Katherine Briggs over the past half century. This tool is used to enhance self-awareness and increase team effectiveness. The theory is that we all possess personality traits in pairs of opposite characteristics. The pairs are Extraversion (E) versus Introversion (I), Sensing (S) versus Intuition (N), Thinking (T) versus Feeling (F), and Judging (J) versus Perceiving (P). When you combine all of the possible combinations of pairs, there are 16 different personality types. Each of these has a preferred communication style. If you sometimes find that you just "click" with someone, it may be because your personality types are similar or compatible. The converse is also true, and it is helpful to realize that different personality types sometimes feel uncomfortable communicating with one another.

Visualize each of these opposing pairs on a continuum, as follows:

How people are energized	
(E) Extraversion ________________	Introversion (I)
The kind of information we naturally pay attention to	
(S) Sensing ________________	Intuition (N)
How we make decisions	
(T) Thinking ________________	Feeling (F)
How we like to organize our world	
(J) Judging ________________	Perceiving (P)

Place an X on each of these scales to indicate where you think you would fall based on your own assessment of your personality type. Look at the typical tendencies of these personality types as shown in Tables 3.1–3.4 (adapted from Tieger and Barron-Tieger, 1998).

Keep in mind that each of us is a blend of each of these four sets of opposites. None of us is pigeon-holed into any category. However, knowing more about our own personality and that of others helps us learn to work more effectively with others who may have personalities different from our own.

Although personality is one of the most important background factors in small group communication, other factors are also involved. *Organismic factors* or variables are those that are part of the organism. These include a number of characteristics, but three seem to be especially pertinent to small group interaction: gender, age, and health.

As we have seen in this section, groups are usually made up of people with different personalities and ways of thinking. Some are left-brain people, some

TABLE 3.1 Extroversion/Introversion

Extraverts	Introverts
Are enthusiastic	Are calm
Talk more	Talk less
Are more animated	Are more reserved
Think out loud	Think, then talk
Talk faster and sometimes louder	Talk slower and usually more quietly
Are easily distracted	Are more focused
Change subjects	Stay with one subject
Like to be around people	Like to be alone
Seek center stage	Avoid the limelight
Act first, think later	Are more cautious and hesitant

TABLE 3.2 Sensing/Intuition

Sensers	Intuitives
Are about 65% of the U.S. population	Are about 35% of the U.S. population
Have clear, straightforward speech patterns	Have complex speech patterns
Have sequential thoughts; one follows the next	Have roundabout thoughts, jump around
Are more literal; use facts, examples	Are more figurative; use analogies and metaphors
Use language as a tool	Use language to express themselves
Are more aware of their bodies	Are more in their heads
Prefer nonfiction reading	Prefer fiction reading
Are direct and to the point	Repeat themselves, recap, and rephrase
Remember the past accurately	Envision the future
Include details and facts	Talk about global issues, the big picture
Tend to listen until others complete their whole thoughts	Tend to finish others' sentences

TABLE 3.3 Thinking/Feeling

Thinkers	Feelers
Act cooler, more distant	Act warmer, friendlier
May seem insensitive	Are more sensitive to feelings
May be blunt	Are more diplomatic
Appear businesslike	Engage in social niceties
May argue for fun	Avoid arguments, conflicts, confrontation
Are more thick-skinned	Have their feelings hurt more easily
Get right to the point	Socialize first
Appear low-key	Appear excited and emotional
Give praise sparingly	Are generous with praise
Usually are very assertive	Are less assertive
Use impersonal language	Use lots of "value" words
Use people's names sparingly	Use people's names frequently
Are more likely to be male (65% chance)	Are more likely to be female (65% chance)

are right-brainers, some prefer the leader role, while some are content being a follower. Regardless of what kind of thinking you do, it's important to include all types of people in a group in order to increase intellectual diversity and avoid what is sometimes referred to as the "comfortable clone syndrome." According to an article in *Harvard Business Online/BusinessWeek,* comfortable-clone syndrome is when you fall victim to surrounding yourself with people who think like you and share similar interests and training. To avoid this syndrome, you need to achieve "creative abrasion." Creative abrasion helps teams rub together in the

TABLE 3.4 Judging/Perceiving

Judgers	Perceivers
Are more formal, conventional	Are more casual, unconventional
Are more serious	Are more playful
Like to take charge and be in control	Are good at adapting
Like to make decisions quickly	Put off decisions
Are definitive, express strong opinions	Are more tentative
Are often in a hurry, like a rapid pace	Like a slower pace
Have a neat appearance, clothes pressed, hair combed	Have a less neat appearance, clothes rumpled, unruly hair
Dress more for appearance	Dress more for comfort
Probably have a neat, tidy desk/workplace	Probably have a messy, cluttered desk/workplace
Like to set and reach goals	Are liable to change goals
Are driven to finish projects	Prefer to start projects
Like rules, structure	Find rules and structure limiting, confining
May have straighter posture	May slouch more
Seek jobs that give lots of control	Seek jobs that are fun

Source: Tables 3.1–3.4. Adapted from Tieger and Barron-Tieger, 1998, pp. 68–85.

right way! To get creative abrasion, you can start by compiling a cognitive profile of your team. Administer a diagnostic tool such as the Myers-Briggs Type Indicator to determine what types of people are in the group. Then focus on which traits are missing, and try to counterbalance your group (Leonard & Straus, 2007).

Gender

Communication between the genders is both the most interesting and sometimes the most challenging of all types of communication. Table 3.5 summarizes some of the research findings on differences in communication between women and men.

One dramatic difference between the genders is that a man in the United States whose weight is 25 pounds below the mean earns *$210,925 less*, on average, across a 25-year career than a man whose weight is at the mean, according to a study by Timothy A. Judge of the University of Florida and Daniel M. Cable of London Business School. But a woman who is 25 pounds below the mean earns *$389,300 more* across the same time span than an average-weight woman. Society rewards people for meeting gender-role expectations on weight, the researchers say (Judge & Cable, 2011). In a humorous comparison between women and men, two groups of people tried to guess the gender of a computer. The women said that computers are definitely masculine for these reasons:

- In order to get their attention, you have to turn them on.
- They have a lot of data but are still clueless.

TABLE 3.5 Gender Differences in Communication

Masculine Speech	Feminine Speech
Choice of words suggests users are:	
logical	emotional
concise	verbose
controlling	vague
dominant	gentle
straightforward	friendly
in control	submissive
competitive	collaborative
adversarial	affiliative
focused on negotiation	focused on connection
attention-demanding	unobtrusive
speaking without connecting to other's ideas	building upon other's ideas
leaping into topic shifts	shifting topics gradually

Source: Gamble and Gamble, 2003, p. 67.

- They are supposed to help you solve the problem, but half the time they ARE the problem.
- As soon as you commit to one, you realize that, if you had waited a little longer, you could have had a better model.

On the other hand, men said that computers are definitely feminine for the following reasons:

- No one but their creator understands their internal logic.
- Even your smallest mistakes are stored in long-term memory.
- As soon as you make a commitment to one, you find yourself spending half your paycheck on accessories for it. (source unknown)

Humor aside, society has branded the Internet "male." Techno-feminist Judy Wajcman, professor of sociology with the London School of Economics, studied gender and the Internet. There is an apparent *digital divide* between men and women and the Internet. The Internet has been classified as appealing more to the needs of males than of females. The Internet itself, as with technology, has historically been a masculine-dominated field, and thus the product, the Internet, meets more masculine needs. Over time, this digital divide will narrow. In fact, there are already signs of this occurring. With the use of the Internet in the workplace and by members of virtual work groups, the Internet has moved into the realm of networking and relationship building, which are defined as more female characteristics. Women constitute a large part of the virtual space, but there is still a small decline in female technical designers. In 2004, the U.S. National Science Foundation found that female involvement in the information technology sector had declined from 28 to 27 percent since 1993. Hopefully this trend will change, thereby narrowing the digital divide from a creation and a usage standpoint (Wajcman, 2004).

Some words in the English language imply a lower status for females. An example that illustrates this is how the English language makes a distinction between "Mrs." and "Miss," which shows that a woman is either married or single. Conversely, males only have "Mr.," which gives no indication of marital status (Lei, 2006).

The following are some examples from Lei (2006) of job titles ending in *-man* that make the presence of women unclear in such positions, as well as some alternative terms:

Policeman—police officer

Businessman—business executive

Chairman—chair, chairperson

Clergyman—member of the clergy

Weatherman—meteorologist

In addition, listed below are more occupations and professions that are used for both genders but are habitually associated with men. As a result, "woman" or "lady" has to be added to the titles. Lei (2006) suggests a few examples:

Doctor—woman doctor

Professor—woman professor

Engineer—woman engineer

Lawyer—lady lawyer

"Women may be scarce in senior management, but here's an intriguing finding: Those who do make it into the executive ranks get there faster than men." So conclude researchers from Dartmouth's Tuck School of Business and Loyola University, who analyzed data on nearly 10,000 Fortune 1,000 executives to create one of the most granular pictures we have of companies' executive makeup. Though nearly half of Fortune 1,000 firms still have no female executive officers, those that do seem to be aggressively hiring and promoting them into the top ranks. As Figure 3.2 shows, a much larger percentage of Fortune 1,000 women have made it to executive officer positions in their thirties, forties, and fifties than have men their age. What's more, these women achieved their executive positions at a younger average age than the men did (46.7 versus 51.1) and have less tenure on average than men in their current positions (2.6 years versus 3.5 years).

Differences in behavior between the sexes have for years been known to be a function of cultural influences and childhood learning experiences. Margaret Mead found as early as 1935 that certain behaviors that the Western world had assumed were innately masculine or feminine were, instead, culturally determined. In her studies of New Guinea tribes, she found certain societies in which women dominated. She wrote: "Among the Tchambuli, the woman is the dominant, impersonal, managing partner, the man the less responsible and the emotionally dependent person" (p. 259). Mead described the husband, on the other

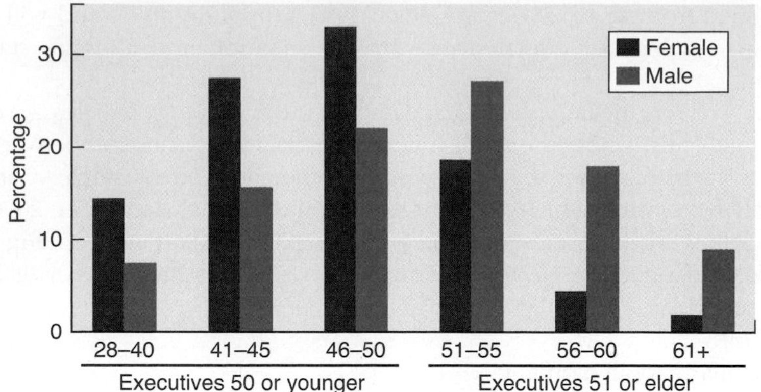

FIGURE 3.2 Percentage of male and female Fortune 1,000 executive officers in each age category (relative to the total number of male and female Fortune 1,000 executive officers)

Source: Adapted from *Harvard Business Review*. 2007.

hand, as being catty toward other men but charming toward women. He danced in the tribal ceremonies, spent hours on his personal makeup, and gossiped about the other men in the village. Obviously, such behaviors cannot be an inherent function of one's sex.

Deborah Tannen's (1995) excellent research has demonstrated that men and women talk differently in group situations. Women tend to offer suggestions but to preface them with disclaimers, such as "You've probably already thought of this, but . . ." or "I don't know if this will work, but. . .". She also notes that other research shows that men talk more often and longer and louder than women. Meeting leaders need to be aware of these possibilities and to strive to allow both sexes to participate equally.

Judy Rosener (1995) conducted a major study, which was published in the *Harvard Business Review,* that asked men and women leaders in diverse professions how they exercised power, what kind of leadership they preferred, and in what kinds of organizations they worked. She found that "women, on average, exhibited and preferred the interactive leadership style, and men the command and control leadership style, and that the interactive style is particularly effective in flexible, nonhierarchical organizations of the kind that perform best in a climate of rapid change" (p. 11).

Morrison, White, and Van Velsor (1990, p. 290) conducted extensive interviews with 76 successful women in Fortune 100 companies. On the basis of this research, they identified six factors associated with women's career success:

1. *Help.* Mentors from above offered advice and inspiration.
2. *Achievement.* They had a track record of proven successes.
3. *Desire.* This was demonstrated through hard work, long hours, and personal sacrifice.
4. *Management.* They had the ability to get people to perform while maintaining their respect and trust.

5. *Risk taking*. They made career moves requiring relocation and travel, for example.
6. *Tough, decisive, and demanding*. They were aggressive, made hard decisions, and were willing to fight for what they believed was right.

It would seem from this list that there is nothing that would differentiate these characteristics from those of successful male executives. However, Loden (1990) found that women approach teamwork and participatory management differently than do men. She found that "they are less likely to 'pull rank' and more likely to stress cooperation than competition" (p. 298).

Two best-selling books focus in depth on the difficulties of male–female communication. One, by John Gray (1992), is titled *Men Are from Mars, Women Are from Venus*. That should give you some idea of the vastness of the communication gap. The other book, by Tannen (1991), is strongly research based. Tannen writes: "Study after study finds that it is men who talk more—at meetings, in mixed-group discussions, and in classrooms . . . [in university faculty meetings]. The men's turns [to talk] ranged from 10.66 to 17.07 seconds, while the women's turns ranged from 3 to 10 seconds" (p. 75). She goes on to say that, nonverbally, "the men sat with their legs stretched out, while the women gathered themselves in" (p. 130).

Female executives and leaders still must face difficult stereotypes that have developed over time. For example, Melissa Thomas-Hunt of Cornell University and Katherine Phillips of Northwestern University (2004) published an article in the *Personality and Social Psychology Bulletin* titled "When What You Know Is Not Enough: Expertise and Gender Dynamics in Task Groups." This study investigated how perception of expertise of group members in groups varied based on the sex of the expert. The study revealed that female experts were viewed by male group members as having less expertise than their male counterparts, even if the level of expertise was equal.

So what are females doing to beat this stereotype? A rising number of women have become highly successful leaders in organizations. The number of female CEOs has increased dramatically since 1995. The number of female CEOs in the 500 largest companies in America increased from 8.7 percent in 1995 to 15.7 percent in 2004. Ilene Lang, president of a nonprofit firm called Catalyst that focuses on the advancement of women, stated that "smart companies know that women are good for the bottom line." Catalyst found that companies with proportionately more women in upper management performed 35 percent better than those with fewer women in upper management (Holmes, 2004d).

Catalyst also conducted a study sponsored by Pricewaterhouse-Coopers of 700 senior-level women and 200 senior-level men within organizations. Contrary to stereotypes, it found that 55 percent of the women and 57 percent of the men had CEO career aspirations. Males and females even shared the elements that they believe are necessary for success. These include performing well above expectation, becoming the subject matter expert, getting the high-profile projects, and managing well. Men also agreed with women that networking and establishing relationships are critical to success (*Pittsburgh Post-Gazette*, 2004b).

Suffice it to say that communication between the sexes will continue to be both complex and interesting.

PRACTICAL TIPS

Because the younger generations are receiving higher degrees earlier, the possibility of working in mixed-aged groups is increasing. In some cases, you might find yourself reporting to a team leader who is younger than you. If you find this difficult, here are some tips to help maintain the cohesiveness of the group:

1. Banish all the soul-searching about what it means professionally to report to someone younger. Being the oldest member of a group should allow you to demonstrate your skills and should reflect your previous work experience and expertise.
2. Avoid showing off your years of acquired knowledge at every opportunity or delivering condescension along with your advice.
3. Share your experience collegially. You'll be considered a major resource rather than a threat.
4. Be careful not to misinterpret a younger person's working methods (say, a preference for email over talking face-to-face) as a sign of disrespect.
5. Be aware that the unease is likely to cut both ways. Younger team members sometimes feel inadequate or guilty when they work with someone of their parents' generation.

Source: Adapted from Sulkowicz, 2007, p. 16.

Age

Obviously, communication patterns differ from childhood through adolescence to adulthood and old age. Older group members in college-age groups (for example, married students, veterans, and so forth) tend to be more influential, on the basis of their relatively greater number of years of experience. Although this may not always hold true, it is usually the case. It generally takes time to develop leadership qualifications.

Zenger and Lawrence (1989) found that age similarity of group members had a positive effect on the communication of information within project groups. This stems from earlier notions that people tend to communicate with those who are similar to themselves. Similar age ranges lead to similar life experiences and interests. Communication channels produced by non-work-related conversations will influence the ease of work-related communications.

One study (Fullerton, Kerch, & Dodge, 1996) found that age was a good predictor of a person's ethics. As age increased, so did one's ethical standards. The researchers classified respondents into four groups: permissives, situationalists, conformists, and puritans. As the names suggest, permissives had a greater tolerance for unethical behavior (such as lying on an insurance report), whereas puritans had the lowest tolerance for such unethical behavior and the other two groups were in between the two extremes.

The age gap for communication may finally be shrinking. Facebook, the social networking website, is helping to make that a reality. Perhaps you thought that the communication tool was only for 20-somethings. According to *Business-Week,* there has been a 113 percent increase since June 2006 in the number of Facebook visitors over the age of 35. The number of visitors 35 and older more than doubled from the previous year! The important thing to note about this is that the age communication gap isn't as large as we may have once thought. Now we can use Facebook as a tool to help bridge that generation gap (Hof, 2007).

Bennis and Thomas (2002) interviewed successful people in two age groups, those under 35 and those over 70 years of age. They found that the older group (the Geezers, as they called them) tended to look to historical figures as their role models or heroes, whereas the younger group (the Geeks, as they called them) tended to cite their parents or other family members as their heroes or role models. One fascinating finding was that those people who continued to be successful regardless of age had what they call "neoteny," or perpetual enthusiasm for learning and for life. People who have neoteny never get cynical; rather, they maintain a positive enthusiasm that is contagious. In a totally separate set of studies, Goleman, Boyatzis, and McKee (2002) found that this same positive characteristic creates what they call "resonance." This is a quality that some leaders exhibit that brings out the best in others. They go on to say, "People in groups at work inevitably 'catch' feelings from one another, sharing everything from jealousy and envy to angst or euphoria. The more cohesive the group, the stronger the sharing of moods, emotional history, and even hot buttons" (p. 7). Your age can reveal a lot about where you are in your career. For example, in high school and college, you may have been successful at every endeavor you attempted. However, the corporate world may be much more challenging than you ever expected. And this can be a major blow to your ego. This is a classic "Hero to Zero" phenomenon that Jack and Suzy Welch write about in *BusinessWeek.* They suggest that many times people "swell" instead of "grow" in their first positions out of college due to their earlier successes in school. They recommend that you commit yourself to being a team player and frequently seek feedback in order to stay on the straight and narrow. This will help you attain a new-found maturity (Welch & Welch, 2007). So, the important lesson is that chronological age is probably much less important than psychological age when it comes to effectively working with others. Finally, you may be pleased to know that

> from age 50 to the mid seventies, happiness and enjoyment tend to rise steadily, while stress, worry, anger, and sadness decline—regardless of employment status, the individual's sex, or whether the person has a partner or has children at home, according to a new study by Gallup. The researchers who studied the findings, which are based on a survey of 340,000 people in the U.S., say it's unclear whether the increase in well-being is due to biology, changes in the individuals' environments, or other factors. (*Harvard Business Review* Daily Briefings, 2010)

<*Source:* HYPERLINK "**http://link.email.hbr.org/r/1AH6/PUK4R/ODKEM/C83N7/NHMW4/XH/h"\t"_blank**"The New York Times>

Health

In his best-selling book *Shadow* (1999), Bob Woodward chronicles the impact of President George H. W. Bush's health on his bid for reelection in 1992:

> In April 1991, Patty Presock, Bush's secretary, reported to Dr. Burton Lee III, the White House physician, that Bush's handwriting had changed. The president's sleep patterns were erratic. He had lost 15 pounds. The next month while jogging at Camp David, Bush collapsed from shortness of breath. His heart was beating irregularly. The diagnosis was Graves' disease, an overactive thyroid. Bush lost some of his zest and stamina. [Presidential aide Marlon] Fitzwater watched for any changes, knowing that the press would notice them. He saw that Bush had some mood swings and was not as engaged in his presidency. The president kept delaying his decision to run for reelection in 1992. . . . On July 24, Bush snapped at a heckler, "Shut up and sit down." Later that day, campaigning in Ohio, Fitzwater was worried: Dr. Lee said Bush had an irregular heart episode that morning. The doctor told Fitzwater that he was having trouble regulating the president's medication. The dosage, he said, affected mental acuity. Fitzwater was shocked. When Bush appeared terrible and pale, the White House photographer confirmed the president seemed to be drained. Later Bush's shirt soaked through and his voice was weak.
>
> The Bush campaign tracking polls showed Bush's chances of turning it around had evaporated. He was cranky, his vitality sapped. When Mary Matalin, a senior spokeswoman, handed him a sheet with some numbers, the president threw it across the table. "I don't want to see them anymore," he snapped.
>
> When Fitzwater questioned Bush about his health, the president claimed everything was perfect, no change. . . . But the staff had to push the president to set up special meetings to get him focused. . . . Regardless of who was to blame, the drive and vitality went out of Bush and his presidency. (pp. 189, 197, 205)

In a more recent example, actor Kirk Douglas (Michael Douglas's father) writes a compelling story of what it is like to go from being normal one day to being handicapped by a stroke the next. His speech was the most severely affected (Douglas, 2002). To learn more about his story, go to www.HarperCollins.com.

Although health may not always be a highly significant factor in your small group experiences, it does play a part. Deficiencies in both the physical and mental health of members seem to impede group performance. A member who fails to attend meetings or who is unable to carry his or her portion of the group workload will sooner or later reduce total group output. Also, physical health frequently affects stamina. Strength and stamina may not be important in relatively short discussions (lasting up to an hour); however, discussions and conferences frequently last for days. Labor–management negotiations may go 20 hours a day for a week or longer. In one case, a local labor dispute was settled after a prolonged strike; the week after the agreement was reached, the local union president died of a heart attack. So physical health and stamina can play an important part in small group interaction.

Clearly, one important aspect of health is personal stress management. It always seems that for college students, stressful events happen right about the time of major exams, term papers, presentations, and so on. Many research studies have shown that too much stress depresses the immune system and causes a host of problems. Modica (1996) reports on research at Stanford University showing that exposure to prolonged stress can actually lead to memory loss similar to that normally seen in people age 70 or older. Other symptoms of stress include the following:

Physical Signs	*Emotional Signs*
Fatigue	Irritability
Tension headaches	Hostility
Upset stomach	Anxiety
Sleep problems	Loss of self-esteem
Backaches	Feelings of helplessness
Weight gain or loss	Withdrawal from friends and family
Muscle tension	Inability to enjoy life
Nervousness	Loss of concentration
Sweaty palms	Substance abuse
Cold hands or feet	

Tropman (1996) argues that high stress levels often become manifest in group meetings. He states, "Under stress, people tend to revert to earlier learned behavior . . . blame becomes rampant, hostility may increase, and nobody wants to devote the time needed to have an innovative type of discussion" (p. 73). Oldham and Cummings (1996) also found that creativity in teams is affected by the psychological climate on the job. A supportive supervisor decreases stress and increases creativity whereas a critical supervisor tends to increase stress, which in turn diminishes creativity.

One incident involving health occurred in the spring of 2008 at a meeting in which a member of the group who had diabetes passed out from low blood glucose (sugar). He had to be taken to the hospital in an ambulance. Those with diabetes have to constantly regulate their blood glucose levels. When their level is too high—for example, if they have just eaten—they may have confused thinking and exhibit impatience and irritability. When their blood sugar is too low, such as in late-morning or late-afternoon meetings, they may become shaky, stop participating, become light-headed, and in some extreme cases, as mentioned above, pass out.

In another incident, a student had an epileptic seizure right in the middle of her group's presentation to the class. Luckily, it was a petit-mal, not a grand-mal, seizure, and she basically went into a deep sleep on the classroom floor following the episode.

One small-company president (Stack, 1992) wrote about the health factor in the following way:

> Several years ago, I took up bass fishing for my health. It was near the end of the first year after the [company's] buyout, and the pressures were getting to me. My hair was falling out in clumps. I couldn't eat or sleep. I missed steps when I walked.

PRACTICAL TIPS

Hinsberg (1996) offers the following 10 practical tips for managing stress:

1. *Exercise.* This relieves muscle tension and may also release beta-endorphins, which are the body's natural way of creating pleasant feelings.
2. *Share it.* Talking things over with friends is often helpful.
3. *Know when to relent.* Remember the wise axiom, "God grant me the serenity to accept the things I cannot change, the courage to change the things I can, and the wisdom to know the difference."
4. *Care for yourself.* Get sufficient rest and eat sensibly. If you can't sleep, see a doctor.
5. *List and delete.* To cut down on the sense of being overwhelmed, make a list of tasks in order of priority. Then tackle each task, complete it, and check it off on the list.
6. *Always right? Wrong.* Nobody is always right. Try cooperation instead of confrontation.
7. *Tears for fears.* Crying is the body's way of helping to relieve some of the tensions of emotions. If that's not practical, try taking some deep measured breaths.
8. *Set a serene scene.* Close your eyes and imagine a beautiful place you love to visit. Play quiet music.
9. *Meditate.* Twenty minutes of silent meditation twice a day does wonders, according to studies at the Harvard Medical School.
10. *Time out.* Be sure to schedule time out for recreation, movies, dancing, or being with friends. All of these help to give a much-needed tension break.

Source: Hinsberg, Claire, "Stress Reversal," *Corporate Detroit Magazine,* June 29, 1996, pp. 70–78. Reprinted by permission of Corporate Detroit, Inc.

> I called a doctor, who told me it was either Lou Gehrig's disease or multiple sclerosis. The next doctor was more encouraging. He said it was stress. (p. 235)

You may want to visit www.MasteringStress.com for an online stress management experience. These are just a few examples of the many ways that the health of individuals may affect their groups.

Attitudes

Over 2,300 years ago, Aristotle wrote about a concept he called "eudaimonia," which scholars today translate as "happiness or well-being" (Wang, 2011, p. D1). Scientists have studied how eudaimonia versus hedonic types of happiness affect health and physical well-being. Eudaimonia refers to doing good for one's fellow person, while hedonic refers to the selfish pursuit of pleasure. They have found the former brings more lasting happiness and the latter becomes somewhat empty and unsatisfying over time (Wang, 2011, p. D6). According to the writers at ChangingMinds.org (2004), *attitudes* are "predispositions towards action, about or towards people and things, evaluative of people, objects and ideas, and made up of emotional reactions, thoughts and beliefs, and action components." Attitudes can be learned or genetic and are sometimes impossible to change. As each of us develops through childhood and adolescence, myriad experiences shape our view of the world. Because we each have different experiences, we would expect our outlooks to differ as well. These experiences are called *developmental factors,* and we will look at three that are related to small group interaction: attitudes, values, and anxieties.

Keith Harrell, a former IBM executive, wrote a book titled *Attitude Is Everything* (2000). If you have ever tried to influence a group whose members seem to have enthusiasm and energy for each and every proposal, you know what he means. Conversely, if you have ever tried to work with a group whose members resist every idea or suggestion, you also know what he means. (See also Tubbs, 2011.)

Over 70 years ago, Gorden Allport defined an *attitude* as "a mental and a neural state of readiness, organized through experience, exerting a directive or dynamic influence upon the individual's response to all objects and situations with which it is related." According to Frymier & Nadler (2010), Triandis (1971), attitudes have three components: (1) a cognitive component, which refers to an idea or a concept, such as "Will Smith is an actor"; (2) an affective component, or the emotion related to the idea (I love Will Smith); and (3) a behavioral component, which is the readiness to act (I will go to see Will Smith's next movie).

Group members may hold several types of attitudes that are relevant to their participation in small groups. For example, they have attitudes toward the task itself, toward the situation within which the group is operating, toward people inside and outside of the group, and toward other issues that may be related to the one under discussion. All these attitudes will ultimately affect their behavior in the group, which in turn will affect the group's results. How many times have you been a member of a project team or group in which either you or others in the group found that you just couldn't seem to get too enthusiastic about accomplishing the task? Or perhaps you would ordinarily have been interested in the task, but it came at a time when you were preoccupied with other things, such as romantic difficulties or financial worries. These illustrations help to indicate the important role that attitudes may play in determining one's actions in the group.

In addition, Fulk (1993) found that group members who had a strong attraction to their group tended to hold similar attitudes on other important topics. She measured attraction to the group on such items as the extent to which members "(1) cooperate with each other, (2) regard each other as friends, (3) know that they can depend on each other, (4) stand up for one another, and (5) work together as a team" (pp. 933–34).

Having the right attitude can make or break a small group. Going into a group situation with a team full of winning attitudes will help the group excel! David Brandon, former chief executive officer of Domino's Pizza, learned this as a college athlete playing football at the University of Michigan under the legendary coach Bo Schembechler. Brandon said in a *Wall Street Journal* interview that he was glued to Coach Schembechler's every move because he was so successful in competing at such a high level. Brandon learned that it was more about getting people with the right attitude and the right character qualities. He learned that Coach Schembechler was never going to bring a young man on the team who had great skills but a bad attitude. This lesson about attitude is what is helping Domino's Pizza build a successful team in order to continue to be a thriving pizza chain (Adamy, 2007). Attitudes are an important part of your success, both on the job and in your personal life. Most people respond better to a person with positive attitudes than to one who chronically complains.

Some of the most intuitive yet provocative theories concerning attitudes are the so-called cognitive consistency theories. These closely related theories are based on the assumption that human beings have a strong psychological need for consistency. Frymier and Nadler (2010) define *consistency theory* as the human need to have all attitudes fit nicely together without contradicting one another. These matching attitudes result in consistent behaviors. In order to maintain a sense of cognitive consistency, people are generally resistant to attitude change, and attitudes best predict behavior when "they are strong and consistent, they are based on and related to personal experience, and they are specifically related to the behavior being predicted" (Underwood, 2003). Heider (1958), the first of the consistency theorists, refers to this as a need to maintain *balance*. He reasons that if we hold an attitude X and another person holds the same value, then we are likely to feel positively toward that person. For example, if Lance likes motorcycles and Brad also likes motorcycles, Lance is likely to have positive feelings toward Brad. This is illustrated in Figure 3.3. If, on the other hand, Brad did not like motorcycles, Lance would feel some imbalance and would be motivated to resolve it in one of several ways. First, he could try to change Brad's evaluation of motorcycles. Second, he could change his feeling toward Brad. Finally, he could change his own evaluation of motorcycles. The specific alternative Lance

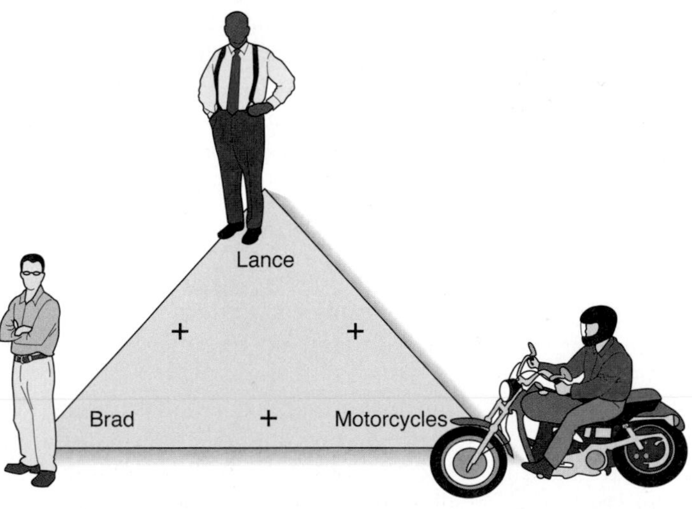

FIGURE 3.3 An Illustration of Attitude Balance

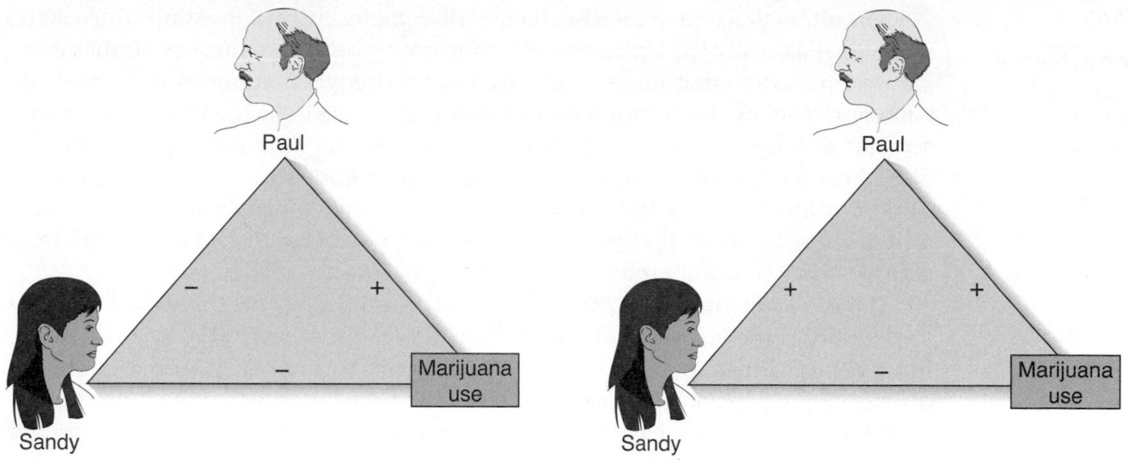

FIGURE 3.4 An Illustration of Attitude Imbalance Versus Balance

chooses would depend on the relative strength of his attitudes toward Brad and toward motorcycles.

Heider predicts that balanced triads are rewarding, or pleasant to experience, whereas imbalanced triads result in pressure to restore balance. An easy rule of thumb for differentiating between balanced and imbalanced triads is that if the algebraic product of the three elements in the triad is positive, the triad is balanced. If the algebraic product is negative, the triad is imbalanced. Which of the triads in Figure 3.4 is imbalanced, thus creating pressure to restore balance? How could balance be restored?

A related consistency theory is called *cognitive dissonance theory* (Festinger, 1957). In order to maintain consistency between our beliefs, attitudes, values, and behaviors, we use certain mechanisms when conflict arises that threatens this consistency. This conflict is known as cognitive dissonance and can result in the following behavior to resolve consistency: denial, rationalization, separation of the issue, belief that no one is perfect, planning for future change, and self-persuasion (ChangingMinds.org, 2004). With this in mind, the theory of cognitive dissonance is the same as Heider's concept of balance, and *dissonance* is equivalent to imbalance in that it serves to motivate a change back to consonance. One of the interesting finds of research in this area is that a severe initiation for attaining group membership creates a high level of dissonance, which is usually resolved by the person's valuing membership in the group more than if the initiation were less severe (Aronson & Mills, 1959).

Fraternities and sororities have used pledging as a device to increase the severity of initiation into membership. The result is usually that one who endures these experiences reduces the dissonance caused by them and begins to believe they are necessary and even desirable for the new pledge class to endure. The traditional pride in being a U.S. marine has also resulted largely from the severity of initiation experienced in Marine Corps boot camps. The movies *A Few Good Men* and *Jarhead* provide good examples of this.

Group interaction may also create dissonance. ChangingMinds.org (2004) believes that our attitudes can predict our behavior. The writers state that there are certain factors that increase the connection between attitudes and predicted behavior. They feel that our attitudes will match our behaviors in most circumstances as long as the circumstances are specific, there is no social-desirability bias, there are few distractions, and the relevant attitudes are deeply rooted. If the subject wants to be socially desirable, he or she may change attitudes to come across a certain way. If there are distractions, the behaviors that spin off from attitudes may be hampered.

If there is dissonance, attitude change is most likely as the individual attempts to return to some level of consistency (ChangingMinds.org, 2004). If you are confronted in a discussion with an opinion contrary to your own, some degree of dissonance will result. The dissonance will increase if you value the other person and if the issue over which you disagree is one of high relevance. According to Festinger and Aronson (1968), you may reduce the dissonance in these five ways (starting with the most likely and going to the least likely approach): (1) devalue the importance of the issue, (2) derogate the disagreeing person, (3) attempt to change his or her attitude, (4) seek additional social support for your view, or (5) change your attitude. Aronson (1973) posits that although people like to think of themselves as rational animals, they are more likely than not "rationalizing animals." It is important to note that we all use these methods of dissonance reduction, and we need to have them. Although rationalizing may sound like something we should avoid, it can be a helpful tool if we are consciously aware of using it.

Values

Attitudes and values are closely linked. Underwood (2003) states that matching attitudes result in cohesive values. Although an overwhelming amount of research has been conducted on attitudes and attitude change, Rokeach (1968, 1971, 1973) and Frymier and Nadler (2010) have argued that people's *values* are also important as a predictor of behavior. The rationale is that we have thousands of different attitudes, but we have only several dozen values. Values, then, are seen as more fundamental than attitudes and are more stable and long-lasting.

With the increasing use of global virtual teams, working in multicultural teams is becoming more prevalent. And because of this, multicultural differences are popping up in more meetings than in the past. For example, *Harvard Business Review* did a feature on managing multicultural teams. They focused on a situation when a major international software developer assembled a team of employees from India and the United States. The software company reported:

> From the start the team members could not agree on a delivery date for the product. The Americans thought the work could be done in two to three weeks; the Indians predicted it would take two to three months. As time went on, the Indian

> team members proved reluctant to report setbacks in the production process, which the American team members would find out about only when work was due to be passed to them. As tensions mounted, conflict over delivery dates and feedback became personal, disrupting team members' communication about even mundane issues. (Brett, Behfar, & Kern, 2006)

Torres (1994) offers an excellent insight into values and value differences through the eyes of followers of the ancient Chinese Taoist philosophy. He writes:

> CLARITY OF VALUES
>
> *The image of moving water suggests an*
> *effortless flow that is yielding while*
> *supporting all things.*
> *Unlike water, values can clash, creating*
> *resentment and mistrust—the ebb and the flow.*
>
> When team members yield, others do not resist.
> When team members insist, others do not yield.
> Evolved team members do not confront opposing
> values; they recognize them as personal beliefs.
> To compete is to challenge, and efforts to win
> yield only loss.
> Learning is in discussion.
> Strength is in collaboration.
>
> *Thus clarity of values contributes to team solidarity.*

We all want different things. This is based on preference, but some of it is shaped early on by our cultural values. For example, research by Coy (2007b) found that workers want different things in different countries:

- U.S. employees want competitive base salaries.
- Brazilian employees want career opportunities.
- Chinese employees want chances to learn.
- Japanese employees want challenges at work.
- Spanish employees want work–life balance.

One promising finding in recent studies is that groups comprising culturally diverse individuals learn to work more effectively over time. Diverse groups were formed of one white American, one African American, one Hispanic American, and a foreign national from another country. The homogeneous groups consisted of four white Americans. Initially, the homogeneous groups were more effective (as measured by quantity and quality of solutions to problems). However, over the course of 17 weeks, the diverse groups became as proficient as the homogeneous groups (Watson, Kumar, & Michaelson, 1993).

With the increase in international trade, it is more than likely that most of you will at some time be involved in a group project with someone raised in a culture different from your own. Also, it is important for you to remember that there are many different cultures in the United States. You don't have to go across the ocean to find someone with cultural values different from your own. As Weisinger (1989) points out, it is important not to force a person to act in a way that contradicts his or her cultural norms. If such a situation arises, make sure that everyone in the group knows each other's cultural rules. Being aware of such differences will help group members learn the best way to respond to one another.

REVIEW OF THE SYSTEMS APPROACH

As noted in Chapter 1, small group interactions are the result of influences that can be labeled inputs, throughputs, and outputs. These factors are in a constant state of simultaneous and reciprocal influence. This chapter has focused on some of the inputs—namely, the relevant background factors of the group members. Through the discussion of personality, we illustrated the role personality plays in shaping individual behavior. For example, those high on inclusion will probably be more inclined to join groups in the first place (if we assume that membership is voluntary). Those high on affection are very likely to smile more; express more feelings, both verbally and nonverbally, than low affiliators; give more direct eye contact to more members of the group; and agree more than low affiliators. We would expect that high-affection members would have higher satisfaction resulting from harmonious group experiences, and greater dissatisfaction with groups that experience a high degree of conflict and disagreement. The person low on need for inclusion will tend to avoid meetings and group memberships whenever possible and will avoid talking in the groups he or she is forced to join. Group interaction is generally viewed by the introvert as threatening and therefore less satisfying than engaging in the same activity alone. However, if the group is conducted by a supportive and nonthreatening leader, the introvert's satisfaction level will increase dramatically.

High-control members tend to enjoy working on task-oriented projects, because they are more task-oriented than most others and find that the group tends to slow down their progress. The exception, of course, is the group composed of a lot of high controllers. In this case, high cohesion or high conflict might result, depending on the way in which the members decide to reward their efforts. Thus, group norms, leadership style, and communication patterns all tend to influence the satisfaction level of group members.

The three organismic factors discussed in this chapter are gender, age, and health. A group with both sexes tends to have more socially oriented communication patterns and fewer task-oriented comments.

Age seems to be somewhat similar to attitudes and values in that the more similar group members are (in age, attitudes, and values), the easier it is for them to communicate (that is, they work more efficiently). However, research on creativity in groups has shown that diversity of age, backgrounds, viewpoint, and so

PRACTICAL TIPS

Value differences may significantly influence the course of any given group discussion. Tropman (1996) identifies several value differences that can influence group discussions:

- *Multipurpose versus unipurpose.* Some individuals bring a very broad perspective to a discussion. They want to look at the big picture and place a problem in its proper context. Others are very focused. They want to get to the bottom line and to concentrate exclusively on the problem at hand and have it solved. Both perspectives have merit. Meeting leaders need to establish the proper balance between the two, as well as those in each of the following.
- *Pragmatism versus excellence.* Some want to get the task done quickly and perhaps inexpensively whereas others want it accomplished only with the greatest attention to high-quality standards. The first value may lead to premature action and the second to slow action or sometimes no action.
- *Status versus class.* Basically, this means emphasizing the individual versus the group. Some will want to see individuals rewarded for good performance, such as with merit increases, sales commissions, or bonuses (status). Others will favor equal treatment for all through across-the-board pay increases (class). Equity is their main concern. Each party will disagree on what is "fair."
- *Personal versus organizational purpose.* Some people want to approach problems from the standpoint "What's in it for me?" Others consider the greater good for the organization. We all can relate to both sides of this value difference.
- *Empirical versus qualitative decision-making bases.* Some people prefer to see things proved "by the numbers." Others approach decisions in a more intuitive or artistic manner. Often good decisions involve a combination of the two. This is the classic left-brain versus right-brain issue.
- *Disposable labor versus intimate concern.* Some see people as interchangeable parts of an organization. When financial need requires that employees be laid off, it is seen as necessary to save the jobs of those who remain. Others see people as the most important asset of any organization and stress their retention at all costs. Some groups have even voted to take pay cuts rather than have other workers laid off.

In each of the situations above, the challenge is to find the appropriate level of balance between the competing value systems. Great skill is required in handling the emotions that often arise in reaction to having one's values challenged.

on, all lead to greater creativity (Leonard & Swap, 1999; Amabile, 1996). Diversity tends to increase a group's divergent thinking (important at the early stages of problem solving) and may retard a group's convergent thinking (important at the latter stages of problem solving) when the group has to come to agreement.

In the first reading at the end of this chapter, Paul Tieger and Barbara Barron-Tieger discuss ways that people with different personality types can communicate more effectively. The second selection, by Teri Kwal Gamble and Michael Gamble, examines the communication patterns between men and women.

PRACTICAL TIPS

Promoting Diversity in the Virtual Space

The Georgia Department of Education recommends tips for facilitating diversity in online environments in its professional development document "Celebrating Diversity: A Facilitator's Guide" (2003). It has put a program in place consisting of four steps. The following is an adaptation of the Georgia Department of Education's steps placed in the context of small work groups.

Step 1: Introduction—Threaded Discussion

- What does diversity mean to you?
- How would you characterize gender interactions in small groups?
- How often have you witnessed gender, age, or ethnic bias in work groups?
- How do you define stereotyping? Can you give a real-life example?
- What have you personally done to promote diversity in work groups?

Step 2: Self-Assessment

- Have you ever subconsciously exhibited prejudice that you realized later?
- In what kind of environment do you roll the windows of your car up or lock the doors?
- What do you think people can do to unlearn subconscious bias?

Step 3: Discussion

- Provide the group with articles about the benefits of small group diversity.
- Discuss challenges of diversity in the virtual space.

Step 4: Strategy Development

- Have small group members set diversity ground rules to follow.
- Create an open environment for discussion of issues as they arise.

EXERCISES

1. Employee Selection Problem

You are a member of a personnel selection committee. You need to hire two people as first-line supervisors in an industrial foundry. The supervisors would be in charge of 30-person (mostly male) work groups who do machining processes (grinding, drilling, polishing) on metal castings made from molten metal in a different part of the foundry. Examine all five information sheets, which describe the candidates who have passed the physical examination and are available for immediate employment.

Group Task: After reviewing all five information sheets, meet as a group for 30 minutes to decide which two candidates should get the jobs. Each of you in the group will be assigned to argue in favor of one of the five candidates. After each of you presents the best case for your candidate, you must work together collectively to determine in the best interests of everyone concerned who should be hired. Your company is an equal opportunity/affirmative action employer.

1

NAME: Sally A. Peterson AGE: 23

MARITAL STATUS: Married NUMBER OF CHILDREN: 0

NUMBER OF DEPENDENTS OTHER THAN SELF (explain relation): 1—husband

EDUCATION:

	Years	Degree or Diploma	Major (where applicable)
Elementary	8	Yes	
High School	4	Yes	College prep.
College	4	Yes (B.A.)	Sociology

CURRENT EDUCATIONAL OR VOCATIONAL SITUATION: Has been management trainee for four months with XYZ Aircraft Company. Began with XYZ immediately after serving two years with Peace Corps.

VOCATIONAL SKILLS OR EXPERIENCE: None other than a few elementary skills learned while in Peace Corps.

POLICE RECORD: None

ADDITIONAL COMMENTS: Currently active in volunteer community social work. Has taken over Junior Achievement group in underprivileged neighborhood.

2

NAME: Thomas Browne AGE: 26

MARITAL STATUS: Married NUMBER OF CHILDREN: 0

NUMBER OF DEPENDENTS OTHER THAN SELF (explain relation): 1—wife

EDUCATION:

	Years	Degree or Diploma	Major (where applicable)
Elementary	8	Yes	
High School	4	Yes	College prep.
College	4	Yes (B.A.)	Economics
	½	(toward M.A.)	Economics

CURRENT EDUCATIONAL OR VOCATIONAL SITUATION: Is completing first year in graduate school working toward M.A. in economics, which should be completed in one more semester. Is classified in top third of his graduate school class. Is currently a research assistant to leading economist in graduate school of business.

VOCATIONAL SKILLS OR EXPERIENCE: None

POLICE RECORD: Arrested with a number of other students involved in campus disturbance—released without charges being made.

ADDITIONAL COMMENTS: None

3

NAME: William Cross — AGE: 20

MARITAL STATUS: Married — NUMBER OF CHILDREN: 0 (expecting first child in 6 months)

NUMBER OF DEPENDENTS OTHER THAN SELF (explain relation): 1—wife

EDUCATION:

	Years	Degree or Diploma	Major (where applicable)
Elementary	8	Yes	
High School	4	Yes	Vocational
College			

CURRENT EDUCATIONAL OR VOCATIONAL SITUATION: Plumber's apprentice completing second year of apprenticeship. Employed by large building contractor.

VOCATIONAL SKILLS OR EXPERIENCE: Plumbing, some automotive repair skills, welding. General construction work.

POLICE RECORD: Two arrests, no convictions.

First arrest while in high school—no details because of juvenile status. Second arrest for disorderly conduct—charges dismissed.

ADDITIONAL COMMENTS: None

4

NAME: Jane Williams — AGE: 24

MARITAL STATUS: Single — NUMBER OF CHILDREN: 0

NUMBER OF DEPENDENTS OTHER THAN SELF (explain relation): 0

EDUCATION:

	Years	Degree or Diploma	Major (where applicable)
Elementary	8	Yes	
High School	4	Yes	College prep.
College	4	Yes (B.A.)	Sociology
	1½	Yes (M.B.A.)	Production Management

CURRENT EDUCATIONAL OR VOCATIONAL SITUATION: Completing second year of graduate school. Has B.A. in sociology, working toward Ph.D., which should be completed in 3 to 4 semesters. Ranks in middle third of graduate class. Working one-half time as a teaching assistant. Doing volunteer work, and beginning research on urban sociology project.

VOCATIONAL SKILLS OR EXPERIENCE: None

POLICE RECORD: None

ADDITIONAL COMMENTS: None

5

NAME: Robert Smith AGE: 21

MARITAL STATUS: Single NUMBER OF CHILDREN: 0

NUMBER OF DEPENDENTS OTHER THAN SELF (explain relation): 0

EDUCATION:

	Years	Degree or Diploma	Major (where applicable)
Elementary	8	Yes	
High School	4	Yes	College prep.
College	3½	B.S. expected at end of semester	Business Administration

CURRENT EDUCATIONAL OR VOCATIONAL SITUATION: College senior expecting degree at end of current (spring) semester. "A–" student.

VOCATIONAL SKILLS OR EXPERIENCE: Typing. Has also worked part-time in selling, construction work, and on farms.

POLICE RECORD: None

ADDITIONAL COMMENTS: Father unemployed for medical reasons. Mother works to support family. It is known that he has worked his way through college and has incurred a small debt in the form of a student loan.

2. Personal Styles Exercise

Read the descriptions of the Tough Battler, Friendly Helper, and Objective Thinker in the table that follows. Then anonymously rate volunteer class members on these three dimensions by placing an "X" inside a triangle as illustrated in the figure.

Personal Styles in Groups and Organizations

Listed below are three characteristic types that may be found in any group or organization.

	Tough Battler	**Friendly Helper**	**Objective Thinker**
Emotions	Accepts aggression, rejects affection	Accepts affection, rejects aggression	Rejects both affection and interpersonal aggression
Goal	Dominance	Acceptance	Correctness
Influences Others by	Direction, intimidation, control of rewards	Understanding, praise, favors, friendship	Factual data, logical arguments
Value in Organization	Initiates, demands, disciplines	Supports, harmonizes, relieves tension	Defines, clarifies, gets information, criticizes, tests

continued

Overuses	Fighting	Kindness	Analysis
Becomes	Pugnacious	Sloppy, sentimental	Pedantic
Fears	Being "soft" or dependent	Desertion, conflict	Emotions, irrational acts
Needs	Warmth, consideration, objectivity, humility	Strength, integrity, firmness, self-assertion	Awareness of feeling, ability to love and to fight

Above are shown characteristic emotions, goals, standards of evaluation, and techniques of influence of each type, and his/her service to the organization.

Each can be overdone and distorted. The *Tough Battler* would be a better manager, a better parent, a better neighbor, and a more satisfied person if he/she could learn some sensitivity, accept his/her inevitable dependence on others, and come to enjoy consideration for them. The Tough Battler would be more successful if he/she recognized that some facts will not yield to pugnacity.

The *Friendly Helper* would be a better manager, parent, citizen, and person if he/she could stand up for his/her own interests and for what is right, even against the pleas of others. This type needs firmness and strength and courage not to evade or smooth over conflicts. He/she must face facts.

The *Objective Thinker* would be a better human being and a better business leader if he/she could become more aware of his/her own feelings and the feelings of others. The Objective Thinker needs to learn that there are times when it is all right to fight and times when it is desirable to love.

Source: This material is adapted from the *Reading Book* of the NTI Institute for Applied Behavioral Science associated with the National Education Association. The papers were originally prepared for theory sessions at the institute's laboratories.

After this has been done, distribute the ratings to the people who have been rated. Class members may ask questions to get more feedback on what behaviors create these impressions of fellow students.

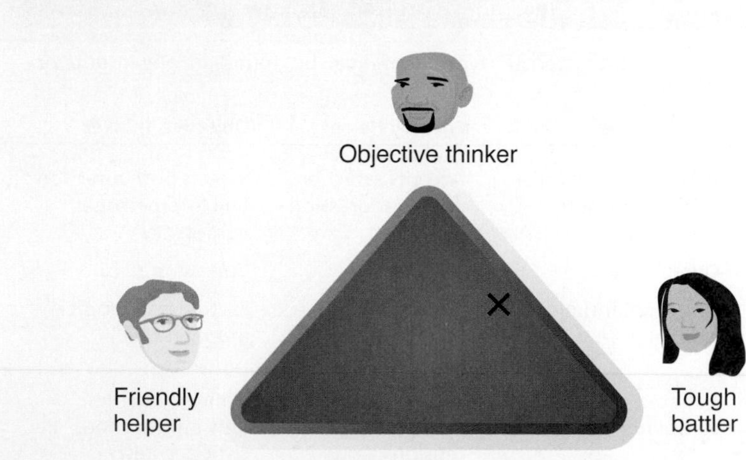

3. The New-Hire Case

Andrea Turner was a new faculty member at a private college (150 faculty members). This was her first teaching job after receiving her Ph.D. from one of the most prestigious graduate schools in the country. She worked in the psychology department, which employed 25 faculty and three secretaries. Andrea commuted from a city 50 miles away. Therefore, she came to work only on the three days she taught classes and on other days worked at home.

When she was at work, she always kept her office door closed. Most others in the department left theirs open. Occasionally, faculty members would go to the student center for coffee breaks in groups of three or four. Andrea was invited along but almost never went. After a while, the others stopped asking her to join them. She was busy writing her first book for a prestigious publishing house.

Andrea was an effective teacher and participated on several faculty committees. She was a prolific writer and scholar. Over the course of three years, Andrea performed well above average for a new faculty member.

When it came time for her review for promotion, a great division was apparent among the other faculty members in their attitudes toward Andrea. A few felt that her work was very strong and that she deserved to be promoted. However, about two-thirds of the professors on the committee felt that she was too much of a loner and did not contribute to the overall needs of the department, only to her own personal success. After much heated discussion, the decision was made not to promote her.

Within three months, Andrea resigned and took a new teaching job at an excellent university. She left without the usual farewell party for departing colleagues. She apparently cleared out her office one night after everyone had left work. Nobody remembered saying good-bye to her.

Postscript: Several other women faculty members had been promoted in this department, and there was a favorable attitude toward affirmative action among the group. So it can be assumed that sex discrimination was not a factor in this case.

DISCUSSION QUESTIONS

1. How would you analyze this case in light of Schutz's theory?
2. How would you analyze it from Andrea's viewpoint? From the department's viewpoint?
3. Would you have done anything about this situation if you had been Andrea's department head?
4. Would you have done anything if you had been one of her colleagues in the department?
5. How typical do you think this case is?

READINGS: Overview

The Myers-Briggs Type Indicator is the most popular personality measure available. In the first article, Paul Tieger and Barbara Barron-Tieger discuss some of the ways that people with different personality types can communicate more effectively.

The second article examines some practical applications of current research on issues having to do with gender and communication.

Reading 3.1 SpeedReaching People: How to Communicate with All Types

Paul D. Tieger and Barbara Barron-Tieger

REWRITING THE GOLDEN RULE

We've all been taught the Golden Rule: "Do unto others as you would have done unto you." However, when it comes to communicating effectively, this really should be modified to read: "Do unto others as *they* would like done unto *them*." In other words, to be effective with others, you need to speak *their* language—to deliver your message in the way *they* want, and will hear it.

Rewriting the Golden Rule means giving up our more egocentric approach to communicating for a more altruistic or responsive approach—one that is more concerned with the other person than with ourselves.

People who communicate egocentrically essentially communicate the same way with everyone, requiring others to adapt to their style. If you think about it, this really makes very little sense. For example, you wouldn't speak the same way to a child of three as you would to an adult with a Ph.D. in philosophy. You would use a different vocabulary and pace, and greatly alter your message so that each person would understand it. Or if you were trying to communicate with someone who was very hard of hearing, you might speak slower and louder to ensure that the person could hear you. Perhaps the clearest example is the change you must make to speak with someone from a foreign country. In order to really communicate well, you would have to speak their language.

Personality type is such an effective tool for enhancing communication because people of different types prefer to communicate in profoundly (and predictably!) different ways. By understanding a person's preferred communication style, you significantly increase your chances of reaching that person. For example, we know that Sensors naturally focus on the facts and details rather than on the big picture and possibilities. Therefore, when trying to connect with a Sensor, it only makes sense to emphasize what they themselves will think is most important.

From Paul D. Tieger and Barbara Barron-Tieger, *The Art of SpeedReaching People* (Boston: Little, Brown, 1998), pp. 139–44. Reprinted by permission.

Simply put, the more similar people are to us, the more comfortable we are with them. Unconsciously, we all want others to be like us, because when they are, we understand them better and are less threatened by them. Evidence of this abounds. For example, most people are uncomfortable with others who have physical or mental disabilities because they are different. And although American culture, legally, is racially integrated, when it comes to socializing most Caucasians choose to be with other Caucasians, just as most African Americans have more close friendships with other African Americans. Similarly, people from very different social classes seldom socialize together.

Most of us tend to surround ourselves with others very much like us. A look at most American companies provides good examples of this: everyone looks pretty much the same. There are clear, if mostly unwritten, rules or norms for everything from the way people dress, wear their hair, speak, and walk, to which hobbies and interests they have.

Norms even extend to the size and shape of our bodies: most of our co-workers are neither extremely tall or short, very heavy or very thin. Aside from the fact that there are admittedly fewer of these individuals in the general population, those that are often don't make it through the interview process for two reasons: most interviewers are personally uncomfortable with them and are concerned they won't fit in.

So what does all this have to do with SpeedReaching People? Quite simply, the more type preferences we have in common with someone, the more similar we are. And the more similar, usually, the easier the communication. (The exception occurs sometimes when people are *too* alike and recognize in someone else a quality they don't like about themselves—not unlike looking in the mirror and seeing a flaw.)

Perhaps you've had the experience where you've met someone and just seemed to "click" with them; although they are strangers, you feel comfortable with them, as if you've known them for a long time. And with other people, perhaps certain family members or co-workers whom you know well, no matter how hard you try, you always seem to be at odds. More than likely, the explanation for both situations has a lot to do with your personality type similarities and differences.

Theoretically, then, communication between two people of the same type should be pretty easy. And it usually is. But what happens when the other person is our type *opposite,* or different on two or three preferences? Although we pay lip service to the notion that differences are good, in reality, most of us tend to see types that are different in negative terms. Recognizing our potential biases is an essential first step in eliminating them. For example:

Extraverts may see *Introverts* as

- secretive; too private
- impersonal and unfriendly
- withholding and self-absorbed
- slow and uncooperative
- socially awkward

While Introverts may see *Extraverts* as

- too talkative; apt to shoot from the lip
- intrusive and pushy
- superficial and disingenuous
- hyperactive and overwhelming
- rude and bossy

These are not always conscious perceptions. Often, they are reflex reactions based on past experience, without the benefit of understanding these fundamental differences in people.

Sensors may see *Intuitives* as

- flighty and erratic
- unrealistic
- impractical
- having their heads in the clouds
- too complicated and theoretical

While Intuitives may see *Sensors* as

- unimaginative and uncreative
- boring; resistant to new things
- stodgy: sticks-in-the-mud
- lacking vision
- simplistic

These are particularly powerful filters, since our preference for Sensing or Intuition reflects the way each of us sees the world. And common sense dictates that if we devalue so central an attribute in someone, it is highly unlikely we will want to identify with them or they with us.

Thinkers may see *Feelers* as

- illogical
- overemotional
- weak
- hysterical
- irrational

While Feelers may see *Thinkers* as

- cold
- insensitive
- uncaring
- inhumane
- hard-hearted

As we touched on earlier, but is worth repeating at this point: many people erroneously assume that all men are Thinkers and all women are Feelers. (Or at least that they *should* be!) Given that mind-set, such people are often uncomfortable with Feeling men and with Thinking women, which can present a particularly difficult obstacle to communication.

Finally, Judgers may see *Perceivers* as

- lazy and/or unproductive
- chronically late; apt to miss important deadlines
- not serious enough
- irresponsible and unreliable
- procrastinators; incapable of making decisions

While Perceivers may see *Judgers* as

- rigid and unyielding
- inflexible and stubborn
- controlling
- apt to regard things as too black and white
- apt to make decisions too quickly

Given the vast number of people in the world, and the fact that there are sixteen distinctly different types, the one thing you can count on is that most of your communications will *not* be with people of your same type. Therefore, the key to communicating effectively lies in your ability to recognize and transcend type differences between you and others. You can do this by learning how to maximize similarities and minimize differences between you.

There are three basic techniques that will help you begin to use your newly acquired understanding of type to reach people who are different from you:

1. Pay attention to others' motivations, values, strengths, and weaknesses, and *follow the rewritten Golden Rule.* Temperament will tell you what they value, their Lead function will identify their greatest strength, and their Least function will generally reveal their greatest weaknesses.
2. *Pay attention to their preferred communication style,* which is greatly influenced by the individual's type preferences as summarized below. For example, suppose you are an ENFP salesperson and the person you are dealing with is an ISTJ—your opposite type. In this case, you would do well to resist your natural ENFP inclination to be clever, funny, and maybe a little irreverent. Remember, her lead is Sensing, so you should pay close attention to the facts and specifics, base your pitch on the logical consequences rather than how important the issue is to you, and make sure to honor any deadlines or schedules that you agree upon.

3. *Use the bridging technique to seek common ground. Bridging* is the process of using the type preferences you have in common with someone else to create a connection. Think of a wooden footbridge built over a raging river to enable people to get from one side to the other. The narrower and weaker the bridge, the more difficult and dangerous the passage. The wider and stronger the bridge, the easier and safer the crossing. In our metaphor, the more preferences people have in common, the wider and stronger the bridge, and the greater likelihood that the message will get across. Here are a few examples of how bridging works:

Example #1: ESTJ and ISTJ

Remember that the more preferences people have in common, the easier the communication process usually is, because there is a wide bridge between these two types. Put another way, there are also several different paths by which these two types might connect—through their shared Sensing, Thinking, and Judging preferences.

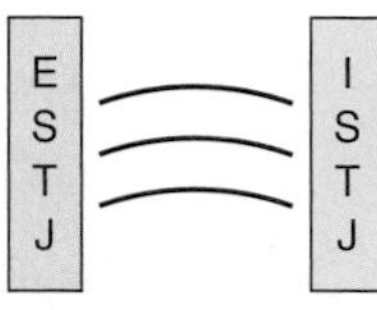

With Extraverts

- Let them talk, and think out loud
- Include a variety of topics
- Communicate verbally
- Expect immediate action
- Keep the conversation moving

With Sensors

- State topic clearly
- Prepare facts and examples
- Present information step-by-step
- Stress practical applications
- Finish your sentences
- Draw on past, real experiences

With Thinkers

- Be organized and logical
- Consider the cause and effect
- Focus on consequences
- Don't ask how they "feel"; ask what they "think"
- Appeal to their sense of fairness
- Don't repeat yourself

With Judgers

- Be on time and be prepared
- Come to conclusions; don't leave issues unresolved
- Be decisive and definitive
- Allow them to make decisions
- Be organized and efficient; don't waste their time
- Stick with plans made

With Introverts

- Ask, then listen carefully
- Talk about one thing at a time
- Communicate in writing, if possible
- Give them adequate time to reflect
- Don't finish their sentences

With Intuitives

- Talk about the "big picture" and its implications
- Talk about possibilities
- Use analogies and metaphors
- Brainstorm options
- Engage their imaginations
- Don't overwhelm them with details

With Feelers

- First mention points of agreement
- Appreciate their efforts and contributions
- Recognize legitimacy of feelings
- Talk about "people" concerns
- Smile and maintain good eye contact
- Be friendly and considerate

With Perceivers

- Expect many questions
- Don't force them to decide prematurely
- Provide opportunities to discuss options and change plans
- Focus on the process, not product
- Give them choices
- Be open to new information

In reality, these two types generally do communicate very well because they see the world in the same way (through Sensing), make decisions using similar criteria (through Thinking), and prefer to live in a decisive, organized way (through Judging). But in addition to having three preferences in common, these two types also share the Traditionalist temperament, which means they have similar core values, making communication even smoother.

Example #2: ENTJ and INTP

These two types relate to each other as Intuitives, as Thinkers, and as Lead Thinkers. And since NTs are Conceptualizers, they share the same temperament as well. This illustrates how types that are similar on only two preferences can still have a significant communication bridge.

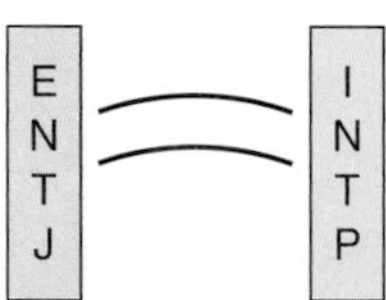

These two people will do best to focus on common values of creativity, competence, and independence. They will best understand one another when they use language that appeals to them both, look at the big picture, and describe things in logical, impersonal terms.

Example #3: ENFP and INTJ

Having only one preference in common, you might assume these two types would form a very narrow, even shaky, bridge. While it's true these two types are very different in many ways, and they share only a preference for Intuition in common, that preference happens to be the lead for both. As a result, they both seek and see possibilities, look for the implications and meaning in things, are creative and open to new ways of doing things. And although they may not agree on everything, the chances are very good they will understand each other. Hence, just their lead Intuition, if used correctly, can be a powerful communication bridge.

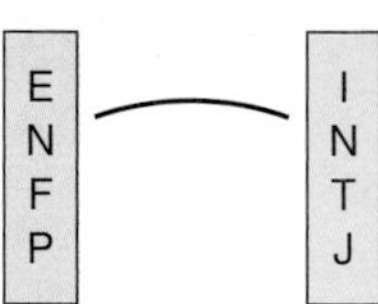

But, as we all have experienced, there are certainly times when you share *no* preferences in common with another person. The key to success here is to start by following the rewritten Golden Rule, working to understand what the other person is all about, and then trying to speak his or her language. Next, look for other, non-type-related, connections. Of course, all human beings share lots of things in common. You may both have children, or work at the same company, belong to the same church, or live in the same town . . . or you may both love photography. There are many more things we have in common that connect us than that separate us. And while they are seldom enough to ensure good communication, these common experiences can form powerful bridges that help the effort.

Reading 3.2 The Gender and Communication Connection

THINKING ABOUT OUR GENDERED WORLD: WHERE WOULD YOU LIKE TO GO FROM HERE?

Teri Kwal Gamble and Michael W. Gamble

Now that we've entered the new millennium, we need to ask ourselves what it is we hope for when it comes to our gendered lives. How we answer such a question will affect what we believe is possible, how we will choose to live, and what we will ultimately become. To be sure, our discussions about gender will certainly continue well into this millennium, especially since much of our communication is filtered consistently through a gendered lens.

We recognize that through the years, gender inequity has assumed many different forms, and we realize the extent to which issues of gender inequality either have or have not been addressed. We are making progress. We have seen the first woman commander of the space shuttle, the first woman candidate for president in the United States, the first woman CEO of a DOW 30 company, and the U.S. National Women's Soccer team attract over 90,000 fans to the Women's World Cup finals. We have also seen that knowledge needs to be produced not just from a man's point of view, but also from a woman's. We have seen men take a larger role in child care, select a woman to head Hewlett Packard, and root for women's sports teams. Most probably, in the years ahead, there will be many more firsts. Certainly, your children may assume different sex role behaviors than the ones you yourself now enact. In addition, if gender categories continue to be challenged, they will probably have even more choices regarding roles believed appropriate for them to fulfill than we currently have.

We also observe that there is healthy diversity among men and among women. All people, regardless of gender, are similar in some ways and different in others, overlapping with each other at different points. Even where we expect to perceive similarities or differences, that expectation is not always borne out. On the other hand, the members of all societies participate in the construction of gender differences. We are taught rules, and we are pressured to adhere to different gendered norms. It is these rules and norms that guide our behavior. How we are gendered depends, in part, on our social class, race, and ethnicity. These variables intersect to give us great diversity among men and women. We can point to examples across cultures, races, and ethnicities such as Chinese Americans, Latin Americans, African Americans, and European Americans, but recognize at the same time there are many more to include and consider.

In the United States, the day-to-day communicative activities of men and women have become more and more similar in the last few decades. The

From Teri Kwal Gamble and Michael W. Gamble, "Thinking About Our Gendered World: Where Would You Like to Go from Here?" in *The Gender Communication Connection* (Boston: Houghton Mifflin, © 2003), pp. 5–21. Reprinted by permission.

founding editor of the journal *Gender and Society,* Judith Lorber, promotes the idea that women and men ought to be socially interchangeable.

In general, men, today, are performing more relational roles than did their fathers. They are more involved as caregivers, home planners, and sounding boards. Today, women are performing more task related roles outside of the home than did their mothers; they are bringing work home from the office, and more of them now see themselves as personally responsible for their economic well-being and for the economic well-being of their families.

Are there guidelines we can use to help us chart our way into the future? What do we see as our options? Who do we believe should perform what tasks? What limits, if any, are we going to enforce?

As we look for answers to these and other questions, we need to use a lens that is unobstructed by our gendered traditions. We need to work to discard any distorted views of men and women that deny us our full physical and emotional potential. We need to understand that there are many ways to be a man and many ways to be a woman. In fact, what is deemed proper or expected for a man or a woman should, from our point of view, be an unanswerable question. If anything, when it comes to responding to that particular question, each individual should be free to give his or her own answer. There should be no response that is viewed as absolute or unequivocal. Of course, it hasn't always been this way.

Thinking About Where We've Been: History/Herstory

To be sure, men's and women's lives have changed over the years. . . . It is important to note briefly here that a number of historical and cultural events have led us to where we are today.

History finds women having been denied a voice, disenfranchised, and not necessarily afforded educational opportunities equal to those of men. In years past, there was even a time when women were perceived to be the property of men. Women fought for the right to vote, fought for job opportunities, and fought to enjoy privileges equal to those of men.

In the United States, men have historically benefited from a patriarchal society. Over time, however, the women's movement challenged traditional perceptions of the male gender role. As a result, men—like women—have had their collective consciousness raised. Like women, men now are afforded the opportunity to reconsider sex roles and to choose whether to be the provider or the emotional caregiver, to work or to stay at home with the children.

So, whether we are calling for equal rights, arguing for fathers' rights, reproductive rights, or job rights, it is by looking at the past that we can understand our present and dream about the future. By understanding the past and by challenging existing assumptions, we pave the way for change.

Exploring Gender Today

Have you ever asked either of these questions? *"Why can't a woman be more like a man?" "Why can't a man be more like a woman?"* If you think about these questions seriously, the answer to each question is not at all simple, since how you respond to them also suggests a great deal about your cultural background, values, and orientation toward the sexes. In fact, how you answer such questions reflects your life experiences, implies a sense of identity, and reveals your point of view regarding the influence of gender.

It is important to understand the roles that *communication* and *gendered communication* play in your life. Communication is at the core of our humanness. It links us with other human beings, and is the tool we rely on to establish connections or relationships with other people. While there are well over 100 published definitions of communication, for the purposes of this [reading], we will define *communication* as the deliberate or accidental transfer of meaning. It occurs whenever someone observes or experiences behavior and attributes meaning or significance to that behavior. Communication is also a process, "a continuous stream in which everything is simultaneously a reaction and an instigation, an instigation and a reaction." In other words, communication is ongoing and ever moving forward. It is virtually impossible to determine when it starts and stops; it is forever changing and cannot be frozen in time.

When we communicate, we simultaneously send and receive messages through multiple channels. Thus, we also conceive of communication as a concurrent exchange of influences. Whenever we communicate with another person, we receive feedback, verbal and nonverbal cues we perceive in reaction to our communication. Communication occurs within a context, which encompasses not only the physical and temporal environment but also the other people present together with their cultural backgrounds. In the context of communication, noise functions as a communication limiter, interfering with or distorting our ability to send or receive messages. Noise can have both internal (personal or psychological) and external (environmental) sources. Communication also has effects, sometimes sought and sometimes unintended. . . .

Communication becomes *gendered communication* when your sex or gender influences your relationships with others—whether those relationships are with persons of the same sex as you or members of the opposite sex. The fact that you are a male or a female may well make a difference in how people communicate with you and how you communicate with them. It may affect not only what you say to others but how you say it. Other people may perceive you through gendered eyes. They may expect you to behave in certain ways simply because of your sex (see Figure A). We may similarly look at others and our world through gendered eyes. Thus, the values and prescriptions that our culture assigns to our gender affect our personal, social, and professional lives. . . .

[T]his [reading] will explore the similarities as well as the differences between men and women. The authors, a husband and wife—or should we say a wife and husband team—do not always use and understand the same verbal and nonverbal messages, but that does not mean we always seem to be speaking different languages or always interpreting messages in disparate ways. If we learn how people both like and unlike ourselves perceive and are affected by gender, work earnestly to comprehend how gender frees us in some ways while it limits us in others, and choose not to be constrained by those who fear or are frustrated by change, we can broaden our life choices and possibilities.

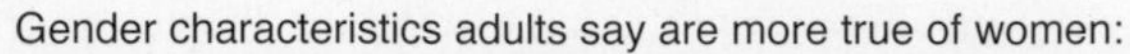

Gender characteristics adults say are more true of women:

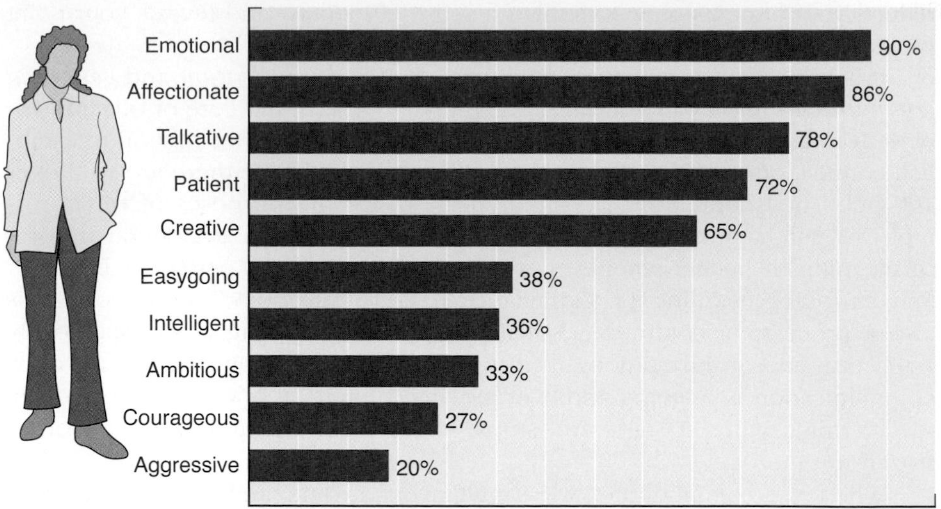

FIGURE A Female Stereotypes

Source: Copyright 2001, *USA TODAY*. Reprinted with permission.

CONCEPTUAL AND PERCEPTUAL FOUNDATIONS

Each of us is unique. We have different viewpoints, and we approach life from different standpoints. *Standpoint theory* informs us that our culture defines people by gender, class, and race, and that a person's location within the culture shapes his or her life. Gender, race, and class affect how we perceive experience, process knowledge, and view the future.

According to both Harding and Collins, because persons in positions of power have an overriding interest in preserving their place in the hierarchy, they tend to develop more distorted views of social life than do persons who gain nothing from their position in the culture. In contrast, persons belonging to a culture's less powerful, subordinate, or marginalized groups develop better insights into how society works because they need to develop these understandings to survive. Thus, while the communication of men and women is similar to one another in some situations, it is quite different in others.

Because standpoint theory recognizes both the similarities and differences among women and men, it provides us with a firm foundation from which we can acknowledge the diversity among women and men as well. "Standpoint focuses on perspectives of women, but could also take the perspectives of African American women, poor white women/men, non-white women and men, and individuals belonging to minority ethnic and religious groups outside modern Western society." Since there is no objective standard for measuring standpoints, and no single perspective on social life, a position taken represents a subjective standpoint. The concept of multiple, albeit partial and incomplete, truths is central to Standpoint theory: Every social group perceives a partial view of society that is based on their experiences.

According to Standpoint theory, the circumstances of women's and men's lives differ in key ways, leading them to develop distinctive identities, perspectives, priorities, views of social life and communication, and ways of interacting. Who we are affects our perception of a situation and our beliefs about how we and others should react. Where we stand shapes what we see and how we understand it. It leads us to personalize what we feel, value, and perceive. It causes us to make choices. For example, because we value equality, we may feel pressured by social expectations and practices, and thus, perceive a need to rebel against inequities based on gender. Or, we may feel relieved by the benefits we perceive our gender to bestow upon us, and we may find ourselves rewarded by a social system that unequally appreciates and values men and women.

Regardless of whether you feel privileged or paralyzed, empowered or disadvantaged by the social evaluations of others, studying how gender influences communication can make a difference in your life. According to Judith Lorber, our task is to move beyond dichotomy and undermine the very basis of gender stratification—that "ubiquitous division of people into two unequally valued categories."

Distinguishing Between Sex and Gender

Before we continue our exploration, it is important to define five key terms: *sex, gender, androgyny, sexism,* and *sexual orientation*. Although the first two terms are sometimes used interchangeably, they do have different meanings.

Sex is a descriptor of the genetic/biological composition or code of an individual. Sex, a distinction based on biological and genetic qualities, accounts for the biological differences between men and women. People do not acquire sex. It is innate; they are born with it.

Gender, while related to one's biological sex, is also a descriptor of "the psychological, social, and cultural features and characteristics strongly associated with the biological categories of male and female." Gender is an acquired, learned, or socially constructed rather than biologically constructed notion, a human invention that identifies the social, psychological, and cultural differentiations between the sexes.

We each have qualities or behavioral tendencies that our culture defines as masculine or feminine; how much of each set we exhibit reveals our gender. Gender makes itself manifest during interaction. The way in which it manifests itself varies across cultures. For example, if you were raised in Saudi Arabia or Japan, your beliefs regarding the rights of women and men in society would probably differ from those you would hold if you were raised in the United States. We should note, however, that we are not just the recipients of culture's gendered messages; we also influence them.

The word *androgyny* is a combination of two Greek words, *andros,* which means man, and *gyne,* which means woman. Persons who are androgynous reject rigid sex role categorizations, preferring instead to embody both masculine and feminine qualities. Thus, an androgynous woman might be both emotional and forceful. An androgynous man might be both deferential and competitive. Androgynous individuals realize that they have more choice than some of us realize in how we define ourselves as males and females. (Note: The etymological basis of the word itself asserts the primacy of male even within a term that is supposed to characterize an individual who possesses both feminine and masculine characteristics.)

The word *sexism* conjures up images of discrimination. Sexism occurs when we assign characteristics to others because of their sex. Typically, it denotes the unfair or inappropriate treatment of others solely based on their sex. While women have been found to be less sexist than men, sexism can pertain to both men and women; also, either a man or a woman may be its victim or the victimizer. What does sexism mean to you?

Persons who are sexist denigrate the members of one sex in order to exalt members of the other sex. They place a significantly higher value on the members of one sex. Examples of sexism include: viewing members of either sex as genetically inferior; supporting discriminatory practices against the members of either sex; or treating the members of either sex as sexual objects. Thus, when we pay women less money than men for the same job, do not vote for a candidate solely because of his or her sex, exhibit hostility toward women and men who fail to fulfill traditional sex roles, do not award a parent custody of a child because of his or her sex, or use women as sex objects in advertising, we display sexism.

Sexual orientation is a characteristic that refers to the sex of the person(s) to whom an individual is sexually attracted, or with whom the individual has sexual relations. Attitudes and behaviors that support heterosexuality as "normal," and as more desirable than homosexuality or bisexuality are *heterosexist*. Labeling a boy as a "sissy" and a girl as a "lesbo" because he or she does not conform to heterosexual expectations is heterosexist.

Communication Cultures

In general, *feminine communication cultures* tend to accentuate expressive goals, less-structured organizations, collective orientations, and cooperative speech patterns. In contrast, *masculine communication cultures* are more apt to accentuate instrumental goals, hierarchical structure, individualistic goals, and competitive speech forms.

Both masculine and feminine communication cultures affect the men and women who adhere to their culture's prescriptions. For example, for many men, the directive *don't be female* becomes the primary cornerstone of their manliness. Men find themselves prompted repeatedly to be aggressive and show what they are made of. In addition, they are expected to be both sexual and self-reliant. Feminine cultures convey very different messages. For example, many women learn that cultural expectations for appearance include being thin, while cultural expectations for behavior require that they be sensitive and caring. It seems that in contrast to men caring for others is integrally connected with being a woman. At this point, we need to stress that we do not mean to draw superficial conclusions about the way that men and women are. The existence of a feminine or masculine communication culture does not mean that all women or all men are perfect representatives of that culture. We do not support *essentializing,* that is, the tendency to reduce the members of either sex to certain essential characteristics. All women are not all alike, and all men are not all alike.

COMMUNICATION AND GENDER: WHICH IS THE CATALYST?

Gender is a communicative process. We construct and communicate our gender to others, and they construct and communicate their gender to us. To what extent do you think that the sex of a person provides you with clues about how to communicate with him or her? Do persons of different sexes react differently to the messages you send? Does knowing a person's sex help you predict how that person will respond to you? In your opinion, what are the proper ways for men and women to communicate and interact with each other?

If communication is the essential human connection, then exploring the gendered nature of that connection is worthy of our consideration. Like communication in general, gendered communication can be accidental or intentional. Any time we accidentally or intentionally send a message that was influenced by our gender or the gender of another person, gendered communication occurs. And whether it is done consciously or unconsciously, our use of gendered communication precipitates reactions in others.

Because of the gendered messages we perceive others to send, we may work to alter or abandon a particular way of thinking or behaving, or we may work to sustain or enhance a particular way of thinking or behaving. Gendered communication can cause us to become dissatisfied with the way others see and respond to us, or it can cause us to experience satisfaction with our identity and the ways others interact with us.

Communication influences our relationships. Gendered communication permeates our relationships. How we act or fail to act when in the presence of other males and females makes a difference in our collective lives. For men, for example, the purpose of talking is primarily instrumental—that is, to gain status, exert control, accomplish a goal, or solve a problem. For women, however, the purpose of talking is to establish connection and gain intimacy. Gender-differentiated patterns of communication may also lead men and women to have different expectations for their interactions and to experience each other in different ways.

An understanding of the standpoints of both men and women is necessary if we are to develop a more complete understanding of gender relations. We need to explore relationships between men and women, among men, and among women. Only by doing this will we be able to identify when gender and not some other variable is functioning as a salient force in our lives.

COMMUNICATION AND GENDER INTERACT

Where did your views of masculinity and femininity come from? More than likely, from the day you were born important people in your life communicated your culture's gender expectations to you. They let you know what was expected from a member of your biological sex. As you matured, you probably became more aware of your feelings about these prescriptions, and you either affirmed their value and validity or you challenged them. Perhaps you questioned their fairness. If you're a woman, you may not have wanted to reroute your career in order to be the primary caregiver for children or elderly parents. If you're a man, perhaps you preferred to be "Mr. Mom" and stay at home and care for your children instead of adhering to a more traditional linear male career path. (By the way, why is such a person referred to as "Mr. Mom" instead of "Mr. Dad"? Could it be that the perception is that dads don't stay at home?) Perhaps you also observed that people from other cultures handle gender issues differently. Perhaps you realized that your gender did not necessarily have to limit your chosen communication style. You might even have made the effort to expand your options and develop a repertoire of diverse communication styles from which you felt free to choose, based upon who you were interacting with.

What gender means to you depends upon how your culture defines masculinity and femininity, and how much of those definitions you accept. All societies promote gender ideologies that specify appropriate gendered behaviors for males and females. In Western culture, at birth boys are generally swaddled in blue blankets, while girls are swaddled in pink blankets. As they grow older, boys are usually given trucks or action figures to play with while girls are given dolls. Even companies target buyers based on gender. For example, Toys "R" Us has different toy sections in its stores, one labeled "Girl's World" and another "Boy's World." Girl's World features plenty of dolls, kitchen toys, and makeup while Boy's World features action figures, trucks, and walkie-talkies.

When they reach adulthood, males are expected to play primary breadwinner while women, whether they work or not, are expected to play primary caregiver. Social practices create different and inequitable socially sanctioned opportunities for males and females. Whether or not you accept a constructed cultural prescription for gender or decide to alter it is up to you. The changing roles of men and women are inescapable. When you reject a cultural prescription, you still influence it, and may even help transform it.

Communicating Our Confusion

Messages regarding gender are not necessarily communicated clearly—or if they are communicated clearly, they are not necessarily accepted by all receiver(s). For example, we might believe that neither men nor women should be judged by appearance. Nonetheless, we may spend hundreds or thousands of dollars a year on beauty and grooming aids and physical conditioning and weight-control regimens, all in an effort to make ourselves more attractive to others. Or we might believe that men and women should have equal career opportunities. Yet, when push comes to shove—whether we are a woman or a man—when asked our personal preference, we are more likely than not to find it more comfortable working for a male manager than for a female one. Similarly, while we believe that both sexes should participate equally in the raising of a child, we may still register surprise when a male takes a sabbatical from work to care for a newborn. And while we believe that all jobs should be open to both sexes, we may still find it amusing to bring our car to a mechanic only to discover that the mechanic is a woman.

While we may have openly voiced our acceptance regarding the roles men and women should play, we may still be marginal when it comes to how deeply ingrained these attitudes actually are in our psyche. We may say, for example, that all people are entitled to the equal protection of the law, but we may protest against changing the law to allow same sex marriages. We may say that all children deserve a secure home life, but we may find it objectionable for same sex partners to adopt a child. We may still find it more comfortable to base societal privileges on arbitrary but traditional categories such as sexual orientation and sex.

Certainly, there are a large number of gender issues for us to sort out and work through. Our ideals and our attitudes may not yet be totally in sync. While this can be unsettling, it does make for some intensely interesting discussions. Communication may help create our gendered image, but it is also through communication that we express our gendered identity. For example, we can perform gender in culturally approved ways, or we can live with the consequences of what others might consider inappropriate gender displays. We can participate in the gender system, or we can rebel against parts of it and change our gender performance accordingly. Through our actions, we can support and go along with the system, we can reveal our gendered confusion to others, or we can imagine and then enact alternatives.

Changing Communication Paradigms

A *paradigm* is a belief structure. For example, we have beliefs about the ways men and women should act and the roles they should perform. When we revise our stereotypical way of thinking about men and women, previous boundaries based upon sex give way, and we make paradigm shifts.

Years ago, for example, it was considered terribly inappropriate for a woman to ask a man out on a date, pay her own way, or to pay for the date altogether. Similarly, in decades passed, a man's worth was measured predominantly by his ability to advance in his career while a woman's was measured primarily by her appearance. While such sex-based stereotypes were once pervasive, rules and standards have changed through the years. Some behavioral standards have been relaxed, while others were totally rejected.

Today, women and men more readily shift positions, which leads them to shift paradigms and learn new ways of thinking and communicating in their new respective roles.

Women and men can occupy positions that develop abilities not socially prescribed for their gender. Women who find themselves in professional positions, for example, may become more confident, competitive, and assertive than women in general—and as much so as their male peers—because they are now called on to perform roles that promote the communication of those qualities. When placed in care-giving roles, men become as nurturing, attentive to others, and emotionally responsive as women are perceived to be. As we see, gender is a relational construct that is clarified through our interaction with others. This is also in accordance with Standpoint theory, which you will recall posits that men and women learn the rules, meanings, and norms of communication of the activities in which they participate. This suggests that if we participate in new activities, then we will learn new rules. So, gendered behavior is not permanently fixed, but can change as individuals find themselves in new situations that allow them to try on new behaviors.

MORE PRINCIPLES OF GENDERED COMMUNICATION

Consider the following additional principles of gendered communication.

Gendered Communication Is Dynamic

When we say that gendered communication is a *dynamic* process we mean that communication about and between men and women is ongoing or continuous. Gendered communication is unpredictable. The norms, rules, and roles sanctioned by society change with time. Many fathers now assume primary responsibility for childcare. Women and men can now sue their employers for sexual harassment. Leave policies for working mothers and fathers have become more lenient. Thus, gendered communication is in a constant state of flux. "Every individual exists in a continually changing world of experience of which s/he is the center." In effect, our present gendered encounters are points of arrival from past encounters and points of departure for future ones.

Gendered Communication Is Systemic

Gender is *relational*. We cannot study gender without studying specific persons in interaction in specific situations with specific other persons. We cannot understand a couple by looking at only one individual. We cannot understand a child without looking at its family. We cannot understand gender's effect on communication without looking at its context, the people involved, and the culture within which an interaction occurs. Every ingredient is connected to every other ingredient. All aspects of our communication with others are interactive and interlinked.

Gendered Communication Is Pervasive

Men and women frequently interact with members of their own sex and with each other. Thus, the likelihood is great that you will regularly exchange ideas and feelings with members of your own sex and with members of the opposite sex. Because of the number of contacts we have with each other, interest continues to grow on how gender affects those interactions. By focusing on social expectations of masculinity and femininity, by exploring the equality (or lack thereof) in the opportunities afforded women and men, and acknowledging how multi-layered messages offered by the media, our families, and religion affect our notions of gender, we become more aware of the gender's *pervasive* impact on our psychological, interpersonal, and professional lives. For example, when it comes to multi-layered messages, how does the New Testament command that wives submit to their husbands resolve itself with the images presented in films and in advertising, and the commitment made by many women to achieve equality in the workforce and on the homefront? Are the majority of our cultural images of women the way men see them, or the way women see themselves? On the flip side, are the majority of our cultural images of men the way women see them, or the way men see themselves?

Gendered Communication Is Learned

Over time, we *learn* which gendered behaviors work for us and which do not. Our interaction with others may be impeded if we remain unconscious of or insensitive to the ways in which our gendered messages affect our relationships with others, and vice versa. Existing gendered prescriptions will limit our communication effectiveness if we fail to confront the experiences of those who reject them or have been hurt by them. We can learn from others whose standpoints may be different from our own. We can explore the anger and pain felt by gay men and lesbians in a society that defines heterosexuality as the norm, recognize the frustration some women experience when they realize they earn approximately 70 percent (on average) of what men do for similar work, and try to understand the anxiety some men feel toward efforts to change "the system." It is we who decide whether or not to accept what society has defined as normal and appropriate behavior. We can learn to challenge disparities that limit our opportunities.

CHAPTER 4

Group Circumstances and Structure

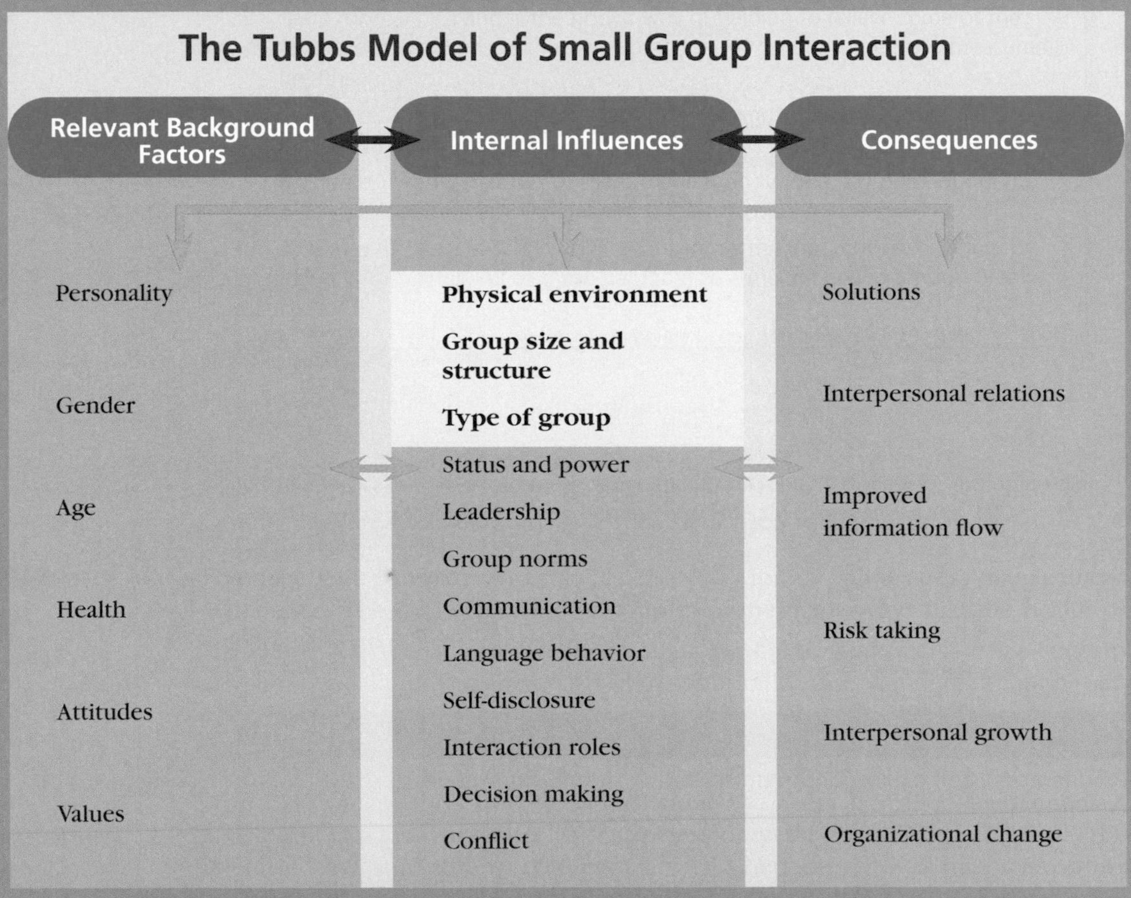

Concepts in **boldface** in gray panels are the emphases of this chapter.

Preview

In Chapter 1, the *internal* influences of the Tubbs Model of Small Group Interaction were introduced briefly. Chapter 4 includes a more in-depth treatment of three of these: physical environment, group size and structure, and group type. Physical environment is the setting in which small group interaction takes place. Territoriality and seating patterns are two aspects of the physical environment. Group size and structure are influences in that people in a group relate to each other in a number of patterns or communication networks. The third internal influence is the type of group. Obviously, groups interact differently depending on what type of group they are. Some examples discussed in this chapter are primary groups, casual and social groups, work groups, educational groups, problem-solving groups, and computer-assisted groups.

Glossary

Casual and Social Groups Casual and social groups include neighborhood groups, fraternities, and even classmates. The impact of these relationships on behavior is often quite profound.

Communication Networks Communication networks are the five patterns of communicating between group members.

Educational Groups Educational groups are groups that interact for the sole purpose of study or instruction.

Primary Groups Primary groups are groups that usually include one's family and closest friends.

Problem-Solving Groups Problem-solving groups are groups that form in order to solve one or more problems.

Seating Patterns Seating patterns often affect the type and volume of interaction in a group.

Territoriality The word *territoriality* was coined by Edward Hall and defined as "the tendency for humans and other animals to lay claim to and defend a particular area or territory."

Work Groups Work groups are the formations of people on the job.

CASE STUDY

HOOTERS

Cassie Smith was threatened with being fired by the Roseville, Michigan, Hooters organization, and she has filed a lawsuit claiming she shouldn't be fired (or threatened to be fired) for being what they consider "too fat." She is 5'8" and weighs 132 pounds.

Hooters is defending their decision, comparing themselves to employers like the Dallas Cowboy Cheerleaders or the Radio City Music Hall Rockettes, who are expected to uphold a specific image. They argue that "our practice of upholding an image standard based on appearance, attitude, and fitness for Hooters girls is both legal and fair."

Smith was told that they would pay for a health club membership and give her 30 days for reevaluation. Failing that, she would be given another 30 days. Failing that, she would be terminated.

continued

In small groups of about five people of a mixture of men and women, discuss the following questions:

1. Do you think a for-profit company has the right to maintain an appearance standard as a condition of employment?
2. Does Cassie Smith look as if she is too fat for this position? How would you go about defining what constitutes being "too fat"?
3. Would this issue influence your likelihood of going to a Hooters restaurant?
4. How would you resolve this case so that it won't keep coming up again?
5. How much agreement is there in your group about the answers to these questions? Why? Does the opinion vary along gender lines?

Below, you can see for yourself what Smith looks like.

After your group discussion check out the following video: http://www.youtube.com/watch?v=-IkcWab98PE

Sources: A. Ayles, "Hooters Waitress Fired for Being Too Fat: Acceptable or Not?" May 21, 2010. http://www.manolith.com/2010/05/21/hooters-waitress-fired-for-being-too-fat-acceptable-or-not/

Dahlia Lithwick, "Our Beauty Bias Is Unfair," *Newsweek,* June 14, 2010, p. 20.

The Hooters case study beautifully illustrates the way groups usually function. In this chapter we will look at several very different types of groups, ranging from the family, or primary, group, to street gangs, encounter groups, and problem-solving groups. Although each type of group differs from the others, some common conceptual links connect all types of groups. The first factor that is relevant to all groups is the so-called *ecology* of the group.

The famous dispute over the size and shape of the negotiating table at the Paris peace talks in 1968 illustrates an example in our nation's history of what we mean by ecology in group discussion. The disagreement lasted eight months and was typical of many with political implications during the negotiations. McCroskey, Larson, and Knapp (1971) explain the reasons for the dispute:

> The United States (US) and South Vietnam (SVN) wanted a seating arrangement in which only two sides were identified. They did not want to recognize the National Liberation Front (NLF) as an "equal" party in the negotiations. North Vietnam (NVN) and the NLF wanted "equal" status given to all parties—represented by a four-sided table. The final arrangement was such that both parties could claim victory. The round table minus the dividing lines allowed North Vietnam and the NLF to claim all four delegations were equal. The existence of the two secretarial tables (interpreted as dividers), the lack of identifying symbols on the table, and an AA, BB speaking rotation permitted the United States and South Vietnam to claim victory for the

two-sided approach. Considering the lives lost during the eight months needed to arrive at the seating arrangement, we can certainly conclude that territorial space has extremely high priority in some interpersonal settings. (p. 97)

In this chapter, we will look more closely at small group ecology, as well as at other internal influences in small group interaction.

Chapter 1 defined *internal influences* on a group as factors that are influenced by the individual characteristics of group members and that in turn influence a group's functioning and its end results. Internal influences are somewhat under the control of group members (that is, members are able to change them). We will examine three major internal influences: (1) physical environment, (2) group size and structure, and (3) type of group.

Physical Environment

For many years, writers have hypothesized that a room's environment influences the interaction within it. Supposedly, warm colors—hues of orange, red, and brown—facilitate interaction, whereas cool hues of blue and green tend to encourage reserved, formal conversation. Research has actually shown support for these commonsense hunches (Leonard & Swaps, 1999).

According to another source, "Working in teams is the hottest concept in the workplace these days, and it's no surprise that office furniture that helps that happen is the hottest seller at area furniture dealers. . . . One hot thing right now is a P-shaped work surface, which allows the person to have meetings in their offices and have people pull up to a round table that is attached to the end of the work surface." The curved part of the P sticks out in the direction where the guests would sit. "It's just a little more inviting to have people sitting around a table than across a desk. There's still the stigma that if a person is behind a desk, that person is in control; where you're around a table, it's more of an equal setting" (Roush, 1996, p. 10). An environment that is conducive to more communication, such as the less traditional "open office," is often more conducive as well to success on group tasks. In another example, the Fallon-McElliott advertising agency's art director and copywriters wheel specially equipped desks out of their cubicles to meet in "flexible space." At Alcoa's world headquarters in Pittsburgh, everyone, including the CEO, works in cubicles without any permanent walls. In many consulting firms, such as the Deloitte Consulting Group and Anderson Consulting, consultants spend most of their time on their client's site. When they do meet at their corporate offices, they use the "hoteling" concept. They occupy a desk and a work space, just for that day, much as they would a hotel room. They do not have regularly assigned offices, nor do they have desktop computers. Everyone uses his or her own laptop (Hamilton, 1996).

The field of *environment psychology* focuses on how people interact with their environment in a variety of contexts. This field is based on the premise that individuals are "active participants in their world." Rob Semper (2004), writer for the Association of Science-Technology Centers (ASTC), notes that learning and performance are highly affected by environment. The *environment* consists of lighting, space, and sounds. Semper says that people search for freedom of choice in thinking and problem solving in their physical spaces. In the small group context, environments that promote creativity and productivity can actually improve group performance. Semper also reports that researchers and theorists in environmental psychology have found that "personal and cultural expectations" affect how an individual interprets and functions in a particular workspace. The study of cultural perceptions of the environment is a growing field that will affect our study of small group dynamics in the future (Semper, 2004).

TERRITORIALITY

Edward Hall (1959) coined the term *territoriality* to describe the tendency for humans and other animals to lay claim to and defend a particular area or territory. We are all familiar with this behavior among dogs, birds, and gorillas, but we may be less aware of our own attempts to defend our territories. It has been estimated that college students begin to identify a particular seat in the class as "their chair" by as early as the second class period. Although we probably would not ask a person to give up the chair, we would feel some annoyance at having to move to another one. This is reminiscent of the home-court advantage in basketball: Teams traditionally play better on the home court than they do at "away" games.

In addition to identifying certain places as our territory, we also move about in a portable space bubble of about 18 inches in each direction that we let only certain people violate. This is referred to as our *personal space*. Sommer (1959) distinguishes personal space from territory in the following way: "The most important difference is that personal space is carried around while territory is relatively stationary. The animal or man will usually mark the boundaries of his territory so that they are visible to others, but the boundaries of his personal space are invisible. Personal space has the body at its center, while territory does not" (p. 248).

Kinzel (1969) conducted a study of inmates at the United States Medical Center for Federal Prisoners. He found that men who had committed violent crimes had a personal space, or "body buffer zone," twice as large as that of prisoners classified as nonviolent. The violent group stated that they felt threatened when a person came close to them, as if the person were an intruder who was "looming up" or "rushing in" at them.

Hall (1959) describes the humorous situation in which people with different-size space bubbles try to communicate. Arabs or South Americans will try to step closer, reducing the distance between them and their listeners. North American or German listeners will then step backward to reestablish what they feel is a comfortable distance for conversation. And so it continues as one individual ends up backing the other all the way around the room. Rosenfeld (1965) found that personality factors influenced the size of one's personal space. Those high in need for affiliation (see Chapter 2) sat an average of 57 inches away from a target person, whereas those low in affiliation averaged 94 inches in distance.

Hall refers to the study of personal space and distance as *proxemics*. Judie Haynes of everythingESL.net writes about proxemics for international students and uses the example of standing on an elevator to teach international students how to ride an elevator in the United States. She describes the complex behavior in the elevator. For example, as the elevator gets more crowded, everyone faces

TABLE 4.1 Distances and Communication

Distance	Content	Vocal Shifts
3–6 inches	Top secret	Soft whisper
8–12 inches	Very confidential topics	Audible whisper
12–20 inches	Confidential topics	Soft voice
20–36 inches	Personal topics	Soft voice
$4\frac{1}{2}$–5 feet	Nonpersonal topics	Full voice
$5\frac{1}{2}$–8 feet	Public information	Loud voice
8–20 feet	Public information to a group	Very loud voice
20–100 feet	Hailing and departing comments	Very loud voice

Sources: Adapted from Hall, 1959, pp. 163–64. Chart from *The Silent Language* by Edward T. Hall.

the front and watches the floor indicator above the door. On a humorous note, Haynes writes, "If you think this behavior is exaggerated, the next time you are on an elevator, don't face the door . . . turn around and face toward the other occupants . . . see what the reaction is." This behavior may be very strange to someone from another culture, but it is very critical to personal distance in the United States (Haynes, 2004).

Hall has identified four zones or distances that seem to influence interaction in North American culture. He points out, however, that these distances do not apply to cultures that have different zones. The four types of distances are intimate, personal, social, and public.

Intimate distance extends from touching to about 18 inches. This distance encourages soft whispers about very confidential matters. It also allows us to use more of our senses in communicating (for example, touching, smelling, and even tasting). *Personal distance* ranges from 18 inches to about 4 feet. Conversation is usually soft, and topics are usually personal. *Social distance* refers to the distance between 4 and 12 feet. At this distance, voices are usually raised, and the topics are nonpersonal public information for anyone to hear. *Public distance* refers to 12 feet and beyond. This requires a loud voice and impersonal topics. As we shall see later in this chapter, different groups may at one time or another involve the use of all four of these distances. Encounter groups frequently include physical touching, whereas large committees may be seated around tables more than 25 feet in diameter. Table 4.1 gives more examples of various distances and kinds of communication.

SEATING PATTERNS

Have you ever noticed the difference in interaction between a group sitting on the grass or the floor and one whose members are seated indoors around a rectangular table? One difference is that sitting on the floor or grass allows greater informality and tends to facilitate interaction. However, research has shown that even the seating patterns around rectangular tables have a major impact on interaction.

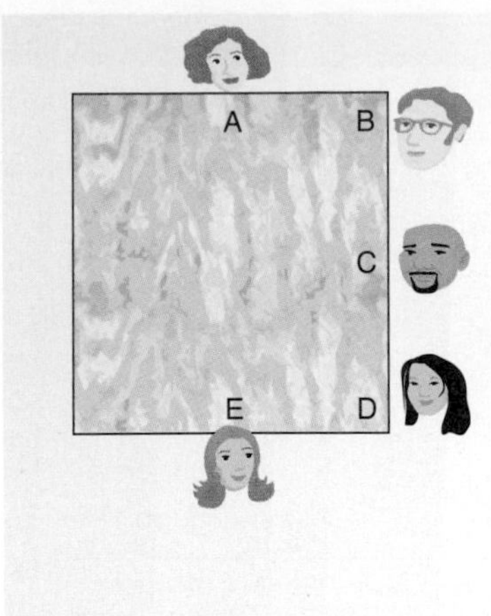

FIGURE 4.1 Seating Pattern

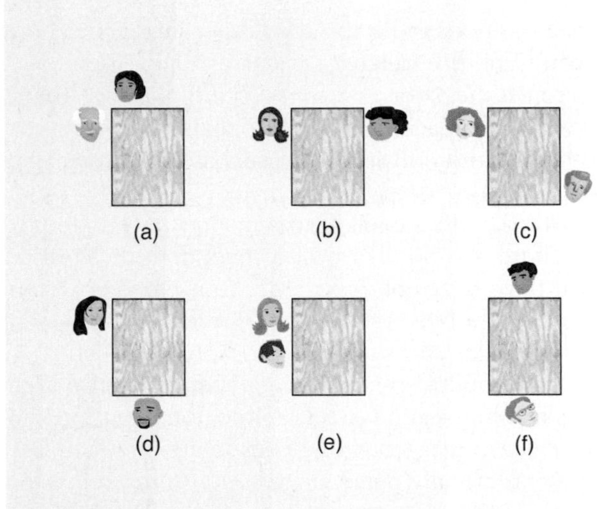

FIGURE 4.2 Seating Patterns at Rectangular Tables: (a) Corner-to-Corner, (b) Face-to-Face, (c) Distant-Opposite, (d) Corner-to-End, (e) Side-by-Side, and (f) End-to-End

Strodbeck and Hook (1961) found that those seated at the head of the table were chosen significantly more often as the leaders. Hare and Bales (1963) found that those seated in positions marked A, C, and E in Figure 4.1 were frequent talkers and frequently scored high on dominance in personality tests.

Sommer (1969) also studied several possible seating patterns (see Figure 4.2). The corner-to-corner or face-to-face arrangements were most often preferred for casual conversation, whereas cooperating pairs (people studying together) preferred the side-by-side arrangement. Competing pairs chose the face-to-face or the distant-opposite arrangements about equally often. Russo (1967) found that people seated in the more distant positions (when all positions around the

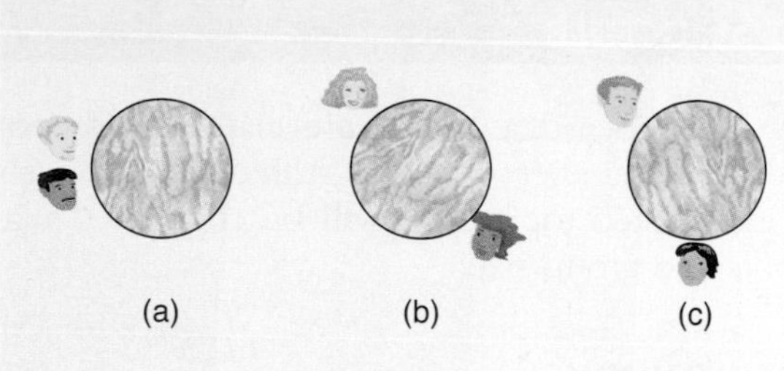

FIGURE 4.3 Seating Preferences at Round Tables: (a) Side-by-Side, (b) Distance-Opposite, and (c) Side-to-End

rectangular table were occupied) were perceived to be less friendly, less well acquainted, and less talkative than those seated closer to the person filling out the questionnaire.

Hearn (1957) verified a phenomenon known as the *Steinzor effect* (Steinzor, 1950), in which members of groups with minimal leadership directed many more comments to those facing them than to those sitting on either side. However, with a dominant, assertive leader, the behaviors were reversed, and significantly more conversation was directed to those sitting next to them.

Sommer (1965) also studied the seating preferences at round tables (Figure 4.3). He found that conversing or cooperating pairs preferred to sit side by side, whereas competing pairs preferred to sit at distant-opposite points. These findings have been corroborated with groups who had no tables at all but simply were allowed to move their chairs to positions they preferred.

All this research taken collectively indicates that groups with differing personalities and tasks will exhibit predictable seating patterns. Also, dominant seating positions at the ends of rectangular tables will tend to give some members a leadership advantage and will result in some frustration and disenchantment for those in the "blind spots" on the sides of the tables.

McCormack (1995) offers an interesting point of view regarding the physical context of one type of small group activity, namely, negotiating. He writes:

> I don't know about you, but my successful negotiations have rarely been conducted sitting around a table. More likely, the nuts and bolts of hammering out agreeable terms have been handled . . . over the course of a friendly meal in a restaurant, or by exchanging letters or faxes, or by middlemen (agents, brokers, attorneys, etc.) employing phones, meals, letters, and faxes.
>
> Almost any negotiation will go more smoothly without a table. A table in a room is a powerful symbol, and none of the symbolism is good. By putting people on opposite sides of the table, a table literally creates a divisive barrier. It formalizes the proceedings, which stiffens people and reminds them to put on their "game face." If it's a big table in a big room, it seems to attract extra people to fill up its many seats—and additional people tend to complicate rather than simplify a negotiation.
>
> I think you can accomplish much more outside of the traditional business environment. That's why I've always liked golf courses, restaurants, sports events, and other hospitable settings for many of my negotiations. The quasi-social environment seems to put people at ease and make them more agreeable. (p. 88)

Group Size and Structure

Group structure refers to the idea that groups are made up of people who are related to one another in a number of ways. Although group structure may include a number of interrelated topics, we will be concerned with only two: communication networks and group size.

COMMUNICATION NETWORKS

The research on communication networks commonly describes five different networks, which are illustrated in Figure 4.4. Lipman-Blumen and Leavitt (1999) found that the central person in a network such as the wheel usually becomes the leader and enjoys the position more than persons on the periphery, whose communication is much more restricted. The central person can communicate with any of them, but they must direct *all* of their comments through the center. Both the chain and the Y networks have characteristics similar to the wheel. In contrast, the circle and the all-channel patterns are much less centralized and are sometimes leaderless.

A person who dominates the discussion will sometimes create a network similar to the wheel. Although this may be more centralized and efficient, it results in dependence on the leader and lower group satisfaction for everyone but the leader. The chain or the Y network allows members to communicate with one or two other persons, but not with all others in the group. This produces subgroups, decreased satisfaction, and a relatively poor amount of idea sharing.

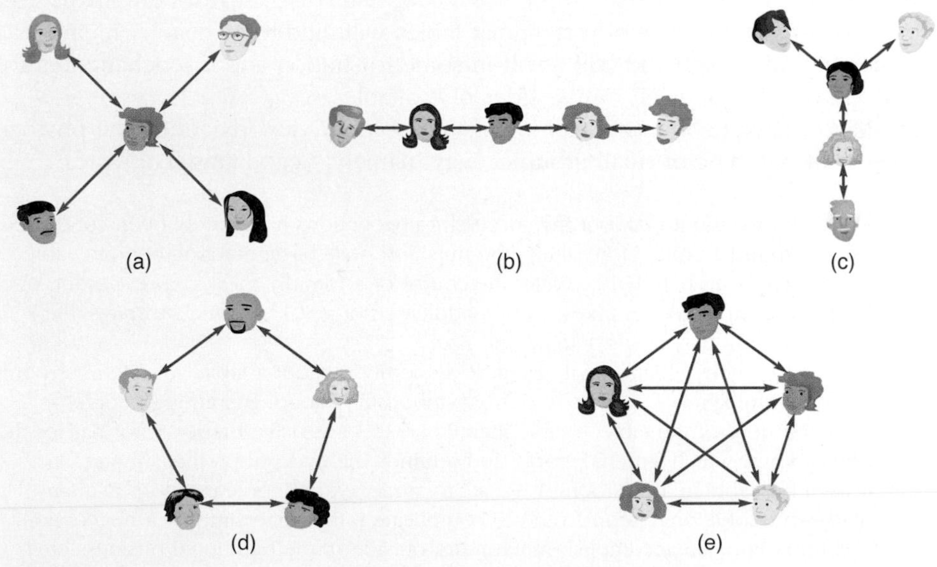

FIGURE 4.4 Communication Networks: (a) Wheel, (b) Chain, (c) Y, (d) Circle, and (e) All-Channel

The all-channel network may be relatively slow, but it is superior in terms of idea sharing and member satisfaction. Feedback is more immediate, and as a result, accuracy of communication is better. Lipman-Blumen and Leavitt (1999) summarized the findings of 18 group network studies by concluding that *centralized networks,* such as the chain and the wheel, are better for solving simple problems, such as identifying colors or picturelike symbols. However, when the problem is complex (as most real-life problems are), the *decentralized networks,* such as the circle and the all-channel, are faster and more accurate and result in higher member satisfaction. Clearly, the all-channel network is the most desirable for most of the problem-solving situations a group is likely to encounter. An example of a centralized network is one in which a boss requires that all information pass through him or her.

The communication networks that we have discussed assume that group members are in the same location, but these networks also have definite applications in the virtual meeting space. The emerging Internet generation has many members who prefer teams and small groups to organize online when distance prevents frequent face-to-face meetings. They must use cell phones and instant messaging to communicate (Network-Centric Advocacy, 2003). The communication networks that we have discussed—the wheel, chain, circle, and all-channel—all apply to virtual meeting technologies as well.

GROUP SIZE

Perhaps one of the questions most frequently asked by students of small group interaction is this: What is the best-size group to work with? On the one hand, it seems that a relatively small group would be more efficient; on the other, larger groups would have more resources. A great deal of research has been conducted on this question, and some fairly clear findings emerge.

Discussion groups of only two people may find themselves deadlocked on many questions. They also suffer the disadvantage of having too few members to contribute ideas. Groups of three are still too small and tend to result in two-against-one coalitions. Groups of four begin to be effective but, because of their even number of members, may end up with tie votes on decisions. Numerous experts advise that the optimum group size appears to be five. This size seems to be small enough for meaningful interaction yet large enough to generate an adequate number of ideas (Kameda et al., 1992).

As groups grow larger than five, members complain that the group is too large and that they are not able to participate as often as they would like. Also, as size gets larger, there is an increasing tendency for subgroups to form, which may carry on side conversations that annoy the rest of the group and detract from the group progress. Groups of 10 or more tend to spend an inordinate amount of time simply organizing themselves, so that more attention is diverted from the task and toward simply maintaining the group's functioning.

The influence of the number of members within a group is mixed with other variables, such as the function of the group and its membership composition. Luft (1984) concludes, "Cohesion tends to be weaker and morale tends to be lower in larger groups than in comparable smaller ones. How often groups meet varies inversely with size and duration and directly with closeness of feelings" (p. 23).

For example, one study found that the top leadership groups of 47 companies averaged 3.39 members each (Haleblian & Finkelstein, 1993). The study also found that companies with a top leadership group that practiced democratic decision making were more profitable than those with a group that was dominated by the boss.

As the group's size increases arithmetically (linearly), the potential number of interactions increases geometrically (exponentially). Bostrom (1970, p. 257) shows how rapidly these interaction patterns multiply. In a dyad (two people), only two relationships are possible, *A* to *B* and *B* to *A*, but in a triad (three people), there are nine possibilities:

A to *B*	*B* to *C*	*A* to *B* and *C*
A to *C*	*C* to *B*	*B* to *A* and *C*
B to *A*	*C* to *A*	*C* to *A* and *B*

As the following figures show (Bostrom, 1970, p. 258), when group size increases from two to eight members, the number of possible interactions increases by more than 1,000:

Number in Group	***Interactions Possible***
2	2
3	9
4	28
5	75
6	186
7	441
8	1,056

Bostrom concludes from his study, "The data here seem to indicate that the individual who sends more than he receives is not only more often chosen as a good discussant but is also more satisfied with the discussion than the member who receives more than he sends; . . . satisfaction apparently comes from talking, not listening" (p. 263). More recently, researchers from Bain & Co., the famous consulting firm, argue that once you've got **7 people** in a decision-making group, each additional member reduces decision effectiveness by **10 percent**. Thus, a group of **17 or more** rarely makes any decisions (Blenko, Mankins, & Rogers, 2010).

Social loafing refers to the decreased effort of each member in the group. This occurs more as the number of people in a group increases. Social impact theory states that when the social pressure for a group member is only to complete a portion of the task, group member motivation is decreased (About.com, 2005b). Research suggests that social loafing occurs because participants perceive that their individual efforts cannot be identified and/or evaluated. This was originally identified in a study in which subjects were asked to pull on a rope in a tug-of-war. When they pulled one against one, they pulled 100 percent. When a second person was added to each side, the effort went down to 93 percent. When a third person was added, the effort went down to 85 percent. If up to 8 people were added on each side, the individual effort went all the way down to 49 percent (Irwin, Hopkins, Payne, & Adams, 2010, p. 150). Perhaps you have experienced this in your teams with class projects. Most students complain that not all members "pull their share" of the work. In situations where our performance can be identified and evaluated, there is interest in doing well (Brutus & Donia, 2010). However, where our performance may be more anonymous, and therefore free from evaluation, apprehension is reduced and social loafing tends to increase. Forsyth (1999) suggests the following guidelines to minimize social loafing:

1. *Increase personal involvement.* When people feel that a poor group performance will affect them personally, they do not loaf.
2. *Minimize free riding.* Free riding tends to decrease as the group size is kept smaller.
3. *Clarify group goals.* Clear goals stimulate more productivity.
4. *Set high standards.* Groups that set high goals tend to outperform those that set lower goals.
5. *Increase collective efficacy.* Motivation is greatest when people think that the goal is within their reach.
6. *Increase unity.* People work harder for groups that are important to them. (pp. 291–94)

In a more recent study, Stark, Shaw, and Duffy (2007) developed a multilevel interactive model for predicting social loafing behavior in groups and tested this model in a study of 367 individuals working in 102 groups during a four-month period. Study results revealed the importance of integrating both personal (preference for group work and winning orientation) and situational (task interdependence) factors in predicting social loafing. Preference for group work was consistently and negatively related to social loafing behavior (self-reported and peer rated), and this relationship was moderated by both winning orientation and task interdependence. As predicted, group members were more likely to self-report social loafing when their preference for both group work and winning orientation was low. Peer-rated social loafing was most likely when preferences for group work, winning orientation, and task interdependence were all low, as predicted.

Further recommendations include recognizing each group member by pointing him or her out and clarifying the member's individual task to the group. Collective rewards for the group will also put more pressure on each individual who is contributing to the end result of the group. This point leads us to the concept of *social facilitation*. Social facilitation theory focuses on the impact an audience has on performance. Some individuals perform their tasks better while in the presence of the group, while others perform better on their own (About.com, 2005b). The key is to find out which context facilitates group member performance to capitalize on this information.

After studying group size in many kinds of groups, Barnard (1991) found that group consensus drops off significantly as the group gets larger than five.

As a result of these findings, it would seem desirable to keep the group size to about five *whenever possible,* unless some other objective, such as increased widespread participation, seems to be worth increasing the group size. Even when increasing participation (for example, including all members of a fraternity or sorority) is the goal, subcommittees of about five allow widespread participation *as well as* the efficiency and satisfaction of working in a small group. This optimal size, however, depends on the type of group. Five is the recommended size for a problem-solving group. Obviously, a work group, a family group, or even some problem-solving groups may require a different number of members, depending on the situation.

Types of Groups

One of the confounding problems in the study of small groups is the variety in the types of groups. It is obvious that certain critical differences will emerge when the term *group* is applied to studies of primitive tribes, street gangs, factory work groups, and artificially formed laboratory groups. Although there may be some important similarities among these groups, we would also expect to find some real confusion resulting from attempts to compare different groups across the board. In addition, it seems likely that differing group types will have differing effects on subsequent interaction and group outcomes or end results. For example, social groups will interact differently than work groups, and the outcomes of their separate group interactions will be different. In this section, we will look at six commonly recognized types of groups.

PRIMARY GROUPS

> *By primary groups I mean those characterized by intimate face-to-face association and cooperation. They are primary in several senses, but chiefly in that they are fundamental in forming the social nature and ideals of the individual.*
>
> —Charles Horton Cooley, 1909

Primary groups usually include one's family and closest friends. Certainly, the vast majority of attitudes and values people hold are a result of the influences of their primary groups. Primary groups influence self-concept as well as personality from childhood to adulthood. The members of our primary groups are sometimes referred to as our *significant others,* because they are probably the most important people in our lives. Although we may sometimes develop deep friendships from associations on the job, in school, and so forth, family members usually remain our most significant others throughout our lives. In fact, Brooks (2011) cites research that our friendship group has even more influence over us than previously thought. For example, if your friends are obese, you are more likely to be obese. If your friends smoke, you are more likely to smoke. If your friends are happy (or lonely), you are also more likely to be like your friends in either case (p. 193).

Obviously, the nuclear family has undergone drastic changes in modern times. For example, the divorce rate has doubled (now at 50 percent) since 1965.

Sixty percent of second marriages also fail. One-third of the children born in the 1990s will live in stepfamilies, and one-fourth of the children in America are being raised by single parents. Over one-fifth of the children born today are born to unwed mothers. "An astonishing two-thirds of all mothers are in the labor force, roughly double the rate in 1955, and more than half of all mothers of infants are in the work force" (Footlick, 1990, p. 16; see also Blankenhorn, 1995).

These statistics are even more dramatic when combined with some other research findings. Research from the *Journal of Pediatrics* shows that "latchkey" children are twice as likely to use cigarettes, alcohol, and marijuana as are youngsters who are cared for by adults after school.

And yet, in spite of all its shortcomings, the family is still one of the most important sources of gratification in our lives. Research reports that 81 percent of those surveyed listed the family as one of their top two sources of pleasure, with friends the next-most-mentioned source.

Families take many forms. In some cultures, *joint families* exist, with many generations of a family living under the same roof. For example, in India, male children generally remain in the family home with their children. Family members equally distribute tasks and share a large common area in their homes. However, this type of family arrangement is becoming less and less common (Wikipedia, 2004).

The annual national survey of incoming college freshmen revealed that 67 percent rated getting married and raising a family as one of the highest of their life goals. Only "becoming an authority in his or her field" (72 percent) and "being very well off financially" (73 percent) rated higher (*Chronicle of Higher Education,* September 6, 1989, p. 17).

CASUAL AND SOCIAL GROUPS

Casual and social groups include neighborhood groups, fraternities, bowling teams, golf foursomes, and, in some cases, street gangs. Although these relationships may be relatively short-lived, their impact on behavior can be quite profound. In 2003, the University of California at Los Angeles conducted a study which revealed that the emotional distress caused by being left out of a social group actually caused blood flow to the portion of the brain that is stimulated by physical pain (Paul, 2005). Belonging to casual and social groups fulfills a need for belongingness, while being excluded from such groups can actually cause physical pain.

Mydans (1990b) reported the following on California street gangs:

> Separating their gang identities from their home lives, the South Bay Family members give themselves nicknames they carry in elaborate tattoos around the backs of their necks. . . . They are "wanna bes," with nothing happening around them to show them it's real dangerous, until they run afoul of real gang members, and then they end up dead.
>
> Bare chests, tattoos, Budweiser beer, . . . seemed to be the fashion. . . . There were knives and a deer rifle in evidence, and some said they had pistols. . . . "Right or wrong, your bros are your bros." (p. B4)

One study by Cherry (1996) of 200 white, middle-class youths in Denver found that students fall into one of four categories: (1) the popular cliques, which consist of as many as 15 members, (2) the "wannabes," who occasionally get invited into the popular groups' activities, (3) the social isolates with few friends, and (4) groups of three or four friends who don't care about attaining social status and enjoy secure relationships with each other. The study found that the popular cliques keep group members dependent on group membership by randomly building up and then tearing down their individual status. The researchers concluded, "Those who attain membership in the elite clique enjoy the benefits of a more expansive social life . . . but pay for this with a greater anxiety about their place within the group" (p. D3). They also found that ridiculing individuals outside the group was a key activity of the popular clique. One member said, "It's a real risk if you want to stick up for someone because you could get rejected from the group" (p. D3). Think about the implications of this research in light of the 1999 shootings at Columbine High School in Colorado and elsewhere.

Cliques are not confined to children and young adults. Marla Paul (2005) of the *Chicago Tribune* wrote an article about cliques among women. Paul discusses the damaging emotional effects of being left out of the social group as an adult woman. Many women take exclusion from a group as if there were something wrong with them personally, thus damaging their self-esteem.

These studies of gangs and friendship groups show the profound influences that social groups have on each of us. It may very well be that we profoundly influence the social groups as well. It is worth keeping in mind that we are all creatures of experience and that these experiences help shape us for a lifetime.

EDUCATIONAL GROUPS

In educational groups (also called learning groups or enlightenment groups), members get together for the primary purpose of study or instruction. These groups may include, for example, management training seminars, orientation meetings, or quarterback clubs. Educational groups may discuss recent books and movies, child rearing, meditation, martial arts, AIDS awareness, or many other topics centering around personal development. An *enlightenment discussion* is one in which members may attempt to solve problems without having the authority to implement their decisions. Small group interaction classes frequently conduct problem-solving discussions concerning national or international issues. Unfortunately, although these groups may develop worthwhile solutions to important real-world problems, they are not usually in a position to implement them. The experience of attempting to improve problem-solving skills, however, is a worthwhile result even if the group's decision does not always affect reality. It is interesting to note that even when we *do* have the authority to implement, the results are sometimes not as dramatic or satisfying as we might like. For example, one group determined an excellent solution to a campus parking problem. The solution was accepted by the university administration. However, because of a major construction program, the parking lot was torn up and replaced by a new classroom building before the new plan could be implemented.

At Harvard Business School, each class consists of 85 people. Kelly and Kelly (1986) describe the extremely competitive class atmosphere in the "B School" classroom:

> In an eighty-minute class, one student is asked to "open" the discussion by presenting the case, analyzing the situation, and recommending an approach to solving the business problem or carrying the company forward toward its stated goals. These openings generally take between ten and twenty minutes.
>
> Then, all hell breaks loose, with eighty-four other students scrambling to argue how they would deal with the situation differently and why their approach would be better. Some teachers gently guide the discussion, others prod, while still others are highly aggressive and intimidating in their questioning. . . . In some sections, students have been known to gang up on less-qualified students, forcing them out of school early—usually between 5 and 10 percent of each section drops out or is forced out in the first year. In other sections, people have worked hard to make sure everyone stays in by making sure that no one student performs badly in more than one or two courses. (pp. 14–15)

The classes are also broken up into smaller study groups of 10 people each. These discussion groups become a class's working units, and each is small enough for members to relate to it effectively. Students learn from each other in discussion groups. Over the course of the term, the discussion groups often become social groups and, for some, surrogate families as well. Whetten and Cameron (2005) argue persuasively on behalf of the use of small groups as a teaching methodology for virtually any subject matter.

In 1985, *The Organizational Behavior Teaching Review Journal* devoted an entire issue to the use of groups in teaching. The editor explained it this way:

> This special issue is devoted to promoting an increased understanding of why groups should be used in teaching and how they can be used effectively. These issues are becoming increasingly important to everyone in higher education, in part because there is a growing recognition that learning groups provide a potential solution to some of our most difficult pedagogical problems. (p. 1; see also Tubbs, 1994b)

Extensive research at Harvard University has shown that learning in groups is both more effective and more fun than learning individually (Light, 1992).

The climate of educational groups has been changing with the advent of online classes and threaded discussion groups. This type of education shows continued promise and is increasing in popularity, from a worldwide market of $4 billion in 1998 to $15 billion in 2002. And the market has increased significantly since then. In the fall semester of 2003, 2 million students took an online class. For example, in 2004, University of North Carolina at Greensboro taught 400 students in online classes between semesters for five weeks. It calls this session *WinterSession* and is continuing to increase the number of courses offered due to the popularity of the flexibility in online coursework (*Greensboro News Record,* 2004).

Software packages such as WebCT and Blackboard and online bulletin boards have allowed educational discussion groups unlimited talking time. Large classes can be broken into threaded discussion groups, which allow five to eight students to discuss a topic in an ongoing discussion page that allows interactive responses. Many discussions can stretch over a week, while lasting only two to three hours in a traditional classroom setting. Students respond more freely without the immediate presence of an authority figure (Higher Education Academy, 2004).

Grand Canyon University (2004) asserts that the critical factors affecting students' "responses to online learning" include *access* to a computer and to the necessary technology, *attitude* toward online learning, and the relevance of assignments and the grading system to the student. The staff there also recommend tips for online discussions. The first day of class should be attended in person if possible, and the online discussion instructions should be:

- Easy to understand
- Technically simple
- Well defined with clear expectations and guidelines
- A community forum
- Combined with individual assignments and related work
- Evaluated and graded

Online classes and discussion groups have many benefits, pulling together a population that would be otherwise unavailable for traditional classes. Proponents say that online courses and discussion groups are flexible enough for students who are currently working or who have otherwise hectic schedules. At-home parents can also log into the online class without having to leave the home. International students can meet in the same virtual space and share their perspectives with other students from around the world. Critics of online classes argue that the experience of the classroom is critical in the learning process. Past research has put this opinion to the test. Grand Canyon University discusses a survey of 200 business administration students who were given the choice of an online or traditional course. The students felt that the traditional classroom experience increased effectiveness of learning and that the pace of learning was more tailored to the individual. However, students in both types of courses rated their "comprehension" of the material, the instructor's availability, and the grading structure equally. Introverted students who would otherwise not usually participate in traditional class discussions felt positive about their ability to respond to questions in online discussion formats. Online students felt that flexibility was the greatest benefit of the online class, allowing students to take classes that would otherwise not be available due to their schedules (Grand Canyon University, 2004). You will read more about other kinds of computer-assisted groups later in this chapter.

WORK GROUPS

Some of the most influential small group research ever to be conducted has occurred in work groups. The now-classic studies conducted by the Harvard Business School in the Western Electric Hawthorne plant in Chicago are a case in point. This company was a subsidiary of AT&T and manufactured telephone equipment for the Bell System.

The studies were originally designed to determine the influence of illumination on industrial productivity. It was hypothesized that improved lighting would improve productivity. The first study showed that productivity increased whether lighting levels were increased or *decreased* to a level darker than moonlight (three foot-candles). This, of course, puzzled the researchers.

A second study was conducted to determine the effect of periodic rest breaks on productivity. Once again, it was found that productivity kept increasing whether a rest break was added or taken out of the work schedule. The researchers hypothesized that the productivity increases resulted from the workers' changed social situation, increased satisfaction, and new patterns of social interaction brought about by creating an experimental condition and paying special attention to the workers. This productivity increase resulting from special attention has been called the *Hawthorne effect.*

In order more carefully to determine the influence of these social factors on productivity, a second set of studies was designed, known as the Bank Wiring Observation Room experiment. Workers were observed as they wired, soldered, and inspected switchboards or "banks" of switches. Workers were on an economic incentive system that allowed them to earn more if they produced more. The experiment showed that workers were producing far below what they were capable of producing, because of the group's social norm enforced by co-workers. The researchers referred to this as artificial restriction of output.

The group norm or unwritten rule was to set a relatively low level of work, which was called a fair day's work for a fair day's pay. Anyone who produced much more was branded a "rate buster" or a "speed king." Those who underproduced were called "chiselers," and those who might tell anything to a supervisor that would get them in trouble were called "squealers." In each case, the person who violated the group's norm was punched hard on the arm or shoulder, a punishment affectionately referred to as "binging." These social practices did, indeed, influence the workers' output more than did the opportunity to earn more money for more work. The major findings of the Hawthorne studies were summarized by Miner (1988, p. 263):

- The level of productivity is set by group norms, not by physiologic capacities.
- Noneconomic rewards and sanctions significantly affect the behavior of workers and largely limit the effect of economic incentive plans.
- Often workers act or react not as individuals but as members of groups.

It was also found that the informally chosen group leader was the best liked and that he or she best represented the values of the group. This leader was often more influential than the appointed leader (the supervisor). On the basis of these studies, management theorists began to stress (1) the importance of communication within the work group, (2) the importance of participation in the decision-making process, and (3) the potential values of democratic leadership. The emphasis on these three factors was later to be referred to as the *human relations* approach to management.

The Quorum Group, an organization dedicated to helping develop reward structures for work teams, has conducted significant research on goal setting and recognizing work group achievement. The leadership of the work group must find a meaningful way to recognize and reward group members to keep them motivated. Research has revealed that team rewards in combination with individual rewards yield positive results. It is also helpful to allow the group members to have a democratic voice in goal setting and the ways in which achievement of the goals within the group will be assessed and rewarded (Brau, 2003).

An innovation in work groups is the self-directed work team (SDWT). An SDWT is defined by Huszczo (1996) as "an intact group of employees who are responsible for a whole work process or segment that delivers a product or service to an internal or external customer" (p. 13). A national study conducted by *Industry Week* magazine in 1995 showed that of the top 25 manufacturing companies in America, 88 percent reported that they had launched SDWTs, up from 80 percent the previous year. In fact, teamwork in general has become so important that many feel that in order to get a good job in the 21st century, you have to have some experience with teams.

Autonomous work teams appear to reduce the potential for interpersonal and group conflict that may be experienced by employees. The reduction in both interpersonal and group conflict may be an operational outcome of SDWTs that encourages open discussion and "constructive controversy" without the suppression of opposing ideas. Team members must afford each other an opportunity to express opposing viewpoints. This enhances the collaborative exchange of ideas and information that may result in highly innovative decisions and improved organizational performance.

Democracy leads to better decisions in the long run because it relies on a diversity of inputs. In addition, autonomous work teams appear to reduce the negative customer experiences in product or service quality that may result from a "suboptimal" combination of technology, people, and work design (Castiglione, 2007).

Along these lines, Nancy Kranz, associate director of the University of New Hampshire Cooperative Extension, wrote a detailed article in the *Journal of Extension* (Kranz, 2004). The Cooperative Extension focuses on "collaboration" in the workplace. Her article was titled "Self-Directed Work Teams: The Antidote for 'Heroic Suicide'" and addresses the shift from the individualistic hero to the team successes of self-directed work teams. According to Kranz, work teams have become more popular with increases in diversity and technology, and these teams actually do better work than could ever be produced by the individual. Teams provide better quality, a stronger customer focus, and a compilation of experts to solve problems. Teams also meet individual needs for belongingness and development. To be successful, these teams must produce meaningful results, strengthen over time, and meet member needs. The time of individual achievement and accolades has certainly shifted and will most likely continue to do so in our global environment (Kranz, 2004).

PROBLEM-SOLVING GROUPS

Although we have looked at other types of groups, by far the greatest emphasis in group discussion textbooks has been on improving problem-solving and decision-making abilities.

The labels *task-oriented, problem-solving,* and *decision-making groups* have been used interchangeably to stress the emphasis on the cognitive end products of group discussion. Although interpersonal relations are often discussed, they are seen as not as important and as merely a means to an end (that is, to solve a problem).

One innovation is the use of *tiger teams*. These are small groups of high-performing people who are challenged by a company's executive team to tackle problems and find workable solutions. They look at issues such as these:

> What is the required solution?
>
> How will it produce superior value?
>
> How large will the potential market be?
>
> What are the costs/benefits to be derived?
>
> What are the critical factors that can make or break this?
>
> How will the company make the transition over the next two to three years? (Treacy & Wiersma, 1995, p. 171)

This is just one of many types of groups being used in organizations today.

Types of Discussion Questions

Problem-solving groups must spend a great deal of time and energy in careful deliberation. Generally, the group will be attempting to provide some answer or answers to the discussion question. Sample discussion questions include these:

1. How can we keep from eliminating the earth's ozone shield?
2. What can be done about the problem of cheating in our school?
3. How do we determine local obscenity and pornography standards?
4. What are the long-term effects of marijuana use?
5. How do we achieve equal opportunity for women and minorities?
6. How can we reduce energy consumption?
7. Should abortion or contraception be made mandatory for families that already have two children?
8. What is an acceptable level of unemployment?
9. Should marijuana be legalized?
10. Should handguns be outlawed?
11. Has the decline of civilization begun in this country?
12. How can we curb drug abuse in industry?

An effective problem-solving discussion begins with an effectively structured discussion question. First, a topic should be limited to one issue. Notice that question 7 includes both abortion and contraception. These two issues may require different answers, so only one should be included in the discussion question. An improved version of number 7 would be, "How can we help curb population growth?"

Questions of Fact. Questions of fact deal with truth and falsity: Is it or is it not so? Or they may question the nature of something. "What are the long-term effects of marijuana use?" is a question of fact. "Can the disease AIDS (acquired immune deficiency syndrome) be transmitted by casual contact in a school classroom?"

is another. "Does the Bermuda Triangle really pose a major threat to ships and planes traveling in the area?" and "Does intelligent life exist in outer space?" are questions of fact. Discussions involving questions of fact require evidence and documentation to establish whether or not the phenomenon exists. Such questions may remain somewhat or wholly unresolvable, but they are interesting to discuss anyway.

Questions of Definition. Questions of definition are fairly narrow but are often quite difficult to answer. The problem of defining obscenity and pornography has been with us for decades. The emotionalism of the debates in several U.S. states over textbook wording is but one of many examples of disagreement over what is obscene. Several years ago, the Supreme Court ruled that no one definition could be established for all communities, so each local community had to define obscenity and pornography for itself.

In the medical arena, lawsuits are arising over differences in the medical definition of death. If accident victims become organ transplant donors, what signs do doctors use to determine if the donor is dead? Cessation of heartbeat is certainly not a reliable sign, because numerous people walking around today have had their hearts stop temporarily. What about cessation of brain activity? The point is that the definition is important and is not as easily determined as it might first appear.

Questions of Value. Questions of value invoke an evaluation of the issues once the facts and the definitions have been determined. Whereas facts can be verified by others, values are personal and cultural and often differ drastically from one individual to another. Perhaps we can agree on a definition of affirmative action as *unequal* opportunity for women and minorities to undo the wrongs that have existed for decades. Yet can we agree that *unequal* opportunity of any kind is desirable? Some judges have ruled that this is still another form of discrimination (against white males) and is inconsistent with the ideals of the Equal Employment Opportunity Commission. Yet others feel strongly that reverse discrimination is required to tip the scales of justice to where they should have been a long time ago.

Differences in values are at the base of the controversies over abortion and contraception as well. Those who believe in the rights of the unborn child may see abortion as murder and may view even contraception as immoral. Those on the other side feel that the right of the individual woman to decide whether she will have a child is sacred and that this decision should not be dictated by the government or others. In such cases, the "right" answer will definitely vary depending on one's own personal and very individual value system.

Questions of Policy. Questions of policy involve finding the facts, establishing definitions, discussing values, and finally determining the ways and means of solving a problem. "What can be done to solve the problems of drug abuse?" "What should our state's policy be toward abortion?" "Should the United States provide more public service jobs for the unemployed?" "How can the misuse of handguns be reduced?" All these are examples of policy questions. Discussions regarding questions of policy are often the most complicated, because they encompass some of the other three types of discussion questions (fact, definition,

TABLE 4.2 Elements Involved in Discussion Questions

	Type of Discussion			
Elements Included	**Fact**	**Definition**	**Value**	**Policy**
Facts	X	X	X	X
Definitions		X	X	X
Values			X	X
Policies				X
Implementation				X

and value). Let us look at one topic (equal rights for women) as it might be discussed in each of the four ways:

1. *Fact:* "Do women have equal rights in this country?"
2. *Definition:* "What do we mean by the phrase *equal rights for women?*"
3. *Value:* "Is it desirable to change women's role in our society?"
4. *Policy:* "How can we achieve equal rights for women in this country?"

As you can see, the policy question assumes, to some extent, that (1) equal rights do not currently exist, (2) agreement on a definition of equal rights can be reached, (3) equal rights for women are desirable, and (4) something ought to be done to bring about equal rights for women. It is important to remember that policy discussions may bog down on these earlier questions if not all group members agree on these assumptions.

In addition to trying to find a solution to the problem, policy questions frequently must deal with the question of how to implement the solution. Should equal rights be dictated by law? Should they evolve through generations of attitude change produced by the mass media and word of mouth? If by law, should they be enforced at the local level, as with obscenity laws, or at the national level, as with laws concerning crimes against the government? Such questions deal with the specifics of how the solution actually gets implemented.

Table 4.2 summarizes the elements involved in various types of discussion questions.

Discussion Group Formats

Discussion questions may be approached in a variety of small group formats. The selection of an appropriate format depends largely on group members' own needs and circumstances. Although there are many possibilities, the following five formats are representative of most problem-solving discussions:

1. *Dialogue.* The dialogue is simply a discussion or conversation between two people. It may be conducted privately or in front of an audience.

PRACTICAL TIPS

Discussion Group Tips

The Pennsylvania Centre County READS (CCR) organization presents discussion group tips for its reading groups. Their tips are general and apply to all forms of discussion groups. An adaptation of these tips is included below (CCR, 2005):

1. Ensure that everyone in the group has some time to get acquainted so that each person can find common cause for being in the group.
2. Make sure to start and end the group at the scheduled times.
3. Let the flow of relevant conversation continue as it may lead back to the question at hand.
4. Give the group time to think before responding.
5. Give each group member equal opportunity to share his or her thoughts by encouraging quiet members while gently discouraging dominant members from monopolizing the discussion.
6. Allow thoughtful introspection time and sharing after completion of the group discussion.

2. *Panel.* The panel discussion usually involves a small number of people (up to five or six) conducting an informal discussion on a topic that they have all thought about and possibly researched beforehand. One person is appointed moderator to help move the group along on its planned agenda. Conversation is mostly spontaneous, and participants may interrupt one another.
3. *Symposium.* The symposium includes several participants, each of whom gives a short formal presentation on a prepared topic, usually built around a central theme. Participants do not interrupt each other during the formal presentations, but a less formal discussion usually follows.
4. *Forum.* A forum is a question-and-answer period designed to allow audience members to interact with the discussion group. A forum period often follows a panel discussion or a symposium. It is customary for the chairperson to introduce the panel or symposium members and to serve as a moderator for the forum.
5. *Colloquy.* A colloquy may take a number of forms, but each involves the questioning of experts by the other experts on the panel, laypersons on a second panel, or laypersons in the audience. This format is very similar to the panel discussion, except that experts are involved and a second panel of laypersons may also be involved.

Discussion Group Techniques

In addition to the major formats discussed above, there are a number of subformats or techniques that may be employed in discussion groups. These techniques are often used for short periods as *part* of a discussion group format. Popular discussion group techniques include the following:

- *Phillips 66.* Phillips 66 is a specific technique developed by J. D. Phillips. It simply allows all the members of an audience to form groups of about six people to discuss a specific topic for about six minutes and then report the group's conclusion through a spokesperson. Realistically, this technique is more useful if longer time limits are allowed (up to an hour or so). The general term for this, when time and group size are not limited to six minutes and six members, is a *buzz group* or *buzz session.* The technique offers the advantage of allowing a lot of people to participate in a fairly efficient manner. The results from all groups are compiled and used to solve the problem faced by the entire assembly.
- *Case discussion.* A case discussion is an educational discussion centered on a real or hypothetical event. The case problem or study is presented to the group, and members attempt to solve it as best they can. A case study is included at the beginning of each chapter in this book to illustrate the ways in which small group theory and research apply to real-life problems.
- *Role playing.* Role playing simply allows participants to adopt a "role" or set of behaviors other than their own. For example, quiet individuals may be assigned the role of leader, or argumentative members may be assigned the role of harmonizer or compromiser. Meek members may be asked to play the role of "devil's advocate." In each case, the individual gets an opportunity to practice a role in an attempt to build his or her group skills. This helps develop role flexibility so that participants can adopt new and different role behaviors as the need arises. Role playing also may be used to demonstrate to the rest of the group what a given role may do to a group discussion. The chronic-nonconformist role can be secretly given to one member to show how the others will react. The typical reaction is that the role player gets a lot of attention from the rest of the group for a while, but will be ignored after a time if she or he continues to deviate (see Chapter 5 for more on deviation).

  Another version of role playing is role reversal. In this case, participants try to take the part of another person (usually one with whom they have a conflict). Biracial groups, labor–management groups, and others frequently use this technique to develop empathy for the other people's points of view. It often results in funny situations, which also help relieve some of the tension. Try some of the role-playing exercises in this book to help get a feel for what role playing is like.
- *Fishbowl.* In the fishbowl technique, one small group attempts to solve a problem for a specified period of time (often 30 minutes), while a second group, seated around the outside of the first group, observes the process. After the discussion, the observer group gives feedback to the first group as to what behaviors they were able to identify as helpful or harmful to the group's progress. Then the two groups reverse positions and roles: The observers become the observed, and vice versa. This technique may be aided by the use of video equipment.

- *Conference.* A conference is a series of meetings on topics of common interest between and among people who represent different groups. For example, representatives from different colleges and universities may gather at a conference to discuss problems of finance, curriculum, community service, and other issues. Conferences often involve hundreds of people and may last several days. For the past several years, different countries have hosted world food conferences in an attempt to plan for the feeding of the world's population. Conferences may also be quite small and last a short time. The critical element is that different groups are represented. An example of the latter type of conference is the plant manager's weekly conference in a manufacturing plant where representatives from production, engineering, maintenance, inspection, personnel, and other departments get together to organize their efforts and to solve common problems.
- *NGT.* The Nominal Group Technique (NGT) was developed by Delbecq, Van de Ven, and Gustafson (1975) as a way to reduce the effects of group conformity pressure. The NGT method has six phases. First is a silent, independent generation of ideas written down on paper. Second is a round-robin listing of ideas on a large sheet of newsprint or on the blackboard so everyone can see. The third step is a clarification of points without any critique. Fourth, everyone individually ranks the ideas. Fifth is a clarification of the vote. Sixth is a final ranking of the ideas. Jarobe (1988) has found that this method results in better decisions than do less-structured group discussions. Clearly, this method incorporates the advantages of a group in that several people's ideas are used. At the same time, it minimizes the disadvantage that often occurs when group members' ideas are subject to self-censorship based on the fear of being rejected by other group members.

COMPUTER-ASSISTED GROUPS

Bill Gates (1999), CEO of Microsoft, has argued persuasively that personal computers, and especially the Internet, will continue to change virtually everything in our lives. Davis and Meyer (1998) in their book *Blur* refer to the rapidly changing speed of change as "Internet time," in which one month is roughly equivalent to one year. According to a national survey (Carr, 2011) virtually 100 percent of U.S. college students own computers and majority of them check out the Web daily. (Horovitz, 1999), nearly 85 percent of the 15 million U.S. college students own computers and more than 60 percent of them check out the Web daily. Many of them report spending up to half their waking hours online. This gives a whole new meaning to the term *campus life.* In fact, one writer has labeled college students as "natives" to digital technology, and their parents as migrants (from previous methods of communicating) (Turkel, 2011, p. 202). this as "e-havior" (Black, 1999).

The Internet permits communication cost reductions, improvements in information management, internal and external communications through comprehensive email facilities, listservs and newsgroups, and access to information from external sources through the searching of websites. Intranets bring benefits such as enabling activities including communication, information retrieval and

PRACTICAL TIPS

Here are 10 of the most common "team traps" to avoid:

1. *Leader abdication.* The leader fails to give the group the needed direction.
2. *Successionless planning.* There is no plan for who will lead the team when the leader leaves.
3. *Downsizing.* The organization lays off members of the team.
4. *Political suicide.* The team supports ideas contrary to the larger organization's best interests.
5. *Team arrogance.* The team thinks that it is more important than the organization of which it is a part.
6. *Undefined accountability.* It is not clear who is responsible for what.
7. *Short-term focus.* This is counter to thinking of the long-term best interests of the organization.
8. *Disruptive team member.* Such a person may ruin the rest of the team.
9. *Poor teamwork habits.* Individuals feel that they are too important for the team.
10. *Decision by default.* Nobody can agree so decisions keep getting put off. No decision becomes a decision. (Rayner, 1996, pp. 15–18)

database access, and their ability to establish a company information system. Companies are making employee profiles, skills inventories, policy manuals and company phone directories available to their employees.

On the basis of 500 mailed survey questionnaires, Ngai and colleagues (2008) made some observations on the extent to which HR professionals use the Internet to support HRM (human resource management) in service and manufacturing organizations in Hong Kong. About 77 percent of the respondents used a computer daily during office hours in relation to HR activities. It seems that many organizations are increasingly using information technology to carry out their HR activities. Over 90 percent of the organizations involved in this study were either fully or partially connected to the Internet, regardless of their size. For many organizations, Internet connection has become a business resource. In particular, many organizations have realized that the Internet can enhance communication and coordination.

"Can absence make a team grow stronger?" According to a 2004 *Harvard Business Review* study, data suggest that group and team members can perform just as effectively spread out across the globe as they do in person. Virtual groups have actually been more productive in some cases than in-person teams when using online meeting or chat rooms. Anytime disagreements arise, a teleconference can be conducted to resolve issues. Virtual groups can also consist of the best experts from around the world rather than those who are readily available with possibly less expertise (Majchrzak et al., 2004).

A common Microsoft advertisement said, "Now you won't cringe when you hear 'We need your team's collective input by noon.'" Through new software, small groups can now do computer-supported cooperative work by means of groupware (such as GroupSystems). If you would like to try this out now, visit www.webex.com. Groupware uses the same input as regular small group communication but changes the mechanics of the interaction. Individuals in the same room type in their ideas on their own computers, which then put the ideas on a large screen for everyone to see. The key difference is that nobody knows whose ideas are whose. In computerized interaction, the group members are freer and less constrained by the social influence we usually feel in the presence of others. Small group software may also have built-in mechanisms for managing feedback.

Rash (1989) explains groupware this way:

> Groupware . . . is designed to enhance the functioning of a group in much the same way that individual productivity software helps the individual. The difference is that groupware, to be effective, must enhance the interaction of the people in a group. Because of the nature of a group of people, groupware faces several challenges. First, people who work together are not necessarily located together. . . . Second, a group consists of individuals who may have their own ideas about what work they need to do and how it should be accomplished. (p. 135)

Much groupware recognizes the problem of group tension. Groupware enables a group of individuals "who have their own ideas" to work together more easily than would be the case if the same people were together in a room.

Group meetings are essential. According to Duarte and Snyder (1999), team members spend most of their working time in group meetings. In addition, people must now absorb more information than in the past, partly because computers contribute more information. The natural response is to use computers to process the information that computers make available. Computers allow the integration of significantly more data and more seamless integration of decisions from group to group. These benefits make computer support particularly attractive to work group participants:

> Those involved in developing or implementing work group support will find more receptive users when they are involved in larger groups, groups with multidepartmental membership, or groups that spend more time in meetings. Additionally, users with positive attitudes toward computers and group work or those who now use some form of support for group work are likely adopters. (Satzinger & Olfman, 1992, p. 105)

Even with the aid of computers, the most common problem that virtual teams face is in their ability to connect with other group members. Individuals in virtual groups have their own tasks in many cases, and if they do not meet online as a group enough, they may have no idea how their work fits into the big picture. It is important to be able to connect with other group members to get a sense of how the project is going overall (McNamara, 2005).

Idea Generation and Anonymity

Groupware (also called *electronic meeting systems,* or *EMS*) has been used in face-to-face settings for a number of years. According to Duarte and Snyder

(1999), there are five different ways that EMS may be used to facilitate face-to-face groups:

1. *Idea generation/brainstorming.* Individuals can generate ideas anonymously from their keyboards and can see all ideas simultaneously on one or more screens. According to Marie Flately of San Diego State University (1999), "The electronic room levels the playing field. Often women are less confident speaking in meetings, but in the electronic room each person is equal. . . . The anonymity is powerful to people who are shy. They can offer ideas and objections, even to the company president" (p. 14) (for further information about SDSU's electronic room, contact george_easton@sdsu.edu).
2. *Idea grouping/issue analyzing.* This function collectively allows groups to move ideas into different categories.
3. *Voting.* Groups can use this to gauge the degree of consensus in the group. We have used this in retreats at our college to allow the entire faculty of 90 to write and revise our college mission statement.
4. *Outlining.* Group members can jointly organize ideas into outlines that the entire group can then review.
5. *Annotating.* Individual group members may comment or make suggestions about any of the ideas generated. (Duarte & Snyder, 1999, p. 36)

"There is an intuitive appeal to the belief that groups, with the diversity of views and experiences that they can bring to a topic, should be effective at generating ideas" (Valicich, Dennis, & Nunamaker, 1992, p. 50). Investigations of structured and unstructured idea-generation techniques have compared the performance of "interacting groups" that use computers with that of individuals working separately whose ideas are pooled. To assess whether "process losses" are inhibitors of verbal, face-to-face idea generation, but not of computer-mediated idea generation, *production blocking, free riding,* and *evaluation apprehension* were evaluated by Valicich and his colleagues in a computerized environment. Production blocking occurs when "only one member of a group can speak at a time. . . . Free riding refers to the tendency of some group members to rely on other group members to accomplish the task without their contributions. . . . Evaluation apprehension refers to the fear of direct reprisals or negative evaluation of contributions that may cause individuals to withhold ideas" (p. 55). The researchers concluded that prior experience within single groups acted to both stimulate new ideas and reduce redundancies.

This study introduced an element of computer-assisted small groups that is not present without the computer anonymity. It is possible that "reduced inhibitions may encourage greater participation of junior or shy group members and the expression of unpopular, novel, or heretical opinions. Anonymity may also lead to the expression of uninhibited comments and the use of strong language" (Valicich et al., 1992, p. 55). One "investigation studying small groups using a computer-mediated idea-generation system found that anonymous [that is, computer] groups generated more unique ideas and had higher levels of participation, yet were more critical and less satisfied than nonanonymous groups" (p. 55).

PRACTICAL TIPS

When to Use Video Conferencing.

Videoconferencing works well when:

- You need the benefit of face-to-face contact and want to save the time and expense associated with traveling to another location.
- Your goal is to provide information such as briefings or training classes.
- You are broadcasting presentations to many employees.

When to Avoid Video Conferencing.

Videoconferencing does not work as well when:

- The time lag will be distracting or detrimental to the communication.
- The added social context of face-to-face communication is needed—for example, if the group members have never met, videoconferencing is not as good for building rapport.
- The success of your meeting relies on short bursts of input from all participants. In videoconferencing, comments are generally longer and come from fewer people. Also, because of the electronic time lag, sometimes participants talk over each other.
- The group must discuss sensitive issues. Participants may be more honest and perceptive in a face-to-face meeting.
- The group misses out on side discussions that often result in new ideas during a face-to-face meeting.

Source: Adapted from Kristen Bell DeTienne, *Guide to Electronic Communication* (Upper Saddle River, NJ: Prentice Hall, 2002), p. 79. (For more on this topic, log onto **http://www.grantbow.com/groupware.html**.)

Another study (Sproull & Kiesler, 1991) also looked at the masking of group participants by a computer. The researchers concluded that "the results [of a test with groups containing both high- and low-status members] confirmed that the proportion of talk and influence of higher-status people decreased when group members communicated by electronic mail." The computer created a group of equals: "People who regarded themselves as physically unattractive reported feeling more lively and confident when they expressed themselves over the network. Others who had soft voices or small stature reported that they no longer had to struggle to be taken seriously in a meeting." These networked groups also "generated more proposals for action than did traditional ones" (pp. 119–20).

A study by Raja and Hwang (1992)—measuring the variables of (1) decision time, (2) number of alternatives generated, (3) satisfaction with the decision, and (4) decision quality—found that large groups (of nine members) had higher-quality results, did not use less time, and did not have enhanced decision satisfaction.

Raja and Hwang conclude, "It is likely that the face-to-face human interaction without the presence of a computer may increase satisfaction with the final decision due to the human and social aspects associated with such interaction" (p. 17).

Leadership

With the advent of computers in every organization, leaders are often "dealing with new or unique decision-making situations, for which there are no standard processes or precedents. In these types of decision-making situations, [leaders] often do not have the breadth or depth of knowledge to make decisions, causing them to operate under greater uncertainty" (Vickers, 1992, p. 790). A recent study by David Pauleen (2004) explored effective leadership and virtual teams. In this study, seven virtual team managers and leaders were surveyed regarding the emphasis that they put on relationship building with their virtual team members. All seven team leaders agreed that developing a relationship is critical prior to embarking on a virtual team project. In another study by Crystal Hoyt (2003), published in *Small Group Research,* transformational and transactional leadership style in small groups were assessed. Transformational leadership, which focuses much more on relationship building, actually increased virtual group unity and satisfaction but inhibited the group's quantitative performance. These results were similar for in-person groups as well. It is interesting that similar leadership styles work for both in-person and virtual groups in similar ways.

In these small group situations, leaders *must* rely on their groups to process the multitude of data. However, they must also be cautious about what they share. Uncertainty can arise from sharing pertinent information, sharing risks, sharing ideas, or sharing commitment. Uncertainty leads to two problems: (1) coping with information complexity, and (2) coping with relatively unstructured know-how or knowledge. The solution for these leaders is to improve the efficiency and effectiveness of decision groups by saving time and resources and producing a "better quality outcome from the group's activity." Vickers suggests that "to maximize process gain and minimize process loss, a group requires collaborative support, such as that offered by GDSS (group decision support systems)" (p. 790). According to Vickers:

> [If] actual effectiveness = potential effectiveness – process losses + process gains, [then] decision quality is reduced when unproductive group conflict (process loss) reduces the quality of information output. Ideally, effective communication within a group is maintained by achieving levels of conflict that are appropriate to the problem being tackled—process gain. (p. 791)

For leaders, computer-aided communication can be an important means of influencing a group's methods and capabilities. Sproull and Kiesler (1991) write:

> [Leaders] are often attracted to networks by the promise of faster communication and greater efficiency. [But it could be that] the real potential of network communication has less to do with such matters than with influencing the overall work environment and the capabilities of employees. [Leaders] can use networks to foster new kinds of task structures and reporting relationships. They can use networks to change the conventional patterns of who talks to whom and who knows what. (p. 116)

These computer-aided communication channels could bring out multiple new resources by tapping individuals who, by virtue of their organizational stature, would not otherwise be tapped. And this same environment can also alleviate leaders' workloads as it nurtures growth.

Numerous organizations have started offering virtual group leadership development programs to help leaders with the challenges of managing computer-assisted and virtual teams. For example, the Fisher Group (2004) from Beaverton, Oregon, introduced a new course called "The Distance Manager." As corporations globalize, the need for virtual interaction and distance expertise is growing, and organizations like the Fisher Group are hot on the trail. The Fisher Group strongly believes that managing virtual teams requires a new and different set of skills than managing groups face-to-face. The coaching and leadership consulting industry will most certainly continue to evolve with the current trend.

Computer-Assisted Groups: Where Are They Going?

What is happening now? Do small group interactions need to be redefined? Some trends are already moving into the mainstream, like intercontinental links, simultaneous work programs, and scientific collaborations. In coming years, computer technology will play an increasing role in group interaction. Opper (1988) writes, "Macro trends in business portend well for the future of groupware. These trends say companies will be trying to do more work faster with fewer people, that the 'time to decision' will be shorter, and that small groups rather than individuals or large committees will be the agents getting things done" (p. 282).

Logistical problems will cease:

> The information marketplace will also change how we work with geographically distant partners. An increasing number of conferences are already conducted over video links, but these conferences still require all the participants to be in the right place at the right time. New approaches to such collaborations will free people to take part in delayed and distributed meetings. (Dertouzos, 1991, p. 66)

Maybe someday Congress will meet electronically, thereby letting senators and representatives remain in the districts they represent.

As small groups foster democracy, so do computers. Dertouzos (1991) claims:

> There is no question . . . that computers and networks will democratize human communication. Nearly everyone would be able to put his or her ideas, concerns and demands before all others. This freedom will undoubtedly bring sociological consequences, including the formation of electronic tribes that can span physical distance. . . . People are neither so naive nor devoid of instincts for self-preservation and control that they will surrender their humanity to their tools.

People will use their tools to make themselves more efficient and productive, but they won't forget what is best done "live."

Computer technology will most help those who know what they want to accomplish. "Investigators say that real gains will come when groups use collaboration technology to reshape the way they work together. . . . [Organizations] employing collaboration technology to 'capture and reflect on' how they make

PRACTICAL TIPS

For Virtual Success

In 2004, Catherine Roseberry offered the following "tips for virtual success" to increase the productivity of virtual teams. The following is an adaptation of her list of suggestions (About.com, 2005b):

1. Build individual relationships with group members, and give them a forum to develop relationships with each other.
2. Get a feel for the motivations of each group member. Will they succeed in a virtual environment? Do they need face-to-face contact?
3. Ask whether each person has worked in a virtual group or team before. If not, it is important to orient them to the norms of the process.
4. Ask whether each team member is independent enough to work successfully on this type of team.
5. Decide up front with your team which communication vehicles will be used. This includes instant messaging, voice mail, email, group chat rooms, teleconferencing, and videoconferencing technologies.
6. Determine the frequency of group meetings. Will the group meet on a regular basis or communicate when necessary on a revolving site?
7. Discuss the modes of communication at the beginning of each meeting. What positive experiences are members having? What negative experiences are they having?
8. Address problems immediately when they arise to reach resolution. Problems for virtual teams can grow exponentially faster than those of face-to-face groups.
9. Always make yourself accessible to the group members.

decisions will find they have a 'learning-curve accelerator' that will hone their competitive edge" (Corcoran, 1988, p. 112).

For excellent summaries of new groupware packages available, see Coleman (1995, 1996), Field (1996), and Lipnack and Stamps (1997).

For a wealth of information on virtual teams, visit Carter McNamara's (2005) website at http://www.mapnp.org/library/grp_skill/virtual/virtual.htm.

REVIEW OF THE SYSTEMS APPROACH

In this chapter, we looked at some of the elements that constitute the internal influences of our model. In systems theory, these elements would be called part of the *throughput* of small groups. Early in the chapter, we examined physical environment, including territoriality and seating behavior in groups. As suggested by the Vietnam negotiations, different cultures have drastically differing perceptions of how to position furniture or whether to have furniture at all. This illustrates the way in which relevant background factors affect internal influences, such as physical environment. For example, in Western culture, we typically place furniture along the walls with open space in the middle of the room. The Japanese tend to cluster furniture in the center of the room, leaving the space along the walls open. Also, imagine conducting a group discussion while seated barefoot on the floor around very low tables. This should help you picture the importance of background factors in relation to seating behaviors.

Probably the most important internal influence in the model is the type of group. Obviously, the procedures, norms, expectations, and outcomes of a work group will be radically different from those of a social group. For example, a norm of openness in both self-disclosure and candid feedback to others exists in many social groups. However, you might find that telling your boss or friend exactly what you do *not* like about him or her is highly inappropriate. The type of group has an enormous impact on the way in which a group functions.

We also looked at the literature on communication networks. We saw that the all-channel network is best for group member satisfaction, whereas the wheel produces the fastest results. As our systems approach suggests, determining the "best" network depends, among other things, on the demands of the situation.

When we discussed the issue of group size, we saw the connection between the type of group and the appropriate group size. All other things being equal, five seems to be the optimum size for a problem-solving group. However, the optimum size for a group discussion in a classroom may be radically different from that of a work group on an assembly line or in a large office. Even the idea of the "right" size family group depends on each of our relevant background factors. Typically, people have quite strong feelings about what the "right" size is for a family. These feelings usually result from a lifetime of attitude formation influenced by parents, friends, and, perhaps, religious affiliation.

Group size is also related to the idea of communication networks. As group size increases, the all-channel network begins to bog down in confusion, and a more controlled network tends to be more appropriate. Group size and the consequences of group interaction are also connected. Larger groups tend to produce lower levels of satisfaction and interpersonal relations among participants. Bostrom's research, cited in this chapter, is very revealing. It showed that most people like to talk far more than they like to listen in groups.

In our examination of problem-solving groups, we looked at different discussion group formats and techniques (for example, panel, symposium, role playing, fishbowl, and conference). Obviously, there is a connection between the type of group and the appropriate format. Can you imagine the U.S. president's cabinet engaging in role-playing and fishbowl simulations? Certainly, educational groups use these formats and techniques with a great deal of success, but work groups would be more likely to use panels, symposiums, and conferences.

The type of group format is also related to the desired group outcome. If personal growth is the goal, then role playing or fishbowls are helpful. On the other hand, if the group goal is to solve a task-oriented problem, such as how to cut energy consumption by 10 percent, the panel discussion or the use of groupware is probably more appropriate. As usual, it all depends.

EXERCISE

1. Case Study Discussion

Divide into five-person groups and discuss the case below.

AGENCIES TIPTOE AMONG LEGAL MINES—ADMINISTRATION ASKS COURT TO RERULE ON GAY CADET

Jim Abrams, Associated Press

WASHINGTON—The administration sought a rehearing Thursday of court orders to commission gay midshipman Joseph Steffan, but sidestepped the larger battle over whether banning gays from the military is constitutional.

The Justice Department, filing the petition on behalf of the Defense Department, focused instead on the narrower issue of whether the U.S. Circuit Court of Appeals in Washington exceeded its authority in ruling that Steffan be given his Naval Academy diploma and commissioned as an officer.

The court, it said, raised "the gravest legal questions" in regard to the principle of separation of powers that holds that military officers must be appointed by the president and approved by the Senate.

The three federal judges on Nov. 16 ruled that expelling Steffan solely on the basis of his sexual orientation violated the equal protection guarantee of the Constitution.

The court considered the old policy banning homosexuals in the military, but its ruling could also raise constitutional questions for the somewhat more liberal policy the Clinton administration has put into effect.

The petition expresses the Pentagon's "profound disagreement" with the opinion that the old policy was unconstitutional. But it states that "it is not necessary to take the extraordinary step of rehearing" the constitutional issue because the court looked only at the old policy.

After one of the most divisive debates of President Clinton's first year in office, the Pentagon earlier this month issued regulations for its new "don't ask, don't tell, don't pursue" policy that forbids homosexual practices but does not necessarily discharge members merely for their sexual orientation.

David Smith, a spokesman for the National Gay and Lesbian Task Force, said the decision not to take up the constitutional question was positive, but said he was angry any appeal was being made.

"Appealing any aspect of this ruling conflicts dramatically with the president's oft-stated position that there should be no discrimination within the services," Smith said.

Steffan's attorney, Evan Wolfson of the Lambda Legal Defense & Education Fund, said they were "disappointed by the government's petty effort to continue denying an outstanding midshipman his commission."

He said Lambda, a gay legal rights organization, and the American Civil Liberties Union will file a court challenge to the Pentagon's new policy on gays within the next few weeks.

Steffan, now 29, is in law school at the University of Connecticut. (*Ann Arbor News,* December 31, 1993, p. A6)

After you have arrived at group agreement, each group should share its reaction and the reasoning behind it. Discuss the different reactions among the groups.

READINGS: Overview

In the first reading, Gibson and Hanna offer some practical tips for participation in groups. In the second reading, Adler and Elmhorst offer some additional sage advice for getting the most out of group meetings.

Reading 4.1 Participating in Groups

James W. Gibson and Michael S. Hanna

The advantages of group decision making cannot have an effect unless individual members make certain commitments to the group. Every member of every group assumes four responsibilities by joining the group. Every time they agree to engage in decision making with other people, they agree to give up some of their individual sovereignty so that the group process can work. They assume an obligation to make decisions by certain ethical standards.

DO YOUR BEST

You have something to offer a group. You have knowledge. You are sensitive and analytical. You think. You feel. You believe. You cannot change your strengths and weaknesses, and you do not need to. You are okay just the way you are, and you can contribute to a group. Give your group the best that you have. Do not hold back.

Sometimes individual group members do hold back. For example, people sometimes decline to take a leadership role because they think someone else might want to do it or because they resent a perceived manipulation by others. If you agree to involve yourself in a decision-making group, commit yourself to help that group to make the best decisions possible. If you give less, you violate a standard of excellence that is widely valued in our society.

BEHAVE RATIONALLY

Keep an open mind, listen to evidence and arguments, and withhold personal decisions until the evidence and the arguments have been presented. Behaving rationally means putting the interests of the group ahead of your own personal interests.

We have all known individuals who were unable to put aside their personal convictions in order to listen to another group member's position. These impatient people bring to the decision-making group their own private truths and their private agendas. For example, a person once served on a committee appointed by the mayor to make recommendations about how the mayor's office could improve two-way communication between the mayor and the community. A member of that group had a personal interest. The person tried to get the group

---

From James W. Gibson and Michael S. Hanna, *Introduction to Human Communication* (Dubuque, IA: Wm. C Brown, 1992). Reprinted by permission of The McGraw-Hill Companies.

to advocate the support for the improvement of the city-owned art museum. The person's idea was that the museum provided the best "out-reach" opportunity for the mayor. Unfortunately, the person did not want to talk or listen to any other ideas. A private agenda such as this interferes with a group's ability to choose the best alternative from a field of possibilities.

Rational behavior implies critical thinking, such as described in the last chapter. Do not behave irrationally. Your responsibilities to the group require that you listen carefully with an open mind, that you consider all the information, and that you work to evolve the most sensible group decisions.

Rational behavior may sometimes require great personal courage. It may mean setting aside personal animosity. It may mean agreeing to work constructively and positively with someone you do not like. It may require you to face and deal with rejection of your ideas. Even so, rational behavior is absolutely necessary. If the members of the group are not rational and do not cooperate, then the group cannot be productive. You take on an ethical responsibility to rational behavior every time you agree to work in a decision-making group.

PLAY FAIR

Group decision making is a cooperative activity. It is not a competitive event at which you champion your viewpoint. This means that group members have the responsibility to seek and to present all of the ideas and evidence, whether or not the information seems contradictory. Every member of the group has a right to expect you to play fair, just as you have a right to expect every other member to play fair. Do not engage in debate in a group decision-making meeting. As a matter of ethical responsibility, you are constrained from competing with other group members.

LISTEN AND PARTICIPATE

When you have prepared carefully and have something important to say, you want other people to listen to you. You have a right to expect them to take you seriously, to listen to you carefully, to ask you questions, to give you feedback, and to evaluate your ideas with an open mind. If they did less than that, they would be mistreating you.

Reading 4.2 A Problem-Solving Meeting

Ronald B. Adler and Jeanne Marquardt Elmhorst

PLANNING A PROBLEM-SOLVING MEETING

Successful meetings are just like interviews, presentations, letters, and memos: they must be planned.

From Ronald B. Adler and Jeanne Marquardt Elmhorst, *Communicating at Work,* 10th ed. (New York: McGraw-Hill, 2010), pp. 266–82. Reprinted by permission of The McGraw-Hill Companies.

When to Hold a Meeting

Given the costs of bringing people together, the most fundamental question is whether to hold a meeting at all. In one survey, middle and upper managers reported that over 25 percent of the meetings they attended could have been replaced by a memo, e-mail, or phone call. Other experts report that roughly half of all business meetings are unproductive. There are many times when a meeting probably isn't justified:

- The matter could be handled just as well over the phone.
- You could send a memo, e-mail, or fax and achieve the same goal.
- Key people are not available to attend.
- There isn't enough time to handle the business at hand.
- Members aren't prepared.
- The meeting is routine, and there is no compelling reason to meet.

Keeping these points in mind, a planner should call a meeting (or appoint a committee) only when all the following questions can be answered yes.

Is the Job beyond the Capacity of One Person? A job might be too much for one person to handle for two reasons: First, it might call for more *information* than any single person possesses. For example, the job of improving health conditions in a food-processing plant would probably require the medical background of a physician or other health professional, the firsthand experience of employees familiar with the work, and a manager who knows the resources available for developing and implementing the program.

Second, a job might take more *time* than one person has available. For instance, even if one employee were capable of writing and publishing an employee handbook, it's unlikely that the person would be able to handle the task and have much time for other duties.

Are Individuals' Tasks Interdependent? Each member at a committee meeting should have a different role. If each member's share of the task can be completed without input from other members, it is better to have the members co-acting under the supervision of a manager.

Consider the job of preparing the employee handbook that we just mentioned. If each person on the handbook team is responsible for a separate section, there is little need for the group to meet frequently to discuss the task: meetings would be little more than "show-and-tell" sessions. A more efficient plan might be for the group to meet at the outset to devise an outline and a set of guidelines about style, length, and so on, and then for a manager or group leader to see that each person completes his or her own section according to those guidelines.

There are times when people who do the same job can profit by sharing ideas in a group. Members of the handbook team, for example, might get new ideas about how the book could be made better from talking to one another. Similarly, sales representatives, industrial designers, physicians, or attorneys who work independently might profit by exchanging experiences and ideas. This is part of the purpose of professional conventions. Also, many companies schedule quarterly or annual meetings of people who do similar but independent work. While this may seem to contradict the requirement for interdependence of members' tasks, there is no real conflict. A group of people who do the same kind of work can often improve their individual performance through meetings by performing some of the complementary *functional roles*. For example, one colleague might serve as reality tester. ("Writing individual notes to each potential customer in your territory sounds like a good idea, but do you really have time to do that?") Another might take the job of being information giver. ("You know, there's a printer just outside Boston who can do large jobs like that just as well as your regular printer, but he's cheaper. Call me, and I'll give you the name and address.") Others serve as diagnosers. ("Have you checked the feed mechanism? Sometimes a problem there can throw the whole machine out of whack.") Some can just serve as empathic listeners. ("Yeah, I know. It's tough to get people who can do that kind of work right.")

Is There More Than One Decision or Solution? Questions that have only one right answer aren't well suited to discussion in meetings. Whether the sales force made its quota last year or whether the budget will accommodate paying overtime to meet a schedule, for instance, are questions answered by checking the figures, not by getting the regional sales managers or the department members to reach an agreement.

Tasks that don't have fixed outcomes, however, are appropriate for committee discussion. Consider the job facing the members of an advertising agency who are planning a campaign for a client. There is no obvious best way to sell products or ideas such as yearly physical examinations, office equipment, or clothing. Tasks such as these call for the kind of creativity that a talented, well-chosen group can generate.

Are Misunderstanding or Reservations Likely? It's easy to see how meetings can be useful when the goal is to generate ideas or solve problems. But meetings are often necessary when confusing or controversial information is being communicated. Suppose, for instance, that changing federal rules and company policy requires employees to document their use of company cars in far more detail than was ever required before. It's easy to imagine how this sort of change would be met with grumbling and resistance. In this sort of situation, simply issuing a memo outlining the new rules might not gain the kind of compliance that is necessary. Only by talking out their complaints and hearing why the new policy is being instituted will employees see a need to go along with the new procedure. "I can write down the vision of the company a thousand times and send it out to people," says Dennis Stamp, chairman of Vancouver's Priority Management Systems, Inc. "But when I sit with them face-to-face and give them the vision, for some reason it is much more accepted."

Setting an Agenda

An *agenda* is a list of topics to be covered in a meeting. A meeting without an agenda is like a ship at sea without a destination or compass: no one aboard

AGENDA

Date:	March 19, 1999
To:	Pat Rivera, Fred Brady, Kevin Jessup, Monica Flores, Dave Cohn
From:	Ted Gross
Subject:	Planning meeting for new Louisville office.
Time/Place:	Tuesday, April 2, from 9:30 to 11:00 A.M. in the third-floor conference room.
Background:	We are still on target for an August 10 opening date for the Louisville office. Completing the tasks below will keep us on schedule—vital if we're to be ready for the fall season.

We will discuss the following items:

1. Office Equipment

   Please come with a list of business machines and other equipment you think will be needed for the office. At the meeting we'll refine this list to standardize our purchases as much as possible. Let's try to start out with compatible equipment!

2. Office Decoration

   Ellen Tibbits of the Louisville Design Group will present a preliminary design for our reaction. She will come up with a final plan based on our suggestions.

3. Promotion

   Kevin wants to prepare a series of press releases for distribution to Louisville media a month or so before the office opens. Please come with suggestions of items that should be mentioned in these releases.

FIGURE A Format for a Comprehensive Agenda

knows where it is or where it's headed. A good agenda contains several kinds of information, all illustrated in Figure A.

Time, Length, and Location. To avoid problems, all three of these details need to be present on an agenda. Without the *starting time,* you can expect to hear such comments as "I thought you said ten, not nine," or "We always started at three before." Unless you announce the *length,* expect some members to leave early, pleading, "I have another meeting," or "I didn't realize we'd run this long—I've got a doctor's appointment." Failure to note the *location* results in members' stumbling in late after waiting in the "usual place," wondering why no one showed up.

Participants. The overall size of the group is important: When attendance grows beyond seven members, the likelihood of some members' falling silent increases. If the agenda includes one or more problem-solving items, it's best to keep the size small so that everyone can participate in discussions. If the meeting is primarily informational, a larger group may be acceptable.

Be sure to identify on the agenda the people who will be attending. By listing who will attend, you alert all members about whom to expect in the meeting. If you have overlooked someone who ought to attend, a member who received the agenda can tell you. It is frustrating and a waste of time to call a meeting and then discover that the person with key information isn't there.

Background Information. Sometimes participants will need background information to give them new details or to remind them of things they may have forgotten. Background information can also provide a description of the meeting's significance.

Items and Goals. A good agenda goes beyond just listing topics and describes the goal for the discussion. "Meetings should be outcome- rather than process-driven," says Anita Underwood, Dun and Bradstreet's vice president of organizational management. Most people have at least a vague idea of why they are meeting. Vague ideas, however, often lead to vague meetings. A clear list of topics and goals like the ones in Figure A will result in better-informed members and more productive, satisfying meetings.

The best goals are *result-oriented, specific,* and *realistic*. Notice the difference between goals that do and don't meet these criteria.

Poorly Worded	*Better*
"Let's talk about how we can solve the sales problems in the northwestern region."	"We will come up with a list of specific ways our product can be shown to be useful in the special climate conditions of the Northwest."
"We're going to talk about the new income-savings plan."	"We will explain the advantages and disadvantages of our two income-savings plans so that employees can decide which best suits their needs."
"Joe Fishman will tell you about his trip to the new supplier's plant."	"Joe will explain the facilities of our new supplier and how we can use them to cut costs."

Goals like these are useful in at least two ways: First, they help to identify those who ought to attend the meeting. Second, specific goals also help the people who do attend to prepare for the meeting, and they help to keep the discussion on track once it begins.

The person who calls the meeting isn't the only one who can or should set goals. There are many times when other members have important business. The planner is often wise to use an "expectations check" to identify members' concerns. Members can be polled before the meeting, so that their issues can be included in the agenda, or at the start of the meeting. The fact that a member wants to discuss something does not mean that the topic should automatically be

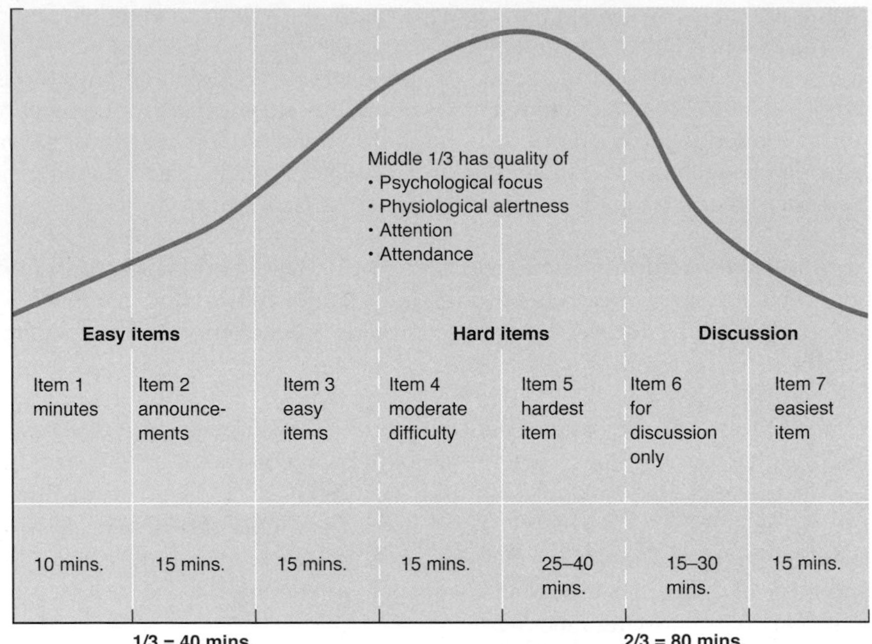

FIGURE B A Bell-Shaped Agenda Structure

Source: From John E. Tropman. "The Agenda," in *Making Meetings Work* (Newbury Park, Calif.: Sage, 1996). Copyright © by Sage Publishing, Inc.

considered. If the issue is inappropriate, the planner may choose to postpone it or handle it outside the meeting.

Premeeting Work. The best meetings occur when people have done all the necessary advance work. The agenda is a good place to tell members how to prepare for the meeting by reading information, developing reports, preparing or duplicating documents, or locating facts or figures. If all members need to prepare in the same way (for example, by reading an article), adding that fact to the agenda is advised. If certain members have specific jobs to do, the meeting organizer can jot these tasks on their individual copies: "Sarah—be sure to bring last year's sales figures"; "Wes—please duplicate copies of the annual report for everyone."

The order of agenda items is important. Some experts suggest that the difficulty of items should form a bell-shaped curve, with items arranged in order of ascending and descending difficulty (see Figure B). The meeting ought to begin with relatively simple business: minutes, announcements, and the easiest decisions. Once members have hit their stride and a good climate has developed, the group can move on to the most difficult items. These should ideally occupy the middle third of the session. Then the final third of the meeting can focus on easier items to allow a period of decompression and goodwill. Table A is a checklist for planning a meeting.

TABLE A Checklist for Planning a Meeting

- **Is membership well chosen?**
  - ❑ Is the size of group appropriate?
  - ❑ Are the necessary knowledge and skills represented?
- **Have unproductive members been excluded (if practical)?**
- **Is enough time allotted for tasks at hand?**
- **Is the meeting time convenient for most members?**
- **Is the location adequate?**
  - ❑ Is the size appropriate?
  - ❑ Are the facilities appropriate?
  - ❑ Is there freedom from distractions?
- **Is a complete agenda circulated?**
  - ❑ Is it distributed far enough in advance of the meeting?
  - ❑ Does it include particulars (meeting data, time, length, location, attendees)?
  - ❑ Does it contain background information as necessary?
  - ❑ Does it list goals for each item supplied?

CONDUCTING THE MEETING

To the uninitiated observer, a well-run meeting seems almost effortless. Time is used efficiently, the tone is constructive, and the quality of ideas is good. Despite their apparent simplicity, results like this usually don't just happen: they grow from some important communication skills.

Beginning the Meeting

Effective openings get the meeting off to a good start. First, they give everyone a clear picture of what is to be accomplished. Second, they define how the group will try to reach its goal. Finally, they set the stage for good teamwork and, thus, good results. The first few remarks by the person who called the meeting can set the stage for a constructive session. They should cover the following points.

Identify the Goals of the Meeting. This means repeating the information listed in the agenda, but mentioning it here will remind everyone of the meeting's goals and help to focus the discussion. For example:

> "We're faced with a serious problem. Inventory losses have almost doubled in the last year, from 5 to 9 percent. We need to decide what's causing these losses and come up with some ideas about how to reduce them."

Provide Necessary Background Information. Background information explains the context of the meeting and gives everyone the same picture of the subject being discussed. It prevents misunderstandings and helps members to understand

Members Can Be Leaders, Too

Good leadership promotes successful meetings, but members can also play an important role in making a meeting successful. The following tips can be used by every person involved in a meeting:

- Ask that an agenda be sent out before the meeting, or agree on an agenda at the beginning of the meeting.
- Ask for help at the beginning of the meeting. Seek clarification on the meeting's goal. Is it to present information? To make a decision?
- Be "tactfully bold" and suggest canceling an unnecessary or badly planned meeting. Convene it when there is a need and an agenda.
- Volunteer to be a record keeper. A written set of minutes reduces the chance for misunderstandings, and keeping notes yourself leads to a record that reflects your perception of events.
- Suggest that a time keeper be appointed, or volunteer yourself. This person advises the group when time for addressing each issue—and the meeting itself—is nearly over and alerts the group when time runs out.
- Ask for help before the meeting closes. Ask "Exactly what have we decided today?" "What do we need to do before our next meeting?"

Source: Adapted from Ana M. Keep, *Moving Meetings.*

the nature of the information the group will consider. Clarifying key terms is often helpful:

> "By 'inventory losses,' we mean materials that are missing or damaged after we receive them. These losses might occur in the main warehouse, en route to the stores, or within the stores themselves."

Show How the Group Can Help. Outline the contributions that members can make during the meeting. Some of these contributions will come from specific people:

> "Tom's going to compare our losses with industry figures, so we can get an idea of how much of the problem is an unavoidable cost of doing business. Chris will talk about his experiences with the problem at Sterling, where he worked until last year. That firm had some good ideas we may be able to use."

Other contributions can be made by everyone present. This is the time to define specifically how each member can help make the meeting a success:

> "We're counting on everybody here to suggest areas where we can cut losses. Once we've come up with ideas, I'll ask each of you to work out a schedule for putting the ideas to work in your department."

Preview the Meeting. If you have not already done so, outline how the meeting will run. For instance:

> "We'll begin by hearing the reports from Tom and Chris. Then we'll all work together to brainstorm a list of ways to cut losses. The goal here will be to get as many ideas as possible. Once we've come up with a list, we can decide which ideas to use and how to make them work."

Identify Time Constraints. Clarify how much time is available to prevent time wasting. In some cases, it's only necessary to remind the group of how much time can be spent in the meeting as a whole. ("We can develop this list between now and eleven o'clock if we keep on track.") In other cases, it can be useful to preview the available time for each agenda item:

> "Tom and Chris have promised to keep their remarks brief, so by ten o'clock we should be ready to start brainstorming. If we get our list put together by ten-thirty, we'll still have a half hour to talk about which ideas to try and how to put them into action."

Following these guidelines will get your meeting off to a good start. Even if you are not in charge of the meeting, you can still make sure that the opening is a good one by asking questions that will get the leader to share the kind of information just listed:

> "How much time do you expect we'll need?"
>
> "How far do you expect we'll get today?"
>
> "What can we do to help solve the problem?"

And so on.

Conducting Business

No meeting will be successful without committed, talented participants. But even the best attendees do not guarantee success. Someone—either the leader or a responsible member—has to be sure that all important business is covered in a way that takes advantage of the talents of everyone present. A number of approaches are available that use meeting time effectively (see Table B).

Encouraging Participation. Loosely structured, informal meetings may appear to give everyone an equal chance to speak out, but because of gender, culture, and style differences, every member may not, in fact, have the same access. Group members' relative status or rank, ages, gender, and cultural backgrounds all influence interaction patterns in groups. Unbalanced participation can cause two sorts of problems: First, it discourages people who don't get a chance to talk. Second, it prevents the group from considering potentially useful ideas. There are several ways to improve participation at meetings.

Use the Nominal Group Technique: One method for giving every member's ideas an equal chance to be considered is the *nominal group technique* (NGT). (The method's name comes from the fact that, for much of this process, the

TABLE B Checklist for Conducting a Meeting

- **Opening the meeting**
  - ❑ Have goals for the meeting been identified?
  - ❑ Has necessary background information been reviewed?
  - ❑ Are expectations for members' contributions clear?
  - ❑ Has the sequence of events for the meeting been previewed?
  - ❑ Have time constraints been identified?
- **Encouraging balanced participation**
  - ❑ Have leader and members used questions to draw out quiet members?
  - ❑ Are off-track comments redirected with references to the agenda and relevancy challenges?
  - ❑ Do leader and members suggest moving on when an agenda item has been dealt with adequately?
- **Maintaining positive tone**
  - ❑ Are questioning and paraphrasing used as nondefensive responses to hostile remarks?
  - ❑ Are dubious comments enhanced as much as possible?
  - ❑ Does the meeting reflect the cultural norms of attendees?
- **Solving problems creatively**
  - ❑ Is the problem defined clearly (versus too narrowly or broadly)?
  - ❑ Are the causes and effects of the problem analyzed?
  - ❑ Are clear criteria for resolving the problem established?
  - ❑ Are possible solutions brainstormed without being evaluated?
  - ❑ Is a decision made based on the previously established criteria?
  - ❑ Are methods of implementing the solution developed?

participants are a group in name only, since they are working independently.) The NGT method consists of five phases:

1. Each member writes down his or her ideas on paper, which is then collected by a discussion leader. This method ensures that good ideas from quiet members will have a chance for consideration.
2. All ideas are posted for every member to see. By keeping the authorship of ideas private at this point, consideration is less likely to be based on personal factors such as authority or popularity.
3. Members discuss the ideas to understand them better, but criticism is prohibited. The goal here is to clarify the possibilities, not to evaluate them.
4. Each member privately ranks the ideas from most to least promising. Individual ranking again prevents domination by a few talkative or influential members.
5. Items that receive the greatest number of votes are discussed critically and thoroughly by the group. At this point, a decision can be made,

using whichever decision-making method (e.g., consensus, majority rule) is most appropriate.

This approach lends itself nicely to computer-mediated meetings. With most groupware packages, members can anonymously input ideas via computer and have their contributions displayed for consideration by everyone. This anonymity can empower normally quiet group members, who might be intimidated to speak up.

The NGT method is too elaborate for relatively unimportant matters but works well for important issues. Besides reducing the tendency for more talkative members to dominate the discussion, the anonymity of the process lessens the potential for harmful conflicts.

Have Members Take Turns: Another approach is to give every member a turn to speak. While it probably isn't wise to conduct an entire meeting this way, the technique can be useful at the beginning of a meeting to start members off on an equal footing, or in the middle if a few people are dominating the discussion, or at the end if some people have not been heard.

Use Questions: Questions that draw out listeners are another way to encourage participation. Four types of questions can balance the contributions of members.

Overhead questions are directed toward the group as a whole, and anyone is free to answer:

> "Sales have flattened out in the western region. Can anybody suggest what's going on?"
>
> "We need to find some way of rewarding our top producers. I'd like to hear your ideas."

As long as overhead questions draw a response from all members, it's wise to continue using them. When a few people begin to dominate, however, it's time to switch to one of the following types.

Direct questions are aimed at a particular individual, who is addressed by name:

> "How would that suggestion work for you, Kim?"
>
> "Greg, how's the new plan working in your department?"

Direct questions are a useful way to draw out quiet members, but they must be used skillfully. Never start a discussion with a direct question. This creates a "schoolroom atmosphere" and suggests the rule "Don't speak until you're called on"—hardly a desirable norm in most meetings. It's also important to give respondents a way out of potentially embarrassing questions. For example, a chairman might ask, "Tony, can you give us the figures for your department now, or will you need to check them and get back to us?"

Reverse questions occur when a member asks the leader a question and the leader refers the question back to the person who originally phrased it:

> "Suppose the decision were up to you, Gary. What would you do?"
>
> "That's a good question, Laurie. Do you think it's a practical idea?"

Reverse questions work well when the leader senses that a member really wants to make a statement but is unwilling to do so directly. It's important to use reverse questions with care: the member could be asking for information, in which case a direct answer is appropriate.

Relay questions occur when the leader refers a question asked by one member to the entire group:

> "Cynthia has just raised a good question. Who can respond to it?"
>
> "Can anyone offer a suggestion for Les?"

Relay questions are especially useful when the leader wants to avoid disclosing his or her opinion for fear of inhibiting or influencing the group. Relays should usually be rephrased as overhead questions directed at the entire group. This avoids the suggestion that one member is smarter than the others. Of course, if a particular person does have special expertise, it is appropriate to direct the inquiry to him or her:

> "Didn't you have a problem like that once with a distributor, Britt? How did you work things out?"

Keeping Discussions on Track. Sometimes the problem isn't too little discussion but too much. Groups often waste time, conducting leisurely discussions when time is short. Even when time is plentiful, members often talk on and on without moving any closer to accomplishing a goal. In other cases, someone may bring up a topic that is unrelated to the task at hand. When problems like these occur, the leader or some other member needs to get the discussion back on track by using one of the following techniques.

Remind the Group of Time Pressures: When the group is handling an urgent topic in a leisurely manner, you can remind everyone about the importance of moving quickly. But when doing so, it is important to acknowledge the value of the comments being made:

> "Radio ads sound good, but for now we'd better stick to the newspaper program. John wanted a copy from us by noon, and we'll never make it if we don't get going."

Summarize and Redirect the Discussion: When members ramble on about a topic after the job is done, you can get the discussion moving again by tactfully summarizing what has been accomplished and mentioning the next task:

> "It seems as if we've come up with a good list of the factors that might be contributing to absenteeism. Can anybody think of more causes? If not, maybe we should move on and try to think of as many solutions as we can."

Use Relevancy Challenges: When a discussion wanders away from the business at hand, summarizing won't help. Sometimes the unrelated ideas are good ones that just don't apply to the group's immediate job. In other cases, they are not only irrelevant but worthless. In either situation, you can get the group back on track by questioning the idea's relevancy. In a *relevancy challenge,* the questioner tactfully asks a member to explain how an apparently off-the-track idea relates to the group's task. Typical relevancy challenges sound like this:

> "I'm confused, Tom, how will leasing new equipment instead of buying it help us to boost productivity?"
>
> "Fran asked us to figure which word processing package to buy. Does the graphics package you mentioned have something to do with the word-processing decision?"

At this point the member who made the original remark can either explain its relevance or acknowledge that it wasn't germane. In either case, the advantage of this sort of challenge is that it isn't personal. It focuses on the *remark* and not on the *person* and thus reduces the chance of a defensive response.

Promise to Deal with Good Ideas Later: Another way to keep the goodwill of a member who has brought up an irrelevant idea is to suggest a way of dealing with it at the appropriate time:

> "That equipment-leasing idea sounds promising. Let's bring it up to Jeff after the meeting and see what he thinks of it."
>
> "A graphics package seems important to you, Lee. Why don't you look into what's available, and we can decide whether the change would be worth the cost."

As with relevancy challenges, your suggestion about dealing with an idea later has to be sincere if the other person is going to accept it. One way to show your sincerity is to mention exactly when you would like to discuss the matter. This might be a specific time (after lunch), or it might be when certain conditions are met ("after you've worked up the cost"). Another way to show your sincerity is to inquire about the idea after the meeting: "How's the research going on the graphics package?"

Keeping a Positive Tone. Almost everyone would agree that "getting along with people" is a vital ingredient in a successful career. In meetings, getting along can be especially tough when others don't cooperate with your efforts to keep the meeting on track—or, even worse, attack your ideas. The following suggestions can help you handle these irritating situations in a way that gets the job done and keeps potential enemies as allies.

Ask Questions and Paraphrase to Clarify Understanding: Criticizing an idea—even an apparently stupid one—can result in a defensive reaction that will waste time and generate ill will. It's also important to remember that even a seemingly idiotic remark can have some merit. Given these facts, it's often wise to handle apparently bad ideas by asking for some clarification. And the most obvious way to clarify an idea is to ask questions:

> "Why do you think we ought to let Marcia go?"
>
> "Who would cover the store if you went skiing next week?"
>
> "What makes you think we shouldn't have a Christmas party this year?"

You can also paraphrase to get more information about an apparently hostile or foolish remark:

> "It sounds as if you're saying Marcia's doing a bad job."
>
> "So you think we could cover the store if you went skiing?"
>
> "Sounds as if you think a Christmas party would be a waste of money."

This sort of paraphrasing accomplishes two things: First, it provides a way to double-check your understanding. If your replay of the speaker's ideas isn't accurate, he or she can correct you: "I don't think Marcia's doing a bad job. I just don't think we need so many people up front." Second, even if your understanding is accurate, paraphrasing is an invitation for the other person to explain the idea in more detail: "If we could find somebody to work a double shift while I was skiing, I'd be willing to do the same thing for her later."

Enhance the Value of Members' Comments: It's obvious that you should acknowledge the value of good ideas by praising or thanking the people who contribute them. Surprisingly, you can use the same method with apparently bad ideas. Even the most worthless comments often have some merit. You can take advantage of such merits by using a three-part response:

1. Acknowledge the merits of the idea.
2. Explain any concerns you have.
3. Improve the usefulness of the idea by building on it or asking others for suggestions.

Notice how this sort of response can enhance the value of apparently worthless comments:

> "I'm glad you're so concerned about the parking problem, Craig [acknowledges merit of comment]. But wouldn't requiring people to carpool generate a lot of resentment [balancing concern]? How could we encourage people to carpool voluntarily [builds on original idea]?"
>
> "You're right, Pat. Your department could use another person [acknowledges merit of comment]. But Mr. Peters is really serious about this hiring freeze [balancing concern]. Let's try to come up with some ways we can get you more help without having to hire a new person [builds on original idea]."

Pay Attention to Cultural Factors: Like every other type of communication, the "rules" for conducting productive, harmonious meetings vary from one culture to another. For example, in Japan problem-solving meetings are usually preceded by a series of one-to-one sessions between participants to iron out issues, a process called *nemawashi*. The practice arises from the Japanese cultural practice that two people may speak candidly to one another, but when a third person enters the discussion, they become a group, requiring communicators to speak indirectly to maintain harmony. By contrast, in countries where emotional expressiveness is the norm, volatile exchanges in meetings are as much the rule as the exception. "I've just come back from a meeting in Milan," stated Canadian management consultant Dennis Stamp. "If people acted the same way in North American meetings you'd think they were coming to blows."

Concluding the Meeting

The way a meeting ends can have a strong influence on how members feel about the group and how well they follow up on any decisions that have been made or instructions that have been given.

When to Close the Meeting. There are three times when a meeting should be closed.

When the Scheduled Closing Time Has Arrived: Even if the discussion has been a good one, it's often best to close on schedule to prevent members from drifting off to other commitments one by one or losing attention and becoming resentful. It's wise to press on only if the subject is important and the members indicate willingness to keep working.

When the Group Lacks Resources to Continue: If the group lacks the necessary person or facts to continue, adjourn until the resources are available. If you need to get cost figures for a new purchase or someone's approval for a new idea, for example, it is probably a waste of time to proceed until the data or go-ahead has been secured. In these cases, be sure to identify who is responsible for getting the needed information, and set a new meeting date.

When the Agenda Has Been Covered: It seems obvious that a meeting should adjourn when its business is finished. Nonetheless, any veteran of meetings will testify that some discussions drag on because no one is willing to call a halt. Unless everyone is willing to socialize, it's best to use the techniques that follow to wrap up a meeting when the job is completed.

How to Conclude a Meeting. A good conclusion has three parts. In many discussions, the leader will be responsible for taking these steps. In leaderless groups or in groups with a weak leader, one or more members can take the initiative. (Table C is a checklist for concluding a meeting.)

Signal When Time Is Almost Up: A warning allows the group to wrap up business and gives everyone a chance to have a final say:

> "We have about fifteen minutes before we adjourn. We still need to hear Bob's report on the Kansas City conference, so let's devote the rest of our time to that."
>
> "It's almost time for some of you to leave for the airport. I'd like to wrap up our meeting by putting the list of suggestions Mr. Moss has asked us to send him into its final form."

Summarize the Meeting's Accomplishments and Future Actions: For the sake of understanding, review what information has been conveyed and what decisions have been made. Just as important is reminding members of their responsibilities:

TABLE C Checklist for Concluding a Meeting

- **Concluding the meeting**
  - ❏ Does the meeting run the proper length of time (versus ending prematurely or continuing after excessive length or wasted time)?
  - ❏ Is a warning given shortly before conclusion to allow wrap-up of business?
  - ❏ Is a summary of the meeting's results and a preview of future actions given?
  - ❏ Does the leader acknowledge contributions of group members?
- **Follow-up activities**
  - ❏ Does the leader build an agenda for the next meeting upon results of the previous one?
  - ❏ Does the leader follow up on assignments of other members?
  - ❏ Do members follow through on their own assignments?

> "It looks like we won't have to meet again until the sales conference next Tuesday in San Juan. We'll follow the revised schedule that we worked up today. Chris will have copies to everyone first thing tomorrow morning. Nick will call the hotel to book the larger meeting room, and Pat will take care of having the awards made up. Let's all plan to meet over dinner at the hotel next Tuesday night."

Thank the Group: Acknowledging the group's good work is more than just good manners. This sort of reinforcement shows that you appreciate the group's efforts and encourages good performance in the future. Besides acknowledging the group as a whole, be sure to give credit to any members who deserve special mention:

> "We really got a lot done today. Thanks to all of you, we're back on schedule. Bruce, I appreciate the work you did on the specifications. We never would have made it without you."
>
> "You were all great about coming in early this morning. The extra rehearsal will make a big difference in the presentation. Those charts are terrific, Julie. And your suggestion about using the slide projector will make a big difference, Lou. Let's all celebrate after we get the contract."

Following Up the Meeting

It's a mistake to assume that even a satisfying meeting is a success until you follow up to make sure that the desired results have really been obtained. A thorough follow-up involves three steps.

Build an Agenda for the Next Meeting. Most groups meet frequently, and they rarely conclude their business in one sitting. A smart leader plans the next meeting by noting which items need to be carried over from the preceding one. What unfinished business must be addressed? What progress reports must be shared? What new information should members hear?

Follow Up on Other Members. You can be sure that the promised outcomes of a meeting actually occur if you check up on other members. If the meeting provided instructions—such as how to use the new long-distance phone service—see if the people who attended are actually following the steps that were outlined. If tasks were assigned, check on whether they're being performed. You don't have to be demanding or snoopy to do this sort of checking. A friendly phone call or personal remark can do the trick: "Is the new phone system working for you?" "How's it going on those sales figures?" "Did you manage to get hold of Williams yet?"

Take Care of Your Own Assignments. Most homework that arises out of meetings needs continued attention. If you wait until the last minute before tackling it, the results are likely to be sloppy and embarrassing.

CHAPTER 5

Leadership and Social Influence Processes

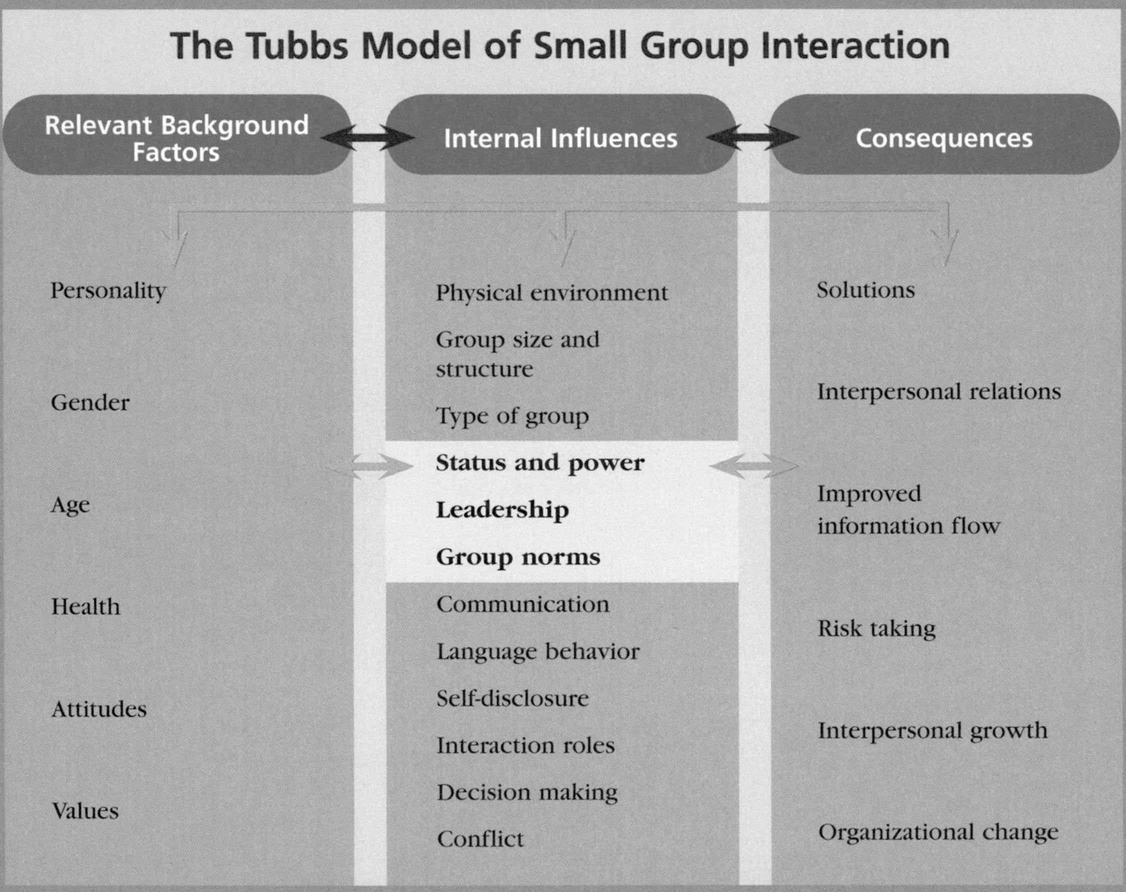

Concepts in **boldface** in gray panels are the emphases of this chapter.

Preview

Chapter 5 covers quite extensively three more of the internal influences in the Tubbs Model of Small Group Interaction: status and power, leadership, and group norms. This chapter examines the two types of status, ascribed and attained, and the five types of power: reward, coercive, legitimate, referent, and expert. The chapter also discusses leadership and several different perspectives on how a leader is developed. Three perspectives are trait theory, circumstances theory, and function theory. Leadership styles and situational leadership are described. Followership styles are discussed briefly, because every successful leader has followers. We then discuss conformity and the processes of social influence. The last subject in Chapter 5 is group development.

Glossary

Ascribed Status Ascribed status is the prestige that goes to a person by virtue of his or her birth.

Attained Status Attained status is the prestige that goes to a person on the merits of his or her own individual accomplishments.

Coercive Power Coercive power is the power an individual has to give or withhold punishment.

Expert Power Expert power is our acceptance of influence from those whose expertise we respect.

Followership Styles Followership styles are behavioral tendencies people have toward authority figures (such as obedient versus rebellious).

Groupthink Groupthink refers to the tendency of group members to share common assumptions, which frequently leads to mistakes.

Legitimate Power Legitimate power is the influence we allow others, such as our bosses, to have over us on the basis of their positions.

Referent Power Referent power is based on identification with the source of power—for example, having admiration for someone.

Reward Power Reward power is the power an individual has to give or withhold rewards.

CASE STUDY

LESSONS FROM A NOBEL LAUREATE

Muhammad Yunus won the 2006 Nobel Peace Prize for his work in establishing microcredit for the extremely poor people of Bangladesh. He learned that the root cause of poverty in his country was not laziness but the inability to get even extremely small loans for small businesses. He turned to the local banks for the solution, but all of them turned him down. So, 30 years ago, he established the Grameen Bank, which has since helped over 100 million people out of poverty. How did he do it?

Yanus requires every loan applicant to submit a business plan. In addition, he requires that applicants form a team with four other people in the business. Each of the others also cosigns for the debt, which means that they are liable

continued

if the applicant does not pay it back. As a result, they become a supercritical group of decision makers who require that every business decision gains the approval of all five members of the team. This key requirement ensures that business decisions are thoroughly reviewed and scrutinized. The teams meet every week and brainstorm as teams. Grameen Bank counts on the synergy resulting from the forced group interaction (Patterson et al., 2008).

1. Why do you think the small groups play such an important part in these successes?
2. Who would you choose for your business partners if you were starting such a business?
3. What is the difference between individuals running a business and groups?

In this case study we see a problem that is not unique to impoverished countries. The problem has to do with being able to develop effective leadership behaviors. Each of us from time to time will be called upon to act in the role of a group leader. For some, the role may seem comfortable; others will have to work hard to grow into it. In any case, leadership is a topic that seems to capture the interest of most students of small group interaction.

The case study clearly illustrates the importance of the systems approach. Hughes, Ginnett, and Curphy (2011) remind us that every leadership act occurs in some context. Our effectiveness depends in large part on the appropriateness of the behaviors to that particular context or situation.

If you have ever tried being a leader, you already know that it is much harder than it looks. White House reporter Leslie Stahl (1999) wrote about her observations of the White House staff:

> The special training I'd had as a teenage girl allowed me to recognize the nest of jealousies and backstabbings. The Reagan White House was more riven with palace intrigue and machinations than anything else I'd ever seen. How enchanting of grown men. While many of the rivalries were personal, they were played out as ideological crusades, with the [Ed] Meese side acting as protectors of holy dogmas against the [Jim] Bakerite infidels. Reagan liked to deflect criticism about all the internal warfare with a joke: "Sometimes in our administration the right hand doesn't know what the far-right hand is doing." (p. 123)

Goleman, Boyatzis, and McKee (2002) put it well when they write:

> Everyone watches the boss. People take their emotional cues from the top. . . . Careful observations of working groups in action revealed several ways the leader plays such a pivotal role in determining the shared emotions. Leaders typically talked more than anyone else, and what they said was listened to more carefully. Leaders were also usually the first to speak out on a subject, and when others made comments, their remarks most often referred to what the leader said than to anyone else's comments. Because the leader's way of seeing things has special weight, leaders "manage meaning" for a group, offering a way to interpret, and so react emotionally to, a given situation. (p. 8)

One example of this is a description of the way President Obama directed his top officials regarding the decision about the number of troops to send to the war in Afghanistan:

> He . . . wanted a decision memorandum that everyone would have to sign. . . . "We're not going to do this unless everybody literally signs on to it and looks me in the eye and tells me that they're for it." The president was as animated as most in the room had ever seen. "I don't want to have anybody going out the day after saying that they don't agree with this." No more gentlemen's agreements. The lawyer in Obama would attempt to deter revisionism with a written document. (Woodward, 2010, p. 305).

A good leader, with good ideas and exciting directions, can generate enthusiasm, support, and cohesion in a group or organization. Compare this orientation with that of the Japanese, whose ancient proverbs include the saying "A nail that protrudes is hammered down" and among whom the idea of standing out above one's peers is considered to be in poor taste. This chapter will examine the process of personal influence and its various ramifications. We begin with a discussion of status and power, then move to the ever-popular topic of leadership, and conclude with an analysis of the uses and abuses of social influence.

Status and Power

Most farmers who have raised poultry are familiar with the chickens' pecking at one another in an attempt to determine which animal dominates. The eventual result is that one chicken rises to the dominant position, a second chicken dominates all others but the top chicken, the third chicken dominates all but the top two, and so on down the line. This order of dominance is generally referred to as the *pecking order*, and when a new chicken is introduced to the barnyard, it must fight all the others to establish its position in the pecking order.

Pecking orders are also found in human interaction. Most often they are informal and adhered to almost unconsciously. They may also be formalized, as on an organizational chart. An example of such a pecking order in the U.S. government is the *order of precedence;* it formally designates who precedes whom in the pecking order (or in order of importance as they might be officially introduced to a visiting dignitary or head of state). James Symington (1971) remarked that, as U.S. chief of protocol, "it was always a humbling reminder to read over this list" (since he was at the bottom) (pp. 94–95). A small part of this list is presented here:

Order of Precedence

The president of the United States
The vice president of the United States
The speaker of the House of Representatives
The chief justice of the United States
Former presidents of the United States
The secretary of state
The secretary-general of the United Nations

TYPES OF STATUS

Status is defined as one's position or rank relative to other members of a group. Those with status are perceived as being more fit to respond regarding a particular subject or experience. Group membership status differences and difference in composition in groups can affect the performance of individual group members. Status within a group is very closely related to the concept of *power*. Those with higher status generally have more power within the group (Sell et al., 2004). High status tends to result in greater personal power or ability to influence others. Increased power, in turn, tends to elevate an individual's status level. Power and status tend to go hand in hand, reciprocally influencing each other.

Social status is the honor or prestige attached to one's position in society (one's social position). The stratification system, which is the system of distributing rewards to the members of society, determines social status. Social status—the position or rank of a person or group within the stratification system—can be determined two ways. Individuals (and groups) can earn their social status by their own achievements, which is known as *achieved status*, or they can be placed in the stratification system by their inherited position, which is called *ascribed status*. Put another way, statuses based on inborn characteristics, such as gender, are ascribed statuses, while statuses that individuals gain through their own efforts are achieved statuses (Newman, 2006, p. 25).

Think of the many ongoing groups you have joined. They often have an established pecking order into which you must insert yourself. How does this pecking order come about in the first place? Ascribed status refers to the prestige that a person has by virtue of some inherited characteristic, such as his or her family wealth, good looks, or age. One man who attended an Ivy League school remarked that it was a bit awesome to be in classes with the children of *the* Rockefellers, *the* Firestones, and *the* Kennedys. In the 2010 movie "The Social Network," the Winkelvoss twins who sued the founder of Facebook, were examples of such very wealthy individuals.

In some cases, being male can result in ascribed status in groups that are discussing topics that are perceived as mostly masculine in nature. McDonald, Toussaint, and Schweiger (2004) wrote about ascribed status of men versus women in small groups. Previous research had also revealed that women are perceived as having a lower ascribed status than men in organizational groups. The study that McDonald et al. conducted looked at 63 undergraduate women who had been told that they were leading a decision-making group. The majority of the decision-making group was male. In one scenario, the woman was not the only female in the group. In the second scenario, the woman was the only female, and in the third scenario, she was the only female but had higher status. Those women who were told that they had higher status in the third scenario were more comfortable and more successful at leading the all-male group. These results are still disturbing, as the ascribed-status perception between genders had to be corrected through fictitious assignment of status.

Differences in status of members of a group may either facilitate or hinder other members' interaction in any type of groups. A study by Sell and colleagues (2004) investigated the use of a handheld computer device to determine if virtual decision-making environments for small groups would have fewer ascribed-status effects. This *group decision support system* (GDSS) can allow anonymous contribution, helping diffuse status differences on handheld wireless devices or through the use of regular computers. In a study by Davis and colleagues (2002), members of a small group were introduced to a computer game and were then instructed to brainstorm names for it. Group members were primarily males who knew a lot about computer games. The females were not likely to respond when their ideas were linked to their names, but idea generation was equal when group members were able to contribute ideas anonymously through a GDSS. Social bias and perceived status of group members were both abolished through this anonymous group decision support system.

In many cases, there is no ascribed status and no established pecking order. How does one get established? What are the effects once it has been set up? Those who rise to positions of status on the basis of their own merits and their own individual accomplishments acquire attained or achieved status. The United States is known as one country in which the Horatio Alger story can and does occur—where a person from humble origins can rise from one socioeconomic class to a higher one—at least more easily than in many other countries.

What kinds of behaviors enable a person to acquire a position of achieved status? Some have hypothesized that power and status are a function of the ratio of the number of successful power acts to the number of attempts to influence:

$$\frac{\textit{Number of successful power acts}}{\textit{Number of attempts made}} = \textit{Power and status}$$

One student stated:

> The impact of this ratio dawned on me during our fraternity's officer elections. One brother tried many times, all unsuccessful, for a variety of positions. He is a good worker, so that was not his problem. His problem was that within the fraternity he did not have any status. The number of attempts made was many, but the number of successful acts was zero. His status fell further with each new failure.

The effects of social status are not limited to an individual's reactions to other people. An individual's status can influence his or her own behavior as well. This is particularly true in group interaction. In one study, Jemmott and Gonzalez (1989) randomly assigned high-status ("boss") and low-status ("helper") labels to grade-school children. These children were randomly assigned to small groups, where only one child in the group was assigned a status level different from the other children. For instance, there would be four bosses with one helper or four helpers with one boss.

As was expected, children who were assigned a high-status label performed significantly better on tasks than did children assigned a low-status label. Moreover, Jemmott and Gonzalez found some interesting interactions among the variously labeled children. The performance of children with low status was even worse if they were alone in their group. The performance of children with high-status labels was either unaffected or further enhanced by the absence of other common-status children.

The authors attribute their findings to the effects of *tokenism*, which occurs when one member of a group is of very different status from other members of the group. Group members tend to minimize the differences among themselves and to emphasize the differences from the token member.

The authors also discuss tokenism in light of what has been described as *chronic status*, a status that people have at all times. Gender, race, and religious affiliation are all examples of chronic status. One interesting case of tokenism and chronic status occurred when a young man was hired into the corporate office of a company run primarily by women. He became the "token male" and was ostracized by his fellow employees. As in other studies, he was not as successful most likely because he was assigned a low-status label and he was alone in his group.

Obviously, the success rate and relative status of any individual will vary from group to group. Most of us find that we have a relatively higher status level in high school than we achieve when we attend college. This is usually because colleges and universities draw from a much larger population than do most high schools, and the competition gets tougher as the size of the population increases.

TYPES OF POWER

Although each of us has encountered situations in which people have power over one another, we may not have been very systematic in identifying the types of power they had. French and Raven (1959) identified five different types of power that can be brought to bear in small groups: (1) reward power, (2) coercive power, (3) legitimate power, (4) referent power, and (5) expert power (see also Pierce & Newstrom, 2000). Another type of power is ingratiation.

Reward power refers to the ability an individual has to give or withhold rewards. A company executive obviously has this type of power, which can take the form of financial rewards through raises and promotions, as well as of social rewards, such as recognition and compliments or praise. The strength of the power increases with the magnitude of the rewards. I once talked to a corporate executive who said that he had the power to award up to $50,000 a year in bonuses for any deserving employee. He said he never had any problem motivating people!

You might not think that *ingratiation* (flattery) is a form of power, but it is! It is a type of interpersonal reward. According to a study published in the *Academy of Management Journal*, flattery will get you everywhere, including a seat on the board of directors of some publicly held companies. The researchers found that the most frequent flatterers got the most seats on the boards. According to the authors (Westphal & Stern, 2007), ingratiation had the strongest effect of all the variables studied for getting a flatterer a seat on the company's board. In fact, ingratiation outranked giving substantive advice and professional counsel as factors in obtaining a board membership (Byrnes, 2007).

When someone flatters you, you have two ways or reacting. You can think that he or she is insincere and is just trying to get something from you. This leaves you feeling badly about that person. Or, you can believe him or her to be sincere, which leaves you feeling good about yourself and that individual. Experts find that the latter often tends to be true, thus the compliment improves the other person's influence (Pfeffer, 2010, p. 34). *Coercive power* (sometimes called *Scrooge power*) is the opposite of reward power in that it utilizes punishment rather than reward. A supervisor can reprimand, discipline, and even fire an employee who does not live up to certain behavioral standards. An IBM employee was once sent home when he showed up for work without a tie. Most organizations reserve the right to set what they believe to be appropriate standards for employees' dress. Coercive power is sometimes used to enforce these standards.

Legitimate power (or *position power*) is defined as the influence we allow others to have over us on the basis of the job they hold or function they perform. For example, we feel that it is legitimate for a judge to determine a sentence in a court case or for a supervisor to determine work schedules or assignments. A person who is elected to office is seen as having a legitimate right to exercise the power of that office. Of course, this right may be abused, and the official may be removed from office. It is critical to remember that leadership and authority are two separate things. People with authority are generally assigned authority through their position level. Some people with assigned authority may not be leaders, and leaders may be the group members without assigned authority who simply emerge in the group due to other characteristics (About.com, 2005a).

Referent power (or *personal power*), perhaps the most nebulous, is extremely potent because it refers to the power a person has to persuade us because we want him or her to admire, respect, or like us. It is based on our identification with the source of power. If you had a teacher you really admired, you would do many things (such as studying hard or putting off social activities) to earn approval or praise from that teacher. Ringwald and colleagues (1971) studied different types of college students and found that one type was especially prone to identifying with the professor and to being a "model student" in the professor's eyes. These students were described as "self-confident, interested, involved; tend to identify with [the] teacher and see him as a colleague. Older than average [mostly upper-classmen]" (p. 47). Although Ringwald et al. studied only undergraduates, this description would also apply to a large segment of graduate students.

Expert power refers to our acceptance of influence from those whose knowledge or expertise we respect. We accept the advice of lawyers on legal matters, of physicians on medical matters, or of others whom we perceive as having credibility on a given topic. In a group discussion concerning the dangers of heroin addiction, for example, the speakers who had the most expert power of persuasion were the former addicts who told tragic stories of how heroin had destroyed parts of their lives.

Yates (1985) makes an interesting point about power:

> Thus, a fundamental shortcoming of organizational behaviorists . . . is that they tend to ignore or underemphasize the importance of power relationships and differing authority roles in the group process. If a decision making group is, in reality, a small representative body comprising a variety of broader interests and institutional claims and statuses, it will function as a group, as a microcosm of larger forces and conflicts, in the organization. To that extent, to treat individual relations in the group as the essential stuff of decision making risks missing the forest for the trees. (p. 123)

In other words, we need to be aware not only of the power relationships that exist within a group context but also of those that grow out of the group and that act as an entity in the larger organizational context.

Pfeffer (2010) offers the following practical advice, "Taking on small tasks [like offering to take minutes of the group meeting] can provide you with power because people are often uninterested in seemingly small, unimportant activities. Therefore, if you take the initiative to do a minor task and do it extremely well, these can become important sources of power." (p. 99). Furthermore, put away your Blackberry, the laptop, the cell phone and other technological gadgets that compete for your time and attention. When you read an e-mail while in a meeting, the message you are sending is clear: I have other things to do that are way more important than paying attention to you (p. 132).

As we think in terms of status and power, we might want to keep in mind that the different types of power usually overlap. A person may be in a position to use reward power as well as coercive power but may prefer to rely on referent power, legitimate power, or expert power. In any event, there are different types of power that can be used (and abused).

Tjosvold, Andrews, and Struthers (1991) found that when a person is seen by others as having power, he or she is also perceived to be effective. So power tends to equate to effectiveness in the eyes of others.

Another application of power in groups is the use of the group itself by a higher authority to develop support for decisions. Imagine that you are asked by your college dean to serve on a student advisory committee. The very fact that you become part of the administration's decision-making structure may be as important in legitimizing the committee's ideas as the substance of the ideas themselves.

Thus the very process of involving groups in making decisions may increase the boss's power to have those decisions implemented.

It also has been found that comments in small groups tend to be directed more often (by direction of eye contact) to higher-status group members than to those of lower status. If you quickly want to determine the high-status members of any group, just notice to whom people direct their comments. Thibaut and Kelley (1986) found this phenomenon in an experimental study and hypothesized that this type of upward communication acts as a substitute for a member's own upward mobility in the group's pecking order. Thus, if we can't be football stars or sorority presidents, we can at least try to become friends with them.

Finally, high status results in a group's being willing to tolerate deviation on the part of a group member (think Lady Gaga). Highly successful people are notoriously idiosyncratic. It has been suggested that a person who is idiosyncratic but not successful is simply considered weird. Albert Einstein and Thomas Edison both were considered eccentric, yet their eccentricities were tolerated because of the magnitude of their contributions. Most groups will tolerate deviations from those who are highly valued in the group. One rule of thumb is that new members are not allowed to deviate nearly as much as those who are old-timers. This is true in college faculties, in companies, in government agencies, and even in prisons. We discuss deviation and conformity pressure in greater detail later in this chapter.

POSITIVE AND NEGATIVE USES OF POWER

Most experts agree that power tactics are amoral. That is, all types of power can be used for good or evil. One of the most provocative writers on the subject of power was the Italian political philosopher Niccolò Machiavelli, whose most famous work is *The Prince*, written in 1513. The most famous concept from this work is "The end justifies the means." In other words, do whatever it takes to get what you want. The term *Machiavellian* has come to mean a manipulator. For example, Korda (1975) describes one person who always sat in meetings with his back to a window so that people looking at him would have to look into the sunlight (to put them at a disadvantage). Some of my students have told me that in their workplaces you are either a "dealer" or one of the "dealt." I've also heard it said that in many organizations you are either a driver, a passenger, or "road kill." It's no small wonder that there is so much interest in the subject of power.

Greene and Elffers (1998) offer numerous examples of uses and abuses of power in their book *The 48 Laws of Power*. For example:

> Law 1: Never outshine the master. Bosses never like to have their subordinates look better than they do. If you are too successful, you will bring out your boss's insecurity.
>
> Law 42: Strike the shepherd and the sheep will scatter. If you take on the most powerful person in the group, others will fear you.
>
> Law 46: Never appear too perfect. People envy [and resent] perfection.

Hillary Clinton actually won the Democratic primary election in New Hampshire just a few days after she lost her composure and cried in front of television cameras. Prior to that, she had been criticized by many for being too cold and calculating (Armour, 2008, p. A10). On the other hand, some still suspected that this too was just part of a politician's Machiavellian act to get elected.

From these laws, you can see that Machiavellianism is alive and well in the 21st century. Power is an ever fascinating subject and those who write about it certainly do stir up the pot of controversy. In fact, that is Law 39: Stir up the waters to catch fish.

Power within groups can bring about or solve conflicts. Sell and colleagues (2004) wrote that group conflict within groups has been described as the "conflict between the motive to compete and the motive to cooperate." This includes conflicts that occur over both "resources" and "information."

Perhaps not surprisingly, recent research **suggests that power reduces the ability to understand how others see, think, and feel. (Galinski, et. al., 2006) In addition, they also discovered that power can inhibit empathy, the ability to perceive another person's emotional states. After being primed with power, participants were shown a set of twenty-four images of faces expressing either happiness, sadness, fear, or anger. For each image, the participants were asked to guess which of these four emotions was being expressed. High-power participants made more errors in judging the emotional expressions of others than were baseline participants who had not been empowered. (Galinski, et. al., 2006)**

Leadership

Definitions of *leader* are numerous, but we prefer the following: "Influencing others to accomplish organizational goals" (Tubbs, 2011, p. vii). An effective leader is essential for optimal group performance. Zenger and colleagues (1994) put it well: "Without skilled leadership, teams can easily flounder, get off course, go too far or not go far enough, lose sight of their mission and connection with other teams, lose confidence, get stymied by interpersonal conflict, and simply fall far short of their enormous potential" (p. 15). Does this sound like some of the groups you have been in? Effective leadership is an international concept.

According to L. Kevin Kelly, the CEO of Heidrick & Struggles, one of the world's largest search firms, years of practical global experience has taught the following,

> One theme that ran consistently through our findings was that requirements have shifted toward . . . "softer" leadership skills. Technical skills are merely a starting point, the bare minimum. To thrive as an executive, an individual needs to be a good communicator, and a strategic thinker. . . . The person today needs to be more team-oriented, capable of multi-tasking continuously, and leading without rank. (Groysberg, Kelly, & McDonald, 2011, p. 68).

With these thoughts in mind, let us examine what people historically have thought about leadership.

HISTORIC TRENDS

Leadership has fascinated humankind for at least 5,000 years! The accompanying diagram shows ancient Egyptian symbols for leadership (Bass, 1995, p. 51). Experts typically identify several leadership principles dating back to the beginning of the common era.

During the 18th and 19th centuries, philosophers argued the relative merits of two viewpoints regarding leadership: (1) the trait, or "great man," theory, and (2) the circumstances theory. Although we have come a long way in our study of leadership, it is still worthwhile to go back and examine the evolution of the different approaches.

Egyptian Hieroglyphics for Leadership, Leader, and Follower

Seshemet–Leadership

Seshemu–Leader

Shemsu–Follower

Trait Theory

Trait theory grew out of the idea that leaders are born, not made. Examples from history include Alexander the Great, Cleopatra Corazon Aquino, John F. Kennedy, Barack Obama, and Angela Merkel, President of Germany. The assumption was that certain physical traits or personality traits enable a person to be a leader.

The physical traits associated with leadership were height, weight, and physical attractiveness and body shape. In our culture, taller people are sometimes associated with higher status, and shorter individuals with power status. In one study (Wilson, 1968), a speaker named Mr. England was introduced to each of five different college classes by a different title:

Class 1—a student from Cambridge

Class 2—a demonstrator in psychology from Cambridge

Class 3—a lecturer in psychology from Cambridge

Class 4—Dr. England, senior lecturer from Cambridge

Class 5—Professor England from Cambridge

When students were asked to estimate the speaker's height, the average estimate increased from Class 1 to Class 5. In other words, the more prestigious England's title, the taller the students thought he was. A study at the University of Pennsylvania showed that height in inches correlated more closely with a graduate's starting salary after graduation than any other index (such as grade-point average, number of extra-curricular activities, or parents' education level). Although correlation does not prove causality, it is still interesting to see the anecdotal evidence supporting the belief that height is viewed positively. As one student aptly put it, "I would define a leader as someone I can look up to, both figuratively and literally."

Another study (Bradley-Steck, 1987) surveyed 1,200 graduates of the University of Pittsburgh. The researchers found that a combination of height and weight predicted starting salary. For example,

> The average salary of those surveyed was $43,000, but a typical six foot professional earned $4,200 more than his 5 foot 5 counterpart. If the taller man was trim and shorter man fat, the difference translated to about $8,200 . . . . Height and weight weren't as important factors among women. It was hypothesized that middle of the road (height and weight) for women was preferred. Men's heights seemed to be an advantage up to about 6-4. However, at 6-6 or 6-7 the height seemed to be a disadvantage. (p. A1)

More recently, a study published in the Harvard Business Review Daily Briefings noted that for every inch of height, candidates gained .41 percent of salary (2010).

What relationship might there be between weight and leadership? The heavier, the better? Actually, the predicted relationship is curvilinear (see Figure 5.1). Thus, people who are too thin or too heavy would be considered either too weak and fragile or too self-indulgent and undisciplined to be good leaders. In one unpublished study conducted in a large company, employees were divided into groups, one whose members weighed within 10 percent of their "desirable" weight (based on a doctor's chart of height and weight) and one whose members

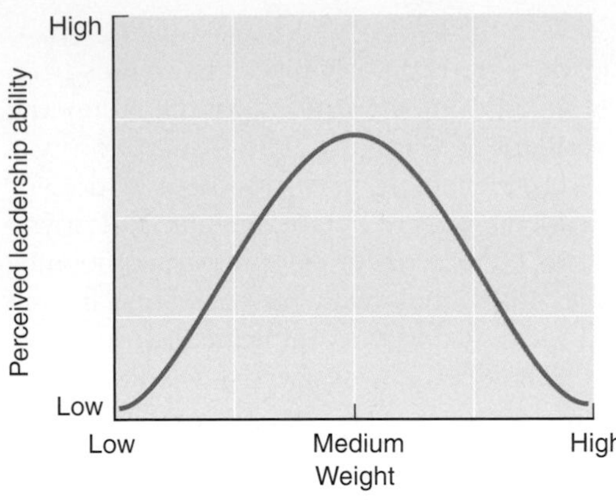

FIGURE 5.1 Hypothetical Relationship Between Weight and Leadership

deviated more than 10 percent above or below their charted body weight. The percentage of promotions was tabulated for the two groups, and it was found that the medium-weight group had more promotions (See also Brooks, 2011).

In a study conducted by a Madison Avenue employment agency with branches in 43 American cities, it was found that overweight persons may be losing as much as $1,000 a year for every pound of fat. According to the agency's president, Robert Hall, the survey showed that among those in the $25,000–50,000 salary group, only 9 percent were more than 10 pounds overweight (according to the standards established by life insurance companies). Hall said that the overweight "are unfairly stereotyped as slow, sloppy, inefficient, and overindulgent. When important, high-paying jobs are at stake and candidates are under close scrutiny, the overweight are less likely to be hired or promoted into them" (p. 1). Hall also stated that companies frequently specify their preference for slim candidates, but only once in 25 years did a company request a plump executive; the company was a manufacturer of oversized clothing.

Closely related to body weight is body type. Sheldon (1940, 1942, 1954) identified three different body types, or *somatotypes*. The very thin person is called an *ectomorph;* the very heavy and soft person, an *endomorph;* and the medium-weight, muscular type, the *mesomorph*. Intuitively, we might expect leaders to come from the mesomorphic body type. Although there are no studies to support or refute this prediction, it is a provocative theory that might someday be tested. For example, those who are successful in political campaigns and in movie careers more often than not seem to be mesomorphic. We also know from several research studies that more attractive people are perceived as having higher credibility (for example, higher expertise and better character) on the basis of their looks alone (Mills & Aronson, 1965; Widgery & Webster, 1969; Widgery, 1974).

In addition to physical traits, certain personality traits are thought to be associated with leadership. A list of some of these traits includes self-confidence, dominance, enthusiasm, assertiveness, responsibility, creativity, originality, dependability, critical-thinking ability, intelligence, and ability to communicate effectively. Although all these traits have some commonsense appeal, Stogdill (1948) surveyed over 200 leadership studies and found that out of all the identified traits, only 5 percent were common to four or more of the studies surveyed. In an update, however, Bass (1995, p. 93) has had somewhat greater success in securing a level

Characteristic	2010
Percentage of Respondents Selecting That Characteristic:	
Honest	85%
Forward-looking	70
Competent	70
Inspiring	69
Intelligent	42
Broad-Minded	40
Supportive	35
Straightforward	34
Dependable	33
Cooperative	28
Determined	24
Imaginative	23
Ambitious	21
Courageous	20
Caring	20
Mature	17
Loyal	14
Self-Controlled	11
Independent	6

FIGURE 5.2 Characteristics of Admired Leaders

Reprinted with permission of John Wiley & Sons, Inc., from James Kouzes and Barry Posner, *The Truth About Leadership*, copyright 2010 by Jossey-Bass, pp. 17–18.

of agreement among leadership trait studies. Kouzes and Posner (2010) found the leadership characteristics shown in Figure 5.2 to correlate across three studies.

In summarizing his latest thoughts on trait theory, Bass (1995) states:

> Although leaders differ from followers with respect to various aspects of personality, ability, and social skills, tests of such traits have been of limited value for selection of leaders. Traits do not act singly but in combination. . . . The leader who acquires leadership status in one group tends to emerge as leader when placed in other groups. Thus, perhaps the best prediction of future leadership is prior success in this role. (p. 413)

On the other side of the coin, Geier (1967) was able to identify five negative behaviors that consistently prevented group members from emerging as leaders. Such members were (1) uninformed about the problem being discussed, (2) nonparticipative, (3) extremely rigid in holding to pet ideas, (4) authoritarian in bossing others around, and (5) offensive and abusive in language style. Although trait theory has not held as many answers as early philosophers and theorists had hoped, it has provided us with some helpful information and insight.

As the old saying goes, "Managers do things right, leaders do the right things."

Being a leader in general can be quite difficult, but being a female leader can present even more challenges. In a *Harvard Business Review* essay, Alice Eagly and Linda Carli, of Northwestern University and Wellesley College, respectively, discuss women's roles in leadership and the eradication of the "glass ceiling." According to Eagly and Carli, the "glass ceiling" phrase can no longer be used to aptly describe the failure to promote women into top leadership roles. Instead, women in the 21st century are facing what Eagly and Carli refer to as a "labyrinth." They believe this is a better image to help organizations understand and address the obstacles to women's progress. Rather than depicting one absolute barrier, as the glass ceiling did, a labyrinth conveys the complexity and variety of challenges that can appear along the way (Eagly & Carli, 2007).

Who is the perfect leader? For thousands of years, leadership scholars have been trying to determine just that. What characteristics or personality traits make up a great leader? None of the studies has ever produced a definite answer. However, a study for the *Harvard Business Review* did find something. After asking 125 leaders ages 23–93, "How can people become authentic leaders?" the study produced 3,000 pages of transcript. The team was startled to see that these people did not identify any universal characteristics, traits, or styles that led to their success. Rather, each of their leadership stories emerged from their life experiences. Therefore, it is important to note that although you may not have the same traits as the leader you idolize, that's quite all right because no two leaders are the same. You can learn from others' experiences, but there is no way you can be successful when you are trying to be just like them. Kevin Sharer, the CEO of Amgen, says, "Leadership has many voices. You need to be who you are, not try to emulate somebody else" (George et al., 2007).

Circumstances Theory

Ira Hayes was a Native American who became famous for having been one of the U.S. marines who lifted the American flag after the battle of Iwo Jima in the South Pacific during World War II. Ira just happened to be standing nearby when the photographer solicited a group to pose for the picture that later became world-famous. He instantly became a national hero and was sent on cross-country U.S. Savings Bond drives to raise money for the American war effort. Ira's pride made him feel so guilty for being a "counterfeit hero" that he began to drink. He eventually died an alcoholic.

Ira Hayes is the classic example of a person's being at the right place at the right (or wrong) time. This is sometimes called the *circumstances theory of leadership*. Another facet of this theory is that a person may be an effective leader in one circumstance but perform poorly in a different circumstance. Therefore, some theorists would argue that the circumstances make the leader. A good example of this is the student/faculty softball, football, and basketball teams that are found on some campuses. Although the professors are usually the leaders in the classroom (because of a relatively higher level of expertise in the subject), the students are usually the leaders on the athletic field, where they often know more about the game and are almost always in better physical shape than the professors.

Like trait theory, circumstances theory seems to have some validity. However, there are many exceptions to the rule. Mitt Romney was the founder of Bain

Capital, a highly successful business. He then was the head of the United States Olympics. Then, he served as governor of Massachusetts, and in 2012 is running for President of the United States. Robert McNamara functioned well as president of Ford Motor Company, U.S. secretary of defense, and head of the World Bank. Matt Damon and Ben Afleck each won an Oscar for writing the screenplay for "Goodwill Hunting." In addition, they have each acted in a slew of successful movies. And in 2011, Afleck directed the successful movie "The Town." Circumstances theory, although somewhat valid, leaves something to be desired in explaining the complex phenomenon of leadership.

Function Theory

A theory that deviates rather dramatically from the first two is *function theory*. Underlying this theory is the notion that leaders are made, not born. That is, leadership consists of certain behaviors or *functions* that groups must have performed. These functions are identifiable behaviors that can be learned by anybody. We can all improve our potential as leaders by learning to perform these key functions more effectively. Whereas trait and circumstance theories assume that there is little we can do to become leaders if we aren't a certain height or if we never seem to be in the right place at the right time, function theory offers hope for those of us who may not have been born into the Bill and Melinda Gates family, or are part of the Walton family, who founded WalMart. or who are not asked to be in photographs that become famous (like Ira Hayes).

The two important functions that have been consistently identified are referred to by a variety of terms but are basically the same concepts: (1) task orientation, and (2) people orientation. Sayles (1993) puts it well when he writes, "Effective leadership requires involvement. . . . Working leadership involves the capacity to make fast-paced trade-offs (each involving embedded people and technology issues)" (p. 13). Certainly, former New York City mayor Rudy Giuliani is a person who rose to great leadership stature after the September 11, 2001, crisis.

With function theory, the emphasis has shifted away from the leader as a person and toward the specific behavioral acts that facilitate group success. Leadership may be "possessed" by any group member who performs these leadership functions. The task-oriented behaviors are those directed toward the group's accomplishing its goal. The people-oriented behaviors are directed toward the maintenance of the interpersonal relationships in the group. It is assumed that people-oriented activities ought to have an indirect effect on helping accomplish the group's task. An analogy would be that of a machine. The machine operates to accomplish a task (producing parts). However, if the machine is not cleaned and lubricated, it will break down sooner or later, thus halting its productivity. Similarly, although task-oriented groups may require a leader who can help them accomplish their goal, they may cease functioning if they become too bogged down in personality conflicts or counterproductive interpersonal friction. Both task-oriented and people-oriented behaviors are required to enable a group to progress. Bales, in Figure 5.3, offers a summary of the 12 types of specific behavioral acts (six task-oriented, six people-oriented) and the average percentage of interaction in any given group discussion that would probably fall into each category. Ross summarizes the work of Bales and others in an extended model of the 12 Interaction Process Analysis (IPA) categories (see Figure 5.4).

	Category	Percentage	Estimated Norms
People-oriented (positive)	1. Seems friendly	3.5	2.6–4.8
	2. Dramatizes	7.0	5.7–7.4
	3. Agrees	18.5	8.0–13.6
Task-oriented	4. Gives suggestions	3.8	3.0–7.0
	5. Gives opinions	24.5	15.0–22.7
	6. Gives information	8.3	20.7–31.2
	7. Asks for information	10.3	4.0–7.2
	8. Asks for opinions	12.5	2.0–3.9
	9. Asks for suggestions	2.3	0.6–1.4
People-oriented (negative)	10. Disagrees	1.0	3.1–5.3
	11. Shows tension	7.8	3.4–6.0
	12. Seems unfriendly	0.5	2.4–4.4
		Total: 100.0	

FIGURE 5.3

Adapted from *Personality and Interpersonal Behavior* by Robert F. Bales. Copyright © 1970 by Holt, Rinehart & Winston, Inc. Reprinted by permission of Harcourt, Inc.

	Major Categories	Subcategories	Illustrative Statements or Behavior
Social-emotional area	Positive reactions	1. Shows solidarity	Jokes, gives help, rewards others, is friendly[f]
		2. Shows tension release	Laughs, shows satisfaction, is relieved[e]
		3. Shows agreement	Passively accepts, understands, concurs, complies[d]
Task area	Attempted answers	4. Gives suggestion	Directs, suggests, implies autonomy for others[c]
		5. Gives opinion	Evaluates, analyzes, expresses feeling or wish[b]
		6. Gives information	Orients, repeats, clarifies, confirms[a]
	Questions	7. Asks for information	Requests orientation, repetition, confirmation[a]
		8. Asks for opinion	Requests evaluation, analysis, expression of feeling[b]
		9. Asks for suggestion	Requests direction, possible ways of action[c]
Social-emotional area	Negative reactions	10. Shows disagreement	Passively rejects, resorts to formality, withholds help[d]
		11. Shows tension	Asks for help, withdraws, daydreams[e]
		12. Shows antagonism	Deflates other's status, defends or asserts self, is hostile[f]
Key:	a. Problems of communication d. Problems of decision	b. Problems of evaluation e. Problems of tension reduction	c. Problems of control f. Problems of reintegration

FIGURE 5.4 Interaction Process Analysis, Categories of Communicative Acts

Based on Robert F. Bales, *Interaction Process Analysis* (Reading, Mass.: Addison-Wesley, 1950), p. 9; A. Paul Hare, *Handbook of Small Group Research* (New York: Free Press of Glencoe, 1962), p. 66; and Clovis R. Shepherd, *Small Groups: Some Sociological Perspectives* (San Francisco: Chandler, 1964), p. 30.

The function theory of leadership seems to hold the most promise for teaching most of us how to improve our own leadership abilities. For example, many students hesitate to participate in discussions for fear of "saying something stupid." Yet several research studies indicate that simply participating at all is one primary requirement of becoming more of a leader. Other studies show that individuals who are able to perform both task- and people-oriented functions in groups are likely to get better results from their groups than those who are less effective in performing these two functions.

Effective leadership on the job emphasizes a high concern for people and a high concern for task in the workplace. There are many objectives of leadership. However, most people would argue that some are better than others. According to John Hamm, leadership coach, strategy consultant, and former CEO, "The real job of leadership is to inspire the organization to take responsibility for creating a better future. . . . Effective communication is a leader's single most critical management tool for making this happen" (Hamm, 2006).

Katzenbach and Smith (1993) emphasize: "Team leaders genuinely believe that they do not have all the answers—so they do not insist on providing them. They believe that they do not need to make all key decisions—so they do not do so. . . . Most important, like all members of the team, team leaders do real work themselves" (p. 131).

Co-leadership is not yet listed in the dictionary but it is becoming a popular style in business. Goldman Sachs is one of many companies that is choosing to use co-leadership. They believe that there are many benefits to co-leadership, with the greatest being diversity of thought and talent. They believe that co-leaders can play to their individual strengths. Where one leader may have exceptional personal relations strengths, the other may be engrossed with task-oriented issues such as financial numbers and statistics. Having both involved in decision making may lead to better-thought-out decisions. As the saying goes, two heads are better than one. Perhaps it won't be long before small groups are running companies and using the strengths of their group dynamics to make even better decisions (Miles & Watkins, 2007).

The final important implication to grow out of the function theory of leadership is that these functions need not be performed by the one person designated as group leader. In fact, the implication is the reverse. To the extent that all group members learn to perform these two functions, overall group leadership will be improved. This is often referred to as *shared* or *democratic leadership*, which we will examine in the next section.

Leadership Styles

The interest in leadership just keeps on getting stronger. Recent changes in the curriculum at the University of Pennsylvania's MBA program are increasing coursework in leadership. Business School Dean Thomas S. Robertson states, "If you talk to alumni 20 years out, they say, 'Ooh boy, I wish I had gotten more in the way of leadership skills, how to manage people.' What's important as a [new] graduate, the set of technical skills that gets them the job, becomes less important as they get into middle and senior management" (Korn, 2011, p. B9). This leads us to the question, What type or style of leadership is best? A great deal of attention has been paid to the different types of available leadership styles. Early studies identified three different styles: autocratic, democratic, and laissez-faire.

The issue in these three leadership styles is the degree and location of control. The *authoritarian*, or *autocratic*, leader has a high need to maintain control of the group him- or herself. Some might even say that the autocratic leader has an obsession for control. When this obsession reaches the extreme, it becomes manifest in the following types of behaviors (written in this classic by Sattler & Miller, 1968, pp. 250–51): (see also Dr. Drew Pinsky's narcisism test at http://www.0eb.com/) (see also Narcissim.com).

- The authoritarian usually plans to get to the conference room when everyone else is assembled. He or she fears getting to the meeting early, for this leader has no interest in carrying on non-task-related conversations. This does not mean that the leader is a latecomer—if the meeting is scheduled to start at 3:10 P.M., you can be sure that the leader will be present and the meeting will start on the proper split second.
- Often the leader will present an extended introduction to start a meeting, in part because he or she wishes others to know how well informed he or she is.
- Sometimes the authoritarian will outline precise procedures on how the discussion is to be conducted. Thus the leader might tell the group that A will comment on item 1; B and C on item 2; and D on item 3. Such advice on procedure is not given in order to be helpful to others; largely, it seems, the authoritarian uses rules of order to make his or her own task easier.
- Authoritarians, more than other leaders, specialize in questions directed to specific persons, such as "Jones, what are your facts?" and "Now I want to hear from Smith." Such leaders do not frequently use open or "overhead" questions that any person in the group may answer.
- Authoritarians appear to be unable to withstand pauses in discussion—if such leaders cannot get rapid verbalization from others, they will themselves supply verbal noises.
- The leader almost invariably maintains strict control over the order and sequence of topics; he or she appears to love placing group members in a "straitjacket" of restrictions.
- The authoritarian interrupts others often, for at least three reasons: to correct errors, whether major or insignificant; to keep people talking about what the leader desires; and in general to show who is in command.
- Clever authoritarians at times encourage group members to discuss irrelevant matters at considerable length. This is true, of course, only when discussing the irrelevant is in keeping with the leader's designs.
- When clarifying contributions, the leader is sometimes guilty of changing the intent of statements to make them more acceptable to him- or herself. (Here, of course, we have both procedural and content control.)

The *laissez-faire* style of leadership goes to the opposite extreme. Not only is there no concern for control, but there is no direction, concern for task

PRACTICAL TIPS

Team Leadership

What is it that leaders do to make the difference? Psychologists have studied these interpersonal dynamics and have found that leaders who are more effective tend to give *at least* 3 times as many positive comments as they do criticisms. Poor leaders have closer to a 1 to 1 ratio. I would take it even farther. I have seen some leaders who offer virtually no positive comments, but frequent criticisms. When you interview these leaders, they say, "People are getting paid to do the work. They don't *need* me to stroke their egos too." Yet, when you talk further, they often will complain about the lack of positive encouragement from their own bosses. Ironically, they do not see the connection between their own psychological needs and those of their team members!

New research has shown that the best leaders have about a 6 to 1 ratio of positive to critical comments to employees, and if the ratio falls below 3 to 1, workplace performance drops noticeably. This line of 3 to 1, good to bad comments, is now known as the Lasoda line after Marcial Lasoda, who discovered this ratio after a decade of research on high and low performance teams (Achor, 2010, pp. 60–61) (see also Seligman, 2011, pp. 290–291).

accomplishment, or interest in interpersonal relationships. The laissez-faire style is not really a style of leadership at all; it is nonleadership.

The *democratic* leadership style represents an attempt to find a reasonable compromise between the other two extremes. The leader does attempt to provide direction and to perform both task and social leadership functions, but at the same time he or she tries to avoid dominating the group with one person's views. Some would argue that no matter how hard an individual tries, some domination cannot be avoided.

Which leadership style is best? In order to answer this question, we must determine the criteria for judging effectiveness. Some criteria are (1) the quality of the group output, (2) the time taken to accomplish the task, (3) the satisfaction of the group members, (4) the absenteeism of group members, and (5) the independence developed by group members. Manz and Sims (2001) reported that (1) the quality of group output was better under democratic leadership, (2) democratic leadership took more time than autocratic, (3) member satisfaction was higher under democratic leadership (in fact, hostility was 30 times as great in the autocratic groups, and 19 out of 20 preferred the democratic group to the autocratic), (4) the democratic group had the lowest absenteeism, and (5) the democratic group fostered more independence, whereas the autocratic style bred dependence and submissiveness among group members (see also Pink, 2009).

The democratic style got better results in each case except in time taken to accomplish the task. However, subsequent studies have shown that the autocratic leader gets fast results in the short run but that these results may be of poor quality or may be resisted by others. The net effect is that the solution may not be enacted, and the problem will have to be dealt with again on future occasions. Because this amounts to less efficiency, the democratic style may even prove to be less time-consuming in the long run (see Chapter 8 for more on this). In addition, the hostility bred by autocratic leadership produces counterproductive results. For example, in industrial groups, absenteeism, grievances, work stoppages, and sabotage are all ways in which employees attempt to get back at what they consider to be harsh leadership. "Goldbricking" in the military is another typical example. An autocratic leadership style fosters group norms that say, "Do as little as possible to get by, and look busy when the boss is around. However, when the cat's away . . ."

Barrett and Carey (1989) note, "History records that Abraham Lincoln sought input from his cabinet officers regarding the appointment of Ulysses S. Grant as commander of the Grand Army of the Republic. When each cabinet member spoke against the appointment, Lincoln responded that the vote was seven nays and one aye—and that the ayes had it" (p. 3). Communication is important to the democratic leader because he or she relies so heavily on the input and support of group members.

In a four-year study of problem-solving teams, Larson (1993) found that the most effective leaders were those who created a process in which people have confidence. He describes some of the other requirements of effective team leaders as follows: "[Successful team leadership] demands great patience. It is accompanied by a willingness to give up control and ego needs and to create ownership by the people involved. . . . It shows itself by a clear focus on the problem and as intense involvement with others in shaping an effective response to the problem" (p. 9). More recently, this finding has been replicated by Wiseman and McKeown (2010). They refer to leaders who support followers emotionally as "Multipliers," and those who dominate followers by minimizing their contributions as "Diminishers" (pp. 149–153).

In summary, leadership is hard work, but it mostly involves sharing the task and allowing others to exert their own leadership too.

SUPERLEADERS

Sims and Manz (2001) have proposed a type of leadership that seems to be the ultimate extension of democratic leadership—*SuperLeadership*. A person who exhibits this type of leadership is called the *SuperLeader*. A SuperLeader who gets a lot of other people involved is said to develop *SuperTeams*. They write, "To bring about successful team development, the leader must first establish the capacity of the . . . group to take on new responsibilities" (p. 212).

Shel Horowitz of the University of Massachusetts Family Business Center (2005) discusses Dr. Charles Manz's concept of the SuperLeader. Manz feels that the emergence of the SuperLeader is critical to contemporary effective leadership. The stereotypical 1950s masculine, authoritative, and directive leader has evolved into a leader who utilizes reward systems to drive motivation. Manz calls this type of leader the *transactor*. He asserts that this type of leadership will not prosper and it encourages group members to achieve only the minimum necessary to reach the reward. Manz also defines the *visionary leader* who inspires with charisma and emotion that dies off when the leader is no longer present. Manz suggests that the pinnacle of this evolution is the SuperLeader, who uses bottom-up leadership, has a democratic and participative leadership style, and has a wealth of experience and knowledge. Organizations with multiple empowered teams become stronger and achieve more as these teams are the foundation for the success of the entire organization.

The SuperLeadership approach seems the most closely relevant to small group interaction and seems to be the trend in leadership development. The philosophy is well summarized in the famous words of Lao-tzu:

A leader is best
When people barely know that he exists,
Not so good when people obey and acclaim him,
Worse when they despise him.
"Fail to honor people,
They fail to honor you";
But of a good leader who talks little,
When his work is done, his aim fulfilled,
They will say, "We did it ourselves."

Manz made a list of suggestions for building oneself into a SuperLeader (Horowitz, 2005). This list includes the following recommendations:

1. Develop yourself into a self-leader.
2. Model this type of leadership.
3. Inspire others in individual and group settings to develop their own goals.
4. Reward positive self-leadership.
5. Provide coaching for self-leadership at all levels of the organization.
6. Become an advocate for groups and teams that lead themselves.
7. Encourage positive thinking in others.
8. Instigate a culture of self-leadership.

The SuperLeader organizes followers into *empowered teams* that can eventually lead themselves (Horowitz, 2005). Manz and Neck (1999) have proposed the idea of *self-leadership*. They contend that ultimately we are each responsible for our own choices. The challenge is to channel those choices in a desirable direction. What are the rewards for making such choices? First, they give us a feeling of competence, which is intrinsically pleasurable. Second, they result in our feeling more in control as opposed to being at the mercy of luck or other natural forces. Third, we gain a feeling of purpose when we choose behaviors that help us achieve what we want. Any leader who can help create a climate that fosters self-leadership is more likely to succeed in life.

Followership

While leadership is written about more than most topics relating to small group interaction, followership is much less frequently discussed. In 2003, Google recorded 19.8 million hits for the search term *leadership* and only approximately 15,000 hits for the term *followership* (Jones, 2004). In February 2005, Google recorded 51.8 million hits on leadership and 34,300 on followership. The gap continues to widen with most research and writing still focusing on leadership. Because leadership is defined as successful attempts to influence, followers are required to make leaders. In fact, leadership and followership go hand in hand. Earlier we saw that one style of leadership—the democratic style—in many cases seems to be best. What style of followership is best? Let us first look at three followership styles.

FOLLOWERSHIP STYLES

Milgram (1974) summarizes almost 15 years of research on followership in his famous book *Obedience to Authority: An Experimental View*. In Milgram's experiments, subjects were told to administer electric shocks to other subjects as part of an experiment in learning associations between word pairs. The victim was strapped in a chair and was unable to escape the shocks. The control panel on the shock generator indicated voltage up to 450 volts (this level was labeled "Danger: Severe Shock"). As the voltage was increased, the victim screamed, "Get me out of here; I can't stand the pain; please, I have a heart condition." These protests were continued for any and all shocks administered above 150 volts. (No actual shocks were given, but the subjects really thought they were shocking the victims.)

A group of psychiatrists was asked to predict how much shock the subject would administer to the victim. They predicted that almost every subject would refuse to obey the experimenter, that those who administered any shocks at all would stop at 150 volts, and that only about 1 in 1,000 would go all the way to 450 volts (the end of the control panel). Out of Milgram's original 40 subjects, however, 26 (65 percent) obeyed the experimenter's orders and administered the shocks right up to the 450-volt limit. However, Milgram found that as situations were changed (for example, if the victim was brought into the same room with the subject), the subject was less willing to shock the victim. The behavior found in Milgram's experiments illustrates what might be termed a *dependent* style of followership.

Large organizations, such as the military, organized religions, and government and industrial organizations, frequently produce a higher level of dependence in people. As discussed earlier, autocratic leadership produces a higher level of dependent followership. Most of us are caught up to some degree in the obedience syndrome, but with much less harmful or dramatic results.

A second type of follower is the *counterdependent* person. Counterdependence is a type of behavior that is rebellious and antiauthoritarian. Although the dependent personality is thought to result from overly punitive parenting, the counterdependent personality is thought to result from overly permissive parenting. People who are used to doing things more or less their own way resent any leader or authority figure who intervenes. This type of person would be dissatisfied with almost any style of leadership. It may not be too much of an exaggeration to say that this group consists of misfits who cause chronic problems. In the industrial workforce, they create major problems for leaders wherever they go. Steinmetz (1969) quoted Edward Cole, former president of General Motors, as stating:

> A research study found that relatively few employees—28%—filed 100% of the grievances and accounted for 37% of the occupational hospital visits, 38% of the

PRACTICAL TIPS

How Fit Are You to Lead?

A recent self-diagnostic from the *Harvard Business Review 2007* will help you to assess your suitability for a leading position. Answering yes and no to the following questions will help you to determine your strengths and weaknesses in terms of leadership. Too many negative answers (without the self-motivation to correct them) might mean that you should abandon your pursuit of the leadership role.

Qualifying Criteria

- Is there a good fit between what I studied and the leadership role?
- Have I taken on jobs and projects whose results can be objectively measured?
- Am I aware of the deficiencies in my training and what I should do about them?

Self-Imposed Standards

- Are the expectations I'm setting achievable?
- Have I taken personal responsibility for the gaps between what I promised and delivered?
- Have I picked a talented team?
- Have I treated friends impartially?

Circumstantial Measures

- Am I willing to take on difficult challenges and crises to demonstrate my ability?
- Have I thought through my strategy for success? Do I have the resources? Can I deliver results in the available time?
- Do I know how to motive others to collaborate with me?
- Am I willing to take responsibility for what goes badly and share the glory for what goes well?
- Am I willing to invest the extra effort necessary to succeed?

Political Parameters

- Can I identify everyone who is threatened by my appointment and my leadership choices?
- Am I aware of what my rivals for the job say and do to undermine me?
- Do I ensure that information flowing to stakeholders is not distorted?
- Would others regard the way I allocate rewards and punishments as fair?
- Am I willing to place the organization's interests above everything else?

Source: Adapted from Lansberg, 2007.

insurance claims, 40% of the sick leaves, 52% of the garnishments, and 38% of the absenteeism experienced at a certain factory. Thus, not only are there a comparatively small proportion of people who are absentee-oriented, but these same people tend also to be the ones who create a significant number of all the other problems generated within the organization. (pp. 10–11)

This type of follower would be hard for any leader to lead. We saw earlier that a democratic leadership style tends to produce higher levels of member satisfaction. However, Runyan (1973) found in an industrial chemical plant that some hourly employees (primarily young workers) did not have high job satisfaction regardless of the type of supervisory style. Even a participative (democratic) style did not produce a high level of satisfaction. Perhaps it is fair to say that some people are simply difficult to lead and that, in dealing with them, one leadership style would be about as good (or bad) as any other. The problem then would be to try to bring the followers to a point where they could accept legitimate leadership from others.

The third followership style is the *independent*. The independent is one who can either take over and lead when the situation demands or follow the lead of others when that role is more appropriate. Benjamin Franklin once said, "He that cannot obey cannot command." This implies the role flexibility required of both an effective leader and an effective follower.

Interestingly, in a totally different context, Stanley Milgram found that when he asked subjects to shock the victims in his studies, psychiatrists (professional group) predicted that they would disobey rather quickly, whereas other middle-class adults (nonprofessional group) predicted that they would obey somewhat longer and give more intense shocks. It appears that, to some extent, education, and perhaps the subsequent self-confidence, tends to correlate with independence of followership and decision making.

To illustrate the contingency aspects of leadership, one student wrote:

> As a second grade instructional aide, I led dependent followers. For these students, who were highly motivated, "gifted" children, I found that a group-centered approach was best, because it forced the students to make decisions which affected them. This improved their academics and matured their thinking processes. As a resident adviser, I led counterdependent followers. The beginning of the year was handled democratically, but after about six weeks, the autocratic method proved more effective. Those students who became dissatisfied changed their followership style, so that they would be treated more democratically; those students who did not change at least accomplished the basic tasks—to establish a community conducive to study and to obey the rules of the school and the laws of Michigan and the U.S., which they were not doing under a democratic style of leadership. Finally, as the vice president of a fraternity, I found a democratic style to be most effective. This provides for personal development and satisfaction, while still accomplishing the tasks which are outlined. However, becoming too group-centered can be a detriment because of the physical size of the membership, and the nature of the tasks which are accomplished.

This is an excellent example of the systems aspect of small group interaction. In each of the situations described above, several factors were acting in combination to influence and determine the most effective leadership style. "If *you* believe in people's abilities, *they* will come to believe in them" (Conger, 1989; emphasis added).

An independent follower requires an empowering leader. Research suggests that the practice of *empowering* employees leads to independent followership styles. Empowerment—instilling a sense of power in subordinates—seeks to

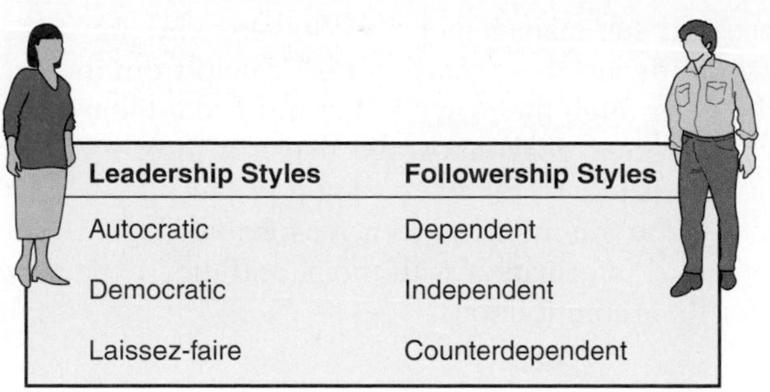

FIGURE 5.5 Leadership and Followership Styles

strengthen an individual's beliefs in his or her sense of effectiveness. Empowering leaders provide a positive emotional atmosphere for their employees, reward and encourage their employees in personal ways, express confidence in their employees, and foster responsibility and initiative among their employees (Hughes, Ginnett, & Curphy, 1996).

In this section, we have looked at three styles of followership: the dependent, the counterdependent, and the independent. On the basis of this discussion, which followership style seems to describe your predominant style? How does your style change in response to different leaders and different situations? Note the styles shown in Figure 5.5.

LEADING THE FOLLOWER

In 2006 the Kravis Leadership Institute at Claremont McKenna College in Claremont, California, opened its 16th annual leadership conference with a somewhat unusual theme. The theme was followership. According to Barbara Kellerman, a research director at Harvard's Kennedy School of Government, the topic of followership hasn't gotten its due. This is partly because of the term itself. *Followership* has a negative connotation that implies sheep being herded. However, much of the focus has always been placed on leaders, and that is only half of the equation. It is important to remember that without followers, there would be no leaders (McGregor, 2006; see also Kellerman, 2008).

Research has revealed that followers contribute 80 percent to the success of the organization; the leader contributes a mere 20 percent. As a result, the follower is an emerging area of focus across organizations. Adrian Walsh Associates (2005) urges organizations to recognize and celebrate the follower. Success depends not only on the leader but also on followers. Followers should be valued and held accountable for the successes of any group, while their leaders should be rewarded for encouraging the followers to reach their full potential. Organizations and groups should set objectives that encourage continuous and positive interaction between the leader and followers, including a relationship built on trust.

Leaders must help their followers find a sense of meaning in their work. Adrian Walsh Associates (2005) summarize recommendations by Bennis and Nanus, who argue that successful leadership depends on "vision, communication, trust, persistence and self-management." Followers who are successful are trustworthy. They work toward their goals and seek help from the leader when they need it. They think through their own work and make their own judgment calls in the framework of their goals and objectives. In turn, followers have certain expectations of their leaders. Followers want a leader who treats them with trust and allows them to be autonomous to a reasonable degree. They expect their leader to share critical information with them, and they expect to be recognized and rewarded for their contributions.

Contingency Theory

Building on the previous theories, two approaches have been offered that are highly consistent with the systems approach taken in this book. Fiedler (1967) has developed a *situational*, or *contingency*, theory of leadership. Hersey, Blanchard, and Johnson (2001) have developed a somewhat different theory. Although these models are both referred to as *situational theories*, the term *contingency theories* also seems appropriate, because the leader's effectiveness is contingent, or dependent, upon the combination of his or her behaviors and the situation.

Fiedler and Chemers (1974) and Potter and Fiedler (1993) argue that a combination of three separate factors determines a leader's effectiveness: (1) leader–member relations, (2) task structure, and (3) position power. Leader–member relations are roughly equivalent to what we have come to know as a person's interpersonal skills or people orientation. If a leader is people-oriented, the leader–member relations are likely to be good. If, on the other hand, his or her orientation is that people are a necessary evil in getting something done, then the leader–member relations are likely to be poor.

Task structure is the second variable in Fiedler's theory. If a group's task is highly structured and the leader has a manual of procedures to be followed, it will be harder for group members to challenge the leader's approach. On the other hand, if the task is highly ambiguous, such as trying to determine policy by predicting future events, then the group members might have quite a bit of legitimate input that could be as good as or better than the leader's idea alone.

Position power, the third variable, can be either strong or weak. If the leader heading a work group has the power to hire and fire, to promote or not, and to determine raises or punishment, then she or he has strong position power. If, on the other hand, the group is composed of volunteers working for a church committee or a student organization, the leader has weak position power to get people to do the task. In the model shown in Figure 5.6, we see the results of Fiedler's research. This model clearly shows that these three variables have a strong influence on the leader's effectiveness; in other words, leadership effectiveness is congruent with these three variables. For example, if a leader is working with a group of volunteers for a student organization and the task is fairly unstructured (without clear guidelines on how to proceed), then the person who is not people-oriented will be very ineffective. In fact, the group members will simply not come back to the next meeting. This theory is fascinating in its

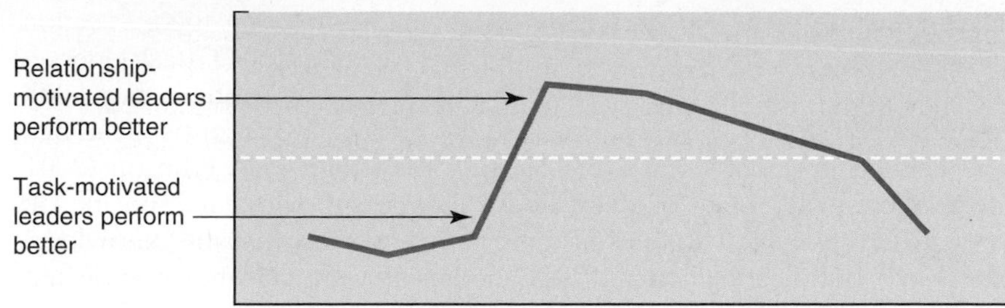

Leader–member relations	Good				Poor			
Task structure	Structured		Unstructured		Structured		Unstructured	
Leader position power	Strong	Weak	Strong	Weak	Strong	Weak	Strong	Weak

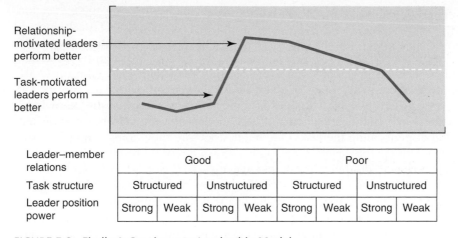

FIGURE 5.6 Fiedler's Contingency Leadership Model

From Fiedler and Chemers, *Leadership and Effective Management* (Glenview, Ill.: Scott, Foresman, 1974), p. 80. Copyright 1974 by Scott, Foresman & Co. Reprinted by permission of Pearson Education Inc., Upper Saddle River, NJ.

implications for leadership, because the same leader acting in the same way would likely be very successful in leading a military group where the operations manual supported "going by the book" and where followers who didn't obey would end up in the guardhouse.

So how do we test a leader's ability to adapt? As previously noted, contingency theory articulates the belief that effective leadership is dependent upon how the leader adapts to particular situations. Fiedler has four primary tests to measure a leader's personality and how it will apply to different situations. The first test, the *Least Preferred Co-workers Scale*, asks leaders to describe the co-worker that they like the least. The type of response given when describing the co-worker actually differentiates *task-* from *relationship-driven* leaders. If the leader describes the least favorable co-worker in a very negative light, then the leader is most likely task-oriented. If there is some positive interjection, then the leader is most likely relationship-oriented. The second test is *Situational Favorableness*, which assesses the relationships between the leader and group members, structure of tasks, and leader position power. In the third test, *Leader–Situation Match and Mismatch*, the aspects of the leadership situation is compared to the leader's strengths. If a strong relationship leader is placed in a task-oriented group, then the leader may not succeed with the same results as a task-oriented leader in that same situation (About.com, 2005a).

Vroom (1993) has studied leadership and participative decision making for over 20 years. He concludes: "We are convinced that the 'bedrock' lies in a situational view of participation, i.e., the most appropriate degree of participation must depend on the circumstances surrounding the participative act. . . . It is more meaningful to talk about autocratic or participative situations than autocratic or participative individuals" (pp. 24, 30).

Building on the ideas we presented earlier in the function theory section, these authors similarly stress the two leadership functions of (1) task-oriented behavior and (2) people-oriented, or relationship, behavior. To these they add a third important variable, (3) the readiness of the followers or groups. Readiness could be defined in various ways, but Hersey, Blanchard, and Johnson (2001) describe it in terms of degrees of ability and willingness to perform a specific job, task, or activity. Followers' abilities are affected by their applicable knowledge and experience, but what matters more is whether they are currently demonstrating skill at performing the task. One might ask, "Are they doing it now at a sustained and acceptable level?" One might also ask a more subjective question, "Do they even want to do the task? Are they willing?" Willingness involves a follower's confidence, commitment, and motivation to perform the task. The concept of readiness is further complicated by the fact that the variables of ability and willingness interact with each other. For instance, as a person's ability to perform a task increases, so might willingness to perform it. Then again, a task may become repetitive and routine over time causing a person to feel less motivated to perform. This can have an effect on that person's ability if he or she starts doing just enough to get by rather than demonstrating skill at the levels he or she should be or were previously performing at. Similarly, one professor gave a motivation test to a group so low in motivation that they would not even complete the test! They simply didn't care about it. For more on determining the Performance Readiness® level of followers, see the reading by Hersey, Blanchard, and Johnson at the end of this chapter.

As we see in Figure 5.7, when the Performance Readiness® of followers is lowest (R1) for a specific job, task, or activity, the leadership style with the highest probability of successfully and effectively influencing others is S1, or *telling*. This involves below average amounts of relationship behavior and above average amounts of task behavior. The follower needs structure and direction from a leader and possibly consequences for nonperformance if necessary. With an R2 level of readiness, the follower is beginning to perform but hasn't reached sustained and acceptable levels of performance yet. The followers at this stage are sometimes referred to as "enthusiastic beginners" because they may not know how to get the job done, but they certainly want to do well. The matching leadership style for this follower would be S2, or *selling*, because it involves above average amounts of relationship and task behavior from the leader. The followers need to know who, what, when, where, and how to do the job, but they also need to know why they are doing it that way and feel rewarded for steps in the right direction. Once followers are performing at a sustained and acceptable level, they don't need the same levels of structure but may understandably feel some anxiety and insecurity about going it "solo." Participating (S3) leader behaviors would be comforting to people at this readiness level (R3) because they need reassurance that they are still on track. At the highest level of the Performance Readiness® continuum is the follower who is not only confident, committed, and motivated to do the task but is currently demonstrating that skill at a sustained and acceptable level. A delegating (S4) leadership style is most appropriate at this juncture, one that involves monitoring or observing but most certainly not abdicating. Low amounts of relationship and task behavior are needed by the leader in this situation.

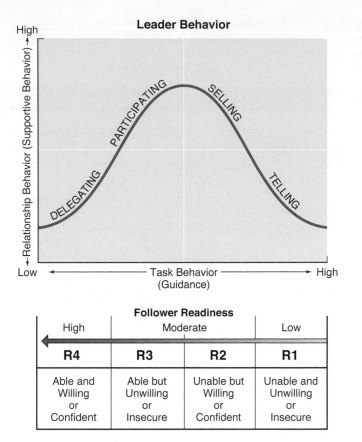

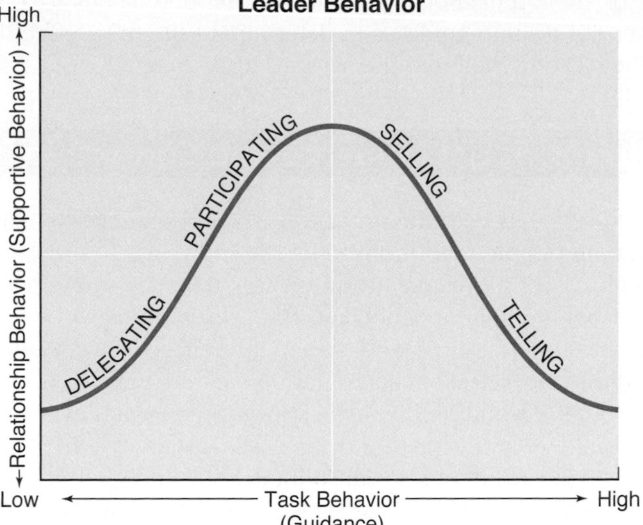

Follower Readiness

High	Moderate		Low
R4	**R3**	**R2**	**R1**
Able and Willing or Confident	Able but Unwilling or Insecure	Unable but Willing or Confident	Unable and Unwilling or Insecure

FIGURE 5.7 Hersey and Blanchard's Contingency Model of Leadership

Source: © Copyright 2006. Reprinted with permission of the Center for Leadership Studies, Inc. Escondido, CA 92025. All rights reserved.

Although it is important to develop some flexibility in our approaches to leadership in different situations, it is also important to realize that we all have limitations. As one colleague remarked, "We can't be a chameleon changing drastically for each situation." Hersey, Blanchard, and Johnson (2001) recognize that each of us tends to prefer one or two of these leadership patterns (that is, telling, selling, participating, or delegating). In most situations, we gravitate toward whichever of these patterns has worked well for us in the past. The difficulty comes when the leadership that is *required* is different from the one we feel comfortable choosing. For example, Donald Trump seems to use a telling style of leadership in managing his companies. Due to his strong personality, it would probably be hard for him to use a delegating style, leaving decisions to his subordinates. (For a good source on this topic, go to www.situational.com.)

In spite of their limitations, contingency models seem to offer the most promising theories to help guide us in determining the most effective leadership behaviors. They also fit well into the systems approach.

Group Norms: Social Influence and Conformity

This entire chapter deals with the process of social influence. In earlier sections, we saw that some people tend more to be the influencers, and others the influencees. In both cases, individuals form groups to attain common goals and to feel a sense of belongingness. Dholakia, Bagozzi, and Pearo (2005) researched small virtual consumer groups and social influence. They found that virtual groups face the same issues of social influences and group norm creation as face-to-face groups. Overall, individuals join groups to achieve group and individual goals, build relationships, and have self-discovery. In this section, we explore some of the results of social influence—namely, conformity pressure. Groups tend to take more risk in their decisions than an individual would. This is called the *risky shift* because the burden of accountability is shared (Nemeth & Goncalo, 2004).

CONFORMITY PRESSURE

Like individuals, groups form habits. When people have been together for a time, they develop standardized ways of managing tasks, procedures, and the environment. Wood, Phillips, and Pedersen (1986) define *norms* as "standardized patterns of belief, attitude, communication and behavior within groups. They grow out of member interaction. Then, in systematic fashion, they influence future interaction" (p. 40). Note this example:

> It had to start somewhere. Every third teenager on the street is wearing them—perfectly good blue jeans ripped to shreds.
>
> The most important determinant of a trend, however, is neither merchandisers nor the media. It's the vast, ineffable plasma of intra-teen peer pressure. At some point between the time the media first transmits the image and the time the merchandisers begin to sell it, peer pressure is critical. Ashley Camron, *Teen* magazine editor Roxanne Camron's 13-year-old daughter, is an eighth grader at Colina Intermediate School in Thousand Oaks, Calif. Ashley picked up on ripped jeans about three years ago, cutting holes in some denim shorts after seeing the look on models and actors. But she didn't have the nerve to wear them to school until her friends started wearing them, too: "If you see it on your friends, then you can wear it in public." Now, she says, everyone's wearing them. (Barol, 1990, pp. 40–41)

Every one of us undoubtedly has felt the pressure to conform at one time or another. One study of players in the National Basketball Association showed that in 1987, 11 percent of the players shaved their heads. However, after Michael Jordan had his head shaved, the rate increased to 63 percent of all the players in the league (source, ESPN).

Although some norms can be described in terms of their functional value to the group, this does not imply that members of the group deliberately develop

PRACTICAL TIPS

How is it that college men started wearing their baseball caps backward, or that college women started saying "awesome," or that binge drinking has become more prevalent on college campuses? Researchers have known for many years that group norms influence individuals to follow the majority (Asch, 1952). But recent research has focused on college students' conforming behavior. Group norms serve to help individuals know how to act. But they also create in-groups and outsiders. Within any group, the most popular individuals tend to set the tone for new behaviors that eventually are adopted by the other group members. In a series of experiments at Princeton University, subjects were placed in two different experimental conditions. One allowed them to rate songs off the Internet without knowing what others thought. The other condition allowed subjects to hear what other people thought of the songs before they rated the songs. As expected, those who saw the ratings of others were significantly influenced by those inputs (Wang, 2011, p. D3). This same process also influences binge drinking in five steps: (1) Students see other students drinking to excess; (2) peers sometimes compliment them on their drinking, which reinforces the belief that drinking is an important factor in student life; (3) students tend not to see the private nondrinking behavior of other students; (4) administrators tell them not to drink so much, but students are more influenced by their peer group norms; and (5) the cycle becomes self-confirming. The more they notice others drinking, the more they believe typical students drink (Wang, 2011, p. D1). On the other hand, brightly colored wrist bands worn by students tend to create a positive loop encouraging healthful behaviors. So group conformity influence can shape behaviors in either a more healthful or a more unhealthful way.

norms with the conscious intention of achieving positive group benefits. According to Thibaut and Kelley (1986):

> The development process underlying the emergence of norms [is] likely to yield rules that have positive functional values for the relationship. As norms are decided upon, imported from other relationships, and tried out, only the more useful ones are likely to be retained. This is not to say that the norms found in any group will be the best solutions to various problems of control, coordination, and synchronization. (p. 141)

One study (Robinson and O'Leary-Kelly, 1998) examined the influence of antisocial group norms on the behavior of group members in work groups. They defined antisocial behaviors as sexual harassment, stealing, sabotage, lying, spreading false rumors, withholding effort, and absenteeism. After studying groups in 20 organizations, they found that the antisocial behaviors of groups tend to promote antisocial behaviors of individuals in the organizations.

Actually, the term *norms* refers to the written or unwritten laws or codes that identify acceptable behavior. Obviously, norms will vary drastically from one group to another. Chen (2001) writes:

> Ren zhe ren ye: "The meaning of person is ren." Embedded in this phrase is a universe of meaning that reveals how the Chinese regard themselves and their relationships with others. The third character, transcribed as ren, means humanity, as well as

> core, or the seed of the fruit. The character ren is composed of the characters for "two" and "person." This etymology ("two people") suggests that in a Chinese context, no person exists except in relationship to another, and that this relationship is the birth of all possibilities. (p. 45)

Historically, important deals have been executed among Chinese firms without any legal contracts of any kind. One striking example is the construction of Asia's fourth-largest building in Hong Kong, which proceeded on a handshake instead of a formal contract (Chen, 2001, p. 80).

Tony Dungy, Super Bowl–winning former coach of the Indianapolis Colts and a devout Christian, writes about his experience with conformity pressure as a player for the Pittsburgh Steelers in the 1970s:

> Early in that first season, the issue of drinking and drugs . . . finally came to a climax for me. During my first road trip as a Steeler, everyone was given two beers as we boarded the flight home . . . I wasn't sure what I would do.
>
> I definitely wanted to fit in and be like everybody else. But I also knew that if I drank the beer, I probably wouldn't be able to drive once we landed in Pittsburgh. Fortunately, I saw a few of the other guys give their beer away, and that little nudge of positive peer pressure helped me to not give in to something I didn't really want to do. (Dungy, 2007, p. 45)

A study reported by Mydans (1990a) found that poor academic achievement by black students was, in part, attributable to group norms. He states, "Many black students may perform poorly in high school because of a shared sense that academic success is a sellout to the white world. . . . The study argues that this grows out of the low expectations that white Americans have of blacks, low expectations that have taken root among blacks themselves." The research was conducted in a predominantly black high school in Washington, DC. Because it was important to the students to maintain a black identity, some black students shunned schoolwork: "They chose to avoid adopting attitudes and putting in enough time and effort in their schoolwork because their peers (and they themselves) would interpret their behavior as 'white.'" Other behaviors considered to be acting "white" were "speaking standard English, . . . going to the opera or ballet, studying in the library, going to the Smithsonian Institution, doing volunteer work, camping or hiking, . . . and being on time" (p. B6). Clearly, group norms serve as a powerful force to inhibit these students' future success.

Even more recently, researchers at Harvard and Tufts Universities have found that these same behavioral norms influence group creativity in corporations (Leonard & Swaps, 1999). They refer to this social influence as "the urge to merge." They find that many groups tend to want to get to the solution prematurely. They suggest that the following guidelines help groups arrive at more creative solutions about 75 percent of the time:

1. Avoid changing your mind only to avoid conflict and to reach agreement and harmony.
2. Withstand pressures to yield, which have no objective or logically sound foundation.
3. View differences of opinion as both natural and helpful. (p. 66)

Thus, training group members about group processes can improve your group's effectiveness.

By now you may have asked yourself, Why do we even need to have norms? Actually, norms often serve to reduce ambiguity and to help us feel more at ease. We may feel uncomfortable when we don't know what behaviors are acceptable in a given situation—for example, when moving from elementary school to junior high or middle school, going from junior high to high school, or graduating from high school and going to college. Remember the uneasiness you felt during your first day in each of these new situations? Only after we have learned some of the common practices or norms can we begin to relax and "be ourselves." One student who went to Harvard a few years ago learned that the norm was to buy expensive sweaters and then take scissors to fray the elbows so that the sweaters didn't look new.

The norms in our society regarding clothing are quite strong. It is interesting to note that even going without clothes involves certain norms. On a nude beach, wearing clothes or even a bathing suit is frowned upon. Jones (1981) writes that at Black's Beach in San Diego, 40,000–50,000 nude bathers gather on a given day. He describes the norms there as follows:

> Nude beaches usually are pretty remote. Gawkers aren't interested in walking very far. . . .
>
> If someone is obnoxious, if some guy keeps his clothes on and stares at the women, it's a matter of peer pressure telling him, hey buddy, what's your problem? Why don't you move on now? This isn't a peep show. (p. C6)

Over a half century ago, psychologist Leon Festinger (1954) hypothesized a fascinating theory of social comparison. This theory pointed out the need each of us has to check out our own ideas with those of others. The more ambiguous the situation, the greater is this need. In addition, when we find ourselves at odds with others, we feel pressure to reduce the discrepancies one way or another. The more we are attracted to the group, the more pressure we will feel to change toward the group norms.

On the hunch that this theory might have some relevance in predicting attitude influence on pot smoking, one student (Unger, 1974) conducted a modest study in which he asked, "What has been the most significant source of influence on your views toward pot smoking?" The largest source of influence (43 percent) was peers; the second largest (37 percent) was authoritative written documents; the next (8 percent) was lectures; and the remainder (12 percent) were other sources. These findings have been replicated many times in varying situations all over the world. Peer groups exert enormous pressure on individuals (Pascale, Sternin, & Sternin, 2010). These data would seem to confirm Festinger's thesis that we are inclined to look to others to help us determine the guidelines for our own opinions and behaviors. It is also significant to note that the value changes we undergo in college are likely to last for a lifetime.

CONFORMITY: RESEARCH AND APPLICATIONS

In the movie *The Firm*, Tom Cruise joins a Memphis law firm only to find out that "the firm" doesn't approve of its employees' spouses working, encourages its employees to have children, has never had one of its employees fail the bar exam, and so on. This film depicts the incredible conformity pressure to which the new lawyers and their spouses are subjected. By the way, as you enter into your career, don't be surprised if you find some more subtle but unmistakably similar conformity pressures placed on you. In fact, one major study of college students found that, "Peer influence is thought particularly potent because it is based on a sense of trust that exists between peers. Peer influence manifests itself through a 'conformity based on personal commitment and choice,' and thus differs from authority-based influence exercised by parents or other adult figures" (Arum & Roksa, 2011, p. 67).

One of the earliest conformity studies was conducted by Muzafer Sherif (1963). He showed subjects a pinpoint of light projected onto a wall in a completely darkened room. The light appeared to move even when the subjects knew that it was stationary. This optical illusion is called the *autokinetic effect*. Subjects were tested alone and in groups. They were told to report when the light appeared to move and to judge about how far it moved. When tested individually, subjects estimated the light's range of movement at 3.6 inches. After they had discussed their experiences in groups of two and three, the average range of estimated movement had been reduced to 0.4 inch. Clearly, the group discussion influenced each person's judgment of the amount of the light's movement, resulting in the reduced range of estimates of that movement. This clearly fits Kiesler and Kiesler's (1969) definition of conformity as "a change in behavior or belief . . . as a result of real or imagined group pressure" (p. 2).

Solomon Asch (1952) also conducted a classic series of conformity studies. Look at the two cards with vertical lines drawn on them shown in Figure 5.8. Which line on card (b) is the same length as that on card (a)? If you had been in Asch's study, you and the other seven subjects would have announced your decisions in order as you were seated in the room. You are the seventh to answer out of eight. For the first two rounds, there is unanimous agreement. However, on the third trial, everyone in the group agrees that line 1 is equal in length to line x. You think it is line 2, instead. What do you do? This goes on through 18 experimental trials. In 12 of the trials, you are the only one disagreeing with the others. Actually, the others in the group were Asch's paid stooges, or confederates. The experiment was designed to create pressure on subjects to conform or yield to the others.

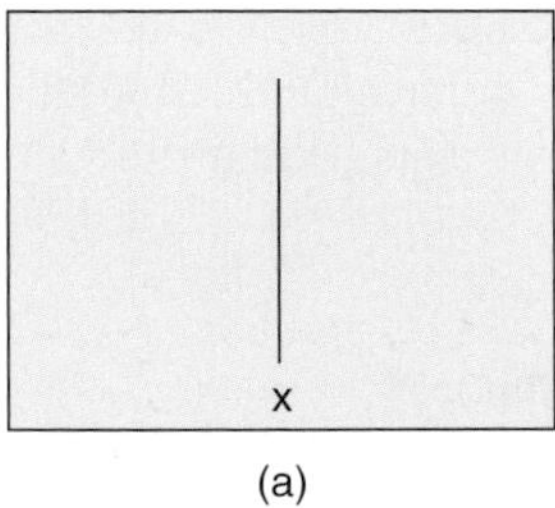

(a)

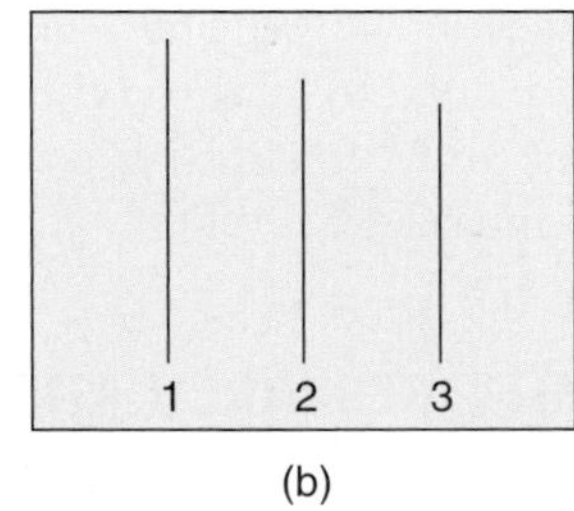

(b)

FIGURE 5.8 Asch's Conformity Study

In several studies, a total of more than 600 people participated as naive subjects. Some of the results are summarized below:

- Group pressure does, indeed, produce conformity.
- Yielding can be induced even in attitudes having personal relevance.
- Yielding is greater on difficult decisions than on easy ones.
- There are large differences in the amounts of yielding for different individuals.
- When subjects are tested again without the group pressure, a major part of the original yielding disappears.

Some situational factors that were found to be pertinent to the conformity process include group size, perceived competence of group members, group unanimity, extremity of group opinion, and group cohesiveness. The size of the group affects conformity in that group pressure increases to a maximum with four people composing the opposing majority. Numbers larger than 4, even up to 15, produce only slightly more yielding. Higher perceived group competence produced more conformity pressure. Group unanimity appears to have a highly significant effect on conformity. Asch (1956) found that when at least one other member of the group reinforced the one-member minority, the resistance to group pressure was significantly increased. With regard to extremity of majority opinion, Tuddenham (1961) found that when the majority opinion lies well outside the range of acceptable judgments, yielding occurs among fewer individuals and to a lesser degree. Group cohesiveness caused an increase in conformity, and the second-higher-status group member conformed the most of anyone in the group.

Individual personal factors also have been studied in relation to conformity (see also Chapter 3). Some of the results of the conformity research include the following (Tuddenham, 1961):

- Conformists are less intelligent.
- Conformists are lower in ego strength and in their ability to work in stress situations.
- Conformists tend toward feelings of personal inferiority and inadequacy.
- Conformists show an intense preoccupation with other people, as opposed to more self-contained, autonomous attitudes of the independent person.
- Conformists express attitudes and values of a more conventional (conservative) nature than nonyielders.

Have you ever noticed what happens to the person who does try to deviate from the group? By definition this person is a *nonconformist.* He or she gets many more comments directed toward him or her as these variables increase (that is, group cohesion and relevance of topic, as well as acting in a noticeably different way). Think of the late Amy Winehouse, the Sex Pistols, and others of the "punk rock" genre as examples.

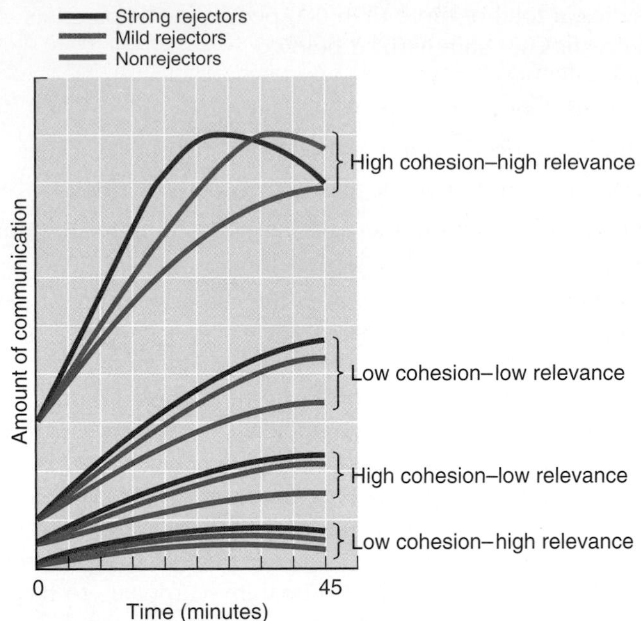

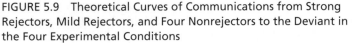

FIGURE 5.9 Theoretical Curves of Communications from Strong Rejectors, Mild Rejectors, and Four Nonrejectors to the Deviant in the Four Experimental Conditions

From Schacter, 1951, Deviation, Rejection, and Communication. *Journal of Abnormal and Social Psychology* 46:202. American Psychological Association, © 1951.

In a quantitative study of the group's reaction to a deviant, Schachter (1951) predicted that the deviant would be talked to the most (frequency of communication) and that the reaction to the deviant would depend upon the (1) relevance of the discussion topic, (2) degree of group cohesiveness, and (3) degree to which the person deviated. These predictions are summarized in the chart in Figure 5.9, which is included because the actual data supported virtually all the predictions.

In other words, we are more likely to get hot under the collar when a person deviates from a neighborhood group discussing cross-district busing of our children (high cohesion, high relevance) than when a person deviates from a group of strangers deciding what color to paint the walls in the school gymnasium (low cohesion, low relevance). Notice that the deviant gets many more comments directed toward him or her as these variables increase (that is, group cohesion and relevance of topic, as well as the degree of deviation on the topic). Notice also that in the most extreme case (the solid curved line at the top), the frequency of communication tends to diminish after about two-thirds of the 45-minute discussion (30 minutes). This leads us to believe that a certain amount of rejection or ostracism results if the deviant doesn't come around.

This study represents a quantitative analysis of a group discussion; Leavitt (1964) and Lipman-Blumen and Leavitt (1999) offer a qualitative analysis of the four stages of conformity pressure. The first stage might be called *reason*. We do not like hearing our ideas disconfirmed, but we are interested in logically convincing the deviant that he or she is wrong. Even at this stage, it is clear that we expect the deviant to change to conform to the group, and not vice versa. The second stage is *seduction*. During this stage, we attempt to appeal to the deviant's social needs. The comments begin to take on the tone of, "Aw, come on, be a sport, we know you don't want to put the whole group on the spot just for the sake of this little issue." It isn't long before the group enters stage 3, *coercion*. During this stage, the group members lose their smiles and good nature. The comments begin to take on the air of threat, something like, "Now look, this has gone far enough. If you won't play ball, then we are going to have to clip your wings but good the next time you want help from us." The fourth and final stage is *isolation*. At this point, the group gives up on and ignores the deviant. This tactic may finally bring conformity if the ostracism is prolonged.

Leavitt (1964) summarizes the four stages as follows: "It's as though the members of the group were saying, 'Let's reason with him; if that doesn't work, let's try to tease him by emotional seduction; and if even that doesn't work, let's beat him over the head until he has to give up. Failing that, then we'll excommunicate him; we'll amputate him from the group; we'll disown him'" (pp. 273–74). One of your author's former students wrote of her painful experience with this conformity influence:

> As a high school band member I experienced all four of these stages when we were to march in the Apple Blossom Parade.
>
> The band master told everyone to wear saddle shoes. When I explained to him that I had none, he said, "Get some, since everybody needs to be dressed the same" (step 1). I told him I had no money. "Then borrow some," another band member suggested. "Come on, we need you" (step 2). I told them I couldn't borrow any because of an unusual foot size. "Then if you don't get them, you can't march in the parade," said someone else (step 3).
>
> I didn't; I hid when the band came down the street. I never returned to the band again. I felt alone, isolated, and ostracized (step 4), and that ended my musical career. Although it was over twenty years ago, it still hurts when I think about it.

On a more personal level, Williams (1989) reports that in spite of all the publicity regarding the dangers of contracting AIDS from unsafe sex, many young people today continue to engage in risky behaviors. She writes, "Even teen-agers who are not sexually active tend to see the matter as a personal choice, . . . and it seems clear that pressure from peers . . . has more impact on teen-agers generally." On the basis of over 900 surveys and interviews nationwide, she reports, "Teenagers say that social pressure is the chief reason why so many do not wait to have sexual intercourse until they are older. Both boys and girls say they are pressured by other teenagers to go further than they wanted to" (p. A1).

John McCain (1999) writes of the severity of the coercive pressure to conform that can be applied toward prisoners of war. In this example, the U.S. POWs had a small American flag that they would keep hidden and bring out once a day to keep their spirits up. When their captors found the flag, this is what resulted:

> Every afternoon, before we ate soup, we would hang Mike's flag on the wall of our cell and together recite the Pledge of Allegiance. No other event of the day had as much meaning to us.
>
> The guards discovered Mike's flag one afternoon during a routine inspection and confiscated it. They returned that evening and took Mike outside. For our

benefit as much as Mike's, they beat him severely, just outside our cell, puncturing his eardrum and breaking several of his ribs. When they finished, they dragged him bleeding and nearly senseless back into our cell, and we helped him crawl to his place on the sleeping platform. After things quieted down, we all lay down to sleep. Before drifting off, I happened to look toward a corner of the room, where one of the four naked light bulbs that were always illuminated in our cell cast a dim light on Mike Christian. He had crawled there quietly when he thought the rest of us were sleeping. With his eyes nearly swollen from the beating, he had quietly picked up his needle and thread and begun sewing a new flag. (McCain, 1999, pp. 335–36)

GROUPTHINK

In 2011, the famous movie producer Harvey Weinstein wrote in *Newsweek* magazine that the greatest mistake in his movie career was listening to his team members who talked him out of buying the movie rights to *The Girl with the Dragon Tattoo*. He wrote, "Everything about it in my gut said, 'Do this.' But my team said, 'No, we should focus on bigger movies,' and I let the committee overwhelm me . . . and that was a big bloody mistake" (Weinstein, 2011, p. 84). Weinstein should have followed his instinct, since he has produced such mega-successes as *The King's Speech*, best picture Academy Award winner for 2011; *The English Patient*, also a best picture Academy Award winner; *The Fighter*, another 2011 Academy Award winner; *Company Men, Shakespeare in Love, Chicago*, and *Blue Valentine*.

Irving Janis, a professor at Yale University, first coined the term *groupthink* (Janis, 1982). He and others have conducted a thorough investigation of the problems that conformity pressure has brought to some major American historical events. He defines groupthink as "a quick and easy way to refer to a mode of thinking that people engage in when they are deeply involved in a cohesive in-group, when the members' strivings for unanimity override their motivation to realistically appraise alternative courses of action" (p. 9). Groupthink represents a form of social influence of the majority that results in a dangerous level of agreement by all members of the group, even if the decided-upon action is obviously wrong. Groupthink results in a close-minded approach to problems and poor decision making. To prevent groupthink, alternative viewpoints should be fostered by the leader instead of hidden. It helps to divide the group into subgroups in hopes that different subgroups will come up with alternative solutions. As mentioned previously, the dissenter is important to groups and teams and can help the leader gain multiple perspectives on problems (Nemeth & Goncalo, 2004).

Janis cites several major political decisions that were characterized by groupthink, including the escalation of the Vietnam War and the 1961 American invasion of Cuba (the Bay of Pigs). Although not included in his book, Watergate is another example that fits his definition. Further studies (Whyte, 1989) have cited the Watergate scandal, the decision to launch the space shuttle *Challenger*, and the Iran-Contra arms scandal as disastrous examples of the groupthink phenomenon. More recently, best-selling investigative reporter Bob Woodward has identified the groupthink that led to the wars in Iraq and Afghanistan (Woodward, 2006, 2010).

Groupthink tends to occur when several factors are operating at once. These are called the *symptoms of groupthink*, and they can occur in any group. The eight symptoms are summarized below:

TYPE I: OVERESTIMATION OF THE GROUP—ITS POWER AND MORALITY

1. An illusion of invulnerability, shared by most or all of the members, which creates excessive optimism and encourages taking extreme risks.
2. An unquestioned belief in the group's inherent morality, inclining the members to ignore the ethical or moral consequences of their decisions.

TYPE II: CLOSED-MINDEDNESS

3. Collective efforts to rationalize in order to discount warnings or other information that might lead the members to reconsider their assumptions before they recommit themselves to their past policy decisions.
4. Stereotyped views of enemy leaders as too evil to warrant genuine attempts to negotiate, or as too weak and stupid to counter whatever risky attempts are made to defeat their purposes.

TYPE III: PRESSURES TOWARD UNIFORMITY

5. Self-censorship of deviations from the apparent group consensus, reflecting each member's inclination to minimize to himself the importance of his doubts and counterarguments.
6. A shared illusion of unanimity concerning judgments conforming to the majority view (partly resulting from self-censorship of deviations, augmented by the false assumption that silence means consent).
7. Direct pressure on any member who expresses strong arguments against any of the group's stereotypes, illusions, or commitments, making clear that this type of dissent is contrary to what is expected of all loyal members.
8. The emergence of self-appointed mindguards—members who protect the group from adverse information that might shatter their shared complacency about the effectiveness and morality of their decisions. (Janis, 1982, pp. 174–75)

Falling into the groupthink pitfall is very easy, especially because the information overload of the new millennium has paralyzed most Americans. We are living in an age of information. There are so many different ways we get our information, from 24-hour news stations like CNN to websites, newspapers, blogs, magazines, and advertisements. However, all of this information isn't necessarily a good thing because we can't process everything we see, read, and hear. That's where groupthink comes into play. It's easier to just follow the crowd instead of forming unique personal opinions (Piazza, 2007).

Certain groups are particularly vulnerable to groupthink. Those with members who are high in need for affiliation (see Chapter 3), those that are very cohesive (see Chapter 8), or those that have an autocratic leadership style (see earlier in this chapter) are likely candidates. However, there are procedures that can be employed to minimize the possibilities of groupthink (Janis, 1982, pp. 260–76). Here are some of the precautions:

- One member should be appointed "devil's advocate" or critical evaluator, to allow disagreements and criticism of the leader.
- Leaders should not reveal their preferences to the group at the beginning of the discussion.
- Several groups with different leaders might work independently on common problems to offer different perspectives.
- Group members should discuss the group's processes with trusted friends and report their reactions to the group.
- Outside experts should be called in periodically as resource persons. They should be encouraged to disagree with the group's assumptions.
- Whenever issues involve relations with rival groups (such as labor and management), time should be spent discussing all warning signals from the rivals and hypothesizing alternative "scenarios of the rivals' intentions."
- After preliminary decisions have been reached, the group should adjourn and hold a "second chance" meeting at a later date to let their ideas "incubate."

Although these suggestions may not always be applicable (even if they are, they may not always work), they do offer a constructive alternative to reduce the dangers of groupthink.

In another study, Whyte (1989) argued that the term *groupthink* is an incomplete explanation for such disastrous occurrences (decision fiascoes). Whyte's contention is that the way choices are "framed in a domain of losses" has more to do with risky groupthink decisions than actual group dynamics.

Whyte examined the events leading up to the space shuttle *Challenger* disaster to illustrate this phenomenon:

> This situation was the product of flawed decisions as much as it was a failure of technology. The pressures on the National Aeronautics and Space Administration (NASA) to launch a space shuttle at the earliest opportunity were intense, despite evidence that this course of action was inadvisable. A decision to delay the launch was undesirable from NASA's perspective because of the impact it would have on political and public support for the program. In contrast, a successful launch would have appeased the public and politicians alike, and would have amounted to another major achievement. NASA engineers claimed that pressure to launch was so intense that authorities routinely dismissed potentially lethal hazards as acceptable risks.

A choice in the domain of losses was involved on either side of this decision. Had the launch of the *Challenger* been delayed any further, the space shuttle program would have undoubtedly suffered consequences. As it stands, the decision to launch the shuttle resulted in even dearer losses. Components of the Whyte study show that the phenomenon of groupthink is not a simple one.

Turner and colleagues (1992) conducted an ingenious set of experiments with college students in which they found that groupthink did in fact occur.

However, the level of groupthink varied along with two other factors. One was the level of cohesiveness (closeness) of the group members. The other was the level of outside threat the group experienced. In the high-threat condition, the groups were told that they were being videotaped and that the tapes would be shown in future classes to demonstrate poor group dynamics. The low-threat conditions had no videotaping.

Recognizing the early warning signs of groupthink is the first step toward stopping that process and regaining your ability to make decisions based on real facts and not the bits and pieces of information that you see in the media and hear from experts, neighbors, and whomever else. This will help you to think twice about forming your own opinions and making decisions based on your own opinions. Avoiding groupthink is always a better alternative because it helps to produce more creative and unique ideas to help groups succeed. "Pulling away and thinking as an individual is no easy task, but you'll be glad when you are no longer subject to the mob's pitfalls" (Rajiva & Bonner, 2007).

Group Development

A number of writers have been interested in the social influence process as it becomes manifest in different stages or phases of group development. Group development seems to be partly the result of individual psychological needs and partly the result of the social influences manifested in the group. The various theories on group phases are somewhat incompatible, in that some writers identify three phases and others identify four. Also, some writers identify the phases that occur during the course of one group discussion (Tuckman, 1965; Fisher, 1980), whereas others identify the phases that occur over the life of a group, including several meetings Blanchard, et. al., 2007; (Bennis & Shepard, 1956; Thelen & Dickerman, 1949). Still another viewpoint is that the phases occur in each meeting and continue to occur throughout the group's life history (Schutz, 1958; Bales & Strodbeck, 1951). This last viewpoint seems the most profound in providing insight into the phenomenon of group development.

With these differing frames of reference in mind, let us look at the four group phases that seem representative of the literature. *Phase 1* (orientation) seems to be a period in which group members simply try to break the ice and begin to find out enough about one another to have some common basis for functioning. It is variously referred to as a period of orientation, inclusion, or group formation. In this phase, people ask questions about one another, tell where they are from, reveal what they like and dislike, and generally make small talk. An excerpt from a student paper describes this phase:

> Even though we had a task to accomplish for the class, we began by talking about ourselves (one guy and girl found they both liked motor-cross racing, and two others found that they had both been to Daytona Beach last spring break). After we had a chance to "break the ice" we were more willing to throw out ideas on how to go ahead with the group project without being afraid of having our ideas shot down in flames.

Phase 1 seems to be characterized by the establishment of some minimal social relationship before group members feel comfortable getting down to work.

However, some executives who have experienced many years of decision-making meetings may begin work with little or no social orientation and only the barest minimum of group orientation. With these exceptions, the vast majority of us feel better having some period in which to build relationships prior to launching into the group's work.

Phase 2 (conflict) is frequently characterized by conflict of one kind or another. After the orientation phase passes, the pressure to accomplish something sooner or later intensifies whatever differences may exist. One student's description illustrates the transition from phase 1 to phase 2:

> We talked about personal interests until some common ground was established, then we found we could talk about the assignment more freely. But after talking about nonsubject things, it was hard to keep the line of talk on the problems at hand. Some wanted to get the assignment accomplished while two guys in the group continually swayed the conversation to things that were easier to talk about, but had nothing to do with the subject (Howard has a big thing for John Deere farm machinery). At first we were constantly trying not to hurt anyone's feelings, so we let the conversation drift. We didn't question or reject each other's ideas, and I feel we often settled for less than we should have. The longer we were in the group together, the more we got to know each other and the more times we voiced our real opinions. That's when the tempers started to flare!

Typically, in phase 2 the group begins to thrash out decisions for procedures as well as for determining the solution to the group task. Conflict over procedures may be one way in which group members fight for influence or control in the group.

After a period of small talk in an encounter group of middle-aged members, one member suggested that they go around the group and introduce themselves in some detail, telling what their jobs were, what part of the country they were from, and so on. Just as they were about to begin, another member suggested that they *not* reveal these things, to avoid the stereotyping that would inevitably result. A heated argument resulted. Eventually, they decided to assume their fantasized identities—that is, they adopted nicknames and behaviors and job titles that represented the type of person they wished they could be. Much later in the course of the group, they decided that the new procedure had been much better in helping them to try out behaviors they normally would have been too inhibited to attempt. For example, one female psychiatrist assumed the identity of "Bubbles," a cocktail waitress, because she had always wondered what it would be like to be a sex object and get outside her role as a professional person. The conflict regarding procedures turned out to be very productive for the group in the long run.

Phase 3 (emergence) involves a resolution of the conflict experienced in phase 2. Group cohesiveness begins to emerge, and the group settles into working more comfortably as a unit. This phase is described by three different sources in the following ways:

> Perhaps the major pitfall to be avoided at this point is that of glossing over significant differences for the sake of harmony. . . . Behavior is essentially a kind of polite behavior which avoids upsetting the group. (Thelen & Dickerman, 1949)

> Resistance is overcome in the third stage in which ingroup feeling and cohesiveness develop, new standards evolve, and new roles are adopted. In the task realm, intimate, personal opinions are expressed. (Tuckman, 1965)

> Social conflict and dissent dissipate during the third phase. Members express fewer unfavorable opinions toward decision proposals. The coalition of individuals who had opposed those proposals which eventually achieve consensus also weakens in the third phase. (Fisher, 1974)

Phase 4 (reinforcement) is the phase of maximum productivity and consensus. Dissent has just about disappeared, and the rule of the moment is to pat each other on the back for having done such a good job. Group members joke and laugh and generally reinforce one another for having contributed to the group's success. Student reactions to a group project in this phase include the following typical comments: "At first I thought this assignment would be a waste of time, but now I think it was the most worthwhile thing we have done in the course so far," and "Everybody I have talked to feels like the group exercise was really good. We are looking forward to doing more of these."

Once a group has gone through the phases and has been established, there are four main rules that apply to all small groups: boundary, aggregation, position, and information rules. *Boundary rules* define members of the group and address the difficulty of exiting and entering the group. If the group is permeable, individuals can enter and leave it at any time. If it is not permeable, then the group members are set and there is very little change in membership over time. *Aggregation rules* outline how decisions are made within the group and how strictly outlined the group norms are. *Position rules* delineate the leadership and authority positions within the group. Last, *information rules* define how information and resources are dispersed and utilized within the group (Sell et al., 2004).

Psychologically, we all need to feel that what we do is somehow justified or worthwhile (this is referred to in Chapter 4 as rationalizing or reducing cognitive dissonance). Thus, even if we have had bad experiences with a group, we tend to repress those and remember the good things we have experienced. The various group development theories are summarized in the chart in Figure 5.10 and in the following quotation from the earliest of the group development theorists:

> Beginning with individual needs for finding security and activity in a social environment, we proceed first to emotional involvement of the individuals with each other, and second to the development of a group as a rather limited universe of interaction among individuals and as the source of individual security. We then find that security of position in the group loses its significance, except that as the group attempts to solve problems it structures its activities in such a way that each individual can play a role which may be described as successful or not in terms of whether the group successfully solved the problem it had set itself. (Thelen & Dickerman, 1949, p. 316)

Although Blanchard and his associates (2007) add a fifth phase, termination, the bulk of the literature seems to point to four actual group phases. Termination is just the ending of the group.

Deadlines and time constraints sometimes offer more initiative than actual accomplishments. In a comprehensive study on models of group development,

	Phase 1	Phase 2	Phase 3	Phase 4	Phase 5
Thelen and Dickerman (1949)	Forming	Conflict	Harmony	Productivity	—
Bennis and Shepard (1956, 1961)	Dependence	Interdependence	Focused work	Productivity	—
Tuckman (1965)	Forming	Storming	Norming	Performing	—
Fisher (1980)	Orientation	Conflict	Emergence	Reinforcement	—
Blanchard et. al. (2007)	Orientation	Dissatisfaction	Integration	Production	Termination
Bales and Strodbeck (1951)	Orientation	Evaluation		Control	—
Schutz (1958)	Inclusion	Control		Affection	—

FIGURE 5.10 Summary of Literature on Group Phases

Gersick (1988) established that a group's progress is triggered more by the group members' awareness of time and deadlines than by completion of an absolute amount of work in a specific developmental stage.

REVIEW OF THE SYSTEMS APPROACH

In this chapter, we examined the complicated and fascinating questions of who influences whom and why. In the discussion of status and power, we saw that the two go hand in hand; that is, high-status individuals tend to have more power. An obvious extension of this is the notion that because of differing group norms, different characteristics bring about status in different groups. On a football team, the best player has the most status. Among college professors, the most extensively published usually has the most status. In street gangs, the toughest member typically has the highest status. And so it goes from one group to another.

A major portion of this chapter dealt with the issues of leadership and followership. Although these two are not always discussed together, they are interrelated. Here the systems principle of *equifinality* applies. In other words, the leadership style that would be appropriate in one situation with one set of followers may not be the most appropriate in a different situation with a different set of followers. Put another way, all leadership occurs in some context. As we change the context, the leader's behaviors also need to change in order to maintain effectiveness (Hughes, Ginnett, & Curphy, 2011). A great deal of study has led to the belief that the democratic leadership style is the most likely to get the best results in a great many cases. However, our systems approach reminds us that some situations require the authoritarian style as the most appropriate. In situations involving life-or-death decisions or in times of crisis requiring rapid decisions, the democratic approach may be too slow or simply impractical. As we saw earlier, two popular theoretical syntheses regarding leadership styles are offered by Fiedler (1967; Fiedler & Chemers, 1974), and Hersey, Blanchard, and Johnson (2001). They all suggest a contingency theory of leadership: The best leadership style is one flexible enough to adapt to the situation. If asked which leadership style is best, they would answer, "It depends."

This chapter also covered the topics of social influence and conformity. Systems theory concepts are beautifully illustrated in the literature. Conformity pressure differs depending on the type of group (for example, military versus the commune), the style of leadership (say, authoritarian versus democratic), the personalities of the group members (dominant versus acquiescent), and a number of other factors. We know from the research literature that conformity is more likely (1) when group membership is highly valued by its participants, (2) when members have dependent, obedient, and acquiescent personalities, (3) when the leader is more authoritarian, (4) when the group is unanimously against a deviant member, and (5) when the goal is to produce public compliance rather than actual private acceptance. Conformity is clearly dependent on an entire constellation of other variables.

One study analyzed conformity in a systems way (although the authors did not identify it as a systems analysis). Rarick, Soldow, and Geizer (1976) looked at conformity as a result of the combination of a person's personality and the situation in which he or she is placed. The personality variable was self-confidence (they called it self-monitoring), and the situational variable was group size (dyad or three- to six-person group). They found that less confident people conform more in three- to six-person groups than do highly confident people. This confirms numerous previous findings. However, they also found that in a dyad, confident people did not conform any more or less than those lacking in confidence. This study very nicely illustrates the systems approach that all these variables (and others) simultaneously influence one another.

The last section of this chapter dealt with group development. We know that groups go through fairly common phases, depending on the type of group. Some writers assume that all the phases occur during the course of one group discussion. Other writers believe that these phases evolve slowly over the group's lifetime. However, the systems theory approach suggests that these phases are simply parts of a recurring *cycle* of events that probably occur during a single meeting and tend to be repeated throughout the group's lifetime as well. This point of view seems to be the most theoretically valid and is supported by other authors who apply the systems approach to the analysis of small group interaction (see, for example, Ellis & Fisher, 1994).

As open and dynamic systems, the key to a successful small group is freedom to be open in the decision-making process. Disagreements should be encouraged to allow for the exploration of alternative viewpoints. Businesspeople agree that openness is the number-one element of a successful team, followed by shared goals, cooperation, information sharing, and access to feedback (Tucci, 2004).

EXERCISES

1. Case Studies Discussion

Break into small groups, and discuss the following case studies. Attempt to reach agreement on each case. Have each group report its decision to the class and the reasons for the choice.

CASE A: "DR. DEATH"

Dr. Jack Kevorkian (also known as "Dr. Death") (see the 2011 HBO movie "You Don't Know Jack') assisted in over two dozen suicides, in violation of a Michigan state law prohibiting doctors from assisting in suicides. Thirty-four other states have such a law.

All the patients Dr. Kevorkian assisted had requested his help. He videotaped the procedure as evidence that he had done nothing wrong.

On the other hand, physicians around the country argued that his behavior was morally wrong and that it violated the Hippocratic oath, in which doctors pledge to help their patients. Opponents also feared that families could abuse this practice. University of Michigan law professor Yale Kasimar argued: "In a climate in which suicide would often be the 'rational' thing to do, or at least a 'reasonable' option, there is a real possibility that it would become the unreasonable thing *not* to do." (Based on David Zeman, "A Question of Control," *The Detroit Free Press*, January 2, 1994, pp. F1, F4.)

CASE B: JACOBS FURNITURE, INC.

You are Bev Stone, manager of the Accounting Department of Jacobs Furniture. The entire company has about 1,700 employees, 15 of whom are in your department. You have just returned from a meeting held by the general manager, Bill Keppler. In this meeting, Bill explained to all the department heads that there was an important task for them to accomplish. The local United Way drive was currently under way. Each year every organization in the city was asked to do what it could to donate money to the United Way, which supports many worthwhile, nonprofit agencies in the community.

Bill explained that last week the brochures and pledge cards had been sent to everyone in the company and that, to date, only 5 percent had responded. Then, Rick Adams, an engineer on loan to the United Way from a local computer company, gave a short presentation telling of the many worthwhile services the United Way provides. Bill Keppler then said that he wanted each department head to go back to his or her employees and see what could be done to raise the participation rate in each department.

You have mixed feelings about this assignment. On the one hand, there is no doubt that the United Way is a deserving organization. On the other hand, because business has been very poor for the past few years, employees have had no raises during that period. Morale is quite low, mostly because of economic pressures. There has been much complaining already about the increases in taxes resulting in less and less take-home pay. Also, with the cost of living on the increase, even the *same* amount of money wouldn't buy as much as it did five years ago. In this context, you feel awkward about asking people in your work group to donate more of their pay to charitable causes.

Your boss has made it clear that he supports this charity to a very strong degree. Therefore, you must do something. Decide what specific steps you will take in carrying out this task.

2. Interaction Analysis Exercise

Observe a group discussion (perhaps one of the two case study discussions from above), and try to use the Bales Interaction Process Analysis scoring sheet (Figure 5.11) to make your observations more systematic. Start by observing

Scoring of Interaction (Bales)	Person 1	Person 2	Person 3	Row Totals
1. *Seems friendly,* raises other's status, gives help, rewards others				
2. *Dramatizes,* jokes, laughs, shows satisfaction				
3. *Agrees,* shows passive acceptance, understands, concurs, complies				
4. *Gives suggestions,* direction, implying autonomy for others				
5. *Gives opinion,* evaluation, analysis, expresses feeling or wish				
6. *Gives information,* repeats, clarifies, confirms				
7. *Asks for information,* repetition, confirmation				
8. *Asks for opinion,* evaluation, analysis; expresses feeling				
9. *Asks for suggestion,* direction, possible ways of action				
10. *Disagrees,* shows passive rejection, resorts to formality, withholds help				
11. *Shows tension,* asks for help, withdraws "out of field"				
12. *Seems unfriendly,* deflates other's status, defends or asserts self				
Column totals				

FIGURE 5.11 Bales Interaction Process Analysis Scoring Sheet

and recording only one person in the group. Simply place a check mark in the appropriate row when a person says something in the group. As you gain more experience, record two or three group members. You may also want to try having several people observe the same person to check the reliability of your observations.

3. Group Development Exercise

Observe a real-life problem-solving group. Listen carefully for statements that indicate the four phases of group development. You might take notes to record exact statements that illustrate the four phases. Notice also if the group does *not* seem to go through these four phases. Compare your observations with those of others who have observed different groups. Do most of the observations correspond to the research findings?

READINGS: Overview

In the first reading, Hersey, Blanchard, and Johnson offer a newly revised elaboration on how to identify the readiness of group members, which influences the choice of an appropriate leadership style.

The second article, by Posner and Kouzes, offers an excellent summary of the top 10 lessons for leaders.

Reading 5.1 Application of Situational Leadership®

Paul Hersey, Kenneth H. Blanchard, and Dewey E. Johnson

In using Situational Leadership®, one should always keep in mind that there is no one best way to influence others. Rather, any leader behavior may be more or less effective depending on the readiness level of the person you are attempting to influence. Shown in Figure A is a comprehensive version of the Situational Leadership® model. It will provide you with a quick reference to assist in (1) diagnosing the level of readiness, (2) adapting by selecting high probability leadership styles, and (3) communicating these styles effectively to influence behavior. Implicit in Situational Leadership® is the idea that a leader should help followers grow in readiness as far as they are able and willing to go. This development

---

From Paul Hersey et al., *Management of Organizational Behavior*, 8th ed. (Englewood Cliffs, NJ: Prentice Hall, 2001). Reprinted by permission of The Center for Leadership Studies, Escondido, CA.

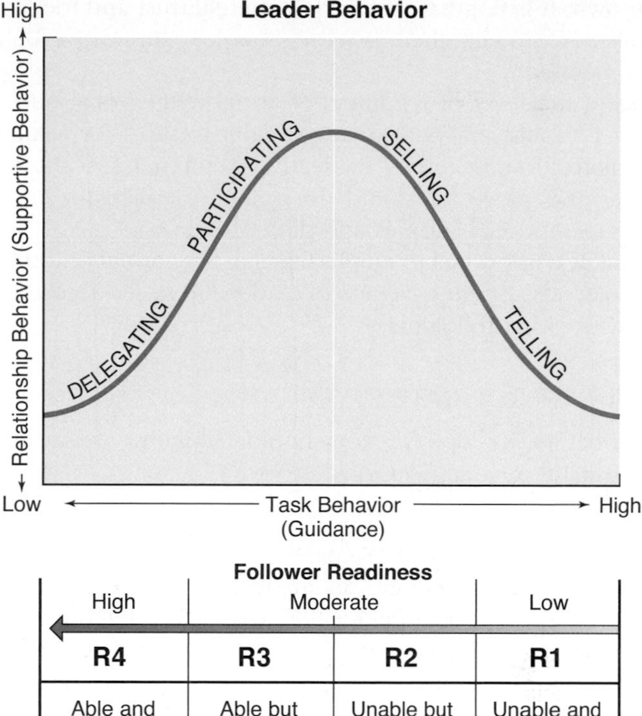

High	Moderate		Low
R4	**R3**	**R2**	**R1**
Able and Willing or Confident	Able but Unwilling or Insecure	Unable but Willing or Confident	Unable and Unwilling or Insecure

FIGURE A Expanded Situational Leadership Model

© Paul Hersey, *The Situational Leader* (Escondido, Calif.: Center for Leadership Studies, 1984), p. 63.

of followers should be done by adjusting leadership behavior through the four styles along the leadership curve in Figure A.

Situational Leadership® contends that strong direction (task behavior) with followers with low readiness is appropriate if they are to become productive. Similarly, it suggests that an increase in readiness on the part of people who are somewhat unready should be rewarded by increased positive reinforcement and socioemotional support (relationship behavior). Finally, as followers reach high levels of readiness, the leader should respond not only by continuing to decrease control over their activities, but also by continuing to decrease relationship behavior. People with high readiness do not need socioemotional support as much as they need greater freedom. At this stage, one of the ways leaders can prove their confidence and trust in these people is to leave them more and more on their own. It is not that there is less mutual trust and friendship between leader and follower—in fact, there is more—but less supportive behavior on the leader's part is needed.

Regardless of the level of readiness of an individual or group, change may occur. Whenever a follower's performance begins to slip—for whatever reason—and ability or motivation decreases, the leader should reassess the readiness level of this follower and move backward through the leadership curve, providing appropriate socioemotional support and direction.

At this point, it is important to emphasize that Situational Leadership® focuses on the appropriateness or effectiveness of leadership styles according to the task-relevant readiness of the followers.

DETERMINING APPROPRIATE STYLE

To determine what leadership style you should use with a person in a given situation, you must make several decisions.

What Objective(s) Do We Want to Accomplish?

First, you must decide what areas of an individual's or a group's activities you would like to influence. Specifically, what objective(s) do you want to accomplish? In the world of work, those areas would vary according to a group's responsibilities. For example, sales managers may have responsibilities in sales, administration (paperwork), service, and group development. Therefore, before managers can begin to determine the appropriate leadership style to use with a group, they must decide what aspect of that group's job they want to influence.

For example, the goal "to ship 100 percent of customer orders within 24 hours of order receipt" is too general and needs to be broken up into specific tasks that can be assigned to a group to accomplish the goal. Developed in association with a customer service unit, it would work like this:

1. The goal is summarized using trigger words, e.g., prompt service.
2. Tasks to accomplish the goal are identified by the people involved.
   a. Answering the phone
   b. Completing the order form
   c. Completing the packing order
   d. Shipping the order
   e. Adjusting service problems

What Is the Group's Readiness?

The sales manager must then diagnose the readiness of the group to accomplish these tasks. The key issue is, How ready or receptive is the group to accomplish these tasks? If the group is at a high level of readiness, only a low amount of leadership intervention will be required. If, on the other hand, the group is at a low level of readiness, considerable leadership intervention may be required.

What Leadership Action Should Be Taken?

The next step is deciding which of the four leadership styles would be appropriate for the group. Suppose the manager has determined that the group's readiness level, in terms of accomplishing all of these tasks, is high—that is, the group is able and willing (R4). When working with this group, a delegating (S4) style (low task–low relationship behavior) should be used. Some members of the group may be lower in readiness than the group as a whole with respect to specific tasks. For example, a team member may be R3 (able but insecure) with regard to responding to service problems on a new line of equipment. The manager would use an S3 (high relationship–low task) leadership style to build that member's confidence and self-esteem.

What Was the Result of the Leadership Intervention?

This step requires assessment to determine if results match expectations. Individuals and groups learn a little bit at a time. Development involves positively reinforcing successive approximations as the individual or group approaches the desired level of performance. Therefore, after a leadership intervention, the manager must assess the result through rechecking the objectives, rediagnosing readiness, and ascertaining if further leadership is indicated.

What Follow-up, If Any, Is Required?

If there is a gap between present performance and desired performance of the individual or group, then follow-up is required in the form of additional leadership interventions, and the cycle starts again. In a dynamic environment, such as the leadership environment, follow-up is almost a certainty. Leadership under modern competitive conditions means hitting moving targets. Tasks, readiness, and results are all continually changing; follow-up is a must. Leading is a full-time job that must be practiced every hour of every day.

EFFECTIVE TASK STATEMENTS

A well-formulated task statement contributes greatly toward the assessment of individual readiness. In contrast, vague and weakly formulated task statements make it difficult to accurately assess task readiness and can lead to unnecessary friction and conflict. Gustav Pansegrouw, president of P-E Corporate Services, a management consulting firm, found the following technique for writing task statements very useful, particularly from the follower's perspective. A key task for a customer order clerk may be stated as follows:

> To answer the phone promptly.

Using this task statement as a guide, the manager may assess the clerk's task readiness level as R2, willing but unable. Using the same task statement as a guide, the clerk may assess the task readiness level as R4, willing and able.

This difference in task readiness assessment between manager and clerk is usually the result of different meanings attached to the word *promptly*. If the task were formulated in the following way the two persons would have a much clearer understanding of the task.

To answer the phone on the first ring.

With such a specific statement of the task as a guide, it becomes much easier to assess task-relevant readiness. The probability of agreement between the two parties' assessments also increases.

The major difference between the two task statements just presented is that the second one contains a clearly defined and measurable performance standard for the task. The expected performance is thus an integral part of the task.

Of all the aspects of accomplishing tasks, individual readiness is the most critical. At any given time, each person is at a variety of task-specific readiness levels, depending on the tasks that must be performed. It is not that an individual is high or low in readiness, but that each person tends to be approximately ready according to a specific task.

It should be remembered that, although readiness is a useful concept for making diagnostic judgments, other situational variables—the supervisor's style (if close by), a crisis or time bind, the nature of the work—can be of equal or greater importance. Yet, the readiness concept is a solid benchmark for choosing the appropriate style with an individual or group at a particular time.

DIRECTION OF READINESS CHANGE

Recent research at the Center for Leadership Studies has indicated that it is useful to measure not only a follower's general level of readiness, such as R1 or R2, but also the direction of this readiness. The primary reason is that there are important differences in leader behavior if the follower's readiness is increasing, decreasing, or static.

For example, place yourself in the role of leader in each of three situations. Recall that one aspect of your role as leader is to diagnose the follower's ability and willingness to respond to your efforts to implement a specific goal. In other words, how receptive is the follower in each of these situations to your leadership efforts?

- *Situation 1.* The follower's confidence, commitment, and motivation are low and are continuing to decline. Knowledge, experience, and skill remain marginal.
- *Situation 2.* The follower's knowledge, skill, and experience are increasing from an entry level, while confidence, commitment, and motivation remain low.
- *Situation 3.* Ability and willingness remain low; the follower is unable and insecure.

After reading the three situations, you can diagnose the appropriate readiness level by looking for the key elements of ability and willingness. Remember that ability has the three components of knowledge, experience, and skill, while willingness has the three components of confidence, commitment, and motivation. One convenient way of assessing these components is to use a scale from + + + for a high level of readiness to - - - for a low level of readiness.

Suppose you have made the correct diagnosis that the follower is R1—unable and unwilling or insecure regarding the goal. You now want to diagnose the direction of the follower's readiness. Does the information in each situation show any elements that seem to be increasing, decreasing, or remaining static?

In situation 1, the follower is declining in readiness; in situation 2, the follower is increasing in readiness; in situation 3, the follower remains static or unchanged in readiness.

What is the implication of this analysis to your leadership efforts? In each situation the follower's general level of readiness is R1. But does that mean that your leadership interventions should be the same? Probably not. Situation 1 suggests action to correct regressive behavior; situation 2 suggests continuing developmental behavior; and situation 3 suggests initiating developmental behavior.

Reading 5.2 Ten Lessons for Leaders and Leadership Developers

Barry Z. Posner and James M. Kouzes

EXECUTIVE SUMMARY

In the early 1980s we set upon a quest to discover what it took to become a leader. We wanted to know the common practices of ordinary men and women when they were at their leadership best—when they were able to take people to places they had never been before. But knowing that the portrait emerging from the study of personal-best leadership experiences was only a partial picture, we also explored the expectations that the constituents have of people they would be willing to follow. Strategies, tactics, skills, and practices are empty (or worse yet, manipulative and exploitative) unless we understand the fundamental human aspirations that connect leaders and constituents.

Our analysis of thousands of cases and surveys from over a dozen years of research has revealed a consistent pattern of exemplary leadership practices and fundamental constituent expectations. What we've learned from studies specifically with college student leaders over the past five years has only strengthened our fundamental appreciation that leadership is not a mysterious, mystical, or ethereal concept—one that is somehow beyond the scope and imagination of the vast majority of people. Leadership is certainly not conveyed in a gene, and it's most definitely not a secret code that can't be understood by ordinary folks. Our research has shown us that leadership is an observable, learnable set of practices. Indeed, the belief that leadership can't be learned is a far more powerful deterrent to development than is the nature of the leadership process itself. In this [reading] we discuss 10 lessons we've learned from thousands of ventures about what it takes to get extraordinary things done in organizations.

Lesson 1: Challenge Provides the Opportunity for Greatness—in Leading and in Learning to Lead

Draw a line down the middle of a piece of paper. Now think of the leaders you admire. Write their names in the left-hand column. In the right-hand column,

---

From Barry Z. Posner and James M. Kouzes, *The Journal of Leadership Studies* 3, no. 3 (1996). Reprinted by permission of the author.

opposite each name, record the events or situations with which you identify these individuals. We predict that you will have associated the leaders from business with corporate turnarounds, entrepreneurial ventures, new product/service development, and other business transformations. For those on the list who are leaders in the military, government, community, arts, church, clubs, and student organizations, we predict a similar association with transforming events and times. When we think of leaders, we recall periods of turbulence, conflict, innovation, and change.

But we need not investigate well-known leaders to discover that all leadership is associated with pioneering efforts. In our research, we asked thousands of individuals, both individual contributors and those in official management positions, to write "personal best leadership" cases. What first struck us about these cases was that they were about significant change. When the participants in our studies—be they college students or senior citizens, from communities or corporations, from the boiler room to the boardroom—recalled doing their "personal best" as leaders, they automatically associated their best with changing, innovating, and overcoming difficulties. These personal best leadership cases were—and still continue to be—unprecedented testimony to the power of challenging opportunities to provide for the expression of extraordinary leadership actions on the part of "ordinary" people. "The biggest lesson I learned from my personal best [involving his college baseball team]," Karl Thompson explained, "is that you will never know if something will work if you don't try it."

A similar realization came when we asked people how they learned to lead. They responded overwhelmingly: "Trial and error." Experience, it appears, is indeed the best teacher—but not just any experience. To describe how their "personal best leadership" and learning experiences felt, people used the words *exciting, exhilarating, rewarding*, and *fun*. Dull, routine, boring experiences—in the classroom or in the boardroom—did not provide anyone anywhere with the opportunity to excel or to learn. Only challenge presents the opportunity for greatness. Leaders are pioneers—people who take risks in innovation and experiment to find new and better ways of doing things. Learners are also venturers.

Lesson 2: Leadership Is in the Eye of the Beholder

Constituents choose leaders. Leaders cannot be appointed or anointed *superiors*. Constituents determine whether someone is fit to lead. The trappings of power and position may give someone the right to exercise authority, but we should never, ever mistake position and authority for leadership. Only when our constituents believe that we are capable of meeting their expectations will we be able to mobilize their actions.

When we view leadership from this perspective, suddenly, and appropriately, the relationship is turned upside down. From this vantage, leaders serve their constituents; they do not boss them around. The best leaders are the servants of others' wants and desires, hopes and dreams. And to be able to respond to the needs of others, leaders must first get to know their constituents. By knowing their constituents, listening to them, and taking their advice, leaders can stand before others and say with assurance: "Here is what I heard you say that you want for yourselves. Here is how your own needs and interest will be served by enlisting in a common cause."

This notion of leaders as servants flies in the face of the leader-as-heroes myth perpetuated so long in comic books, novels, and movies. Yet it is the single most important factor in the dynamic relationship between leader and constituent. Unless we are sensitive to subtle cues, we cannot respond to the aspiration of others. And if we cannot respond to their aspirations, they will not follow.

Lesson 3: Credibility Is the Foundation of Leadership

We also researched the expectations people have of those whom they would be willing to follow. We asked more than 25,000 people from a range of organizations, around the globe, to tell us what they admired and looked for in their leaders. According to these data, people want leaders who are honest, forward-looking, inspiring, and competent.

While these results aren't terribly surprising, they are extraordinarily significant to all leaders, because three of these four characteristics comprise what communications experts refer to as *source credibility*. When determining whether or not we believe someone who is communicating with us—whether that person is a teacher, newscaster, salesperson, manager, parent, or colleague—we look for trustworthiness (honesty), expertise (competence), and dynamism (inspiration). Credibility is the single most important asset a leader has, and it should be protected and nurtured at all costs. Personal credibility is the foundation on which leaders stand. We call this the First Law of Leadership—If you don't believe in the messenger, you won't believe the message. This is precisely what Michael Cole learned as a 16-year-old T-ball coach: "Once the kids [ages 4–8] saw that I wanted what was best for them, as well as sharing in their excitement, they became a lot more trusting of me."

Lesson 4: The Ability to Inspire a Shared Vision Differentiates Leaders from Other Credible Sources

While credibility is the foundation, leaders must envision an uplifting and ennobling future. The one admired leadership quality that is not a criterion of source credibility is *forward-looking*. We expect leaders to take us to places we have never been before—to have clearly in mind an attractive destination that will make the journey worthwhile. "Leadership isn't telling people what to do," says Anthony Bianchi, who as a college sophomore organized a ski trip to the Italian Alps for American college students studying abroad in Florence: "It's painting a picture of an exciting possibility of how we can achieve a common goal."

To distinguish ourselves as leaders, we must be concerned with the future of our groups, organizations, and communities. If there is no vision, there is no business. The domain of leaders is the future. The leader's unique legacy is the creation of valued programs and institutions that survive over time.

Equally important, however, is the leader's capacity to enlist others to transform the vision into reality. In our leadership studies, we found that the ability to inspire others to share the dream—to communicate the vision so that others come to embrace it as their own—was what uplifted constituents and drew them forward. Leaders in any endeavor, whether they occupy the formal role of manager or not, must demonstrate personal enthusiasm for the dream. Only passion will ignite the flames of our constituents' desires.

Lesson 5: Without Trust, You Cannot Lead

While we ask people to tell us about their "personal best leadership" experiences, they typically come to the realization that it wasn't really "my best; it was our best. Because it wasn't me; it was us." Leaders can't do it alone! In fact, no one ever achieved an extraordinary milestone all by themselves—it is a team effort (and notice that the letter "I" does not appear in the word *team*).

At the heart of these collaborative efforts is trust. Leaders possess the genuine desire to make heroes and heroines of others. Without trust, people become self-protective. They are directive and tightly hold the reins on others. Similarly, when there is low trust, people are likely to distort, ignore, and disguise facts, ideas, conclusions, and feelings. People become suspicious and unreceptive. A trusting relationship between leader and constituents is essential to getting extraordinary things done.

Leaders create a caring climate—a climate of trust. For people to disclose their needs and feelings, to make themselves vulnerable, to expose their weaknesses, to risk failing, they must truly believe that they are safe. Take learning to parachute jump as an example. It is unlikely that people will be eager to jump if they do not trust the instructor or the equipment. The beginning phase of all effective learning processes has to be the establishment of a climate of trust, one in which people will want to take the risk associated with learning something new.

Another primary task of leadership is to create a climate in which others feel powerful, efficacious, and strong. In such a climate, people know they are free to take risks, trusting that when they make mistakes the leader will not ask, "Who's to blame?" but rather, "What did we learn?"

Involvement and participation are absolutely essential if this climate is to be created. Giving free choice and listening to others are also important elements of a trusting environment. Leaders focus on fostering collaboration, strengthening others, and building trust—on giving their power away—as the most effective strategy for synergistically enhancing the power of everyone.

Lesson 6: Shared Values Make a Critical Difference in the Quality of Life at Home and at Work

Credibility—that single most important leadership asset we mentioned earlier—has at its root the word *credo*, meaning "a set of beliefs." Every leader must begin by asking, "What do I stand for? What do I believe in? What values do I hold to be true and right?" Through our research, we found that people who reported greater compatibility between personal values and values of their organizations also reported significantly greater feelings of success in their lives; had greater understanding of the values of their managers and co-workers; were more willing to work longer and harder hours; and felt less stress at home and on the job. Shared values are essential for personal and business health.

Shared values provide a sense of alignment, so that, just like a rowing team, everyone is pulling in the same direction. Feeling aligned is an empowering feeling, creating a sense of freedom and personal integrity. When people feel that their personal values are in sync with those of their organization, our research indicates they are personally more successful and healthier. They feel liberated and in control of their lives. Shared values enable everyone to experience ownership in their organization.

Lesson 7: Leaders Are Role Models for Their Constituents

When we asked people to give us a behavioral definition of credibility the most common response was "do what you say you will do." People believe in actions more than in words, in practices more than in pronouncements. It's simply not sufficient to clarify and communicate values and beliefs. We must live them, and leaders are expected to set the example for others.

Mindy Behse, for example, reported that when she was captain of her high school swim team her teammates watched what she did, and, so, she said: "I couldn't ask anybody to do anything I wasn't willing to do. I had to take practices very seriously." Blain Thomas learned quickly that being captain of his baseball team meant that people not only watched what he did on the field, but off the field as well. And, he pointed out, "I couldn't be one kind of a leader, with certain standards on the field, and then be some other kind of person or leader off the field with different, especially lower, standards." As the team leader of a group of student painters during the summer, Mike Burciago observed that it was his willingness to do his share of the "grubby work" that made it easier to get others to voluntarily do their share as well.

Credibility is earned—minute by minute, hour by hour, day by day, week by week, month by month, year by year—through actions consistent with stated values leaders profess. Values are often considered the soft side of management, but, based on our research, we would say that nothing is more difficult than to be unwaveringly true to one's guiding beliefs.

Lesson 8: Lasting Change Progresses One Hop at a Time

When we asked Don Bennett, the first amputee to reach the 14,410-foot summit of Mt. Ranier, how he was able to climb to that height, he replied, looking down at his one leg and foot, "One hop at a time." He said that, when he was preparing for the climb, he would imagine himself on top of the mountain 1000 times a day. But when he started to climb, he'd look down at his foot and say, "Anybody can hop from here to there. So I did."

Big results from small beginnings. "Our goal seemed enormous; so we broke it down into parts and gave one part to each member," is how Richard Cabral accounts for the success of their high school organization in organizing a dinner for 300-plus people, including their parents and the city's mayor. Progress is always incremental. The key to lasting improvement is small wins. Choosing to do the easy things first—those that can be accomplished quickly and inexpensively by a team with a local champion—is the only sure way to achieve extraordinary things in organization. Referring to his own struggles against the seemingly insolvable problem of South Africa's apartheid, Bishop Tutu noted: "You eat an elephant . . . one bite at a time!"

Lesson 9: Leadership Development Is Self-Development

Leaders take us to places we have never been before. But there are no freeways to the future, no paved highways to unknown, unexplored destinations. There is only wilderness. If we are to step out into the unknown, we must begin by exploring the inner territory.

Leadership is an art—a performing art. And in the art of leadership, the instrument is the self. A musician may have a violin, an engineer a work station, and an accountant a computer. But a leader has only himself or herself as the medium of expression. Leadership development, then, is essentially a process of self-development.

Through self-development comes the self-confidence to lead. Self-confidence is really awareness of and faith in our own powers. The self-confidence required to lead comes from learning about ourselves—our skills, prejudices, talents, and shortcomings. Self-confidence develops as we build on strengths and overcome weaknesses. As Larry Olin, captain of his college tennis team, learned: "You must be confident in yourself before you can expect others to be confident in you."

People frequently ask, "Are leaders born or made?" We firmly believe that leadership can be learned. Certainly, some people are more predisposed to lead than others. But this is true of anything. Leadership is definitely not a divine-like grace given to a few charismatic men and women. It is a set of learnable practices. We believe it is possible for ordinary people to learn to get extraordinary things done. There is a leader in everyone, and the greatest inhibitor to leadership development is the belief that leadership cannot be learned.

Developing ourselves as leaders requires removing the barriers, whether self-imposed or imposed by the organization, and understanding that development is a continuous improvement process, not an event, a class, a book, or series of programs.

Lesson 10: Leadership Is Not an Affair of the Head—It Is an Affair of the Heart

Leadership is emotional. Period. To lead others requires passionate commitment to a set of fundamental beliefs and principles, visions and dreams. The climb to the summit is arduous and often frightening. Leaders encourage others to continue the quest by inspiring them with courage and hope.

In our study of leadership, we often asked our interviewees to tell how they would go about developing leaders, whether in school, business, government, or volunteer organizations. Major General John Stanford, then Commander of the U.S. Army's Military Traffic Management Command, gave a memorable reply: "When people ask me that question, I tell them I have the secret to success in life. The secret to success is to stay in love." Not the advice we expected from a military officer or, for that matter, from any of the people we interviewed. But the more we thought about it, the more we realized that leadership is an affair of the heart. Constituents will not follow unless they are persuaded that their leader passionately believes in his or her view of the future and believes in each of them.

In Conclusion: Leadership Is Everyone's Business

In our classes and workshops we regularly ask people to share a story about a leader they admire and whose direction they would willingly follow. From this exercise we hope they will discover for themselves what it takes to have an influence on others. We have another objective as well: we want them to discover the power that lies within each of us to make a difference.

Veronica Guerrero, then a graduate student, made us realize just how extraordinary those around us can be. She selected her father, Jose Luis Guerrero, as the leader she admired. Guerrero told the story of her father's leadership in the Union Nacional Sinarquista (UNS) back in the early 1940s. She related, in detail, what her father did and summed it up with this observation from Jose Luis: "I think the work that I did back then helped me extend myself and others to levels that I didn't know we could reach. . . . If you feel strongly about anything, and it is something that will ultimately benefit your community and your country, do not hold back. Fear of failing or fear of what might happen does not help anyone. . . . Do not let anyone or anything push you back."

Veronica Guerrero closed her description of her father (who was then dying of pancreatic cancer) with this observation: "As I heard his story and I saw a sick, tired, and weak man I could not help thinking that our strength as humans and as leaders has nothing to do with what we look like. Rather, it has everything to do with what we feel, what we think of ourselves. . . . Leadership is applicable to all facets of life." That is precisely the point. If we are to become leaders, we must believe that we, too, can be a positive force in the world. It does have everything to do with what we think of ourselves.

Decision-Making Processes

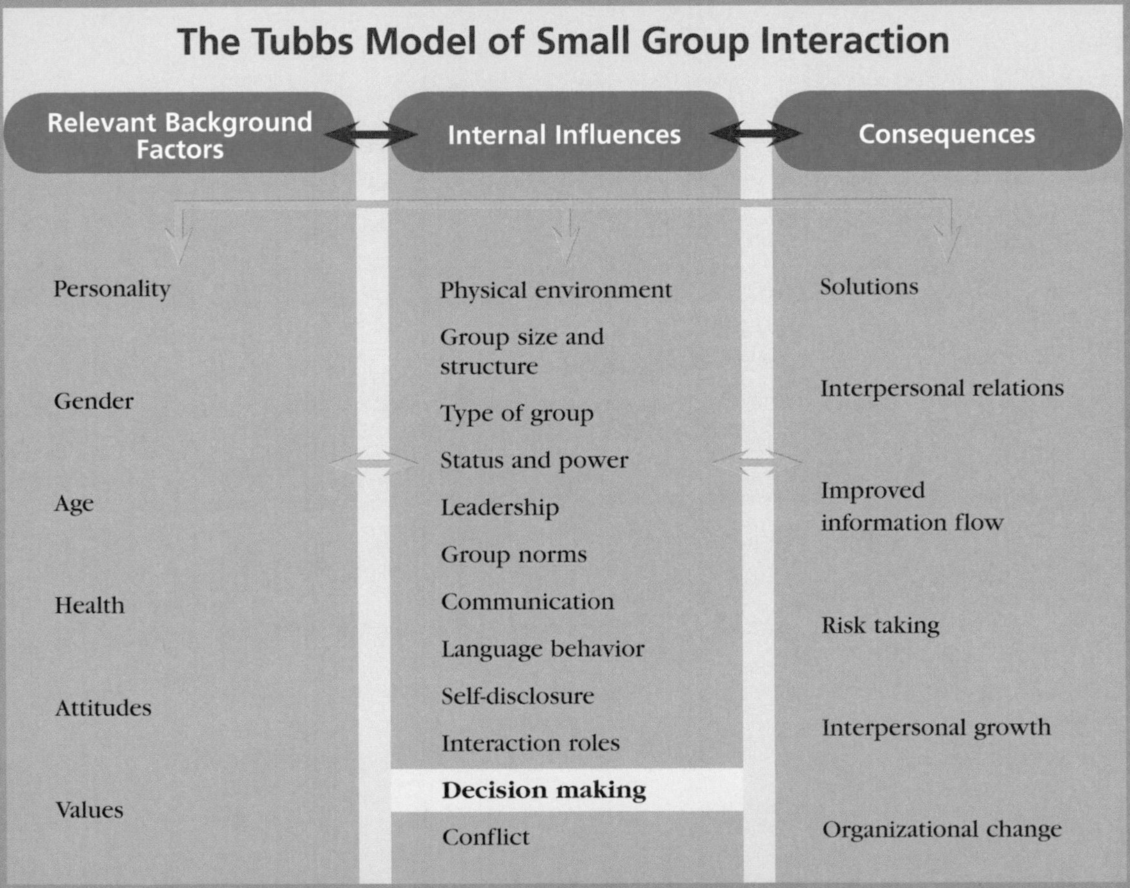

The Tubbs Model of Small Group Interaction

Relevant Background Factors	Internal Influences	Consequences
Personality	Physical environment	Solutions
Gender	Group size and structure	Interpersonal relations
Age	Type of group	Improved information flow
Health	Status and power	Risk taking
Attitudes	Leadership	Interpersonal growth
Values	Group norms	Organizational change
	Communication	
	Language behavior	
	Self-disclosure	
	Interaction roles	
	Decision making	
	Conflict	

Concepts in **boldface** in gray panels are the emphases of this chapter.

Preview

Our analysis of the internal influences of the Tubbs Model of Small Group Interaction continues in Chapter 6. Several different decision-making processes are presented. We begin with a discussion of ways to improve creativity. The reflective thinking process, which is one of the oldest and most-often-used decision-making methods, is described. We also examine the Kepner-Tregoe approach, a variation of the reflective thinking process based mainly on the criteria phase. The fishbone technique, brainstorming, incrementalism, mixed scanning, and tacit bargaining are the other methods for decision making discussed in this chapter. By examining each of these problem-solving strategies, we hope to help you become a better problem solver.

Glossary

Brainstorming A technique used to generate ideas. It emphasizes brain activity. It can be applied as part of the problem-solving process.

Convergent Thinking A form of thinking in which ideas come together to form a solution.

Divergent Thinking A form of thinking in which many different aspects of an idea are explored. Brainstorming is one technique of divergent thinking.

Fishbone Technique A method of examining cause and effect using a fishbone diagram.

Incrementalism The process of making decisions that result in change by increments.

Kepner-Tregoe Approach A variation of the reflective thinking sequence. Its most important contribution is the way in which a group works through the criteria phase, differentiating between the musts and the wants of a solution.

Mixed Scanning A decision-making strategy that combines examining a problem comprehensively (the rational approach) and part by part (the incremental approach).

Reflective Thinking Process A pattern for small group problem solving that includes six components:

1. What is the problem?
2. What are its causes and limits?
3. What are the criteria for an acceptable solution?
4. What are the available solutions?
5. What is the best solution?
6. How can it be implemented?

Tacit Bargaining Bargaining in which communication is incomplete or impossible.

CASE STUDY

THE AIRBUS 380

Airbus, one of the world's leading commercial jet manufacturers, planned to launch its newest and biggest jet, the A380, in 2007. At 239 feet long and with a capacity for 555 passengers, this is the largest passenger airliner ever built. With the plane's wings made in Britain, the horizontal stabilizer in Spain, the nose section and center fuselage in France, and the forward fuselage and vertical tail stabilizer in Germany, this plane illustrates one of the most modern and advanced uses of global teams in the world. There are also over 348 miles of

continued

bundled electric wiring in each plane. When the final assembly was attempted for the first time, Airbus found that the wires from the front to the back of the plane were too short to connect. It turns out that engineers in Hamburg, Germany, were initially drawing on a two-dimensional computer program, while their counterparts in Toulouse, France, were working in 3-D. The plane is now scheduled to debut in 2010. The delays caused Airbus enormous headaches and losses in the billions of euros and even more in dollars. One of the fallouts has been that FedEx canceled an order for 10 planes, at a loss of over $30 billion. The plane, now labeled the "Toulouse Goose," has resulted in still further organizational problems for Airbus. CEO Christian Streif was forced to resign after only three months in the position.

Airbus and FedEx are now negotiating over penalty payments, which could reach as high as $100 million. In the meantime, UPS has ordered 10 Boeing 747s, which will be delivered before the A380 is ready. The new software systems needed to allow the engineering teams in Toulouse and in Hamburg to work together were not available until late 2008. Airbus executive John Leahy says that customers are "past the point of yelling. They just sit there and stare, speechless, and then ask, 'How could this have happened?'" (Burke, 2007, p. 98).

1. What does this case tell you about working in virtual teams?
2. What would you do if you were John Leahy?
3. What group or team experiences have you had that are similar to the ones illustrated in this case?
4. What lessons from this case apply to your life?

Perhaps one of the most frequent criticisms of committees is that they are a waste of time. By this, people usually mean that groups often require a lot of effort without achieving positive results. Therefore, it is important to know that several problem-solving techniques are available that can help us get better results from our problem-solving groups or committees. Keep in mind that numerous research studies have shown that no matter which decision-making method groups may use, the group tends to become more committed to their decision as they get closer to completing their task, so much so that they begin to ignore warning signs and new information that they may be making a mistake by continuing with their decision (Jensen, Conlon, Humphrey, & Moon, 2011).

Neurobiologists have found that our decision-making processes are quite complex (Lehrer, 2009). In order to keep it simplified, ancient writers such as Plato argued that mankind is like a person driving a chariot pulled by two horses. The rational brain is the charioteer. It holds the reins and decides where the horses should run. If the horses get out of control, the charioteer uses the whip to change direction to get the chariot back on track. One of the horses is well bred and behaves. The other horse is not so well behaved and tends to lead us astray. According to Plato, "this obstinate horse represents negative, destructive emotions. The job of the charioteer is to keep the dark horse from running wild and to keep both horses moving forward" (Lehrer, 2009, p. 10). If you have ever tried to keep a group discussing their agenda, you will surely identify with this analogy. There is often the tendency for members to get away from their agenda and to discuss other things, which is a lot more fun, but doesn't usually lead to accomplishing the group's goals.

Small group interaction must include decision-making techniques, discussion, an outlet for quiet members, time, and values to meet the needs of all different types of decision makers. This chapter will explore ways for small groups with members having diverse decision-making styles to increase creativity, find the right problem, generate ideas, and find the right solution that fits with the problem.

Bo Schembechler, the late legendary football coach at the University of Michigan, once observed:

> Having attended countless meetings, it never ceases to amaze me how few leaders know how to conduct one.
>
> First, if you don't have anything important to say, don't schedule a meeting. . . . When you do have something worthwhile to address, know what your message is—and just as important, know what you want them to get out of it. Otherwise, you're just wasting everyone's time—and people hate that.
>
> The person who knows how to run a meeting will get twice as much out of his [or her] people, because when the meeting's over they'll be ready to act. . . . That's what a meeting's supposed to accomplish! (Schembechler & Bacon, 2007, p. 65)

Bob Iger, president and CEO of Disney, says the following about how he sees meetings: "Meetings need to start on time. I'm zealous about that because my day needs to be managed like clockwork. If people are late for meetings, the meetings tend to go late, which throws off my agenda thereafter. I frequently start the meeting even if all the people expected to be in attendance aren't there. I don't need to say to people, 'Be on time.' They know" (Iger, 2007, p. 38). So, if you want people to come on time for meetings, it is wise to start and end meetings on time. People will eventually get the message.

Improving Creativity

Creativity is a "soft" skill that is not usually a major focus in college studies. However, it is becoming more and more important in today's business world. No longer can organizations stay stagnant; rather, they need to be assured that their future leaders will have creative ideas to continue to boost the company into higher levels of success! IBM released its global study based on face-to-face interviews with over 1,500 CEOs spanning 60 countries and 33 industries. Some key points from the study are:

1. 79% of CEOs expect the business environment to become more complex in coming years.

2. More than half of CEOs doubt their ability to manage this escalating complexity.
3. A majority of CEOs cite creativity as the most important leadership skill required to cope with the growing complexity. (IBM, 2010, pp. 8–10)

This is becoming more apparent in the application process for some business schools. For example, in 2008 and beyond, the University of Chicago Graduate School of Business requires applicants to submit up to four PowerPoint slides about themselves in order to be admitted. This will allow applicants to use their creativity to portray themselves, unlike in the "formulaic" application process of yesterday. Therefore, students who would rely on "just the facts" are going to have to come up with creative, unique, and exciting ways to describe themselves, their extracurricular activities, and their educational experiences (Damast, 2007).

One of the most exciting developments in problem solving in recent times has been the realization that creativity needs to be unleashed and nurtured in order for team members to become more effective problem solvers. Taylor (2011), in his book *Practically Radical*, suggests using a technique called vuja de, the opposite of deja vu. Vuja de is "looking at a familiar situation ([like] a product you have been working on for years) as if you've never seen it before, and with that fresh line of sight, developing a distinctive point of view of the future" (Taylor, 2011, p. 13). Some examples are the Lincoln MKS, the Cadillac CTS, the Chevy Volt, and the Ford Eco-boost engine that has the power of a V8 with the fuel economy of a V6. These are products that have resulted from very creative problem solving—when someone comes up with an idea, ask "why" five times. This technique derives from the Japanese and is designed to get to a deeper level of understanding of both the problem and its possible solutions.

Tubbs (2011) cites the example of Gerber baby foods. For many years its jars were round and made of glass. More recently, it has squared off the shape for easier storage and has made the jars out of plastic so that they won't break. This is another illustration of "vuja de" (or déjà vu backwards). It involves seeing old things in new ways. Another example is the famous Post-it notes. 3M now makes these on chart-size paper so that people can write on the chart paper and then tear the pages off and stick them on the wall for further use, thus eliminating the need for masking tape. Experts also suggest using "retrograde inversion" (or turning ideas upside down and backwards). One example is using a device that plugs into the cigarette lighter of your car while the other end is in the cigarette lighter of another car to jump start your car when the battery goes dead. Instead of getting power from your battery, you give power to your battery. Another example is Motorola's FreeCharge cell phone, which has a hand crank on the side to recharge your cell phone battery. The cell phone is a high-tech device, but the source of power is the old-fashioned hand crank (Tubbs, 2011).

Creative thinking is often characterized as thinking "outside the box." This refers to the classic puzzle in which one is asked to connect nine dots with four straight lines without lifting the pencil (see Figure 6.1). The only way this can be done is to think outside the box. Vance and Deacon (1995) write that when Walt Disney was building Disney World, he wondered how to entertain guests during the frequent rain showers that occur in Florida. He and his colleagues decided

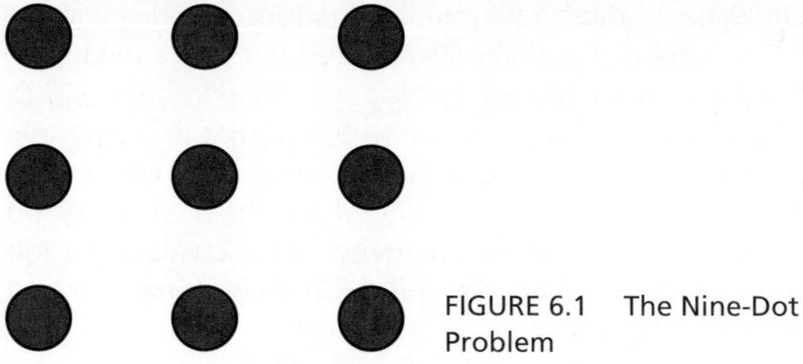

FIGURE 6.1 The Nine-Dot Problem

to have a "rain parade." They didn't really know what they had in mind, but the result was the electric-light parades that entertained people nightly for years. They also encourage us to think with all five of our senses. For a fun example of cybercreativity, see www.acmevaporware.com.

Creativity can be divided into two phases of thinking. In the first phase, called *divergent thinking*, people try to think of as many ideas as possible. Brainstorming is the technique most often used to generate numerous ideas for later consideration. In the second phase, referred to as *convergent thinking,* the ideas are evaluated against predetermined criteria and then prioritized. One author has pointed out that the word *decide* means "to resolve difficulties by cutting through them." The word's roots literally mean to "murder the alternative" (Isaacs, 1999, p. 45).

Some groups spend too much time on the divergence phase. This may then leave too little time for the convergence phase, and decisions may be rushed. The explosion of the space shuttle *Challenger* on January 28, 1986, is considered one of the most noteworthy examples of this (see Chapter 5). Some recent writers have referred to this as an example of *forced convergence* (Leonard & Swap, 1999). Other groups may spend too little time on the divergence phase, which then limits the number of ideas to be considered in the convergence phase. This is referred to as *premature convergence.* The best approach is to balance both of these phases, with appropriate time and consideration given to each. This will be discussed in greater detail in the section on the reflective thinking process.

In a totally different context, Russian scientist Genrikh Altshuller developed a method of problem solving called TRIZ (from the Russian acronym for theory of inventive problem solving). He began by studying patents, looking for common principles of innovation in order to apply those principles to finding ways to increase problem-solving creativity and efficiency. He found common formulas based on his analysis of 1.4 million patent descriptions, 400,000 of which are some of the most significant inventions from history's most ingenious thinkers, including Leonardo da Vinci, Thomas Edison, the Wright brothers, and Albert Einstein.

This method, which is now available on a computer software system called Invention Machine, can work on any type of problem. Basically, it looks at the inherent contradictions in solving the problem. For instance, a product needs to be thin for one reason and thick for another. Or it needs to be both light and heavy, or both fast and slow. The TRIZ method seeks radical ways to discover answers. An example is to make automobile parts out of a moldable composite material that is one-third of the weight of steel and yet as strong. The parts are also easier and cost less to manufacture. The research on "new generation" vehicles coming out of Detroit promises to have cars that will get 60–80 miles per gallon with performance similar to or better than that of current automobiles (Chowdhury, 2002).

One interesting study (Oldham & Cummings, 1996) found that those people who were the most creative (as measured by how many patents they applied for and how many suggestions they contributed) depended for their creativity on several factors: (1) their own personal level of creativity, (2) a challenging job situation, and (3) a supportive, noncontrolling supervisor. The combination of all three of these factors stimulated the greatest creativity.

As you no doubt know, decision making is hard work. The decision-making models in textbooks are often extremely simplified compared with the actual cases that confront us in real life. Additionally, group decision-making process research has been difficult to apply to real-world scenarios. In the past, subjects have been mostly students who were put together in groups or observed in preformed groups. Student motivations in small groups may be very different from those in the workplace. In groups that are assembled for the purposes of experimentation, the tasks assigned to them may be too simple to compare to the complicated tasks that most groups in the real-life setting face (Ngwenya, 2003). Research is helpful in understanding group decision-making processes and continues today.

Some fascinating material has been published revealing that, even within our own brains, we use two different models or methods for decision making. The left hemisphere of the brain is more prone to logical, factual, sequential, and systematic thinking and decision making. The right hemisphere tends to function more in a holistic, intuitive, emotional manner. For example, one advertisement for a sports car stated that the left side of our brains would like its craftsmanship, fuel economy, and high resale value, whereas the right side of our brains would like the fact that it goes like a "bat out of hell" or, as Lutz (1998) puts it, "goes from zero to jail in four seconds." The right side of the brain would enjoy pictures and cartoons, whereas the left side would like charts that organize concepts. The chart in Figure 6.2 compares the right- and left-brain functioning methods.

Michalko (2006) discusses some of the terms that are used to describe the right-brain and left-brain decision-making processes. The term *rational* or *logical* is often applied to decision making that is consciously analytical, or what we have described as *left brain*. The term *irrational* is applied to decision-making behaviors that are more intuitive and respond to the emotions, as right-brain processes have been described.

Nonrational decision making can be both intuitive (right brain) and judgmental (left brain). This occurs when, under pressure, people arrive at sound analytical solutions for complex problems at the snap of a finger. The decision seems to have been made intuitively but is analytical in nature. Simon (1987) described the expert problem solver, who will arrive at a problem diagnosis and decision quickly and intuitively without being able to report how he or she attained the result. This ability is best explained by a judgmental recognition and retrieval process that employs thousands of patterns stored in long-term memory.

Think of, for instance, champion chess players who can take up to 30 minutes to make a move in a tournament. Yet, when as part of a fund-raiser, these professionals go up against 50 opponents simultaneously, making a move every 30 seconds, their effectiveness is only mildly reduced. As Simon (1987) argued,

	Left	Right	
1	Logical, more like a computer analyzing component bits of information in a systematic manner and sequence, then drawing a conclusion from the premises.	Intuitive, more like an artist looking for an *overall* image, concept, or Gestalt. The conclusions are often reached in a flash of insight, rather than in a systematic method.	1
2	Either/or thinking, one correct answer (such as in mathematics).	Many alternatives, numerous shades of gray, subtle gradations or nuances of meaning.	2
3	Precise, literal meaning, such as in legal documents.	Nonliteral comparisons, such as in metaphors and analogies (for example, comparing a group's leader to a ship's rudder).	3
4	Verbally oriented.	Nonverbally oriented, uses graphic or pictorial descriptions.	4
5	Explicit, carefully defined, and fully explained.	Implicit, impressionistic, like a sketch rather than a photograph.	5
6	Controlled, disciplined.	Emotional, sensual, like reacting to music or to fragrances or colors.	6
7	Pragmatic, very practical real-world orientation.	Imaginative, nontraditional, innovative, uses fantasy.	7
8	Dominant.	Passive.	8
9	Intellectual, cerebral.	Sensually oriented, prefers experiencing to intellectualizing.	9
10	Careful with time and the use of time.	Casual with time and the use of time.	10
11	Scientific.	Artistic.	11
12	Preprogrammed, organized.	Ambiguous, nebulous.	12
13	Objective, verifiable.	Subjective, personal, unique.	13
14	Skeptical, preferring evidence and factual proof.	Accepting, preferring intuition and gut-level impressions.	14
15	Comparison against standards of performance.	Comparison against internal private standards.	15

FIGURE 6.2 Left- and Right-Brain Functions

nonrational kinds of decision-making processes occur in both simple and complex decision making.

Gibson and Hodgetts (1986) identify four different kinds of creativity that may be applied to group problem solving:

> *Innovation* is original thinking. This is probably the most difficult since by definition it is something never created before. Reportedly, the flip top can was invented by a can opener company which was going broke and needed to think up a new product line.

PRACTICAL TIPS

The following are some mental flexibility exercises that should help you improve your creativity, adapted from Katz and Rubin (1999):

1. Use your nondominant hand for brushing your teeth, writing, or using the remote.
2. Vary your usual routine.
3. Take a different way to work or class.
4. Seek out social stimulation, especially with people you don't already know.
5. Put your watch on the other wrist.
6. Turn pictures on your desk upside down.
7. Randomly move your wastebaskets, stapler, penholder, and so on.
8. Shop at different stores.
9. Vary your usual route through the grocery store.
10. Look at magazines written for the opposite sex.

> *Synthesis* is the combining of information from other sources into a new pattern. A kaleidoscope is somewhat like this. The colored pieces of glass are combined and recombined to make new patterns.
>
> *Extension* is the expansion of ideas beyond their current boundaries. McDonald's decided a few years back to add breakfast to their existing product lines. This increased their profits by 40 percent!
>
> *Duplication* is to copy good ideas. Japanese companies have become famous for taking original ideas from American companies and copying them and improving on them. The motorcycle, electronics, watch, and auto industries are but a few examples. (pp. 155–56)

Recent research on innovation and creativity has shown that imitation has a much higher chance of success than groundbreaking innovation. For example, Procter & Gamble has made over 70 improvements in its Tide detergent rather than begin a new product. Miller Lite has long since put the first light beer innovator (Rheingold/Gablinger's) out of the picture. Similarly, Wrigley's chewing gum has pushed American Chicle out of the picture, and Visa and Mastercard copied the credit card model and quickly outpaced the innovator, which was Diner's Club (Shenkar, 2010).

As you look at several decision-making models in this chapter, you will notice that implied in each approach is a bias toward the left brain or the right brain. It is probably good to remember that both sides of the brain should be used in concert, because their functions complement one another.

Finally, some of the following models are prescriptive—that is, they prescribe a desired way to solve problems. Other models are more descriptive and describe how we tend to solve problems rather than tell us how we should do so. Each model has some research evidence suggesting that it is helpful in improving the decisions that people make. However, our ability to solve problems will probably be helped most if we become familiar with several of these approaches and gain what we can from each instead of picking only one.

Reflective Thinking Process

The famous *Washington Post* reporter Bob Woodward writes in his book *Obama's Wars* that one way high-level Washington officials tried to force others to accept their favorite option on a decision was as follows:

> Bruce has done the classic Henry Kissinger model, referring to the military options [in Afghanistan]. "You have three options, two of which are ridiculous, so you accept the one in the middle.". . . It was a vintage White House trick, one that offered the illusion of choice. (Woodward, 2010, pp. 103–104)

Undoubtedly, the best-known pattern for small group problem solving is the reflective thinking sequence first proposed by John Dewey (1910). It emphasizes the left-brain functions. Although the method has several variations, there are six basic components: (1) What is the problem? (2) What are its causes and limits? (3) What are the criteria for an acceptable solution? (4) What are the available solutions? (5) What is the best solution? and (6) How can it be implemented? A more detailed outline is presented below.

I. *Define Problem*
   A. Identification of problem area, including such questions as:
      1. What is the situation in which the problem is occurring?
      2. What, in general, is the difficulty?
      3. How did this difficulty arise?
      4. What is the importance of the difficulty?
      5. What limitations, if any, are there on the area of our concern?
      6. What is the meaning of any term that needs clarifying?

II. *Analyze Causes*
   A. Analysis of the difficulty
      1. What, specifically, are the facts of the situation?
      2. What, specifically, are the difficulties?
   B. Analysis of causes
      1. What is causing the difficulties?
      2. What is causing the causes?

III. *Identify Criteria*
   A. What are the principal requirements of the solution?
   B. What limitations must be placed on the solution?
   C. What is the relative importance of the criteria?

IV. *Generate Solutions*
   A. What are the possible solutions?
      1. What is the exact nature of each solution?
      2. How would it remedy the difficulty? By eliminating the cause? By offsetting the effect? By a combination of both?

B. How good is each solution?
   1. How well would it remedy the difficulty?
   2. How well would it satisfy the criteria? Are there any that it would not satisfy?
   3. Would there be any unfavorable consequences? Any extra benefits?

V. *Select a Solution*
   A. How would you rank the solution?
   B. Would some combination of solutions be best?

VI. *Implement Solution*
   A. What steps would be taken to put the solution into effect?

The Kepner-Tregoe Approach

A variation of the reflective thinking sequence has been proposed by two business consultants (Kepner & Tregoe, 1992). The Kepner-Tregoe approach is very effective across industries, countries, and cultures. The analytic troubleshooting (ATS) approach focuses mostly on problem solving through two key steps: identification of root causes and action steps. For example, Kepner-Tregoe's approach is very useful in production and manufacturing environments. It works well with self-managed work groups that are attempting to solve problems or resolve issues through troubleshooting. First, identification of root causes starts with deciding which problem is most critical, outlining the problem, and attempting to assess potential causes. Causes are proven through testing and analysis before action is taken. Next, when action steps are taken, the best solutions and options are considered, including any peripheral elements that might be affected. Potential problems are brainstormed, and appropriate preparations are made (Edison Community College, 2005).

The overall format is similar to the reflective thinking sequence; however, the most important contribution seems to be the way in which a group works through the *criteria phase*.

Let's say that the group is trying to figure out how to cut its departmental spending by 10 percent. When we select the best solution, several criteria must be considered. There are certain required elements and other desired elements to any solution. Kepner and Tregoe (1992) refer to these as the *musts* and *wants*, respectively. For example,

Musts	*Wants*
The budget must be reduced by 10 percent.	We would like to avoid laying people off.
We must have it accomplished within a year.	Sooner would be better.
Any changes must be in line with existing company policies.	We would like to involve people in the decision.
Any changes must not violate our union contract.	We would like people willingly to cooperate.

If we use the method described above, the criteria for an acceptable decision could be assigned a numerical value and ranked in order of importance. Then a grid could be constructed on which you could evaluate different solutions against the relevant criteria.

Magner (1988) described the process the federal government used to decide which state would receive the multibillion-dollar contract for the Superconducting Super Collider (SSC), a high-powered atomic research facility. The process used was exactly that described in this text. For example, the competing states (alternative solutions) were listed according to the major criteria and were evaluated along the scale: outstanding, good, satisfactory, and poor. The actual ratings appear in Figure 6.3 (Magner, 1988, pp. A1, A4). You can see why Texas won the competition. (In late 1993, Congress canceled funding for the project.)

In 2004, Kepner and Tregoe enhanced their famous problem-solving approach through the release of the collaborative eThink Enterprise, which is an online system that allows users to walk through the analysis of the problem, research possible decisions and resulting problems, list barriers and opportunities, and assess the possible solutions. It assists in collection of data and management of problem-solving steps, and captures institutional knowledge for each problem assessed (Kepner & Tregoe, 2004). This update to the Kepner-Tregoe approach will keep it as a front-runner in reflective thinking techniques.

	Ariz.	**Col.**	**Ill.**	**Mich.**	**N.C.**	**Tenn.**	**Texas**
Geology	S	G	O	S	G	O	O
Reg. Resources	S	S	O	O	G	S	O
Environment	G	O	G	G	G	G	O
Setting	G	G	P	S	S	O	O
Reg. Conditions	S	O	G	O	G	O	G
Utilities	G	G	G	G	G	G	G

O—outstanding S—satisfactory
G—good P—poor

Geology: geologic suitability, operational stability, operational efficiency, and construction risk.

Regional resources: community resources, accessibility, industrial base, and institutional support for the project.

Environment: environmental impacts, compliance with regulatory requirements, and ability to mitigate any adverse impacts.

Setting: real estate, flexibility for changes in site plan, and natural and artificial features.

Regional conditions: vibrations, noise, and climate.

Utilities: availability of electricity, water, and other utilities.

FIGURE 6.3 SSC Ratings for Competing States

From Mike Magner, "Geology Blamed for State's Loss of Atom Smasher," *Ann Arbor News*, November 11, 1988, pp. A1, A4.

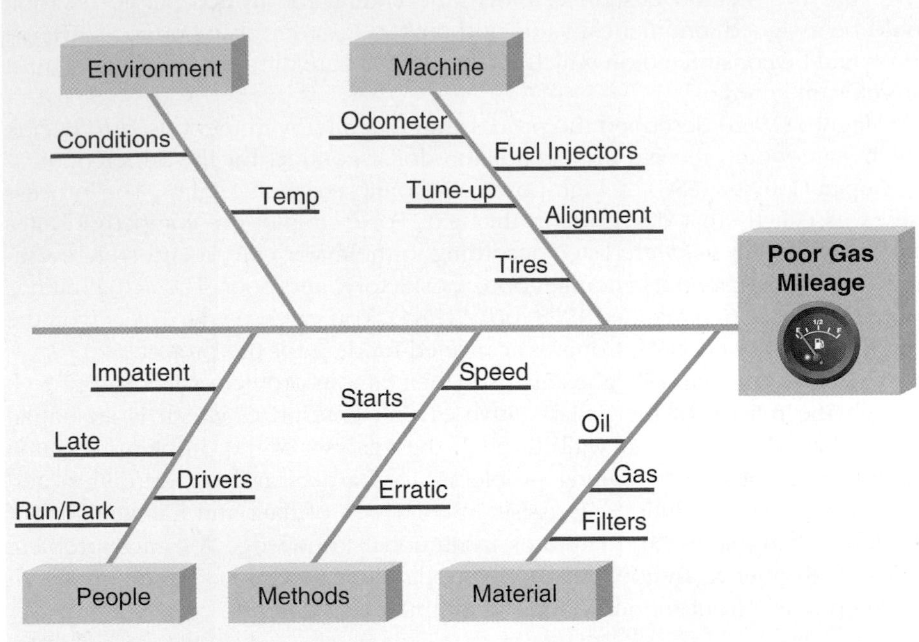

FIGURE 6.4 The Fishbone Technique

The Fishbone Technique

The fishbone technique is so called because its outline resembles the skeleton of a fish. It helps graphically to identify the underlying causes of a problem. In the diagram in Figure 6.4, in the box at the far right (the fish head), the problem is briefly stated. To the left of the fish head, the major causes are identified along the large bones, and the subordinate causes are listed on the smaller bones (Graban, 2009; Tapping et al., 2009).

Each of the problem-solving methods described thus far (that is, reflective thinking, the Kepner-Tregoe approach, and the fishbone technique) will probably offer you and your group a way to get better results than if you used no systematic method at all. Try using each of these methods in solving some of the exercises in this book. Don't give up—most problems can be solved if we work at them long enough.

Brainstorming

Another popular technique that can be applied to problem solving is brainstorming (Osborn, 1953). This technique is primarily used to generate ideas and can be applied as *part* of the problem-solving process. It emphasizes right-brain activity. For example, groups frequently dwell on only one or two proposed solutions to a problem, when many more solutions may be available. Brainstorming is one way to generate more alternative solutions for the group to consider.

PRACTICAL TIPS

One way to get at the root causes of problems is to ask "why" five times. For example, some team members don't follow through on a team's decision.

> *Why?* Because team members weren't really committed to the decision in the first place.
>
> *Why?* Because the team didn't spend enough time exploring the problems in implementing the solution.
>
> *Why?* Because it didn't want to spend the time.
>
> *Why?* Because it didn't think the problem was that important.
>
> *Why?* Because no one thought through the team's mission clearly when it was formed.

Try using the five why's to help your problem solving. (Carr, 1996, p. 66)

Brainstorming is a *lateral thinking process.* Lateral thinking processes encourage the thinker to think outside of his or her regular framework to gain a new perspective. Brainstorming is an excellent method for doing this. Brainstorming encourages open and random thinking and communication. In groups, when one member starts to run out of ideas, other group members can continue the process. The group generally has more brainstorming success than the individual. However, there are some initial obstacles to group brainstorming. Group members may feel apprehensive about presenting free-range ideas out of fear of seeming silly (Mind Tools, 2005).

Brainstorming can be applied to any of the phases of the reflective thinking sequence discussed earlier. The problem identification phase includes the need to determine the factors causing the problem; the criteria phase requires identification of the requirements for an appropriate solution; the solution phase requires some alternatives from which to choose; and the implementation phase requires creative application of the chosen solution. Guidelines (adapted from Osborn, 1953) for using the brainstorming technique are given here:

RULES FOR BRAINSTORMING

1. *Put judgment and evaluation aside temporarily.*
   a. Acquire a "try anything" attitude.
   b. Forbid faultfinding, which stifles ideas, halts association.
   c. Know that today's criticism may kill future ideas.
   d. Recognize that all ideas are at least thought starters.
2. *Turn imagination loose, and start offering the results.*
   a. Remember, the wilder the ideas are, the better.
   b. Be aware that ideas are easier to tame down than to think up.
   c. Encourage freewheeling; ideas can be brought down to earth later.
   d. Recognize that a wild idea may be the only way to bring out another really good one.

3. *Think of as many ideas as you can.*
   a. Remember that quantity breeds quality.
   b. Know that the more ideas there are to choose from, the more chance there is of a good one.
   c. Be aware that there is always more than one good solution to any problem.
   d. Try many different approaches.
4. *Seek combination and improvement.*
   a. Recognize that your ideas don't all have to be original.
   b. Improve on the ideas of others.
   c. Combine previously mentioned ideas.
   d. Remember that brainstorming is a group activity. Take advantage of group association.
5. *Record all ideas in full view.*
6. *Evaluate at a later session.*
   a. Approach each idea with a positive attitude.
   b. Give each idea a fair trial.
   c. Apply judgment gradually.

Osborn offers a few additional tips to further stimulate the creation of ideas (ideation). After ideas are generated, think of adding, subtracting, multiplying, and dividing as ways of modifying the ideas you already have. For example, effective toothpaste was improved by adding fluorides. Radios were made portable by subtracting size through the use of printed circuits. The common razor blade market was revamped by the creation of a double-edged razor (multiplying). Ford Motor Company decided to divide the production of the 2008 Ford Focus among several assembly plants, because the single plant in Wayne, Michigan, could not expand fast enough to keep up with demand.

The Massachusetts Institute of Technology (MIT) conducted a survey which revealed that 20 percent of individuals say they do their most effective brainstorming during their daily commutes while another 20 percent name the office or school. The majority of survey respondents also felt that they brainstorm best in a quiet environment and brainstorm worst in a crowded and noisy context. The latter findings were understandable, but MIT researchers focused on the intriguing concept that so many people think creatively in the car. Lemelson-MIT program director Merton Flemings believes that the car might foster creativity since it "may be one of the last environments in which we can escape from our over-stimulated lives and just be alone with our thoughts" (Schorow, 2005). So how can we translate effective brainstorming into the group session? Perhaps a period of quiet individual reflection after the initial brainstorming session would provide new idea generation that could continue in the group setting the next day.

One aspect of brainstorming that may be less obvious is the incubation of ideas—allowing ideas to develop during a period of relative relaxation. Sometimes allowing ideas to incubate, or "set," leads to new insight into a problem. Many company executives, as well as politicians, prefer to be alone before

PRACTICAL TIPS

Brainstorming: The Hybrid Method

Based on research at Wharton School of Business at the University of Pennsylvania, researchers found that if individuals went through brainstorming on their own before doing it in the group, they got even better results. So, next time, have group members try using the brainstorming rules shown above in private, then again in the group. (Terwiesch, 2010, pp. 591–605)

making important decisions. This period of solitude may help you let all the facts sink in before you commit yourself to a decision.

The brainstorming process has a success record that is hard to ignore. Cocks (1990) cites a well-known product innovation that resulted from brainstorming:

> In Minneapolis 3M encourages employees to devote about 15% of their work schedule to non-job-related tasks, or doing "skunkworks" duty, as it's known around the

PRACTICAL TIPS

While Brainstorming

1. ***Systematize.*** Take 3 × 5 index cards, and have each member of the team follow this sequence: Say it, write it, toss it (on the table). When you say it, you stimulate every other team member's creativity. When you write it, you record it for later evaluation. When you toss it on the table, you are ready to come up with a new idea.
2. ***Categorize.*** After you have generated as many ideas as you can, group similar ideas into several categories. This will allow you to weed out overlapping ideas.
3. ***Classify.*** Take each index card, and evaluate it against the four-way classification grid shown below. Spend only a minute per card.

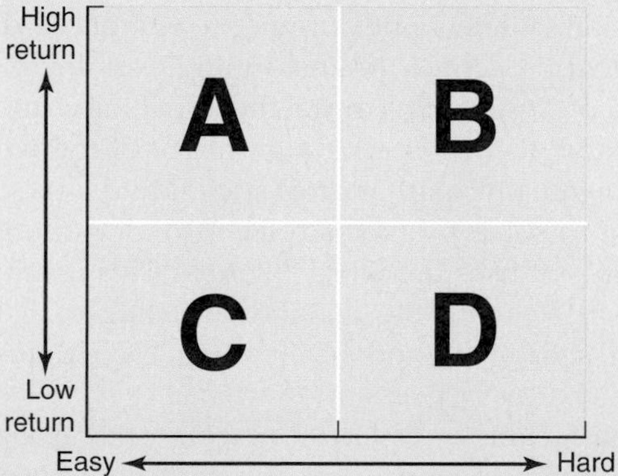

4. ***Prioritize.*** Once you have classified each idea as either an A, B, C, or D, then you can prioritize the best ideas for your proposal. Usually, the A ideas will be the ones to emerge as the top priorities. However, some A's will be better than others.

office. One skunkworking engineer came up with the idea for those neat adhesive Post-it notes while letting his imagination roam. This and other employee-generated brainstorms, from three-dimensional magnetic recording tape to disposable masks, have encouraged 3M to set a goal of 25% in total revenues from new products developed in the past five years. Currently those revenues are running closer to 30%, and 3M figures that nearly 70% of its annual $12 billion in sales comes from ideas that originated from the work force.

One writer (Csikszentmihalyi, 1996) studied 90 highly creative people to look for the common denominators of creativity. We can summarize his findings on creative individuals as follows:

- They exhibit a great deal of energy.
- They tend to be smart yet naive at the same time. This leads them to ask many questions.
- They exhibit playfulness with ideas and yet have great discipline when it comes to working hard.
- They are remarkably humble and proud at the same time.
- Creative women are tougher than average, and creative men are more sensitive than average.
- Their behavior is consistent with the values of the culture, but they are also somewhat rebellious and independent.
- They are passionate about their work and yet can be extremely objective about it as well.

Perhaps you can see some characteristics here that will help you and your groups gain greater creativity.

Alternative Brainstorming Techniques

There are several techniques that can add flavor and structure to a small group brainstorming session. When brainstorming a complicated problem or issue, the *random input* approach to brainstorming can increase creativity. This approach involves picking nouns from the dictionary and starting to brainstorm from these random words. Although many of the words may be meaningless, one may eventually spark a great idea. Mind Tools offers the example of a group working to solve problems related to air pollution. After a number of meaningless words, it uses the word "plants." This results in a discussion of the role of plants in cleaning the air and releasing oxygen. The brainstorm eventually ends in a new method of cleaning car exhaust in the air (Mind Tools, 2005).

A brainstorming technique called *reframing* asks group members to view problems from the perspective of someone with entirely different life experiences. To do this, the problem is put in the form of a question and written in the middle grid. The different perspectives are written in the surrounding grid boxes. In a business, groups can use four main perspective grids, in what is called the *4Ps* approach: the "product, pricing, placement, and promotion" perspective. Another type of reframing matrix is the *professions* technique. In this approach, the grid boxes surrounding the problem are filled with the perspective that people from different professions and specializations would take (Mind Tools, 2005).

Provocation is another brainstorming technique that allows group members to break free from their normal way of thinking. The individual thought process is bolstered by things that we have experienced in life. Human beings see patterns in their experiences and make decision based on these patterns. To use the provocation process, patterns are broken and bold statements are made that are intended to contradict the direction that the decision-making process should go in. When a contradictory statement is made, group members are asked to look at this statement and its benefits, barriers, and consequences. For example, if a work group is trying to create a new performance appraisal system for employees, a provocative statement would be something like "Employees shouldn't be rewarded for their performance." Analyzing the consequences of this statement will allow an understanding of why employees *should* be rewarded. This is called a *lateral thinking* technique because it breaks the boundaries of expected thinking (Mind Tools, 2005).

When making decisions on new ideas and options, the *SCAMPER* system may also be very useful. SCAMPER is used to create new ideas out of existing things. Tubbs (2011) defines the acronym as noted below:

S = Substitute
C = Combine
A = Adapt
M = Modify
P = Put to another use
E = Eliminate
R = Reverse

For example, if a group is trying to find a new type of food to add to the menu of a fast-food restaurant, it would take an existing product, such as a milkshake, and substitute something else, such as frozen yogurt. Then two products could be combined, such as a milkshake and apple pie. To adapt the milkshake, maybe it could be put in a spill-proof container. Then to modify the product, maybe the milkshake could be adapted to a milkshake with cookies and candy mixed in. To put the product to another use, the milkshake could be used to keep other things cold. If the milkshake were eliminated, what would the consequences be? For reversal, think of the opposite of what you are trying to do. What if a new product is not launched? What would be the consequences of that?

When all brainstormed possible solutions have been ruled out, a technique called the *concept fan*, developed by Edward DeBono (1985), can be useful. This technique encourages group members to get away from the details and see the bigger picture. To create a concept fan, draw a circle on the middle of a sheet of paper or flip chart and write the problem question in the middle of it. Then possible solutions, even a step removed from the problem, should be brainstormed and written on lines radiating out from the circle. Broaden the problem by drawing another circle near the first with a larger problem. Continue writing solutions on radiating lines, and make the problem as broad as needed to regenerate ideas (Mind Tools, 2005).

Gamestorming (Gray et al., 2010) involves using various creativity games to help improve problem solving. Although their book is loaded with dozens of useful games, "Dot Voting" is one example. Once participants have brainstormed various ideas, the ideas are listed on a board. Then, each participant is given three sticky notes or colored dots. Each person then places a sticky note or dot next to the idea he or she likes best. In a very short time, ideas can be prioritized based on the number of paper votes on the board. We have used this in faculty meetings that usually take much longer due to people advocating for their pet idea. However, this dot voting technique quickly demonstrates which ideas are more valuable to the group (Gray et al., 2010, pp. 63–64). For more Gamestorming ideas see http://gogamestorm.com

A combination of these techniques can add fuel to any small group brainstorming session, increasing the number of potential solutions to problems and therefore the effectiveness of the eventual solution.

Six Thinking Hats

Another classic method for decision making in groups originated with DeBono (1985). It is an intuitive way to keep your thoughts focused while problem solving. Each role or type of thinking is represented by a different-colored hat.

The white hat is emotionally neutral. This type of thinking stresses logic and objectivity. The analogy would be a judge in a courtroom, or perhaps a computer. It is objective and focuses on facts and figures.

The red hat represents emotions, gut instincts, intuitions, and feelings, as well as passion and heartfelt concerns. Comments like "I love it" or "I hate it" are extreme examples.

The black hat represents careful and analytical thinking. It can also be somber and serious and is concerned with what may be the limitations or the cons of an idea—that is, what might be wrong with it.

The yellow hat represents sunny, optimistic, and positive thinking, as well as the desire to make things happen. It can also include being hopeful for positive outcomes.

The green hat represents creativity, new ideas, alternatives, and possibilities. It can also include change and nontraditional approaches.

The blue hat represents coordination, control, and the discipline to know when to use which hat. It is often used by the group leader but may be used by any member when needed.

This method is quite easy to use and is often applied in engineering fields when the subject matter is highly complex. It is just one of the alternatives available for you to master. For more on this subject, log onto Six Thinking Hats—Edward DeBono.

Checklists

Although people have been using checklists for many years, one physician and surgeon has formalized the process for teams in a book entitled *The Checklist Manifesto* (Gawande, 2009).

He got the idea from watching pilots prepare for flying. They have an extensive preflight checklist in order to ensure a safe flight. No pilot would ever think of taking off without following this checklist each and every time. One exception is Northwest Airlines flight #255, which crashed in Detroit in 1987. Investigations revealed that the pilot and copilot skipped some parts of their preflight checklist and accidentally forgot to deploy the flaps and slats in the proper position for takeoff, killing all but one person aboard.

Similarly, surgical teams have been known to leave surgical instruments and even a sponge inside their patients when sewing them up after surgery, leading to severe complications and death.

The actions of most groups don't have such severe consequences, but Gawande (2009) asserts that virtually all groups can benefit from using checklists to ensure that all important practices and procedures are followed. It would seem that checklists would be especially helpful for virtual teams who have the additional complexity of working without actually being in the same room.

Gawande (2009) writes,

> Nonetheless, that know-how is often unmanageable. Avoidable failures are common and persistent, not to mention demoralizing and frustrating, across many fields from medicine to finance, business and government. And the reason is increasingly evident: the volume and complexity of what we know has exceeded our individual ability to deliver its benefits correctly, safely, or reliably. Knowledge has both saved us and burdened us. (p. 13)

(See, for example, the Airbus case at the beginning of this chapter.)

Incrementalism

Braybrooke and Lindblom (1963) have pointed out that many economists, social scientists, political analysts, and other decision makers generally resort to a style of decision making that is far from the rational models described earlier in this chapter. They argue that numerous decisions concerning governmental policies, such as welfare and Social Security, are arrived at partially as a result of adapting to political pressure rather than as a result of rational analysis of the available alternatives. Because environmental obstacles frequently prevent groups from choosing a "best" alternative, other alternatives may result by default. For example, a Supreme Court vacancy may be filled by a "compromise candidate," one who is clearly not the most outstanding contender but who is the only one upon whom the politicians can agree. This is an example of a nonrational decision.

The term *incrementalism* refers to the process of making decisions that result in change. Some decisions result in vast amounts of change, whereas other decisions progress toward change by small bits, or *increments*. A second variable is the

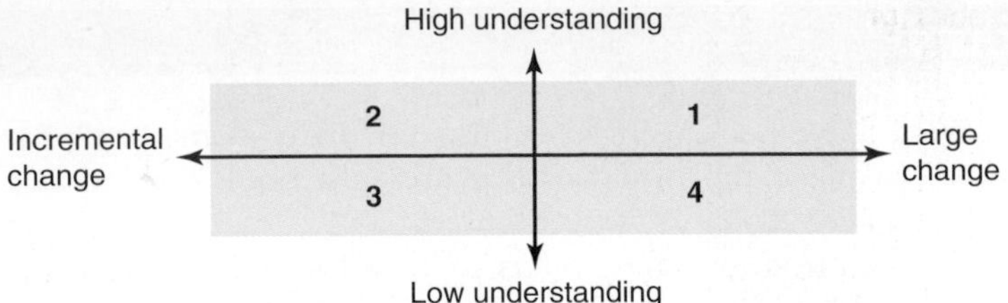

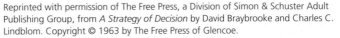

FIGURE 6.5 Model of Decision Making

Reprinted with permission of The Free Press, a Division of Simon & Schuster Adult Publishing Group, from *A Strategy of Decision* by David Braybrooke and Charles C. Lindblom. Copyright © 1963 by The Free Press of Glencoe.

amount and quality of knowledge or understanding underlying a decision. When these two factors are taken in combination, the model shown in Figure 6.5 results.

Braybrooke and Lindblom's analysis is primarily centered on political decisions resulting in societal change. With respect to quadrant 1 in the diagram in Figure 6.5, the researchers contend that few decisions resulting in major social changes can be made with a high level of intellectual understanding of a problem. Numerous "think tanks" are devoted to analyzing what we should be doing to prepare ourselves for the year 2020 and beyond. Yet even the best estimates are "guesstimates" that must be continually revised on the basis of new data. The decision to enact forced busing of schoolchildren to achieve a racial balance in public schools was an attempt to bring about a major social change. Yet the magnitude of resistance to this move was severely underestimated. In another context, the decision to have year-round daylight saving time was implemented in an attempt to save fuel. However, because of the threat that children might be run down by cars in the dark early-morning hours, more parents drove their children to school, thus using more energy than daylight saving time was saving. These decisions illustrate the point that attempts to make major changes are not always accompanied by a full realization of the consequences. Thus, the majority of decisions resulting in large changes would be depicted in Figure 6.5 as falling in quadrant 4.

Quadrant 2 refers to the daily decisions of most groups that result in relatively small changes. Decisions to change the prime lending rate of a bank, to increase Social Security benefits, or to add a few employees to a payroll are all examples of such decisions. Obviously, defining "small" changes is a matter of judgment. These types of decisions frequently result from the careful study of experts in finance, economics, and management. Thus, the chances are increased that the decision will be made with a high level of understanding of the problem. However, this may not always be the case. If the decision results in unwanted or unanticipated problems, such as inflation or unionization, the decision is defined as falling into quadrant 3. Braybrooke and Lindblom (1963) offer the following explanation for the tendency toward incremental change (see also Zakaria, 2008):

> For a democracy like the United States, the commitment to incremental change is not surprising. Nonincremental alternatives usually do not lie within the range of choice possible in the society or body politic. Societies, it goes without saying, are complex structures that can avoid dissolution or intolerable dislocation only by meeting certain preconditions, among them that certain kinds of change are admissible only if

> they occur slowly. Political democracy is often greatly endangered by nonincremental change, which it can accommodate only in certain limited circumstances. (p. 73)

Their point is that we make group decisions on the basis of relatively limited information on and understanding of the consequences of those decisions. By implication, it would seem that this calls for problem-solving strategies that are flexible and subject to change on the basis of feedback indicating the change is desirable. For example, the U.S. automakers at one time committed large amounts of money to the development of a rotary engine as a possible alternative to the piston engine. However, when the demand for more energy-efficient engines became greater, the work on the rotary engine was permanently halted. This type of bit-by-bit planning is representative of the exploratory decision making sometimes required in a continually changing environment.

Mixed Scanning

Etzioni (1968) offers a decision-making strategy that he asserts is neither reflective thinking nor incrementalism. Actually, it is a combination of the two approaches. Rather than examine a problem comprehensively (reflective thinking approach) or part by part (incremental approach), we can combine elements of both of these approaches into a so-called mixed-scanning strategy. Patler (1999) calls it being able to see the forest and the trees simultaneously (p. 105).

The basic idea is to combine an analysis of the "big picture" with an appropriate amount of attention to detail. In an employment decision, several candidates may be assessed according to specific ratings on several criteria relevant to the job. This would be an example of paying attention to detail. It may be that one person meets all the criteria very well, and he or she would be a suitable replacement for the employee who is leaving. However, at the same time, perhaps a completely different level of scanning is needed to anticipate the type of employee that might be best several years from now. In one such case, a decision to replace a college debate coach resulted in the hiring of a professor in interpersonal and small group communication, because the debate program was getting smaller while the interpersonal and small group curriculum was increasing in size and scope.

Etzioni claims that this alternating between levels of analysis enables us to "see the forest for the trees." Many groups seem to have trouble either coming down from the clouds of ambiguities and abstractions or climbing up out of the quagmire of trivia long enough to see the overview. This ability to maintain a balance between attention to the general and attention to the specific appears to be a major factor in successful problem solving.

Tacit Bargaining

Yet a third strategy for decision making that is considered an alternative to the rational thinking approach is advanced by Murnighan (1992). This strategy is referred to as "tacit bargaining," or "bargaining in which communication is incomplete or impossible" (pp. 35–36). Examples of such situations include the following:

1. Name heads or tails. If you and your partner name the same, you both win a prize.
2. Circle one of the numbers listed in the line below. You win if you all succeed in circling the same number.
   7 100 13 26199555
3. You are to divide $100 into two piles, labeled A and B. Your partner is to divide another $100 into two piles labeled A and B. If you allot the same amounts to A and B, respectively, that your partner does, each of you gets $100; if your amounts differ from your partner's, neither of you gets anything. (pp. 35–36)

In his research, Murnighan found that in the first problem, 36 participants chose heads and only 6 chose tails. In problem 2, the first three numbers got 37 out of 41 votes (7 got the most, then 100, then 13). In problem 3, 36 out of 41 split the money into two equal piles of $50 each. The data suggest that people can cooperate fairly successfully in some problem-solving situations if it is to their advantage to do so. However, numerous situations exist in which the participants have divergent interests. For example, suppose several fraternity representatives meet together on an interfraternity council; each member is interested in promoting the entire Greek system, but his primary loyalty is to his own fraternity. This divided loyalty creates an arena of "politicking" such that most members will choose *not* to communicate in a completely open and honest way.

This is often referred to as a *mixed-motive* situation: There is simultaneous pressure to cooperate and to compete. Thus, many proposed solutions are likely not prompted by the most honorable intentions but motivated by the interests of a single person. Similar situations exist in congressional committees, which often split according to partisan (Republican and Democrat) affiliations. In these situations, decisions are frequently based on compromises and a philosophy of "I'll support you on this issue, but you owe me support on the next issue." Rational and objective choices are less likely to prevail under these circumstances. These bargaining situations imply communication procedures that are distinctly different from those in other kinds of problem-solving situations.

Negotiations between union and management are often characterized by each side's making highly publicized statements of extreme positions in order to strengthen its respective bargaining position. Thus, the union president will call for a minimum wage increase of 10 percent, and the company's representative will state flatly that 3 percent is all the company can afford to give. In reality, both parties exaggerate their public position and privately acknowledge that a 6 or 7 percent agreement is what they are really trying to achieve.

If we assume that in these bargaining situations it would be naive to advise participants simply to give in, still some reasonable suggestions can be made to increase the effectiveness of communication, as well as the quality of decisions made. A good negotiator should learn to master the following abilities.

1. Try to gauge your own strength or weakness:
   a. If you're strong, make sure your counterpart knows it.
   b. If you're weak, work hard to keep him from realizing it.

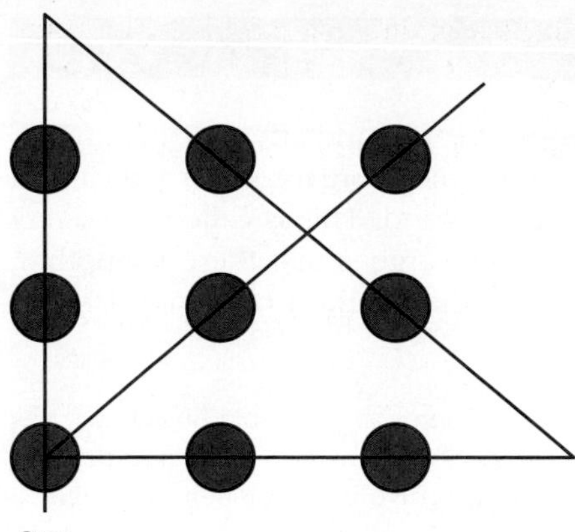

FIGURE 6.6 One Solution to the Nine-Dot Problem

2. Try to gauge your counterpart's actual strength or weakness.
3. Surmise whether his perception of his strength or weakness accords with your reality:
   a. If your counterpart believes he's stronger than he actually is, educate him to the real facts.
   b. If he thinks he's weaker than he actually is, don't say a word. (Fruend, 1992, p. 46)

In concluding this chapter on problem solving, we should point out that, to some extent, the situation will affect the strategy of decision making chosen. In some situations, one of the rational thinking approaches will be most appropriate; in other, more tentative, situations, the incremental approach may be preferable. The mixed-scanning strategy seems to have application in most situations, and in situations allowing little or no free communication among participants, the tacit-bargaining strategy will be most likely. In using any strategy, you should know which one you are using and understand the underlying assumptions and requirements of each. You should also expect some problems with each and realize the communication requirements inherent in each. Also, as you attempt to make decisions, you will undoubtedly encounter many types of conflict, which is the subject of the next chapter. (See Figure 6.6 for one solution to the nine-dot problem.)

Recent research at Harvard University has shown that one of the most important factors in motivating team members is for leaders to maintain a sense of group progress (Amabile & Kramer, 2011). This consists of four types of communication behaviors. *First*, acknowledge each person's contributions to the group's progress. When group members feel that their ideas are ignored, they lose motivation. *Second*, keep members on the same team for the duration of a project. When they are switched in the middle of projects, they tend to lose motivation. *Third*, let group members know that their ideas will be used and not discarded. This keeps the group members motivated to keep contributing. *Fourth*, keep the group informed about how their work will contribute to the project they are working on. Sometimes groups don't see the results of their work and eventually may lose motivation (Amabile & Kramer, 2011, pp. 70–80).

Obliquity

Most of our lives we are taught to think in terms of cause and effect. For example, if we have an agenda, the meeting will usually be more organized. If we call on someone to participate, the person will usually respond. This is called the direct approach. However, John Kay, a British economist, argues that there is another, indirect way that is often effective, too. He calls this method obliquity. He has observed the following examples of obliquity:

> Happiness is not through the pursuit of happiness. The most profitable businesses are not the most profit-oriented [they are the ones who work to meet a need, and profit follows]. The wealthiest people are not those most assertive in the pursuit of wealth. The greatest paintings are not the most accurate representations of their subjects [think impressionism];... Soviet planners managed the economy far less successfully than the adaptive, disorganized process of [free] market economies.... Problem-solving is iterative and adaptive rather than direct.... The most complex systems come into being without anyone having knowledge of the whole. (Kay, 2011, p. 13)

Basically, Kay argues that many overarching, high-level goals are often accomplished in counterintuitive ways. For example, happiness is often achieved as a by-product of our daily activities. Going to college and studying are daily activities. But graduating, getting a good job, and making money all contribute to life happiness. Since there are so many examples of this, he calls it "the ubiquity of obliquity" (Kay, 2011, p. 53). The primary lesson in this context is to become aware that high-level, overarching goals may best be achieved through an oblique or indirect method, rather than through the direct method.

Virtual Decision Making

The increase in virtual small group technologies has resulted in increased focus on decision-making processes in the virtual environment. One of the most useful tools in the virtual environment is one of the simplest: brainstorming. David Gould (2004) wrote an article for *Virtual Organization* in which he discussed decision-making processes that are useful in virtual team environments, giving special attention to brainstorming. In the virtual group or team environment, ideas are written down by each member and the online chat is saved for the record. The online brainstorming process follows the same process as a face-to-face brainstorming session, except that the computer acts as the flip chart.

Decision making in the virtual environment is a thoughtful and time-consuming process. When groups and teams make decisions, they should make a "decision log" to capture and institutionalize the work that they have done. The decision log includes the context of the decision, date of the decision, details of the decision, process used, and consequences of the decision. This type of log not only captures institutional knowledge but also provides upcoming groups and teams with a reference to help them determine which methodologies are best in making their own decisions (Gould, 2004).

Humphries (2008) offers some insight by identifying the fundamental evolution of the group decision support model from the single "decision spine," which focuses on a single procedural context, to provide comprehensive group communication and decision support (GDACS). They showed how GDACS can boost creative decision making through *collaborative authoring of outcomes* within a large group of decision spines and also within the structure that constitutes the body-without-organs (which they refer to as the *decision hedgehog*) in which these spines are rooted. They explain decision making through the construction of narratives with the fundamental aim of enriching the understanding of decision making.

Many groups combine virtual technologies with face-to-face interactions. There is abundant research that highlights the benefits of this approach over groups that are only face-to-face or strictly virtual. The online tools that help groups make decisions are called *decision support systems* (DSSs). The concept of DSS technology has been evolving since the advent of computer technology. DSS began with efforts to capture information and ideas. In the late 1950s, the Massachusetts Institute of Technology began the study of decision support mechanisms. Articles in the 1960s and 1970s explored the importance of computer programs as tools to facilitate complex decision making through data storage, compilation, and analysis capabilities. In the 1980s, group software emerged to assist groups in decision-making processes (Power, 2003).

Djamasbi and Loiacono (2008) investigated the effect gender has on the use of computer-based feedback and the impact that this feedback has on group members' moods. The decision-making processes of men and women were investigated in a laboratory experiment using a previously validated DSS and commonly used and negatively framed feedback. Previous research showed that men and women react to negative feedback differently. So, the authors argued, the commonly used outcome feedback in DSS studies would influence both the decision accuracy of male and female users and their moods differently. The results, which support their theoretical argument, indicated that outcome feedback (in particular, the more negative outcome feedback) improved the decision-making accuracy of the female users compared to their male counterparts. The results also indicated that the outcome feedback affects the overall mood of men and women differently. The overall moods of the female subjects were significantly less positive before and after completing the task (receiving this commonly used negative form of feedback), while the moods of the male subjects before and after completing the task (receiving the same negative feedback) did not change. It appears that women react more negatively to this form of computer-based negative feedback than men.

In common terms, DSS technology changes the decision-making climate of small groups. For example, Reply wireless response systems allow voting on group decisions to be anonymous and free of social bias. By voting on a computerized keypad device that does not capture names, group members can participate and share their ideas even in a face-to-face setting without linking their ideas to themselves (Reply Systems, 2005). This type of technology-assisted group decision making is continuing to evolve, and research continues to prove the effectiveness of the face-to-face meeting with DSS combination.

Unintended Consequences

One of the most unusual and difficult challenges with decision-making is to solve a given problem without causing unintended consequences. Steven Levitt and Stephen Dubner (2009) cite government policies intended to do one thing that end up doing just the opposite. For example, the Americans with Disabilities Act (ADA) was designed to help people with disabilities. However, the data show that fewer disabled people were hired as a result of the act, because employers were so worried that they would not be able to fire bad workers, who happened to have a disability, that they didn't hire them (p. 139). They also cite numerous other examples. So, all groups need to be aware that any solutions that they develop to solve problems may actually create new problems that are worse.

REVIEW OF THE SYSTEMS APPROACH

In this chapter, we have examined the very difficult task of improving our ability to make decisions. Most untrained groups do not follow a disciplined path toward a decision. Instead, we frequently find ourselves either off the track or bogged down in conflicts that keep us from accomplishing a task. The focus in this chapter has been biased toward problem-solving groups. However, other types of groups also have to make decisions. Certainly these issues arise for families, learning groups, social groups planning events, and work groups solving organizational problems.

It is probably apparent by now that the decision-making process in most groups can be improved. In this chapter, we examined twelve alternative problem-solving strategies: (1) the reflective thinking process, (2) the Kepner-Tregoe approach, (3) the fishbone technique, (4) brainstorming, (5) alternative brainstorming techniques, (6) six thinking hats, and (7) checklists, (8) incrementalism, (9) mixed scanning, (10) tacit bargaining, (11) obliquity, and (12) virtual decision making. You might want to become familiar enough with each of these methods so that you will be able to use whichever one seems most appropriate for a given problem and a given group. Again, this illustrates the systems principle of *equifinality* in that several alternative methods may be used to reach the same desired end result—namely, the solution to the group's problem.

By now you may be wondering how one *does* decide which of the twelve problem-solving strategies to use. Should you use a rational strategy, such as the reflective thinking process or brainstorming, or should you use incrementalism or tacit bargaining? The systems approach suggests that the appropriateness of any method will depend on the demands of the specific situation. Therefore, we need to be familiar with all the alternatives in order to increase our tool kit of behavioral science "tools."

The rational problem-solving methods work well in most cases but seem particularly suited to an autonomous group trying to satisfy its own needs while being allowed to do so by a democratic leader. By comparison, governmental groups are not autonomous and must answer to the taxpayers. Thus, incrementalism may be appropriate, because major changes may be demanded without the luxury of enough time to gather exhaustive amounts of data on the problem. It's a little like the old story about how, when you are up to your hips in a swamp full of alligators, you don't want a systematic estimate of the probability of danger; you want somebody to throw you a rope!

Tacit bargaining seems to be primarily appropriate in the mixed-motive situations we described earlier. Notice the assumptions and viewpoints expressed in the following quotations. Karrass (1994), in his book on negotiating, writes, "In a successful negotiation both parties gain, but more often than not one party wins more than the other" (p. 6). In a similar vein, Korda (1975) writes, "No matter who you are, the basic truth is that your interests are nobody else's concern, your gain is inevitably someone else's loss, your failure someone else's victory" (p. 4). The viewpoint expressed in these two quotations reflects some of the attitudes and values relevant to the mixed-motive situation. These statements also describe the outcomes or consequences of bargaining types of problem-solving situations. Obviously, such competitive situations suggest very different communication behaviors and skills than would the encounter group, which stresses trust, mutual self-disclosure, and risk taking. Thus, the demands of the situation play a large role in suggesting which problem-solving strategy we want to employ.

EXERCISES

1. Problem-Solving Discussion Assignment

Each group should decide on a topic and formulate a discussion question that cannot be answered yes or no. A sample question would be, What can be done about current marijuana laws? This form of discussion question is preferable because it poses a problem to be answered by the group. A less desirable discussion question would be, Should marijuana be decriminalized? Notice that this question can be answered yes or no and is less open-ended and, therefore, less helpful in prompting discussion.

Each group may want to gather some preliminary information on the topic. (This is optional.) Select a moderator, and work up an agenda for your discussion, including the following:

1. Define the nature and limits of the problem.
2. Analyze causes and important aspects of the problem.
3. Determine the criteria by which to judge an acceptable solution to the problem.
4. Identify several alternative solutions to the problem.
5. Decide which is the best solution (on the basis of the criteria you have identified).
6. Determine how this solution might be implemented.

Application of this pattern depends upon such factors as

- Whether the discussion is one of fact, value, or policy
- The general scope of the problem
- The amount of time available
- The knowledge of the participants

The discussion should be approximately 30 minutes long. Moderators will be responsible for introducing and concluding the discussion, as well as for moving the group along on the agenda.

As a guide, you may want to review the following questions, which show in greater detail the various issues to be encountered at each phase of the agenda.

I. *Define Problem*
   A. Identification of problem area, including questions:
      1. What is the situation in which the problem is occurring?
      2. What, in general, is the difficulty?
      3. How did this difficulty arise?
      4. What is the importance of the difficulty?
      5. What limitations, if any, are there on the area of our concern?
      6. What is the meaning of any terms that need clarifying?

II. *Analyze Causes*
   A. Analysis of the difficulty:
      1. What, specifically, are the facts of the situation?
      2. What, specifically, are the difficulties?
   B. Analysis of causes:
      1. What is causing the difficulties?
      2. What is causing the causes?

III. *Identify Criteria*
   A. What are the principal requirements of the solution?
   B. What limitations must be placed on the solution?
   C. What is the relative importance of the criteria?

IV. *Generate Solutions*
   A. What are the possible solutions?
      1. What is the exact nature of each solution?
      2. How would it remedy the difficulty? By eliminating the cause? By offsetting the effect? By a combination of both?
   B. How good is each solution?
      1. How well would it remedy the difficulty?
      2. How well would it satisfy the criteria? Are there any that it would not satisfy?
      3. Would there be any unfavorable consequences? Any extra benefits?

V. *Select Solution*
   A. How would you rank the solution?
   B. Would some combination of solutions be best?

VI. *Implement Solution*
   A. What steps would be taken to put the solution into effect?

2. Adjunct of Exercise 1

In conjunction with Exercise 1, some members of the class may want to fill out the evaluation forms (Figures 6.7 and 6.8) on the discussion group. These forms can serve as the basis of a postdiscussion feedback session in which the group can analyze its own strengths and weaknesses in conducting the assignment.

3. Brainstorming Exercise

Using the rules for brainstorming given in this chapter, try to answer the following question: How can we limit growth in population, industrial pollution, and use of natural resources in such a way as to ensure the preservation of the human race?

For further practice, try brainstorming other topics.

4. Web Resources

FINDING GROUPWARE

Here are some of the more popular groupware products, listed according to category. (Remember that most programs perform more than one function. Lotus Notes, for example, does just about everything.)

Knowledge Sharing

Lotus Notes, Lotus Development Corp., Cambridge, MA (800-828-7086, http://www.lotus.com). Cost: Notes Mail Client, $55; Notes Desktop, $69; single-processor server, $495; multiprocessor server, $2,295; each client, $27.

Microsoft Exchange Server, Microsoft Corp., Redmond, WA (800-426-9400, http://www.microsoft.com/exchange). Cost: Microsoft Exchange Server Enterprise Edition, $1,970; Microsoft Exchange Server, $699; each client, $54.

Group Calendaring and Scheduling

CaLANdar, Microsystems Software Inc., Framingham, MA (800-489-2001, http://www.microsys.com). Cost: $595 for 10 users (includes server cost); Web Scheduler, $995 per CaLANdar network.

OnTime Enterprise, FTP Software Inc., Andover, MA (800-559-5955, http://www.ontime.com). Cost: $994 for 10 users (includes server cost).

OnTime for Networks, FTP Software Inc., Andover, MA (800-559-5955, http://www.ontime.com). Cost: $828 for 10 users (includes server cost).

Real-Time Meetings

Enhanced CU-SeeMe, White Pine Software Inc., Nashua, NH (800-241-PINE, http://www.cuseeme.com). Cost: $69–$99; software server, $395.

GroupSystems, Ventana Corp., Tucson, AZ (800-368-6338, http://www.ventana.com). Cost: $895 per user (volume discounts available).

RoundTable, ForeFront Group Inc., Houston, TX (800-867-1101, http://www.ffg.com). Cost: $500 for five-user server; up to $5,000 for unlimited number of users.

Bulletin Boards

FirstClass, SoftArc Inc., Markham, Ontario, Canada (800-SOFTARC, http://www.softarc.com). Cost: $495 for five users (includes server cost).

TeamTalk, Trax Softworks Inc., Culver City, CA (800-367-8729, http://www.traxsoft.com/traxsoft). Cost: $59 per user.

WebBoard, O'Reilly & Associates, Sebastopol, CA (800-998-9938, http://www.webboard.ora.com). Cost: $149.

Group Document Handling

Face to Face, Crosswise Corp., Santa Cruz, CA (408-459-9060, http://www.crosswise.com). Cost: $59 per user.

Work Flow

ActionWorkflow Enterprise Series (includes **Process Builder-Analyst Edition, Builder-Developer Edition, Process Manager,** and **Software Developer Kit**), Action Technologies Inc., Alameda, CA (800-WORKFLOW, http://www.actiontech.com). Cost: Process Builder-Analyst Edition, $495 per user; Builder-Developer Edition, $3,995 per user; Process Manager, $4,995 for 10 users (includes server cost); Software Developer Kit, $4,495 per developer.

FormFlow, Symantec Corp., Cupertino, CA (800-441-7234, http://www.symantec.com). Cost: $399 for starter kit (one designer component and three fillers [users]).

JetForm Filler Pro, JetForm Corp., Ottawa, Canada (800-538-3676, http://www.jetform.com). Cost: $149 per user.

Name of leader ______________________________

Evaluator ______________________________

Assign one of the following ratings for each criterion:

5—Superior
4—Excellent
3—Average
2—Below average
1—Poor

Criteria	*Rating*
1. *Attitude.* Impartiality, fairness; ability to help group maintain discussion attitude.	________
2. *Knowledge.* Understanding of the problem. Knowledge of discussion method.	________
3. *Thinking.* Ability to think quickly, to see relationships.	________
4. *Introducing.* Skill in getting the discussion off to a good start.	________
5. *Speaking.* Ability to express ideas clearly, rephrase unclear contributions.	________
6. *Guiding.* Ability to keep discussion "on the track"; maintain progress; make internal summaries.	________
7. *Regulating.* Ensuring evenness of contribution, maintaining equanimity.	________
8. *Ending.* Summarizing group effect.	________

General comments

____

FIGURE 6.7 Judge's Evaluation Report on the Leader

Name of participant ______________________________

Evaluator ______________________________

Assign one of the following ratings for each criterion:

5—Superior
4—Excellent
3—Average
2—Below average
1—Poor

Criteria	*Rating*
1. *Attitude.* Objectivity, open-mindedness; willingness to modify views in light of new evidence.	________
2. *Knowledge.* Information on the problem.	________
3. *Thinking.* Analysis, ability to reason about the problem.	________
4. *Listening.* Ability to understand and interpret view of others.	________
5. *Speaking.* Ability to communicate ideas clearly and effectively; adaptation to the speaking situation.	________
6. *Consideration for others.* Tact, courtesy, cooperation, evenness of contribution.	________

General comments

____

FIGURE 6.8 Judge's Evaluation Report on Participants

READINGS: Overview

Probably one of the most troublesome issues in small group interaction is how to use time effectively and efficiently. In the first reading, Michalko discusses some novel ways to improve group creativity. In the second reading, Martin discusses the application of team concepts from sports to teams of all kinds.

Reading 6.1 Finding What You're Not Looking For

Michael Michalko

Whenever we attempt to do something and fail, we end up doing something else. As simplistic as this statement may seem, it is the first principle of the creative accident or "serendipity." We may ask ourselves why we have failed to do what we intended, and this is the reasonable, expected thing to do. But the creative accident provokes a different question: What have we done? Answering that question in a novel, unexpected way is the essential creative act. It is not luck but creative insight of the highest order.

The discovery of the electromagnetic laws was a creative accident. The relationship between electricity and magnetism was first observed in 1820 by Hans Ørsted in a public lecture at which he was demonstrating the "well-known fact" that electricity

From Michael Michalko, *Cracking Creativity* (Berkeley, CA: Ten Speed Press, 1998), pp. 227–35. Reprinted by permission.

and magnetism were completely independent phenomena. This time the experiment failed—an electric current produced a magnetic effect. Øersted was observant enough to notice this effect, honest enough to admit it, and diligent enough to follow up and publish. Maxwell used these experiments to extend Newton's methods of modeling and mathematical analysis in the mechanical and visible world to the invisible world of electricity and magnetism and derived Maxwell's Laws, which opened the doors to our modern age of electricity and electronics.

Even when people set out to do something purposefully and rationally, they wind up doing things they did not intend. John Wesley Hyatt, an Albany printer and mechanic, worked long and hard trying to find a substitute for billiard-ball ivory, then coming into short supply. He invented, instead, celluloid—the first commercially successful plastic.

B. F. Skinner advised people that when they were working on something and found something interesting, they should drop everything else and study it. In fact, he emphasized this as a first principle of scientific methodology. This is what William Shockley and a multidiscipline Bell labs team did. They were formed to invent the MOS transistor and ended up instead with the junction transistor and the new science of semiconductor physics. These developments eventually led to the MOS transistor and then to the integrated circuit and to new breakthroughs in electronics and computers. William Shockley described it as a process of "creative failure methodology."

Richard Feynman had an interesting practical test that he applied when reaching a judgment about a new idea: Did it explain something unrelated to the original problem? That is, "What can you explain that you didn't set out to explain?" and "What did you discover that you didn't set out to discover?" In 1938, twenty-seven-year-old Roy Plunkett set out to invent a new refrigerant. Instead, he created a glob of white waxy material that conducted heat and did not stick to surfaces. Fascinated by this unexpected material, he abandoned his original line of research and experimented with this interesting material, which eventually became known by its trade name, "Teflon."

In principle, the unexpected event that gives rise to a creative invention is not all that different from the unexpected automobile breakdown that forces us to spend a night in a new and interesting town, the book sent to us in error that excites our imagination, or the closed restaurant that forces us to explore a different cuisine. But when looking for ideas or creative solutions, many of us ignore the unexpected, and consequently, lose the opportunity to turn chance into a creative opportunity. You have to give yourself the freedom to see what you are not looking for. In 1839 Charles Goodyear was looking for a way to make rubber easier to work and accidentally spilled a mixture that hardened but was still usable. By allowing himself to go in an unanticipated direction, he invented a practical vulcanization process. By focusing on the "interesting" aspects of the idea, he discovered its potential. Alexander Fleming was not the first physician to notice the mold formed on an exposed culture while studying deadly bacteria. Less gifted physicians would routinely trash this seemingly irrelevant event but Fleming noted it as "interesting" and wondered if it had potential. This interesting observation led to penicillin, which has saved millions of lives. Thomas Edison, while pondering how to make a carbon filament, was mindlessly toying with a piece of putty, turning and twisting it in his fingers, when he looked down at his hands and the answer hit him between the eyes: twist the carbon like a rope.

What makes it possible to turn the unlooked-for event into novel fortune? We have to prepare our minds for chance. This is difficult to do when we are looking at a subject, because of our existing emotions and prejudices. Consider the following situation: Susan is twenty-eight years old, single, outspoken and very bright. She majored in sociology and minored in philosophy. As a student, she was deeply concerned with issues of racial discrimination and social justice and also participated in antinuclear demonstrations. Which statement is the most probable?

A. Susan is an office manager.

B. Susan is an office manager and is active in the feminist movement.

On any rational account, it is more probable that Susan is an office manager than Susan is both an office manager and active in the feminist movement. The probability of x, after all, is always greater than the probability of independent event x and independent event y. Yet more than 80 percent of subjects, including those who are sophisticated in statistics, assent more readily to the statement that Susan is an office manager and is active in the feminist movement than to the statement that Susan is an office manager.

Asked the abstract question "Which is more probable, x alone or x and y?" subjects readily consent that x alone is more probable. Moreover, when confronted with the apparent contradiction between this abstract response and the Susan question, they readily admit that they have made an error. This seems to reflect a deep-seated bias in human judgment. Given information that Susan is a certain kind of person, subjects readily fit in other events that have, in the past, been representative of such persons, and in the process, intellectually ignore what they otherwise know about probability. People are emotionally prejudiced to the likelihood that someone with certain characteristics will also exhibit other ones (to the extent that if someone is a social activist, she is likely to be a feminist).

Generally, we use our intelligence to support and rationalize our emotions and prejudices about a particular subject or idea. Suppose, for example, that you are about to buy a sweater for $125 and a desk organizer for $15. The desk organizer salesman tells you that the organizer you want to buy is on sale at the other branch of the store, twenty minutes away, for $10. Would you make the trip? Most people say they will. Another group is asked a similar question. This time the cost of the sweater is changed to $15, and the cost of the desk organizer is discounted from $125 to $120 at the branch. Of respondents presented with this version, the majority said that they would not make the extra trip. Note that in both cases the total purchases are the same: the choice is always whether to drive twenty minutes to save $5. But apparently respondents evaluate the saving of $5 in relation to the price of the desk organizers. In relative terms, a reduction from $15 to $10 (33 percent) is emotionally less resistible than a reduction from $125 to $120 (less than 5 percent).

Instead of using our intelligence to support our emotions and prejudices, we need to use our intellect to explore our subject before we apply our existing emotions and prejudices. If the above respondents had done that, they would have instantly realized that the choice is the same—whether to drive twenty minutes to save $5. To explore a subject with our intellect, we need to will ourselves to do so.

EXPLORING

Most people describe the unusual illustration below as a group of ten circles forming a triangle, and the three stars as a separate group. Few people spontaneously would describe the illustration as a six-pointed Star of David, which it represents as well. To see the Star of David, you need to consciously focus on it in a different way.

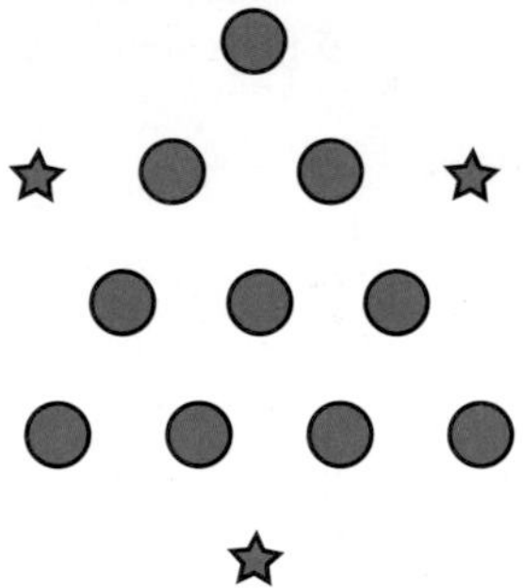

Similarly, to explore a subject with our intellect, we need to "will" ourselves to direct our attention in a different way. A tool to help you achieve this is the PMI (Plus, Minus, Interesting). The PMI is an attention-directing tool that was first introduced by Edward De Bono, an international authority on thinking. It is designed to deliberately direct your attention to all the positive, negative, and interesting aspects about your subject. Carrying out a PMI is simple. What is not simple is to deliberately concentrate your attention in one direction after another when your emotions and prejudices have already decided how you should feel about your subject. In the diagram on the next page, when an idea is emotionally rejected, all creative exploration stops.

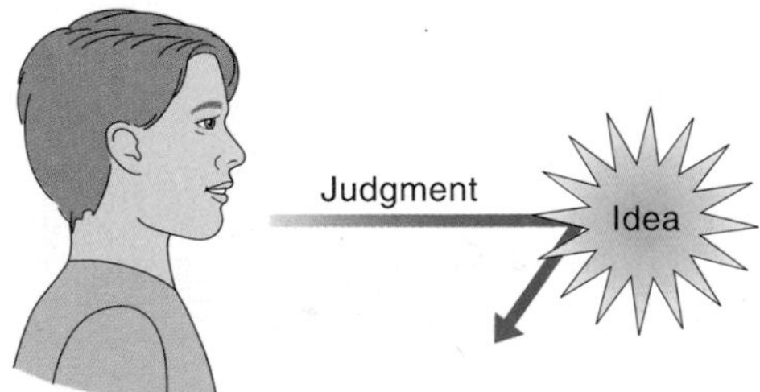

You need to will yourself to look in different directions. Once you have the will to do a PMI, then the natural challenge to your intelligence is to find as many positive, negative, and interesting points as you can. Instead of using intelligence to support your emotions and prejudices, you are now using it to explore the subject matter.

The guidelines for doing a PMI are

1. Make three columns on a sheet of paper. Title the columns "Plus," "Minus," and "Interesting."
2. Under the "Plus" column, list all the positive aspects about the subject that you can.
3. Under the "Minus" column, list all the negative aspects that you can.
4. Under the "Interesting" column, list all those things that are worth noting but do not fit under either "Plus" or "Minus." The "Interesting" items help

us to react to the interest in an idea and not just to judgment feelings and emotions about the idea. "I do not like the idea but there are interesting aspects to it…."

With the PMI, you use your intelligence to explore the subject matter. At the end of the exploration, emotions and feelings can be used to make a decision about the matter. The difference is that the emotions are now applied after the exploration instead of being applied before and so preventing exploration. With a PMI, one of three things can happen:

- You may change your mind about the idea and decide that it is a viable alternative.
- You may still reject the idea as unsound.
- You may move from the idea to another idea. By exploring the "positive" and "interesting" aspects of an idea, you may be able to recycle it into something else.

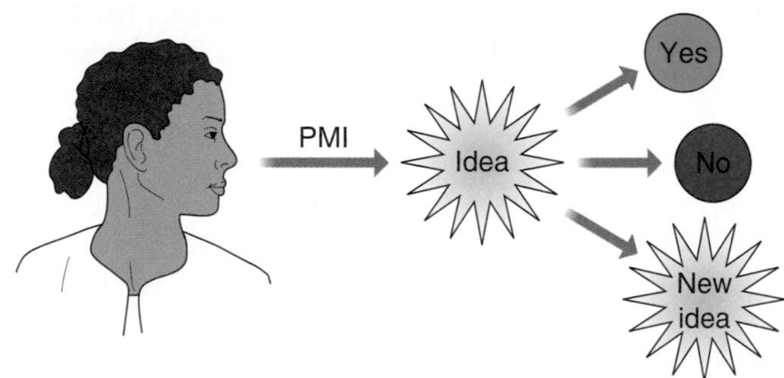

When you put down the P, M, and I points, you react to what you put down and your feelings change. Once a point has been thought and put down under any of the headings, that point cannot be "unthought," and it will influence the final decision.

A while back, a group of designers brainstormed for a new umbrella design. One of the participants suggested a combination umbrella with holster. The holster would be worn on a person's belt. A trigger mechanism in the umbrella handle would release the springloaded umbrella when unholstered.

The group thought this was a terrible idea, because everyone would look armed and dangerous. They decided to do a PMI on the idea, and one of the interesting aspects they focused on was the idea of using the umbrella for protection. This triggered the idea of incorporating a stun gun into the umbrella. If attacked, one touches the attacker with the tip of the umbrella, pulls a trigger, and renders the attacker helpless with a nonlethal shock.

By focusing on the "interesting" aspects of the umbrella idea, they provided themselves with material to look at what they might not have looked for. Just as a carefully designed experiment is an attempt to hurry along the path of logical investigation, so focusing on "interesting" aspects of subjects is an attempt to encourage the chance appearance of ideas that would not have been sought out. Years back, 3M invented a new adhesive for industry. No industry was interested, and management ordered an engineer to burn the samples. The engineer, instead, thought the adhesive had "interesting" aspects and took some samples home. He observed his teenage daughters setting their hair with it and using the adhesive in various other ways. He went to management and convinced them that what they had was a consumer product, not an industrial one, which was manufactured and marketed as Scotch tape.

When thinking of creativity, one usually associates it with the generation and evaluation of new, fresh, and original ideas, but there is more to it than that. You can use your intellect to profoundly change the way you perceive any subject or idea through prolonged inspection, thus furthering the creative process. The studies of the Gestalt psychologists concluded that prolonged study of any subject will bring about spontaneous perceptual changes in the subject. The mind, through prolonged inspection of a subject, becomes bored with it and will explore alternative ways of perceiving it by decomposing the whole into parts and looking for the interesting parts. In the early steps of this process, the effects of these changes remain below the level of awareness. After a while, they penetrate consciousness as new ideas and insights. Some great artists, such as Cézanne and Rodin, often spent a long time looking at their subjects before they painted or sculpted them. They were creatively profiting from the disintegration of a subject into something different, brought about by prolonged inspection.

Groups

An interesting exercise is to deliberately present a valueless or dumb idea to a small group. Ask the participants to write a paragraph opinion (yes or no and why) of the idea on a sheet of paper. Discuss the opinions and then ask each participant to do a PMI on the idea. Finally, combine the PMIs into one master PMI. This forces the group to subject the idea to a prolonged inspection. You'll discover that sometimes participants will change their opinion or will discover that an "interesting" aspect will lead to some other idea. This process is not passive but essentially active because the changes are the result of the mind's manipulative operations when exploring the interesting aspects of a subject. This intellectual exploration sometimes makes it possible to turn a valueless idea or some aspect of it into a novel idea.

LATENT POTENTIAL

Latent potential exists in every subject. We now throw out a large range of objects—from watches to automobile tires—and buy new things, rather than fix them. We rarely rebuild materials for radically different uses. Third World countries, out of necessity, must be more creative and often find a strikingly different purpose for material too worn out to perform its original role. In Nairobi, they recycle worn tires and manufacture sandals. Durability for sandals is a latent potential of auto tires, and the production of sandals defines a functional shift. The Nairobi recycling market is an example of the principle of Darwinian continuous adaptation that led to a quirky shift of function and a new idea.

Evolution works like the Nairobi sandal makers, not like the throwaway society we live in. Species can evolve further only by using what they have in a new and interesting way. Organisms have no equivalent to currency for acquiring something new; they can reconstruct only from their own innards. If organisms could not reuse old material in strikingly new ways, how could evolution ever produce anything novel?

Similarly, every new subject or idea produces a host of creative by-products, initially seen as irrelevant, but available for fashioning in novel new directions.

Much of creative genius hinges on the willingness to creatively observe the seemingly irrelevant and find the latent potential.

There are six irregular shapes in the illustration below that can be initially seen as irrelevant. However, you can use your imagination to fashion these irrelevant shapes into meaningful ones. The V-shaped figures can be fashioned by your imagination to form one large triangle, or closed opposite the apex to form three separate white triangles with an apex in each circle, or you can form one large upside-down white triangle. You can also form a six-pointed star by combining the large white upside-down triangle and the one formed by the Vs. Using your imagination, you created a variety of different-sized triangles and stars out of some irrelevant shapes.

In the same way, you can take a seemingly irrelevant subject and use your imagination to find its latent potential and refashion it into something else. Consider the Walkman radio. Sony engineers tried to design a small, portable stereo tape recorder. They failed. They ended up with a small stereo tape player that couldn't record. They gave up on the project and shelved it. One day Masaru Ibuka, honorary chairman of Sony, discovered this failed product and decided to look for its potential. He remembered an entirely different project at Sony where an engineer was working to develop lightweight portable headphones. "What if you combine the headphones with the tape player and leave out the recorder function altogether?"

Ibuka was mixing up functions. The idea that tape players also record was so well established that no one had considered reversing it. Even after Ibuka made his creative association, no one at Sony believed they could market it. Ibuka was not discouraged and plowed ahead with what he called a new concept in entertainment. Ibuka took a failed idea and by combining, eliminating, and reversing found the latent potential and created a brand new product. The Walkman radio became Sony's best-selling electronic product of all time and introduced all of us to "headphone culture."

Ibuka took what existed (a failed product) and recycled it into something new. Similarly, Michelangelo's masterpiece, *David*, was the result of another sculptor's failed attempt. Back in 1463, the authorities of the cathedral of Florence acquired a sixteen-foot-high chunk of white marble to be carved into a sculpture. Two well-known sculptors worked on the piece and gave up, and the badly mangled block was put in storage. Other sculptors were brought in and asked to carve a statue. They refused to work with the mangled block and demanded a new block. They said they couldn't possibly produce art out of the mangled block. Their demands were not economically feasible, so the project was scrapped by the cathedral. Forty years later, Michelangelo took the mangled block of marble from storage and carved it into the youthful, courageous *David* within eighteen months. He took what existed and sculpted it into one of the world's greatest statues.

Reading 6.2 TeamThink

Don Martin

By conducting only meetings that are necessary, well prepared, and well organized, you set the pattern for business efficiency throughout your organization.

Antony Jay, chairman of London's Video Arts Ltd., says, "Certainly a great many meetings waste a great deal of everyone's time and seem to be held for historical rather than practical reasons; many long-established committees are little more than memorials to dead problems."

Effective meetings serve a number of worthwhile functions. First, they give your staff a chance to be brought up to date, as a group, on what's happening. Second, meetings can become a main focal point for decision making where consensus is necessary. Finally, meetings can create a commitment to decisions which become binding on the group.

But too often meetings are unproductive and waste valuable time for everyone. A survey of 200 executives conducted by Accountemps indicated that executives waste an average of 288 hours a year attending unnecessary meetings. Here are some suggestions on meetings that can help you use time more effectively and productively.

- Start every meeting on time. If all your staffers aren't present, they will be for the next one. Notre Dame's Lou Holtz says, "I normally will walk into a meeting at precisely the proper time. The first thing we do on a continuous basis is set our watches. We go by LLH time. This stands for 'Louis Leo Holtz' time."

  When Vince Lombardi coached Green Bay, he instituted "Lombardi time," which meant fifteen minutes early. Often when the team bus was scheduled to leave at 10:00, he would direct the driver to pull out at 9:45. If you missed the bus, you had to find your own way of catching up with the team.

  General Electric's Medical Health Group in Milwaukee always has one less chair in the room than people invited to the meeting. The purpose is to get people to the meetings on time.

  The CEO of Southland Corp., which operates the 7-Eleven stores, starts every meeting at seven or eleven minutes after the hour. The CEO figures the odd starting time ups the chances of punctual attendance.
- Clearly define the purpose of the meeting. If you can't state the purpose, don't have the meeting. Recognize that there are two types of meetings—the kind where ideas are generated and the kind where decisions are made. It's difficult to mix the two successfully.
- Always have an agenda. The agenda should be completed and distributed enough in advance that all participants can prepare for the meeting.

High-priority items should appear first on the agenda. The early part of a meeting tends to be livelier and more energetic. The top of the meeting is also the place to approach the tough problems—you'll have the time to deal with them.

The more detailed the agenda, the better everyone can prepare. Terms such as "discuss new venture" are too vague.

- Control the timing of the meeting. Besides setting the starting time, it's important to fix the ending time. You control the meeting so that it ends on schedule. The participants will appreciate this; they have their own schedules to maintain. Set a time limit beforehand on discussion of less important items on the agenda.

  If meetings have gone on too long in the past, try scheduling them one hour before lunch or one hour before the end of the day. Everyone will develop a strong motivation to see them end.

- Limit the number of meetings within a certain period. Don't schedule several meetings consecutively. People need mental breaks, time to deal with their own pressing issues and return important phone calls. If possible, limit your normal meetings to one hour.

  Check the meeting schedules of your key managers. Holding too many meetings in a short time makes it difficult for them to prepare and may disrupt their own work patterns.

- Never leave a meeting without writing a list that defines all actions agreed upon. Send it to all attendees, asking for additions or corrections. This way, everyone essentially signs off on the list and acknowledges the actions and deadlines.

- All potential interruptions should be eliminated. Telephone calls to participants, papers to be signed, or people walking in with questions should only be allowed if the situation absolutely cannot wait until the end of the meeting.

- Use breakfast and lunch for meetings with people in your firm. Breakfast meetings have a built-in deadline, as most people are anxious to get back to their offices. Since it's the first meeting of the day, people are fresh and focused. I've found breakfasts seem to be more oriented to specific business problems, while lunches seem to focus on more general topics and building personal and social relationships. In both cases, the no-interruption rule must hold.

  Our boardroom often functions as a lunch-meeting room. My own office has a table and chairs that accommodate lunch for four. Lunch meetings there eliminate travel time and waiting in restaurants.

- Schedule a meeting with yourself. Create "discretionary" or "disposable" free time. This allows you to sit down and think. Management consultants McKinsey & Company, in a recent study titled "Leveraging CEO Time," recommended blocking out at least two "CEO Time Alone" sessions a week, each two hours long.

CHAPTER 7

Conflict Management

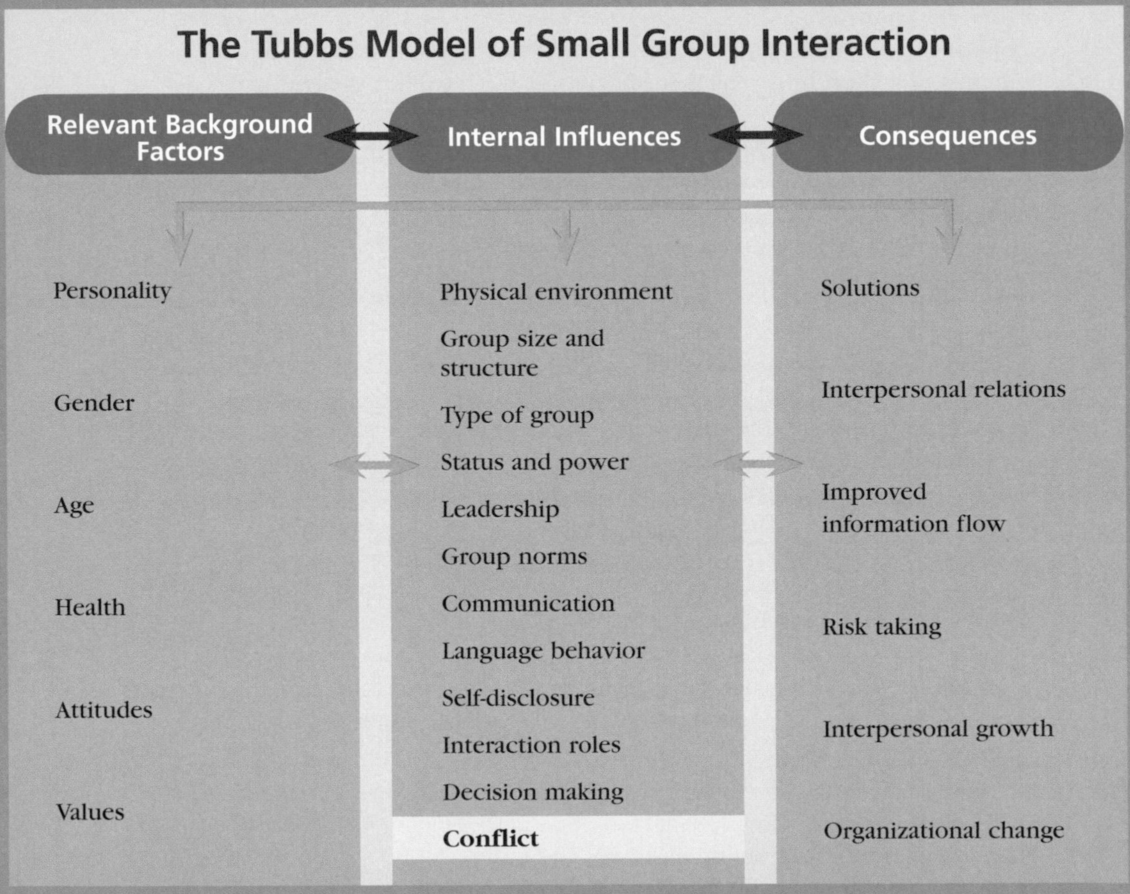

Concepts in **boldface** in gray panels are the emphases of this chapter.

Preview

This chapter focuses on the important topic of conflict management. Conflict is a natural part of the discussion process. However, conflict can sometimes become so intense that a group's functioning is damaged. In this chapter we examine sources of conflict, the desirability and undesirability of conflict, types of conflict, and some methods for conflict management. Blake and Mouton's Conflict Grid is discussed as one possible model for conflict management. Don't forget: "Rudeness is contagious" (Goleman, Boyatzis, & McKee, 2002, p. 16).

Glossary

Conflict of Feelings When people's ideas come into conflict, the participants often begin to have negative feelings toward one another. These conflicts of feelings can damage the group's functioning.

Conflict Grid The Conflict Grid, a model of conflict management developed by Robert Blake and Jane Srygley Mouton, is a framework for developing conflict management skills.

Conflict of Ideas Many ideas are generated in group discussions. Sometimes different people's ideas may conflict. It is important to remember that a variety and diversity of ideas is usually desirable in the process of problem solving.

Conflict Management This is the ability to manage conflict so that there is a healthy conflict of ideas without the unhealthy conflict of feelings.

CASE STUDY

CONFLICT IN THE MOTION PICTURE INDUSTRY

The famous director and former child actor Ron Howard was negotiating with Disney Studios some time back over the movie *The Alamo*. Howard wanted his standard $10-million fee plus a percentage of the profits starting from the first day the movie came out. Disney wanted to first recoup all the costs of the movie before paying Howard a share of the profits. They ultimately stalemated, and *The Alamo* was made without Ron Howard. *The Missing* with Tommy Lee Jones and Cate Blanchett is the western that Ron Howard made instead. According to *The Wall Street Journal*, Disney's decision not to agree with Howard's terms hinged on a disagreement between the financial and the creative departments at Disney.

The financial people cited the box-office failure of *Windtalkers*, starring Nicholas Cage, despite a big-name star and a $115-million budget. They felt that Disney should hedge against another failure by refusing to agree to Howard's financial guarantees.

The creative people argued that *Splash, Apollo 13, A Beautiful Mind*, and Howard's other movies were all great financial sucesses. But in the end they were overruled.

continued

The Alamo, with a well-known story, turned out to be a box-office flop. *The Missing* turned out to be more successful, even with an unknown story, once again proving Ron Howard's worth as a director.

1. How typical does this case seem based on your experience (that is, creative versus financial pressures)?
2. What would you have done differently if you had been the head of Disney?
3. Are there any other suggestions or recommendations that you have for situations like this that happen at work?
4. What material in this chapter can help prepare you to deal with such situations?

A survey of executives and managers conducted at Northwestern University found that "team conflict is one of the top three concerns of team management" (Thompson, 2000). It has been said that conflict is an inevitable part of people's relating to one another. Some would even go as far as to say that a conflict-free relationship is probably a sign that you really have no relationship at all. It has also been said that where there is movement, friction results, and where there is friction, heat is produced. Certainly, many small groups involve movement, especially if their task is to solve and act on problems. Obviously, in such cases the heat referred to is the emotional heat that results from conflicts. In fact, Wall, Solum, and Sobol (1992) state, "After 15 years of observation, we have reluctantly come to the conclusion that working together in harmony does not come naturally for human beings" (p. 132).

In our society, conflict is usually considered to be bad—that thing that results in wars, divorces, worker strikes, and bloody noses. However, most experts agree that conflict within and among groups has some *desirable* effects. Both the desirable and undesirable aspects of conflict will be discussed in this chapter. However, we look first at the sources from which conflicts arise.

Sources of Conflict

Wilmot and Hocker (2010) define *conflict* as "an expressed struggle between at least two interdependent parties who perceive incompatible goals, scarce resources, and interference from others in achieving their goals" (p. 34). Conflict exists whenever incompatible activities occur. An incompatible action prevents, obstructs, interferes with, injures, or in some way reduces the effectiveness of the other action. Incompatible actions may occur within a single person (intrapersonal), a single group (intragroup), between two or more people (interpersonal), or between two or more groups (intergroup). Conflicts may originate from a number of different sources, including (1) differences in information, beliefs, values, interests, or desires; (2) a scarcity of some resource, such as money, power, time, space, or position; and

(3) rivalries in which one person or group competes with another. To these sources could be added the difficulty of the task, the pressure to avoid failure, the relative importance of a group's or individual's decision, and differences in skill levels that may cause more skilled individuals to become irritated at the less skilled, which often leads to a reciprocal irritation. In an earlier chapter, we discussed personality differences. These differences lead to incompatibilities among certain members of a group. Members may be incompatible because of their differences—or they may be incompatible because of their similarities, such as in the need to achieve or dominate others. All these factors tend to instigate conflict.

Desirability of Conflict

An iconoclast is someone who tends to create conflict by arguing against long-held beliefs. The term was coined "when Leo III, Roman emperor of Constantinople, destroyed the golden icon of Christ over his palace gates in 725 AD. Leo's act of defiance against the church was to consolidate his power, but the word iconoclast, which means literally 'destroyer of icons,' stuck" (Berns, 2009, p. 10). As mentioned above, many writers believe that conflict in a group is desirable. For example, in Chapter 5 we discussed the very real problem of groupthink, which can occur in any group. Conflict helps eliminate or reduce the likelihood of groupthink. Clearly, there are significant benefits to conflict, or it would not be the prominent characteristic of human relationships that it is. Conflict has been described as the engine of social learning. Without conflict, attitudes, behavior, and relationships will always stay the same, regardless of whether they are fair. Conflict helps to reveal problems and encourages the people involved to deal with them. Whether conflict is constructive or destructive depends on how it is handled. Conflict can also help to build team cohesiveness and to construct group boundaries by helping individuals recognize their common interest. For example, a team working together to fight the opposition begins to realize that they are working toward a common goal. This one thing they have in common is the building block to more commonality and, ultimately, more group cohesiveness. It has been said that groups may actually seek enemies to maintain internal cohesion. For example, it has been argued that the United States had to find an enemy to replace the Soviet Union once the Cold War ended, and Iraq was the unlucky choice (Brahm, 2004).

Gamero, González-Romá, and Peiró (2008) analyzed whether relationship conflict mediates the link between task conflict and shared affect at the team level of analysis. Moreover, we tested the hypothesis that the relationship between these two types of intrateam conflict would be moderated by team members' interaction. The sample was composed of 156 bank branches. Data were gathered at two points in time, and two affect dimensions (tension and enthusiasm) were measured. The results obtained supported their hypotheses. Relationship conflict fully mediated the link between task conflict and team affect. Team members' interaction about team issues moderated the relationship between task conflict and relationship conflict, so that when team members' interaction was low, the relationship enhanced, whereas when team members' interaction was high, the relationship weakened.

Alfred Sloan was one of the early executives who helped make General Motors successful. He recognized the importance of idea conflict in decision making. Once Sloan was chairing a meeting of the GM board of directors in which someone presented an idea for buying a small company. After the presentation, Sloan asked each member around the table for an opinion. Not one objected to the proposal; they all agreed the company should buy at the earliest possible moment. Finally, Sloan looked at the other board members and said, "Gentlemen, I don't see any reason not to adopt the idea either. Therefore, I suggest we postpone this decision for thirty days while we do some more thinking." Thirty days later, the board decided against the plan—after finding out many negatives they had not known earlier (Cosier & Schwenk, 1990, p. 69).

Peterson and Behfar (2003) studied the relationship between group performance and types of conflict. They found that a moderate level of conflict across tasks within a group resulted in improved group performance, while conflict among personalities resulted in poorer group performance. Also, if group members experience any type of conflict early in their experience of working together, they tend to have a higher chance of future failure. Those groups whose members have less conflict early on and have high levels of intragroup trust have a higher chance of future success.

Conflict clearly plays an important role in small group interaction. However, it is a double-edged sword, as we shall see.

Types of Conflict

Many people fail to differentiate between two very different types of conflict—namely, *conflict of ideas* and *conflict of feelings* (often called *personality conflict*). As we saw in the example above, Alfred Sloan recognized the importance of idea conflict in making a decision. If there is too little conflict of ideas, groupthink can occur, as we saw in Chapter 5. Idea conflict, however, can very easily turn into conflict of feelings. We call this *personal conflict.* Notice the difference between the conflicts in these two conversations in a group discussion:

Conversation 1

JUDY: Why don't we have our next meeting at my sorority house?

DAVE: I think the campus center meeting room might have fewer interruptions. I know how hard it is to have meetings at my fraternity house.

Conversation 2

JUDY: Why don't we have our next meeting at my sorority house?

DAVE: And have people interrupting us all the time? No, thanks, I'd rather meet in the campus center.

In the first situation, there was a conflict of ideas. In the second, the conflict could have escalated to the personal level depending on Judy's reaction. The personal animosity that may have been created by Dave is the kind that tends to get in the way of group success. As shown in Figure 7.1, our goal in using conflict successfully is to avoid turning idea opponents into personal opponents.

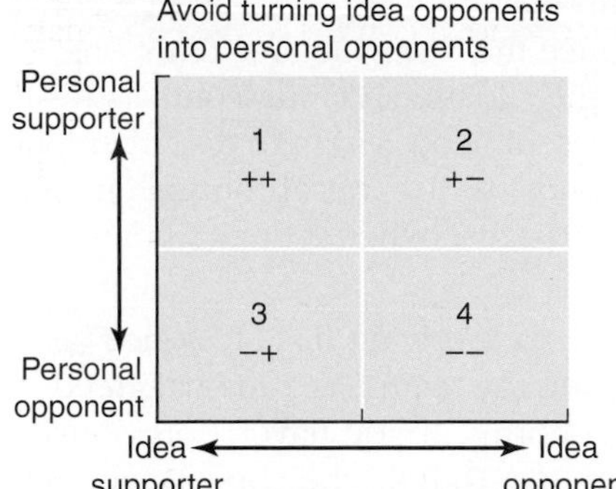

FIGURE 7.1 Opposition and Support

Undesirability of Conflict

You don't want to go to bed at night with more enemies than you started with in the morning.

—Sun Tzu, ancient Chinese general, *The Art of War*

Our society frequently considers conflict to be undesirable. Millions of dollars are lost each year because of work stoppages and strikes. Thousands of divorces result from unchecked marital conflicts. And every once in a while, a disaster like the Los Angeles riots following the Rodney King verdict means that conflict has gotten out of control. Even in meetings, discussions, and conferences, conflict may cause reactions similar to that of one student who said, "I don't even want to go to publication council meetings anymore. Every week it is just one hassle after another. Nothing ever gets accomplished because every time we end up arguing."

Conflicts are often hard to keep under control once they have begun. There is a definite trend toward escalation and polarization. Once conflict escalates to a point at which it is no longer under control, it almost always yields negative results. In this same vein, one conflict tends to lay the groundwork for further conflicts at a later time. Part of this is because of defensive reactions. Defensiveness leads us to distort our perceptions so that ambiguous acts are more frequently misconstrued as threatening when they may, in fact, not be intended that way.

Woolf (1990), in his outstanding book *Friendly Persuasion,* offers 101 tactics for negotiating and resolving conflict. Here are a few examples:

- Almost everything is negotiable.
- It doesn't hurt to ask.
- Don't be intimidated just because it's printed.
- Don't take anything personally.
- It never works for one . . . to insult another's intelligence.
- Start high but don't be ridiculous. (pp. 162–87)

According to communication expert Amy Gallo (2010), regardless of why your team is fighting, following a few simple guidelines can help you resolve disputes quickly.

Intervene early. When two or more team members are engaged in a conflict, the sooner you step in, the better. Once the dispute starts, emotions can run high, making it harder to diffuse the situation. Letting conflicts fester can result in hurt feelings and lasting resentment. A simple disagreement can turn into a serious conflict in milliseconds, so it's critical for team managers to be aware of the team dynamics and sense when a disagreement is percolating.

Focus on team norms. The best approach to resolving disputes once they've erupted is to refer back to something the team has already agreed on. These may be explicit or implicit team norms. If you haven't previously discussed norms as a team, now is a good time to hold the conversation. Be careful not to frame the discussion around the dispute but to focus it on setting rules of engagement for going forward.

Identify a shared agreement. Your job as a team member is to help the fighting team members reach an accord. The only way to do this is to talk it through. Most teams cut short dialogue or don't do it well. Once the cards are on the table, you need to facilitate an outcome that takes into account both parties' points of view. Compromise often has a bad connotation in the business world, but the resolution should integrate both parties' interests. Whenever possible, connect the resolution back to shared purposes, values, or identity that can help both parties see eye to eye (Gallo, 2010).

Needless to say, it is extremely important to fine-tune our conflict management skills.

Game Theory

Before you read this section, try out Exercise 1 at the end of this chapter.

The movie *A Beautiful Mind* tells the story of Nobel Prize–winning Princeton professor John Nash, who was the founder of game theory. His theory has had wide-ranging applications around the world. In this case, we will be looking at game theory from the standpoint of conflict resolution.

If you tried Exercise 1 at the end of this chapter, then you have had the chance to experience an example of game theory. Let's take a look at what is behind the exercise. First, game theory puts people into the mixed-motive situation discussed in Chapter 6. That is, you are simultaneously tempted to both cooperate and compete. How did you interpret the phrase "Win as much as you can"? Did you think of it as winning as much as you can as an individual? That is the most popular way to think of and play the "game." However, you can also interpret this as the team of two people winning as much as they could compared to all the other pairs in the class. The third way to interpret the game is to see how much the entire class can win by employing a strategy that allows everybody in the class to maximize their profits. Now you can see what is meant by the term *mixed motives*. Most people have some desire to win as much as they can individually. However, these other two approaches also have some distinct appeal.

Game theory originated with a specific exercise called the *Prisoner's Dilemma* (Deutsch, 1958). Suppose you are one of two prisoners who have been taken into custody by the police. You have been kept apart so that you cannot coordinate your stories. The police offer each of you prisoners a deal. If one of you confesses to the crime (such as a burglary) and the other doesn't, the confessor can go free. The police don't care which person takes the "rap." The downside is that the burglar who doesn't confess gets 10 years of prison. However, if both of you confess, you will both be convicted but will get a reduced sentence (eight years) for cooperating with the police. Finally, if both of you refuse to confess, you will both get a sentence of two years in prison (Murnighan, 1992).

In this scenario, each prisoner has four possible outcomes:

	He Keeps Quiet	*He Confesses*
I Keep Quiet	We each get 2 years.	He goes free; I get 10 years.
I Confess	I go free; he gets 10 years.	We each get 8 years.

If you happened to be one of the prisoners, what do you think you would do? Keep in mind that you have no way of knowing what the other prisoner will do. The interesting thing about this mixed-motive situation is that both parties can do well if they cooperate, or they can try to gain an advantage by competing. This is very typical of many life situations. The game theory situation is a microcosm of real life.

Psychological game theory seeks to discover strategies for success in which the best option depends upon what other people are going to do, when you have no advance knowledge of what the other party is going to do. The Prisoner's Dilemma is regarded as a branch of game theory. The essential question asked by the Prisoner's Dilemma is this: Can people be naturally cooperative, or do our individual genes mandate a selfish response to life situations? This question is intriguing to mediators because variations of the Prisoner's Dilemma are played out in all conflict resolutions. The dilemma is whether to testify against a friend in order to get a lighter sentence or to stay loyal and deny the charge, hoping that the other party will also deny rather than testify, in which case they will both be set free.

And there are other versions of the Prisoner's Dilemma including one invented by Hammerstein and Selten, one invented by John Maynard Smith called Hawk and Dove, and one invented by Hofstadter called the Wolf's Dilemma. At the heart of each of these game theory exercises is the same question: Are we motivated by selfishness, or can we be naturally cooperative? And what you find out is that you can't escape the dilemma; all you can do is try to maximize whatever advantage you are offered.

Social scientists have been playing with these theories for years and have still not come up with an exact formula for why people make the choices they do. However, some research has shown that cooperation breeds cooperation and competition breeds competition. So, if you want to foster a cooperative climate, try cooperating to set the climate of the relationship (Parselle, 2007).

Suppose you are a new hire in a work team. How do you get off on the right foot? Do you try to make yourself look good as an individual? Most experts suggest that you are much more likely to be successful if you try to be a good team player rather than put yourself ahead of the other team members. Kelley (1998) conducted extensive research and found that those who learn how to work successfully as team players tend to go much further in their careers than those who try to compete with their fellow team members. He cites the Boeing 777 project that employed 100 separate teams that worked together over a six-year period to create this new jetliner. This achievement boosted company profits by 20 percent for that year and doubled its stock price (p. 184). When a company has a profit-sharing plan, each employee also benefits from the company's success. For example, in the past, Chrysler Corporation employees have averaged over $7,500 per year in profit-sharing bonuses. Many other companies are moving in this direction. This approach is analogous to having the entire class win in the "Win as Much as You Can" exercise.

The Prisoner's Dilemma is also an example of a non–zero sum game. A *zero sum game* is where I take 10 from 10 and so leave you with zero. This is also known as the *fixed-pie situation*. If you or I cut a piece out of a pie, the bigger our piece, the less is left for the other person. This is because the size of the pie is fixed. However, if we create a pie that is bigger, then we can each have more without harming the other. This latter situation is referred to as a *non–zero sum game*. Steven Covey (1990) in his famous book *The Seven Habits of Highly Successful People* refers to these two approaches as the scarcity mentality versus the abundance mentality. The scarcity mentality leads us to resent the success of others. However, the abundance mentality allows us to think of situations in which everybody can win. This is the so-called win–win approach.

The purpose of a study conducted by Pearsall, Ellis, and Evans (2008) was to use faultline theory to examine the effects of gender diversity on team creativity. Results from 80 teams working on an idea-generation task indicated that the activation of gender faultlines negatively affected the number and overall creativity of ideas. However, gender faultlines that were not activated had no effect. Results also indicated that the relationship between activated gender faultlines and team creativity was partially mediated by the level of conflict within the team. In other words, when teams had an overall higher level of conflict, men and women tended to argue based on male versus female viewpoints.

However, many individuals and organizations have difficulty applying these concepts. Many people as well as organizations still run on the principle of competition and the scarcity mentality. In the next section, we will examine some of the ways that conflicts can be managed in order to allow for greater mutual gains among all of the parties involved.

Toward Conflict Management

Building Collaborative Solutions, Inc. (BCS), defines conflict management as "the opportunity to improve situations and strengthen relationships" (BCS, 2004). It presents the concept of conflict management in two parts. The first is *proactive conflict management*, which prevents conflict through proactive programs, such as relationship-building and team exercises. The second is *collaborative conflict management*, which helps diffuse any conflicts that come up through development of a process for working through conflict. Conflict management is "cooperative, balanced, and empathic." In other words, group members in a conflict must rally together to solve the conflict, express individual and group viewpoints freely and openly, and take the time to understand the points of view of other group members. As a result, conflict that is managed effectively results in open sharing of thoughts, feelings, and ideas; increased group and individual productivity and creativity; and personal satisfaction, positive relationships, and less future conflict. Conversely, conflict that is not managed effectively results in group members who withhold their thoughts, feelings, and ideas; decreased group productivity and creativity; and personal dissatisfaction, ineffective communication channels, and an increase in future conflict (BCS, 2004).

A number of systems have been proposed for improving our abilities to resolve conflict. Two well-known psychologists (Blake & Mouton, 1970) have proposed a scheme whereby we can try to avoid win–lose situations and, when possible, apply a win–win approach. This can best be illustrated with their model, the Conflict Grid (see Figure 7.2).

The Conflict Grid clearly illustrates the possibility of having *both* concern for results and concern for people at the same time. Intuitively, it would seem difficult to "have your cake and eat it, too" when it comes to conflict resolution. Alternative strategies of dealing with conflict are also depicted on the grid. Try to identify where your style would fit.

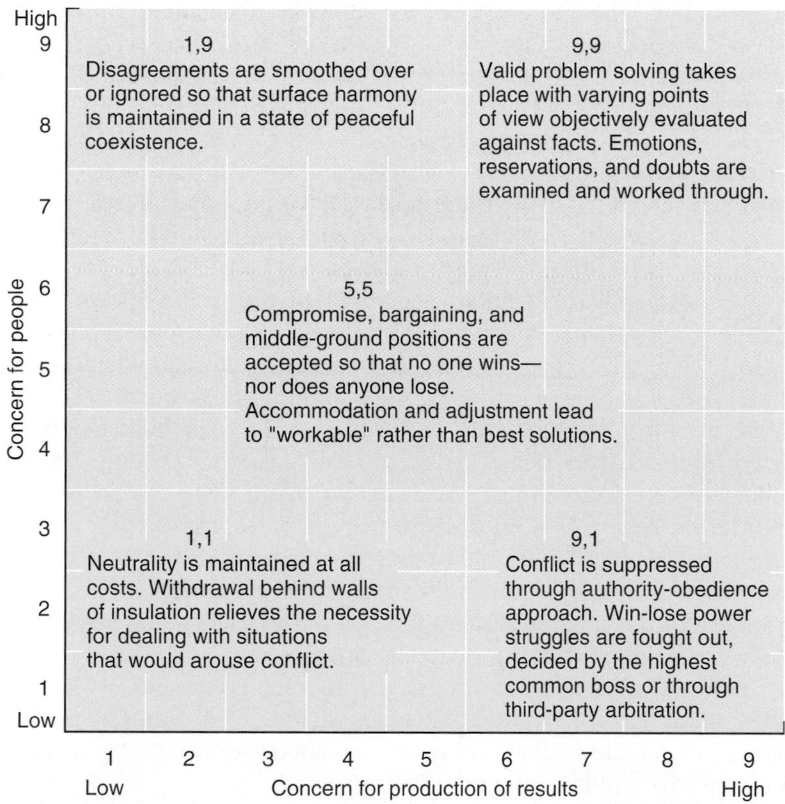

FIGURE 7.2 Blake and Mouton's Conflict Grid

Reproduced by permission from "The Fifth Achievement," Robert R. Blake and Jane Srygley Mouton. *Journal of Applied Behavioral Science* 6(4), 1970.

PRACTICAL TIPS

Walker and Harris (1995) offer the following practical tips for implementing the 9,9 style of encouraging behavior among team members:

1. Avoid feelings or perceptions that imply the other person is wrong or needs to change.
2. Communicate a desire to work together to explore a problem or seek a solution.
3. Exhibit behavior that is spontaneous and destruction-free.
4. Identify with another team member's problems, share feelings, and accept the team member's reaction.
5. Treat other team members with respect and trust.
6. Investigate issues rather than taking sides on them.

The same principles can be applied to negotiating with others outside your team, or with a supplier or customer (p. 102).

The 1,1 style is the hands-off approach, also called *avoidance*. With this approach, conflict is simply avoided. Neutrality is maintained with the attitude "the less said about it the better." The 1,9 position, also called *accommodation*, is excessively person-oriented. Its goal is to maintain the *appearance* of harmony at all costs. In reality, deep conflicts exist but are never dealt with. An uneasy state of tension exists, which is frequently characterized by lots of smiling and nervous laughter (but members avoid looking at each other). In this style, people suppress their substantive needs in order to give in to the other person's needs. The 5,5 position represents the willingness to compromise. Although compromise may be a viable alternative in some cases, it should not be a chronic way of avoiding deeper levels of conflict resolution. The problem with the 5,5 style is that both parties settle for less than a fully satisfying agreement. This approach is sometimes referred to as "cutting the baby in half," from the Bible story in which two women are fighting over a baby and the wise King Solomon offers to cut the baby in half to settle the dispute. Obviously, this is a terrible solution. The bullheaded approach is depicted by the 9,1 position. This style is also called *competing*. People attack each other verbally and will use whatever tactics are necessary in order to gain the upper hand. This style is even worse than the compromise. Because absolute stalemates often occur, a group full of these types may get nowhere fast.

The optimum style for reducing conflict is the 9,9 approach, also called *collaboration*. Here the members attempt to be both person- and results-oriented. Conflicts are not ignored, but individuals don't go around with a chip on their shoulder either. Differences are discussed with such comments as "I don't agree with the position that . . . " At the same time, personally insulting statements, such as "Anybody who believes that is nuts," are avoided. Tubbs and Moss (2008) offer four guidelines for implementing the 9,9 style:

1. Make sure you agree on the use of your terms or definitions.
2. Build on areas of mutual agreement.

3. Determine the specific changes necessary for a satisfactory resolution of the issues.
4. Avoid personal attacks, and stick to the issues.

Reporter Lesley Stahl (1999) writes about one of her contract negotiations with CBS in the following way: "My negotiation for a new contract brought with it the usual ego blandishments. Joe Peyronnin mass-mailed a computer message: 'From here on Lesley Stahl will be known as CHIEF White House Correspondent.' The technical term for that is contract foreplay; the supposition: the longer the title, the smaller the raise" (p. 348). The important point here is that there are financial and nonfinancial bargaining chips that may be used in a negotiation.

One qualitative study of 57 autonomous teams (Behfar et al., 2008) suggests that groups that improve or maintain top performance over time share three conflict resolution tendencies: (1) focusing on the content of interpersonal interactions rather than delivery style, (2) explicitly discussing reasons behind any decisions reached in accepting and distributing work assignments, and (3) assigning work to members who have the relevant task expertise rather than assigning by other common means such as volunteering, default, or convenience. The authors' results also suggest that teams that are successful over time are likely to be both proactive in anticipating the need for conflict resolution and pluralistic in developing conflict resolution strategies that apply to all group members.

One famous conflict-reducing method known as *principled negotiation* has been developed at Harvard University by Fisher and Ury (1991), Fisher and Ertel (1995), and Fisher et al. (1999). The authors outline four principles that compose the method:

> *Separate the people from the problem.* The natural tendency in any conflict situation is to get angry with the other party. A more effective method is to use the approach described as "hard on issues, soft on people." If possible, treat the other party with respect, and avoid sarcastic comments and nonverbal behaviors.
>
> *Focus on interests, not positions.* I once had a disagreement with the full professors in a department that centered on which candidate to hire. They wanted Tom, and I wanted Harry. We absolutely could not agree. I wanted Harry because of his distinguished publication record, which would strengthen our position regarding reaccreditation. They did not like his personality. We focused on the common interest of reaccreditation. They agreed as a group (of twenty) to each publish one article in the next year, which would be more publications than Harry would have brought to our organization. I agreed to let them hire Tom, with the provision that if they did not live up to their promise of publishing twenty articles, I would select the next new hire. The agreement was satisfactory to all parties and was based on the common interest rather than on the position (in this case Tom or Harry). At the end of one year they had published ten articles (not twenty), so I selected a new professor to hire who had several high-quality publications. Again, all parties were satisfied, and the case for reaccreditation was strengthened.
>
> *Invent options for mutual gain.* All the material discussed regarding brainstorming and creative problem solving applies here. For example, CMS Energy in Michigan established a joint venture with Oxford Energy in England. They built a plant in California that burns used automobile tires as a source of energy. With electrostatic precipitators, they also eliminate any air pollution. Tires contain so much petroleum that a ton of tires has more BTUs of energy than a ton of coal. This is an ingenious

innovation to rid the overcrowded landfills of old tires and create clean, low-cost energy at the same time (Morris, 1999).

Seek objective criteria. Striving for objective criteria is often useful. For example, in determining prices for houses, usually the bank will require an appraisal done by an objective third party. Some of the data used in setting the value are the recent selling prices of several "comparables," which are other houses in a similar location with comparable features. This method of valuing a property is a common technique of using objective criteria.

These steps represent an assertive way to manage conflict. However, many people run away from conflict. That can make the situation worse, because differences do not simply disappear with time; sometimes they get worse. It is important to confront conflict.

Tubbs, Kryska, and Cooper (1997) propose that one frequent source of conflict is the leadership struggle between superior and subordinate in decision making. They assert that the leader has to be flexible enough to modify his or her decision-making style to fit the "followership" of the group. This discussion focuses primarily on the business setting, but the implications are valid for any small group setting in which conflict arises from a leadership struggle. The continuum of decision-making styles can serve as a model for the leader (in conjunction with the group) so that the group can choose the style that is most appropriate for its situation and that would reduce unnecessary conflict. This model (see Figure 7.3) has also been described as including four styles of decision making: (1) tells, (2) sells, (3) consults, and (4) joins.

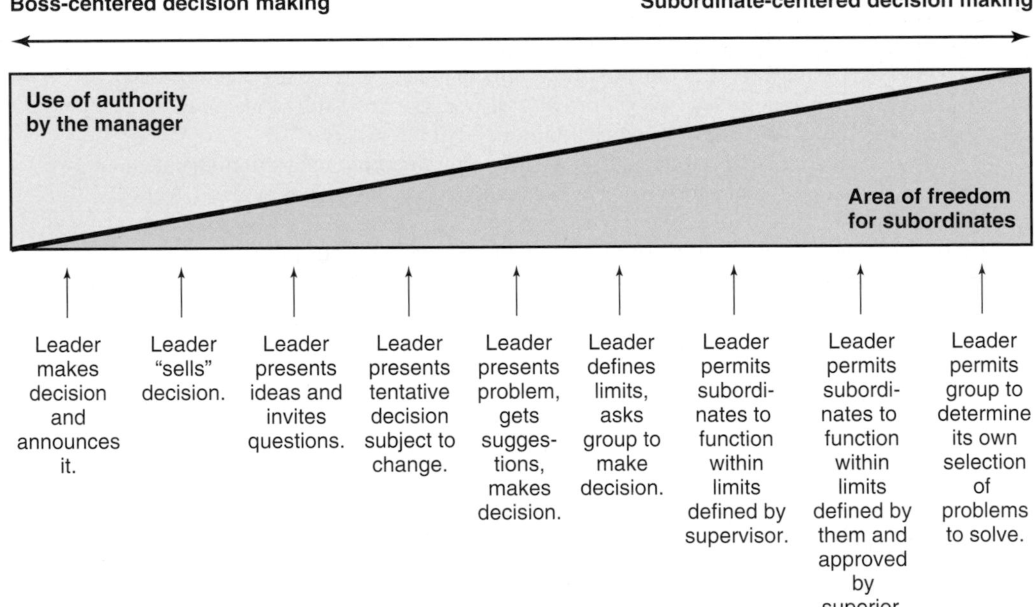

FIGURE 7.3 A Continuum of Decision-Making Behavior

From Stewart L. Tubbs, *Empowerment* (Ann Arbor, Mich.: U-Train, Inc., 1993), pp. 5–9. Adapted from R. Tannenbaumt and H. W. Schmidt, "How to Choose a Leadership Pattern," *Harvard Business Review*, March–April 1958.

A related system of conflict prevention through better decision making includes four other styles: (1) railroading, (2) teaming up, (3) majority vote, and (4) consensus. *Railroading* occurs when one or more group members force their will on the group. This technique is very likely to produce resentment and result in unnecessary conflict. *Teaming up* refers to a situation in which various minority members within a group form a coalition to help each other achieve mutually advantageous goals. This pattern is frequently used in Congress when politicians make trades through which they agree to support each other's bills. This may lead to short-term success, but may also result in further conflict once the scheme is discovered. *Majority vote* represents the wishes of at least 51 percent of a group's members. However, the remaining minority may be bitterly opposed to the decision. This bitterness often results in conflict at a later time. *Consensus* denotes agreement among all members of a group concerning a given decision. Consensus is generally considered to yield the best resolution of conflict in a group decision. Few groups are as concerned as they should be about trying to reach consensus on decisions. Juries represent one of the few types of groups that are required to reach consensus. Those that don't—hung juries—are dismissed.

Consensus does not come quickly or easily. Agreement generally results from careful and thoughtful interpersonal communication between group members. If we are to achieve complete group consensus, some individual preferences of group members must be surrendered. The group as a whole must decide if consensus can be achieved. If several members are adamant in their positions and refuse to change their minds in agreement with the others, the group may decide that reaching complete consensus is not worth the effort. In this case, it may be better to postpone the group decision—particularly if the group making the decision will also be implementing the decision. If several group members are not in favor of the solution, they will be less anxious to put it into practice.

Conflict resolution seems to improve as we engage in certain types of behaviors. These can be summarized as follows:

1. Set the stage for dialogue. Move to a neutral environment.
2. Disengage your fight–flight response, clear your mind of everything you think you already know about the conflict, and listen empathically to the other parties.
3. State, clearly and without anger, your needs and self-interests, and listen carefully to those expressed by others.
4. Look below the surface of what is being said to resolve the underlying reasons for the dispute.
5. Separate the person from the problem, the future from the past, and positions from interests.
6. Brainstorm all potential solutions to your conflict, listing as many as possible, and ask the others to work with you to develop criteria to resolve it.
7. Discuss collaboratively rather than aggressively, and look for values, standards, or rules that will help resolve the dispute fairly, to your mutual satisfaction.

8. Use informal problem solving, mediation, and other conflict resolution techniques to overcome impasse, clarify areas of agreement, and reach closure.
9. Let go of your judgments about the others and focus instead on improving your own skills at handling their difficult behaviors. Then let go, forgive yourself and others, and move on with your life.
10. Don't surrender just so the conflict will go away. The point is not to avoid but to turn it into a collaboration and an opportunity.
11. Recognize the larger organizational and social issues that express themselves through conflict, and discover how your committed actions and acceptance of responsibility contribute to a more peaceful world.
12. Search for completion. Summarize what you think has been agreed to and ask the others to see if this fits their understanding of the agreement.
13. Modify the agreement if necessary. (These guidelines are adapted from Cloke and Goldsmith, 2011, pp. 14–18.)

Although these are not hard-and-fast rules, and they may not work in all cases, they should improve a group's chances for keeping conflict at a manageable level so that the group can move forward toward its goal.

Questions about how to resolve conflicts regarding organizational development and culture issues, customer service problems, or struggling sales often surface when working with clients. To help with problems such as these, Scott (2008) offers the ERI model. The ERI (emotions, reason, intuition) model uses a step-by-step approach to help you think about ways to resolve a problem. To resolve any conflict, you first have to rid the situation of any negative emotions, such as feelings of anger, resentment, mistrust, or fear. The second step in ERI is to use reasoning techniques to better understand the conflict and discern the appropriate resolution strategies. The final step in the process is to use your intuition. The intuition phase has you brainstorm new possibilities and alternatives for resolving a conflict, and intuitively decide the best approach to use in a particular situation. Let your intuition, which may come to you as a sense of knowing or gut feeling, help you find win–win solutions.

Daniel Robin (2004), of Daniel Robin & Associates, encourages individuals to understand their own personal triggers to better deal with conflict situations in the workplace. In the group setting, Robin encourages members to think about the other group members early in the meeting process and to privately identify those individuals and subsequent behaviors that are more apt to "push their buttons." Awareness of these issues up front will help group members minimize their reactions to buttons. To promote further awareness, Robin presents a list of behavior patterns that generally push buttons:

- *Person with a bad attitude:* complains constantly.
- *Space invader:* has no personal distance boundaries.
- *Knee-jerk resister:* is always one-sided.
- *Permanent hijacker:* hijacks all situations with anger.

- *Ruthless critic:* never stops criticizing.
- *Verbally compulsive type:* won't stop talking.
- *Avoider:* hides from commitment on projects.
- *Accommodator:* says yes even when thinking no.
- *Authoritarian bully:* must always be right.

Robin recommends helping groups release their buttons by brainstorming in a group about things that generally help or hinder them in group settings. This session should be free and without criticism and will result in the creation of group norms and ground rules (Robin, 2004).

Conflict resolution is much easier with a clear head. Once tensions and tempers start to rise, it's difficult to speak rationally. Temper and tension are not the way to resolve conflicts within your group. Research tells us that it takes 15–30 minutes for the chemicals in our body to deplete after a highly emotional situation. This calming-down period has the added effect of allowing us to see the situation more clearly and come up with a wider variety of possible solutions. And the best solutions come when there are the most options available. Therefore, when tensions start to rise, take a 15-minute break. This can make a major difference in group decisions and the success of the team (Barthel, 2007).

In a recent article titled "What the Bleep Does Spirituality Have to Do with Conflict Resolution," the question is raised, Where do spirituality and emotion fit into this mess? Far too often, the emphasis is on thinking rather than feeling, on the head instead of the heart. This may actually be hurting our chances for conflict resolution. Underneath the veneer of what may formally be presented

PRACTICAL TIPS

- **Identify common ground.** To start a difficult conversation the right way, it's important for you and your co-worker to identify something you agree on. This may be a common goal or a set of operating rules that you consent to. Try saying something like: "We both want to develop a plan that will take our company to the next level," or "We said we would be thorough about this decision."
- **Hear your coworker out.** Even if you think you already understand your co-worker's perspective, you should hear what she has to say. Ask questions that help you fully understand her point of view and determine whether your disagreement is a function of differing interests or differing perceptions. For example, if she says she is just trying to keep her boss happy, you can help her articulate how a resolution is aligned with her boss's concerns.
- **Propose a resolution.** After all of the data is on the table, offer a resolution. Say to your coworker, "You've said A, and I've said B, perhaps we can consider solution C."

Source: Amy Gallo, "The right way to fight," *Harvard Business Review Daily Briefing*, May 12, 2010.

as sophisticated business, we are still dealing with *human* conflict (which includes many of the feelings and emotions that go along with being human). Sometimes conflict resolution needs to go deeper than the clear-cut options. Sometimes we need to consider the intellectual, psychological, and emotional needs of people as well. In the end, we may benefit from using our hearts and not just our heads (Barker, 2007).

Verbal Judo

As we have seen, understanding motivations and communication styles as critical elements of personality is crucial to effective group performance. Tactical communication techniques like *verbal judo* have increased in popularity as a method for diffusing conflict. Verbal judo is an international phenomenon that started with training for police officers and moved into the workplace as a critical technique in diffusing all types of conflict. George J. Thompson, president and founder of the Verbal Judo Institute, defines verbal judo as "the gentle art of persuasion that redirects others behavior with words and generates voluntary compliance" (2004). Verbal judo is not just a business technique. This method, introduced by George Thompson in his book *Verbal Judo: The Gentle Art of Persuasion*, is being used by many different professions now. For example, it helps local police officers settle disputes and gets people to comply with their requests by redirecting people's energy to achieve a goal. The verbal judo style allows the officers to use their words instead of brute force to defuse situations (Fortney, 2007).

Verbal judo also takes its principles from the physical art of judo. "Presence" and "words" are the two elements necessary for successful verbal judo conflict resolution and negotiation (Hikaru Dojo Martial Arts Academy, 2001). Words are used as instruments to facilitate cooperation instead of as weapons to feed a conflict. Personal feelings are held at bay so that situations can be assessed objectively. Individuals in professional settings learn how to help others understand why cooperation will help them meet their objectives (Karpela, 2003).

Verbal judo consists of two primary principles. The first is to learn how to take a verbal beating from another person with class and finesse. The second is to "walk a mile" in the aggressor's shoes to really understand where he or she is coming from and what the key motivations for the conflict are. Thompson recommends controlling the situation with words and reaching common ground, making the opponent a partner in achievement of a goal. He discourages hiding behind policies and rules, using phrases such as "calm down" or "be reasonable," or telling someone that he or she is wrong. These activities merely feed the conflict. Thompson further emphasizes the importance of active listening in diffusing conflict, even when it means listening to the objections of others. Listening aids in the understanding of the perspective and motivation of others.

Tactical communication skills like verbal judo are critical in a variety of settings and can be especially helpful when group conflict arises. Conflicts are dissolved, and situations rather than people are assessed, resulting in higher levels of group cooperation (Hikaru Dojo Martial Arts Academy, 2001) and higher levels of group performance.

Verbal judo may have started out as a concept, but it is slowly becoming a phenomenon. In fact, anyone can take courses at the Verbal Judo Institute. There you will learn to use presence and words to calm difficult people, redirect the behaviors of hostile people, diffuse potentially dangerous situations, perform professionally under all conditions, and achieve the desired outcome of the encounter. You can visit the institute's website at www.verbaljudo.org.

Conflict in Virtual Groups

Before we conclude, it is important to mention conflict in virtual group environments. Virtual groups often pull together people of very diverse backgrounds from across the globe to set and attain goals. Conflict in these groups primarily arises from communication style differences, technological problems with the meeting medium, and lack of sufficient trust built between group members.

Virtual groups, like in-person groups, face two primary types of conflict: task-oriented and relationship-oriented. Task-oriented conflict tends to help groups explore alternatives and make better decisions. Relationship-oriented conflict tends to negatively impact the performance of the group. Virtual groups differ from in-person groups in that they have less opportunity for relationship-oriented conflict; however, they exhibit more task-related conflict (Paul, Seetharam, & Samarah, 2005). This task-related conflict can result in more alternative solutions but can also result in communication gaps and other difficulties that might negatively impact group performance.

REVIEW OF THE SYSTEMS APPROACH

This chapter dealt with conflict and conflict management. It should be emphasized that conflict may have some desirable consequences for the group. However, conflict that gets out of control may be destructive. Also, conflict between ideas is usually more productive than conflict between personalities.

As for personality and its relation to conflict, we would expect more conflict-producing behaviors from those high in aggression, dominance, and need for autonomy. Conversely, we would expect less conflict and more conflict-resolving attempts from those high in need for affiliation and nurturance. Other background factors that would probably relate to conflict include the degree of difference or heterogeneity in group members' ages, sex, values, attitudes, and beliefs. Consistency theories would lead us to believe that the greater and more numerous these differences are, the greater the group conflict and the lower the satisfaction level resulting from the discussions.

Perhaps one of the most important factors related to conflict is the style of leadership and the resulting group norms regarding conflict. In this chapter, we examined Blake and Mouton's Conflict Grid model, which suggests practical methods for developing some leadership expertise in resolving conflicts.

EXERCISES

1. Conflict Management Exercise: "Win as Much as You Can"

Directions: For 10 successive rounds, you and your partner will choose either an X or a Y. The "payoff" for each round depends on the pattern of choices made in your cluster.

Strategy: You should confer with your partner on each round and make a joint decision. Before rounds 5, 8, and 10, you should confer with the other dyads in your cluster.

INSTRUCTIONS FOR PARTICIPANTS

1. This is a learning exercise. There are 10 rounds, and there are other teams with which you are playing.
2. The purpose of the exercise is to win as much as you can.
3. When the timekeeper says, "Begin round 1," your team will decide on its vote for the first round. Your vote may be either X or Y and should be recorded secretly on a small piece of paper. The payoff for each round will be determined by how your team's vote relates to the votes of all the other teams. The payoff possibilities are shown below.

4 X's:	Lose	$1.00 each
3 X's:	Win	$1.00 each
1 Y:	Lose	$3.00
2 X's:	Win	$2.00 each
2 Y's:	Lose	$2.00 each
1 X:	Win	$3.00
3 Y's:	Lose	$1.00 each
4 Y's:	Win	$1.00 each

4. When all votes are collected, the timekeeper will announce the total vote but will *not* disclose how each individual team voted.
5. As shown on the tally sheet (see Figure 7.4), you will have two minutes to cast your vote for the first round. For all the other rounds, you will have one minute to cast your vote, except for rounds 5, 8, and 10, which are bonus rounds.
6. During each bonus round, your team will select as many representatives as it wishes to send to a meeting of the teams. The representatives from all teams will then meet separately for three minutes to discuss their strategy.

Round	Strategy: Time Allowed	Strategy: Confer with	Choice	$ Won	$ Lost	$ Balance	
1	2 mins.	Partner					
2	1 min.	Partner					
3	1 min.	Partner					
4	1 min.	Partner					
5	3 mins. + 1 min.	Cluster Partner					Bonus round: pay is multiplied by 3
6	1 min.	Partner					
7	1 min.	Partner					
8	3 mins. + 1 min.	Cluster Partner					Bonus round: pay is multiplied by 5
9	1 min.	Partner					
10	3 mins. + 1 min.	Cluster Partner					Bonus round: pay is multiplied by 10

FIGURE 7.4 "Win as Much as You Can" Tally Sheet

7. After the representatives have met, your team will then have one minute to make its final decision about your vote. At the end of each round, when all the votes are in, you will be told the total outcome of the vote (2 X's, 2 Y's; 4 Y's; and so on).
8. There are three key rules to keep in mind:
   a. You are not to talk to the other teams or signal them in any way. You may communicate with them, but only during rounds 5, 8, and 10 through your representatives.
   b. All members of your team should agree on your team's vote or at least be willing to go along with it.
   c. Your team's vote must be reported on a small slip of paper when it is called for at the end of each round.

2. Conflict Resolution Exercise: "Gun Control"

Read the following excerpts from an article on gun control.

POLL FINDS WIDE SUPPORT FOR TIGHTER CONTROL ON GUNS

Lawrence L. Knutson

The USA Today-CNN-Gallup Poll found that six out of 10 people oppose an outright ban on handguns, but the reverse was true when questions referred to "cheap" handguns.

> The poll comes a day after the *USA Today*, the nation's second-largest daily after the *Wall Street Journal*, devoted a significant portion of the paper to articles focusing on gun violence in America.
>
> . . . 15,377 people were killed in firearms homicides in 1992—12,489 of them with handguns. That is twice the number killed by handguns in 1966 . . . . Homicides among Americans under 18 rose by 143 percent over six years, from 602 deaths in 1986 to 1,468 in 1992.
>
> On the other hand, the National Rifle Association argues that every citizen has the right to bear arms. If you add laws limiting these rights, only those who obey the laws will be affected. Those who are criminals will continue to have and use guns. (*Ann Arbor News*, December 30, 1993, p. A1. Reprinted by permission of the Associated Press.)

Form groups of five and discuss this controversy. See if you can reach consensus in your group. Each group should report the results of its discussion to the class.

For another source of excellent exercises, see www.mhhe.com/shani.

READINGS: Overview

In the first reading, Goleman outlines the reasons why people with good conflict management skills are so successful in their lives and careers. In the second reading, Acuff describes several methods for improving conflict reduction skills. He shows how conflict can be managed more effectively across cultures. Both articles provide a useful extension of the ideas presented in the chapter.

Reading 7.1 Conflict Management

Daniel Goleman

People with this competence:

- Handle difficult people and tense situations with diplomacy and tact.
- Spot potential conflict, bring disagreements into the open, and help de-escalate.
- Encourage debate and open discussion.
- Orchestrate win–win solutions.

"A banker wanted to sell a copper company to investors, and he needed a research person expert in mining to write about it so he could convince people in sales to pitch the deal. But the researcher refused outright, upsetting the banker. I was director of research, so the banker complained to me," says Mark Loehr, of Salomon Smith Barney.

From Daniel Goleman, *Working with Emotional Intelligence* (New York: Bantam Books, 1998), pp. 178–83. Reprinted by permission.

"I went to the researcher, who told me he was overwhelmed. He was already working seventy to eighty hours a week, had to finish analyses of eighteen companies by the end of the month, make a hundred phone calls, run off to meetings in Boston—and this report would have taken him another forty hours to do. After we talked, he went back to the banker and explained how swamped he was, but added, 'If you want me to do it, I will.'"

"Once the banker understood the researcher's predicament, he decided to find another way to get the job done. But there could have been a blowup. Everyone is so busy and overwhelmed, their listening abilities dwindle to nothing. And they tend to just assume that no one is as busy as they are, so they make imperious demands."

"It's so hard to get people to take the time to be good listeners. It's not just about being nice—until you're a good enough listener, until you can sense what the other person is going through, you won't be able to make a reasonable suggestion, to come up with something they'll buy."

One talent of those skilled at conflict resolution is spotting trouble as it is brewing and taking steps to calm those involved. Here, as Loehr points out, the arts of listening and empathizing are crucial: Once the investment banker understood the researcher's perspective, he became more accommodating—and the conflict ended.

Such diplomacy and tact are qualities essential for success in touchy jobs like auditing, police work, or mediation—or *any* job where people depend on each other under pressure. One of the competencies sought in tax auditors by the U.S. government is the ability to present an unpopular position in a way that creates little or no hostility and preserves the other person's sense of dignity. The word for this skill is *tact*. At American Express, the ability to spot potential sources of conflict, take responsibility for one's own role, apologize if need be, and engage openly in a discussion of each person's perspective is prized in their financial advisors.

READING THE SIGNS

Charlene Barshefsky had finally gotten the Chinese government, after months and months of negotiation, to agree to clamp down on the piracy of American movies, compact discs, and computer software. How? Barshefsky had refused to accept their "final" offer, just another in an ongoing series, all of which she felt were inadequate. But this time, the head of the Chinese delegation thanked her for her work, told her he would respond at a later date, and then moved his shoulders back in a slight shrug. That simple and subtle gesture indicated she had won their cooperation.

Barshefsky had been closely studying the faces across the table from her that day, and she had sensed far less acrimony than before in the endless, tedious meetings. That day, reactions were muted and questions few—a striking change from the combative, sharply challenging dialogue that had marked the early rounds of the negotiations.

Barshefsky's reading of those subtle signals proved right: That was the day the Chinese delegation stopped fighting and started moving toward the trade agreement the countries later signed.

The ability to read the feelings of the opposition during a negotiation is critical to success. As one of my lawyers, Robert Freedman, says about negotiating contracts, "It's mainly psychological. Contracts are emotional—it's not just what the words say, but how the parties think and *feel* about them, that matters."

Those who have mastered the art of the deal realize the emotionally charged nature of any negotiation. The best negotiators can sense which points matter most to the other party and gracefully concede there, while pressing for concessions in points that do not carry such emotional weight. And that takes empathy.

Skill at negotiation obviously matters for excellence in professions like law and diplomacy. But to some extent everyone who works in an organization needs these abilities; those who can resolve conflict and head off trouble are the kind of peacemakers vital to any organization.

In a sense, a negotiation can be seen as an exercise in joint problem solving, since the conflict belongs to both parties. The reason for the negotiation, of course, is that each side has its own competing interests and perspective and wants to convince the other to capitulate to its wishes. But the very act of agreeing to negotiate acknowledges that the problem is a shared one and that there may be a mutually satisfying solution available. In this sense negotiation is a cooperative venture, not just a competitive one. Indeed, as Herbert Kelman, a Harvard psychologist who specializes in negotiations, points out, the process of negotiation itself restores cooperation between conflicting parties. Solving their problems together transforms their relationship.

That resolution requires that each side be able to understand not just the other's point of view, but their needs and fears. This empathy, Kelman observes, makes each side "better able to influence the other to their own benefit, by being responsive to the other's needs—in other words, to find ways in which both parties can win."

NEGOTIATING CHANNELS

Negotiations, mostly informal, happen all the time. Take the negotiation between a manufacturer and the retail stores that sell its products, like this one: "I've been cut off from carrying one of our main lines of women's jewelry," a boutique owner explained. "I wanted to negotiate a better deal with the distributor—we've been a good outlet for them. But he got a better offer from a store across town. So I made a counterproposal. But the other store got the account—and the company only wants one outlet in a town this size. So now I'm out of luck."

Such channels of distribution are essential for manufacturers' very survival, just as the retailers depend on the manufacturers for their stock. But each party has an array of choices. The result is an ongoing negotiation over such issues as how large markups will be, the terms of payment, and timeliness of deliveries.

Most "channel relationships" are long-term and symbiotic. And in any long-term relationship, problems simmer and boil to the surface from time to time. When they surface, those involved on either side of manufacturer–retailer disputes typically use one of three styles of negotiation: problem solving, in which both parties try to find the solution that works best for each side; compromise, where both parties give in more or less equally regardless of how that serves their needs; and aggression, where one party forces unilateral concessions from the other side.

In a survey of retail buyers in department store chains, each of whom handled merchandise worth $15 million to $30 million, the style of negotiating was an accurate barometer of the health of the manufacturer–retailer relationship. Predictably, when negotiations were typically aggressive, revolving around threats and demands, it boded poorly for the future of the relationship; buyers ended up embittered and dissatisfied and often dropped the product line. But for those relationships in which aggressiveness was ruled out in favor of problem solving or compromise, the longevity of the relationship increased.

Threats and demands poison the waters of negotiation. As the survey showed, even when one party is far more powerful than the other, a magnanimous spirit may be a winning strategy in the long run, particularly when the parties will have continued dealings. And this is why even when a retailer was completely dependent on a single manufacturer, negotiations were most often noncoercive; given the desire for a long-term relationship and their mutual dependence, a spirit of cooperation always worked best.

RESOLVING CONFLICT—CREATIVELY

One evening Linda Lantieri was walking down a desolate, dangerous block lined with abandoned, boarded-up buildings when suddenly, out of nowhere, she was surrounded by three boys about fourteen years old. One pulled out a knife with a four-inch blade as they pressed in around her.

"Give me your purse! Now!" the boy with the knife hissed.

Though frightened, Lantieri had the presence of mind to take some deep breaths and reply coolly, "I'm feeling a little uncomfortable. You know, guys, you're a little into my space. I'm wondering if you could step back a little."

Lantieri studied the sidewalk—and, to her amazement, she saw three pairs of sneakers take a few steps back. "Thank you," she said, then continued, "Now, I want to hear what you just said to me, but to tell you the truth, I'm a little nervous about that knife. I'm wondering if you could put it away."

After what seemed an eternity of silence and uncertainty, the knife went back into a pocket.

Quickly reaching into her purse, Lantieri took out a $20 bill, caught the eye of the one with the knife, and asked, "Who should I give it to?"

"Me," he said.

Glancing at the other two, she asked if they agreed. One of the two nodded.

"Great," she said, handing the leader the $20 bill. "Now here's what's going to happen. I'm going to stay right here while you walk away."

With puzzled looks on their faces, the boys slowly started to walk away, glancing over their shoulders at Lantieri—and then they broke into a run. *They* were running from *her*.

In a sense, that small miracle of turning the tables is no surprise: Lantieri is the founder and director of the New York City–based Resolving Conflict Creatively Program, which teaches these skills in schools. Lantieri has immersed herself in the crafts of negotiation and handling conflict amicably. While she learned her trade as a teacher—for a while in a Harlem school not far from that desolate block—she now trains others in more than four hundred schools throughout the United States.

Lantieri does more than just promote education in conflict resolution—she first convinces skeptical school boards to approve her program. In fact, when the school board of one California town was paralyzed by two bitterly bickering factions, both sides were so impressed by her negotiating skills they asked Lantieri to come in and help them heal the split.

Lantieri's maestro performance on the street illustrates some classic moves for cooling down conflicts:

- First, calm down, tune in to your feelings, and express them.
- Show a willingness to work things out by talking over the issue rather than escalating it with more aggression.
- State your own point of view in neutral language rather than in an argumentative tone.
- Try to find equitable ways to resolve the dispute, working together to find a resolution both sides can embrace.

These strategies parallel those espoused for win–win solutions by experts at Harvard's Center for Negotiation. But while following these strategies may seem simple, implementing them as brilliantly as Lantieri did requires the prerequisite emotional competencies of self-awareness, self-confidence, self-control, and empathy. Remember, empathy need not lead to sympathetically giving in to the other side's demands—knowing how someone feels does not mean agreeing with them. But cutting off empathy to hold a hard line can lead to polarized positions and deadlocks.

Reading 7.2 World-Class Negotiating Strategies

Frank L. Acuff

If I listen, I have the advantage: if I speak, others have it.

—From the Arabic

There are many negotiating strategies that tend to work very well in one culture but are ineffective in other cultures. A case in point is the Miami-based project manager who put together a very detailed, thorough, research-oriented proposal and presentation for his Brazilian client. "I felt good that we had done our homework," he later noted. "I was very disappointed, however, to find that the Brazilian representatives were flatly uninterested in the details I was prepared to explain. A similar approach worked extremely well in Germany only four months earlier."

In spite of the many different negotiating approaches required among cultures, there are five strategies that tend to be effective anywhere in the world. While there may be local variations in how these strategies are applied, their basic premises remain viable. . . .

From Frank L. Acuff, *How to Negotiate Anything with Anyone, Anywhere* (New York: Amacom, 1997), pp. 96–119. Used by permission of Amacom, conveyed through Copyright Clearance Center.

NEGOTIATING STRATEGIES THAT WILL WORK ANYWHERE

The strategies that tend to be effective in negotiations throughout the world are as follows:

1. Plan the negotiation.
2. Adopt a win–win approach.
3. Maintain high aspirations.
4. Use language that is simple and accessible.
5. Ask lots of questions, then listen with your eyes and ears. . . .

Strategy 1: Plan the Negotiation

Everybody wants to get a good deal, to get a sizable share of the pie, and to feel good about the negotiation. Everybody wants to be a winner. Yet not everyone is willing to do the homework necessary to achieve these ends. . . . The essential steps necessary to plan your negotiation [are]: (1) identify all the issues; (2) prioritize the issues; (3) establish a settlement range; and (4) develop strategies and tactics. Make this preparation a habit and you will set the stage for getting what you want.

There are other factors to consider prior to global negotiations. You can use the Tune-Up Checklist to ensure that you put yourself in the strongest possible position before the negotiation.

The Tune-Up Checklist: Prior to the Negotiation

This is the data-gathering stage where you should get background information related to the other side (TOS), to his or her culture and its effects on the negotiating process, to TOS's organization and other potential players in the negotiation, and to the history of any past negotiations. What do you know about:

TOS

- ❑ Family status (e.g., married, single, children)?
- ❑ Leisure or recreational activities?
- ❑ Work habits (e.g., long hours, early to work)?
- ❑ Behavior style (e.g., perfectionist, "big picture" oriented, task-oriented, people-oriented)?
- ❑ Number of years with current organization?
- ❑ Stability in current position?
- ❑ Overall reputation as a negotiator?
- ❑ What special interest groups might affect the negotiator?

TOS's Culture and Its Effects on Negotiations

- ❑ Are meetings likely to be punctual?
- ❑ What can you expect the pace of negotiations to be?
- ❑ How important is "saving face" likely to be?

- ❑ Are differences of opinion likely to be emotional or argumentative?
- ❑ Will TOS bring a large team?
- ❑ Will you need an agent or interpreter?
- ❑ Should you prepare a formal agenda?

TOS's Organization

- ❑ What is the organization's main product or service?
- ❑ What is its past, present, and projected financial status?
- ❑ What organizational problems exist (e.g., downsizing, tough competition)?
- ❑ Who is TOS's boss, and what do you know about him or her?
- ❑ Is the organization under any time pressures?

Past Negotiations

- ❑ What were the subjects of past negotiations?
- ❑ What were the main obstacles and outcomes of the negotiations?
- ❑ What objections were raised?
- ❑ What strategies and tactics were used by TOS?
- ❑ How high were the initial offers compared with the eventual settlement?
- ❑ How was the outcome achieved, and over what period of time?

There are many ways to plan negotiations. One study identified five approaches skilled negotiators share when planning their negotiations:

1. They consider twice as wide a range of action options and outcomes as do less-skilled negotiators.
2. They spend over three times as much attention on trying to find common ground with TOS.
3. They spend more than twice as much time on long-term issues.
4. They set range objectives (such as a target price of $50 to $60 per unit), rather than single-point objectives (e.g., $55). Ranges give negotiators flexibility.
5. They use "issue planning" rather than "sequence planning." That is, skilled negotiators discuss each issue independently rather than in a predetermined sequence or order of issues.[1]

Strategy 2: Adopt a Win–Win Approach

We don't adopt the win–win approach simply because we are wonderful human beings. It helps us get what we want. There is a difference between how skilled and unskilled negotiators prepare for the win–win approach. Skilled negotiators, for example, tend to spend less time on defense/attack behavior and in disagreement. They also tend to give more information about their feelings and have fewer arguments to back up their position.[2] This last point may seem odd. It might seem that the more arguments one has for one's position, the better. Skilled negotiators know, however, that having only a few strong arguments is more effective than having too many arguments. With too many arguments, weak arguments tend to dilute strong arguments, and TOS often feels pressured or manipulated into settlement.

To achieve a win–win situation, you must tune in to the frequency with which TOS can identify: WIIFT ("What's In It For Them"). This means different things in different cultures. For example, in Saudi Arabia a certain amount of haggling back and forth on terms may indicate your sincerity about striking a deal. To refuse a somewhat expressive give-and-take would be an insult to many Saudi negotiators. A Dallas-based, commercial building contractor now experienced in Saudi Arabia discovered this on his first trip there. "I really got off-base in our early discussions in Riyadh. I felt we were being extremely polite as we patiently explained the reasonableness of our proposal. We fell flat on our faces. The Saudis felt we were inflexible and not serious about doing business. The next project we bid had a lot of fat built into it. We haggled back and forth for four meetings, and they ended up loving us. That's what they wanted—someone to bargain with back and forth. It showed them we cared." This negotiator adds, "I still get a knot in my stomach sometimes when I go through a Saudi negotiation, but at least I know what works now."

Fortunately for this negotiator, he quickly learned the win–win approach for his Saudi client. Yet the very idea of haggling would be a sure win–lose proposition in many parts of the world. In England, for example, it would be hard to come up with a worse idea than to engage TOS in an emotional afternoon of haggling back and forth. The British idea of win–win is a somewhat formal, procedural, and detailed discussion of the facts.

Achieving a win–win result also requires careful scrutiny of both parties' overall goals. You may be seeking short-term profit and cash flow, while your Japanese counterparts may be more interested in long-term viability. In many cases, different goals can lead to overall win–win results. Consider the company president negotiating a joint venture in Hungary in order to take advantage of a skilled, inexpensive workforce, while her TOS is motivated to find business linkages outside eastern Europe.

Wherever you negotiate, focusing on win–win results sharply increases your chances for success, particularly in the long term.

Strategy 3: Maintain High Aspirations

In the spring of 1978, the International Air Transport Association (IATA) discontinued its policy of airline ticket price compliance. IATA had been for many years a powerful enforcer that had maintained a firm grip on the airline ticket prices of the world's domestic and international airlines. Immediately after this announcement was made, Leroy Black, my boss, suggested I contact the airlines to determine what, if any, ticket price concessions we might extract as a result of this policy change. The Middle East Division where we worked was located in Dubai, United Arab Emirates, a small oil sheikdom adjoining Saudi Arabia. Our 3,500 workers and many of their family members collectively logged millions of air miles per year.

"That's a good idea," I remember telling Leroy. Shaving 5 or 10 percent—perhaps even 15 percent—would amount to substantial savings on our $4 million annual airline expenses. I was stunned, though, when Leroy suggested we ask for a 50 percent price decrease in ticket costs.

"Are you kidding?" I asked, quite shocked.

"I think that 50 percent is about right," Leroy said serenely.

Our first appointment was with representatives from British Airways. They told us, in a reserved, nice kind of way, to take a hike.

Then KLM, in a not particularly nice kind of way, suggested the same recourse as British Airways. The same with Lufthansa. "We really are being a bit chintzy on this thing," I thought to myself.

"Leroy, let's try asking for a little less and see what happens," I suggested.

"I don't know. Let's hang in there awhile longer," Leroy insisted.

Next was Alitalia. As in our appointments with the other airlines, I went through a short prologue explaining the company's position, and assertively put forth that we would like to see a 50 percent reduction in future fares. This caused quite a commotion with the Alitalia representatives, who waved their arms and with great conviction gave us several reasons why this was not possible.

"This is really a little embarrassing," I thought.

They then asked if they could privately telephone their regional headquarters staff. They returned in about ten minutes in a solemn mood.

"Mr. Acuff," one of the representatives said with a grave look on his face. "What you ask is quite impossible. The very most we can offer you is a 40 percent reduction," he said apologetically.

"Excuse me?" I asked. He repeated his offer.

"Unbelievable," I thought to myself. "Give us some time to think about it," I replied.

As soon as they were out of earshot, Leroy and I almost jumped for joy. As it turned out, this was the first of several key concessions we received from the various airlines, ranging from 15 to 45 percent discounts. British Airways, KLM, Sabena, and Lufthansa all soon after reduced their rates well beyond my initial expectations.

This situation was a valuable lesson with regard to aspiration levels in negotiations. What at first seemed like a brash, overbearing approach to business turned out to be very positive. But was it win–win? you ask. Didn't you just bleed the airlines at a time when they were vulnerable? Not at all. We later found out that the airlines were quite pleased with the new arrangements. They thought discounts might be greater than they were, and, of course, some of the airlines were delighted that they had negotiated better terms than their competitors.

We have all kinds of negative fantasies about high initial demands (HIDs):

"They won't like me anymore. I'll make them really mad and it will hurt the relationship."

"I'll price myself out of the market."

"Maybe we aren't being reasonable."

"This is embarrassing."

In spite of these concerns, there are compelling reasons to go for it, which are summarized in the following World-Class Tips.

World-Class Tips: Seven Reasons Why You Should Have High Initial Demands (HIDs)

1. Don't take away your own power. TOS may do it to you, but don't do it to yourself.
2. HIDs teach people how to treat you.
3. They lower the expectations of TOS.
4. HIDs demonstrate your persistence and conviction.
5. You can always reduce your asking offer or demand. HIDs give you room to make concessions.
6. Remember that time is on your side. Making HIDs gives you more time to learn about your counterpart, and time heals many wounds.
7. There is an emotional imperative for TOS to beat you down. It's important for TOS to feel that they've "won."[3]

World-Class Tip 7 is especially important. Many negotiators find it hard to accept that there is an emotional imperative for TOS to beat you down. To illustrate this point, let's get in the other person's shoes to see how TOS might feel. You are in Germany to negotiate the purchase of the Drillenzebit, a precision tool-making machine from a Munich-based firm. You say to yourself, "This time won't be like the other times. This time I'm going to do my homework—I will read appropriate industry periodicals and talk to consultants, clients, suppliers, and others who know a lot about the Germans, the German business environment, and the competitive market for precision tool-making machines." So you do your homework and begin to negotiate with the Germans for the Drillenzebit machine. When the subject of price arises, you are ready. You've got the facts, figures, and some savoir-faire about German negotiating practices. So you say, "Mr. Dietrich, today I'm going to offer you one price and one price only for this fine Drillenzebit machine. That final price is $74,000—that's U.S. dollars."

Dietrich looks at you for a moment and says, "Let me see if I have this right. That's $74,000—in U.S. dollars?"

"That's right," you repeat, proud that you're sticking by your guns.

"Seventy-four thousand dollars. You've got it. The machine is yours!" he beams.

How would you feel in this situation? Wonderful? Exuberant? If you are like most people, you would have a morbid, sinking feeling that you had just been taken. Your first thought would probably be, "Damn. I should have offered less." Is this reaction logical? No. You did, after all, get what you asked for. You reacted as you did because only part of your needs were met—the logical part—while the emotional part was not.

There are cultural differences as to how high our aspiration level should be with our foreign counterparts, but as a rule of thumb, go for it! If you really want $30,000 for your widget machine, don't ask for $30,500. Ask for $60,000. Put TOS in the position of saying to his or her boss, "You know, this woman came in asking $60,000. This price was completely off-the-wall. Excellent negotiator that I am, I got her down to $38,000. I saved us $22,000." And if you are in a

Don't use this . . .	when this will do.
annual premium	annual payment
accrued interest	unpaid interest
maturity date	final payment date
commence	start
utilize	use
acquaint	tell
demonstrate	show
endeavor	try
modification	change
proceed	go
per diem	daily

EXHIBIT A Simplifying English Words and Terms

competitive bidding situation, stress the quality, service, and other aspects that make your price an excellent value.

Strategy 4: Use Language That Is Simple and Accessible

American English is filled with thousands of clichés and colloquialisms that make it very hard for others to understand. Phrases such as "getting down to brass tacks," "getting down to the nitty gritty," wanting to "zero in on problems," or "finding out where the rubber meets the road" only clog communication channels.

Don't assume that because your foreign counterpart speaks English, he or she fully understands it. This individual may know English as it was taught in school but may not be able to speak it or understand it in conversation with an American. An American executive who regularly travels to Taiwan makes this point. "When I first asked my Taiwanese client if he spoke English, he told me yes. I found out the hard way that his understanding was very elementary and that I used way too many slang expressions. We still do business together, but now I speak more slowly and simply, and I'm learning some Chinese."

This doesn't apply only to slang. Make sure you use the simplest, most basic words possible. Exhibit A provides examples of simplified words and terms you should use, even if you're speaking English.

Strategy 5: Ask Lots of Questions, Then Listen with Your Eyes and Ears

Asking good questions is vital throughout the negotiation, but particularly in the early stages. Your main goal is receiving information. Making a brilliant speech to TOS about your proposal may make you feel good, but it does far less in helping you achieve your ends than asking questions that give you data about content and the emotional needs of TOS.

Exhibit B illustrates the importance of asking questions. Skilled negotiators ask more than twice the number of questions of unskilled negotiators. They also engage in much more active listening than those who are less skilled.

There is one important consideration when asking questions: Don't do anything that would embarrass your international counterpart. Questions can be much more direct and open in such cultures as the United States, Canada,

Negotiating Behavior	Skilled Negotiators	Average Negotiators
Questions, as a percentage of all negotiating behavior	21.3%	9.6%
Active listening		
▪ Testing for understanding	9.7	4.1
▪ Summarizing	7.5	4.2

EXHIBIT B Questioning and Listening in Skilled and Average Negotiators

Source: Neil Rackham, "The Behavior of Successful Negotiators" (Reston, Va.: Huthwaite Research Group, 1976), as reported in Ellen Raider International, Inc. (Brooklyn, N.Y.) and Situation Management Systems, Inc. (Plymouth, Mass.), *International Negotiations: A Training Program for Corporate Executives and Diplomats* (1982).

Australia, Switzerland, Sweden, and Germany than in Japan, Taiwan, Brazil, or Colombia, where indirectness is prized.

> *Judge a man by his questions rather than by his answers.*
>
> —Voltaire

Effective listening is especially challenging when different cultures are involved. This can be the case even when English is the first language of TOS. Mike Apple, an American engineering and construction executive, found this to be the case in England and Scotland. Apple notes that even though English is spoken, one must listen very carefully to English and Scottish negotiators because of their dialects. "When I first got to Scotland, I wondered if some kind of challenge was in the making when a union negotiator told me he was going to 'mark my card.' I asked a colleague about it. As it turned out, the term is one used by Scottish golfers to explain the best approach to the course for those who haven't played there before. The union negotiator was only trying to be helpful," Apple notes. "The lesson learned here? When in doubt, ask for clarification."

If the communication pattern is from low-context countries, such as Japan, China, Saudi Arabia, Greece, or Spain, listening is even more challenging for Americans. In these cultures the message is embedded in the context of what is being said. Mike McMahon, a former managing director for National Semiconductor's Singapore plant, found Singaporeans reluctant to respond directly to questions. He notes, "I had to listen very carefully to figure out what was really on their minds."[4]

Here are some additional tips for effective listening:

- Limit your own talking.
- Concentrate on what TOS is saying.
- Maintain eye contact (but don't stare).
- Paraphrase and summarize TOS's remarks.
- Avoid jumping to conclusions. Be postjudicial, not prejudicial, regarding what TOS is saying.
- Watch for nonverbal cues.

- Listen for emotions.
- Ask for clarification: Assume differences, not similarities, if you are unsure of meaning.
- Don't interrupt.
- Pause for understanding; don't immediately fill the voids of silence.

Some of the rituals of international negotiating serve dual purposes of entertainment and information gathering. Foster Lin, director of the Taiwanese Far East Trade Service Office in Chicago, considers formal Taiwanese banquets and other entertainment as a prime opportunity to gain information on one's negotiating counterpart. Says Lin, "Entertainment demonstrates courtesy toward our foreign guests. It also helps us find out more about the individual person. Is this someone we can trust and want to do business with?" Such occasions can help you as well. Careful listening in this "offstage" time, away from the formal negotiating sessions, can give you another side to the negotiators. Use this time to gather additional data on your counterpart.

A key part of listening relates to body language. TOS may encode messages, making sophisticated, cogent arguments. However, one thing almost always happens during a moment of insecurity or deception: body movements change (e.g., the person literally squirms in his or her seat or blinks more rapidly). Also, be aware of the impact of your own nonverbal behavior. For example, if your gestures are quite expressive and TOS is from Sweden and quite reserved, tone it down a bit. Alternatively, if your facial and arm gestures are unexpressive and you are meeting a Brazilian who is very expressive, loosen up a bit—smile and use expressive hand and arm gestures.

World-Class Tips: Five Positive Things You Can Do Without Saying a Word

1. Smile! It's a universal lubricant that can help you open the content of the negotiation. A genuine smile says very loudly, "I'd appreciate doing business with you."
2. Dress appropriately and groom well. Shined shoes, combed hair, clean nails, and clothes appropriate for the occasion show that you respect yourself and your counterpart. It also communicates that you are worthy of your counterpart's business.
3. Lean forward. This communicates interest and attention in almost every culture.
4. Use open gestures. Crossed arms in front of your chest may be viewed as disinterest or resistance on your part. More open gestures send a signal that you are open to your counterpart's ideas.
5. Take every opportunity to nod your head. Don't you like it when people agree with you? Let TOS know that you are listening by this simple action.

NOTES

1. Neil Rackham, "The Behavior of Successful Negotiators" (Reston, Va.: Huthwaite Research Group, 1976), as reported in Ellen Raider International, Inc. (Brooklyn, N.Y.) and Situation Management Systems, Inc. (Plymouth, Mass.), *International Negotiations: A Training Program for Corporate Executives and Diplomats* (1982).
2. Ibid.
3. See Phil Sperber, *Fail-Safe Business Negotiating: Strategies and Tactics for Success* (Englewood Cliffs, N.J.: Prentice Hall, 1983), pp. 40–41; and Roy J. Lewicki and Joseph A. Litterer, *Negotiation* (Homewood, Ill.: Richard D. Irwin, 1985), pp. 75–79.
4. Frank L. Acuff, "What It Takes to Succeed in Overseas Assignment," *National Business Employment Weekly* (August 25, 1991): pp. 17–18.

CHAPTER 8

Consequences

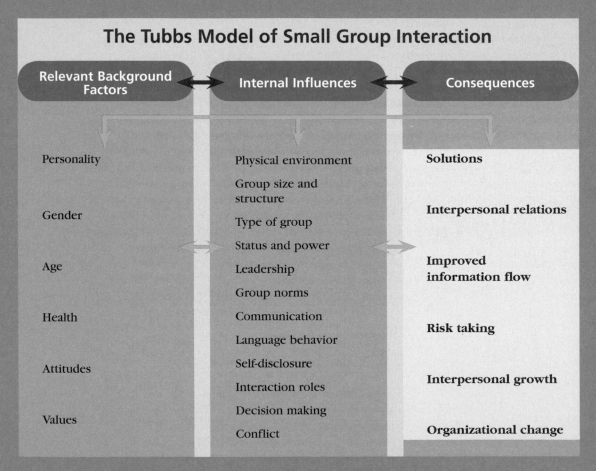

The Tubbs Model of Small Group Interaction

Relevant Background Factors	Internal Influences	Consequences
Personality	Physical environment	**Solutions**
Gender	Group size and structure	**Interpersonal relations**
Age	Type of group	**Improved information flow**
Health	Status and power	**Risk taking**
Attitudes	Leadership	**Interpersonal growth**
Values	Group norms	**Organizational change**
	Communication	
	Language behavior	
	Self-disclosure	
	Interaction roles	
	Decision making	
	Conflict	

Concepts in **boldface** in gray panels are the emphases of this chapter.

Preview

Chapter 8 is devoted entirely to the consequences section of the Tubbs Model of Small Group Interaction. These consequences are the potential outcomes or end results of group interaction. One consequence, solutions to problems, is discussed, along with the quality and acceptance of solutions. Another end result of group interaction is the improvement of intergroup relations. This is often a way of clearing up and reducing misunderstandings. An improvement in information flow often results from group discussion. Organizational change can also be a consequence of group interaction.

Glossary

Acceptance of Solutions There are three different types of solutions for problems: (1) high quality, low acceptance, (2) high acceptance, high quality, and (3) high acceptance, low quality.

Quality of Solutions Groups have the potential to make better-quality decisions than the same individuals in those groups would make if working alone.

CASE STUDY

NORTHWEST AEROSPACE

Northwest Aerospace is a global $8-billion diversified industrial manufacturer headquartered in the Seattle/Tacoma area and a leader in fluid power systems for the aerospace industry. It makes components for commercial and military jet aircraft and helicopters. The organization is unionized.

When Robert Kline, manager of manufacturing for North America, took over, the East Avenue Facility in Cleveland, Ohio, was on the verge of being shut down and in dire need of improvement. It was losing $6–8 million a year.

The East Avenue Facility is a 200,000-square-foot facility with over 300 employees. This facility had over 50 years of culture associated with it, and Kline knew that bringing about change was going to be a difficult task.

The East Avenue Facility had annual sales of $30 million and performed functions such as hose assemblies, tube fittings, and bent tube assemblies.

Initial Situation

Imagine walking into a plant with poor lighting; torn-up, dingy walls; broken, oil-soaked wood floors; and blaring radios (that is, every tenth worker had a radio playing). Further, instead of operating a machine many workers were sitting on reclined swivel chairs reading the newspaper. This is what the initial environment was like, and this is what Kline witnessed.

Besides the plant appearance and all the distractions, there were other things that needed to change. For example, there was a lot of nonproductive

continued

movement on the floor, and when one looked down an aisle, there were people walking around, probably going to get a tool, a part, or material. There were garbage cans on either sides of the aisle. The place looked like a really dumpy supermarket.

The facility also had the traditional method of manufacturing, that is, one person per machine. Robert remembers seeing a worker who appeared to be operating two machines. He went up to the worker and told him he was happy to see one worker handling two machines. The worker replied that his buddy was operating the second machine, but after switching the machine on, he had gone for a walk and would be returning soon.

The only time the employees got together was about once every two years, usually when there was some news about an impending crisis. As a result, there were lots of rumors flying around since the employees were chronically uninformed and frequently misinformed. There were three departments with high-seniority members, resulting in significant overtime (the lowest seniority in the entire plant was 25 years). The three departments were machining, maintenance, and tool room; therefore, in order to incorporate change, Robert needed to convince the entire leadership team. Besides overtime, problems with productivity and scrap existed.

Even though the products produced by Northwest Aerospace were some of the best in the industry, and the company had a great reputation with over 60 percent market share and customers like Boeing and Airbus, the facility was hemorrhaging money. The facility was producing a variety of products, but when Northwest analyzed the product lines, it discovered that there was really only one product line that was making all the money.

There was a crisis at hand. The only choices Robert and his team had were either to close down the facility or to incorporate major changes for improvement. The employees were well aware of the existing problems, and almost everyone was willing to bring about the much-needed changes for improvement.

1. What would you do if you were Robert?
2. What would you do first?
3. Whom would you talk to to get things started?
4. What will be the consequences if you are not successful?
5. What lessons from this case can you apply to your own work experience?

The case study above illustrates a real-life example of a need to make major organizational changes. Even skilled, well-intentioned leaders sometimes live to see their best efforts fail. This chapter deals with the potential outcomes or consequences of group interaction. These are sometimes referred to as the *end results*. However, our systems theory perspective reminds us that groups are ongoing and that today's end results are simply the new inputs for tomorrow's activities.

After reading seven chapters on small group interaction, you should be able to answer such questions as, Why use groups anyway? Wouldn't it be easier to just do the job yourself? Certainly, by now you are more aware of the many difficulties and complexities associated with group behavior. Before you throw up your hands and give up, read this chapter. We begin our elaboration on the advantages of group interaction by determining the end results or potential consequences of group discussion. In this chapter, we will examine four of these end results: (1) solutions to problems, (2) changes in interpersonal relations, (3) improved information flow, and (4) organizational change.

Solutions to Problems

QUALITY OF SOLUTIONS

A clear finding of small group research is that groups have the potential to make better-quality decisions than the same individuals would make if working alone. Recent research by Brutus and Donia (2010) found that students who were asked to evaluate each other in classroom groups increased their effectiveness in exhibiting such team skills as assisting teammates when needed, suggesting ideas, tying ideas together, contributing to the organization of the work, respecting teammates, and respecting deadlines as a few examples of 22 different team skills (Brutus & Donia, 2010, p. 659). Peter Senge (1990), in his best-selling book *The Fifth Discipline,* argues that even the most talented person can benefit from teamwork. He cites Einstein, who said that he often got his best insights from discussions with other professionals. Senge states that this illustrates "the staggering potential of collaborative learning—that collectively we can be more insightful, more intelligent than we can possibly be individually" (p. 239). More recently, Brooks (2011) writes, "Human beings evolved to work in small bands. And in fact there's a great deal of evidence to suggest that much of the time groups think better than individuals. In one study 75 percent of groups solved a complicated task, compared to 9 percent of individuals" (p. 260) (remember the case study at the beginning of Chapter one)?.

Group performance does not always surpass individual performance. In those instances when it doesn't, the group *process* has been counterproductive. In 2008, the New York Giants football team won the Super Bowl over the highly favored New England Patriots. Giants coach Tom Coughlin had not been very successful just a year or two earlier. However, he decided to create a player's council of team leaders to help him work better with the team. Many attributed the Super Bowl victory and the year's successes to the new group processes resulting from these changes. This is supported by studies on communication in project groups (Lipman-Blumen & Leavitt, 1999). Reports have generally agreed that frequent communication among colleagues both inside and outside their project group is vital to high project performance. This notion has been stated in the following formula (Steiner, 1972, p. 9):

Actual productivity = Potential productivity − Losses due to faulty process

The *Wall Street Journal* reported that value engineering teams at Ford Motor Company once found ways to take $180 out of the cost of each car. One cost-reducing measure was the redesign of a bent hose in the heating system into a straight hose. The net savings was 50 cents per part. Another example was the use of a new integrated bracket for the air conditioner's accumulator bottle. This resulted in a $4 savings per car. Most recently, they have done away with the gas cap in favor of a new opening that does not require a gas cap, thus saving millions of dollars. When parts are manufactured by the millions, the cost savings are certainly worth the effort.

The mechanism they used to find these savings is called "value engineering/value analysis teams." Value engineering activities are based on this simple formula:

Value = Function/Cost

The Ford examples show how a firm can increase value by performing the same function at a lower cost. Teams can help increase value in three additional ways.

1. *By increasing function while reducing costs.* For example, the new Ford Escort was introduced with substantially upgraded styling and electronic features, but at a lower price than its predecessor. This was where Ford originally went wrong with the new cars: They increased functions but at considerably higher costs.
2. *By increasing function while increasing cost by a proportionally smaller amount.* The Chevrolet Malibu has a lot more features than its predecessor but at a relatively modest price increase. This increases its value.
3. *By decreasing function while decreasing cost by a proportionally greater amount.* Ford recently began taking out some of the electronics in its 2010 Lincoln town car to reduce the base price. Such items as moon roofs and built-in car phones have been removed to get the car's price down to a more attractive level. Sales of the new Town Car had been well below preproduction estimates, primarily because of the high price tag. So Ford was looking for ways to get the car back into the customer's price comfort zone.

Whereas value engineering applies to the design of parts or products, value analysis applies to the design and analysis of processes. For example, in the banking industry, it has historically taken about six weeks to get a mortgage loan approved. By using value analysis, the cycle time from application to approval has been reduced in some banks to less than one hour (www.wingsanbank.com, for example). This is a phenomenal improvement in service to the customer. It is easy to see a competitive advantage for the company that can provide dramatically better service.

It has also been found that groups are better at solving complicated tasks requiring reasoning and elimination of poor solutions. In addition, it would seem that simply having several individuals solve a problem would increase the probability that a good solution would emerge.

Another example of this type of decision-making process is the use of credit committees in lending institutions, such as banks and credit unions. These committees are made up of individuals who have a high degree of technical knowledge—yet the committees must meet to consider all applications for loans larger than a certain dollar amount. Another good example would be surgical teams in hospitals. Here again, each person is highly educated, yet the collective wisdom of the group is superior to that of any one of the members acting alone.

The Boeing Corporation decided to design the entire Boeing 777 using virtual groups entirely online. The airplane was so complex that the paper documentation for the service manuals alone would have filled an entire Boeing 777 (Patler, 1999).

Finally, most large corporations are run by executive committees made up of top-level executives. Here again, the reasoning is that committees make better decisions than do individuals.

One ancient author stated the point eloquently when he wrote, "Nowadays I make it a practice to call my workers into consultation on any new work. . . . I observe that they are willing to set about on a piece of work on which their opinions have been asked and their advice followed" (Columella, A.D. 100).

Finally, the research on this issue shows that group members together can achieve more than even the most superior member can achieve alone.

Groups are altering their form with changes in geography, tighter budgets, increased technology, and the global search for the very best subject matter experts. Virtual groups have evolved, and specific team skills and dynamics are necessary to achieve high-quality solutions. Refer to the Practical Tips section on this page titled "Virtual Group Competencies for High-Quality Solutions" for more information.

As we saw in Chapter 6, there are four methods for reaching decisions: (1) railroading, (2) teaming up, (3) majority vote, and (4) consensus. Consensus typically is the best method, because it optimizes good-quality decisions as well as a high degree of acceptance.

PRACTICAL TIPS

Virtual Group Competencies for High-Quality Solutions

Virtual Connection (VirtualConnection.biz, 2003b) has listed virtual group member competencies necessary for the achievement of high-quality solutions. Foir more information, visit the Virtual Connection website at www.virtualconnection.biz.

Group Member Competencies

1. Develop trust with fellow virtual group members.
2. Value differences between people.
3. Work both on your own and with other people.
4. Learn and adapt to new and current technologies.
5. Manage time effective.
6. Effectively manage projects.
7. Create expectations for yourself and others.
8. Share in the development of group norms.
9. Be held accountable and hold others accountable.

ACCEPTANCE OF SOLUTIONS

The plant manager of a large manufacturing plant decided that the supervisors were using far too many pens and that this was an unnecessary cost. He wrote a memo to all supervisory personnel indicating that each one would have to turn in a completely empty pen to an assistant plant manager in order to get a new pen. The intent was to save money. However, the pens cost about 50 cents apiece, and the supervisor's salary was about $20 per hour, so if a supervisor had to spend more than six minutes searching for the assistant plant manager, the cost was actually *greater* than if the supervisor had just gotten a new pen from the immediate area. The supervisors determined that it usually took them about 30 minutes to find the assistant plant manager. Thus, under the new policy, the cost of replacing the pen was 20 times higher than the old-policy cost. An even greater cost was the supervisors' loss of positive attitude toward the plant. They felt that they were being treated like children, and several went out of their way to do a poor job in retaliation. After less than one month, the plant manager rescinded the new policy in favor of the old practice for replacing pens.

As of 2008, Toyota Motors was the world standard in the auto industry. Its market capitalization (number of shares multiplied by the value per share) was more than that of General Motors, Ford, and Chrysler combined! One of the reasons that Toyota is so successful is its outstanding use of continuous-improvement teams. These teams constantly look for ways to improve every aspect of their business. As a result, Toyota is able to develop new cars like the top-selling Camry, the top-selling hybrid Prius, and the Yaris, which sells for just over $11,000, in addition to their other vehicles, such as the Lexus, the top-selling luxury brand, and the Scion, the edgy new brand that looks like nothing else on the road. Morgan and Liker (2006) and Liker and Merer (2007) attribute Toyota's runaway success to its consistently effective use of continuous-improvement teams to bolster every aspect of its business.

John Kotter at Harvard Business School had published a book titled *The Heart of Change* (2002) in which he documented interviews with over 200 leaders in more than 90 U.S., European, Australian, and South American organizations. He discussed the importance of people's acceptance in creating organizational changes. He summarized the findings in his book in the following way: "Our main finding, put simply, is that the central issue is never strategy, structure, culture, or systems. All those elements, and others, are important. But the core of the matter is always about changing the behavior of people, and behavior change happens in highly successful situations mostly by speaking to people's feelings."

Duke basketball coach Mike Krzyzewski (Coach K for short) offers the following example of how he implements Kotter's theory in his own book titled *Leading with the Heart:*

> Another time when the team was struggling and had lost a few games in a row near the end of the regular season, the team was gathered in the locker room for my standard pregame talk.
>
> Well, I turned out the lights and walked in with a lighted candle in my hand.
>
> "I'm just an old Polish coach looking for a few players with heart," I said.
>
> That was my entire pregame oration. And all of the players who were in the locker room that day still talk about it. (Krzyzewski, 2000, p. 156)

These cases illustrate one of the most common problems suffered by organizations—namely, employees' rejection of solutions to problems. For solutions to be effective, they must be of high quality and they must be accepted by those who must carry them out. If a solution is weak on either of these dimensions, its overall effectiveness is reduced (see Tubbs, 2011). Maier (1963, p. 5) offers the following formula and explanation for determining a decision's effectiveness:

$$ED = Q \times A$$

where *ED* represents effective decision, *Q* represents quality, and *A* represents acceptance.

Three types of problem situations can be identified from this frame of reference. The first includes problems requiring *high quality but low acceptance.* These problems are best solved by persons with a high level of technical knowledge and expertise. They might include important financial decisions involving setting prices, determining expenditures, and so on.

Second, some solutions require *high acceptance but low quality.* These might include fair ways of distributing new equipment, vacation schedules, undesirable work assignments, new offices or office equipment (such as the newest computer), or a new vehicle such as a truck. Decisions such as these may include all individuals who may be affected by the results of the decision.

Third, some decisions require both *high quality and high acceptance.* It would appear that the majority of problems falls into this category. Because this is the case, Maier recommends that problem-solving groups rather than isolated individuals be used, because the acceptance of the solution is likely to be higher when people are involved in formulating a solution and because we have already seen that groups tend to produce better-quality solutions than do individuals.

Participative decision making (PDM) not only can result in high-quality decisions and increased acceptance of the solutions but also may result in increased levels of satisfaction, commitment, and loyalty to the solution and to the group. Let us return to the pen replacement problem. The chances are that if the supervisors had been made aware of the problem and been asked to help find a way to reduce costs, several things would have occurred. First, they might have suggested a good solution. Second, they would have been more likely to accept the new solution. Third, they probably would have put peer pressure on one another to see that the new solution was followed. In each case, the result would probably have been better than what actually happened.

See the reading at the end of this chapter in which Norman Maier more fully explains the use of the $ED = Q \times A$ formula. This reading also shows the relevance of small group interaction to organizations and their effectiveness.

Literally thousands of modern organizations are learning a lesson from group theory and research. Google is just one example of an organization that highly values teams and a team culture. According to Murray (2007), Google has some of the following team-building elements in its culture: free catered lunches; a cafeteria stocked with candy, soft drinks, and cereal; leather massage chairs; garage doors instead of walls; lava lamps; Mr. Potato Heads; balloons; and workers in jeans with their dogs. Teams are encouraged to liven up their cubicles with Chinese lanterns and super action heroes. New employees are called Nooglers and are greeted with balloons and other welcoming celebrations (Murray, 2007, p. A1). Fisher (2000) offers the following explanation for the superiority of group decision making:

> Competitive advantage comes from fully utilizing the *discretionary effort* of the work force, not from buying the latest gadget or using the latest management fad. Voluntary effort comes from employees' commitment, and commitment comes from empowerment. It is simple human nature. Why? In the words of Weyerhaeuser Human Resources manager Doug King, "It's hard to resist your own ideas." (p. 13)

Dell Computers has been one of the fastest-growing and most successful companies in history. Michael Dell, the company's founder, cites the use of teams and teamwide accountability as one of the major factors in the company's phenomenal success. He uses a team-based reward system so that people are rewarded financially for working together (Dell, 1999).

These studies indicate two things. First, people generally are resistant to changes that affect their lives, especially if these changes are initiated by others. Second, group decision making and "people involvement" can be powerful assets in increasing satisfaction and overcoming resistance to change. Let us look at each of these in more detail.

Resistance to change is a phenomenon that some would argue begins with the so-called birth trauma in which the fetus resists being plucked from the warm, dark security of the womb and exposed to the shock of the cold, bright, noisy world outside. Over time and with experience, most of us develop a "separation anxiety" when we are forced to leave (or be separated from) any place or set of circumstances in which we feel comfortable. Each time we move or change schools or jobs, a certain amount of this is experienced. Try to remember how threatening your first day of high school (or college) was compared with the comfortable security of your immediate past. Resistance to change is normal and tends to increase when we do not understand the need for change or if we are not instrumental in bringing about the change.

Paul Beebe (1986) cites three of the hundreds of companies that are successfully using teams to overcome resistance to change:

> *Problem:* A mountain of paperwork was building on desks at CH2M Hill's Boise office last year. Employees were slow to file reports and other documents in loose-leaf binders favored by the consulting engineering firm. The forms were not pre-punched.
>
> *Solution:* A volunteer group of workers suggested to the company that it switch to pre-punched forms. Doing so would relieve employees of an annoying chore and speed filing, they said.
>
> *Savings:* Pre-punched forms save the Boise office 60 man-days a year, said Edward Sloan, CH2M Hill's district coordinator of construction management services. Companywide it probably saves 2,400 man-days, he said.
>
> *Problem:* It took 15 to 20 minutes to unload each potato truck that entered the Ore-Ida Foods Inc. processing plant at Ontario, Ore. Employees estimated hundreds of hours were being wasted as potatoes moved down truck-mounted conveyors into the building.
>
> *Solution:* A group of Ore-Ida workers in Ontario last year recommended to managers that belly-dump trucks should be used to haul potatoes to the plant. Potatoes could be unloaded into bays in only a few minutes.

Savings: Within one year, Ore-Ida realized $130,000 in labor savings and lost time, said John Walhof, the company's productivity manager.

Problem: Could the error rate of machines that place electrical components on printed circuit boards at Hewlett-Packard Co.'s disc memory division in Boise be improved?

Solution: The employees who operate the machines thought so. One group suggested a series of modifications that improved the manufacturer's error rating of its machines from 3,000 improperly mounted components per million to 500 parts per million, a sixfold improvement.

Benefit: Far fewer components are being mounted incorrectly. Board rejection rates are down and employee morale is up, said Jim Stinehelfer, manufacturing manager in H-P's disc memory division. (p. A3) (Reprinted with permission of *The Idaho Statesman*.)

The Ore-Ida and CH2M Hill teams consist of 6–10 people who meet once a week. Hewlett-Packard teams contain up to 30 people. Most of the groups are composed of workers from the same area of the company. "We wanted to create an environment where employees are free to offer suggestions about their working environment, ideas on ways our products are produced, [and] new products," said Ore-Ida's productivity manager of the company's People-Excellence-Products (PEP) program. Ore-Ida has organized 138 PEP teams in all of its U.S. operations, including 35 at its Ontario plant and 35 at its Burley plant. Teams tackle everything from safety issues to product quality. Hewlett-Packard spokespersons report that their company has seen big increases in morale and productivity that can be related to quality teams. Line inspectors have been eliminated in many areas, because employees now monitor the quality of their work. The manufacturing manager of Hewlett-Packard stated that the fundamental reason for the quality teams was to "make the people on the lines feel responsible for the quality of the product. The best way to have them feel that responsibility is to give it to them."

There are several important factors to remember in *overcoming resistance to change*. First, people will accept changes that they have a part in planning. Obviously, it is much easier to live through the trauma of going to college if we choose to go and if we like the college or university than if we are forced by our parents to go or to go someplace we don't like. Second, changes will be accepted if they do not threaten people's security. Many office work groups resist innovations, such as computer systems, for fear that the computer will eventually take away some of their jobs. Third, changes will be more readily accepted when people are involved in gathering facts that indicate the need for change. Farmers who notice decreasing crop yields will be more receptive to farming innovations than will those who are prospering. Finally, greater acceptance and commitment will result when the changes remain open to further revision based on the success or failure of the new procedures. None of us is very enthusiastic about adopting changes for a lifetime. However, if we feel the changes are on a trial basis, subject to modification, we are usually more willing to give them a try. Obviously, to the extent that these conditions are *not* met, resistance to change will be increased.

Many firms are beginning to take a major step toward the use of self-directed work teams. Wellins, Byham, and Wilson (1991) define a *self-directed work team* as "an intact group of employees who are responsible for a 'whole' work process or segment that delivers a product or service to an internal or external customer" (p. 3). This organizational innovation has as its fundamental theme the attempt to place a remarkably high degree of decision-making responsibility and behavior control in the hands of the work group itself.

A self-managing team usually elects its own leader, and often management appoints an external leader who acts as a coordinator-facilitator rather than a supervisor. Teams frequently take on responsibilities that have not traditionally been the topic for work groups in the past. These include (1) preparing the annual budget, (2) performing timekeeping functions, (3) recording quality control statistics, (4) solving technically related problems, (5) adjusting production schedules, (6) modifying or redesigning production processes, (7) setting team goals, and (8) assessing internal performance.

For long-term success, teams must function in a responsible manner, and management must possess a high degree of trust and confidence in the system. To help ensure successful teams, organizations typically design them with "well defined physical and task boundaries, sometimes using socio-technical design concepts to ensure an appropriate match between technical systems and the conventions, rules, and norms governing interaction. Task interdependence within teams is usually higher than between teams" (Wellins et al., 1991, p. 5). Sophisticated computerized information systems are frequently used in measuring inputs and outputs across team boundaries. This provides extensive and rapid feedback about the quantity and quality of team performance while reducing secrecy between teams. Teams are provided with as much information as possible.

Management typically initiates the self-managing work concept while striving for additional productivity, improving quality, reducing overhead, and limiting conflict. For the employee, the concept provides the opportunity to exercise more control over aspects of daily work life. Are these teams successful? There is no single conclusive answer to this question, but according to Zenger and colleagues (1994), literally thousands of organizations have instituted self-directed teams because of the success of this approach. Many other benefits of the team approach seem to manifest themselves. Teams become very flexible and adapt well to changing conditions and new start-ups. Also, organizations with the team concept generally have very positive responses on job satisfaction and attitude surveys.

Katzenbach and Smith (1993) put it well: "Unbridled enthusiasm is the raw motivating power for teams" (p. 265). They also write, "Teams will be the primary building blocks of company performance in the organization of the future" (p. 173). There is a high probability that you will find it very useful to learn more about teams and teamwork as you progress in your career.

Changes in Interpersonal Relations

As we saw in the case of Grameen Bank's loans to small groups of entrepreneurs in Bangladesh (see Chapter 5), the practice of loaning money to five women rather than to just one borrower significantly increased the success of the borrowers' businesses (Patterson et al., 2007). This was not only because of the shared accountability but also due to the increased closeness of the women who worked together in the business. This was also true in the case of Netflix (see Chapter 3). By using a team of friends, the business was more successful (Shell & Mousa, 2007). So, improvements in interpersonal relations can often lead to improvements in the organization's overall performance as well.

In Chapter 7, we examined the positive and negative aspects of conflict. Group discussion may improve interpersonal relations through the successful resolution of conflict. Conflict may be intragroup or intergroup. In either case, resolving conflict tends to affect interpersonal relations favorably.

A common technique for improving intergroup relations is to have members of each group get together and write down their perceptions of (1) themselves, (2) other members, and (3) how they think the others view them. Production and service groups in manufacturing plants frequently need to have such meetings to coordinate their activities more effectively. The production groups often feel that a service department (such as maintenance) does not act quickly enough to get defective machinery working. On the other hand, maintenance people feel as if they are always put under unreasonable pressures, because every time a piece of machinery breaks down, each production supervisor wants immediate attention to his or her problems, even though several machines require repair simultaneously.

Meetings designed to share members' perceptions of one another and to inform each other of particular problems can potentially clear up areas of misperception and misunderstanding. After one such meeting, one man said to another from a different department, "After drinking coffee with you and hearing your side of the story, it's going to be hard for me to cuss you out tomorrow the way I usually do." This comment reflects the increased quality of interpersonal relations that can come out of group problem solving conducted in an atmosphere of support and mutual gain. However, if the meetings take place in an atmosphere of blame placing and faultfinding, the relations are likely to be even worse than if the meetings had not been held. In other words, the intermediate influences discussed in Chapters 2, 5, 6, and 7 have a significant influence on the end results.

A subset of interpersonal relations is group cohesion. *Cohesiveness* has been defined as morale or feelings of belongingness. Group cohesion can also be a byproduct or end result of group activity. Generally, a prestigious or successful group is more attractive to belong to and results in higher levels of cohesion. The 2008 New York Giants and the U.S. Olympic teams that won medals in Beijing are two examples of successful groups that could be expected to have high levels of cohesion.

Cohesion is a result of group interaction, but it in turn influences other things. As we saw in Chapter 5, cohesive groups tend to have stricter norms and to tolerate smaller amounts of deviance from the group values. Cohesive groups may have high or low productivity, depending on the group norm regarding productivity. Cohesiveness increases the loyalty of each member to that particular group but frequently breeds deeper cleavages *between* groups. This may become a problem if the groups happen to be part of a single organization in which integration of several groups is necessary. In a study on predictors of performance in project groups (Keller, 1986), group cohesiveness was found to be the strongest predictor of the project groups' performance both initially and over time. The findings suggested that "cohesive project groups were able to achieve high project quality and meet their goals on budgets and schedules." Similarly, Barnard and colleagues (1992) found that the higher the cohesion among group members, the more likely they were to share attitudes.

In a seven-year study, Tubbs, Kryska, and Cooper (1999) measured satisfaction before and after introduction of a program to develop employee work teams in a company of about 100 people. The results showed that people's satisfaction with their peers was significantly higher after the program. In fact, the improvements were still there seven years later. In addition, the company's productivity and profitability more than doubled. It is clear that working together in teams can dramatically increase feelings of closeness and, at the same time, increase group output.

Similarly, Reinig, Horowitz, and Whittenberg (2011, p. 27) used a team-based learning approach in several sections of their accounting course. They found that this approach increased student satisfaction and students' perceived professional skills. They also found that a systems approach was the best way to view the concept of teams. So, research in university classes as well as in business has shown that attitudes can and do improve as a result of using team methods to achieve personal and organizational goals. (Reinig, Horowitz and Whittenberg, 2011).

In summary, it is important to note that small group interaction has the potential to increase interpersonal relations and cohesiveness. The strong emphasis on team building in management training illustrates the usefulness of this concept. In terms of learning theory, the behaviors of talking and cooperating rather than avoiding and competing with one another have been reinforced, and the cooperating behaviors are therefore more likely to occur again. Thibaut and Kelley (1986) put it this way: "The selectivity observed in interaction reflects the tendency for more satisfactory interactions to recur and for less satisfactory ones to disappear. The consequences of interaction can be described in many different terms, but we have found it useful to distinguish only between the rewards that a person receives and the costs he [or she] incurs" (p. 12). The critical element in improving interpersonal relations through group interaction is to make the experience as rewarding as possible.

TEAM BUILDING

Note the following analogy between a computer keyboard and a team:

> Xvxn though this kxyboard is old, it works wxll xxcxpt for onx kxy. I havx wishxd many timxs that it workxd pxrfxctly. It is trux that thxrx arx forty-onx kxys that function wxll xnough. But just onx kxy not working makxs thx diffxrxncx.
>
> Somxtimxs an organization or community is likx this kxyboard—all thx pxoplx but onx arx working propxrly. You may say to yoursxlf, "Wxll, only onx won't makx or brxak a projxct." But it doxs makx a diffxrxncx. Any projxct, to bx xffxctivx, nxxds thx participation of xvxry mxmbxr.
>
> So thx nxxt timx you think you arx thx "only onx" and that your xfforts arxn't nxxdxd, rxmxmbxr this kxyboard and say to yoursxlf, "I am an important pxrson in thx organization and community, and I am nxxdxd vxry much." (source unknown)

The analogy touches on a special case of group interpersonal relations referred to as *team building*. As we saw in the case of Google, extensive efforts to build teams has led to impressive organizational success (Murray, 2007). Larson and LaFasto (1989) report the results of their research investigating over 30 leaders of high-performance teams like these:

The Boeing 747 project team

The Rogers Commission (*Challenger* disaster investigation)

Cardiac surgical teams

A Mount Everest expedition

The Centers for Disease Control epidemiology teams

New York stage production teams

The McDonald's Chicken McNuggets team

Championship football teams

All these teams have something in common. Team Technology (2004) defines three critical team-building stages. First, the goals of the group or team must be clarified. Second, barriers to goal achievement must be brainstormed and identified. Third, the barriers should be peeled away so that the group or team goal can be effectively achieved. On the basis of Larson and LaFasto's (1989) fascinating research, eight dimensions of team excellence emerged:

1. *Clear, elevating goal:* For example, the purpose of the Rogers Commission was to determine the causes of the *Challenger* disaster within 120 days. Paul Lazarus, a Broadway producer, is quoted as saying, "It is better to have a clear idea and have it fail than to be unclear in conception, because you can learn from a failure and go on to the next clear idea" (p. 29).
2. *Results-driven structure:* The Mt. Everest team had as its objective getting one or two team members to the top of the mountain. The group's structure was to use the other members strictly as support for getting the one or two strongest members to the summit. The McDonald's Chicken McNuggets team was purposely structured as a separate entity from the rest of the company and reported directly to Bud Sweeney, the project director. The purpose was to cut through the corporate bureaucracy.
3. *Competent team members:* The team members for the Centers for Disease Control are selected for their outstanding talent along the following dimensions: (1) technically competent, (2) friendly and outgoing, (3) politically astute, (4) willing to subordinate his or her own interests in favor of the group goal, (5) willing to spend a lot of time on the task, (6) imaginative, (7) honest, and (8) interested in challenge (p. 60).
4. *Unified commitment:* Dr. Don Wukasch, a member of both the famous Michael DeBakey and Denton Cooley cardiac surgical teams, described his level of dedication to his teams: "Nothing was as important for me as being on that team and making it through the 10 years to get there. It was total commitment, and when I got married, that was part of the deal with my marriage. We looked at it and never had any questions as to what came first. It was the job" (p. 74).
5. *Collaborative climate:* Working well together is the basic building block of teamwork. Trust turns out to be the main ingredient. Anthony Rucci, a Baxter-Travenol Corporation team leader, states: "You need to clearly define the expectations, leaving people with the sense that you trust them enough to do things on their own, that you trust their judgment enough to let them take some personal initiative, that you are not looking over their shoulder. That is the quickest way that I know of

for a manager of a team to demonstrate trust and to build a climate of trust" (p. 87).

6. *Standards of excellence:* Director Paul Lazarus describes the level of excellence exemplified by one Broadway star: "Angela Lansbury did one song, and yet she requested more rehearsal time than anybody else simply because she would not go out on the stage unless she was prepared within an inch of her life. . . . She rehearsed 'Send in the Clowns' . . . once a week for 10 weeks. We could have done it in one rehearsal, but that's the kind of perfectionism that someone like that strives for, and that's why Angela Lansbury is a major star" (p. 102).
7. *External support and recognition:* Emotional support from top leaders above the team followed by financial incentives is the strongest combination to ensure that the team continues to give its best.
8. *Principled leadership:* Although leadership was discussed in Chapter 5, suffice it to say that Larson and LaFasto (1989) identify effective leaders as those who (1) establish a vision, (2) create change, and (3) unleash talent (p. 121).

In case you are wondering how to develop this high level of team spirit, Heathfield (2005) offers 12 tips for successful team building:

1. *Clear expectations:* Define clear outcomes.
2. *Context:* Help team members understand their role as a team.
3. *Commitment:* Ensure that all team members are committed to the team.
4. *Competence:* Make sure that the team has all necessary skills/resources.
5. *Charter:* Define a mission and vision and values specifically for the team.
6. *Control:* Help team members understand boundaries and barriers.
7. *Collaboration:* Develop group norms to assist working relationships.
8. *Communication:* Make sure that a group communication process exists.
9. *Creative innovation:* Encourage calculated risk taking within the group.
10. *Consequences:* Build a culture of accountability within the team.
11. *Coordination:* Ensure that management and departments are on board.
12. *Cultural change:* Have an organization that encourages and empowers change.

In some cases, groups with many highly capable members can actually underachieve by an unfortunate chain of events. This phenomenon is called the *Apollo syndrome.* Dr. Meredith Belbin coined this term to describe teams that did not effectively form into teams. These teams did not behave constructively, failed to compromise, held individualistic opinions and goals, avoided conflict, and couldn't make good decisions. The most important observation by Belbin is that groups and teams that are more effective are those that have varied expertise and skills (Team Technology, 2004).

Although all of these are important misconceptions to consider when examining a group-building communication process, it is important to emphasize one particular misconception—that of viewing the group as if it were a closed system. A group's performance is a function of its collective abilities, motivations, and opportunities. It is important for group members to improve the way they relate to each other, the roles they play, the relationships between these roles, and the norms that help group members work effectively.

Quite often, group members forget that they are part of a larger system (an organization), which itself can define roles, goals, and norms for the group. At times, changes in an organization will create changes in a group that make it difficult for the group to work effectively. An effective group will create constructive external relationships with its broader system. Group members will have an understanding of the group's role in the organization and learn to recognize threats from the larger system, as well as the opportunities it affords.

VIRTUAL TEAM BUILDING

All types of groups can benefit from team building. This includes virtual groups and teams. In the increasingly multinational environment, businesses are trying to save money and cut down on travel costs. This increases the use of virtual teams and groups (VirtualConnection.biz, 2003b). For virtual teams, an initial face-to-face team-building session is optimal, but if this is impossible, then a virtual team–building session can be helpful. This type of interaction can help group members develop relationships and understand the communication styles of other group members. If a face-to-face meeting is not possible, a video or Web conference can allow team building. Virtual Connection (VirtualConnection.biz, 2003a) gives an example of a team-building conference for the members of a small acquired company across the globe. The SARS epidemic prevented the conference from occurring face-to-face, so a virtual meeting was planned in its place. First, each team member shared something about him- or herself that would help colleagues work well with the individual. The shared items included pet peeves or other such characteristics. Second, playing work-related Pictionary gave members insight into the group's task. Third, question games helped group members get to know one another. Describing favorite things, hobbies, and so on can build relationships and enhance trust between group members. Fourth, sharing photos online helped to build relationships among virtual team members (VirtualConnection.biz, 2003a).

Virtual Connection (VirtualConnection.biz, 2003b) has listed tips for successful team building within virtual teams. First, set ground rules for the virtual group or team that include working patterns and communication planning. Second, focus on relationship dynamics within the group as well as task and goal dynamics. Third, share information and resources among the virtual team. The compilation of information and resources is much more useful when shared among members. Fourth, spend time developing understanding for each group member's work pattern and style. Doing this will help members work more effectively together in the virtual environment.

Group support systems (GSS) have been the subject of many investigations over the past decade. One study by Fjermestad (2004) analyzed the results of

145 experiments that used communication mode as an independent variable. The research showed that the modal outcome for GSSs compared to face-to-face (FtF) methods was no different, while the overall percentage of positive effects for results that compare GSS to FtF was 29.2 percent. These findings suggest that the use of a GSS improves decision quality, depth of analysis, equality of participation, and satisfaction over manual methods. Additionally, more detailed analysis suggests that task type, GSS type, and the interaction of both have a moderating effect on adaptation and outcome factors. Specifically, groups working on idea-generation tasks using GSS decision room technology improved to 39.6 percent (GSS > FtF) effect, while asynchronous computer-mediated communication (CMC) groups working on decision-making tasks improved to 46.4 percent (GSS > FtF) effect. FtF groups showed higher levels of consensus and perceived quality, communicated more, and were more efficient (requiring less time to complete the tasks). No differences were observed between FtF and GSS groups on satisfaction and usability (Fjermestad, 2004).

There are many benefits to virtual team building. In most cases, there are more attendees than would have been possible in a face-to-face meeting. Morale is raised through the enhanced and continued communication that virtual meetings make possible. Many virtual groups and teams evolve to save money, to pull together global talent into a cohesive group that would otherwise be impossible to create, and to create a channel for continual communication (VirtualConnection.biz, 2003b). Virtual teams use team-building meetings to enhance their performance and ensure positive information flow between group members.

Improved Information Flow

As we saw in the case of team-based breast cancer treatments (see Chapter 2), it is far superior to conduct diagnoses within a team of doctors than to go from one to another getting a second or third opinion. (Bakalar, 2006). This is but one example of improved information flow as a result of group work. Tubbs, Husby, and Jensen (2008) studied dozens of teams in hospitals and found that teams more often than not improved information sharing compared to the routine hospital practices (Tubbs, Husby, & Jensen, 2008).

Communication in small groups also can result in an increased knowledge level and increased coordination among group members based on the sharing of information. Information may be distorted severely if passed along serially from one person to the next through 10 people. However, the distortion will be significantly reduced if the same 10 people hear the information simultaneously in a meeting. In addition, active discussion by participants will help them remember the information better than if they heard it in an announcement or read it in a memo.

Rogers (1995) has discovered over many years of research that there are various predictable patterns of the "diffusion of innovations." He notes that some people by nature are earlier adopters of new ideas whereas others are more resistant to change. His pattern of adopter categories is shown in Figure 8.1 (p. 262).

Another factor is the tendency for subgroups to form so that information that passes *between* groups is restricted. This is especially true in complex

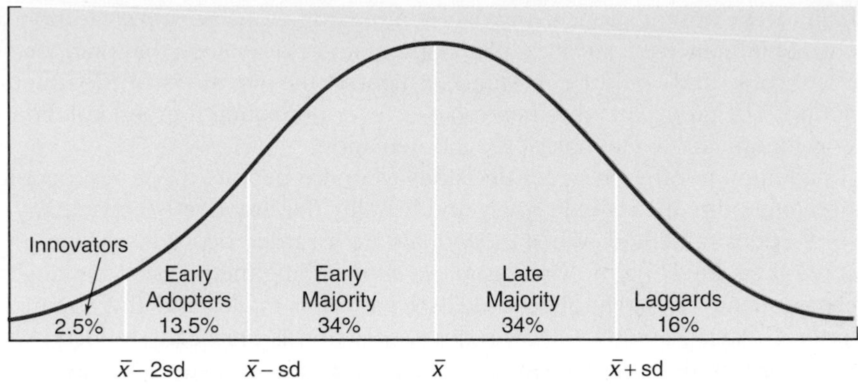

FIGURE 8.1 Adopter Categorization on the Basis of Innovativeness

organizations. Lawrence and Lorsch (1969) referred to problems of this nature as *differentiation–integration* problems. Organizations require specialization (differentiation) in order to operate effectively. Thus, different groups become specialists in such departments as production, finance, legal, research and development, data-processing inspection, master mechanics, engineering, accounting, sales, and personnel. At the same time, these groups must cooperate and coordinate their efforts to keep from working at cross-purposes and generally harming organizational success.

Hammer and Champy (1993) argue persuasively that the barriers created by the high degree of differentiation in organizations have created the need to, in their terms, "reengineer the corporation." This involves breaking down and reexamining traditional ways of doing things. They use the example of Taco Bell. Before 1983, the chain's typical restaurant was 70 percent kitchen and 30 percent eating area. By 1993, those percentages had reversed (p. 177). Changes like these come directly from greater teamwork and communication across functional areas of the company.

Coordination problems certainly occur among members of a single group as well as among multiple groups in an organization. Almost invariably, groups of students assigned to work on class projects have at least some difficulty in finding (1) each other, (2) a free hour in common in which to meet, (3) the materials necessary to conduct the research for their assignments, and sometimes (4) a suitable place in which to conduct their discussion. In addition, group members may forget that they were supposed to meet, or they may get too busy to prepare for the meeting. A host of other tangential problems may add to the coordination difficulties. Not all of these problems will be solved by group discussions, but they will probably at least be reduced. In some circles, this is known as letting the right hand know what the left hand is doing.

Patterson and colleagues (2008) point out that group decision making tends to lead to a different type of solution than does person-to-person decision making. In the one-on-one setting, the focus of the solution is on the person perceiving an individual problem. In an organization, this approach frequently solves one person's problem while *creating* new problems for others. Suppose that five supervisors all want to take their vacations in June and July. Assuming that not all of them can be absent at once, any decision regarding one person's vacation will potentially influence the vacation plans of the others. It may be that one person's plan is flexible and could be modified in light of the situations of the others in the group. The group method then focuses on coordinating the best solution for all, considering the limitations of the job demands.

In addition to offering better decisions for more people, the group decision-making method reduces the jealousy and hostility that frequently accompany the person-to-person method. When individuals are awarded decisions in their favor without others knowing the circumstances surrounding the decision making, the others frequently feel that special deals have been made, and the superior is accused of playing favorites. However, this reaction is drastically reduced when all interested parties are witness to the decision and the surrounding circumstances. Although the group method may be time-consuming, the end results of increased knowledge and increased coordination are frequently worth the time spent. In fact, the total time expenditure may be less, because the related problems of jealousy and resentment do not arise as often and do not have to be solved as offshoots of the original problem.

CASE STUDY

THE TEDDY BEAR NAMED MUHAMMAD

In 2007, Khartoum, Sudan, was catapulted into the news after a British teacher, Gillian Gibbons, brought a teddy bear into her classroom. Gibbons started the teddy bear project with her class of six- and seven-year-olds to teach the behaviors and habitats of actual bears. The teddy bear was supposed to go on adventures with each of the students, be dressed up, provide a learning experience for the students, and have its very own journal of its outings (Crilly, 2007). However, an innocent learning experience caused political and religious outrage after the class voted to name the teddy bear "Muhammad." The students very strategically chose the name Muhammad to reflect the first name of the most popular student in the class. Twenty out of the 23 students voted on the name (Fox News, 2007). Muhammad is one of the most popular names in that part of the world. Unfortunately, it is also the name of the revered Muslim prophet (Pitts, 2007).

After a group of parents (not from this particular class) found out that a teddy bear was given the name Muhammad, they became outraged. They raised concerns with school officials, and it quickly became a legal issue. Sudan, which is ruled by religious conservatives, was deeply offended that a teacher would allow her class to name a teddy bear Muhammad (Fox News, 2007). Officials said that it showed blatant disregard for Islam's prophet and was unacceptable. Gibbons was arrested and jailed, accused of insulting Islam's prophet, and charged with blasphemy (Crilly, 2007). The penalty was, potentially, six months in jail and 40 lashes of a whip or cane. Large groups of protestors formed outside the jail demanding her execution. Fortunately, she was pardoned by the president of Sudan and deported to England. This incident resulted in a change in practices not only in classrooms in Sudan but also around the world in predominantly Muslim countries.

1. What is your reaction to this incident?
2. How does culture influence the parents' reactions?
3. How do you think parents in the United States might have reacted if the teddy bear had been named Jesus?
4. What can we learn from this case about the importance of culture as students of communication?
5. What communication behaviors can we draw upon to potentially resolve such differences?

Organizational Change

Change occurs within groups and within organizations. It is just a difference of scale. In most cases, groups and teams are in charge of implementing organizational change across the organization.

It has been said that the only person who likes change is a baby with a wet diaper. Changes that are initiated by someone else are particularly hard for us to accept. In this regard, former General Electric CEO Jack Welch writes, "Change has no constituency. People like the status quo. They like the way it was. When you start changing things, the good old days look better and better" (Welch, 2001).

Historically, organizational change has had a rough reception. Research indicates that 75 percent of organizational change attempts reported by CEOs have not been effective. In 2011 alone, Blockbuster Video and Borders Books both filed for Chapter 11 bankruptcy due to their inability to change fast enough to compete with Netflix and Amazon.com. Unsuccessful change results in reactionary behavior instead of proactive behavior. The unexpected consequences of organizational change consume all the critical time necessary to make change succeed. Employees who are resisting change turn against one another and disengage from the organization (Wheatley, 2004). Effective change results in employees who collectively have a stronger sense of ownership of the future of the organization and who help drive change. For example, **recent research by McKinsey & Company found that 100 percent of successful change efforts allowed employees to contribute ideas. Nearly 25 percent of those "extremely successful" transformations were planned by fifty or more people, compared to just 6 percent of the unsuccessful transformations (Harvard Daily Briefings, 2010).**

On the basis of a rapidly increasing rate of change, modern organizations have been put under ever greater pressure to adapt or go under. Certainly, the policies and practices of colleges and universities have to be different today than they were just a few years ago. For example, online registration, online courses, and Web pages showing curricula and textbooks are now common place. Numerous attempts have been made to help "ease the squeeze" felt by organizations. These attempts usually fall under the general label of *organizational development (OD),* which is another name for planned organizational change.

One excellent example of group thinking that made a difference is shown in a comparison of Xerox Corporation and Apple Computers. Xerox was the leading paper copier company in the 1970s, and it saw its business as chemicals on paper. Its engineers developed electronic computing capabilities, but the company executives rejected the innovations since they did not fit with the company's self-image. Apple, on the other hand, was in the microcomputer business; it obtained the technology from Xerox, and the rest is history (Rogers, 1995). More recently, Nokia has also fallen victim to Apple and Motorola in the cell phone business. Nokia was a market leader until Apple introduced the iPhone and Motorola introduced the Droid. These so-called "smart phones" do so much more than a simple cell phone that sales of Nokia's phones fell immediately. So one of the lessons of change is that we have to be willing to look past our conceptual blinders to see the possibilities. (In mid 2011 Google, which invented the Droid technology, bought Motorola's cell phone business, as one more example of organizational change).

Over fifty years ago, Kurt Lewin (1951) wrote about the problem of trying to get people to change. He called his analysis *force field analysis,* and it states basically that any situation occurs as a result of the combination of various competing forces. If you have ever tried to live up to your New Year's resolutions, you have experienced this. Figure 8.2 illustrates the concept further. Your motivation to live up to your New Year's resolutions represents one of the arrows labeled "driving forces." If you are thinking about exercising more or losing some weight, several arguments can add to your motivation (better-fitting clothes, more dates, better health). The restraining forces would be all the reasons why you don't live up to your resolutions (it's fun to eat, it's too cold to exercise, you hate to exercise alone).

Just as this force field analysis can be applied to individuals, it also can be applied to groups and to organizations. In most groups, some members may want to get the job accomplished (task-oriented behavior), whereas others may be much more interested in socializing with an attractive group member. In fact, they may have joined the group just to meet that person. How much work actually gets accomplished is the status quo where these competing sets of forces meet. If the socializing couple leaves, the restraining forces will go up. Change can occur through either a reduction in the restraining forces or an increase in the driving forces, or both. Various methods of organizational development are designed to move the status quo in the more positive direction.

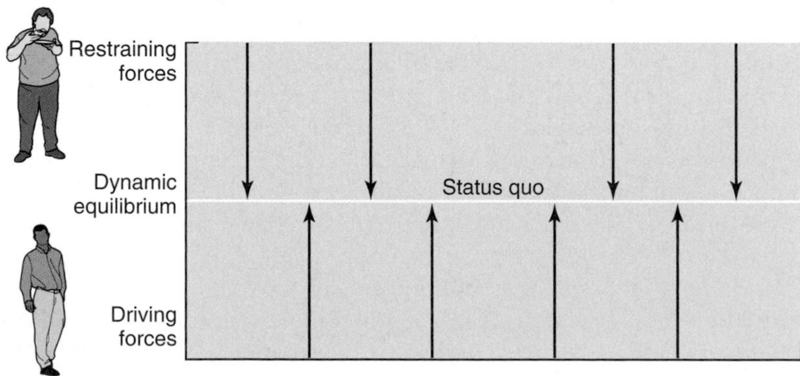

FIGURE 8.2 An Illustration of Force Field Analysis

Let's say that you have been elected to an office in your sorority, fraternity, or church group, or in some other organization. If you have identified things that you think need to be changed, then you are faced with the challenge of creating and implementing organizational change. Now what do you do? Jick (1993) offers the following helpful advice:

THE TEN COMMANDMENTS OF IMPLEMENTING CHANGES

1. Analyze the organization and its need for change.
2. Create a shared vision and common direction.
3. Separate from the past.
4. Create a sense of urgency.
5. Support a strong leader role.
6. Line up political sponsorship.
7. Craft an implementation plan.
8. Develop enabling structures.
9. Communicate, involve people, and be honest.
10. Reinforce and institutionalize change. (p. 195)

By the way, these 10 steps are very similar to Kotter and Whitehead's (2010) eight steps for organizational change.

Henry Ford Health System in Michigan, an organization of over 21,000 employees and 1,000 doctors, used a step-by-step method to introduce ground-breaking organizational change. First, CEO Nancy Schlichting brought in best practices from the hotel industry by hiring Gerard van Grinsven, who had had a long career at Ritz-Carlton, to become CEO of their new West Bloomfield Hospital. They trained all their staff extensively using a Leadership Academy for doctors and top administrators, then had extensive employee involvement to plan the new facility. Among other things, all rooms are private, and every patient has 24-hour room service from a gourmet menu created by celebrity chef Matt Prentice from Bingham Farms. Having all private rooms significantly reduces infection, which is the leading cause of death in hospitals. Henry Ford Health System has become one of the best hospitals in the United States (Taylor, 2011, pp. 74–81).

Nadler, Shaw, and Walter (1995) have created two interesting cyclical models. One shows creative changes in response to organizational needs (see Figure 8.3), and the other shows how to perpetuate the status quo (see Figure 8.4) (p. 123).

Excellence comes in all sizes. Not only can giant corporations, such as Xerox, benefit from using principles of group dynamics, but small companies, such as Fernco, Inc., of Davison, Michigan, also benefit from these innovations (Tubbs, Kryska, & Cooper, 1999). Fernco manufactures plastic pipe products and employs 100 people. Several years ago, the company began to implement an employee involvement program based on the principles in this book. This author was asked to design and conduct the program. We began by measuring employee attitudes with a survey to diagnose the strengths and weaknesses in the organization. Several offsite training programs were held with all the

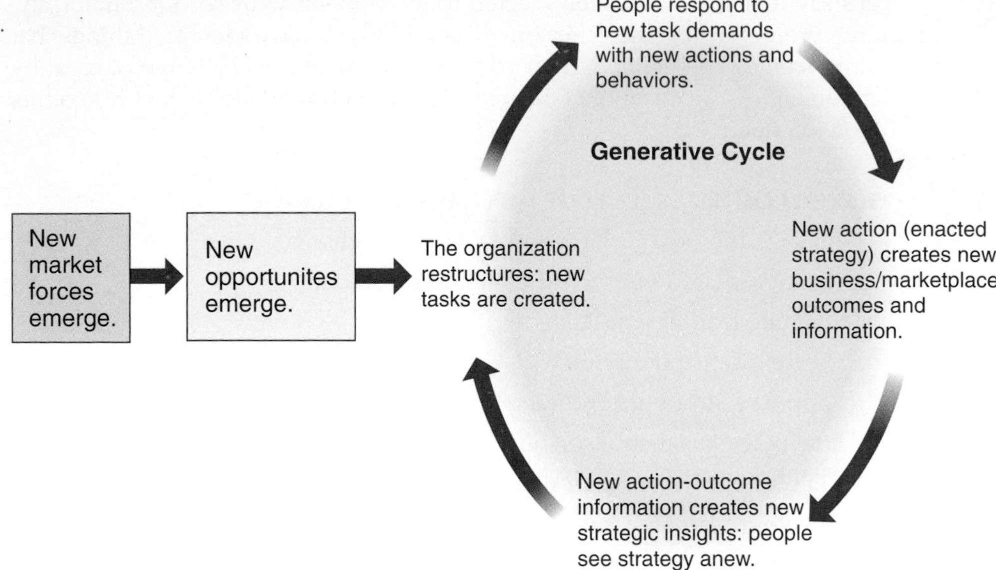

FIGURE 8.3 The Generative Strategy Cycle

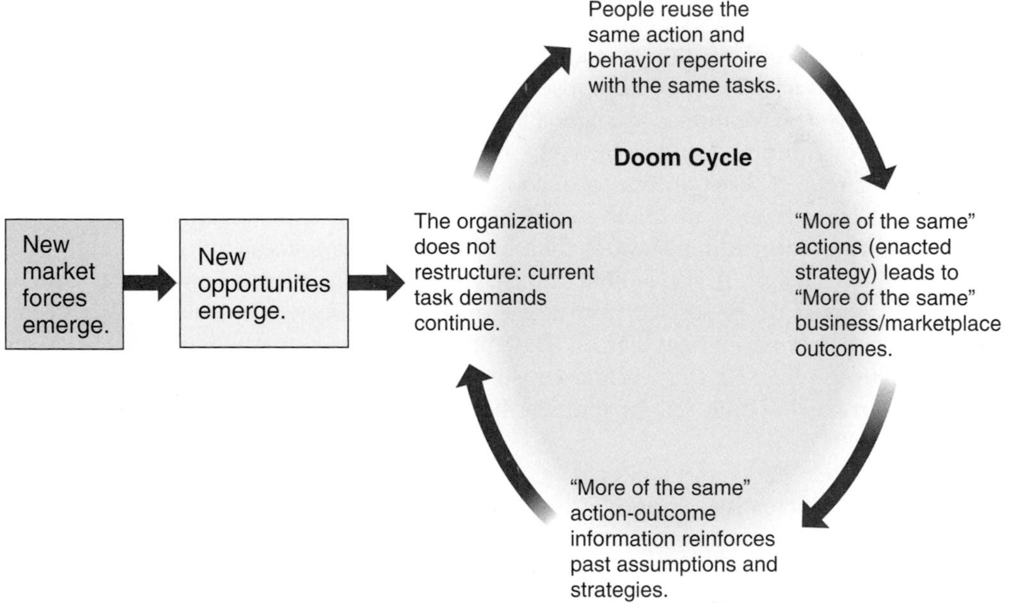

FIGURE 8.4 The Strategic Doom Cycle

company management and the employees who volunteered to join the TAG Teams, as they became known. A set of company guidelines was developed in collaboration with an advisory committee made up of managers and employees. Four TAG Teams were formed to work on problems of their choice. After

PRACTICAL TIPS

Kotter and Whitehead (2010) have identified more than 20 common objections to organizational change. Here are few, with some useful responses:

1. "We've been successful, so why change?"

   RESPONSE: "True. But surely we have all seen that those who fail to adapt eventually become extinct."

2. "There's no money."

   RESPONSE: "We are limited only by our imagination."

3. "Your proposal leaves too many details unanswered."

   RESPONSE: "We purposely left this broad to allow for maximum input and ideas from you and your colleagues."

(Kotter & Whitehead, 2010, pp. 108–122)

one year, employee attitudes showed significant improvement, and the teams had proposed numerous innovations that management strongly supported and quickly implemented. The company is the leader in its industry and is widely recognized in the region as an outstanding organization for which to work. Fernco has almost no employee turnover, and there is a long waiting list to get a job there. This is but one more example of the use of groups to improve an already excellent organization.

The famous Peter Drucker (1999) has offered the following advice for leaders on managing change:

1. *Introduce change on a small scale.* James Watt designed and patented the steam engine in 1769, and it was only used for running steam engines to pump water out of coal mines. It was several years later that the engines were used for widespread purposes.
2. *Budget for change.* Have one budget for maintaining your operation (85–90% of your total budget), and another budget to finance the changes for the future (10–15% of the total budget). Most organizations cut their budgets in bad times and don't protect their investment in the future.
3. *Balance change and continuity.* Change requires constant information to people to help them understand what is going on. Also, innovators need to be promoted and rewarded with pay raises and bonuses. At the same time, those who keep the organization's routine operations running smoothly also need to be recognized and rewarded appropriately. This is a delicate balancing act. (pp. 70–72)

Numerous studies of organizational change have been discussed by Heath and Heath (2010).

All change occurs in a context of interconnected systems. Heath and Heath (2010) recommend that we think of a journey riding on an elephant. Our logical component is the rider, our emotional component is the elephant, and the situation we are in is the path. These are the three critical subsystems. In order to bring about change, we should do the following:

1. *Direct the rider.* What looks like resistance is often a lack of clear goals. So provide crystal-clear goals.
2. *Motivate the elephant.* Find mostly carrots and some sticks to motivate people to change the status quo. The elephant is much bigger than the rider and will usually ignore the rider when the two are in conflict.
3. *Shape the path.* Change the situation to remove obstacles to change. For example, Amazon.com has transformed the book business by creating an online order form that is so simple that it is much easier to order from your home than to go to the trouble of going to a bookstore. Now, they have expanded into other retail products, so that they are even robbing sales from such extremely successful companies as Wal-Mart.

Rogers (1995) and his colleagues have conducted over 4,000 studies on people's acceptance and resistance to change. The research is described in his classic book *Diffusion of Innovations.* Rogers and colleagues have found that people accept change along a distribution that is a bell-shaped curve (see Figure 8.1). We fall into five categories depending on the innovation we are considering adopting—for example, the DVD or iPhone—as summarized below. Those at the innovation end of the distribution tend to be higher in intelligence, better educated, more socially connected, more tuned in to information sources, and better off financially.

- ***Innovators.*** This includes only 2.5 percent of the population. They are the first on the block to embrace a new innovation. Venturesomeness is almost an obsession with innovators. Their interest in stimulation leads them into a wider and more diverse circle of people and experiences. Innovators tend to be so far ahead of the rest of us that they are sometimes thought to be a bit bizarre. For example, Bill Gates dropped out of Harvard to pursue his dream of starting Microsoft, and Mark Zuckerberg did the same to start Facebook.
- ***Early adopters.*** This group includes 13.5 percent of the population. These people are also ahead of the curve when it comes to accepting change. They like change and get bored easily. Early adopters are often called opinion leaders. They tend to be influential in getting others to accept innovations. They are often role models for the rest of us. Recent research by Bain & Company found that some customers who are eager to be seen as "eco-prestigious" are willing to pay as much as $13,500 more for an electric car, to encourage others to buy electric vehicles (Harvard Business Review Daily Briefings, 2010). In his book *The Tipping Point* (2000), Malcolm Gladwell calls these people "connectors, mavens and salesmen." They are highly instrumental in influencing others to adopt new ideas.

- ***Early majority.*** This group consists of 34 percent of the population, constituting what might be called the critical mass that makes an innovation really catch on—in other words, "the tipping point." However, they seldom hold positions of opinion leadership in a social system. They may deliberate some time before adopting a new innovation.
- ***Late majority.*** This is another 34 percent who begin to accept change a little later, but still within a reasonable period of time. These folks are skeptical of change. They may adopt change out of necessity or due to increasing pressure from peers. They do not adopt an innovation until the majority of others have already done so.
- ***Laggards.*** The last 16 percent of the population resists change more than any of the others. They tend to possess almost no opinion leadership and to be isolates in a social system. They look to the past rather than to the future. They are suspicious of innovations and of those who promote them.

In working with organizations trying to implement change, I have found that it is helpful to share the above information with leaders and associates to help them better understand the dynamics of change. When organizational change is a goal, "participation is not a choice." The key is to involve as many people as possible, to make them part of the process (Wheatley, 2004). Most of us resist change to some extent. The more we have control in choosing the changes, the more comfortable we are with them. If we can't choose the changes, then the more we are able to participate in how changes are implemented, the more likely we are to accept the changes. A friend of mine frequently says, "It is hard to resist something that you have helped to create."

Recent research findings show that some methods of creating change (such as autocratic methods) can elicit only the minimum begrudging response from people. However, Patterson and colleagues (2008) have found that using teams also increases group members' willingness to do more than just the minimum required.

See the reading by Schlesinger, Sathe, Schlesinger, and Kotter at the end of this chapter for a comprehensive discussion of the methods for accomplishing organizational change.

REVIEW OF THE SYSTEMS APPROACH

This chapter dealt with the consequences of group interaction. In Chapter 1, our model indicated that all the other variables tend to culminate in the consequences. However, in ongoing groups, the outcomes or consequences of earlier group interactions tend to have a continuing influence on subsequent activities.

In this chapter we looked at four potential consequences of group interaction: (1) solutions to problems, (2) changes in interpersonal relations, (3) improved information flow, and (4) organizational change. Each of these potential consequences may vary considerably depending on the particular combination of the other variables depicted in the model. For example, the quality and acceptance of solutions will vary depending on the degree of group member participation.

A great deal of material has been written about member acceptance of group-derived solutions. The term *consensus* is typically used in this context. Consensus means unanimous agreement with the solution. Conceptually, consensus and acceptance of the solution appear to be roughly equivalent.

All the studies cited in this chapter confirm our thesis that small group interaction must be viewed as a system of interrelated variables in which a change in any one variable creates changes in the other variables in the system.

The second section of this chapter dealt with interpersonal relations. We saw that group member relations may be improved as a result of group interaction. However, groups composed of members with highly incompatible personalities or value systems may, in fact, become even more polarized as a result of small group interaction. This outcome would depend on the style of leadership and quality of conflict resolution in the group. Information flow may be improved as a result of interaction; but with a highly structured communication network and authoritarian leadership, communication flow might actually diminish. Similar points also can be made regarding organizational change. Each of the potential consequences depends to a considerable degree on the quality of the mix of other relevant variables in the model.

Hackman (1990) has identified three consequences for measuring the effectiveness of groups. He writes:

> First, is the degree to which the group's productive output . . . meets the standards of quantity, quality, and timeliness of the people who receive . . . that output.
> . . . The second dimension is the degree to which the [group] process . . . enhances the capability of members to work together interdependently in the future.
> . . . The third dimension is the degree to which the group experience contributes to the growth and personal well-being of team members. (pp. 6–7)

This seems a good way to measure the ultimate success or effectiveness of the groups to which you belong.

Numerous studies have shown that it takes a comprehensive (systems) approach to successfully create large-scale organizational change. Pfeffer (1998) and Pfeffer and Veiga (1999) identified seven practices of successful organizations: (1) employment security, (2) selective hiring of new personnel, (3) self-managed teams and decentralized decision making, (4) comparatively high compensation based on organizational performance, (5) extensive training, (6) reduced status distinctions including dress, language, and office arrangements, and (7) extensive sharing of financial and performance information. The use of teams, extensive training, and reduction of status barriers are just a few of the issues covered in this book.

What we have attempted to do in this chapter and throughout the book is to indicate ways to better understand and improve your functioning in small groups. The considerable research cited earlier leads us to believe there is a distinct probability that you can and will become a more effective group participant if you are able to implement the ideas we have discussed. Keep in mind that to be an effective participant or leader you should "choose exploration over exploitation, rallying others over ruling, imagination over inventory, achievement over compliance, and giving over taking" (Patler, 1999, p. 217).

Liker and Franz (2011) correctly emphasizes that organizational change cannot be sustained without the proper philosophy and values that are consistently applied before, during, and after the change efforts. For example, many organizations publish statements like, "People are our most valuable resource." However, when times get tough, they lay people off as the first way to save money. Such inconsistencies in philosophy and values will undermine any efforts to change, because the organization's leadership lacks believability and credibility (Liker and Franz, 2011, p. 411).

In Chapter 1 we showed some of the reasons why studying small group interaction would be valuable to your life and to your career. As you complete this book, it is worthwhile to note some of the most recent developments in higher education. As of 2011, several major universities are changing their curricula to include more small group, leadership, and interpersonal communication courses in their business school curricula. Such top schools as Columbia, Harvard, MIT, Stanford, University of Michigan, University of Southern California, and University of California–Berkeley all have changed their curricula along these lines. The changes are as a result of advice from business leaders from such companies as Google, BASF, and Deloitte LLP.

Previously, these companies looked for expertise in such functional areas as accounting, finance, engineering, and chemistry. However, "'Job candidates with stronger people skills ended up leading better no matter what their functional background,' said Michael Kannisto, head of staffing at BASF, North America" (Korn & Light, 2011, p. B6). In addition, a recent study conducted at DePaul University also found that decision making and giving effective feedback were most important to managers. However, these subjects were covered in only about 10 percent of the 373 business schools surveyed. The study's author stated that, "Business schools are falling short where it matters most" (Korn & Light, 2011, p. B6). So, you can be assured that the information that you have learned from this book and in this course is some of the most important of any that you will study in your entire college career.

The readings in this chapter help show how you can improve several small group consequences. Directly or indirectly, these articles touch on how to improve all four consequences discussed in this chapter. The article by Norman Maier even proposes a contingency model consistent with systems theory that suggests which types of problems are more likely to be solved using group decisions and which can be solved by the leader acting alone.

EXERCISES

1. Getting the Car Home

Divide the class in half. Let one half attempt to solve this problem individually, with no conversation allowed between and among participants. Record the number who solve the problem correctly as well as the average amount of time taken to solve it (sum the times of all persons and divide by the number of persons). Have the other half of the class form into groups of four or five people. Record how many groups correctly solve the problem and the average length of time taken per group.

Problem: You are stranded with a flat tire. In attempting to change the tire, you step on the hubcap containing the lug nuts (which hold the wheel on), and all five nuts are lost down a storm drain. How do you get the car home?

2. Case Study Discussion

Read the following excerpts from an article on the use of aborted fetus eggs.

> UPROAR ERUPTS OVER FUTURE USE OF ABORTED FETUSES' EGGS
> William Tuohy
>
> Another controversy over fertilization techniques erupted Sunday in Britain amid reports that a method of producing test-tube babies from aborted fetuses is on the horizon.
>
> Researchers said the technique, which has sparked intense ethical debate, might be able to produce a human baby within three years if the British Medical Association's ethics committee gives it the go-ahead as expected next month.
>
> The latest developments in fertilization come after a 59-year-old woman gave birth to twins in a London clinic after undergoing artificial fertilization in Rome. Many doctors and officials argued that women past menopause are unsuitable mothers because of the vast differences between them and their offspring.
>
> Last week a British fertility clinic was embroiled in another controversy over implanting a white woman's egg into a black woman, following reports that the woman and her husband, a man of mixed race, wanted to ensure the color of the child.
>
> Member of Parliament David Alton . . . [said of] the new treatment, "This consumerist approach to the creation of life puts it on a par with an American fast-food outlet." (*Ann Arbor News,* January 3, 1994, p. A1)

In groups of five, discuss the ethics of these practices. See if you can agree as a group on what should be done. Each group should report its results to the rest of the class.

3. Personal Feedback Exercise

On the basis of the case study discussion in Exercise 2, answer the questions in Figure 8.5 for each person in the class (while every other person in the class does the same thing). Ultimately, you will receive feedback from every other class member. These can be anonymous, or you may sign your name if you wish.

Comments for ______________________________

Following are some general impressions I have formed of your performance over the course of the semester.

1. In the task or problem-solving areas, you seem to have the following
   strengths:

   weaknesses:

2. In terms of your ability to *communicate clearly and effectively* on an interpersonal level, you seem to have the following
   strengths:

   weaknesses:

3. In terms of your ability to work *with others on a social-emotional level,* you seem to have the following
   strengths:

   weaknesses:

4. In the following areas you seem to have improved during the semester:

5. Additional comments:

FIGURE 8.5 Personal Feedback Exercise Form

READINGS: Overview

Most of us who work in small groups are interested to one extent or another in getting results. In the first reading, Norman Maier offers a very practical discussion of the formula $ED = Q \times A$ briefly described in this chapter. This article also bridges the gap between communicating in small groups and applying those concepts and skills to meeting the needs of an organization. In the second reading, Schlesinger, Sathe, Schlesinger, and Kotter offer a comprehensive spectrum of seven methods for dealing with resistance to change.

Reading 8.1 Improving Decisions in an Organization

Norman R. F. Maier

THE PRAGMATIC TEST OF DECISIONS

Most management situations are sufficiently complex so that solutions to problems or decisions that are to be made cannot be classified into correct and incorrect categories. Rather the alternative possibilities have relative merits, and the standards by which they are to be judged are not agreed upon. Frequently the criteria for judging them are unclear, or there is a lack of agreement on the correct standards to use. People may favor certain decisions because they fit the facts, because they like them, because they get support from those who must execute them, because they are the only ones that came to mind, because making a change in preference may cause them to lose face, because they like the person who suggested a particular decision, because the alternative favored is their brain child, because they participated in reaching it, and for a variety of other reasons. Some of these reasons may be of assistance in the reaching of effective decisions while others may be a hindrance.

Regardless of why people favor certain solutions or decisions over others, the test of a decision's value is quite a different matter. If the pragmatic test is to be used, an effective decision would be the one that produced the desired objectives most completely, achieved the desired objective most efficiently (costwise, energy-wise, and with the least undesirable side effects), and carried with it the most valuable by-products. These three measures of success might sometimes be in conflict, but in any event they would all be dependent on the outcome of the decision.

In other words, decisions can best be evaluated in terms of subsequent events, and unfortunately it is then too late to change the decision. For example, General Eisenhower's decision to invade the French coast at a time when the weather report was doubtful is regarded as a good one because it turned out that the weather did not interfere with the plans. Had the weather turned out to be sufficiently unfavorable and created great losses, his decision would have been open to criticism. In this instance the weather information indicated that invasion was risky on the date set for the invasion. However, the alternative was to set another date and go through the costly preparation process again.

Decisions of this sort may be regarded as lucky, or we might suppose that the decision maker has some kind of intuition, some special wisdom, or some special information that guides him. Regardless of how we view such decisions, the factor of chance plays a part. Some people are wealthy because their ancestors happened to settle along a river bank that later became a thriving city. Even if we view the ancestors as having the intuition to settle at the right place, the payoff on these decisions did not occur in their lifetimes. It seems unlikely that potential real estate values were factors influencing these decisions, and hence it would be more appropriate to attribute the successes of the decisions to luck than to wisdom.

Granting that chance plays a part in successful decisions, we also must concede that some people seem to be lucky more often than others and that the difference exceeds what one would expect from the laws of probability. Some

---

From Norman R. F. Maier, *Problem-Solving Discussions and Conferences* (New York: McGraw-Hill, 1963), pp. 1–9. Reprinted by permission of the estate of Norman R. F. Maier and Ayesha A. Maier.

executives seem to have an uncanny way of making decisions that turn out to be highly successful; others may go through several bankruptcies. Although the borderline between luck and decision-making aptitude may sometimes be narrow, it is important to do what we can to reduce the chance factors to their bare minimum if we are to examine the factors that make for decision-making ability.

Since the final evaluation of the decision is only possible some time after the decision has been made, and since the evaluation of alternatives is often not available, we must confine our speculation to the ingredients of the decision that have high probabilities for success. In examining alternate decisions we may appraise them from the point of view of their probable effectiveness.

For example, if a first-place baseball team is to play the seventh-place team, an even-money bet placed on the first-place team would be wiser, even if it turned out that the seventh-place team won. One cannot take unknowns into account in appraising decisions before the actual test. However, failure to consider all the factors and influences that are available before the decision is made will reduce its possibility for success. Thus, the illness of two star players on the first-place team should not be overlooked.

THE DIMENSIONS OF EFFECTIVE DECISIONS

Two different dimensions seem to be relevant in appraising a decision's potential effectiveness. One of these is the objective or impersonal quality of the decision; the other has to do with its acceptance or the way the persons who must execute the decision feel about it. The usual conception of effective decisions has emphasized the quality dimension. This approach leads to a careful consideration of the facts of the case. The advice is to "get the facts; weigh and consider them; then decide." It is this emphasis that causes one to assume that there is a correct answer to a problem, a right decision to make. Although this position is sound in technological matters that do not involve people, one cannot assume that it is universally sound. It is this position that causes us to concentrate on getting more information and to assume that when decisions do not work out there must have been some oversight. Thus, nations may debate peace plans for the world, attempting to improve the decision, when the fault may lie elsewhere. It is quite possible that any number of plans would be adequate if they received international acceptance. As soon as the behavior of people is involved, opinions and feelings introduce a second dimension.

It is important to clearly separate these two dimensions since, as we shall see, the ways for dealing with them are very different. Failure to differentiate the dimensions leads to complications in discussion because one person may be using terms such as "good" to describe the quality of the decision, another to describe its acceptability, and a third may be thinking in terms of the outcome, which depends on both.

Decisions may have varying degrees of acceptance by the group which must execute them; and it follows that, quality remaining constant, the effectiveness of decisions will be a function of the degree to which the executors of the decision like and believe in them.

For example, let us suppose that there are four ways to lay out a job and that the quality of these methods, from best to poorest, is in the following order: method A, method B, method C, and method D. Suppose further that the persons who must use these methods have a preference order as follows: method D, method B, method C, and method A. It is conceivable under these circumstances that method B would yield the best results even though it is not the decision of highest objective quality. Naturally one must consider the degrees of difference between each alternative; nevertheless, the fact remains that an inferior method may produce better results than a superior one, if the former has the greater support.

The formula for an effective decision (*ED*) therefore would require consideration of two independent aspects of a decision: (1) its purely objective or impersonal attributes, which we are defining as quality (*Q*); and (2) its attractiveness or desirability to persons who must work with the decision, which we are defining as acceptance (*A*). The first depends upon objective data (facts in the situation); the second on subjective data (feelings which are in people). Simply stated, the relationship may be expressed as follows:

$$ED = Q \times A$$

This separation of quality and acceptance somewhat alters the meaning of such expressions as "good" decisions and "correct" decisions. The term "goodness" might be used to describe degrees of quality, acceptance, or effectiveness and hence has little meaning when applied to decisions. The term "correct" similarly has different dimensions and in addition is limited because it is an absolute term and suggests that there are no moderately effective decisions, medium-quality decisions, and partially acceptable decisions.

It must also be recognized that the effect of acceptance on performance will vary from one problem to another. It is clear that when the execution of a decision is independent of people, the need for acceptance is less than when the execution is influenced by the motivations and attitudes of the people who must carry it out. Nevertheless, a respect for acceptance may be a worthwhile consideration in all group problem solving since a concern for a participant's satisfaction may influence his motivations and attitudes, which in turn would influence his contributions. For example, a marketing plan may have high quality and still have poor acceptance by a group of persons involved in designing the visual appearance of a package. Since the execution of the design and its reception by the public are independent of the initial planning group, it can be assumed that the success of the decision will be independent of the degree of acceptance of the decision-making group. However, what effect will such a decision have on a group if it has been railroaded through? If some members of the planning group are dissatisfied with the decision, may not this make them less valuable participants in the future? When we take the long-range point of view, dissatisfaction with a perfectly good decision can depress a group's future performance, whereas high satisfaction with a decision may serve to upgrade future performance.

If we can assume the position that the acceptance of a decision by the group that must implement it is a desirable ingredient, what are the problem issues? First of all, we must examine how this ingredient is related to the other desired ingredient—quality.

It is one thing to say that in striving for effective decisions two criteria must be satisfied, but can one achieve both of these objectives simultaneously? High-quality decisions, on the one hand, require wisdom, and wisdom is the product of intelligence and knowledge. Decisions of high acceptance, on the other hand, require satisfaction, and satisfaction is the product of participation and involvement in decision making. Thus, the method for achieving quality differs from the method for achieving acceptance; as a matter of fact they are in conflict.

Figure A describes this basic problem in aiming at two objectives. If we aim for both objectives, we may achieve neither. The traditional leadership approach is to aim for quality first, as in Figure B. This means that the man responsible for decisions uses whatever resources he feels are needed in obtaining facts and opinions, and he may make free use of experts or consultants. However, the actual decision-making function resides in the leader who finally weighs the evidence and decides. Once a satisfactory quality has been achieved, the next step in this process is to obtain acceptance of the decision.

Traditional methods for achieving this secondary objective have ranged through (1) imposing the decision on subordinates who must execute it (dictatorial methods, using the motivation of fear); (2) playing the father figure and gaining acceptance through a sense of duty and trust (paternalistic methods, using the motivation of loyalty); (3) using persuasion types of approach which explain the virtues of the decision (selling methods, in which personal gains are stressed); and (4) using participative approaches which encourage discussion of decisions by subordinates but leave the final decisions to the superior (consultative management, in which the motivation is based on a limited degree of participation in which there is opportunity to discuss but no right to make a decision). Although this evolution of the decision-making process reveals improvement, the change has been confined to the aspect that is concerned with obtaining acceptance of decisions by subordinates. Throughout the history of the decision-making process, the quality ingredient has remained in the hands of the top man or group leader. Management philosophy is that

FIGURE A Quality and Acceptance as Targets

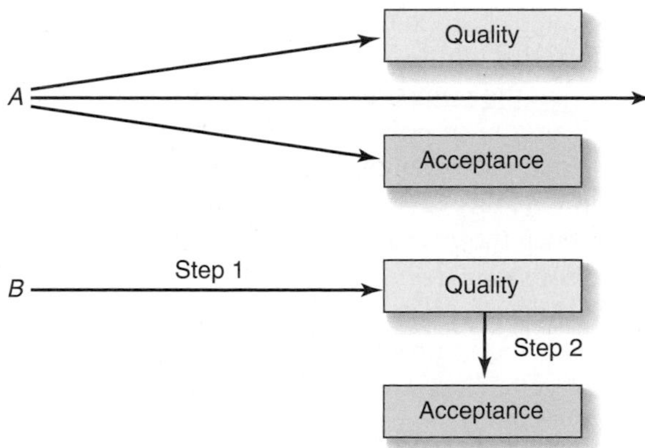

FIGURE B Acceptance as Primary Objective

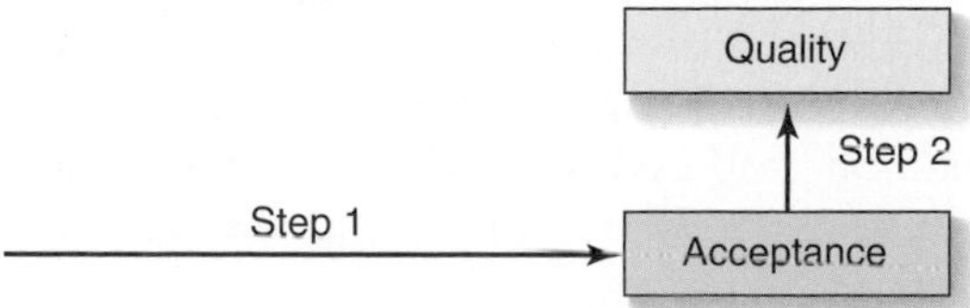

the person held accountable for the decision should be the one who makes it. The fact that changes in methods for obtaining acceptance have occurred, however, suggests that the adequacy of the acceptance ingredient still leaves something to be desired. Patching up an old method may improve things, but it lacks elegance.

Suppose for the moment we make a fundamental change in our thinking and regard acceptance as the initial objective. This approach is shown in Figure B. To ensure success with this objective it is necessary to share the decision making with the subordinates who must execute the decision. Group decision, a method in which problems are solved and group differences are resolved through discussion, now emerges as the appropriate approach. It immediately becomes apparent that in attempting to be sure of obtaining acceptance, one risks the ingredient of quality. At least, that is the first concern of leaders and superiors when the question is raised. This notion of group decision becomes even more threatening when the leader discovers that he is to be held responsible for decisions made by his immediate subordinates. It is for this reason that he wishes to retain a veto power; yet such a safeguard tends to destroy the value of group problem solving. Yes-men are the products of a superior's tendency to disapprove of decisions made by subordinates.

It appears then that the second objective is endangered whenever the appropriate method for obtaining the first is used. If this conflict is inevitable, it may be well to conclude that there is no one best approach to the problem of effective decision making. Perhaps problems, as well as approaches, should be analyzed. It is possible that the best approach may be a function of the nature of the problem.

BASIC DIFFERENCES IN PROBLEMS

Problems may be examined with respect to the degree in which quality and acceptance are implicated. For example, in pricing a product it is apparent that a price may be so low that the loss will increase with the volume of business, or it may be so high that the company will be priced out of business. These two fates are possible, regardless of how acceptable the price is to the persons who make or sell the product. Establishing a proper price, therefore, is an illustration of a problem where the quality of the decision is a prime consideration. Although acceptance may influence the manufacture or sale of the product, it is quite clear that satisfaction with company decisions would not depend primarily upon problems of this type.

In contrast, let us select a problem involving the issue of fairness. What is fair is largely a matter of feeling, and it would be difficult for anyone to find an objective criterion that would ensure the achieving of fairness in a group. For example, when a new typewriter is introduced into an office group to replace an old one, who should get it? Should it be the person whose typewriter is replaced, the person with most seniority, the person who is most skilled, the person who is least skilled, the person who does the most work, or should some other criteria be found? Each member of the group might advocate a different scale of values, and invariably the criterion proposed is found to favor the person who advocated it. Thus, when people want something, they select the facts and the values that tend to favor their feelings.

If a problem of this kind were solved by group decision, the supervisor would hold a meeting and conduct a group discussion to determine the fair way to introduce the new typewriter into the group. Usually this type of discussion resolves itself into a reshuffling of typewriters so that several persons stand to gain. Furthermore, different groups will solve the same problem in different ways, and each group will be most satisfied with its own solution. Solutions of this kind cannot be generalized, and their merit lies in the fact that they are tailored to fit the groups who make them.

The question of quality is a minor one in such instances. The supervisor need not be concerned with which of several possible solutions is objectively the best; his primary concern is to have a decision that is acceptable. Future performance of the group will depend more upon the way the members accept decisions on such matters than upon their objective qualities. As a matter of fact, it might be difficult to find measures of quality that would be acceptable to everyone.

If we follow this approach to distinguishing between problems, the first step in decision making is to analyze the problem in terms of the important objective—quality or acceptance. Three classifications of problems would seem to emerge.

High-Quality, Low-Acceptance Requirement

These are problems in which the quality of the decision is the important ingredient and the need for acceptance is relatively low. Such problems can be solved effectively by the leader with the aid of experts. The ingredient of acceptance should come up for consideration only after concern with the quality of the decision has been satisfied. Thus, the procedure for obtaining acceptance may be regarded as secondary, though necessary.

We shall see later that the quality of decisions often can be improved by the effective use of group participation. This use of the group has additional objectives and raises new problems. For the present we will confine the discussion to the types of problems that can adequately be solved by experts and do not create major acceptance problems. These include:

Decisions regarding expansion, new products, decentralization, plant sites, etc.

Problems concerned with setting prices, determining costs, etc.

Decisions regarding the purchase of materials

Solutions to problems requiring specialized or technical knowledge

Although persons may disagree on the relative importance of the quality and acceptance requirements, this evaluation must be made by the person who is responsible for the decision. If he feels that a particular decision is required, he is in no condition to permit participation without directly or indirectly imposing his views. In this state of mind he is in a better condition to supply the solution and make acceptance the secondary objective. When the leader strongly favors a particular decision, he is a more effective persuader than conference leader. Thus, regardless of whether quality is the most important factor in a decision or whether the leader thinks it is the most important, the procedure is the same—protecting quality by the effective utilization of the knowledge and intelligence of the decision maker.

Certain decisions that involve acceptance but for which there are no acceptable solutions may also be included in this classification of problems. For example, an airline had the problem of choosing a uniform for stewardesses when the company's new jet plane was introduced. The solution to this problem involves a quality aspect in that the uniform should artistically conform to the design of the plane's interior, and it involves an acceptance decision from the stewardesses, who would have to wear the uniforms. In this instance, the reaction of the stewardesses to the company-imposed decision was quite unfavorable, so that it seemed that the approach used may have been a poor one. On the other hand, could stewardesses have agreed on a solution even if effort had been made to hold group meetings with such a large population?

If we assume that blondes, brunettes, and redheads are favored by different color combinations, it is quite unlikely that all women would be satisfied with the same uniform, so that any group decision would tend to favor the predominant group. Would such an outcome be a good group decision? Until we know more, it might be best to confine the group decision method to situations that permit a resolution of differences. However, it is important not to assume that all conflicts in a group resist resolution. It is conceivable that if group discussion had been used the women would have:

1. Evolved a compromise that was artistic.
2. Adopted a uniform that permitted variation in some part (such as a scarf) so that complexion differences would have been recognized.
3. Been more satisfied because of having had some opportunity to influence the decision.

Whether the cost of such meetings would offset the cost of the discontent, which would be temporary, is a decision that the responsible person must make.

High-Acceptance, Low-Quality Requirement

These are problems in which poor acceptance can cause a decision to fail and in which the judgment of quality is influenced by differences in position, experience, attitudes, value systems, and other subjective factors. Problems of this type can best be solved by group decision.

An illustration of a problem falling into this group arose when a supervisor needed two of the three women in his office for work on a Sunday. He asked them individually, and each claimed that she had made a date that she could not break. The fact that Sunday work paid double did not interest them.

He decided to try the group decision method he had just learned about in the company training program. He asked the women to meet in his office on Friday morning and told them about the emergency job. Since he needed the help of two of them, he wondered what would be the fairest way to handle it. The women readily entered into the discussion. It turned out that all had dates, but one had a date with some other women, and all three agreed that a date with other women was not a "real" date. Thus, this woman agreed that it was only fair that she should work.

One more woman was needed. Further discussion revealed that one woman had a date with the man to whom she was engaged, and the third had a date with a new boyfriend. All women agreed that a date with a fiancé was a real date, but it was not a "heavy" date. It was decided that the third woman who had the date with a new conquest, should be excused from Sunday work. Thus, she was not required to work, even though she had least seniority, because this was considered fair.

The quality issue does not enter into this problem for two reasons: (1) All women were qualified to do the work. Had this not been true, the supervisor might have been more reluctant to try out this method. However, it remains to be seen whether the women would have placed an incompetent woman on the job. (2) The problem was stated in such a way as to limit it to the matter at stake. Had he posed the problem in terms of whether or not anyone should be forced to work on Sunday, the answer might have been "no." We shall see later that a problem should be so stated as to keep it within the bounds of the supervisor's freedom of action. If he has no authority to set such matters as pay rates, he cannot expect the group to solve this type of problem through group decision.

In using group decision the superior serves as the discussion leader and presents the problem to his subordinates. His objective is to have the group resolve their differences through discussion while he remains neutral. He confines his activities to clarifying the problem, encouraging discussion, promoting communication, supplying information that may be at his disposal, and making appropriate summaries. His objective is to achieve unanimous agreement on a decision that is the product of the interaction in a group discussion.

Problems that fall into the high-acceptance category have to do with:

The fair way to distribute something desirable, be it a typewriter, a truck, office space, or office furniture.

The fair way to get something undesirable accomplished, be it unpleasant work, unattractive hours, or shifts.

The scheduling of overtime, vacations, coffee breaks, etc.

The fair way to settle disciplinary problems that involve violations of regulations, lack of cooperation, etc.

High-Acceptance, High-Quality Requirement

These are the problems that do not fall into the other two categories. At first this may seem to be the largest category of all, so that little seems to have been achieved by extracting the other two. However, in working with group problem solving, it soon becomes apparent that group decisions are often of surprisingly good quality. It is not uncommon for a supervisor to volunteer the information that the group's solution surpassed not only what he had expected, but what he could have achieved by himself. The fear that group decisions will be of poor quality appears to be greater than the hazard warrants. However, if the supervisor is anxious about the outcome, he is likely to interfere with the problem-solving process, rather than facilitate it. For this reason this category of problems should be handled by group decision only when the leader is experienced. Thus, it is a category for which either group decision or leader decision is recommended, depending upon the supervisor's skills.

The fears of people frequently determine the motives they ascribe to others, particularly if they are members of an opposition group. For example, if a manager fears a drop in production, he unjustly assumes that his employees are motivated to produce less. Actually the motivational forces in employees form a complex pattern. They include not only what the employees want, but ways of protecting themselves from what they fear management wants to accomplish. With fear removed by the opportunity to participate, the outcome of a discussion often differs greatly from what is anticipated. Obstacles that seem insurmountable frequently disappear in thin air.

THE DYNAMICS OF GROUP PROBLEM SOLVING

In order to illustrate the types of forces at work in a problem-solving interaction, it may be best to describe a case in the use of group decision. Specific incidents serve to bring theories and generalizations in closer contact with reality.

This case is selected because it is characteristic of the manner in which men solve problems involving attitudes toward prestige and seniority rights. At the same time it illustrates how the men on the job are aware of company objectives and do not take advantage of the company or of each other when the need for protective behavior is removed.

The problem arose because repair foremen in the telephone industry had a persistent problem in getting their men to clear "wet-weather drops."[1] A wet-weather drop is a defective line that runs from a pole to a building. These lines have to be replaced from time to time because water can seep through a break in the insulation and create a short. After a heavy rain there are reports of trouble, but since the difficulty is present only when the line is wet, the problem is a purely temporary one. During periods of expansion or when replacement material is at a minimum, many lines suffer from this wet-weather difficulty. If a station is out of order for this reason, the loss of service corrects itself and is not as serious as if the station were completely out of order. Hence the company, as well as the men, regards wet-weather drops to be minor and routine jobs in contrast to emergency jobs. Furthermore, repair men do not like to do this unimportant work, and they feel that anyone can do it without thinking. As a consequence, the men make little effort to get these jobs done. If the foreman decides to pressure men into bringing in a few wet-weather drops, he finds himself at a disadvantage. The men may promise to pick up one or two and then fail to do so. When asked why, they claim that they ran into extra difficulty on an emergency job and say, "You wanted me to do a good job on the other first, didn't you, boss?" Although the foreman may know the men are shirking, he never knows on what occasion the excuse is justified. It thus comes about that wet-weather drops are a headache to the foreman. When he gets far enough behind, he puts one man on the job full-time and lets him clear wet-weather drops. The man in question feels degraded and wonders why he is picked on. To be as fair as possible, this job is usually given to the man with the least seniority. He may complain violently, but invariably the man with least seniority is in the minority. Among supervisory groups this practice is considered the fairest way to handle the situation, and they believe that the men want seniority to be recognized this way. They are completely unaware of the fact that this practice turns an undesirable job into one that has low status as well.

In a particular crew of 12 men the number of wet-weather drops was gradually increasing, and the time was approaching when something would have to be done about the matter. The foreman decided that this was a good problem on which to try group decision. He told his men that he realized no one liked to clear wet-weather drops and that he wanted to have their reactions on how the problem should be handled.

Of interest is the fact that no one in the group felt that the man with the least seniority should do the whole job. The man with most seniority talked against the idea of picking on the fellow with least seniority, saying that he had hated being stuck with the job when he had the least seniority and that he couldn't see why everybody shouldn't do a share of it. It was soon agreed that the job should be evenly divided among the crew. This crew divided up the job by assigning a work area for each man. In this way each man was to be responsible for the wet-weather drops in his area, and he was to be given a list of those. Each morning the local test desk was to designate for each man the wet-weather drop most in need of replacement. It was understood that he was to clear this one, if at all possible. This condition took care of clearing up the drops that were most essential from the point of view of the office. In addition, all agreed that each man should clear as many additional drops as his load permitted. However, when a man had cleared up all the wet-weather drops in his area, it was specifically understood that he should not be asked to help out another. This last condition clearly reveals an attitude built up over the years. It is evident that the reluctance to clear wet-weather drops hinged on the idea that when a man was conscientious, advantage was taken of him. Soon he got to be the "sucker" in the group or perhaps the foreman's pet. It was evident that all men were willing to do their parts but they did not wish to run the risk of being made a sucker. (Other foremen have testified that this defensive reaction made sense from the manner in which the job is frequently handled. The foreman wants to get the job done, and he begins to rely on those individuals who have cooperated in the past. Soon these men find they are doing all the undesirable jobs. It is just a matter of how long it takes a man to find out that he is losing out with the group.)

The results of this solution were immediately apparent. During the three-month period previous to the discussion, a total of 80 wet-weather drops had been cleared; during the week following the discussion, 78 wet-weather drops were cleared and without any letup on the rest of the work. Within a few months the problem was practically nonexistent. The reaction of the men also bore out the effectiveness of the decision. Men discussed the number of drops they had cleared and showed a friendly competitive spirit. They discussed the time when they expected to be caught up and would only have to take care of wet-weather drops as they arose.

It should be noted that the men's notion of fairness was quite different from what the supervisor had anticipated. Although men strongly urge seniority privileges, they do not wish to give junior men a hard time. Rather, advantage is taken of junior men only when seniority rights are threatened. It is of special interest to note the protective reactions against the possibility that cooperation will lead to abuse. Once the protection was ensured, the men considered customer service. This recognition of the service is apparent from the fact that the crew wanted to clear the drops in the order of their importance. With defensive behavior removed, it is not uncommon for good quality solutions to emerge.

DEPENDENCE OF THE SOLUTION'S QUALITY ON THE LEADER'S SKILLS

The quality of group decisions can further be enhanced by improving the skills and the attitude of the discussion leader. Even with a minimum of skills the group decision approach can be effective with problems such as the following:

Setting standards on tardiness and absenteeism

Setting goals for production, quality, and service

Improving safety, housekeeping, etc.

Introducing new work procedures, changing standards, introducing labor-saving equipment, etc.

It is apparent that both quality and acceptance are needed in solving problems of this type, and for this reason they are the areas of greatest conflict in labor–management relations. However, the requirement of skill is more than methodology because it is something that cannot be decided, adopted, or purchased. It requires additional training in conference leadership, and this means an increase in a company's investment in management talents.

CONCLUSIONS

Problems may be divided into the following three types:

Type 1. Q/A problems: those for which the quality of the decision is clearly a more important objective than its acceptance. These may be successfully solved by the leader.

Type 2. A/Q problems: those for which acceptance of the decision is clearly a more important objective than its quality. These may be successfully handled by the group decision method in which the decision is made by the subordinates with the superior serving as a discussion leader.

Type 3. Q/A problems: those for which both quality and acceptance of the decision become major objectives. These problems may be handled in either of two ways, each requiring a different set of skills on the part of the leader. The alternatives are as follows:

Leader decision plus persuasive skills to gain acceptance or

Group decision plus conference leadership skills to gain quality

[We emphasize] the second alternative because conference skills permit the effective use of a greater range of intellectual resources, thereby achieving high-quality decisions as a by-product.

NOTE

1. Taken from N. R. F. Maier, *Principles of Human Relations,* Wiley, New York, 1952.

Reading 8.2 Organizational Change Strategies and Tactics

Phylis F. Schlesinger, Vijay Sathe, Leonard Schlesinger, and John P. Kotter

Solving and avoiding organizational problems inevitably involves the introduction of organizational change. When the required changes are small and isolated, they usually can be accomplished without major problems. However, when they are large and involve many people and subunits, they often can cause significant problems.

Managing the change process is a critical skill for any manager. Very few organizations exist in a static state; the world is constantly changing. Outside the organization, in the space of a fiscal year, product development cycles go from two years to six months, because customers demand new products, better and faster. Governments impose new regulations, and/or remove others. The financial environment becomes difficult to predict. Communication across organizations is intense and rapid, as the business environment becomes more global.

This kind of change in the competitive environment has an effect on organizations as well. They must seek and adopt more effective ways to set strategies, to market and manufacture products, to work effectively in an ever changing environment. Most organizations have to make major changes in their management style, beliefs, systems, and perhaps even culture in order to meet this challenge. Whereas some companies make changes in their design factors and their management styles very easily, most do it with great difficulty. They become accustomed to their proven ways of managing, even if those ways are no longer as effective as they once were.

A MODEL FOR ASSESSING THE NEED FOR CHANGE

Several factors need to be examined before one begins a change process. Managers can use the concepts of "fit" . . . to analyze the organization's design problems. The ideas presented in this [reading] will address ways to assess the need for organizational change, develop the "vision" for change, design implementation plans for change, and manage the change process. The ideas presented here can apply equally to managers at any organizational level.

Most organizations have a difficult time in preparing the organization for change. Once the organization is ready to change, it is often difficult to implement and sustain the process. Managers who are supporters of the change often meet resistance from many fronts. One president of a hotel company, for example, believes that the managers should be more attentive to the levels of service in their units. He exhorts them to change in a speech at the annual meeting; they all leave convinced that their unit will offer the best service imaginable. Once they return to their units, however, the speeches and new ideas fade in the day-to-day processes of the organization. Clearly, the change effort was not effective. If we look at the above example in terms of the model presented on next page, we can understand why.

From Phylis F. Schlesinger, Vijay Sathe, Leonard Schlesinger, and John P. Kotter, *Organization,* 3rd ed. (Homewood, IL: Irwin, 1992). Reprinted by permission of The McGraw-Hill Companies.

There are many ways to conceptualize the change process.[1] We have found that change is more likely to be effective when the costs of making the change are outweighed by factors which create the motivation to change. The relationship can be explained as follows:[2]

$$Change = D \times M \times P > C$$

where D = the levels of dissatisfaction with the status quo, M = the new model for managing implicit in the change, P = the planned implementation process for making the change, and C = the cost of the change to the relevant stakeholders, the individuals, and groups in the organization.

Change can occur only when sufficient dissatisfaction (D) with the status quo is present in key individuals or groups, such as the hotel president in our example. These individuals have to articulate the new way of managing (M) which is necessary to make the changes. In our previous example, it was to pay more attention to customer service as a management tool. While most companies have articulated some kind of vision statement, the model for management is the way that managers have to put the vision into managerial practice. Finally, the organization has to have a process (P) for managing the change that is sufficiently well-planned, anticipates that resistance to the change will occur, understands where that resistance will come from, and outlines effective intervention methods for dealing with these changes. Unfortunately for our hotel president, this is the piece he missed. Exhortation through speeches will not suffice. All of these variables combined must be greater than the cost (C) of the change economically and emotionally to the organization in question.

Creating Dissatisfaction

Most dissatisfaction comes when key organizational members recognize a crisis. A major customer suddenly shifts to another supplier. The bottom falls out of the market and managers are forced to make layoffs. Examples of organizational crises are as numerous as examples of the often traumatic change that results. However, a prescient manager is always looking for ways for the organization to improve continuously. She or he is constantly on the lookout for ways to make the organization more effective, and looks to communicate these ideas as a way to generate dissatisfaction with the status quo.

Often these ideas come from many sources. One source is from the competitive environment. Perhaps the hotel staff does not see the effects of poor service on customers—what difference can one angry customer make? Another source is the employees within the organization itself; the annual employee attitude surveys can be a powerful tool for diagnosing the culture and style of the organization. If the employees seem to be demoralized, dissatisfaction is present. In order to spread the word about the dissatisfaction present, to make it more known around the organization so as to arouse people to change, managers must communicate this concern through their letters, memos, actions, and expectations.

Developing a New Model for Managing

A vision of the future state, the structures and systems of the organization as well as the behaviors and attitudes of the employees, is essential for a change to occur.

The vision a manager has of his/her unit or company's future can energize change, by uniting the people in a common goal. It also serves as a road map for change; establishing this model across the organization can be a planning exercise on just what the organizational problems are and the solutions for them. Managers arrive at this vision through discussion, analysis, and observation. It should specify the "fit" of all the organization's elements, and be viable and adaptable over the long term.

At times the vision originates in a small part of the organization which itself serves as the role model for change. For example, one manufacturing company had a group of employees who focused on improving the cross-functional processes involved while they worked on developing a new product. Their results were so successful that they not only cut the introduction time from two years to one, but also improved cross-functional communication at the same time. Senior managers were so impressed by their efforts that they developed a "vision" of the organization as one which focused on process as well as on product, and developed a detailed model and plan for implementing process and product teams across the organization.

Managing the Process for Change

Having a vision of what ought to be does not translate directly into organizational life, however. Managers must work to develop a process for the implementation of the model they hold. This process is the sequence of events, meetings, speeches, communiqués, celebrations, and design factor changes (personnel decisions, reward system changes, structural changes) directed at helping the model become a reality.

[There are a number of methods that] managers can use to implement the process of change. These include[3] building a coalition of backers and supporters, articulating and communicating the shared vision through symbols, signals, and rewards, assigning responsibility and accountability, ensuring communication, education, and training, and constantly monitoring the process as it goes forward. The particular strategies one uses to implement the desired change depend on many factors, most notably the amount and kind of resistance encountered, the position of the change initiator relative to the resistors, the sources of data and the energy of the change initiators for managing the implementation, and the stakes involved. These can be partially understood by looking at the costs of the change to those affected by it.

Costs of the Change

Change does not occur without costs to some parts of the organization. For example, the employee who has been used to performing one job the same way for years, who has developed a routine for work, may be terrified at the prospect of becoming a member of a self-managing work team where s/he is required to perform many tasks. The costs can be expressed in terms of the losses those with a stake in the change feel will occur. For some it is power, or a sense of competence, or a key relationship, or a sense of identity or perhaps a key intrinsic or extrinsic reward. For whatever reason, understanding the costs to key individuals is crucial to planning the process of change.

It is useful for the change initiator to perform an assessment of each stakeholder affected by a change.

What is that person's "stake" in the status quo? What do they believe they will lose? How can the cost of the change be decreased for that stakeholder? What techniques can one use to deflect the resistance that stakeholder will present? These data should be used in the planning of the change process itself.

Taken together, this model becomes a powerful tool for making sure a manager has considered all of the aspects of a change before embarking on one. Most managers can see the places where misfits or mismatches occur, and most have a particular view of where they would like to see the organization (or division or unit) be in the future. By understanding the nature and source of the resistance to the new model, the manager can plan the process to deal with that resistance.

HUMAN RESISTANCE TO CHANGE

Human resistance to change takes many forms—from open rebellion to subtle, passive resistance. It emerges for many reasons—rational and irrational. Some reasons are primarily self-centered; others are selfless.

Politics and Power Struggles

One major reason that people resist organizational change is that they see they will lose something of personal value due to the change. Resistance in these cases is often called "politics" or "political behavior" because people focus on their own interests and not the total organization.[4]

After years of rapid growth, for example, the president of one organization decided that its size demanded the creation of a new staff function—new-product planning and development—to be headed by a vice president. Operationally, this change eliminated most of the decision-making power that the vice presidents of marketing, engineering, and production had over new products. Inasmuch as new products were important in this organization, the change also reduced the status of marketing, engineering, and production VPs. Yet, status was important to those three vice presidents. During the two months after the president announced his idea for a new-product vice president, the existing vice presidents each came up with six or seven reasons why the new arrangement might not work. Their objections grew louder and louder until the president shelved the new job idea.

In another example, a manufacturing company traditionally employed a large group of personnel people as counselors to production employees. This group of counselors exhibited high morale because of the professional satisfaction they received from the helping relationships they had with employees. When a new performance-appraisal system was installed, the personnel people were required to provide each employee's supervisor with a written evaluation of the employee's emotional maturity, promotion potential, and so on, every six months. As some personnel people immediately recognized, the change would alter their relationship with most employees—from a peer helper to more of a boss/evaluator. Predictably, they resisted the new system. While publicly arguing that the new system was not as good for the company as the old one, they privately put as much pressure as possible on the personnel vice president until he significantly altered the new system.

Political behavior emerges in organizations because what is in the best interests of one individual or group is sometimes not in the best interests of the total organization or of other individuals and groups. The consequences of organizational change efforts often are good for some people and bad for others. As a result, politics and power struggles often emerge through change efforts.

While this political behavior sometimes takes the form of two or more armed camps publicly fighting it out, it usually is subtle. In many cases, it occurs completely under the surface of public dialogue. In a similar way, although power struggles are sometimes initiated by scheming and ruthless individuals, they are fostered more often by those who view their potential loss as an unfair violation of their implicit, or psychological, contract with the organization.[5]

Misunderstanding and a Lack of Trust

People also resist change when they incorrectly perceive that it might cost them considerably more than they will gain. Such situations often occur when people are unable to understand the full implications of a change or when trust is lacking in the change initiator–employee relationship.[6]

For example, when the president of a small midwestern company announced to his managers that the company would implement a flexible work schedule for all employees, it never occurred to him that he might run into resistance. He had been introduced to the concept at a management seminar and decided to use it to make working conditions at his company more attractive, particularly to clerical and plant personnel. Shortly after the announcement to his managers, numerous rumors began to circulate among plant employees—none of whom really knew what flexible working hours meant and many of whom were distrustful of the manufacturing vice president. One rumor suggested that flexible hours meant that most people would have to work whenever their supervisors asked them to—including weekends and evenings. The employee association, a local union, held a quick meeting and then presented the management with a nonnegotiable demand that the flexible hours concept be dropped. The president, caught completely by surprise, decided to drop the issue.

Few organizations can be characterized as having a high level of trust between employees and managers; consequently, it is easy for misunderstandings to develop when change is introduced. Unless misunderstandings are surfaced and clarified quickly, they can lead to resistance.

Different Assessments of the Situation

Another common reason people resist organizational change is that their analysis of the situation differs from that of persons initiating the change. In such cases, their analysis typically sees more costs than benefits resulting from the change, for themselves and for their company.

For example, the president of one moderate-sized bank was shocked by his staff's analysis of their real estate investment trust (REIT) loans. Their complex analysis suggested that the bank could easily lose up to $10 million and that possible losses were increasing each month by 20 percent. Within a week, the president drew up a plan to reorganize the bank division that managed REITs. However, because of his concern for the bank's stock price, he chose not to release the staff report to anyone except the new REIT section manager. The reorganization immediately ran into massive resistance from the people involved. The group sentiment, as articulated by one person, was "Has he gone mad? Why is he tearing apart this section of the bank? His actions have already cost us three very good people [who quit] and have crippled a new program we were implementing [which the president was unaware of] to reduce our loan losses."

Persons who initiate change sometimes incorrectly assume that they have all relevant information required to conduct an adequate organizational analysis. They often assume that persons affected by the change have the same basic facts, when they do not. In either case, the difference in information that groups work with often leads to differences in analysis, which can lead to resistance. Moreover, insofar as the resistance is based on a more accurate analysis of the situation than that held by persons initiating the change, that resistance is good for the organization, a fact that is not obvious to some managers who assume resistance is always bad.[7]

Fear

People sometimes resist change because they know or fear they will not be able to develop the new skills and behaviors required. All human beings are limited in their ability to change their behavior, with some people more limited than others.[8] Organizational change can inadvertently require people to change too much, too quickly. When such a situation occurs, people typically resist the change—sometimes consciously but often unconsciously.

Peter Drucker has argued that the major obstacle to organization growth is managers' inability to change their attitudes and behaviors.[9] In many cases, he points out, corporations grow to a certain point and then slow down or stop growing because key managers are unable to change as rapidly as their organizations. Even if they intellectually understand the need for changes in how they operate, they sometimes cannot make the transition.

All people who are affected by change experience some emotional turmoil because change involves loss and uncertainty—even changes that appear positive or "rational."[10]

For example, a person who receives a more important job as a result of an organizational change will probably be happy. But, it is possible that such a person feels uneasy. A new and different job will require new and different behavior, new and different relationships, and the loss of some current activities and relationships that provide satisfaction. It is common under such circumstances for a person to emotionally resist giving up certain aspects of the current situation.

Still Other Reasons

People also sometimes resist organizational change to save face; to go along with the change would be an admission that some of their previous decisions or beliefs were wrong. They may resist because of peer pressure or because of a supervisor's resistant attitude. Indeed, there are many reasons why people resist change.[11]

Because of all the reasons for resistance to organizational change, it is hardly surprising that organizations do not automatically and easily adapt to environmental, technological, or strategic changes. Indeed, organizations usually adapt only because managers successfully employ strategies and tactics for dealing with potential resistance.

TACTICS FOR DEALING WITH RESISTANCE

Managers may use a number of tactics to deal with resistance to change. These include education/communication, participation, facilitation and support, negotiation, co-optation, coercion, and manipulation.[12]

Education/Communication

One of the most common ways to deal with resistance to change is education and communication. This tactic is aimed at helping people see the need for and logic of a change. It can involve one-on-one discussions, presentations to groups, or memos and reports. For example, as a part of an effort to make changes in a division's structure, measurement system, and reward system, the division manager put together a one-hour audiovisual presentation that explained changes and their reasons for changes. Over a four-month period, he made this presentation a dozen times to groups of 20 or 30 corporate and divisional managers.

Education/communication is ideal when resistance is based on inadequate or inaccurate information and analysis, especially if the initiators need the resister's help in implementing the change. But, this tactic requires at least a good relationship between the initiators and the others, or the resisters may not believe what they hear. It also requires time and effort, particularly if many people are involved.

Participation

Participation as a change tactic implies that the initiators involve the resisters or potential resisters in some aspect of the design and implementation of the change. For example, the head of a small financial services company once created a task force to help design and implement changes in the company's reward system. The task force was composed of eight second- and third-level managers from different parts of the company. The president's specific request was that they recommend changes in the company's benefits package. They were given six months and were asked to file a brief progress report with the president once a month. After making their recommendations, which the president largely accepted, they were asked to help the firm's personnel director implement them.

Participation is a rational choice of tactics when change initiators believe they do not have all the information they need to design and implement a change or when they need the wholehearted commitment of others in implementing a change. Considerable research has demonstrated that participation generally leads to commitment, not just compliance.[13] But participation has drawbacks. It can lead to a poor solution if the process is not carefully managed, and it can be time consuming.

Facilitation and Support

Another way for managers to deal with potential resistance to change is through facilitation and support. As a tactic, it might include providing training in new skills, giving employees time off after a demanding period, or simply listening and providing emotional support.

For example, one rapidly growing electronics company did the following to help people adjust to frequent organizational changes. First, it staffed its human resource department with four counselors who spent most of their time talking to people who were feeling "burned out" or who were having difficulty adjusting to new jobs.

Second, on a selective basis, it offered people "minisabbaticals," which were four weeks in duration and involved some reflective or educational activity away from work. Finally, it spent money on in-house education and training programs.

Facilitation and support are best suited for resistance due to adjustment problems. The basic drawback of this approach is that it can be time consuming and expensive and still fail.[14]

Negotiation

Negotiation as a change tactic involves buying out active or potential resisters. This could mean, for example, giving a union a higher wage rate in return for a work rule change, or it could involve increasing an individual's pension benefits in return for early retirement.

Effective use of negotiation as a change tactic can be seen in the activities of a division manager in a large manufacturing company. The divisions in this company were highly interdependent. One division manager wanted to make some major changes in the division's organization. Yet, because of interdependencies, she recognized that she would be forcing some inconvenience and change on other divisions. To prevent top managers in other divisions from undermining her efforts, she negotiated with each division a written agreement that promised certain positive outcomes (for them) within certain time periods as a result of her changes and, in return, specified certain types of cooperation expected from the divisions during the change process. Later, whenever other divisions began to complain about changes or the process, she pulled out the negotiated agreements.

Negotiation is particularly appropriate when it is clear that someone will lose out as a result of a change and yet has significant power to resist. As a result, it can be an easy way to avoid major resistance in some instances. Like the other tactics, negotiation may become expensive—and a manager who once makes it clear that he or she will negotiate to avoid resistance opens up the possibility of being blackmailed by others.[15]

Co-optation

A fifth tactic managers use to deal with potential or actual resistance to change is co-optation. Co-opting an individual usually involves giving him or her a desirable role in the design or implementation of the change. Co-opting a group involves giving one of its leaders, or someone it respects, a key role in the design or implementation of a change. A change initiator could, for example, try to co-opt the sales force by allowing the sales manager to be privy to the design of the changes and by seeing that the most popular salesperson gets a raise as part of the change.

To reduce the possibility of corporate resistance to an organizational change, one division manager in a large multibusiness corporation successfully used co-optation in the following way. He invited the corporate human relations vice president, a close friend of the president's, to help him and key staff analyze some division problems. Because of his busy schedule, the corporate VP was not able to do much information gathering or analysis, thus limiting his influence on the diagnoses. But, his presence at key meetings helped commit him to the diagnosis and the solution designed by the group. The commitment was subsequently important because the president, at least initially, did not like some of the proposed changes. Nevertheless, after discussion with his human resource VP, he did not try to block them.

Co-optation can, under certain circumstances, be an inexpensive and easy way to gain an individual's or a group's support (less expensive, for example, than negotiation and quicker than participation). Nevertheless, it has drawbacks. If people feel they are being tricked into not resisting, they may respond negatively. And, if they use their ability to influence the design and implementation of changes in ways that are not in the best interests of the organization, they can create serious problems.

Manipulation

Manipulation, in this context, refers to covert influence attempts. Co-optation is a form of manipulation. Other forms do not have specific names but involve, for instance, the selective use of information and the conscious structuring of events so as to have some desired (but covert) impact on participants.

Manipulation suffers from the same drawbacks as co-optation, but to a greater degree. When people feel they are not being treated openly or that they are being lied to, they often react negatively. Nevertheless, manipulation can be used successfully—particularly when all other tactics are not feasible or have failed.[16] With one's back to the wall, with inadequate time to use education, participation, or facilitation, and without the power or other resources to use negotiation, coercion, or co-optation, a manager might resort to manipulating information channels to scare people into thinking there is a crisis coming that they can avoid only by change.

Coercion

The seventh tactic managers use to deal with resistance is coercion. They essentially force people to accept a change, explicitly or implicitly threatening them with the loss of jobs, promotion possibilities, raises, or whatever else they control. Like manipulation, coercion is a risky tactic because people resent forced change. Yet, coercion has the advantage of overcoming resistance quickly. And, in situations where speed is essential, this tactic may be the only alternative.

For example, when assigned to "turn around" a failing division in a large conglomerate, the chosen manager relied mostly on coercion to achieve the organizational changes she desired. She did so because she felt, "I did not have enough time to use other methods and I needed to make changes that were pretty unpopular among many of the people."

Using Change Tactics

Effective organizational change efforts are almost always characterized by the skillful use of a number of these change tactics. Conversely, less effective change efforts usually involve the misuse of one or more of these tactics.

Managers sometimes misuse change tactics simply because they are unaware of the strengths and limitations of each tactic (see Figure A). Sometimes they run into difficulties because they rely only on the same limited number of tactics regardless of the situation (e.g., they always use participation and persuasion or coercion and manipulation).[17] Sometimes they misuse the tactics simply because they are not chosen and implemented as a part of a clearly considered change strategy.

Tactic	Best for	Advantages	Drawbacks
Education/ communication	Resistance based on lack of information or inaccurate information and analysis.	Once persuaded, people will often help with implementing the change.	Can be very time consuming if large numbers of people are involved.
Participation	Situations in which initiators do have all the information needed to design the change and where others have considerable power to resist.	People who participate will be committed to implementing change. Any relevant information they have will be integrated into the change plan.	Can be time consuming. Participators could design an inappropriate change.
Facilitation and support	Dealing with people who are resisting because of adjustment problems.	No other tactic works as well with adjustment problems.	Can be time consuming, expensive, and still fail.
Negotiation	Situations where someone or some group will lose in a change and where they have considerable power to resist.	Sometimes it is an easy way to avoid major resistance.	Can be too expensive in many cases. Can alert others to negotiate for compliance.
Co-optation	Specific situations where the other tactics are too expensive or are not feasible.	Can help generate support for implementing a change (but less than participation).	Can create problems if people recognize the co-optation.
Manipulation	Situations where other tactics will not work or are too expensive.	Can be a quick and inexpensive solution to resistance problems.	Costs initiators some credibility. Can lead to future problems.
Coercion	When speed is essential and the change initiators possess considerable power.	Speed. Can overcome any kind of resistance.	Risky. Can leave people angry with the initiators.

FIGURE A Tactics for Dealing with Resistance to Change

Change Strategies

In approaching an organizational change situation, managers explicitly or implicitly make strategic choices regarding the speed of the effort, the amount of preplanning, the involvement of others, and the relative emphasis of different change tactics. Successful change efforts are those in which choices are both internally consistent and fit some key situation variables.

The strategic options available to managers exist on a continuum.[18] (See Figure B.) At one end of the continuum, the strategy calls for a rapid implementation of changes, with a clear plan of action and little involvement of others. This type of strategy mows over any resistance and, at the extreme, would involve a fait accompli. At the other end of the continuum, the strategy would call for a slower change process that is less clearly planned from the start and that involves many people in addition to the change initiators. This type of strategy is designed to reduce resistance to a minimum.[19]

With respect to tactics, the farther to the left one operates on the continuum in Figure B, the more one uses coercion and the less one uses other tactics—especially participation. The opposite is true the more one operates to the right on the continuum—less coercion is used and other tactics are used more.

Rapid changes	Slow changes
Clearly planned	Not clearly planned initially
Little involvement of others	Lots of involvement of others
Attempt to overcome any resistance	Attempt to minimize any resistance

Key Situational Variables

- The amount and type of resistance that is anticipated.
- The position of the initiators vis-à-vis the resisters (in terms of power, trust, etc.).
- The locus of relevent data for designing the change and of needed energy for implementing it.
- The stakes involved (e.g., the presence or absence of a crisis, the consequences of resistance and lack of change).

FIGURE B Strategic Options for the Management of Change

Exactly where a change effort should be strategically positioned on the continuum in Figure B is a function of four key variables:

1. *The amount and type of resistance anticipated.* The greater the anticipated resistance, other factors being equal, the more appropriate it is to move toward the right on the continuum.[20] The greater the anticipated resistance, the more difficult to simply overwhelm it and the more one needs to find ways to reduce it.
2. *The position of the initiator vis-à-vis the resisters, especially regarding power.* The greater the initiator's power, the better the initiator's relationships with the others; and the more the others expect that the initiator might move unilaterally, the more one can move to the left on the continuum.[21] On the other hand, the weaker the initiator's position, the more he or she is forced to operate to the right.
3. *The locus of relevant data for designing the change and of needed energy for implementing it.* The more the initiators anticipate they will need information from others to help design the change and commitment from them to help implement it, the more they must move to the right.[22] Gaining useful information and commitment requires time and the involvement of others.
4. *The stakes involved.* The greater the short-run potential for risks to organizational performance and survival, the more one must move to the left.

Organizational change efforts that are based on an inconsistent strategy, or ones that do not fit the situation, run into predictable problems. For example, an effort that is not clearly planned but quickly implemented will almost always have unanticipated problems. Efforts that attempt to involve large numbers of people and at the same time try to move quickly will always sacrifice either speed or involvement. Efforts in which the change initiators do not have all the information that they need to correctly design a change but which nevertheless move quickly and involve few others sometimes encounter enormous problems.

IMPLICATIONS FOR MANAGING ORGANIZATIONAL CHANGE

Organizational change efforts are aided by an analysis and planning process composed of the following three phases:

1. Conducting a thorough organizational analysis—one that identifies the current situation, any problems, and the forces that are possible causes of problems. The analysis must clearly specify:
   a. The actual significance of the problems.
   b. The speed with which the problems must be addressed if additional problems will be avoided.
   c. The types of changes needed.
2. Conducting a thorough analysis of factors relevant to implementing the necessary changes. This analysis focuses on questions of:
   a. Who might resist the changes, why, and to what extent.
   b. Who has information that is needed to design the change and whose cooperation is essential in implementing it.
   c. The position of the change initiator vis-à-vis other relevant parties in terms of power, trust, normal modes of interaction, and so forth.
3. Selecting a change strategy based on the analysis in Phases 1 and 2, a set of change tactics, and then designing an action plan that specifies:
   a. What must be done.
   b. By whom.
   c. In what sequence.
   d. Within what time frame.

When initiating and managing an organizational change, it is conceivable that some or all of these steps will need to be repeated if unforeseen events occur or if new and relevant information surfaces. At the extreme, in a highly participative change, the process might be repeated a dozen times over a period of months or years. The key to successful organizational change is not whether these steps are repeated once or many times but whether they are done competently and thoroughly.

NOTES

1. See Michael Beer, *Organization Change and Development,* Scott, Foresman and Company, 1980; Richard Beckhard and Reuben T. Harris, *Organizational Transitions,* Addison-Wesley Publishing Company, 1987; and Rosabeth Kanter, *The Change Masters,* Simon and Schuster, 1983, for three examples.
2. Michael Beer, *Organizational Change and Development,* Scott, Foresman and Co., 1980.
3. Rosabeth Kanter, *The Change Masters,* Simon and Schuster, 1983.
4. For a discussion of power and politics in corporations, see Abraham Zaleznik and Manfred F. R. Kets De Vries, *Power and the Corporate Mind* (Boston: Houghton Mifflin, 1975), chap. 6; and Robert H. Miles, *Macro Organizational Behavior* (Santa Monica, Calif.: Goodyear Publishing, 1978), chap. 4.
5. Edgar Schein, *Organizational Psychology* (Englewood Cliffs, N.J.: Prentice Hall, 1965), p. 44.

6. See Chris Argyris, *Intervention Theory and Method* (Reading, Mass.: Addison-Wesley Publishing, 1970), p. 70.
7. See Paul R. Lawrence, "How to Deal with Resistance to Change," *Harvard Business Review,* May–June 1954.
8. For a discussion of resistance that is personality based, see Goodwin Watson, "Resistance to Change," in *The Planning of Change,* ed. Warren Bennis, Kenneth Benne, and Robert Chin (New York: Holt, Rinehart & Winston, 1969), pp. 489–93.
9. *The Practice of Management* (New York: Harper & Row, 1954).
10. See Robert Luke, "A Structural Approach to Organizational Change," *Journal of Applied Behavioral Science,* 1973.
11. For a general discussion of resistance and reasons for it, see Gerald Zaltman and Robert Duncan, *Strategies for Planned Change* (New York: John Wiley & Sons, 1977), chap. 3.
12. There are many ways to label change tactics. This list of seven tactics is one useful approach. Other writers use variations of this list.
13. See, for example, Alfred Marrow, David Bowers, and Stanley Seashore, *Management by Participation* (New York: Harper & Row, 1967).
14. Zaltman and Duncan, *Strategies for Planned Change,* chap. 4.
15. For an excellent discussion of negotiation, see Gerald Nierenberg, *The Art of Negotiating* (New York: Cornerstone, 1974).
16. See John P. Kotter, "Power, Dependence, and Effective Management," *Harvard Business Review,* July–August 1997, pp. 133–35.
17. Ibid., pp. 135–36.
18. See Larry E. Greiner, "Patterns of Organizational Change," *Harvard Business Review,* May–June 1967; and Larry E. Greiner and Louis B. Barnes, "Organization Change and Development," in *Organization Change and Development,* ed. Gene Dalton and Paul Lawrence (Homewood, Ill.: Richard D. Irwin, 1970), pp. 3–5.
19. For a good discussion of an approach that attempts to minimize resistance, see Renato Tagiuri, "Notes on the Management of Change," Working Paper, Harvard Business School.
20. Jay Lorsch, "Managing Change," pp. 676–78.
21. Ibid.
22. Ibid.

APPENDIX A

Small Group Presentations to an Audience

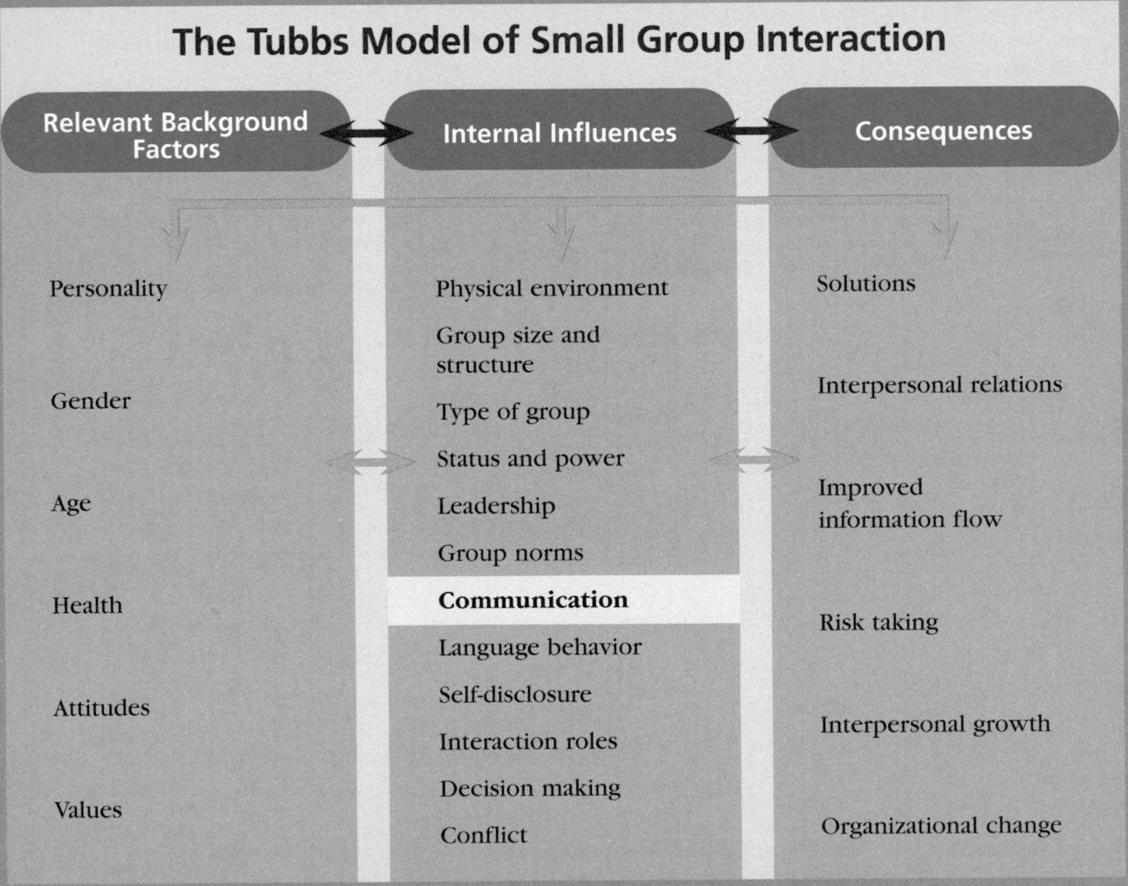

Concepts in **boldface** in gray panels are the emphases of this appendix.

Preview

Appendix A discusses the three major forms of group presentations: the panel discussion, the symposium, and the forum. It also offers some practical advice for preparing an oral presentation. The steps in preparing an oral presentation are (1) determine your purpose, (2) determine your topic, (3) analyze your audience, (4) gather supporting materials, (5) organize your materials, (6) prepare visual aids, and (7) practice your delivery.

Glossary

Forum Discussion A group presentation in which audience members have an opportunity to ask questions and comment on panel members' presentations.

Symposium Discussion A group presentation where individual speakers give presentations in front of an audience. It is more structured than a panel discussion and may also be followed by a forum discussion.

Small Group Presentations to an Audience

The vast majority of your small group discussions will be private, involving only the members of your group. However, on some occasions, you may be asked to present your group's recommendations to a larger audience. In fact, some groups are designed to conduct their discussions in front of an audience. Think of the many examples you see on television each week. These can be excellent models for both what to do and what not to do. There are three small group presentation formats that will be discussed in the following sections: (1) panel discussions, (2) symposium presentations, and (3) forum discussions.

PANEL DISCUSSIONS

A panel discussion is basically a conversation in front of an audience. Think of the ABC Sunday morning talk show *This Week* with Christiane Amanpour. This is a modified version of a panel discussion. It has one moderator, Christiane Amanpour, who introduces the panel members, presents the topic, and leads the discussion. Often the panel members will have some special area of expertise, or they may hold opposing opinions on the topic. Past panel members have included George Will, a syndicated news columnist who usually has a Republican viewpoint, and Cokie Roberts, an ABC News analyst who is also a Republican. Their roundtable also includes Donna Brazile, who is a Democrat, and Ron Brownstein also a Democrat. As moderator, Amanpour often asks questions and tries to allow each person an opportunity to speak. Amanpour also acts as a gatekeeper or conversational "traffic cop." She may ask clarifying questions or may restate issues needing further clarification. She usually makes some closing remarks at the end of the discussion as well.

Because of the spontaneous nature of the discussion, it is usually interesting and can be quite lively for both panelists and audience members. Panelists should feel free to disagree with one another. That is one of the advantages of this format. However, keep in mind what we said in Chapter 7, and try to avoid having idea opponents become personal opponents. The panel does not lend itself to structured presentations of a group's recommendation, so this format is seldom used for problem-solving groups.

When you participate in a panel discussion, keep in mind that you should prepare for the presentation much as you would any public communication event. Although you will be speaking impromptu, you should know the topic, conduct the appropriate background research, study the major issues, identify some of the reasoning on both sides of any controversy, and jot down any key points that you would like to make during the discussion. Each panel member should plan to participate as evenly as possible. It is important that members help the moderator balance member participation.

SYMPOSIUM PRESENTATIONS

A symposium is much more structured than a panel discussion. It consists of a moderator and several speakers seated in front of an audience. The moderator introduces the topic and each of the speakers. The topic is divided into segments, and each speaker gives an uninterrupted speech on one portion of the topic. In a symposium, as in a panel discussion, speakers are informing or, in some cases, persuading members of the audience. The symposium format is often used in classes for group reports. Each speaker could, for example, give his or her view on violence in public schools. One speaker could discuss the role of the family. Another could discuss preventative methods such as guidelines for student tolerance. Another could discuss the role of guns and gun control laws. Another could discuss various security methods used. In each case, each presentation should be carefully planned. Each speaker should coordinate his or her presentation with the others to ensure that all the important aspects of the topic are covered.

PRACTICAL TIPS

Jonah Lehrer, in his book, How We Decide (2009) offers the following insights with regard to group problem solving:

- The early stage of problem solving requires *divergent thinking.* This means that the group should try to think of as many different ideas as possible.
- Once the ideas are identified, the second phase of problem solving requires *convergent thinking.* Convergent thinking requires that group members come together in their thinking behind one or more alternative solutions.
- It is important to balance the needs for *divergent* and *convergent* thinking.
- Too little divergent thinking results in shallow analysis of the problem and too few alternatives for consideration.
- Too little convergent thinking results in lack of focus and follow through.
- Too much divergent thinking has the same result as too little convergent thinking.
- Too much convergent thinking results in what is commonly referred to as *group-think.* For more on this, see www.hbsp.harvard.edu.

Symposium presentations are sometimes followed by a forum discussion. This allows audience members to interact with the discussants and to raise questions not covered in the presentations. It also allows presenters to address comments and questions to the other speakers.

FORUM DISCUSSIONS

A forum is not really a group presentation. Instead, it is a format in which audience members have an opportunity to ask questions and/or to comment on the speaker or speakers' presentations. If you have ever seen the movie *Wall Street,* you will remember the stockholders meeting in which Gordon Gekko, a stockholder played by Michael Douglas, asks questions of the company's board of directors. This is an example of a forum. When the president of the United States holds a press conference, he opens with a prepared statement followed by a question-and-answer period with reporters. This is another example of a forum. Many communities have open forums during which citizens are allowed an opportunity to discuss important issues with city leaders.

One of the important aspects of a forum is to allow all points of view to be heard. Therefore, no one person should be allowed to dominate the "air time." In stockholder meetings like the one described above, companies sometimes have a time limit imposed for each speaker. When the time is up, the microphone is turned off and the next speaker is given the floor. If you ever decide to attend a Board of Regents or Board of Trustees meeting on your campus, you will probably find that there is an open forum scheduled on the agenda, with a time limit given to each speaker. Sometimes forum participants are required to submit questions in advance of the meeting. In other situations, the participant needs to simply request the opportunity to ask questions or to make comments. One of the most exciting forums I ever witnessed on a campus was when students organized a campaign to encourage the Board of Regents to support a proposal for a new library. Several years later, the library opened and was dubbed a "cybrary" because it was so much more electronic than the traditional library it replaced. But the sincere, constructive, and eloquent comments from the students were the powerful catalyst for this wonderful new campus building.

TECHNOLOGY AND PRESENTATIONS

Technology is utilized in almost all presentations given within organizations today. Panel discussions, symposium presentations, and forum discussions can all occur utilizing multimedia technology. For example, many organizations utilize videoconferencing centers to have meetings and give presentations to individuals across the globe. These high-tech centers contain multiple microphones, cameras, scanners, and presentation technologies to give life to the meeting across distance. In videoconferencing, a television projects images for the presentation. Here, several aesthetic elements need to be considered. First, videoconferencing on the computer screen has an *aspect ratio*. Aspect ratio refers to the proportion and orientation of the images on the screen. If you are attempting to show something that is too vertical or horizontal, your viewers will not benefit. Second is *color choice*. The color red does not work well as backgrounds for videoconference material. Dark letters against light backgrounds are usually the best bet. If you are utilizing *document cameras* to show sequential loose documents, make sure to number your documents. Failing to do so can result in confusion if the pages become mixed up. Finally, you should *test* the microphones or speaker phone to make sure that they are working effectively and that they are placed in the most useful manner (Twice, 2003).

Many organizations conduct "webinars" and utilize the virtual space as a common ground for group members across the globe. PowerPoint is currently the medium most utilized for webinars. PowerPoint webinars can be a very useful tool if used correctly. First, as speaker, you must remember that the medium is intended to reinforce your critical points. Graphics that are too complex or intriguing may distract your audience from your message (Feierman, 2005). Second, webinars can often sound scripted unless steps are taken to make them more natural, to give them a face-to-face feel. There are training programs available such as those hosted by Coreography (Rosario, 2003) that actually help companies gain this face-to-face feel in webinars. The demand in this area of expertise is growing.

Many media technologies are also used in the original face-to-face meeting. In this setting, the presenter must make sure not to hide behind the computer or stand in front of the screen. The presentation must be in order and contain clear and concise information that supplements the speech. Last, the presenter must make sure to have a backup plan in case of power failure (PowerPublicSpeaking, 2001).

Preparing an Oral Presentation

There are seven steps that you need to follow in preparing an oral presentation. If you follow these, you will find it less threatening and difficult than you might have imagined. Most people feel less than energized about the thought of speaking in front of an audience, and many are downright uncomfortable with the idea. The more thoroughly you prepare, the easier it will be.

DETERMINE YOUR PURPOSE

Typically, presentations serve one of four purposes: to inform, to entertain, to persuade, or to actuate. The informative presentation emphasizes increasing the audience members' knowledge and understanding of the topic. The presentation to entertain is less often used. However, you may be called upon occasionally to "roast" or to "toast" someone. The persuasive presentation attempts to convince or to influence people's opinion. If you have ever tried this, you know that it is often a formidable task. The hardest purpose is to actuate, that is, to convince someone to actually do something. A salesperson tries to convince us to buy something. A politician tries to get us to vote for him or her. A doctor tries to get us to lose weight or to exercise more. All of these are attempts to get us to act. The first step is to decide which of the four is the primary purpose of your presentation.

DETERMINE YOUR TOPIC

Sometimes your topic will be assigned to you. This is especially likely in a classroom situation or on the job. However, if you have the choice of selecting a topic, one

PRACTICAL TIPS

What Audiences Want

All audiences are different, but there are some expectations that all audiences have in common. Awareness of these expectations will help you in your oral presentation to any audience. PowerPublicSpeaking (2001) lists these audience expectations:

- The audience wants to learn something previously unknown.
- The audience wants you to be yourself during the presentation.
- The audience wants to be respected.
- The audience wants to feel secure and comfortable.
- The audience wants to understand what you are saying.
- The audience wants to be told the truth.
- The audience expects you to follow through on your promises.
- The audience wants an agenda and a finish time that is honored.

of the best ways is to brainstorm several possible subjects or topics. Think of your experiences. It is much easier to talk about things that you have personally experienced than about things that are unfamiliar to you. Once you have decided on a general subject—health, for example—you need to narrow your subject to fit the time allowed. Perhaps you would like to discuss health problems associated with weight. This may still be too broad. You might want to pick one particular disorder, such as anorexia nervosa. Keep in mind that it is important to pick a topic that is of interest to your audience and then to narrow the topic to fit your time limitations.

ANALYZE YOUR AUDIENCE

What are your audience demographics? Are they mostly college age or older? Are they educators or businesspeople? Are they mostly from one geographic location or from all over the country or the world? Are they from all kinds of professions, or are they all from one type of profession, such as social workers? Just about all audiences have some reason for attending the event. Can you determine what are their reasons and interests from their demographics? From these known characteristics, you can make deductions about their beliefs, attitudes, and values. Thinking about the audience ahead of time will allow you to try to establish "common ground" with them. It is always important to adapt your presentation to fit the audience. You can often accomplish this with a story, joke, or comment that identifies you with them. For example, Senator John McCain of Arizona spoke to several veterans groups in his bid for the presidency in 2000. According to one source, McCain said, "I wanted to join the Marine Corps when I graduated from the Naval Academy. But they turned me down when they learned my parents were MARRIED" (loud guffaws from the Army and Navy vets) (Perry, 1999, p. A28).

Audience trust in the speaker is absolutely critical to effective presentations. Dr. Steve Boyd (2005) of the Presenters University says that the one tenet of presenting that should never be ignored is to "treat each audience member as you would like to be treated if you were in your audience."

GATHER SUPPORTING MATERIALS

The difference between a 3-minute and a 30-minute presentation is in how many supporting materials you use. The supporting materials will often make the speech come alive. The audience may not remember exactly what you said, but they will remember how you made them feel. Supporting materials include the examples, statistics, quotations, and analogies.

Examples

The use of examples is so much a part of daily conversation that we may forget that this is one of the best types of supporting materials for a speech. If you were talking about air safety, you might use the examples of the deaths of John F. Kennedy, Jr., his wife Caroline, and her sister to illustrate a tragic plane crash that all of your audience members could relate to. The more vivid the examples, the more likely they are to stay in the minds of your listeners. If you are talking about world conflict, what better example than to discuss war-torn Iraq? The most effective examples will be the ones that listeners can relate to from their own personal experience.

Statistics

Sometimes numbers can be used to make points in a dramatic way. For example, 80 percent of college students log onto the Internet every day, or 50 percent of all marriages end in divorce. You may have even heard in your college orientation that you could look to your left and look to your right, and only one of the three of you would be sitting at graduation four years from now. Statistics lend themselves to graphic presentation in line diagrams, bar graphs, and pie charts. These are natural ways to introduce visual aids and computer graphics into your presentation. Visual aids also increase listener attention and interest. A very effective way to use statistics is to relate them to the audience in the room. For example, you could say, "Statistically, half of you in this room will have your marriage end in divorce."

Quotations

Sometimes, people have said things in such an eloquent way that we can use some of their words to make the point more dramatically. Mark Antony's famous quote in *Julius Caesar,* "Friends, Romans, countrymen, lend me your ears," is one such example. If you want to make an emotional appeal, it is sometimes effective to quote passages that the audience may already be familiar with. The funeral speech of W. H. Auden, used in the movie *Four Weddings and a Funeral,* is a well-known example.

> He was my North, my South, my East and West.
> My working week and my Sunday rest;
> My noon, my midnight, my talk, my song;
> I thought that love would last forever; I was wrong.

As you can see, most of us do not use language so eloquently.

Analogies

A speaker who draws an analogy makes a comparison between two things or situations on the basis of their partial similarities. Analogies help make points in a dramatic way. For example, a college president might say that he was the shepherd of his flock or the captain of the ship. In another analogy, one speaker displayed an advertisement from *Inc.* magazine showing a Jack Russell terrier with his rear leg up in the air, marking a nearby tree. The speaker said, "The Jack Russell terrier marks the tree high up so that other dogs think he is a much bigger dog. When you are in a small business you have to be more innovative." This is referred to as a *figurative analogy,* since a dog is mostly not similar to a small business. So, she is speaking figuratively. A *literal analogy* is a more nearly similar comparison. For example, on the issue of handgun control, former Senator Bill Bradley pointed out that in the United States, in the past year, over 9,000 people had been killed by handguns. In Great Britain, the number was fewer than 10 people. In Japan it was fewer than 10 people. This is a literal analogy or comparison between the countries, implying that the countries should be comparable.

Analogies are very effective, but they can also be refuted if the listener is inclined to be critical. Sooner or later, every analogy breaks down because of the partial similarities between the two things being compared. For example, one faculty member didn't like being compared to a sheep when the university president said that he was the shepherd of his flock. With the handgun comparisons, a member of the National Rifle Association would certainly argue that Japan and Great Britain are very different from the United States and shouldn't be used as a basis for comparison. However, keeping this note of caution in mind, analogies can often be very useful as supporting material.

ORGANIZE YOUR MATERIALS

Most untrained speakers suffer from poor organization. Every speech should have an introduction, body, and conclusion. The introduction is used to gain attention, to lead into your subject, and, if possible, to build rapport with your audience. There are several standard methods for introducing a speech: using humor, asking a question, using a dramatic quotation, using a startling statement, or telling a story.

In the summer of 1999, President Clinton gave a speech to a group at the New York State Fair in Syracuse. He opened his speech this way:

> In 1990, at the state fair, I was thinking about running for a fifth term [as governor] . . . This good old boy in overalls came up to me and said, "Are you going to run again?" I said, "Well if I do, will you vote for me?" He said, "Yes, I guess so, always have." I said, "Well aren't you sick of me after all these years?" He said, "No, I'm not. But everybody else I know is." (*Detroit Free Press,* September 3, 1999, p. A5)

Note how he used self-deprecating humor to build rapport with his audience. This introduction was also good at gaining the listeners' attention. But he still needed to lead into whatever his subject was going to be.

The body of the speech consumes most of your speaking time. This is where your organization needs to be especially strong. There are several standard types of organizational patterns that you can use: chronological, spatial, problem-solution, causal, and topical. The *chronological* method allows you to use time as the organizing method. For example, you could cite the stages of preparing for a wedding. You start with the early preparations of securing a church or synagogue, and then securing the reception hall. Then you must decide on whom to have in the wedding party. Then you buy the dress, rent the tuxedos, order the flowers, decide on the music, and so on. An interesting twist would be to use a reverse chronological order beginning with the latest event and moving backward to the earliest.

The *spatial* method follows positions in space as a method of organizing. For example, you could talk about a trip you took and discuss where you visited. First we went to Paris, then to the Loire valley to tour French castles, then south to the French Riviera, then along the coast from Cannes, east toward Italy to Nice, and then to Monaco.

The *problem-solution* pattern is very useful. In the new campus library example, you could begin by citing the problem mentioned of the overcrowded and out-of-date campus library. Then you could propose a new library with the idea of making it more electronic, thereby connecting it to all the libraries in the world. This is exactly the presentation method that students used on one campus.

The *causal* method refers to the cause-and-effect or effect-to-cause organizational pattern. In discussing student violence in the schools, many speakers have attempted to link what they think are the causes, with the effects being school shootings. Another example would be citing smoking as the cause of cancer of the lips, gums, esophagus, and lungs. There is a great deal of evidence available to support these claims.

The fifth method of organizing is *topical*. With this method, you put together different topics that don't lend themselves to any of the other methods. For example, you could discuss the stages of a group's development: forming, storming, norming, and performing. What's important is that you clearly show how the topics logically flow from one to another.

The body of the presentation also needs to be organized. Organizational patterns usually follow an outline pattern, which looks like this:

- Main point 1
  - Subordinate point 1
    - Supporting materials
  - Subordinate point 2
    - Supporting materials
- Main point 2
  - Subordinate point 1
    - Supporting materials
  - Subordinate point 2
    - Supporting materials
- Main point 3
  - Subordinate point 1
    - Supporting materials
  - Subordinate point 2
    - Supporting materials

The number of main and subordinate points will vary depending on your topic, and the number of supporting materials will vary depending on the amount of time you have for your presentation.

Once you have completed the body of the speech, you need to plan the conclusion. If you are giving an informative speech, then it is often good to go back and review the main points that you want the audience to remember. If you are entertaining, then you probably want to save your very best joke for last. If you are persuading, you may want to end with a gripping story or quote. If your purpose is to actuate, then you can use the conclusion for a final call to action. There is no formula for giving an effective presentation. It is very much an artistic endeavor. What works for one audience may not work for another.

PREPARE YOUR VISUAL AIDS

Most speakers can improve the quality of their presentations by the effective use of visual aids. With PowerPoint this has become much easier than in the past. PowerPoint provides access to color and graphics that used to be much harder to create. One very effective method for using PowerPoint slides is called "Presentation Zen." Based on the book of that title by Garr Reynolds (2008) The rule of thumb is to keep the number of words on each slide to fewer than ten (except for quotes and/or definitions). The following are a few rules of thumb for preparing visual aids:

1. Prepare the aids well in advance and get used to using them.
2. Keep them simple (remember "Presentation Zen").
3. Be sure they can be seen and heard.
4. Make sure that the necessary equipment is available in advance.
5. Be sure the aids really enhance the verbal part of the speech.
6. Talk to your audience and not to the screen.

Keep in mind that the visual aids need to be audience- and situation-specific. What works for one audience may not be appropriate for another. To accommodate all participants, you should utilize your multiple media to meet all audience needs. For example, videos should contain captions, print on slides and in presentations should be reasonably sized, and handouts should be provided. And you should speak clearly and in an audible tone. These elements are key to reaching all members of your audience.

To really gain and hold your audience's attention, you should make your visual aids as interesting and clear as possible. Martin Eppler and Ralph Lengler, professors at the Institute of Corporate Communication at the University of Lugano in Switzerland, have created an extremely helpful online tool that clearly organizes 100 classic types of visual aids. It is similar to the periodic table of the elements used in chemistry (see Jana, 2007; see also http://www.visual-literacy.org/periodic_table/periodic_table.html#).

PRACTICE, PRACTICE, PRACTICE YOUR DELIVERY

Inexperienced speakers underestimate the amount of time and preparation that goes into an effective presentation. When practicing your presentation, you should actually imagine yourself giving the speech and have note cards available to keep you on track (even if you think you don't need them). If you are utilizing multimedia devices for your presentation, make sure that they are working in advance, and prepare backup methods in case of technology failure. Dress to fit the tone of your meeting, and if you are really running short on time, focus on rehearsing the first part of your presentation since catching your audience's attention quickly is critical.

Just remember that ending the presentation is as important as starting it. The ending should remind audience members why they are there and what they have gained from the session. Plan your presentation to have a captivating beginning and a memorable ending, and you will surely impress your points upon your audience.

For a symposium presentation, there are four modes of delivery that can be employed: (1) impromptu, (2) extemporaneous, (3) manuscript, and (4) memorized. The impromptu speech is one in which the speaker does not prepare in advance and tries to think up the presentation on the spot. This is usually not effective. The extemporaneous method is one that is most often recommended by experts. With this method you follow the seven oral presentation steps in this chapter and practice ahead of time. When giving the speech, you use a keyword outline, usually with the notes on note cards. However, you choose the exact words at the time of delivery so that it doesn't become too rehearsed. The manuscript speech requires much too much time and effort to write every word ahead of time. It also has the distinct disadvantage of tying you to reading the manuscript and causes you to lose significant eye contact and spontaneity with the audience. Finally, the memorized speech requires the extensive work of writing the manuscript and then committing it to memory. If you have any speech anxiety at all, you will forget some or all of the speech and will be very disappointed with the results. To maximize the best of all these choices, we strongly encourage you to use the extemporaneous approach.

Finally, no matter how much you plan and practice, you will very likely end up with three different speeches: (1) the one you planned, (2) the one you gave, and (3) the one you wished you had given.

The Adult Learner

When you deliver an oral presentation within the organizational context, you are speaking to an *adult* audience. Adult learners have unique characteristics that enrich discussions and shared learning. The way that adults learn also suggests that certain presentation styles will be more effective. Feierman (2005) makes several statements regarding adult learners that are important to consider:

- Adult learners have various roles and want to understand the practicality and applications of information that they learn.
- Adult learners are interested in outcomes rather than the details leading up to those outcomes.

- Adult learners do not like circuitous presentations and want to get to the bottom line sooner rather than later.
- Adult learners deem time as precious and need to understand the relevance of the meeting or presentation to them.
- Adult learners have a wealth of experience and like to share this experience.

Additionally, all learners tend to remember no more than five key points from any presentation (Feierman, 2005). As noted in the previous sections, analyzing your audience is critical to your success. Is it also very important to diversify your style and your visual aids.

APPENDIX B

Observing Group Process

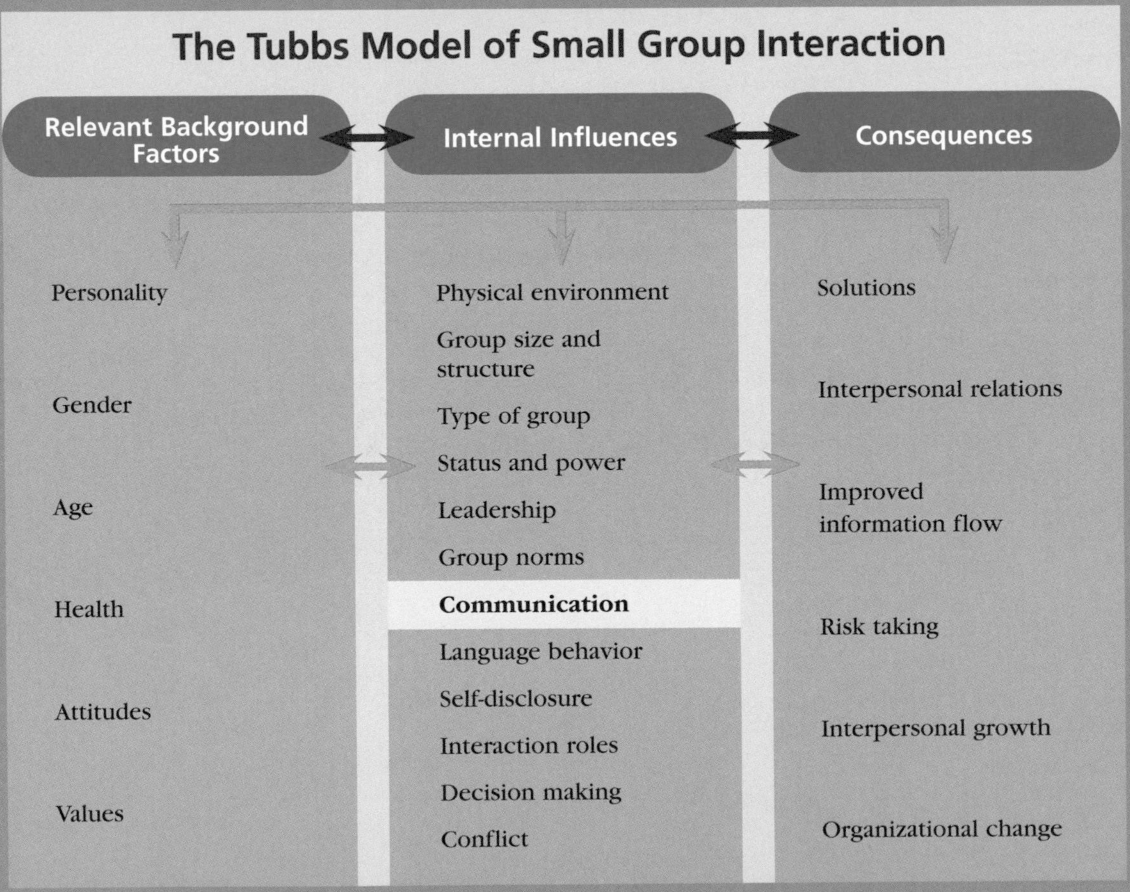

Concepts in **boldface** in gray panels are the emphases of this chapter.

Preview

One of the most intriguing and difficult challenges in learning group dynamics is the phenomenon of learning while doing. When we are engaged in group activities, we are usually fairly absorbed in what is going on (that is, the group's purpose or discussion content). However, to improve our competencies to work and play more effectively in groups, we also need to be able to observe the group's processes. Scholars have worked for years developing instruments designed to help us structure our observations. This appendix is intended to acquaint you with some of the methods for observing groups. As Yogi Berra once said, "You can observe a lot by watching." Once we learn how to better observe group process, our goal is to use those insights to help us perform better in groups.

Perhaps an illustration will help.

I was once in a very intensive group dynamics class that met for a semester and got into some very deep issues about people's feelings, hopes, and dreams for their future. As a result, the group members all developed a high degree of cohesion and team spirit. On the night of the last class, the topic of death and dying seemed to be raised by one person after another. The group's leader then made a very insightful observation. He said, "Do you think it is possible that we are all feeling something about the fact that this class is, in effect, 'dying' tonight? Some of us will go off to other countries, and we may never see each other again."

At first, everyone said that they didn't think that was true. But as with many really penetrating observations about human behavior, one by one the group members started to admit that they did have strong feelings about the class ending that night. So, by observing the group members' behaviors and then by sharing his observation, the leader changed the course of the conversation for the remainder of that last class. This is just one example of how effective group observation can enhance our group experiences.

Glossary

Analyzing Group Process This is a method for group members to report their views of the group's process.

Functional Task Roles of Discussants This is a method of recording which group members made comments that were task-oriented.

Interaction Diagram This is a graphic method for showing who talks to whom in a group discussion.

Participant Rating Scale Form This is a method for group participants to rate their group on a number of different dimensions.

Postmeeting Reaction Form This is a method for allowing participants to assess their view of the group's effectiveness after a meeting.

Progress Report on Group Interaction This is a method for measuring each group member's perceptions of a group meeting.

Self-Centered Roles of Discussants This is a method of recording which group members made comments that were more self-promoting than group promoting.

Socioemotional Roles of Discussants This is a method of recording which group members made comments that were more socially oriented. These comments often build the group members' feelings.

Team Diagnostic Questionnaire This is a method of determining a group's strengths and weaknesses from the viewpoint of the group members.

The Collaborative Team Leader—Leader Version This is a method for team leaders to assess their own group leadership effectiveness.

The Collaborative Team Leader—Team Version This is a method for team members to assess their group leader's effectiveness.

Observation Instruments

All of us benefit from periodic observation and feedback. Imagine how much less fun and interesting it would be if you went bowling and there was a curtain covering the pins so that you couldn't see which pins you knocked down and you couldn't hear any sound from the ball hitting the pins. Similarly, groups often meet and spend countless hours together without benefit of observation, feedback, and modification of their behavior.

The instruments shown in this chapter are designed to structure your observations in such a way as to help you learn more about how your group is performing.

Analyzing Virtual Group Processes—Emerging Research

Research has begun to emerge investigating group processes in the virtual setting. Group processes in virtual groups appear to mirror those in face-to-face group interactions in many cases, but continued research is needed to investigate the nuances between the two group formats. Common sense tells us that virtual group members may have more trouble developing relationships without the face-to-face component, and research has begun to attempt to identify the real issues and recommend solutions to build virtual teams that equal their face-to-face counterparts.

The members of DecisionPoint (2004) believe that there are many pieces to the group process effectiveness puzzle. These include shared goals and vision, clarity in role definition, productive meeting formats, effective and defined leadership, effective conflict resolution, cohesion, and collaboration.

It is commonly thought that virtual groups can lack effectiveness in development of group member relationships, group member roles, and team building without any type of face-to-face interaction. Balthazard, Waldman, Howell, and Atwater (2004) put this idea to the test through the study of differences in processes between virtual teams and face-to-face teams. Balthazard and colleagues concluded that the speculation is correct. Virtual teams are more likely to suffer from a lack of sufficient relationship building between group members, resulting in trust and cohesion issues. These issues affect the group's effectiveness and result in less satisfied group members. Overall, virtual teams must have more clearly outlined processes to make up for the relationship and cohesion gaps in order to perform as effectively as face-to-face teams.

Date ______________			Group ______________		
Time ______________			Observer ______________		
Group Characteristic	**5 Excellent**	**4 Good**	**3 Average**	**2 Fair**	**1 Poor**
Organization of discussion					
Equality of opportunity to speak					
Cooperative group orientation					
Listening to understand					
Evaluation of ideas					
Comments:					

FIGURE AB.1 All-Purpose Discussion Rating Scale
From Galanes, Adams, and Brilhart, 2000 p. 263.

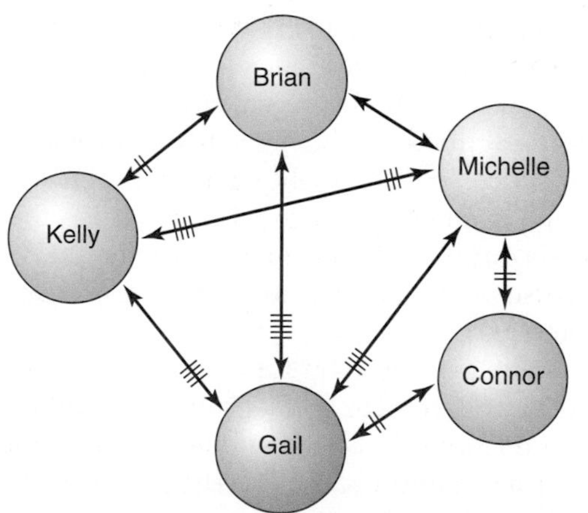

FIGURE AB.2 Interaction Diagram
From Wilson, 2002, pp. 295–96.

Furthermore, Dr. Allan Jeong (2004), assistant professor in instructional systems at Florida State University, proposed a study of virtual group processes through the coding and analysis of email conversational sequences within virtual groups. The purpose of this study was to analyze strings of email; categorize each string as "position statement, agreement, disagreement, argument, negotiation, and evaluation"; and see how the emerging communication patterns mimicked the discussion patterns of face-to-face groups in the pursuit of solutions. Jeong developed a computerized tool to calculate the percentage of each type of conversation string utilized by virtual groups versus face-to-face groups. His conclusions are fascinating. He found that virtual group performance suffers as a result of abbreviated position statement discussions. Virtual groups must spend more time on defining the position statement of the group than they currently do on average in order to be effective. Developing the position statement should involve group member viewpoints, collaboration, and information gathering. Unlike virtual groups, face-to-face groups spend substantial time on this portion of the communication sequence, which leads to higher rates of face-to-face group effectiveness.

So how do we address these issues? They all fall into the categories of communication and cohesion. Young and Coleman (2003) studied *group decision support systems* (GDSS) for virtual groups to enhance communication. You will remember reading about GDSS solutions earlier in this textbook as supplements to face-to-face group interactions. GDSS enables members of groups to report their thoughts and views anonymously, allowing for more open communication. Even in virtual groups, it is always known who is sharing their thoughts based on email addresses and user names. GDSS allows for more open communication, creativity, and collaboration in virtual groups. More importantly, group members do not hold back their views, resulting in more creative and effective solutions. Both virtual and face-to-face group members report higher group member satisfaction ratings when GDSS is utilized. The communication gap is bridged significantly in this case.

However, the problem of cohesion remains. In order to ensure that the virtual group is functioning properly and relationships are built, outside help might be necessary. Most virtual groups require facilitation to ensure that their processes are effective and that they reach their prescribed goals. A facilitator provides assistance in key areas of virtual group processes. She or he can aid the group in building relationships and trust with other members. She or he also helps the group develop ground rules, roles, and accountabilities. The facilitator should be prepared to support group processes, assist with communication, and help channel conflict in a positive direction (White, 2004).

To be successful, the online facilitator must abide by four principles. First, she or he must have knowledge about the differences in facilitation for virtual groups and face-to-face groups and foster relationship and trust building. Second, he or she must understand group organization and processes. Third, she or he must understand the group's purpose. Finally, the facilitator must be prepared with helpful instruments to guide the group to success (White, 2004).

In addition to the facilitator, the virtual group may need members to take on additional roles to ensure effective processes. For example, the "cybrarian" is

Functional Task Roles	Participants' Names							
1. Initiator								
2. Information seeker								
3. Information giver								
4. Opinion seeker								
5. Opinion giver								
6. Elaborator–clarifier								
7. Coordinator								
8. Diagnostician								
9. Orienter								
10. Energizer								
11. Procedural technician								
12. Recorder								
13. Evaluator								

FIGURE AB.3 Functional Task Roles of Discussants
From Wilson, 2002, p. 298. Based on K. D. Benne and P. Sheats (1948).

the virtual group member who researches and provides new information to the group. The "help desk" is the individual who manages the technical aspects of the group and orients new members. The "referee" makes sure that the group's ground rules are followed. The "janitor" helps archive group information and weed out irrelevant topics. These roles are critical, whether formally appointed or naturally assumed. Nevertheless, these roles must be defined in order for the virtual group to benefit from the work that these individuals provide.

Social-emotional Roles	Participants' Names							
1. Supporter-encourager								
2. Harmonizer								
3. Tension releaser								
4. Compromiser								
5. Gatekeeper								
6. Feeling expresser								
7. Standard setter								
8. Follower								

FIGURE AB.4 Functional Socio-Emotional Roles of Discussants

From Wilson, 2002, p. 301. Based on K. D. Benne and P. Sheats (1948).

Self-centered Roles	Participants' Names							
1. Blocker								
2. Aggressor								
3. Deserter								
4. Dominator								
5. Recognition seeker								
6. Self-confessor								
7. Playboy/playgirl								
8. Special-interest pleader								

FIGURE AB.5 Self-Centered Roles of Discussants

From Wilson, 2002, p. 301. Based on K. D. Benne and P. Sheats (1948).

Directions: Use the questions provided in the checklist below to insure that the broad range of possible dynamics are looked for during your observation of a team. Familiarize yourself with this checklist in advance so that you do not miss noticing these things if they arise.

1. **Participation levels**
   Who participated the most? The least? How were the silent members treated? Were there any shifts in participation levels? Who talked to whom?
2. **Leadership**
   Who had the most influence? Over which issues?
   How did various members gain influence?
   Who would you say was the *task* leader?
   Who would you say was the *social* (relationship oriented) leader?
3. **Group roles**
   Who would you say played which of the following task-oriented roles: Idea initiator? Information/opinion giver? Coordinator? Topic gatekeeper? Consensus tester? Clarifier/summarizer? Task accomplishment evaluator?

   Who would you say played which of the following social (relationship oriented) roles: Harmonizer? Person gatekeeper? Encourager/support giver? Team spirit captain? Team member relations evaluator?

   Who would you say played which of the following dysfunctional roles: Avoider? Dominator? Attention seeker? Dependent member? Blocker? Attacker? Clown? Standards reducer? Topic jumper? One upper?
4. **Decision-making procedures**
   What styles of group decision making were used: Self-authorized? Handclasp? Majority rule? Compromise? Consensus?
   Did the group openly decide how it would make its decisions?
5. **Group norms and sanctions**
   Where were ground rules stated? What "rules" (spoken and unspoken) influenced how the group actually worked? What norms were established regarding standards of performance? Group cohesion? Risk taking? What rewards and punishments were used to maintain the group's norms? (Hint: Look for subtle clues, including uses of humor.) What rewards and punishments were used to reinforce changes in the behavior of group members?
6. **Group heterogeneity**
   How did the group celebrate/capitalize on the differences that existed between its members? To what extent did this group make full use of its human resources?
7. **Group procedures**
   Did the group clarify the purpose and agenda for the meeting? Did it follow the agenda? Did the group follow a systematic approach to problem solving? Did the group assign responsibilities to particular individuals to ensure that actions would be taken on decisions made by the group? How was this handled? Did the group manage its time well?
8. **Group effectiveness**
   How well did this group do on its task? Overall, what are the strengths and weaknesses of this group?

FIGURE AB.6 Analyzing Group Process

From Huszczo, 1996, pp. 47–48.

(Quick Scoring Form)

Directions: Each team member should complete this questionnaire. In order to help identify your team's strengths and weaknesses, honest and independent responses of every member of your team are needed. Each person's individual responses will be kept strictly confidential. Each individual will receive a copy of the team's average response to each question and how this team compares with a sample of other teams who have used this instrument.

Name of team: ______________________________

For each of the following items, you will be asked, How true is the statement for your team now? For all items, circle the rating that is currently most accurate for the situation described regarding your team, with 0 not at all, 1 = a little bit, 2 = somewhat, 3 = to a large extent, and 4 = very much.

1a. The goals of our team are appropriate and clearly stated,

0 1 2 3 4

1b. The members of our team are committed to the accomplishment of our shared team goals.

0 1 2 3 4

1c. Our team accomplishes its goals.

0 1 2 3 4

2a. Our team collectively contains the full range of talents we need to be an effective unit.

0 1 2 3 4

2b. The talents of the members of our team are fully utilized.

0 1 2 3 4

3a. The role of leadership is competently fulfilled by one or more people on this team.

0 1 2 3 4

3b. Each member of our team clearly understands the role he or she is to play for us to be an effective unit.

0 1 2 3 4

3c. Each member of our team clearly fulfills the role he or she is expected to play.

0 1 2 3 4

4a. Our team uses effective and efficient procedures to work together to complete our tasks.

0 1 2 3 4

4b. Our team uses effective and efficient procedures to identify and resolve problems as they occur.

0 1 2 3 4

4c. Our team holds effective and efficient meetings.

0 1 2 3 4

FIGURE AB.7 Team Diagnostic Questionnaire
From Huszczo, 1996, pp. 43–45.

4d. Our team uses effective and efficient procedures to ensure that information is shared and received.

0 1 2 3 4

4e. Our team uses effective and efficient planning procedures.

0 1 2 3 4

4f. Our team effectively monitors its progress.

0 1 2 3 4

5a. Our team members deal with conflict in a constructive manner.

0 1 2 3 4

5b. Our team members provide enough support to each other to encourage a sense of belonging to the team.

0 1 2 3 4

5c. Team members provide enough positive challenge to each other to encourage high levels of performance.

0 1 2 3 4

5d. Team members get along with each other quite well.

0 1 2 3 4

6a. Team members provide each other with enough recognition for our working together as a team.

0 1 2 3 4

6b. Our team receives enough recognition from sources outside our team for our working together as a team.

0 1 2 3 4

7a. Our team recognizes and actively pursues opportunities available in its external environment.

0 1 2 3 4

7b. Our team recognizes and actively addresses the threats it is facing in its external environment.

0 1 2 3 4

7c. Our team has good constructive relationships with the other teams and individuals that we interact with.

0 1 2 3 4

Finally, please provide two overall ratings of your team:

8a. Overall, on a 0 to 100 percent scale, how effective would you rate your team?

____

8b. Overall, on a 0 to 100 percent scale, how satisfied are you to be a member of this team?

_______________%

FIGURE AB.7 Team Diagnostic Questionnaire—Continued

True	More True Than False	More False Than True	False	
I. Focus on the Goal				
❑	❑	❑	❑	1. I clearly define our goal.
❑	❑	❑	❑	2. I articulate our goal in such a way as to inspire commitment.
❑	❑	❑	❑	3. I avoid compromising the team's objective with political issues.
❑	❑	❑	❑	4. I help individual team members align their roles and responsibilities with the team goal.
❑	❑	❑	❑	5. I reinforce the goal in fresh and exciting ways.
❑	❑	❑	❑	6. If it's necessary to adjust the team's goal, I make sure the team understands why.
II. Ensure a Collaborative Climate				
❑	❑	❑	❑	7. I create a safe climate for team members to openly and supportively discuss any issue related to the team's success.
❑	❑	❑	❑	8. I communicate openly and honestly.
❑	❑	❑	❑	9. There are no issues that I am uncomfortable discussing with the team.
❑	❑	❑	❑	10. There are no chronic problems within our team that we are unable to resolve.
❑	❑	❑	❑	11. I do not tolerate a noncollaborative style by team members.
❑	❑	❑	❑	12. I acknowledge and reward the behaviors that contribute to an open and supportive team climate.
❑	❑	❑	❑	13. I create a work environment that promotes productive problem solving.
❑	❑	❑	❑	14. I do not allow organization structure, systems, and processes to interfere with the achievement of our team's goal.
❑	❑	❑	❑	15. I manage my personal control needs.
❑	❑	❑	❑	16. I do not allow my ego to get in the way.
III. Build Confidence				
❑	❑	❑	❑	17. I ensure that our team achieves results.
❑	❑	❑	❑	18. I help strengthen the self-confidence of team members.
❑	❑	❑	❑	19. I make sure team members are clear about critical issues and important facts.
❑	❑	❑	❑	20. I exhibit trust by giving team members meaningful levels of responsibility.
❑	❑	❑	❑	21. I am fair and impartial toward all team members.
❑	❑	❑	❑	22. I am an optimistic person who focuses on opportunities.
❑	❑	❑	❑	23. I look for and acknowledge contributions by team members.

FIGURE AB.8 The Collaborative Team Leader—Leader Version

From LaFasto and Larson, 2001, p. 151.

True	More True Than False	More False Than True	False	
IV. Demonstrate Sufficient Technical Know-How				
❑	❑	❑	❑	24. I understand the technical issues we must face in achieving our goal.
❑	❑	❑	❑	25. I have had sufficient experience with the technical aspects of our team's goal.
❑	❑	❑	❑	26. I am open to technical advice from team members who are more knowledgeable than I am.
❑	❑	❑	❑	27. I am capable of helping the team analyze complex issues related to our goal.
❑	❑	❑	❑	28. I am seen as credible and knowledgeable by people outside our team.
V. Set Priorities				
❑	❑	❑	❑	29. I keep the team focused on a manageable set of priorities that will lead to the accomplishment of our goal.
❑	❑	❑	❑	30. Team members and I agree on the top priorities for achieving our goal.
❑	❑	❑	❑	31. I communicate—and reinforce a focus on priorities.
❑	❑	❑	❑	32. I do not dilute the team's effort with too many priorities.
❑	❑	❑	❑	33. If it's necessary to change priorities I make sure the team understands why.
VI. Manage Performance				
❑	❑	❑	❑	34. I make performance expectations clear.
❑	❑	❑	❑	35. I encourage the team to agree upon a set of values that guides our performance.
❑	❑	❑	❑	36. I ensure that rewards and incentives are aligned with achieving our team's goal.
❑	❑	❑	❑	37. I assess the collaborative skills of team members as well as the results they achieve.
❑	❑	❑	❑	38. I give useful, developmental feedback to team members.
❑	❑	❑	❑	39. I am willing to confront and resolve issues associated with inadequate performance by team members.
❑	❑	❑	❑	40. I recognize and reward superior performance.
❑	❑	❑	❑	41. What are my strengths as team leader? ____________________ ____________________ ____________________
❑	❑	❑	❑	42. What one or two changes are most likely to improve my effectiveness as team leader? ____________________ ____________________ ____________________

FIGURE AB.8 The Collaborative Team Leader—Leader Version—Continued

True	More True Than False	More False Than True	False	
I. Focus on the Goal				
❑	❑	❑	❑	1. Our team leader clearly defines our goal.
❑	❑	❑	❑	2. Our team leader articulates our goal in such a way as to inspire commitment.
❑	❑	❑	❑	3. Our team leader avoids compromising the team's objective with political issues.
❑	❑	❑	❑	4. Our team leader helps individual team members align their roles and with the team goal.
❑	❑	❑	❑	5. Our team leader reinforces the goal in fresh and exciting ways.
❑	❑	❑	❑	6. If it's necessary to adjust the team's goal, our team leader makes sure we understand why.
II. Ensure a Collaborative Climate				
❑	❑	❑	❑	7. Our team leader creates a safe climate for team members to openly and supportively discuss any issue related to the team's success.
❑	❑	❑	❑	8. Our team leader communicates openly and honestly.
❑	❑	❑	❑	9. There are no issues that our team leader is uncomfortable discussing with the team.
❑	❑	❑	❑	10. There are no chronic problems within our team that we are unable to resolve.
❑	❑	❑	❑	11. Our team leader does not tolerate a noncollaborative style by team members.
❑	❑	❑	❑	12. Our team leader acknowledges and rewards the behaviors that contribute to an open and supportive team climate.
❑	❑	❑	❑	13. Our team leader creates a work environment that promotes productive problem solving.
❑	❑	❑	❑	14. Our team leader does not allow organization structure, systems, and processes to interfere with the achievement of our team's goal.
❑	❑	❑	❑	15. Our team leader manages his/her personal control needs.
❑	❑	❑	❑	16. Our team leader does not allow his/her ego to get in the way.
III. Build Confidence				
❑	❑	❑	❑	17. Our team leader ensures that our team achieves results.
❑	❑	❑	❑	18. Our team leader helps strengthen the self-confidence of team members.
❑	❑	❑	❑	19. Our team leader makes sure team members are clear about critical issues and important facts.
❑	❑	❑	❑	20. Our team leader exhibits trust by giving us meaningful levels of responsibility.
❑	❑	❑	❑	21. Our team leader is fair and impartial toward all team members.
❑	❑	❑	❑	22. Our team leader is an optimistic person who focuses on opportunities.
❑	❑	❑	❑	23. Our team leader looks for and acknowledges contributions by team members.

FIGURE AB.9 The Collaborative Team Leader—Team Version

From LaFasto and Larson, 2001, p. 153.

True	More True Than False	More False Than True	False	
IV. Demonstrate Sufficient Technical Know-How				
❑	❑	❑	❑	24. Our team leader understands the technical issues we must face in achieving our goal.
❑	❑	❑	❑	25. Our team leader has had sufficient experience with the technical aspects of our team's goal.
❑	❑	❑	❑	26. Our team leader is open to technical advice from team members who are more knowledgeable.
❑	❑	❑	❑	27. Our team leader is capable of helping the team analyze complex issues related to our goal.
❑	❑	❑	❑	28. Our team leader is seen as credible and knowledgeable by people outside our team.
V. Set Priorities				
❑	❑	❑	❑	29. Our team leader keeps our team focused on a manageable set of priorities that will lead to the accomplishment of our goal.
❑	❑	❑	❑	30. Our team leader and the members of our team agree on the top priorities for achieving our goal.
❑	❑	❑	❑	31. Our team leader communicates and reinforces a focus on priorities.
❑	❑	❑	❑	32. Our team leader does not dilute our team's effort with too many priorities.
❑	❑	❑	❑	33. If it's necessary to change priorities our team leader helps us understand why.
VI. Manage Performance				
❑	❑	❑	❑	34. Our team leader makes performance expectations clear.
❑	❑	❑	❑	35. Our team leader encourages the team to agree on a set of values that guides our performance.
❑	❑	❑	❑	36. Our team leader ensures that rewards and incentives are aligned with achieving our team's goal.
❑	❑	❑	❑	37. Our team leader assesses the collaborative skills of team members as well as the results they achieve.
❑	❑	❑	❑	38. Our team leader gives useful, developmental feedback to team members.
❑	❑	❑	❑	39. Our team leader is willing to confront and resolve issues associated with inadequate performance by team members.
❑	❑	❑	❑	40. Our team leader recognizes and rewards superior performance.
❑	❑	❑	❑	41. What are the strengths of the team leader? ______ ______ ______
❑	❑	❑	❑	42. What one or two changes are most likely to improve the effectiveness of the team leader? ______ ______ ______

FIGURE AB.9 The Collaborative Team Leader—Team Version—Continued

Instruction: Circle the number that best indicates your reactions to the following questions about the discussion in which you participated:

1. *Adequacy of Communication.* To what extent do you feel members were understanding each others' statements and positions?

0	1	2	3	4	5	6	7	8	9	10

Talked past each other; Misunderstanding — Communicated directly with each other; Understanding well

2. *Opportunity to Speak.* To what extent did you feel free to speak?

0	1	2	3	4	5	6	7	8	9	10

Never had a chance to speak — Had all the opportunity to talk I wanted

3. *Climate of Acceptance.* How well did members support each other, show acceptance of individuals?

0	1	2	3	4	5	6	7	8	9	10

Highly critical and pushing — Supportive and receptive

4. *Interpersonal Relations.* How pleasant and concerned were members with interpersonal relations?

0	1	2	3	4	5	6	7	8	9	10

Quarrelsome, status differences emphasized — Pleasant, empathic, concerned with persons

5. *Leadership.* How adequate was the leader (or leadership) of the group?

0	1	2	3	4	5	6	7	8	9	10

Too weak or dominating — Shared, group-centered and sufficient

6. *Satisfaction with Role.* How satisfied are you with your participation in the discussion?

0	1	2	3	4	5	6	7	8	9	10

Very dissatisfied — Very satisfied

7. *Quality of Product.* How satisfied are you with the discussions, solutions, or learnings that came out of this discussion?

0	1	2	3	4	5	6	7	8	9	10

Very displeased — Very pleased

8. *Overall.* How do you rate the discussions as a whole apart from any specific aspect of it?

0	1	2	3	4	5	6	7	8	9	10

Awful; waste of time — Superb; time well spent

FIGURE AB.10 Postmeeting Reaction Form

From Galanes, Adams, and Brilhart, 2004, p. 267.

Date ______________________

______________________ Observer ______________________

(Name of participant)

1. Contributions to the *content of the discussions?* (well prepared, supplied information, adequate reasoning, etc.)

5	4	3	2	1
Outstanding Quality and quantity		Fair share		Few or none

2. Contributions to *efficient group procedures?* (agenda planning, relevant comments, summaries, keeping on track)

5	4	3	2	1
Always relevant, Aided organization		Relevant, no aid in order		Sidetracked confused group

3. *Degree of cooperating?* (listening to understand, responsible, agreeable, group centered, open-minded)

5	4	3	2	1
Very responsible				Self-centered

4. *Speaking?* (clear, to group, one point at a time, concise)

5	4	3	2	1
Brief, clear, to group				Vague, indirect, wordy

5. *Value* to the group? (overall rating)

5	4	3	2	1
Most valuable				Least valuable

Suggestions:

FIGURE AB.11 Participant Rating Scale Form

From Galanes, Adams, and Brilhart, 2004, p. 267.

Your code no. or initials: ____________________

Instructions: Please circle the number in front of the phrase which best describes your answer to the particular question.

1. How do I feel about this group as of now?
   a. Worst possible group.
   b. Moderately poor group.
   c. Slightly more poor than good.
   d. Slightly more good than poor.
   e. Moderately good.
   f. Best possible group.
2. How clear were the group's goals today?
   a. Completely unclear.
   b. Moderately unclear.
   c. Slightly more unclear than clear.
   d. Slightly more clear than unclear.
   e. Moderately clear.
   f. Completely clear.
3. How well did the group work at its task?
   a. Coasted, loafed, made no progress.
   b. Made little progress, most loafed.
   c. Progress was slow, spurts of effective work.
   d. Above average in progress and pace work.
   e. Worked well, achieved definite progress.
   f. Worked hard, achieved its goal.
4. To what extent was our discussion up in the clouds, unrealistic, out of this world, or down to earth, practical, and concrete?
   a. Almost completely in the clouds.
   b. Somewhat in the clouds.
   c. A little more in the clouds than down to earth.
   d. A little more down to earth than in the clouds.
   e. Moderately down to earth.
   f. Almost completely down to earth.
5. To what extent did we talk about our own functioning as a group and to what extent did we talk about other topics?
   a. Almost completely on outside problems or topics.
   b. A lot more outside than about ourselves.
   c. A little more outside than about ourselves.
   d. A little more on ourselves than about outside topics.
   e. A lot more ourselves than about outside problems.
   f. Almost all ourselves and our own group.
6. To what extent were group members out to win their own points as opposed to considering the merits of the issue?
   a. Almost completely out to win own points.
   b. Moderately out to win own points.
   c. Slightly more out to win own points than to consider merits of issue.
   d. Slightly more considering merits of issues than out to win own points.
   f. Moderately considering merits of issues.
   g. Almost completely considering merits of issues.
7. To what extent did I have private thoughts and unexpressed feelings and opinions, which I would not feel comfortable in bringing out?
   a. I felt almost completely under wraps.
   b. Somewhat under wraps.
   c. Slightly more under wraps than free and expressive.
   d. Slightly more free and expressive than under wraps.

FIGURE AB.12 Progress Report on Group Interaction

Source: Unknown.

e. Somewhat free and expressive.
f. I felt almost completely free and expressive.

8. Did I get as much help as needed from other members of my group?
   a. No, they disregarded my needs completely.
   b. Disregarded quite a bit.
   c. More disregarded than recognized.
   d. More recognized than disregarded.
   e. Recognized quite a bit.
   f. Almost completely recognized my needs.
9. To what extent did I feel a real part of the group?
   a. Completely a part of the group all the time.
   b. Mostly a part of the group.
   c. A little more a part of the group than outside.
   d. A little more outside of the group than a part.
   e. Mostly on the outside of the group.
   f. Completely on the outside, not part of the group at all.
10. To what extent were the minority views listened to with respect?
    a. Most were disregarded, or ignored.
    b. Some were disregarded.
    c. A few more were disregarded than given serious thought.
    d. A few more were given serious thought than disregarded.
    e. Some were given serious thought.
    f. Most were given serious thought and consideration.
11. How strong were the group's needs to depend on the instructor?
    a. Group has strong need to depend on instructor.
    b. Group has moderately strong need to depend on instructor.
    c. Group has some need to depend on instructor.
    d. Group has little need to depend on instructor.
    e. Group has practically no need to depend on instructor.
    f. Group needs to depend on instructor only as much as on any other member.
12. What did the group generally do when the group was confronted with differences in feelings and ideas?
    a. Denied there were any differences.
    b. Avoided discussion of apparent differences.
    c. Recognized differences but moved to other issues.
    d. Attempted to deal with differences but not openly.
    e. Faced conflicts but could not resolve them.
    f. Faced conflicts and worked them through.
13. How would you characterize the quality of communication in the group?
    a. Very poor, members don't listen to each other and don't understand at all.
    b. Poor, members listen and understand very little.
    c. Slightly more poor than good.
    d. Slightly more good than poor.
    e. Good, members listen some and understand some.
    f. Very good, members really listen to each other and understand.
14. How would you characterize the intellectual level of problem-solving in the group meeting?
    a. Creative, imaginative, logical, critical—can't imagine a better situation.
    b. Highly competent but lacking in some regards.
    c. Routine, ordinary level of problem-solving.
    d. Less than routine level.
    e. Quite incompetent but some good thinking.
    f. Flat, unimaginative, many illogical ideas, uncritical.

FIGURE AB.12 Progress Report on Group Interaction—Continued

Glossary

Acceptance of Solutions There are three different types of solutions for problems: (1) high quality, low acceptance; (2) high acceptance, high quality; and (3) high acceptance, low quality.

Affection Affection refers to the friendship and closeness between people.

Analyzing Group Process This is a method for group members to report their views of the group's process.

Appropriateness Appropriateness includes several factors that help determine the timing and extent of self-disclosure.

Ascribed Status Ascribed status is the prestige that goes to a person by virtue of his or her birth.

Attained Status Attained status is the prestige that goes to a person on the merits of his or her own individual accomplishments.

Attitudes An attitude is a mental state that exerts influence over an individual's behaviors. Attitudes have three components: (1) a cognitive component, which refers to a concept; (2) an affective component, which is emotion; and (3) a behavioral component, which is the readiness to act.

Brainstorming A technique used to generate ideas. It emphasizes brain activity. It can be applied as part of the problem-solving process.

Bypassing Bypassing is a misunderstanding that occurs when "the sender . . . and receiver . . . miss each other with their meaning."

Casual and Social Groups Casual and social groups include neighborhood groups, fraternities, and even classmates. The impact of these relationships on behavior is often quite profound.

Coercive Power Coercive power is the power an individual has to give or withhold punishment.

Communication Networks Communication networks are the five patterns of communicating between group members.

Conflict of Feelings When people's ideas come into conflict, the participants often begin to have negative feelings toward one another. These conflicts of feelings can damage the group's functioning.

Conflict Grid A model of conflict management developed by Robert Blake and Jane Srygley Mouton. It is a framework for developing conflict management skills.

Conflict of Ideas Many ideas are generated in group discussions. Sometimes different people's ideas may conflict. It is important to remember that a variety and diversity of ideas is usually desirable in the process of problem solving.

Conflict Management The ability to manage conflict so that there is a healthy conflict of ideas without the unhealthy conflict of feelings.

Consistency Theories Consistency theories are all based on the assumption that human beings have a strong psychological need for consistency. This is often referred to as a need to maintain cognitive balance.

Content and Process Content of a group discussion includes comments about the *topic* of the discussion. Process is the *manner* in which the discussion is conducted.

Control Control is our need to influence, lead, and develop power over others or to be influenced, be led, or have others exert power over us.

Convergent Thinking A form of thinking in which ideas come together to form a solution.

Cycles A cycle is characterized by the results of group interaction being fed back to the group and becoming input for future interactions. For example, a team's success adds strength to the group's cohesion in future activities.

Defensive–Supportive Communication Defensive communication occurs when a psychological barrier is created, known as a *defense mechanism*. This barrier acts to reduce effective communication. Supportive communication minimizes these types of problems.

Differentiation Differentiation is the specialization that occurs among people in small group communication.

Divergent Thinking A form of thinking in which many different aspects of an idea are explored. Brainstorming is one technique of divergent thinking.

Dynamic Equilibrium Dynamic equilibrium is reached at a point at which the forces to change and the forces to resist change are equal.

Educational Groups Educational groups are groups that interact for the sole purpose of study or instruction.

Emotional Intelligence Personal and interpersonal skills that enable one to induce desired responses in others.

Empowerment Empowerment is a leadership style that enables group members to utilize their talents, abilities, and knowledge more effectively.

Equifinality Equifinality is the potential for adaptation that groups possess. This allows for various possible approaches to achieve a goal.

Expert Power Expert power is our acceptance of influence from those whose expertise we respect.

Feedback Feedback is information groups receive and use to modify themselves.

Fishbone Technique A method of examining cause and effect using a fishbone diagram.

Followership Styles Followership styles are behavioral tendencies people have toward authority figures (for example, obedient versus rebellious).

Forum Discussion A group presentation in which audience members have an opportunity to ask questions and comment on panel members' presentations.

Functional Task Roles of Discussants This is a method of recording which group members made comments that were task-oriented.

Group-Building and Maintenance Roles Group-building and maintenance roles help the interpersonal functioning of the group and alter the way of working by strengthening, regulating, and perpetuating the group.

Group Task Roles Group task roles are identifiable behaviors that are directed toward accomplishing the group's objective.

Groupthink Groupthink refers to the tendency of group members to share common assumptions, which frequently leads to mistakes.

Inclusion Inclusion is our need for belonging, feeling a part of, and being together with others.

Incrementalism The process of making decisions that result in change by increments.

Individual Roles Individual roles are roles that are designed to satisfy an *individual's* needs rather than to contribute to satisfying the needs of the group.

Inference Making Inference making refers to going beyond observations and what we know. Inferences have only a low probability of coming true.

Input Input is the raw material of small group interaction. It includes the six relevant background factors: personality, gender, age, health, attitudes, and values. It also includes information the group receives from outside the group.

Integration Integration in small group communication is synonymous with organization. It is the coordination of the various parts of the group.

Intentional–Unintentional Communication Intentional communication occurs when we communicate what we mean to. Unintentional communication occurs when we communicate something different from what we intend, as when we accidentally offend someone.

Interaction Diagram An interaction diagram is a graphic method for showing who talks to whom in a group discussion.

Kepner-Tregoe Approach A variation of the reflective thinking sequence. Its most important contribution is the way in which a group works through the criteria phase, differentiating between the musts and the wants of a solution.

Legitimate Power Legitimate power is the influence we allow others, such as our bosses, to have over us on the basis of their positions.

Mixed Scanning A decision-making strategy that combines examining a problem comprehensively (the rational approach) and part by part (the incremental approach).

Negative Entropy Entropy is characterized by all systems moving toward disorganization or death. Negative entropies are the forces that maintain the organization of a system.

Output Output includes solutions, interpersonal relations, improved information flow, risk taking, interpersonal growth, and organizational change. It is sometimes called the end result of group interaction.

Participant Rating Scale Form This is a method for group participants to rate their group on a number of different dimensions.

Polarizing Polarizing is the exaggeration that occurs when people attempt to make a point.

Postmeeting Reaction Form This is a method for allowing participants to assess their view of the group's effectiveness after a meeting.

Primary Groups Primary groups are groups that usually include one's family and closest friends.

Problem-Solving Groups Problem-solving groups are groups that form to solve one or more problems.

Progress Report on Group Interaction This is a method for measuring each group member's perceptions of a group meeting.

Quality of Solutions Groups have the potential to make better-quality decisions than the same individuals in those groups would make if working alone.

Referent Power Referent power is based on identification with the source of power—for example, having admiration for someone.

Reflective Thinking Process A pattern for small group problem solving that includes six components:

1. What is the problem?
2. What are its causes and limits?
3. What are the criteria for an acceptable solution?
4. What are the available solutions?
5. What is the best solution?
6. How can it be implemented?

Reward Power Reward power is the power an individual has to give or withhold rewards.

Seating Patterns Seating patterns often affect the type and volume of interaction in a group.

Self-Centered Roles of Discussants This is a method of recording which group members made comments that were more self-promoting than group promoting.

Signal Reactions Signal reactions are learned responses to certain stimuli, such as emotional reactions to offensive swear words or racial slurs.

Socioemotional Roles of Discussants This is a method of recording which group members made comments that were more socially oriented. These comments often build the group members' feelings.

Symposium Discussion A group presentation where individual speakers give presentations in front of an audience. It is more structured than a panel discussion and may also be followed by a forum discussion.

Tacit Bargaining Bargaining in which communication is incomplete or impossible.

Team Diagnostic Questionnaire This is a method of determining a group's strengths and weaknesses from the point of view of the group members.

Territoriality The word *territoriality* was coined by Edward Hall and defined as "the tendency for humans and other animals to lay claim to and defend a particular area or territory."

The Collaborative Team Leader—Leader Version This is a method for team leaders to assess their own group leadership effectiveness.

The Collaborative Team Leader—Team Version This is a method for team members to assess their group leader's effectiveness.

Throughput Throughput refers to all the actual verbal and nonverbal behaviors that occur in the course of a group discussion.

Values Values are fewer in number than attitudes and serve as important predictors of behavior. They appear to be more stable and long-lasting than attitudes.

Verbal–Nonverbal Communication Verbal communication is the use of words to get across a message. Nonverbal communication is the use of physical actions, such as facial expression or tone of voice, to get across a message.

Virtual Teams A virtual team is one in which members communicate with each other through computers and may or may not be located near one another.

Work Groups Work groups are the formations of people on the job.

References

About.com. 2005a. Leadership theories: Definitions and framework. From http://psychology.about.com/library/weekly/aa040102a.htm.

———. 2005b. Organizational psychology: Group performance. From http://psychology.about.com/library/weekly/aa031502.htm.

Achor, Shawn. 2010. *The happiness advantage: The seven principles of positive psychology that fuel success and performance at work.* New York: Crown Business.

Acuff, Frank L. 1997. *How to negotiate anything with anyone anywhere around the world*, 2nd ed. New York: American Management Association.

Adams, Scott. 1996. *The Dilbert principle.* New York: HarperBusiness.

Adams, W. A., Cindy Adams, and Michael Bowker. 1999. *The whole systems approach.* Provo, UT: Executive Excellence.

Adamy, Janet. 2007. The value of pie: Domino's David Brandon talks about the challenge of running a national brand that depends on a local decision. *The Wall Street Journal*, April 16.

Adelman, Ken. 1999. The real Reagan. *The Wall Street Journal*, October 5: A26.

Adler, Ronald B., and Jeanne M. Elmhorst. 1996. *Communicating at work*, 5th ed. New York: McGraw-Hill.

Adrian Walsh Associates. 2005. The case for promoting followership within business. From http://adrianwalsh.com.au/followership.htm.

Albrecht, Karl. 2004. 50 tips for better thinking. From http://karlalbrecht.com/bptips.htm.

Amabile, Theresa. 1996. *Creativity in context.* Boulder, CO: Westview Press.

Amabile, Theresa, and Steven Kramer. 2011. The power of small wins. *Harvard Business Review*, May, pp. 70–80.

Anderson, Terry D. 1998. *Transforming leadership*, 2nd ed. Boca Raton, FL: St. Lucie Press.

Aranda, Eileen K., Luis Aranda, and Kristi Conlon. 1998. *Teams.* Upper Saddle River, NJ: Prentice Hall.

Arends, Brett. 2011. A tip for financial advisors: When possible, use English. *The Wall Street Journal*, May 2, p. R1.

Argenti, Paul A. 1998. *Corporate communication*, 2nd ed. New York: Irwin/McGraw-Hill.

Argyle, Michael. 1967. *The psychology of interpersonal behavior.* Baltimore: Penguin.

Armano, David. 2010. A deep dive on Facebook groups and their potential. *Harvard Business Review Daily Briefings*, October 12.

Armour, Stephanie. 2008. Think twice before crying on the job. *The Detroit Free Press*, January 21: A10.

Aronson, Elliot. 1973. The rationalizing animal. *Psychology Today* 6: 46–52.

Aronson, Elliot, and Judson Mills. 1959. Effect of severity of initiation on liking for a group. *Journal of Abnormal and Social Psychology* 59: 177–81.

Arum, Richard, and Josipa Roksa. 2011. *Academically adrift.* Chicago: The University of Chicago Press.

Asch, Solomon. 1952. *Social psychology.* Englewood Cliffs, NJ: Prentice Hall.

———. 1956. Studies of independence and conformity: A minority of one against a unanimous majority. *Psychological Monographs* 70(9): (Whole No. 416).

Ashkenas, Ron. 2010. Why we secretly love meetings. *Harvard Business Review Daily Alert*, October 5.

Associated Press. 1990a. Avianca pilots not trained to say "fuel emergency." *Detroit Free Press*, June 23: A4.

———. 1990b. City manages to get itself out of a (man) hole. *Ann Arbor News*, June 23: A2.

———. 1992. Nose rings? No. *Ann Arbor News*, July 6: A5.

———. 1998. Crayola's "chestnut" replaces "Indian red." *Ann Arbor News*, July 27: A4.

———. 2004. Complaint filed against Peterson attorney. *The Grand Rapids Press*, November: A2.

Avolio, Bruce, and Fred Luthans. 2006. *The high impact leader*. New York: McGraw-Hill.

Axelrod, Alan. 2003. *Profiles in leadership*. New York: Prentice Hall.

Axtell, Roger E. 1991. *Gestures: The do's and taboos of body language around the world*. New York: Wiley.

Babcock, Charles. 2007. Chambers sees virtual teams competing with virtualized resources. *Information Week*, September 12. From http://www.informationweek.com/story/showArticle.jhtml?articleID=201805858.

Bakalar, Nicholas. 2006. A team approach may help in treating breast cancer. *International Harold Tribune*, December 6: 1.

Bales, Robert F. 1950. *Interaction process analysis*. Reading, MA: Addison-Wesley.

———. 1970. *Personality and interpersonal behavior*. New York: Holt, Rinehart & Winston.

Bales, Robert F., and Fred Strodbeck. 1951. Phases in group solving. *Journal of Abnormal and Social Psychology* 46: 485–95.

Balthazard, P., D. Waldman, J. Howell, and L. Atwater. 2004. Shared leadership and group interaction styles in problem-solving virtual teams. Proceedings of the 37th Hawaii International Conference on System Sciences. From http://www.csdl.computer.org/comp/proceedings/hicss/2004/2056/01/205610043b.pdf.

Banes, T. J. 2005. Kids say the darndest things . . . ; Parents can avoid sting of remarks/Youngsters should learn words can hurt. *Seattle Times*, January: p. D10.

Barker, Eileen. 2007. What the bleep does spirituality have to do with conflict resolution? From www.mediate.com.

Barnard, William. 1991. Group influence and the likelihood of a unanimous majority. *Journal of Social Psychology* 131: 607–13.

Barnard, William, Carol Baird, Marilyn Greenwalt, and Ray Karl. 1992. Intragroup cohesiveness and reciprocal social influence in male and female discussion groups. *Journal of Social Psychology* 132: 179–88.

Barnlund, Dean. 1968. *Interpersonal communication: Survey and studies*. Boston: Houghton Mifflin.

Barol, Bill. 1990. Anatomy of a fad. *Newsweek*, September: 40–41.

Barrett, Marty W., and Thomas A. Carey. 1989. Communicating strategy: The best investment a CEO can make. *Mid-American Journal of Business* 4(1): 3–6.

Barthel, Trip. 2007. A practical process for reciprocal negotiation. From www.mediate.com.

Bar-Yam, Y. 2004. Complexity rising: From human beings to human civilization, a complexity profile. From http://necsi.org/Civilization.html.

Bass, Bernard. 1995. Concepts of leadership: The beginnings. In *The Leader's Companion*, ed. J. Thomas Wren. New York: Free Press, pp. 49–52.

Bauduin, E. Scott. 1971. Obscene language and source credibility: An experimental study. Paper presented at the annual conference of the International Communication Association, Phoenix, Arizona.

Bazerman, Max H., and Margaret A. Neale. 1993. *Negotiating rationally*. New York: Free Press.

BCS. 2004. Conflict management FAQ's. Online learning center: Conflict management. Building Collaborative Solutions, Inc. From http://www.bcsolutions.org/olccmfaq.html.

Beamer, Lisa. 2002. *Let's roll*. Wheaton, IL: Tyndale House.

Beck, Joan. 1990. 2 Live Crew is more offensive than obscene. *Detroit Free Press*, June 25: A7.

Beebe, Paul. 1986. Going in circles. *The Idaho Statesman*, May 11.

Behfar, Kristin, Randall Peterson, Elizabeth Mannix, and William Trochim. 2008. The critical role of conflict resolution in teams: A close look at the links between conflict type, conflict management strategies, and team outcomes. *Journal of Applied Psychology*, January: 170.

Bellew, Charles, and Alexander Todorov. 2007. Predicting political elections from rapid and unreflective face judgments. *Proceedings of the National Academy of Science of the United States of America*, 104, no. 46 (November 13, 2007), pp. 17948–53.

Bellinger, G. 2004. Management & leadership: A systemic perspective. From http://www.systems-thinking.org/malasp.htm.

Benne, Kenneth D., and Paul Sheats. 1948. Functional roles of group members. *Journal of Social Issues* 4: 41–49.

Bennett, William J. 1994. *The index of leading cultural indicators*. New York: Simon & Schuster.

Bennis, Warren, 1994. *On becoming a leader*. Reading, MA: Addison-Wesley.

Bennis, Warren, and Burt Nanus. 1985. *Leaders: The strategies for taking charge*. New York: Harper & Row.

Bennis, Warren, and Herbert Shepard. 1961. Group observation. In *The planning of change*, ed. Warren Bennis, Kenneth Benne, and Robert Chin. New York: Holt, Rinehart & Winston, pp. 743–56.

Bennis, Warren G., and Robert J. Thomas. 2002. *Geeks & Geezers*. Boston: Harvard Business School Press.

Benton, D. A. 1996. *How to think like a CEO*. New York: Warner Books.

Berns, Gregory. 2009. *Iconoclast*. Boston: Harvard Business School Press.

Berryman, R. 1995. Systems thinking and organizations: An initial inquiry into the subject. *CSWT Papers*. From http://www.workteams.unt.edu/reports/rberyman.htm.

Beyerlein, Michael, and Douglas Johnson. 1994. *Theories of self-managing work teams*. Greenwich, CT: JAI Press.

Bisoux, Tricia. 2002. The mind of a leader. *Biz Ed*, September/October: 26–32.

Black, Mathew. 1999. Kao's theory. *Business 2.0*, September: 145–54.

Blackburn, Richard, and Benson Rosen. 1993. Total quality and human resource management: Lessons learned from Baldrige award–winning companies. *Academy of Management Executive* 7: 49–66.

Blair, Gwenda. 1988. *Almost golden: Jessica Savitch and the selling of television news*. New York: Simon & Schuster.

Blake, Robert, and Jane Mouton. 1970. The fifth achievement. *Journal of Applied Behavioral Sciences* 6: 413–26.

Blanchard, Ken. 1999. *The heart of a leader*. Tulsa, OK: Honor Books.

———. 2007. *Leading at a higher level*. Upper Saddle River, NJ: Prentice Hall.

Blankenhorn, David. 1995. *Fatherless in America*. New York: Basic Books.

Blenko, Marcia, Michael C. Mankins, and Paul Rogers. 2010. *Decide & deliver: 5 steps to breakthrough performance in your organization*. Boston: Harvard Business School Publishing.

Block, Peter. 1987. *The empowered manager*. San Francisco: Jossey-Bass.

Bloom, Benjamin S., and Lois J. Broder. 1961. Problem-solving processes of college students. In *Selected readings in the learning process*, ed. Theodore L. Harris and Wilson E. Schwahn. New York: Oxford University Press, pp. 31–79.

Bluedorn, A. C., and R. L. Standifer. 2006. Time and the temporal imagination. *Academy of Management Learning & Education* 5: 196–206.

Boone, Louis E., and David L. Kurtz. 1994. *Contemporary business communication*. Englewood Cliffs, NJ: Prentice Hall.

Borisoff, Deborah, and David A. Victor. 1998. *Conflict management: A communication skills approach*, 2nd ed. Boston: Allyn & Bacon.

Bostrom, Robert, 1970. Patterns of communicative interaction in small groups. *Speech Monographs* 37: 257–63.

Bostrom, Robert, and Charles Rossiter. 1969. Profanity, justification, and source credibility. Paper presented at the annual conference of the International Communication Association, Cleveland, Ohio.

Bott, Jennifer. 1999. Taking delivery. *Detroit Free Press*, August 9: F6–F7.

Bounds, Wendy, Rebecca Quick, and Emily Nelson. 1999. In the office, it's anything goes. *The Wall Street Journal*, August 26: B1–B4.

Boyatzis, Richard E., Scott S. Cowan, and David A. Kolb. 1995. *Innovation in professional education*. San Francisco: Jossey-Bass.

Boyd, S. 2005. Ethics in speaking: A practical point of view. *InFocus: Presenters University*. From http://presentersuniversity.com/delivery_Ethics.php.

Bracey, Hyler, Jack Rosenblum, Aubrey Sanford, and Roy Trueblood. 1993. *Managing from the heart*. New York: Dell Books.

Bradenburger, Adam M., and Barry J. Nalebuff. 1996. *Co-opetition*. New York: Doubleday.

Bradford, David L., and Allan R. Cohen. 1997. *Managing for excellence: The guide to developing high performance in contemporary organizations*. New York: Wiley.

Bradley-Steck, Tara. 1987. High overhead: Tall and thin executives receive fatter paychecks, university study reports. *Ann Arbor News*, March 3: A1.

Brahm, Eric. 2004. Benefits of intractable conflict. In *Beyond Intractability*, ed. Guy Burgess and Heidi Burgess. From http://www.beyondintractability.org/essay/benefits/.

Brants, K., and V. Frissen. 2003. Inclusion and exclusion in the information society final deliverable. The European Media and Technology in Everyday Life Network. From http://www.lse.ac.uk/collections/EMTEL/reports/brants_2003_emtel.pdf.

Brassard, Michael, et al. 1995. *The team memory jogger*. Methuen, MA: Goal/QPC.

Brau, J. 2003. Self directed work teams. The Quorum Group. From http://www.jbrau.com/qg-7.html.

Braybrooke, David, and Charles E. Lindblom. 1963. *A strategy of decision*. New York: Free Press.

Brenner, R. 2004. The ties that bind. *Point Lookout: An E-mail Newsletter from Chaco Canyon Consulting* 4(29). From http://www.chacocanyon.com/pointlookout/040721.shtml.

Brett, Jeanne, Kristin Behfar, and Mary C. Kern. 2006. Managing Multicultural Teams. *Harvard Business Review*, November.

Brokaw, Tom. 2007. *Boom! Voices of the sixties*. New York: Random House.

Brooks, David. 2011. *The social animal*. New York: Random House.

Brown, Donald, and Don Harvey, 2006. *An experiential approach to organizational development*, 7th ed. Upper Saddle River, NJ: Pearson/Prentice Hall.

Brutus, Stephane, and Magda Donia. 2010. Improving the effectiveness of students in groups with a centralized peer evaluation system. *Academy of Management Learning & Education*, December, pp. 652–662.

Buckingham, Marcus, and Curt Coffman. 1999. *First break all the rules*. New York: Simon & Schuster.

Burke, Doris. 2007. Anatomy of an A380: Missed connections," *Fortune*, March 5: 101–8.

Burley-Allen, Madelyn. 1995. *Listening: The forgotten skill*, 2nd ed. New York: Wiley.

Butler, Dore, and Florence L. Geis. 1990. Nonverbal affect responses to male and female leaders: Implications for leadership evaluations. *Journal of Personality and Social Psychology* 58(1): 48–59.

Byrnes, Nanette. 2007. Profiles in sycophancy. *BusinessWeek*, August 13: 12.

Campbell, Don. 1997. *The Mozart effect*. New York: Avon Books.

Canfield, Jack, and Mark Victor Hansen. 1996. *A 3rd serving of chicken soup for the soul*. Deerfield Beach, FL: Health Communications.

Canfield, Jack, Mark Victor Hanson, and Les Hewitt, 2000. *The Power of Focus*. Deerfield Beach, FL: Health Communications.

Capezio, Peter, and Debra Morehouse. 1993. *Taking the mystery out of TOM*. Hawthorne, NJ: Career Press.

Carey, B. 2004. Fear in the workplace: The bullying boss. *The New York Times*, June: F.1.

Carney, Dana. 2010. Powerful people are better liars. *Harvard Business Review*, May, pp. 32–33.

Caroselli, Marlene. 1995. *Meetings that work*, 2nd ed. Mission, KS: Skillpath Publications.

Carr, Clay. 1996. *Team leader's problem solver*. Englewood Cliffs, NJ: Prentice Hall.

Carr, Nicholas. 2011. The Shallows: What the Internet is Doing to Our Brains. New York: Norton & Co.

Carville, James, and Paul Begala. 2002. *Buck up, suck up . . . and come back when you foul up*. New York: Simon & Schuster.

Case, John. 1995. *Open book management*. New York: HarperBusiness.

Castiglione, James. 2007. Self-managing work teams and their external leadership: A primer for library administrators. *Library Management* 28: 379–93.

CCR. 2005. Tips on leading a discussion. Centre County Reads, Pennsylvania. From http://www.ccr.minitab.com/2005/discussionGroupTips.aspx.

ChangingMinds.org. 2004. Theories. From http://www.changingminds.org/explanations/theories.

Charan, Ram. 2008. *Leaders at all levels*. San Francisco: Wiley.

Charan, Ram, Stephen Drotter, and James Noel. 2001. *The leadership pipeline*. San Francisco: Jossey-Bass.

Chen, Ming-Jer. 2001. *Inside Chinese business*. Boston: Harvard Business School Press.

Cherniss, Gary, and Daniel Goleman, eds. 2001. *The emotionally intelligent workplace*. San Francisco: Jossey-Bass.

Cherry, Susan Spaeth. 1996. Kids find lessons, pain in cliques. *Ann Arbor News*, October 22: D3.

Cho, J., and D. Struck. 2003. S. Koreans complain of exclusion. *Seattle Times*, April: A2.

Chopra, Deepak. 1994. *The seven spiritual laws of success*. San Rafael, CA: Amber-Allen.

Chowdhury, Subir. 2002. *Design for six sigma*. Dearborn, MI: Dearborn Trade.

Christenson, Clayton M. 1997. *The innovator's dilemma*. Boston: Harvard Business School Press.

Cialdini, Robert B. 2001. *Influence*, 4th ed. Boston: Allyn & Bacon.

Cissna, Kenneth. 1976. Interpersonal confirmation: A review of current theory and research. Paper presented at the annual convention of the Central States Speech Association, Chicago, April.

Clawson, James G. 2003. *Level three leadership*, 2nd ed. Upper Saddle River, NJ: Prentice Hall.

Cloke, Kenneth, and Joan Goldsmith. 2011. *Resolving conflicts at work*, 3rd ed. San Francisco: Jossey-Bass.

Cocks, Jay. 1990. Let's get crazy. *Time*, June 11: 40–41.

Cohen, Arianne. 2008. Scuttling scut work. *Fast Company*, February: 42–43.

Cohen, Dan. 2005. *The heart of change field guide*. Boston: Harvard Business School Press.

Cohen, Herb. 1996. *You can negotiate anything*. Seacaucus, NY: Lyle Stewart.

Coleman, David. 1995. *Groupware: Technology and applications*. Englewood Cliffs, NJ: Prentice Hall.

———. 1996. *Groupware: Collaborative strategies for corporate LANS and intranets*. Englewood Cliffs, NJ: Prentice Hall.

Collington, J. 2004. Rolling thunder: Kerry wins nonverbal communication prize with Kennedy-esque gesture. *Tulsa World*, October: D.8.

Collins, James C., and Jerry I. Porras. 1994. *Built to last: Successful habits of visionary companies*. New York: HarperBusiness.

Communiqué: News & Views of Interest to All from Media Training. 2003. Interpersonal communication. From http://www.mediatraco.com/interper.html.

Conger, Jay A. 1989. Leadership: The art of empowering others. *Academy of Management Executive* 3(1): 17–24.

Conner, Daryl. 1993. *Managing at the speed of change*. New York: Villard Books.

Connors, Roger, and Tom Smith. 2011. *Change the culture: change the game*. New York: Portfolio/Penguin.

Cooley, C. 1909. Primary Groups. *Social organization: A study of the larger mind*. New York: Scribner, pp. 25–31. From http://www2.pfeiffer.edu/~lridener/courses/primgrp.html.

Cooper, Jim. 1998. Cooperative learning in college science, mathematics, engineering, and technology. *Cooperative Learning and College Teaching*, Spring: 8, 1–8.

Cooper, Robert K., and Ayman Sawaf. 1997. *Executive EQ*. New York: Grosset/Putnam.

Copley News Service. 2004. Technology Communication tips for the digital age; E-mail, faxes, cellular phones, Oh my! Springfield, Illinois, *State Journal Register*, March: A28.

Corcoran, Elizabeth. 1988. Groupware: Beyond number crunching, computers aid management. *Scientific American*, July: 110–12.

Cosdon, C. 2004. Experts to share tips on detecting terrorists. *St. Petersburg Times*, April: 1.

Cosier, Richard A., and Charles R. Schwenk. 1990. Agreement and thinking alike: Ingredients for poor decisions. *Academy of Management Executive* 4(1): 69–74.

Costin, Harry. 1996. *Management development and training: A TQM approach*. Orlando, FL: Dryden Press.

Cotton, John L. 1993. *Employee involvement*. Newbury Park, CA: Sage.

Coulter, Ann. 2002. *Slander*. New York: Crown.

Courtwright, John A., Gail T. Fairhurst, and L. Edna Rogers. 1989. Interaction patterns in organic and mechanistic systems. *Academy of Management Journal* 32(4): 773–802.

Cousins, Norman. 1980. *Anatomy of an illness*. New York: Norton.

Covey, Stephen. 1990. *The seven habits of highly effective people*. New York: Simon & Schuster.

———. 1991. *Principle-centered leadership*. New York: Simon & Schuster.

———. 1994. *First things first*. New York: Simon & Schuster.

Coy, Peter. 2007a. Ten years from now . . . *BusinessWeek*, August 20 and 27.

———. 2007b. Cog or co-worker. *BusinessWeek*, August 20 and 27.

Crane, Loren, Richard Diecker, and Charles Brown, 1970. The physiological response to the communication modes: Reading, listening, writing, speaking, and evaluating. *Journal of Communication* 20: 231–40.

Crilly, Rob. 2007. The blasphemous teddy bear. *Time*, December 9. From http://www.time.com/time/world/article/0,8599,1687755.00.html.

Cross, Rob, Andrew Hargadon, Salvatore Parise, and Robert J. Thomas. 2007. Together we innovate. *The Wall Street Journal*, September 15: R6.

Csikszentmihalyi, Mihaly. 1996. *Creativity*. New York: HarperCollins.

Culbert, Samuel A. 1968. *The interpersonal process of self-disclosure: It takes two to see one*. New York: Renaissance Editions.

Daily Herald. 2004. Fence Post. Arlington Heights, Illinois, *Daily Herald*, March: 19.

Damast, Alison. 2007. PowerPoint: Is there no escape? *BusinessWeek*, August 13: 14.

Dance, Frank E. X., and Carl E. Larson. 1972. *Speech communication: Concepts and behavior*. New York: Holt, Rinehart & Winston.

———. 1976. *The functions of human communication*. New York: Holt, Rinehart & Winston.

Davis, J., M. Zaner, S. Farnham, C. Marcjan, and B. McCarthy. 2002. Wireless brainstorming: Overcoming status effects in small group decisions. Computers in Human Interaction. From http://research.microsoft.com/scg/papers/Wireless%20Brainstorming.pdf.

Davis, Sammy, Jr., and Jane and Burt Boyar. 1989. *The Sammy Davis, Jr. story: Why me?* New York: Warner Books.

Davis, Stan, and Christopher Meyer. 1998. *Blur*. Reading, MA: Addison-Wesley.

Dean, Peter. 2006. *Leadership is for everyone*. New York: McGraw-Hill.

DeBono, Edward. 1985. *Six thinking hats*. Toronto: MICA Management Resources.

DecisionPoint. 2004. Team effectiveness. From http://www.decpoint.com/teameffectiveness.html.

Deep, Sam, and Lyle Sussman. 1998. *Yes you can*. Reading, MA: Addison-Wesley.

De Janasz, Suzanne, Karen Dowd, and Beth Schneider. 2009. *Interpersonal skills in organizations*. New York: McGraw-Hill.

Delbecq, André L., Andrew H. Van de Ven, and David H. Gustafson, 1975. *Group techniques for program planning: A guide to nominal group and Delphi processes*. Glenview, IL: Scott, Foresman.

DeLisser, Eleena. 1999. Firms with virtual environments appeal to workers. *The Wall Street Journal*, October 5: B2.

Dell, Michael. 1999. *Direct from Dell*. New York: HarperBusiness.

Denison, Daniel, Stuart Hart, and Joel Kahn. 1996. From chimneys to cross-functional teams: Developing and validating a diagnostic model. *Academy of Management Journal* 39: 1005–23.

DePree, Max. 1989. *Leadership is an art*. New York: Doubleday.

Dertouzos, Michael L. 1991. Communications, computers and networks. *Scientific American*, September: 62–69.

Dertouzos, Michael L., Richard K. Lester, and Robert M. Solow. 1989. *Made in America*. New York: Harper Perennial.

DeTienne, Kristen Bell. 2002. *Guide to electronic communication*. Upper Saddle River, NJ: Prentice Hall.

Deutsch, Morton. 1958. Trust ad suspicion. *Journal of Conflict Resolution* 2: 215–79.

Dewey, John. 1910. *How we think*. New York: Heath.

Dholakia, U., R. Bagozzi, and L. Pearo. 2005. A social influence model of consumer participation in network and small-group-based virtual communities. *International Journal of Research in Marketing*. From http://papers.ssrn.com/sol3/papers.cfm?abstract_id=534523.

Djamasbi, Soussan, and Eleanor Loiacono. 2008. Do men and women use feedback provided by their Decision Support Systems (DSS) differently? *Decision Support Systems*, March: 854

Doehrman, M. 2003. Creating leadership ranks high on the list. *The Colorado Springs Business Journal*, March: 1.

Donaldson, Thomas, and Patricia Werhane. 2008. *Ethical issues in business*, 8th ed. Upper Saddle River, NJ: Pearson Prentice Hall.

Donnellon, Anne. 1996. *Team talk*. Boston: Harvard Business School Press.

Donoghue, Denis. 2008. *On eloquence*. New Haven, CT: Yale University Press.

Dooley, Robert S., and Gerald E. Fryxell, 1999. Attaining decision quality and commitment from dissent: The moderating effects of loyalty and competence in strategic decision-making teams. *Academy of Management Journal*, August: 42, 389–402.

Douglas, Kirk. 2002. *My stroke of luck*. New York: HarperCollins.

Downey, L. 2004. Making workplaces FIT. *Corporate Report Wisconsin*, September: 40.

Drucker, Peter. 1990. The emerging theory of manufacturing. *Harvard Business Review*, May–June: 94–102.

———. 1999. Change leaders. *Inc.*, June: 65–72.

Duarte, Deborah, and Nancy Tennant Snyder. 1999. *Mastering virtual teams*. San Francisco: Jossey-Bass.

Dumaine, Brian. 1990. Who needs a boss? *Fortune*, May 7: 52–60.

———. 1993. The new non-manager managers. *Fortune*, February 22: 80–84.

Dungy, Tony, with Nathan Whitaker 2007. *Quiet strength*. Carol Stream, IL: Tyndale House.

Dunlap, Albert. 1996. *Mean business*. New York: Times Business.

Durre', Linnda. 2010. *Surviving the toxic workplace*. New York: McGraw-Hill.

Eagly, Alice H., and Linda L. Carli. 2007. Women and the labyrinth of leadership. *Harvard Business Review*, September: 63–71

Edison Community College. 2005. Kepner-Tregoe. Business and Industry Center. http://www.edison.cc.oh.us/business/KepnerTregoeAnalytic.htm.

Edwards, Allen, and L. E. Acker. 1962. A demonstration of the long-term retention of a conditioned galvanic skin response. *Psychosomatic Medicine* 24: 459–63.

Eisenberg, Eric M., and Marsha G. Witten. 1987. Reconsidering openness in organizational communication. *Academy of Management Review* 12(3): 418–26.

Ellis, Donald G., and B. Aubrey Fisher. 1994. *Small group decision-making*, 4th ed. New York: McGraw-Hill.

Ellison, S. 2004. Powerful non-defensive communication; More than a technique—a new way of being. From http://www.pndc.com/exercises/NonDefWdList.htm.

Engardio, Pete. 2007. Managing the new workforce. *BusinessWeek*, August 20 and 27.

Envision Software. 2004. Maslow's hierarchy of needs. From http://www.envisionsoftware.com/Articles/Maslows_Needs_Hierarchy.html.

Epstein, Robert. 1996. *Creativity games for trainers*. New York: McGraw-Hill.

Erard, M. 2004. Just like, er, words, not, um, throwaways. *The New York Times*, January: B7.

Etzioni, Amatai. 1968. *The active society*. New York: Free Press.

Falkoff, R. 2004. Linguistic faux pas knows no bounds. Monster.com Work Abroad. From http://workabroad.monster.com/articles/linguisticfaux/.

Feierman, A. 2005. The art of communicating effectively: Tips about all aspects of pulling off a successful presentation! Projector Solution: An Alliant Solutions, Inc. Company. From http://www.projectorsolution.com/effectivepresentations.asp?.

Ferdman, B. 2003. A matter of difference: Accounts of inclusion (and exclusion). Society for Industrial and Organizational Psychology, Inc. From http://siop.org/tip/backissues/Apr03/09ferdman.htm.

Fernandez-Araoz, Ignacio. 1999. Hiring without firing. *Harvard Business Review*, July–August: 109–20.

Festinger, Leon. 1954. A theory of social comparison processes. *Human Relations* 7: 117–40.

———. 1957. *A theory of cognitive dissonance*. Stanford, CA: Stanford University Press.

Festinger, Leon, and Elliot Aronson. 1968. Arousal and reduction of dissonance in social contexts. In *Group dynamics: Research and theory*, 3rd ed., ed. Dorwin Cartwright and Alvin Zander. New York: Harper & Row, pp. 125–36.

Fiedler, Fred. 1967. *A theory of leadership effectiveness*. New York: McGraw-Hill.

Fiedler, Fred, and Martin Chemers. 1974. *Leadership and effective management*. Glenview, IL: Scott, Foresman.

Field, Anne. 1996. Groupthink: Today's groupware. *Inc. Technology* 3: 38–44.

Finney, D. 2004. A real lip-locker. *St. Louis Post–Dispatch*, August: E1.

FIRO-B. 2004. From http://www.cpp.com/products.firo-b/index.asp.

Fisher, B. Aubrey. 1974. *Small group decision making: Communication and the group process*. New York: McGraw-Hill.

———. 1980. *Small group decision making*, 2nd ed. New York: McGraw-Hill.

Fisher Group. 2004. Home page. From http://www.thefishergroup.com.

Fisher, Kimball. 2000. *Leading self-directed work teams*. New York: McGraw-Hill.

Fisher, Roger, and Danny Ertel. 1995. *Getting ready to negotiate*. New York: Penguin Books.

Fisher, Roger, and Scott Brown, 1988. *Getting together*. Boston: Houghton Mifflin.

Fisher, Roger, and William Ury. 1991. *Getting to yes*. Boston: Houghton Mifflin.

Fisher, Roger, John Richardson, and Alan Sharp. 1999. *Getting it done*. New York: HarperBusiness.

Fiske, Edward. 1990. Of learning and college: How small groups thrive. *New York Times*, March 5: A1.

Fishman, Charles. 2007. What drives Toyota? *Fast Company*, January: 82–90.

Fjermestad, Jerry. 2004. An analysis of communication mode in group support systems research. *Decision Support Systems* 37: 239–63.

Flately, Marie. 1999. Electronic boardroom of the future is here today. *SDSU Business*, Spring: 14.

Fleming, John H., and Jim Asplund. 2007. *Human sigma*. New York: Gallup Press.

Folger, Joseph P., Marshall Scott Poole, and Randall K. Stutman, 1998. *Working through conflict*, 3rd ed. Reading, MA: Addison-Wesley.

Footlick, Jerrold K. 1990. What happened to the family? *Newsweek*, Winter/Spring: 15–20.

Foreman, Janis. 1999. Management communication and MBA education: An argument for management literacy. *Selections*, Spring/Summer: 9–16.

Forsyth, D. n.d. Guest lecture: Groups in places. Virginia Commonwealth University, Don Forsyth's web page. From http://www.has.vcu.edu/psy/faculty/fors/glamy.htm.

Forsyth, Donelson R. 2009. *Group dynamics*, 5th ed. Belmont, CA: Wadsworth.

Fortney, Sarah. 2007. Academy gets verbal judo lesson. *Frederick News Post*.com, October 20.

Fox News. 2007. British teacher faces 40 lashes for naming class teddy bear "Muhammad." Retrieved December 11, 2007, from http://www.foxnews.com/story/0,2933,312895,00.html.

Francis, Dave, and Don Young. 1992. *Improving work groups*, 2nd ed. San Diego, CA: Pfeiffer.

French, John, and Bertram Raven. 1959. The bases of social power. In *Studies in social power*, ed. Dorwin Cartwright. Ann Arbor, MI: Institute for Social Research, 150–67.

Fried, Jason, and David Hansson. 2010. *Rework*. New York: Crown Publishing.

Friedlander, John. 2007. Abstract, concrete, general and specific terms. Retrieved January 20 from http://faculty.southwest.tn.edu/jfriedlander/abstract_and_concrete.htm.

Fruend, James C. 1992. *Smart negotiating*. New York: Simon & Schuster.

Frymier, Ann and Margorie Nadler. 2010. Persuasion. New York: Kendall-Hunt.

Fulk, Janet. 1993. Social construction of communication technology. *Academy of Management Journal* 36: 921–50.

Fullerton, Sam, Kathleen B. Kerch, and H. Robert Dodge. 1996. Consumer ethics: An assessment of individual behavior in the marketplace. *Journal of Business Ethics* 15: 805–14.

Fulmer, Robert M., and Marshall Goldsmith. 2001. *The leadership investment*. New York: AMACOM.

Galanes, Gloria J., Katherine Adams, and John K. Brilhart. 2000. *Comunicating in Groups*, 4th ed. New York: McGraw-Hill.

Galinsky, Adam D., Joe C. Magee, M. Ena Inesi, and Deborah H. Gruenfeld. 2006. Power and perspectives not taken. *Psychological Science*, 17(12): 1068–1074.

Gallo, Amy. 2010. The right way to fight. *Harvard Business Review Daily Alert*, May 12, 2010.

Gallo, Amy. 2010. Get your team to stop fighting and start working. *Harvard Business Review Daily Alert*, June 9.

Gamble, Teri Kwai, and Michael W. Gamble. 2003. *The gender communication connection*. Boston: Houghton Mifflin.

Gamero, Nuria, Vicente González-Romá, and José Peiró. 2008. The influence of intrateam conflict on work teams' affective climate: A longitudinal study. *Journal of Occupational and Organizational Psychology* 81: 47.

Gannon, J. 2003. At Heinz, it's hoped openness begets oneness at renovated Gimbels quarters. *Pittsburgh Post–Gazette*, February: F1.

Gardner, John W. 1990. *On leadership*. New York: Free Press.

Gates, Bill. 1995. *The road ahead*. New York: Penguin Books.

———. 1999. *Business @ the speed of thought*. New York: Warner Books.

Gawande, Atul. 2009. *The checklist manifesto: How to get things right*. New York: Metropolitan Books.

Geier, John. 1967. A trait approach to the study of leadership. *Journal of Communication* 17: 316–23.

George, Bill, Peter Sims, Andrew N. McLean, and Diana Meyer. 2007. Discovering your authentic leadership. *Harvard Business Review*, February.

George, Bill. 2007. *Authentic Leadership*. New York: McGraw-Hill.

George, Maryanne, and David Morrow. 1992. Union was key in GM plant decision. *Detroit Free Press*, December 17: A1, A4.

Georgia Department of Education. 2003. Celebrating diversity: A facilitator's guide. Professional Development Center, Georgia Department of Education. From http://www.glc.k12.ga.us/passwd/trc/ttools/attach/pdc/CelebratingDiversity.pdf.

Gerdes, Lindsey. 2007. The best places to launch a career. *BusinessWeek*, September 24.

Gersick, Connie J. G. 1988. Tune and transition in work teams: Toward a new model of group development. *Academy of Management Journal* 31(1): 9–41.

Giacomin, Joe. 1995. The top 12 list—What automotive suppliers seek most in the salespeople they hire. Southfield, MI: The Giacomin Group.

Gibb, Jack. 1961. Defensive communication. *Journal of Communication* 11: 141–48.

Gibson, Jane Whitney, and Richard M. Hodgetts. 1986. *Organizational communication: A managerial perspective*. New York: Academic Press.

Gladwell, Malcolm. 2000. *The tipping point*. New York: Little, Brown.

Glencoe.com. 2004. Thinking critically: Observing and inferring. Glencoe.com. From http://www.glencoe.com/sec/science/sc_interaction/si4/skill_handbook/tc.shtml.

Glickman, Jodi. 2010. How to interject in a meeting. *Harvard Daily Briefings*, November 3.

Goldberg, Bernard. 2002. *Bias*. Washington, DC: Regnery.

Goldman, Alan. 2009. *Transforming toxic leaders*. Stanford, CA: Stanford Business Books.

Goleman, Daniel. 1997. *Emotional intelligence*. New York: Bantam Books.

———. 1998a. *Working with emotional intelligence*. New York: Bantam Books.

———. 1998b. What makes a leader? *Harvard Business Review*, November–December: 93–102.

Goleman, Daniel, Richard Boyatzis, and Annie McKee. 2002. *Primal leadership*. Boston: Harvard Business School Press.

Gordon, Judith R. 2002. *Organizational behavior: A diagnostic approach*, 7th ed. Upper Saddle River, NJ: Prentice Hall.

Gordon, William I., Erica L. Nagel, Scott A. Myers, and Carole A. Barbato. 1996. *The team trainer*. Chicago: Irwin.

Gould, D. 2004. Methods and technologies. Virtual Organization. From http://www.seanet.com/~daveg/technolo.htm.

Graban, Mark. 2009. *Lean hospitals*. New York: Productivity Press.

Grand Canyon University. 2004. Watching trends in education—Evaluations: Online and traditional classes. From http://www.gcu.edu/education-news/online-degrees/online-classes.htm.

Gray, David, Sunni Brown, and James Macanufo. 2010. *Gamestorming: A playbook for innovators, rulebreakers and changemakers*. Sebastopol, CA: O'Reilly Media.

Gray, John. 1992. *Men are from Mars, women are from Venus*. New York: HarperCollins.

Greene, Robert, and Joost Elffers. 1998. *The 48 laws of power*. New York: Viking Penguin.

Greensboro News Record. 2004. Winter break studying works for UNCG students; Popular online wintersession classes fill the void between semesters as more students turn to the cyber-classroom to meet their needs. *Greensboro News Record*, December: A12.

Gregory, Hamilton. 1999. *Public speaking.* New York: McGraw-Hill.

Griffin, A. M., and J. H. Langlois. 2006. Stereotype directionality and attractiveness stereotyping: Is beauty good or is ugly bad? *Social Cognition* 24 (2). From pubmedcentral .nih.gov.

Gross, Steven E. 1995. *Compensation for teams.* New York: AMACOM.

Groysberg, Boris, L. Kevin Kelly, and Bryan McDonald. 2011. The new path to the C-suite. *Harvard Business Review*, March, pp. 61–68.

Grunska, J. n.d. The art of verbal judo. From http://members.shaw.ca/calgarysoftballumpires/ art_of_verbal_judo.htm.

Hackman, J. Richard, ed. 1990. *Groups that work (and those that don't).* San Francisco: Jossey-Bass.

Haleblian, Jerayr, and Sydney Finkelstein. 1993. Top management team size, CEO dominance, and firm performance: The moderating roles of environmental turbulence and discretion. *Academy of Management Journal* 36: 844–63.

Hall, Edward T. 1959. *The silent language.* Garden City, NY: Doubleday.

Hamel, Gary, and C. K. Prahalad. 1994. *Competing for the future.* Boston: Harvard Business School Press.

Hamilton, Joan. 1996. The new workplace. *Business Week*, April 29: 106–17.

Hamilton, William L. 2006. Low down, repulsed, yet watching all the same. *The New York Times* [electronic version], December 6: section 4, 5.

Hamm, John. 2006. The five messages leaders must manage. *Harvard Business Review*, May.

Hammer, Michael, and James Champy. 1993. *Reengineering the corporation.* New York: HarperCollins.

Hampden-Turner, Charles, and Fons Trompenaars. 2000. *Building cross-cultural competence.* New Haven, CT: Yale University Press.

Haney, William V. 1992. *Communication and organizational behavior*, 6th ed. Homewood, IL: Irwin.

Hare, A. Paul. 1962. *Handbook of small group research.* New York: Free Press.

Hare, A. Paul, and Robert Bales. 1963. Seating position and small group interaction. *Sociometry* 26: 480–86.

Harms, W. 2003. Discovery of inheritability of social behavior traits has human implications. *The University of Chicago Chronicle*, 23(6). From http://www.chronicle.uchicago .edu/031211/monkey.shtml.

Harper, Bob, and Ann Harper. 1993. *Succeeding as a self-directed work team.* Mohegan Lake, NY: MW Corp.

Harrell, Keith. 2000. *Attitude is everything.* New York: HarperCollins.

Harvard Business Review Daily Alert. 2010. Height and salary relationship. August 18.

Harvard Business Review Daily Alert. 2010. Fifty plus is the mellowest time of life. June 4.

Harvard Business Review Daily Alert. 2010. Successful change efforts involve people. May 10.

Harvey, Don, and Donald R. Brown. 1996. *An experiential approach to organizational development.* Upper Saddle River, NJ: Prentice Hall.

Haynes, J. 2004. Proxemics and U.S. culture. everythingESL.net. From http://www.every thingesl.net/inservices/proxemics_elevator.php.

Hearn, G. 1957. Leadership and the spatial factor in small groups. *Journal of Abnormal and Social Psychology* 54: 269–72.

Heath, Chip, and Dan Heath. 2010. *Switch: How to change things when change is hard.* New York: Broadway Books.

Heathfield, S. 2005. Twelve tips for team building: How to build successful work teams. About: Human Resources. From http://www.humanresources.about.com/od/involvementteams/a/twelve_tip_team.htm.

Heider, Fritz, 1958. *The psychology of interpersonal relations*. New York: Wiley.

Henrickson, Lorraine Uhlander, and John Psarouthakis. 1992. *Managing the growing firm*. Englewood Cliffs, NJ: Prentice Hall.

Herman, Roger E. 1995. *Turbulence*. Akron, OH: Oakhill Press.

Hersey, Paul, Kenneth H. Blanchard, and Dewey E. Johnson. 2001. *Management of organizational behavior*, 8th ed. Upper Saddle River, NJ: Prentice Hall.

Higher Education Academy. 2004. Online discussion groups—How to set them up. Subject Centre for History, Classics, and Archaeology. From http://hca.ltsn.ac.uk/resources/Briefing_Papers/bp8.php.

Hikaru Dojo Martial Arts Academy. 2001. Verbal judo Australia: Negotiations training and tactical communication. Hikaru Dojo Martial Arts Academy. From http://ninjado.com/verbaljudo.html.

Hinsberg, Claire. 1996. Stress rehearsal. *Corporate Detroit*, June: 29.

Hitchcock, Darcy E., and Marsha L. Willard, 1995. *Why teams can fail*. Chicago: Irwin.

Hocker, Joyce, and William Wilmot. 2010. *Interpersonal conflict*, 6th ed. New York: McGraw-Hill.

Hof, Robert D. 2007. Facebook's new wrinkles. *BusinessWeek*, August 20 and 27.

Holmes, T. 2003a. Creating a culture of inclusion. From http://www.bostonworks.boston.com.

———. 2003b. The multicultural marketplace: Diversity at work. BostonWorks.boston.com. From http://www.bostonworks.boston.com.

———. 2004a. Asian-Americans fastest-growing ethnic group. BostonWorks.boston.com. From http://www.bostonworks.boston.com/diversity/032004/moreinfo.shtml#boardseats.

———. 2004b. Diversity in the workplace. BostonWorks.boston.com. From http://www.bostonworks.boston.com.

———. 2004c. DiversityWorks: Institutions that value diversity must plan for it. BostonWorks.boston.com. From http://www.bostonworks.boston.com.

———. 2004d. Number of female corporate officers in America's largest 500 companies. BostonWorks.boston.com. From http://www.bostonworks.boston.com/diversity/032004/moreinfo.shtml#boardseats.

Holpp, Lawrence. 1999. *Managing teams*. New York: McGraw-Hill.

Holtz, Lou. 2006. *Wins, losses, and lessons*. New York: HarperCollins.

Hoober III, J. 2004. 3 charged in separate "road rage" incidents. *Lancaster New Era*, September: 1.

Hood, James. 2006. AT&T plans to kill Cingular name. *Consumer Affairs*, May 4.

Horovitz, Bruce. 1999. Wired on campus e-mail. *USA Today*, August 19: B1, B2.

Horowitz, S. 2005. Manz: Turn leaders into "superleaders." The University of Massachusetts Family Business Center. From http://www.umass.edu/fambiz/superleadership.htm.

Hosmer, LaRue. 2008. *The ethics of management*, 6th ed. New York: McGraw-Hill.

Hoyt, C. 2003. Transformational and transactional leadership in virtual and physical environments. *Small Group Research*, 34(6): 678.

Hudson, Frederic M. 1999. *The adult years*, rev. ed. San Francisco: Jossey-Bass.

Hudson, R. 2004. The open spaces of a futuristic office are better workplaces *St. Louis Post-Dispatch*, March: C1.

Hughes, Richard L., Robert C. Ginnett, and Gordon J. Curphy. 2002. *Leadership: Enhancing the lessons of experience*, 4th ed. New York: McGraw-Hill/Irwin.

Humphreys, Patrick, and Garrick *Jones*. 2008. The decision hedgehog for creative decision making. *Information Systems and eBusiness Management*, March: 117–37.

Hurst, David. 1995. *Crisis & renewal.* Boston: Harvard Business School Press.

Huszczo, Gregory E. 1990. Training for team building: How do you avoid the 10 common pitfalls of team-training approaches? *Training and Development Journal*, February: 37–43.

———. 1996. *Tools for team excellence*. Palo Alto, CA: Davies-Black.

IBM. 2010. *Capitalizing on complexity*. Somers, NY: IBM Corporation.

Iger, Bob. 2007. How I work. *Fortune*, December 10: 38.

Insko, Chester, John Schopler, Stephen M. Drigotas, Kenneth A. Graetz, James Kennedy, Chante Cox, and Garry Bornstein. 1993. The role of communication in interindividual-intergroup discontinuity. *Journal of Conflict Resolution* 37: 108.

Institute of General Semantics. 2004. General semantics. From www.generalsemantics.org.

Irwin, Jacqueline, Pamela Hopkins, Holly Payne, and Tyrone Adams. 2010. *Competent communication at work*. Dubuque, IA: Kendall Hunt.

Isaacs, William. 1999. *Dialogue*. New York: Currency.

Ivy, Diana K., and Phil Backlund. 1994. *Exploring genderspeak*. New York: McGraw-Hill.

Jana, Reena. 2007. Inside Innovation section. *BusinessWeek*, September 10: 2.

Janis, Irving. 1982. *Victims of groupthink*, 2nd ed. Boston: Houghton Mifflin.

Jarobe, Susan P. 1988. A comparison of input-output, process-output, and input-process-output models of small group problem-solving effectiveness. *Communication Monographs* 55: 121–42.

Jemmott, John B. III, and Elida Gonzales. 1989. Social status, the status distribution, and performance in small groups. *Journal of Applied Social Psychology* 19(7): 584–98.

Jensen, J. M., D. E. Conlon, S. E. Humphrey, and H. Moon. 2011. The consequences of completion: How level of completion influences information concealment by decision makers. Journal of Applied Social Psychology 41: 401–428.

Jeong, A. 2004. Methods and tools for the computational analysis of group interaction and argumentation in asynchronous online group discussions. Proposal for AERA 2005 Symposium (June 29, 2004). Methodological issues in Computer Mediated Communication Research. From http://dev22448-01.sp01.fsu.edu/Research/Proposals/AERA-2005_CMCResearchMethods(Jeong)_v2.pdf.

Jick, Todd D. 1993. *Managing change*. Homewood, IL: Irwin.

Johnson, A. 2003. People succeed at sarcasm through sneer determination. *Houston Chronicle*, December: 6.

Jones, Richard P. 1981. Nude sunbathing. *Flint Journal*, September 6: C6.

Jourard, Sidney M. 1964. *The transparent self: Self-disclosure and well-being*. Princeton, NJ: Van Nostrand.

Judge, Timothy, and Daniel Cable. 2011. Thin men get lower pay than average-weight men. *Harvard Daily Stat*, March 4.

Kameda, Tatsuya, Mark F. Stasson, James H. David, Craig Parks, and Suzi Zimmerman. 1992. Social dilemmas, subgroups, and motivational loss in task-oriented groups: In search of an "optimal" team size. *Social Psychology Quarterly* 55: 47–56.

Kane, Yukari Iwatani, and Jennifer Valentino-DeVries. 2011. Jobs tries to calm iPhone imbroglio. *The Wall Street Journal*, April 28, pp. A1, A2.

Kao, John. 1996. *Jamming*. New York: HarperBusiness.

Kaplan, Robert D. 2002. *Warrior politics*. New York: Random House.

Karpela, T. 2003. Verbal Judo. Verbal Judo Europe. From http://verbaljudoeurope.com/etusivu/index.php.

Katz, Daniel, and Robert Kahn. 1978. *The social psychology of organizations*, 2nd ed. New York: Wiley.

Katz, Lawrence C., and Manning Rubin. 1999. *Keep your brain alive*. New York: Workman.

Katzenbach, Jon R., and Douglas K. Smith. 1993. *The wisdom of teams*. Boston: Harvard Business School Press.

Kay, John. 2011. *Obliquity: Why our goals are best achieved indirectly*. New York: Penguin Press.

Keller, Robert T. 1986. Predictors of the performance of project groups in R&D organizations. *Academy of Management Journal* 29(4): 715–26.

Kellerman, Barbara. 2008. *Followership*. Boston: Harvard Business School Press.

Kelly, Francis J., and Heather Mayfield Kelly. 1986. *What they really teach you at the Harvard Business School*. New York: Warner Communications.

Keltner, John. 1970. *Interpersonal speech communication*. Belmont, CA: Wadsworth.

Kenyon, R. 2004. General semantics. Xenodochy.org. From http://www.xenodocy.org/gs/.

Kepner, Charles H., and Benjamin B. Tregoe. 1992. *The rational manager: A systematic approach to problem solving and decision making*. New York: McGraw-Hill.

———. 2004. eThink systems support and enhance the acclaimed Kepner-Tregoe processes for problem solving and decision making—long considered the gold standard throughout the world. From http://www.kepner-tregoe.com/ethink/eThink.cfm.

Kets De Cries, Manfred. 2001. *The leadership mystique*. Upper Saddle River, NJ: Prentice Hall.

Kibler, Robert, and Larry Barker. 1969. *Conceptual frontiers in speech communication*. New York: Speech Association of America.

Kidwell, Roland E., and Nathan Bennett. 1993. Employee propensity to withhold effort: A conceptual model to intersect three avenues of research. *Academy of Management Review* 18: 429–56.

Kiesler, Charles, and Sara Kiesler. 1969. *Conformity*. Reading, MA: Addison-Wesley.

Kinzel, Augustus. 1969. Toward an understanding of violence. *Attitude* 1.

Kirkman, Bradley L., and Benson Rosen. 1999. Beyond self-management: Antecedents and consequences of team empowerment. *Academy of Management Journal* 42: 58–74.

Klein, Gary. 2007. Performing a project premortem. *Harvard Business Review*, September: 18–19.

Knapp, Mark L. 1972. *Nonverbal communication in human interaction*. New York: Holt, Rinehart & Winston.

Korda, Michael. 1975. *Power! How to get it, how to use it*. New York: Random House.

Korn, Melissa. 2011. As world turns, Wharton adapts. *The Wall Street Journal*, February 3, p. B9.

Korn, Melissa, and Joe Light. 2011. On the lesson plan: Feelings. *The Wall Street Journal*, May 5, p. B6.

Korzybski, Alfred. 1948. *Selections from science and sanity: An introduction to non—Aristotelian systems and general semantics*. Lakeville, CN: Institute of General Semantics.

Kotter, John P. 1986. *Power and influence: Beyond formal authority*. New York: Free Press.

———. 2002. *The heart of change*. Boston: Harvard Business School Press.

Kotter, John, and Lorne Whitehead. 2010. *Buy in*. Boston: Harvard Business School Press.

Kouzes, James M., and Barry Z. Posner. 1995. *Credibility*. San Francisco: Jossey-Bass.

———. 2002. *The leadership challenge*, 3rd ed. San Francisco: Jossey-Bass.

Kouzes, James, and Barry Posner. 2010. *The truth about leadership*. San Francisco: Jossey-Bass.

Kranz, N. 2004. Self-directed work teams: The antidote for "heroic suicide." *Journal of Extension* 42(2). From http://www.joe.org/joe/2004april/tt1.shtml.

Krol, B. 2004. The SpeechGuard is the luxury of multilingual communication for travelers. *PR Newswire*, December: 1.

Krzyzewski, Mike, 2000. *Leading with the heart*. New York: Warner Books.

Kuczmarski, Susan Smith, and Thomas D. Kuczmarski. 1995. *Values based leadership*. Englewood Cliffs, NJ: Prentice Hall.

Kusy, Mitchell, and Elizabeth Holloway. 2009. *Toxic workplace*. San Francisco: Jossey-Bass.

LaFasto, Frank, and Carl E. Larson. 2001. *When teams work best*. Thousand Oaks, CA: Sage.

Langan-Fox, Janice, Gary Cooper, and Richard J. Klimoski. 2007. *Research companion to the dysfunctional workplace: Management challenges*. New York: Edward Elgar.

Lansberg, Ivan. 2007. The tests of a prince. *Harvard Business Review*, September: 92–101.

Larson, Carl E. 1969. Forms of analysis and small group problem solving. *Speech Monographs* 36: 452–55.

———. 1993. The leader as problem-solver. *Teamworks* 3: 9.

Larson, Carl E., and Frank M. J. LaFasto. 1989. *Teamwork*. Newbury Park, CA: Sage.

Lawler, Edward E., III. 1992. *The ultimate advantage: Creating the high-involvement organization*. San Francisco: Jossey-Bass.

Lawrence, Paul, and J. Lorsch. 1969. *Developing organizations: Diagnosis and action*. Reading, MA: Addison-Wesley.

Leathers, Dale. 2002. *Nonverbal communication systems*, 3rd ed. Boston: Allyn & Bacon.

Leavitt, Harold. 1964. *Managerial psychology*, 2nd ed. Chicago: University of Chicago Press.

Lefkowitz, M., R. Blake, and J. Mouton. 1955. Status factors in pedestrian violation of traffic signals. *Journal of Abnormal and Social Psychology* 51: 704–6.

Lehrer, Jonah. 2009. *How we decide*. Boston: Houghton-Mifflin.

Lei, Xiaolan. 2006. Sexism in language. *Journal of Language and Linguistics*, 5(1).

Lencioni, Patrick. 2002. *The five dysfunctions of a team*. San Francisco: Jossey-Bass.

———. 2005. *Overcoming the five dysfunctions of a team: Field guide*. San Francisco: Jossey-Bass.

———. 2007. *The five dysfunctions of a team: Team assessment*. San Francisco: Jossey-Bass.

Lennick, Doug, and Fred Kiel. 2005. *Moral intelligence*. Upper Saddle River, NJ: Wharton School.

Leonard, Dorothy, and Susan Straus. 2007. Putting your company's whole brain to work. *Harvard Business Online/Business Week*, September 13.

Leonard, Dorothy, and Walter Swaps. 1999. *When sparks fly: Igniting creativity in groups*. Boston: Harvard Business School Press.

Leviton, Richard. 1995. *Brain builders*. Paramus, NJ: Prentice Hall.

Levitt, Steven, and Stephen Dubner. 2009. *Superfreakonomics*. New York: William Morrow.

Lewicki, Roy J., Joseph A. Litterer, John W. Minton, and David M. Saunders. 1998. *Negotiation*, 3rd ed. Chicago: Irwin/McGraw-Hill.

Lewin, Kurt. 1951. *Field theory in social science*. New York: Harper & Row.

Light, Richard. 1992. The Harvard assessment seminars.

Liker, Jeffrey, and David Meier. 2007. *Toyota talent*. New York: McGraw-Hill.

Liker, Jeffrey, and James Franz. 2011. *The Toyota way to continuous improvement*. New York: McGraw-Hill.

Likert, Rensis. 1967. *The human organization*. New York: McGraw-Hill.

Lipman-Blumen, Jean, and Harold J. Leavitt. 1999. *Hot groups*. New York: Oxford University Press.

Lipnack, Jessica, and Jeffrey Stamps. 1997. *Virtual teams*. New York: Wiley.

Locke, Edwin A. 2007. The case for inductive theory building. *Journal of Management* 12(33): 867–90.

Loden, Marilyn. 1990. Feminine leadership: Or how to succeed in business without being one of the boys. In *Manager's bookshelf*, ed. Jon L. Pierce and John W. Newstrom. New York: Harper & Row, pp. 295–301.

Lorsch, Jay, and Paul Lawrence. 1972. *Managing group and intergroup relations*. Homewood, IL: Irwin.

Los Angeles Times. 2004. Think they need to spend more time together? *Seattle Times*, September: F6.

Louis, Meryl Reis. 1990. The gap in management education. *GMAT Selections* 6: 1–12.

Lovins, Amory B., and L. Hunter Lovins. 1995. Reinventing the wheels. *Atlantic Monthly*, January: 77–86.

Lublin, J. 2004. To win advancement, you need to clean up any bad speech habits. *The Wall Street Journal*, October: B1.

Lucas, Stephen E. 1998. *The art of public speaking*. New York: McGraw-Hill.
Luft, Joseph. 1969. *Of human interaction*. Palo Alto, CA: National Press.
———. 1984. *Group processes: An introduction to group dynamics*, 3rd ed. Palo Alto, CA: National Press.
Lundin, William, and Kathleen Lundin. 1993. *The healing manager*. San Francisco: Berrett-Koehler.
Luntz, Frank. 2007. *Words that work*. New York: Hyperion.
Luntz, Frank. 2011. *Winning*. New York: Hyperion.
Lutz, Robert A. 1998. *Guts*. New York: Wiley.
Madjar, Nora, Greg R. Oldham, and Michael G. Pratt. 2002. There's no place like home? The contributions of work and nonwork creativity support to employees' creative performance. *The Academy of Management Journal*, August 4: 757–67.
Magner, Mike. 1988. Geology blamed for state's loss of atom smasher. *Ann Arbor News*, November 11: A1, A4.
Maier, Norman R. F. 1963. *Problem-solving discussions and conferences*. New York: McGraw-Hill.
Maier, Norman R. F., and A. R. Solem. 1952. The contributions of a discussion leader to the quality of group thinking: The effective use of minority opinions. *Human Relations* 5: 277–88.
Majchrzak, A., A. Malhotra, J. Stamps, and J. Lipnack. 2004. Can absence make a team grow stronger? *Harvard Business Review* 82(5): 131.
Mann, Tana. 2003. Relationship between metacommunication among romantic partners and their level of relationship satisfaction. *Journal of Undergraduate Research, 6.*
Manz, Charles C. 1999. *The leadership wisdom of Jesus*. San Francisco: Berrett-Koehler.
Manz, Charles C., and Christopher P. Neck. 1999. *Mastering self-leadership*. Upper Saddle River, NJ: Prentice Hall.
Manz, Charles C., and Henry P. Sims. 1990. *Super leadership: Leading others to lead themselves*. New York: Berkeley Books.
———. 1993. *Business without bosses*. New York: Wiley.
———. 2001. *The new SuperLeadership*. San Francisco: Berrett-Koehler.
Maslow, Abraham. 1970. *Motivation and personality*, 2nd ed. New York: Harper & Row.
McCain, John, with Mark Salter. 1999. *Faith of my fathers*. New York: Random House.
McCain, John. 2002. In *The right words at the right time*, ed. Marlo Thomas. New York: Atria Books, pp. 213–16.
McCall, Morgan, and George Hollenbeck. 2002. *Developing global executives*. Boston: Harvard Business School Press.
McCauley, Cynthia, Russ Moxley, and Ellen Van Velsor, eds. 1998. *Handbook of leadership development*. San Francisco: Jossey-Bass.
McCormack, Mark H. 1984. *What they don't teach you at Harvard Business School*. New York: Bantam Books.
———. 1995. *On negotiating*. Beverly Hills, CA: Dove Books.
McCroskey, James. 1971. Human information processing and diffusion. In *Speech communication behavior: Perspectives and principles*, ed. Larry Barker and Robert Kibler. Englewood Cliffs, NJ: Prentice Hall, pp. 167–81.
McCroskey, James, Carl Larson, and Mark Knapp. 1971. *An introduction to interpersonal communication*. Englewood Cliffs, NJ: Prentice Hall.
McDonald, T., L. Toussaint, and J. Schweiger. 2004. The influence of social status on token women leaders' expectations about leading male-dominated groups. *Sex Roles*, 50(5/6): 401.
McGrath, Joseph E., and Irwin Altman. 1966. *Small group research: A synthesis and critique of the field*. New York: Holt, Rinehart & Winston.
McGraw, Phillip C. 1999. *Life strategies*. New York: Hyperion.
McGregor, Jena. 2006. How to play follow the leader. *BusinessWeek*, February 13.

Mehrabian, Albert. 1971. Nonverbal betrayal of feeling. *Journal of Experimental Research in Personality* 5: 64–73.

Meister, Jeanne C. 1994. *Corporate quality universities*. Burr Ridge, IL: Irwin.

Merx, Katie. 2008. GM to roll out vision of cleaner, safer ride. *Detroit Free Press*, January 8: A1.

Metcalf, Lynn E., Allan Bird, Mahesh Shankarmahesh, Zeynep Aycan, Jorma Larimo, and Dídimo Dewar Valdelamar. 2006. Cultural tendencies in negotiation: A comparison of Finland, India, Mexico, Turkey, and the United States. *Journal of World Business* 41: 382–94.

Michaelson, Gerald A. 2001. *Sun Tzu: The art of war for managers*. Holbrook, MA: Adams Media Corp.

Michalko, Michael. 1998. *Cracking creativity*. Berkeley, CA: Ten Speed Press.

———. 2006. *Thinkertoys*, 2nd ed. Berkeley, CA: Ten Speed Press.

Middleton, Diana, and Joe Light. 2011. Harvard changes course: School's curriculum overhaul part of a push to alter elite B-school cultures. *The Wall Street Journal*, February 3, p. B8.

Miles, Stephen A., and Michael D. Watkins. 2007. The leadership team: Complementary strengths or conflicting agendas? *Harvard Business Review*, April.

Milgram, Stanley. 1974. *Obedience to authority: An experimental view*. New York: Harper & Row.

Miller, C. W. 2004. Body language can speak volumes. *Roanoke Times & World News*, October: 1.

Mills, Judson, and Elliot Aronson. 1965. Opinion change as a function of the communicator's attractiveness and desire to influence. *Journal of Personality and Social Psychology* 1: 73–77.

Mind Tools. 2004. Creativity tools—Develop creative solutions to the problems you face. Mind Tools. From http://www.mindtools.com/pages/main/newMN_CT.htm.

———. 2005. Decision making techniques—How to make better decisions. Mind Tools. From http://www.mindtools.com/pages/main/newMN_TED.htm.

Miner, John B. 1988. *Organizational behavior: Performance and productivity*. New York: Random House.

Modica, Peter. 1996. Stress takes a toll on memory. *Detroit Free Press*, August 13: F10.

Mohr, William L., and Harriet Mohr. 1983. *Quality circles: Changing images of people at work*. Reading, MA: Addison-Wesley.

Moran, Richard A. 1993. *Never confuse a memo with reality*. New York: HarperBusiness.

Morgan, James, and Jeffrey Liker. 2007. *The Toyota product development system*. New York: Productivity Press.

Morris, Betsy. 1999. Addicted to sex. *Fortune*, May 10: 66–80.

Morrison, Ann M., Randall P. White, and Ellen Van Velsor. 1990. Breaking the glass ceiling: Can women reach the top of America's largest corporations? In *Manager's bookshelf*, ed. Jon L. Pierce and John W. Newstrom. New York: Harper & Row, pp. 289–94.

Morrison, Elizabeth (2010), "From the editors, OB in AMJ: what is hot and what is not?" Academy of Management Journal, October, 2010, 53, 932–936.

Morrison, Elizabeth Wolfe, and Corey C. Phelps. 1999. Taking charge at work: Extrarole efforts to initiate workplace change. *Academy of Management Journal* 42: 403–19.

Murnighan, Keith. 1992. *Bargaining games*. New York: Morrow.

Murphy, Kevin J. 1993. *Effective listening*. Salem, NH: ELI Press.

Murray, Stephanie. 2007. A look inside Google. *The Ann Arbor News*, September 23: A1.

Mydans, Seth. 1990a. Academic success seen as selling out, study on blacks says. *San Francisco Chronicle*, April 25: B6.

———. 1990b. Wanna-be's: Youth gangs spread from the inner city. *Ann Arbor News*, May 6: B1, B4.

Myers, Isabel B. 1993. *Introduction to type*, 5th ed. Palo Alto, CA: Consulting Psychologists Press.

Myers, Laura L., and Mary L. Tucker. 2005. Increasing awareness of emotional intelligence in a business curriculum. *Business Communication Quarterly* 68: 44.

Myser, Michael. 2006. When brainstorming goes bad. *Business 2.0*, October: 76.

Nadler, David A., Robert B. Shaw, and A. Elise Walton. 1995. *Discontinuous change*. San Francisco: Jossey-Bass.

Nadler, Gerald, Shozo Hibino, and John Farrell. 1999. *Creative solution finding*. Rocklin, CA: Prima.

Nahavandi, Afsaneh. 2003. *The art and science of leadership*. Upper Saddle River, NJ: Prentice Hall.

———. 2000. *The art and science of leadership*. Upper Saddle River, NJ: Prentice Hall.

Naisbitt, John. 1982. *Megatrends: Ten new directions transforming our lives*. New York: Warner Books.

Nakane, Hisao, and Rita Darga. 1995. *Building a continuous improvement culture from the bottom up*. Mt. Clemens, MI: Gold Leaf Press.

Nanus, Bert. 1992. *Visionary leadership*. San Francisco: Jossey-Bass.

National Oceanographic and Atmospheric Administration. 2004. Diversity dimensions. NOAA. From http://www.rdc.noaa.gov/~divdimensionstxt.html.

———. 2007. NOAA's managing diversity strategy. NOAA. From http://www.rdc.noaa.gov/~Diversity/newdivindex/mdstrategy.html.

Neeley, Tsedal, and Paul Leonardi. 2011. Effective managers say the same thing twice (or more). *Harvard Business Review*, May, pp. 38–39.

Nelson, Bob. 1994. *1001 ways to reward employees*. New York: Workman.

Nemeth, C., and J. Goncalo. 2004. Influence and persuasion in small groups. Institute of Industrial Relations Working Paper Series: University of California, Berkeley. From: http://repositories.cdlib.org/cgi/viewcontent.cgi?article=1100&context=iir.

Network-Centric Advocacy. 2003. NetGen wants small group organizing. From http://www.network-centricadvocacy.net/2003/10/netgen_wants_sm.html.

Newman, David M. 2006. *Sociology: Exploring the architecture of everyday life*. New York: McGraw-Hill.

Newstrom, John, and Edward Scannel. 1998. *The big book of team building games*. New York: McGraw-Hill.

Newsweek Beauty Poll, June 30, 2010. Retrieved from the Harvard Daily Briefing, September 30, 2010.

Ngai, Eric, Chuck Law, Simon Chan, and Francis Wat. 2008. Importance of the Internet to human resource practitioners in Hong Kong. *Personnel Review* 37: 66–84.

Ngwenya, J. 2003. The effects of augmenting face-to-face meetings with web-based asynchronous group support systems. *Journal of Information Technology Theory and Application*. From http://www.findarticles.com/p/articles/mi_qa4008/is_200301/ai_n9216855.

Odell, C. 2003. Emotional intelligence, communication skills, initiative marks of star workers. *Colorado Springs Gazette*, June: BUS.4.

O'Hair, Dan, Gustav W. Friedrich, and Lynda Dixon Shaver. 2010. *Strategic communication in business and the professions*, 7th ed. Boston: Houghton Mifflin.

Ohmae, Kenichi. 1999. *The borderless world*. New York: HarperBusiness.

Oldham, Greg R., and Anne Cummings. 1996. Employee creativity: Personal and contextual factors at work. *Academy of Management Journal* 39: 607–34.

Opper, Susanna. 1988. A groupware toolbox. *Byte*, December: 275–82.

Ornstein, Suzyn. 1989. The hidden influences of office design. *Academy of Management Executive* 3(2): 144–47.

Osborn, Alex. 1953. *Applied imagination: Principles and procedures of creative thinking*. New York: Scribner.

O'Toole, James. 1999. *Leadership A to Z.* San Francisco: Jossey-Bass.

Ouchi, William. 1981. *Theory Z: How American business can meet the Japanese challenge.* Reading, MA: Addison-Wesley.

Palus, Charles J., and David M. Horth. 2002. *The leader's edge.* San Francisco: Jossey-Bass.

Parselle, Charles B. 2007. No way out: Negotiation and the prisoner's dilemma. From www.mediate.com.

Pascale, Richard, Jerry Sternin, and Monique Sternin. 2010. *The power of positive deviance.* Boston: Harvard Business Press.

Patler, Louis. 1999. *Don't compete…tilt the field.* Oxford: Capstone.

Patterson, James. 1996. *How to become a better negotiator.* New York: AMACOM.

Patterson, Kerry, Joseph Grenny, David Maxfield, Ron McMillan, and Al Switzler. 2008. *Influencer: The power to change anything.* New York: McGraw-Hill.

Paul, M. 2005. Left out of the in crowd: Cliques sometimes form among grown women. Results can be painful. *Chicago Tribune*, January: 3.

Paul, S., P. Seetharaman, and P. Samarah. 2005. Understanding conflict in virtual teams: An experimental investigation using content analysis. From http://csdl.computer.org/comp/proceedings/hicss/2005/2268/01/22680044aabs.htm.

Pearsall, Matthew, Aleksander Ellis, and Joel Evans. 2008. Unlocking the effects of gender faultlines on team creativity: Is activation the key? *Journal of Applied Psychology*, January: 225.

Pearson, Christine, and Christine Porath. 2009. *The cost of bad behavior.* New York: Portfolio/Penguin.

Perry, James M. 1999. War hero McCain focuses on VFW to boost campaign. *The Wall Street Journal*, September 6: A28.

Peters, Tom. 1994. *Liberation management.* New York: Fawcett Columbine.

Peterson, R., and K. Behfar. 2003. The dynamic relationship between performance feedback, trust, and conflict in groups: A longitudinal study. *Organizational Behavior and Human Decision Processes*, 92(1/2): 102.

Pfeffer, Jeffrey. 1981. *Power in organizations.* Marshfield, MA: Pitman.

———. 1998. *Human equation.* Boston: Harvard Business School Press.

Pfeffer, Jeffrey. 2010. *Power.* New York: HarperBusiness.

Pfeffer, Jeffrey, and Christina T. Fong. 2002. The end of business schools? Less success than meets the eye. *Academy of Management Learning and Education*, September: 78–95.

Pfeffer, Jeffrey, and John F. Veiga. 1999. Putting people first for organizational success. *Academy of Management Executive* 13: 37–48.

Phillips, Donald T. 1992. *Lincoln on leadership.* New York: Warner Books.

Phillips, Katherine W., Katie A. Liljenquist, and Margaret A. Neale. 2009. Is the pain worth the gain? The advantages and liabilities of agreeing with socially distinct newcomers. *Personality and Social Psychology Bulletin* 35: 336–350.

Piazza, Judyth. 2007. Not-so-merry: Five ways to tell if mob mentality is driving your decisions. Newsblaze.com, October 19.

Pierce, Jon L., and John W. Newstrom. 2000. *Leaders and the leadership process*, 2nd ed. New York: McGraw-Hill.

Pink, Daniel. 2009. *Drive: The surprising truth about what motivates us.* New York: Riverhead Books.

Pitts, Leonard. 2007. God and the fuzzy teddy bear. *Detroit Free Press*, December 8: A12.

———. 2004b. Leadership aspirations show regard to gender. *Pittsburgh Post-Gazette*, November: C11.

Pittsburgh Post-Gazette. 2004a. Forget IQ and EG. Best entrepreneurs have high BQ. *Pittsburgh Post-Gazette*, October: F2.

Popkey, Dan. 1986. NFL football sacks Monday meetings of Boise Council. *The Idaho Statesman*, March 1: 1.

Portnoy, Bill. 1992. The empowered knowledge worker. *Enterprise* 6: 26–29.

Post-Tribune wire report. 2004. E-mail not always effective communication. *The Gary, Indiana Post-Tribune*, December: E1.

Potter, Earl H., and Fred E. Fiedler. 1993. Selecting leaders: Making the most of previous experience. *Journal of Leadership Studies* 1: 61–70.

Power, D. J. 2003. A brief history of decision support systems. DSS Resources. From http://dssresources.com/history/dsshistory.html.

PowerPublicSpeaking. 2001. Public speaking tip and trick links. From http://www.powerpublicspeaking.com.

PR Newswire. 2003. Inaugural speech fitness institute challenging executives to "flex" communication "muscles." *PR Newswire*, April: 1.

———. 2004. Global crossing drives collaboration, productivity with Microsoft Office Live Meeting. *PR Newswire*, August: 1.

Pritchett, Price. 1996. *Mindshift*. Dallas: Pritchett & Associates.

Pritchett, Price, and Ron Pound. 1995. *The stress of organizational life*. Dallas: Pritchett & Associates.

Proenca, Jose. 2007. Team dynamics and team empowerment in health care organizations. *Health Care Management Review* 32: 370.

Puente, M. 2004. Most "voice lifts" don't fit "vanity surgery" label: Cases of physical damage outnumber those who just want to sound younger. *USA Today*, June: D5.

Quinn, Robert. 1973. *Job satisfaction: Is there a trend?* Washington, DC: U.S. Department of Labor.

Raja, M. K., and Hsin-Ginn Hwang. 1992. Computer-aided decision-making in large groups. *Journal of Information Technology Management* 3: 13–18.

Rajiva, Lila, and Bill Bonner. 2007. *Mobs, messiahs, and markets: Surviving the public spectacle in finance and politics*. New York: Wiley.

Ramundo, Bernard A. 1992. *Effective negotiating*. New York: Quorum Books.

Rarick, David, Gary F. Soldow, and Ronald S. Geizer. 1976. Self-monitoring as a mediator of conformity. *Central States Speech Journal* 27: 267–71.

Rash, Wayne, Jr. 1989. Groping for groupware. *Byte*, April: 135–38.

Rath, Tom, and Jim Harter. 2010. *Well-being: The five essential elements*. New York: Gallup Press.

Ray, Michael, and Rochelle Myers. 1989. *Creativity in business*. New York: Doubleday.

Rayner, Steven R. 1996. *Team traps*. New York: Wiley.

Reed, C. 2004. School's nose stud ban won't wash. *Rocky Mountain News*, May: E7.

Rehfeld, John E. 1994. *Alchemy of a leader*. New York: Wiley.

Reichheld, Frederick. 1996. *The loyalty effect*. Boston: Harvard Business School Press.

Reinig, Bruce, Ira Horowitz, and Gerald Whittenberg. 2011. The effect of team-based learning on student attitudes and satisfaction. *Decision Sciences Journal of Innovative Education* 9 (January): 27–47.

Reply Systems. 2005. Reply. Fleetwood Group Inc. From http://www.replysystems.com.

Reynolds, Garr. 2008. Presentation Zen: Simple Ideas for Presentation Design and Delivery. Berkeley, CA.: New Riders.

Richmond, Virginia, and James C. McCroskey. 2000. *Nonverbal behavior and interpersonal relations*. New York: Allyn & Bacon.

Robbins, Harvey, and Michael Finley. 1995. *Why teams don't work*. Princeton, NJ: Peterson's/Pacesetter Books.

Robin, D. 2004. I hate it when you do that! (Do what?): Strategies for handling difficult workplace behaviors, part 3. Daniel Robin & Associates. From http://www.abetterworkplace.com/difficult3.html.

Robinson, Alan G., and Sam Stern. 1997. *Corporate creativity*. San Francisco: Berrett-Koehler.

Robinson, G. 2004. The behavior of genes [Op-Ed]. *The New York Times*, December 23: A27.

Robinson, Sandra L., and Anne M. O'Leary-Kelly. 1998. Monkey see, monkey do: The influence of work groups on the antisocial behavior of employees. *Academy of Management Journal* 41: 658–72.

Rodes, Joy. 1992. Personal correspondence, November 18.

Rodin, Robert. 1999. *Free, perfect, and now.* New York: Simon & Schuster.

Rogers, Carl R., and F. J. Roethlisberger. 1952. Barriers and gateways to communication. *Harvard Business Review* 30: 48.

Rogers, Everett M. 1995. *Diffusion of innovations*, 4th ed. New York: Free Press.

Rokeach, Milton. 1968. *Beliefs, attitudes, and values.* San Francisco: Jossey-Bass.

———. 1971. Long-range experimental modifications of values, attitudes, and behavior. In *Human behavior and its control*, ed. William A. Hunt. Cambridge, MA: Schenkman, pp. 93–105.

———. 1973. *The nature of human values.* New York: Free Press.

Romig, Dennis A. 2001. *Side by side leadership.* Atlanta: Bard Press.

Rosario, N. 2003. Ten tips every webinar presenter needs to know. *Coreography.* From http://www.coreography.com/docs/pr_TenTips.pdf.

Roseberry, C. 2004. Management tips for virtual success: Help keep your mobile teams productive. About.com. From http://mobileoffice.about.com/od/getmobilized/qt/mngtips.htm.

Rosen, Robert, Patricia Digh, Marshall Singer, and Carl Phillips. 2000. *Global literacies.* New York: Simon & Schuster.

Rosener, Judy B. 1995. *America's competitive secret: Utilizing women as a management strategy.* New York: Oxford University Press.

Rosenfeld, Howard. 1965. Effect of approval-seeking induction on interpersonal proximity. *Psychological Reports* 17: 120–22.

Roush, Matt. 1996. Working with team concept extends to office furnishings. *Crain's Detroit Business*, May 6: 10–11.

Ruch, Richard S. 1972. An analysis of the Freudian slip and errors in speech communication. *Journal of Technical Writing and Communication* 2: 343–52.

Runyan, Kenneth. 1973. Some interactions between personality variables and management styles. *Journal of Applied Psychology* 57: 288–94.

Russell, D. 2004. Golden rule: Rewarding top performers. Envision Software, Incorporated. From http://www.envisionsoftware.com/Articles/Break_the_Golden_Rule.html.

Russo, N. F. 1967. Connotations of seating arrangements. *Cornell Journal of Social Relations* 2: 37–44.

Safon, Vincente. 2007. Factors that influence recruiters' choice of B-schools and their MBA graduates: Evidence and implications for B-schools. *Academy of Management Learning & Education* 6: 217–33.

Sager, K. L., and J. Gastil. 2006. The origins and consequences of consensus decision making: A test of the social consensus model. *Southern Communication Journal*, informaworld.com.

St. Martin's College. 2003. Decision making styles. Career Pages. From http://www.ucsm.ac.uk/careers/student/decisionStyles.php.

Sample, Steven. 2002. *The contrarian's guide to leadership.* San Fancisco: Jossey-Bass.

Sattler, William, and N. Edd Miller. 1968. *Discussion and conference.* Englewood Cliffs, NJ: Prentice Hall.

Satzinger, John, and Lorne Olfman. 1992. A research program to assess user perceptions of group work support. *Proceedings of the Association for Computing Machinery* 7: 99–106.

Sayles, Leonard R. 1993. *The working leader.* New York: Free Press.

Schachter, Stanley. 1951. Deviation, rejection, and communication. *Journal of Abnormal and Social Psychology* 46: 190–207.

Schembechler, Bo, and John U. Bacon. 2007. *Bo's lasting lessons*. New York: Business Plus.

Schembechler, Bo, and Mitch Albom. 1989. *Bo: Life, laughs, and lessons of a college football legend*. New York: Warner Books.

Schnake, Mel E. 1990. *Human relations*. Columbus, OH: Merrill.

Schorow, S. 2005. Gridlock unlocks brain's potential. *Boston Herald*, January: 4.

Schutz, William C. 1958. *FIRO: A three-dimensional theory of interpersonal behavior*. New York: Holt, Rinehart & Winston.

———. 1967. *Joy: Expanding human awareness*. New York: Grove.

———. 1971. *Here comes everybody: Bodymind and encounter culture*. New York: Harper & Row.

Scott, Cynthia D., and Dennis T. Jaffe. 1991. *Empowerment: A practical guide for success*. Los Altos, CA: CRISP Publications.

Scott, Gini Graham. 2008. Take emotion out of conflict resolution. *Training and Development*, February: 84–85.

Scotti, Anna, and Paul Young. 1997. *Buzzwords: L.A. freespeak*. New York: St. Martin's Press.

Seebach, L. 2004. Communication styles wear many faces: What is said often carries less weight than how it's said. *Rocky Mountain News*, July: A46.

Seglin, Jeffrey L. 1996. The happiest workers in the world. *Inc*. Special Issue, "The state of small business": 62–74.

Seligman, Martin. 2011. *Flourish*. New York: Free Press.

Sell, J., M. Lovaglia, E. Mannix, C. Samuelson, and R. Wilson. 2004. Investigating conflict, power, and status within and among groups. *Small Group Research* 35(1): 44–72. From http://sgr.sagepub.com/cgi/reprint/35/1/44.

Semper, R. 2004. The importance of place. Association of Science-Technology Centers, California Science Center. From http://www.astc.org/resource/education/learning_semper.htm.

Senge, Peter M. 1990. *The fifth discipline*. New York: Doubleday.

Shani, A. B., and James Lau. 2000. *Behavior in organizations*, 7th ed. Homewood, IL: Irwin.

Shaw, Marvin E. 1981. *Group dynamics: The psychology of small group behavior*, 3rd ed. New York: McGraw-Hill.

Sheldon, William. 1940. *The varieties of human physique*. New York: Harper & Row.

———. 1942. *The varieties of temperament*. New York: Harper & Row.

———. 1954. *Atlas of man: A guide for somatotyping the adult male of all ages*. New York: Harper & Row.

Shell, G. Richard, and Mario Mousa. 2007. *The art of WOO*. New York: Penguin Group.

Shellenbarger, Sue. 1999. *Work and family*. New York: Ballantine Books.

Shenkar, Oded. 2010. Copycats: How smart companies use imitation to gain a strategic edge. Boston: Harvard Business Press.

Shepard, James A. 1993. Productivity loss in performance groups: A motivation analysis. *Psychological Bulletin* 113: 67–81.

Sherif, Muzafer. 1963. *The psychology of social norms*. New York: Harper & Row.

Sherman, Joe. 1994. *In the rings of Saturn*. New York: Oxford University Press.

Shriberg, David, and Arthur Shriberg. 2011. *Practicing leadership*, 4th ed. New York: John Wiley & Sons.

Shula, Don, and Ken Blanchard, 1995. *Everyone's a coach*. New York: HarperBusiness.

Siakas, Kerstin, and Errikos Siakas. 2008. The need for trust relationships to enable successful virtual team collaboration in software outsourcing. *International Journal of Technology Policy and Management* 8(1): 59.

Simon, Herbert A. 1987. Making management decisions: The role of intuition and emotion. *Academy of Management Executive*, February: 57–64.

Sims, Henry P., Jr., and Charles C. Manz. 1996. *Company of heroes*. New York: Wiley.

Sims, Henry P., Jr., and Peter Lorenzi. 1992. *The new leadership paradigm*. Newbury Park, CA: Sage.

Smith, R. 2003. How design affects the mind. *Wall Street Journal*, June: B8.

Sommer, Robert. 1959. Studies in personal space. *Sociometry* 22: 247–60.

———. 1965. Further studies of small group ecology. *Sociometry* 28: 337–48.

———. 1969. *Personal space: The behavioral basis of design*. Englewood Cliffs, NJ: Prentice Hall.

Sproull, Lee, and Sara Kiesler. 1991. Computers, networks and work. *Scientific American*, September: 116–23.

Stack, Jack. 1992. *The great game of business*. New York: Doubleday-Currency.

Stahl, Lesley. 1999. *Reporting live*. New York: Simon & Schuster.

Stanley, A. 2004. Candidates most telling when they aren't talking. *New York Times*, October: A18.

Stanwick, Peter, and Sarah Stanwick. 2009. *Understanding business ethics*. Upper Saddle River, NJ: Pearson.

Stark, Eric, Jason Shaw, and Michelle Duffy. 2008. Preference for group work, winning orientation, and social loafing behavior in groups. *Group & Organization Management* 32: 699–723.

Staub, Robert E., II. 1996. *The heart of leadership*. Provo, UT: Executive Excellence Publishing.

Stech, Ernest, and Sharon A. Ratliffe. 1985. *Effective group communication: How to get action by working in groups*. Lincolnwood, IL: National Text Book.

Stein, Debra. 2007. Sending the right signals: Honesty, respect, and power. *Public Management* 89(3): 30–32.

Steiner, Ivan D. 1972. *Group process and productivity*. New York: Academic Press.

Steinmetz, Lawrence. 1969. *Managing the marginal and unsatisfactory performer*. Reading, MA: Addison-Wesley.

Steinzor, B. 1950. The spatial factor in face-to-face discussion groups. *Journal of Abnormal and Social Psychology* 45: 552–55.

Stockdale, S. 2004. General semantics. ThisIsNotThat.com: From http://www.ThisIsNotThat.com.

Stogdill, Ralph. 1948. Personal factors associated with leadership. *Journal of Psychology* 25: 35–71.

———. 1993. *Handbook of leadership: A survey of theory and research*. New York: Free Press.

Stoltz, Paul G. 1997. *Adversity quotient*. New York: Wiley.

Stoney, Patty. 1993. The Saturn story. Paper presented at the International Conference on Self-Managed Work Teams, September 23.

Strodbeck, Fred, and L. H. Hook. 1961. The social dimensions of a twelve-man jury table. *Sociometry* 24: 397–415.

Strongman, K., and B. Champness. 1968. Dominance hierarchies and conflict in eye contact. *Acta Psychologica* 28: 376–86.

Sulkowicz, Kerry. 2007. My boss, the whippersnapper. *BusinessWeek*, August 20: 16.

Sullivan, Gordon R., and Michael V. Harper. l996. *Hope is not a method*. New York: Random House.

Sulloway, Frank J. 1996. *Born to rebel*. New York: Pantheon Books.

Sutton, Robert I. 2002. *Weird ideas that work*. New York: Free Press.

Symington, James W. 1971. *The stately game*. New York: Macmillan.

Tannen, Deborah. 1991. *You just don't understand*. New York: Ballantine Books.

———. 1995. *Talking from 9 to 5*. New York: Avon Books.

Tapping, Don, Sue Kozlowski, Laura Archibold, and Todd Sperl. 2009. *Value stream management for healthcare*. Chelsea, MI: MCS Media.

Taylor, Marisa. 2010. Businesses focus on critical thinking. *The Wall Street Journal*, September 12.

Taylor, William. 2011. *Practically radical*. New York: HarperCollins.

Team Technology. 2004. Team building. Team technology. From http://www.teamtechnology.co.uk/tt/h-articl/tb-basic.htm.

Terwiesch, Christian. 2010. Idea generation and the quality of the best idea, *Management Science* 56, no. 4: 591–605.

Thelen, Herbert, and Watson Dickerman. 1949. Stereotypes and the growth of groups. *Educational Leadership* 6: 309–16.

TheScienceDesk.com. 2004. Observations and inferences. TheScienceDesk.com. From http://www.thesciencdesk.com/pdffiles/ObservationsInferencesMeasu.pdf.

TheWorkingManager.com. 2005. The dean: Control and power. From http://www.theworkingmanager.com/articles/detail.asp?ArticleNo=32.

Thibaut, John W., and Harold H. Kelley. 1959. *The social psychology of groups*. New York: Wiley.

———. 1986. *The social psychology of groups*, 2nd ed. New Brunswick, NJ: Transaction Books.

Thomas-Hunt, M., and K. Phillips. 2004. When what you know is not enough: Expertise and gender dynamics in task groups. *Personality and Social Psychology Bulletin*, 30(12): 1585–98. From http://psp.sagepub.com/cgi/content/abstract/30/12/1585.

Thompson, G. 2004. Verbal judo. Verbal Judo Institute, Inc. World Headquarters. From http://www.verbaljudo.com.

Thompson, Leigh. 2000. *Making the team*. Upper Saddle River, NJ: Prentice Hall.

———. 2001. *The mind and heart of the negotiator*. Upper Saddle River, NJ: Prentice Hall.

Tichy, Noel, and Eli Cohen. 1997. *The leadership engine*. New York: HarperBusiness.

Tichy, Noel M., and Stratford Sherman. 1993. *Control your destiny or someone else will*. New York: Doubleday.

Tieger, Paul D., and Barbara Barron-Tieger. 1998. *The art of speedreading people*. Boston: Little, Brown.

Tierney, John. 2007. Smart doesn't equal rich. *New York Times*, April 25.

Tjosvold, Dean, and Mary Tjosvold. 1991. *Leading the team organization*. New York: Lexington Books.

Tjosvold, Dean, I. Robert Andrews, and John T. Struthers. 1991. Power and independence in work groups. *Group & Organizational Studies* 16: 285–99.

Todd, Morgan. 2005. Eastern Michigan University.

Toogood, Granville. 1997. *The inspired executive*. New York: Carroll & Graf.

Torres, Cresencio. 1994. *The tao of teams*. San Diego: Pfeiffer.

Tracy, Brian. 1995. *Maximum achievement*. New York: Fireside Books.

———. 2000. *The 100 absolutely unbreakable laws of business success*. San Francisco: Berrett-Koehler.

Treacy, Michael, and Fred Wiersma. 1995. *The discipline of market leaders*. Reading, MA: Addison-Wesley.

Triandis, Harry C. 1971. *Attitude and attitude change*. New York: Wiley.

Tropman, John E. 1996. *Meetings that work*. Thousand Oaks, CA: Sage.

Tubbs, Stewart L. 1993a. *Empowerment*. Ann Arbor, MI: U-Train.

———. 1993b. *Self-directed teams*. Ann Arbor, MI: U-Train.

———. 1993c. *Team leadership*. Ann Arbor, MI: U-Train.

———. 1993d. Implementing self-managed work teams: A case of organizational success. *Proceedings of the 1993 International Conference on Self-Managed Work Teams* 3.

———. 1994a. The evolution of self-managed teams in the twentieth century. In *Theories of self-managed work teams*, ed. Michael Beyerlein and Douglas Johnson. New York: JAI Press.

———. 1994b. Team leadership: A systems approach. *Journal of Leadership Studies* 1: 27–45.

———. 2011. *Keys to leadership: 101 tips for success, 9th ed.* New York: Learning Solutions, a division of McGraw-Hill.

Tubbs, Stewart L., and John Baird. 1980. *Self-disclosure and interpersonal growth*. Columbus, OH: Special Press.

Tubbs, Stewart L., and Sylvia Moss. 2010. *Human communication: Principles and contexts*, 12th ed. New York: McGraw-Hill.

Tubbs, Stewart L., Husby, Brock, and Jensen, Laurie. 2008. Using continuing improvement teams in health care organizations for improved performance. Association for Global Business Conference, *Proceedings*.

Tubbs, Stewart L., Joseph H. Kryska, and Darrell H. Cooper. 1997. Teams turn round Fernco. *Teams Magazine*, February: 57–60.

———. 1999. Sustaining teams. In *Developing high-performance work teams*, ed. Steven D. Jones and Michael M. Beyerlein. Alexandria, VA: American Society for Training and Development, 181–89.

———. 2008. *Human communication*, 11th ed. New York: McGraw-Hill.

Tucci, L. 2004. Psychologist teaches companies how to be better. *St. Louis Post-Dispatch*, December: C5.

Tuckman, Bruce. 1965. Developmental sequence in small groups. *Psychological Bulletin* 63: 384–99.

Tuddenham, R. D. 1961. The influence upon judgment of the apparent discrepancy between self and others. *Journal of Social Psychology* 53: 69–79.

Turkle, Sherry. 2011. Alone Together. New York: Basic Books.

Turner, Marlene E., Anthony Pratkanis, Preston Probasco, and Craig Leve. 1992. Threat, cohesion, and group effectiveness: Testing a social identity maintenance perspective on groupthink. *Journal of Personality and Social Psychology* 63: 781–96.

Twice. 2003. Tips to make your presentation better. Two Way Interactive Connections in Education, Michigan. From http://www.twice.cc/projpres.html.

UCLA Center for Society and Genetics. 2005. Behavior, evolution and genetics. From http://www.societyandgenetics.ucla.edu/evolution.htm.

Ulrich, Dave. 1997. *Human resource champions*. Boston: Harvard Business School Press.

Underwood, M. 2003. Psychology of communication: Consistency theory. From http://www.cultsock.ndirect.co.uk/MUHome/cshtm1/psy/consist/html.

Unger, Mark. 1974. Unpublished behavioral science term paper. Flint, MI: General Motors Institute.

University of California at Santa Cruz. 2004. Exploring nonverbal communication. University of California at Santa Cruz. From http://zzyx.ucsc.edu/~archer/intro.html.

University of Colorado Conflict Research Consortium. 2004. Escalation problems. International Online Training Program on Intractable Conflict. From http://www.colorado.edu/conflict/peace/!overlay_problems.htm.

Urner, K. 2004. A contribution to general systems theory (GST): Version 1.15. Synergistics on the Web. From http://www.grunch.net/synergetics/gstwork.html.

Ury, William. 1993. *Getting past no*. New York: Bantam Books.

Valicich, Joseph S., Alan R. Dennis, and J. F. Nunamaker, Jr. 1992. Group size and anonymity effects on computer-mediated idea generation. *Small Group Research* 23: 49–73.

Vance, Mike, and Diane Deacon. 1995. *Think out of the box*. Franklin Lakes, NJ: Career Press.

Van Velsor, Ellen, and Jean Brittain Leslie. 1995. Why executives derail: Perspectives across time and cultures. *Academy of Management Executive* 9: 62–72.

Varney, Glenn H. 1989. *Building productive teams*. San Francisco: Jossey-Bass.

Viceri, Albert A., and Robert M. Fulmer. 1997. *Leadership by design*. Boston: Harvard Business School Press.

Vickers, Brent. 1992. Using GDSS (group decision support systems) to examine the future European automobile industry. *Futures* 24: 789–812.

VirtualConnection.biz. 2003a. Virtual work: The new business reality: Current trends. From http://www.virtualconnection.biz.

———. 2003b. Tip of the month: Virtual Connection. From http://www.virtualconnection.biz/pages/TipOfMonth.html.

———. 2003c. Virtual work facts. From http://www.virtualconnection.biz.

Vroom, Victor H. 1993. Two decades of research on participation. *Yale Management* 5: 22–32.

Wahrhaftig, S. 2004. Language, listening, and learning in an age of polarization: The Middle East Peace Forum of Pittsburgh. From http://www.mediate.com.

Wajcman, J. 2004. Gendered by design: Comment on "an evolving gender digital divide?" Sonia Liff and Adrian Shepherd, OII Issue Brief No. 2, July 2004. *OII Internet Issue Brief No. 2.1*. From http://www.oii.ox.ac.uk/resources/publications/OIIIB2C1_200407.pdf.

Waldroop, James, and Timothy Butler. 2000. *The 12 bad habits that hold good people back*. New York: Currency/Doubleday.

Walker, E. L., and R. W. Heynes. 1967. *An anatomy for conformity*. Belmont, CA: Brooks/Cole-Wadsworth.

Walker, Michael A., and George L. Harris. 1995. *Negotiations: Six steps to success*. Upper Saddle River, NJ: Prentice Hall.

Wall, Bob, Robert Solum, and Mark Sobol. 1992. *The visionary leader*. Rocklin, CA: Prima.

Walster, E., V. Aronson, D. Abrahams, and L. Rohmann. 1966. Importance of physical attractiveness in dating behavior. *Journal of Personality and Social Psychology* 4: 508–16.

Wang, Shirley. 2011. Happiness overrated? *The Wall Street Journal*, March 15, pp. D1, D6.

Wang, Shirley. 2011. Under the influence: How the group changes what we think. May 3, pp. D1, D3.

Wang, Ying. 2008. Eastern Michigan University, personal correspondence.

Watson, Warren E., Kamalesh Kumar, and Larry K. Michaelson. 1993. Cultural diversity's impact on interaction process and performance: Comparing homogeneous and diverse task groups. *Academy of Management Journal* 36: 590–602.

Weinstein, Harvey. 2011. My favorite mistake. Newsweek, March 14, p. 84.

Weintraub, Arlene. 2003. Online extra: Roger Permutter: Teamwork is key. *BusinessWeek*, June 2.

Weisinger, Hendrie. 1989. *The critical edge: How to criticize up and down your organization and make it pay-off.* Boston: Little, Brown.

Welch, Jack. 2001. *Jack: Straight from the gut*. New York: Warner Business Books.

Welch, Jack, and Suzy Welch. 2007. From hero to zero. *BusinessWeek*, September 3.

Wellins, Richard S., William C. Byham, and Jeanne M. Wilson. 1991. *Empowered teams*. San Francisco: Jossey-Bass.

West, D. 2005. The nature of power. TheWorkingManager.com From http://www.theworkingmanager.com/articles/detail.asp?ArticleNo=97.

West, Phil. 1993. UAW, Saturn laud union approval vote. *Ann Arbor News*, January 15: B7.

Whetton, David A., and Kim S. Cameron. 2010. *Developing management skill*, 8th ed. Upper Saddle River, NJ: Prentice Hall.

White, Erin, Joann Lublin, and Phred Dvorak. 2007. It's about time—literally. *The Wall Street Journal*, December 31: B3.

White, N. 2004. Facilitating and hosting a virtual community. Full Circle Associates. From http://www.fullcirc.com/community/communityfacilitation.htm.

Whyte, Glen. 1989. Groupthink reconsidered. *Academy of Management Review* 14(1): 40–56.

Widgery, Robin. 1974. Sex of receiver and physical attractiveness of source as determinants of initial credibility perception. *Western Speech* 38: 13–17.

Widgery, Robin, and Bruce Webster. 1969. The effects of physical attractiveness upon perceived initial credibility. *Michigan Speech Journal* 4: 9–19.

Wikipedia: The Free Encyclopedia. 2004. Complex family. From http://en.wikipedia.org/wiki/Complex_family.

Williams, Hank. 1996. *The essence of managing groups and teams.* Hertfordshire, England: Prentice Hall Europe.

Williams, Lena. 1989. Counter culture: Despite AIDS, report finds teens voicing entitlement to sex. *Ann Arbor News*, February 27: A1, A5.

Williams, R. 2003. Experience shapes biology: New tool support learning about child development. Voices for Children. Regional Niagara Health Department. From http:\\www.voicesforchildren.ca/report-Feb2003-1.htm.

Wilmot, William. 1975. *Dyadic communication: A transactional perspective.* Reading, MA: Addison-Wesley.

Wilmot, William, and Joyce Hocker. 2010. *Interpersonal conflict*, 6th ed. New York: McGraw-Hill.

Wilson, Gerald L. 2002. *Groups in context*, 6th ed. New York: McGraw-Hill.

Wilson, Gerald L., and Michael S. Hanna. 1993. *Groups in context*, 3rd ed. New York: McGraw-Hill.

Wilson, Jeanne M., and Jill A. George. 1994. *Team leader's survival guide.* Pittsburgh: Development Dimensions International.

Wilson, Jeanne, Paul Goodman, and Matthew Cronin. 2007. Group learning. *Academy of Management Review* 32: 1041–59.

Wilson, Paul. 1968. Perceptual distortion of height as a function of ascribed academic status. *Journal of Social Psychology* 74: 97–102.

Wire Feed. 2004. CPP enhances FIRO-B product line with new profile. *PR Newswire*, May: 1.

Wiseman, Liz, and Greg McKeown. 2010. *Multipliers: How the best leaders make everyone smarter.* New York: HarperCollins.

Wood, Dana. 1993. Fitness rage: Some class members add a little boxing to all that jumping. *Ann Arbor News*, October 12: D1–D2.

Wood, Julia T., Gerald M. Phillips, and Douglas J. Pedersen. 1986. *Group discussion: A practical guide to participation and leadership.* New York: Harper & Row.

Wood, Robert, and Albert Bandura. 1989. Social cognition theory of organizational management. *Academy of Management Review* 14(3): 361–83.

Woodward, Bob. 1999. *Shadow: Five presidents and the legacy of Watergate.* New York: Simon & Schuster.

Woodward, Bob. 2006. *State of denial.* New York: Simon & Schuster.

Woodward, Bob. 2010. *Obama's wars.* New York: Simon & Schuster.

Woolf, Bob. 1990. *Friendly persuasion.* New York: Berkeley Books.

Yarbrough, Bonnie T. 2003. *Leading groups and teams.* Mason, OH. South-Western.

Yates, Douglas. 1985. *The politics of management.* San Francisco: Jossey-Bass.

Young, J., and D. Coleman. 2003. Optimize the collaboration process and speed innovation. Facilitate.com. From http:\\www.facilitate.com/resource/files/article_Collaborate.html.

Younger women at the top. 2007. *Harvard Business Review*, April.

Zakaria, Fareed. 2007. *The Post-American World.* New York: W.W. Norton.

Zenger, John H., Ed Musselwhite, Kathleen Hurson, and Craig Perrin. 1994. *Leading teams.* Homewood, IL: Irwin.

Zenger, Todd R., and Barbara S. Lawrence. 1989. Organizational demography: The differential effects of age and tenure distributions on technical communication. *Academy of Management Journal* 32(2): 353–76.

Zeus, Perry, and Suzanne Skiffington. 2002. *The coaching at work toolkit*. Sydney: McGraw-Hill Australia.

Credits

CHAPTER 1 Table 1.2 Source: Frank L. Acuff, *How to Negotiate Anything with Anyone Anywhere Around the World* (New York: American Management Association, 1997), p. 70. Reprinted by permission of the American Management Association via Copyright Clearance Center. Group Consensus, page 29: "Cloning Clamor" by Connie Cass from *Ann Arbor News*, October 26, 1993, p. A4. Reprinted by permission of the Associated Press; Reading 1.1, page 30: From Gerald L. Wilson, *Groups in Context*, 5th ed. (New York: McGraw-Hill, 1999). Reproduced with permission of the McGraw-Hill Companies; Reading 1.2, page 34: From Jessica Lipnack and Jeffrey Stamps, *The Teamnet Factor*, © 1993. Reprinted by permission of John Wiley & Sons, Inc.

CHAPTER 2 Figure 2.6, page 85: From *Group Processes: An Introduction to Group Dynamics*, by Joseph Luft, Mayfield Publishing Company. Copyright © 1963, 1970 by Joseph Luft. Reproduced with permission of The McGraw-Hill Companies. Reading 2.1, page 98: From *Faith of my Fathers* by John McCain and Mark Salter. Copyright © 1999 by John McCain and Mark Salter. Used by permission of Random House, Inc.; Reading 2.2, page 100: From Anne Donnellon, *Team Talk* (Boston: Harvard Business School Press, 1996), pp. 25–39. Copyright © 1996 by the President and Fellows of Harvard College; all rights reserved.

CHAPTER 3 Figure 3.2, page 132: Adapted from Constance E. Helfat et al., "The Pipeline to the Top: Women and Men in the Top Executive Ranks of U.S. Corporations" from *Academy of Management Perspectives*, 20(4), November 2006. Box, page 138: Source: Hinsberg, Claire, "Stress Reversal," *Corporate Detroit Magazine*, June 29, 1996, pp. 70–78. Reprinted by permission of Corporate Detroit, Inc. Reading 3.1, page 152: From Paul D. Tieger and Barbara Barron-Tieger, *The Art of Speadreaching People*, pp. 139–144. Copyright © 1998 by Paul D. Tieger and Barbara Barron-Tieger. Reprinted by permission of Little, Brown and Co., Inc. Reading 3.2, page 159: From Teri Kwai Gamble and Michael W. Gamble, "Thinking About Our Gendered World: Where Would You Like to Go from Here?" in *The Gender Communication Connection*, pp. 5–21. Copyright © 2003 by Houghton Mifflin Company. Reprinted with permission. Figure A, page 162: Copyright © 2001 *USA Today*. Reprinted with permission.

CHAPTER 4 Table 4.1, page 175: Adapted from Hall, 1959, pp. 163–64. Chart from *The Silent Language* by Edward T. Hall. Copyright © 1959, 1981 by Edward T. Hall. Used by permission of Doubleday, a division of Random House. Box, page 198: From Detienne, Kristen, *Guide to Electronic Communication*, 1/e, p. 79. Copyright © 2002. Reprinted by permission of Pearson Education, Inc., Upper Saddle River, NJ. Exercise, page 203: From Jim Abrams, "Agencies Tiptoe Among Legal Mines—Administration Asks Court to Rerule on Gay Cadet." Reprinted with permission of The Associated Press. Reading 4.1, page 204: From James W. Gibson and Michael S. Hanna, *Introduction to Human Communication*. Copyright © 1992 William C. Brown. Reproduced with permission of The McGraw-Hill Companies. Reading 4.2, page 205: From Ronald B. and Jeanne Marquardt Elmhorst, *Communicating at Work*, 6th ed. Copyright © 1999 The McGraw-Hill Companies. Reproduced with permission of The McGraw-Hill Companies. Figure B, page 210: From John E. Tropman, "The Agenda," in *Making Meetings* Work. Copyright © 1996 by Sage Publications, Inc. Reprinted by permission of Sage Publications, Inc.

CHAPTER 5 Figure 5.1, page 234: Copyright © 1971 Henry R. Martin. Reprinted with permission of Meredith Corporation and Henry Martin; Figure 5.2, page 235 From James Kouzes and Barry Posner, *The Leadership Challenge*, 3rd ed. Copyright © 2002 by John Wiley & Sons, Inc. This material is used by permission of John Wiley & Sons, Inc.; Figure 5.3, page 238: From *Personality and Interpersonal Behavior* by Robert F. Bales. Copyright © 1970 by Holt, Rinehart & Winston, Inc. Reprinted by permission of the author; Figure 5.6, page 249: *Leadership in Effective Management* by Fiedler and Chemers, p. 80. Copyright © 1974 by Scott Foresman & Co. Reprinted by permission of Pearson Education Inc., Upper Saddle River, NJ; Figure 5.7, page 251: From *Management of Organizational Behavior*, 8th ed., p. 186 by Hersey et al. Copyrighted material. Reprinted with permission of Center for Leadership Studies, Escondido, CA 92025. All Rights Reserved; Figure A, page 271: From *The Situational Leader* by Paul Hersey, p. 63. © Copyrighted material. Reprinted with permission of Center for Leadership Studies, Escondido, CA 92025. All Rights Reserved. Reading 5.1, page 270: From *Management of Organizational Behavior*, 8th ed by Hersey et al. Copyrighted material. Reprinted with permission of Center for Leadership Studies, Escondido, CA 92025. All Rights Reserved. Reading 5.2, page 275: From Posner & Kouzes in Journal of Leadership and Organizational Studies, 1996, Vol. 3, No. 3. Reprinted with permission.

CHAPTER 6 Figure 6.3, page 293: From Mike Magner, "Geology Blamed for State's Loss of Atom Smasher" as reprinted in *The Ann Arbor News*, November 11, 1988, pp. Al, A4. Figure 6.5, page 302: Reprinted with the permission of The Free Press, a Division of Simon & Schuster Adult Publishing Group, from *A Strategy of Decision: Policy Evaluation as a Social Process* by David Braybrooke and Charles E. Lindblomp. 57. Copyright © 1963 by The Free Press. Copyright renewed © 1991 by David Braybrooke and Charles E. Lindblom. Box, page 300: From Six Thinking Hats by Edward DeBono. Copyright © 1985 The McQuaig Group, Inc. Reprinted with permission. Reading 6.1, page 313: From Michael Michalko, *Cracking Creativity* (Berkeley, CA: Ten Speed Press, 1998), pp. 227–235. Reprinted by permission. Reading 6.2, page 320: From Don Martin in Team Think. Copyright © 1993 Dutton Book. Reprinted by permission of Cowan, Liebowitz & Latman.

CHAPTER 7 Figure 7.2, page 331: From Robert R. Blake and Jane Srygley Mouton in *Journal of Applied Behavioral Science*, Vol. 6, No. 4. Copyright © 1970 by Sage Publications, Inc. Reprinted by permission of Sage Publications, Inc.; Figure 7.3, page 334: Adapted and reprinted by permission from *Harvard Business Review*, "How to Choose a Leadership Partner" by H. W. Schmidt, May–June 1973. Copyright © 1973 by The Harvard Business School Publishing Corporation. All rights reserved; Figure 7.4, page 334: Reprinted in *The Ann Arbor News*, December 30, 1993, p. Al; Reading 7.1, page 342: From *Working with Emotional Intelligence* by Daniel Goleman. Copyright © 1998 by Daniel Goleman. Used by permission of Bantam Books, a division of Random House; Reading 7.2, page 346: Republished with permission of American Management Association from Frank Acuff, *How to Negotiate Anything with Anyone Anywhere Around the World*, 2nd ed., 1997. Reprinted by permission of the American Management Association via Copyright Clearance Center.

CHAPTER 8 Reading 8.1, page 386: Reprinted by permission from Sage Publications Ltd. from Norman R.F. Maier and A.R. Solem, "The Contributions of a Discussion Leader to the Quality of Group Thinking: The Effective Use of Minority Opinions," in *Human Relations* 5:277–288. Copyrigh © The Tavistock Institute 1952. Reading 8.2, page 397: From Phylis F. Schlesinger, Vijay Sathe, Leonard Schlesinger, and John P. Koter in *Organization*, 3rd ed. Copyright © 1992 The McGraw-Hill Companies. Reproduced with permission of The McGraw-Hill Companies.

APPENDIX B Appendix AB.1, page A-16: From Effective Group Discussion, 10/e by Galanes, Adams, and Brilhart, 2000, p. 263. Reproduced with permission of The McGraw-Hill Companies. Appendix AB.2, page A-16: From Gerald L. Wilson, *Groups in Context*, 6th ed., pp. 295–296. Copyright © 2002 The McGraw-Hill Companies. Reproduced with permission of The McGraw-Hill Companies.

Index